One Tragic Night

'We are told that a saint is a sinner who keeps on trying to be clean. One may be a villain for ¾ of his life and be canonised because he lived a holy life for the remaining ¼ of that life. In real life we deal, not with gods, but with ordinary humans like ourselves: men and women who are full of contradictions, who are stable and fickle, strong and weak, famous and infamous, people in whose bloodstream the muckworm battles daily with potent pesticides.'

— NELSON MANDELA, *Conversations with Myself*, page 234

'M'Lady, what happened behind that door, you will never know.'

— WOLLIE WOLMARANS, defence expert witness

One Tragic Night

The Oscar Pistorius
Murder Trial

Mandy Wiener
and Barry Bateman

St. Martin's Press
New York

Floor plan by Stephane de Sakutin/AFP/Getty Images

www.stmartins.com

The Library of Congress Cataloging-in-Publication Data is
available upon request.

ISBN 978-1-250-04617-8 (hardcover)
ISBN 978-1-4668-4631-9 (e-book)

St. Martin's Press books may be purchased for educational,
business, or promotional use. For information on bulk
purchases, please contact Macmillan Corporate and Premium
Sales Department at 1-800-221-7945, extension 5442, or write
specialmarkets@macmillan.com.

First published in South Africa by Pan Macmillan South Africa

First U.S. Edition: October 2014

10   9   8   7   6   5   4   3   2   1

Contents

Valentine's Day

The battered meranti door stands ajar, a crude gap stretching from its mid-point towards its upper reaches. Three of the four panels in the top two-thirds of the door are missing, leaving a gaping hole in the structure. A key with an apple-green plastic tag dangles from the brass lock next to the handle. One long shard of wood lies inside the toilet cubicle, a half-moon bullet hole along the spine of the plank and a chip on the side. Several splinters litter the floor of the tiny space, which measures only an arm's length in each direction.

A large rectangular piece of meranti – the bulk of the missing panels – lies discarded on the bathroom floor, where it had been flung in a moment of desperation. It has come to rest next to a buckled silver plumbing access panel of the corner Jacuzzi bath, and squares of broken tile have fallen off the wall adjacent to the hinge of the door, testament to the force with which the door was bashed down.

The deep reddish-brown grain of the wood is marred by bullet holes, blood-stains and garish cracks. What appears to be a tiny fragment of human bone has come to rest on the timber. Later, as they reassemble the broken pieces, investigators will tack strips of police marking tape near the holes as indicators of where the bullets cracked through the wood.

Behind the door lies the real horror. A congealing Rorschach-like pattern of crimson has formed on the mottled beige marbled tiles. On the wall tiles, rivulets of blood have trickled down to the floor where more wood splinters and bits of black metal from the bullet jackets came to lie, the detritus of the devastating events that played out in this bathroom pre-dawn. On the back wall, three separate ricochet points mark where bullets struck the ceramic and shattered the tiles. An old-fashioned dark-wood magazine rack with a heavy, curved handle, packed with glossy titles, stands against the wall, one leg resting in the puddle.

The square porcelain toilet is on the left of the space, the lid up against the cis-tern. The right half of the seat is smeared in a thin film of red, cascading into the bowl below in thick ribbons, separated by strips of white where it appears run-ning water has washed it clean. The macabre sight of the dark red water in the bowl, where one would expect to see sanitised blue, jars. Floating on top of the water are globules of varying sizes, creating the appearance of oil in the water. So murky is the liquid in the bowl that a spent bullet projectile would not be vis-ible to investigators and would be missed during an initial inspection of the site.

The trail leads out past the toilet door, alongside the shower, across the tiles towards a crumpled charcoal bathmat and a pile of soaked pebble-grey towels and on to a worn cricket bat with its perished rubber grip partly torn from the handle.

The trail has settled in various shapes – there are smears, drops, crowns and larger puddles where it seeps away into the grouting. There are flecks on the screen of a black iPhone 4 and its metallic cover, partially hidden under the bathmat, and droplets on the handle of the silver-and-black Taurus 9 mm fire-arm, which has been abandoned on the mat with its hammer cocked and the safety off. Droplets crowd around the cricket bat, itself marked by squiggled wisps along the blue-and-yellow 'Lazer' text and the chevron logo. The signa-tures of famous cricketers along the face of the bat have not been saved from the indignity of being tarnished, but investigators only discovered that when turn-ing the bat over hours later.

Nearby is a fragment of a hollow-point, strands of hair entangled in its jag-ged metal claws. There are three spent cartridges on the tiles in the bathroom: one near the bath, one near the cricket bat and a third at the entrance. A fourth lies in the passage near the cupboards, its copper casing marked by the black residue of spent gunpowder and its distinctive head stamp 'WCC +P+' identi-fying the bullet as Winchester-produced hollow-point ammunition.

There are dark red spots on the two square white basins, where his and hers toothbrushes rest neatly alongside each other, and on a toilet roll parked in the cabinet of the dark-wood vanity. While the flecks on the basins could be missed at a glance, there is no ignoring the blatant smear on the tiled pillar alongside. The streaks mark where her soaked blonde hair swept past as he carried her out of the bathroom, her head resting on his left arm. He had to navigate his way over the towels, wood panels and splinters as he rushed through the doors and then down the passage lined with clothes cupboards into the bedroom. The trail bears testament to this journey that was her last.

At the end of the passage, the trail makes a sharp turn through the bedroom after passing a tall four-tiered bookshelf, a washbasket and a pair of smart black suit shoes. On the left it avoids a chocolate-brown leather couch, her white flip-flops and her black-and-white Virgin Active kitbag, a black bra peeking out from the unzipped opening. There is no spatter on the side table that holds an extreme sports magazine, a silver damask lamp, a squeezed tube of Voltaren gel, and a white coffee mug holding the dregs of the previous night. But, inexplicably, there are a couple of stray drops on the wall above the bed and the ebony headboard.

The spatter also does not make it as far as the right side of the bed alongside the sliding doors that lead out to the balcony, where an iPad, its cover and a grey T-shirt have been left on the floor next to a pair of men's hair clippers. The contents of the drawer on this side of the bed include an array of sexual lubricants, pellets for a pellet gun, playing cards, Mickey Mouse plasters, a USB stick and a spare firearm magazine containing Ranger ammunition.

His rushed exit from the bathroom, with her in his arms, left several marks on the contents of the bedroom. Experts suggested this was the result of so-called arterial spurt – sprays from the devastating wounds to her body as her heart continued to beat. One spurt, likely occurring as he rounded the bend from the bathroom passage towards the bedroom door, reached around a metre and a half along the carpet onto a grey duvet, which had a pair of inside-out jeans resting on a corner.

An open leather-wrapped watchcase containing eight high-end timepieces was spattered and four streaks of red, resembling cracks in the glass, show where her hair flicked past, while speckles are visible on the watches themselves. The box rests on a dark chest of drawers, next to a silver amplifier with an iPhone cable dangling from it, two BlackBerry phones, a silver Tiffany & Co. bracelet, a packet of syringes in a plastic bag and a plastic container, along with several boxes. Spatter also landed on the tall aluminium-and-glass Oakley stand next to the drawers, housing in excess of 40 pairs of sunglasses in varying shades and shapes. Next to the cabinet rests a black air rifle and a small blue baseball bat, indicators perhaps of his heightened security awareness.

The trail is more obvious again where carpet meets tile at the doorway and there has been no opportunity for it to soak away. The bedroom door itself is damaged – not only from speckles of blood but there is also a small hole in the top third of the door caused by a projectile, scuff marks near the spine and a section of the wood is cracked at the bottom near the latch.

The horrifying path of arterial spurts – vertical lines on the walls and tiles – trace the route he followed out the double doors of the bedroom, across the upstairs lounge past the TV unit, the flat screen, surround-sound amp and headphones on the left and the tawny faux-suede couch and ottoman on the right. A red line stretches from the ottoman across to the L-shaped couch. It follows his route past an open linen cupboard stacked with towels and sheets that have been left dishevelled as a result of a scramble to find something, anything, to stop the haemorrhaging. A blue hand towel lies abandoned on the floor next to the cupboard.

The trail follows his route across the landing towards the stairs, past two paintings of bushveld savanna in heavy wooden frames and a tall wooden sculpture on a metal stand. All along the cream eggshell-coloured walls are sprays in a serpentine pattern. The splotches are reminiscent of cuttlefish, with their bulbous heads and long twisted tentacles.

Some of the spray reached over the silver balustrade down to the lounge below where drops landed on the beige leather bucket chairs and couch, raw-wood wine rack, animal-skin ottoman and pillow, and Nguni-hide rug. It is in this room that the trophies are paraded, witnesses to years of success and achievement. Their polished sheen has escaped blemish.

There are maroon drops on every step leading down to the ground floor – on the mottled tiles, the walls and streaked on the balustrade as if a paintbrush has been flicked deliberately and violently. Finally, the trail stops at the bottom of the stairs where the body lies. The woman, once a paragon of beauty and grace, now lies broken and damaged, drained of life.

She lies on her back, stretched out with her head closest to the main entrance of the house. Those who were amongst the first to arrive on the scene were met by this harrowing sight as they threw open the doors. Her legs are splayed, revealing the cursive 'Lioness' tattoo on her left ankle and the shimmering pink polish on her toes. The light-grey Nike basketball shorts are soaked red on her right side where a bullet struck her hip. Her head is cocked to the left, away from the staircase, and her left hand rests on her exposed navel, showing the wound on the webbing between her index and middle fingers. Her black vest has been pulled up to below her chest and a white ECG electrode pad peeks through on her right breast. The white stickers from the ECG pads have been discarded near the staircase where paramedics left them in their haste. Her right arm, destroyed by a wound to the elbow, is bent unnaturally at her side and a light towel has been draped over her bicep – a hasty tourniquet abandoned when it became clear that any attempt at stemming the flow was in vain. There is another towel at the wood skirting and several black plastic bin bags to the side. Her head, devastated by the wound high above her right ear, lies on a black-and-white patterned towel. Her right eye is bruised grey over the lid, reminiscent of the smoky eye shadow she was painted with for model shoots. Her manicured eyebrow has halted a trickle of blood from her forehead onto the bridge of her nose. The rim of her nostril is bright red and a thick line runs at a 90-degree angle across to her left cheekbone, as if it has been drawn across her face with a stick of lipstick gone awry. Her lips are pale.

She lies where he left her. It is here, at the foot of the staircase, where others tried to help her, where the paramedics came, scrambled and then had to walk away. In the pre-dawn hours following her death, police officers arrived on the scene to investigate. They made their way through the house following the trail from her body up to the primary crime scene in the toilet cubicle where she was shot. A photographer recorded the images for posterity. The spatter, the bullet jackets, the cellphones, the cricket bat, the gun and the door would all later be scrutinised as investigators hunted for the truth.

And then finally, only once the sun was already high in the sky over Silver Woods estate, would members of the pathology services arrive to remove her from where she had died, leaving a bloody chaos at the bottom of the stairs where the trail had gone cold.

• • •

The narrative that follows up to page 30 is based on the court testimony of witnesses and is in line with each individual's interpretation of events, not necessarily fact.

Estelle van der Merwe glanced over at the clock. It was 1:56am and she was irritated. She had had barely five hours' sleep and knew that her 11-year-old son was writing an exam in the morning and was probably also being kept up by the disturbance. Her husband Jacques lay asleep in the bed alongside her, apparently oblivious to the voice wafting over the warm night air across the Silver Woods estate.

Estelle couldn't hear what the fight was about or even what language the woman was speaking, but to her it sounded like an argument. The voice was loud and the breaks and pauses suggested she was speaking to someone else – who was it? Estelle couldn't hear a second voice.

She got out of bed to peer out of a window, looking towards the Farm Inn, a small nature reserve neighbouring the estate, but she couldn't see anything and went back to bed. Out of desperation and annoyance, she folded a pillow and put it over her head, hoping it would shut out the persistent voice. She heard it go on and on for about an hour before she finally dozed off.

An hour later, four '*plof geluide*' ('thuds' or 'bangs') shook her awake again. Then there was silence.

This time her husband had also been jolted awake and Estelle anxiously asked him what the noise had been.

'Gunshots,' he responded. Jacques got out of bed to look out of the windows, but could see nothing out of the ordinary. He climbed back under the covers next to her. But then the sounds of a commotion caught their attention once again. Jacques called the estate security to establish what was going on and moments later they both heard what sounded like someone crying in the distance.

'Who's crying?' asked Estelle. She was in shock, felt paralysed and too scared to get up herself to see what was happening.

'It's Oscar,' said Jacques, which confused her because it sounded like a woman who was sobbing.

The couple didn't know Oscar well, but Jacques had occasionally chatted to the athlete when they happened upon each other in the street. He was a friendly neighbour, always willing to offer a smile and a wave when leaving his house. When the men did talk, the topic was usually cars.

Terrified, Estelle slowly climbed out of bed and joined her husband at the window. Together they watched as several cars began to arrive at 286 Bush Willow Crescent. Eventually an ambulance pulled up and they saw it drive off again minutes later, lacking the urgency with which it had arrived.

· · ·

Michelle Burger shot up in bed just after 3am, jolted awake by what she believed to be the blood-curdling screams of a woman in distress. Her husband Charl Johnson heard them too and lifted his head from his pillow to make sure what he had heard was real and not a dream. Charl leapt out of the bed and ran onto the balcony to focus his ear on what had pierced the early-morning silence. The couple had left the windows wide open – it was a warm evening and the lack of air conditioning made the bedroom stiflingly uncomfortable.

They had lived on the Silver Stream estate, adjacent to Silver Woods, for about two years and their house was 177 metres from Oscar's home. Standing on the balcony, Charl heard what he thought to be a terrified woman calling into the night, clearly distressed and in trouble. 'Help ... Help,' he heard. Then what sounded like the voice of a man, also calling for help three times. Was this an armed robbery gone wrong? Both Charl and Michelle wondered.

'Charl! It's no use standing there, call security!' shouted Michelle to her husband out on the balcony. As he rushed back inside, Michelle reached for her cellphone on the bedside table. Frantically she scrolled through her phone's contact book and dialled the number saved under 'Security'. It was 3:16am when she passed the handset to Charl.

They hoped the estate's security officers could call their colleagues at the neighbouring complex to alert them to what seemed to be a terrible attack in progress.

When the call was answered, Charl rapidly explained that there were people being attacked, but he was met with confusion on the other end of the line. The guard who had answered handed over to a colleague and Charl repeated the story. When the second guard still didn't respond, the penny dropped. Charl realised that the number Michelle had dialled was for security at the Strubenkop estate, several kilometres away, where they had previously lived. Realising the error, Charl ended the call, which had lasted 58 seconds, and ran back out on to the balcony.

All that separated their house from the source of the noise was a few spindly poplar trees and an open field, and from the bed, Michelle could hear the screams becoming increasingly intense. She could only think about how scared the woman sounded. Charl sensed the fear in the voice escalate and to him it was clear that the woman was in imminent danger.

And then, just as the screaming reached a climax, it was brought to an end by four cracks.

First one shot, a slight pause, and then three more.

Bang. Bang, bang, bang.

The couple heard the woman scream again and then the final scream fading out after the last crack. Alarmed and shocked by what he had heard, Charl stepped back through the balcony door into the bedroom.

'I hope that woman didn't see her husband being shot in front of her,' said Michelle to her husband.

They did not hear the voices again that night but the memory of the shrill scream stayed with them, haunting them.

· · ·

Annette Stipp was feeling slightly fluish and was battling a troublesome cough that woke her up just after 3am on Valentine's Day. The occupational therapist, her radiologist husband Johan and their three children live in the Silver Woods estate, with a clear line of sight of the home of Oscar Pistorius. The kids had gone to bed at around 8:30pm the previous night and the couple settled in to watch a few episodes of a TV series before going to bed at 10:30pm.

Nearly four and a half hours later, Annette's cough woke her. She looked at the digital clock radio on her husband's bedside table. It was 3:02am but she knew that the clock was set three or four minutes fast.

Annette lay in bed contemplating what to do about her cough, wondering if she should bother getting up to have a drink of water or just ignore it. Finally, she resolved to get up to fetch a drink. She didn't want her husband to be disturbed by her coughing.

As she was climbing out of bed, she was startled by what sounded to her like three gunshots.

'What was that?' Annette asked her husband.

'I think it's gunshots,' he responded as he jumped out of bed and rushed out onto their balcony.

Annette looked across to the row of houses directly opposite their own. She could see the lights on in two of the homes. She sat on the edge of her side of the bed and focused her eyes on Oscar Pistorius's house and noticed the light was on in his bathroom.

Moments later, they heard the screaming. Three, four times, they heard what to them sounded like a woman screaming, loud and fearful. The type of screaming that made the doctor think the woman must be scared out of her mind. Johan knew that there was a serious problem and looked around, trying to establish where the noise was coming from. From the balcony he was standing on, he could clearly see the houses in the row opposite his own, separated by an open stand.

He focused his eyes on Oscar's house and he could clearly see the window of the athlete's bathroom, where the lights were on.

Together the couple stood on the small bedroom balcony, trying to ascertain the source of the screaming. They then moved onto a bigger balcony, which they hoped would give them a better view. The screaming continued and Annette couldn't help but think there was a family murder playing out in one of the neighbouring homes.

Johan knew he had to alert someone quickly and hurried back into the bedroom, grabbed his phone and called the estate's security number. There was no answer.

He punched in 10111, the police's emergency number, and hit the call button but he had no luck with that either. There was an unusual dialling tone, as if the number was out of order. Annette went inside and tried to raise the alarm using her own phone.

Meanwhile, Johan Stipp was still trying to get through to the police and get dressed at the same time. He was worried that children might be in danger and he wanted to go out to help. As he battled to think what number to dial next, he heard three loud bangs ring out.

The doctor didn't know if the same shooter had opened fire again or if someone else had begun shooting. 'Get away from the windows!' he shouted at Annette, trying to keep her out of harm's way.

The Stipps' domestic worker Osterella Ntombenkosi Mkhwanazi also heard the gunshots. She was in her room on the ground floor, at the back of the house. Osterella was woken up by what she first thought was a baby crying next door. She listened carefully and realised it sounded as if it was a woman crying. She was still trying to work out where the noise was coming from when she heard 'boom, boom, boom'.

Johan Stipp's phone finally connected to security and he told the guard on the other end to please come quickly; there was an emergency. As he put the phone down he heard a man scream for help three times.

$\bullet \bullet \bullet$

Mike Nhlengethwa slept right through the bang that woke his wife Rontle. She nudged him awake, asking him if he had heard the noise. The electrical engineer, his wife and their daughter live to the left of Oscar's house in Bush Willow Crescent in the Silver Woods estate. Both homes are of a similar design and the same putty-grey colour. The balcony off their main bedroom is just 18 metres from Oscar's balcony and a mere 11 metres from his bathroom window.

Mike momentarily lay still, waiting to see if he could hear another bang, but all was quiet. His immediate concern was that the noise was emanating from inside his house and he worried about his daughter who was sleeping in her room, across the passage from theirs.

Unable to hear any further noises, Mike got out of bed and went straight to his daughter's room. The family has a habit of locking all the bedroom doors when they are asleep and he was relieved to find her door still securely locked. Mike thoroughly checked the rest of the house on the upper and ground floors, ensuring that the doors and windows were all still secure. Satisfied that all was as it should be, he returned to his wife in the master bedroom.

While her husband had been out checking the house, Rontle had heard someone shouting for help three times. She had heard the voice loudly and was certain it was a man. Just then Mike walked back in to the room and peeked through the blinds.

'No, there's nothing in the house. So it means it is outside,' he told her. As he widened the blinds to get a better look, he heard the piercing cry of a man – the voice of someone who sounded as if he was in shock. The Nhlengethwas both thought the person must have been badly hurt and needed urgent help. They could tell the cry was different to that of a man who was merely sad – this person was in danger. The high-pitched wailing stopped for a short while and then continued again. 'Hey, I wonder, maybe it was a security guard that was patrolling. Maybe something happened to him?' Mike asked his wife.

All he had heard was, 'No, please. Please, no.'

Mike continued to peer through the blinds but he was cautious not to switch on the lights in his house. He didn't want to give his position away and was alert to whatever danger might be lurking right outside his window.

A similar scene was unfolding in the Motshuanes' house, which neighbours Oscar's on the right. Rika Motshuane had been woken by what seemed to her to be the sounds of a man crying in pain. She roused her husband Kenneth, urgently asking him if he had heard what she had.

'Yes, I heard, but I thought I was dreaming,' he responded.

'The crying is real,' she told him, beginning to panic.

Like the Nhlengethwas, Rika thought it might be a security guard who had been injured. Dogs were barking and the crying was very loud and very close – so close, in fact, that she thought it could even be inside her own house.

The couple couldn't work out where the noise was coming from. Stricken by panic, they lay frozen in their bed and didn't dare reach for the lights.

Back at the Nhlengethwas' place, Rontle remained seated on the edge of her bed, frightened into silence. But when Mike decided he was going outside to investigate, she found her resolve.

'There's no way I'll allow you to go out,' she told him.

But together they reached a compromise and agreed that Mike should phone security, and at 3:16:13 he dialled the number from his cellphone. The first attempt didn't connect so he tried a second time at 3:16:36. The call lasted 44 seconds.

'It's Michael from number 287. Can you quickly come up and check what is going on here? There is a person desperately crying and I'm sure he needs help,' Mike told the security guard on the other end. He also asked security to check the houses of his surrounding neighbours. The guard confirmed they would investigate.

As Mike ended the call, he continued to peer through the window. He could still hear the crying and in the distance a car driving up the street. He assumed it must be the estate security already responding to his call.

• • •

Pieter Jacob Baba reported for duty at 6pm on 13 February. He had been working at the Silver Woods estate for nearly two years and had assumed a position of seniority there. Baba was the shift leader and one of five security guards working the night shift. He was responsible for a supervisor who patrolled the estate in a dedicated vehicle, a guard who patrolled on a bike, another who worked the gate and a fourth person who was responsible for general duties.

Not long after Baba clocked in for work, a beautiful blonde pulled up to the boom in her Mini Cooper. Baba knew her as Oscar Pistorius's girlfriend and they shared a brief joke and a smile before she drove through into the estate. A few minutes later, the Olympic athlete drove up in his white BMW, chatting on his cellphone at the time.

At 8pm, as per normal, Baba and his colleagues closed one of the access gates to the estate and then an hour later, at 9pm, they shut all the gates. They needed to ensure the safety of the complex and this was the optimal way of doing so. As part of this function, the guards on duty also had to comply with a 'guard track' that saw them check in at various points around the estate a certain number of times per hour.

That particular night, a guard by the name of Nyiko Maluleke was responsible for doing this clock-in patrol. Having completed a circuit of the estate, Maluleke came to fill Baba in on the situation in the estate that evening. He told his supervisor that the Van der Merwes' gate was open, the Stipps' balcony sliding door hadn't been closed and a small gate leading to another resident's home was ajar. It was a hot night, which explained why the Stipps had left their balcony door open, but Baba thought it best to send the other residents text messages from his official phone, telling them about their open gates.

In the early hours of the morning Baba decided to patrol with Maluleke. At around 2:20am they drove down Bush Willow Crescent and checked in at Guard Track Point Two, located right outside Oscar Pistorius's neighbour's house. Everything was as it should have been that night; at this point there was nothing unusual to be seen or heard, and Baba and Maluleke returned to the gatehouse just before 3am.

Minutes later, Phillemon Ndimande, the guard on bike duty, entered the gate to report that he had heard gunshots. It wasn't long before the official phone line began to ring with residents reporting having heard gunshots in the estate.

Phone records showed that the first call came at 3:15:51 from Dr Johan Stipp, who said he had heard gunshots and told Baba to come and see what was going on. The second was from Mike Nhlengethwa, Oscar's direct neighbour at 3:16. His first call did not go through, but his second attempt connected. He called to say that he had heard bangs. None of the residents could say which house was the source of the action.

Baba immediately sprang into action and sent Ndimande back out on his bike to try to gauge where the gunshots were coming from. He also phoned Jacob Makgoba, who was patrolling in the official security vehicle, ordered him back to base and told him he wanted to drive around the estate with him to try to find the source of the shots.

They drove straight to the Stipps' house, where they found the doctor standing on the small balcony outside his bedroom, waving them down and pointing across at Oscar's house.

• • •

Through his bedroom window, Mike Nhlengethwa had a clear view of the open plot at the back of his house. Across the field, he saw a white security vehicle pulling up to a house he would later find out belonged to the Stipps. Mike watched as the security guards stepped out of the car and he could see them talking to the owner of the house.

Standing on the balcony, Johan Stipp explained to Baba that he believed the shots and screams were coming from Oscar's house and they should investigate. As the guards drove off, Stipp moved on to the bigger balcony and watched as they made their way towards the row of houses opposite. Stipp looked towards Oscar's house where the lights were on in the bathroom and noticed a figure moving in the bathroom, from right to left. He had the distinct impression that it was a man.

Meanwhile, as Baba drove away from the Stipps' house, the guard's phone rang. It was Oscar. Phone records show that the athlete phoned security at 3:21:33 and that Baba called him back at 3:22:05. But despite this, Baba maintained that he made the first call to Oscar. He also recalled the runner saying to him, 'Security, everything is fine.' The athlete's version is different, saying he told the guard, 'I am fine.'

During the call Baba realised that Oscar was crying. He turned to his colleague Makgoba and told him that everything was not in order but before he could say anything further, the phone line went dead. Moments later the guards pulled into the driveway of the athlete's house.

Johan Stipp still felt compelled to act despite security already being en route to the scene. He was concerned that there might be children involved in the incident and, having kids of his own, he was worried it could be a family tragedy.

He quickly dressed, climbed into his SUV, drove first to the guardhouse at the entrance to the estate, to check if it was safe, and then proceeded to Oscar's home.

Mike Nhlengethwa had watched the exchange between the Stipps and Baba. Initially he remarked to his wife that the crying must be coming from the Stipps' house. But then he saw the security vehicle speed away. It made a left turn and did a loop, passing his own house. Moments later, a white SUV also pulled out from the Stipps' house and made a right turn, doing a loop in the opposite direction.

Mike realised that the disturbance must be closer to his own home and moved to another room in the house to see if he could get a better look. His study looks onto Bush Willow Crescent and, peeking through the horizontal wooden blinds in that room, he saw the security vehicle pull up in front of Oscar's house.

He knew his neighbour relatively well. They often greeted each other on the street and just days before Oscar had introduced Reeva Steenkamp to Mike as his fiancée.

Mike knew he wouldn't be able to get back to sleep and now that security had arrived, it seemed safe to go outside. Like Johan Stipp, he felt the need to go to see what was happening. He threw on some clothes, switched on the lights and went downstairs.

Rika Motshuane heard a car pass by her home and turn into the street outside Oscar's house. Overcoming her fear, she got out of bed and looked through a window that faced in that direction. From the window she saw a Mini Cooper coming to a stop in Oscar's driveway.

Rika climbed back into bed but struggled to sleep. She was still shaken and wondered what had happened. Then she heard another car. Again, she looked out the window and saw that a security vehicle had also arrived at the house.

Rika urged Kenneth to phone security to find out what was going on. The guard told him they were taking care of the situation but offered no further details about what was unfolding at their neighbour's house. But the Motshuanes knew the situation was grave. The screams had been terrifying.

· · ·

It was 3:19:03 when Johan Stander's cellphone rang. He looked at the handset and saw that the caller was Oscar Pistorius. At that hour of the morning, he knew it must be urgent.

'Oom Johan, please, please, please come to my house. Please. I shot Reeva. I thought she was an intruder. Please, please, come quick,' was how Stander would later recall the conversation.

The voice on the other end of the line was desperate.

Stander and Oscar first met in May 2009 when the Standers moved into the Silver Woods estate. The athlete arrived at their home in Summerbrook Close, several blocks from his own house, and offered to help them move their furniture in. Over the years they became increasingly friendly – Oscar and Stander's daughter Carice Viljoen became friends, occasionally meeting for coffee, and Stander looked after Oscar's dogs when the athlete travelled overseas to train and compete.

Stander's wife woke up as he scrambled out of bed and headed for the bedroom door. As he opened it, Carice came out of her bedroom.

'I heard someone screaming for help. Someone's in trouble,' she said to her father.

'It must have been Oscar,' Carice's mother explained. 'He called your dad and said he shot Reeva.'

It was the screams for help and not the phone call to her father that woke Carice. The petite blonde, a legal adviser by profession, had gone to bed at around 8 or 9pm the previous evening, as per usual. It was a hot summer night and she left the sliding door to her balcony open and the room's blinds pulled all the way up. In the early hours of the morning, she was startled by her dogs barking in her room where they usually sleep. Annoyed and tired, she lay in bed thinking about how she would have to get up and close the sliding door so that her dogs didn't rush out onto the balcony and wake the neighbours. But she could hear other dogs in the neighbourhood barking too.

Just as she was about to roll out of bed, Carice heard a person shouting, 'Help! Help! Help!' It was a man's voice, she was sure.

Carice froze. Her first thought was that she had to close the sliding door because someone could climb up to her balcony and she could be in danger. The neighbours' dogs began to bark even more and Carice slipped out of bed and went to stand at the sliding door. She dropped the blinds, leaving them tilted very slightly and left the door open a crack. She kept her ear at the opening to hear where the sound came from – she couldn't tell, but she knew someone needed help.

Her heart pounding, Carice shut the door and latched it. She closed the blinds and climbed back into bed. The dogs remained restless, and she was afraid. She contemplated what to do next. Her heart was beating furiously and she knew she wouldn't be able to settle back to sleep. Her dogs were at the foot of her bed and continued to bark madly so she reached for them and brought them close to her in the hope of calming them down. She pulled the covers back over herself.

As she lay in bed, she suddenly picked up movement in her parents' bedroom, which she could see into from her own room. She saw the lights going on and that her mother and father were both awake.

Again, Carice quickly got out of bed and ran to find out what was going on and to tell her parents she had heard someone screaming for help. In the passage, Johan and his daughter decided they needed to get to Oscar's house as quickly as possible and that she would drive them.

Carice raced downstairs, pulled her silver Mini Cooper out of the garage and waited for her father in the street. When he finally appeared, she was so anxious she struggled to push in the clutch to change gears.

She chose the quickest route, driving fast around the corners to Oscar's house nearly 600 metres away. The trip was so short that Carice later estimated that only three minutes passed between Oscar's phone call to her father and the time they arrived at his house.

As Carice pulled up outside the house, she brought the Mini to an abrupt halt in the street and she and her father rushed up the driveway. There were already men standing on the pavement and she asked them what was going on, but they were confused and didn't know.

Frank Chiziweni, the man who works at Oscar's house, was there. So too were the three security guards, Baba, Makgoba and Ndimande. Baba could see on the neighbours' faces they were worried that something serious had taken place.

Through the two vertical glass panes alongside the large double wooden front doors, Carice could see the lights on in the house. She could also see that one of the doors had been left slightly open. As she rushed up the narrow tiled pathway, between rectangular ponds on either side, she glimpsed a man making his way down the staircase inside, a woman in his arms, her head and limbs dangling lifelessly.

Her father and the three security guards trailing behind her saw him too. Carice put her hand on the wooden door and, without much effort, it swung open, revealing something of the nightmare that had unfolded inside.

• • •

From the second Carice walked into the house, she could see that Oscar was distraught. He was walking fast down the second flight of stairs from the landing; Reeva was in his arms, her bloodied head resting on his left forearm.

Johan Stander noticed the immediate relief on the runner's face as they stepped through the door, perhaps because help had arrived. Stander could tell that Reeva had suffered a terrible head wound.

Baba, the security guard, was in shock. He was so flabbergasted he couldn't quite grasp what he was seeing and only regained 'consciousness', as he put it, when he heard Carice shout 'Oscar!' According to Baba, the athlete had told him on the phone that everything was fine and yet what he saw now was in direct contrast to what he recalled the man saying to him. He chose to remain outside the front door rather than rush in to help.

'Carice, please, Carice, please, can we just put her in the car and get her to the hospital?' Oscar begged.

'No, can you please just put her down so we can see what's wrong?' she responded.

Oscar placed Reeva at the foot of the stairs. All Carice could see was blood. Oscar was, however, desperate for them to put Reeva in a car and rush her to hospital.

'He was a young man, walking down the stairs with a lady, with a young woman in his arms and the scene you see, the expression on his face … the expression of sorrow, the expression of pain. He is crying. He is praying. He is asking God to help him. He was torn apart. Broken, desperate, pleading. It is difficult really to describe and his commitment to save the young lady's life. How he begged her to stay with him. How he begged God to keep her alive,' Stander later recalled about the events. 'I saw the truth there that morning. I saw it and I feel it.'

Oscar put his fingers in Reeva's mouth to try to keep her airway open so that she could breathe. He was kneeling on one side of Reeva with Carice on the other. He continued to plead with Carice to rush Reeva to the hospital. Stander stepped outside to phone for help and call for an ambulance.

On the pavement outside, Stander instructed Baba to call the police and paramedics. He also issued instructions to Makgoba and Ndimande. Makgoba was to wait at the gate to escort the police and ambulance to the scene while Ndimande was responsible for keeping the area outside the house clear. Then Stander got on his own phone and tried to call for help.

Inside the house, the scene was frantic.

'Oscar, we're phoning the ambulance. Just wait. Let's see what we can do,' Carice responded to Oscar's persistent requests to get Reeva to a hospital. She knew they had to stem the bleeding and that she needed towels to do this.

Carice ran upstairs to the landing and, in the dark, grabbed a bundle of towels from the linen cupboard, dropping one on the floor in her haste.

She could hear Oscar praying, pleading with God to save Reeva's life and also pleading with Reeva. 'Stay with me, my love … Stay with me,' he begged.

Carice scrunched up the towels and pushed them down on the wounds to try to stop the bleeding. She then tried to make a crude tourniquet with one of the towels to stem the flow on Reeva's right arm. She knew she had to tie it as tight as possible and asked Oscar to help her by holding one side while she pulled the other.

Then she lifted the elastic of Reeva's white shorts and, like a sea, a rush of blood was released. Oscar put pressure down on the towel, trying to dam the flow.

In the frenzy of trying to stop the bleeding, Carice glanced up at her friend and asked, 'Oscar, what happened?'

He looked back at her and said, 'I thought she was an intruder.' She chose not to ask him any more questions.

The towels, however, weren't stemming the flow so Carice asked Oscar for bags and tape in order to tie the fabric even tighter. At this point he still had his fingers in Reeva's mouth, trying to help her breathe, so when he stood up to fetch bags and tape, he asked Carice to take over.

By the time he returned with bags and tape, Oscar was still desperate for the paramedics to arrive and kept asking, 'Where is the ambulance? Where are they?' So Carice decided to go outside to her father to find out how far away help was, although she must have known that in reality it was already too late for help.

· · ·

As Johan Stipp navigated his Prado around the corner into Bush Willow Crescent, he took in the scene on the pavement outside the modern grey double-storey home. He had no idea who the house belonged to but had gathered that this must be where the screams and shots he and his wife had heard earlier had originated. It was also in this house that he believed he saw a man walking behind a lit bathroom window, from right to left.

There was a car parked in the street outside the house and he pulled up behind it. A man was leaning against a white BMW in the driveway. The man motioned him nearer and directed him towards the door. A woman was standing in the doorway.

'I'm a doctor. Can I maybe be of assistance? Can I help?' Dr Stipp said to Johan and Carice.

Stander instantly suggested Stipp go in to see if he could help. As Stipp made his way inside, he stopped and turned back to Stander. He thought it important to clarify his status, just in case.

'I'm actually a radiologist,' said Stipp, before walking through the door.

Back inside the house Carice explained to Oscar, 'There's a gentleman, he's a doctor.' They were both relieved that someone with medical expertise had arrived.

Stipp saw a woman lying on her back at the bottom of the staircase. He also noticed a man he didn't recognise to her left, kneeling over her on the side closest to the kitchen. He had his left hand on her groin and the second and third fingers of his right hand inside her mouth. Stipp bent down next to the woman.

'I shot her. I thought she was a burglar and I shot her,' was the first thing Oscar said to him as he knelt down.

Stipp's medical training kicked in. He tried to open the woman's airway and look for signs of life. She had no pulse in her neck. He checked her wrist but there was no peripheral pulse either. He was positioned on the side of her badly damaged, broken right arm. The woman showed no signs of breathing and she seemed to be clenching down on Oscar's fingers as he was trying to open her airway.

Stipp thought to try what is known in medical circles as a 'jaw lift manoeuvre' in order to open her airway but he struggled because her jaw was still clenching down on Oscar's fingers.

He could find no signs of life at all. Stipp opened the woman's right eyelid and could immediately see that the pupil was fixed and dilated and that the cornea was milky. This was the telltale sign for him. It was already drying out so it was obvious that the woman was mortally wounded.

During Stipp's attempts to revive Reeva, Oscar was still praying and crying. He prayed to God please to let her live. She could not die. He vowed to dedicate his life and her life to God if she would only live and not die that night.

Now that the urgency had dissipated, Stipp took time to look over the woman's body and assess her injuries. He noticed the wound on her right thigh and hip and another on her right upper arm. As he searched further, he noticed the blood in her hair and what appeared to be brain tissue around the right area of her skull. It was obvious to him that there was nothing left for him to do for her.

Mike Nhlengethwa had dressed and walked over to see what the commotion was about at his neighbour's home, leaving his wife Rontle in bed. In the street he identified the security vehicle he had watched driving away from the Stipps' house and he could hear crying coming from inside Oscar's home.

He recognised Johan Stander standing in the driveway, greeted him and asked, 'Johan, is Oscar okay?'

'Hey, Oscar's okay, but I think it is better you go and check yourself inside,' was the best response Stander could muster.

Mike walked towards the front door. Inside he could see Oscar kneeling next to a woman who was covered in blood. Oscar was crying and there was another man with him. Oscar was pleading with the man to help him, repeating, 'Please, please help.'

Mike couldn't handle the scene playing out before him and retreated to the door where Stander was still trying to get hold of emergency services.

Stipp stood up and walked outside, leaving Oscar kneeling on the floor next to his girlfriend's body. 'Ja, it's very bad,' said Stipp to Carice. He then reached for his own phone and called the trauma unit at Wilgers Hospital. They instructed him to phone private ambulance service Netcare and he gave the number to Stander.

At 3:27:06 Stander dialled 082 911. Stipp took the phone and spoke to the dispatcher, describing the injuries. At one point, Carice took the phone and attempted to give the dispatcher directions to the scene.

In the meantime the security guard, Baba, had made several calls of his own. He had alerted the police at the Boschkop police station and had contacted the control room of his security company. He had also tried to get hold of an ambulance.

It took less than 20 minutes for the emergency services to arrive at Silver Woods estate. Oscar and Carice stayed at Reeva's side during the agonising wait, while Stipp periodically went inside to check on her status. Her condition did not change.

Stander, who had not heard any of the shots or the screams and had simply responded to Oscar's distressed early-morning call, asked Stipp what had happened. Had he heard anything? Stipp explained he had heard four shots, silence, screams and then another four shots. And while he had initially been baffled as to what had led to the screams and the shots, he now had a better understanding, having witnessed the scene first-hand. He also knew there was nothing more he could do to help the woman lying inside the house.

When the Netcare ambulance finally pulled up, Carice dashed outside to the pavement, shouting, 'Just come quick, just come quick!' The emergency workers offloaded a stretcher but they struggled to get it through the doors to the house.

Once inside, the paramedics rushed to assess the patient. They lifted her black vest and placed white ECG electrode pads on her chest to check for any signs of life.

Oscar was in a state. He kept asking the paramedics to do whatever they could to save Reeva's life. 'Let's just step aside so that they can work on her,' Carice said to Oscar and the two retreated to the kitchen nearby. Emergency officials followed them into the kitchen to make sure Oscar was all right and to check whether they could phone anyone for him.

At the foot of the staircase, the frenzy had calmed. It had soon become apparent to the paramedics, as it had been to Dr Stipp, that there was nothing more they could do.

The paramedics asked for Reeva's ID and Carice explained to Oscar they needed Reeva's handbag so they could get her driver's licence or ID book. Oscar said it was upstairs and went off to fetch it while Carice remained downstairs with the medics.

From the doorway, Stipp realised what was playing out and turned to Stander. 'Do you know where the gun is?' he asked. It was obvious to him that Oscar was overwrought and he was concerned that the athlete might hurt himself. Stander had no idea where the firearm was. He went inside and asked his daughter, 'Where's Oscar going?'

Carice noticed that Oscar had disappeared and then she too clicked. She remembered him telling the paramedics that the gun was upstairs in the bathroom. She too thought he might shoot himself. Carice looked at her father, leapt up and raced up the stairs, calling Oscar's name. She stood at the top of the stairs, which was still in darkness, shouting, 'Oscar, please just bring the bag quickly!'

She could hear him walking across the tiled lounge and then his footsteps fell silent as he stepped onto the carpet in the bedroom.

'Oscar, please just bring the bag,' she panicked, fearing the worst.

Moments later, he came back out, handed her the bag and walked down the stairs.

Reeva Steenkamp was declared dead at 3:50am.

• • •

'Please, Oscar, just let me know who I can phone for you. Somebody needs to come,' Carice urged her neighbour and friend. She could see he was fumbling with his phone. They were standing in the kitchen area and his attempts to make phone calls were punctuated by bouts of vomiting.

Finally, however, Oscar managed to dial his friend Justin Divaris, but seemed to be making no sense. Carice took the handset from him and explained to Justin what had happened. The same thing happened with his call to Peet van Zyl, his agent. Oscar then called his brother, Carl.

Mike Nhlengethwa waited for the paramedics to leave before departing himself. He watched as the paramedics carried the stretcher back out and loaded it into the ambulance, empty. It was then that he knew the woman was 'no more'.

When he got back home, all he could tell his wife was that he didn't know what had happened, but somebody had died.

Johan Stipp hung around for a while, exchanged numbers with Stander and then drove home. He walked back into his bedroom at around 4:20am. Stipp told Annette that a man had killed his girlfriend. She asked him what the man looked like. He explained that he was very muscular and had tattoos on his back but he hadn't paid much attention because his primary concern was the woman. It was only later that day that Stipp worked out who the shooter was and the scale of what he had witnessed.

• • •

As he pulled up to the Boschkop police station at around 3:30am on Valentine's Day, Lieutenant-Colonel Schoombie van Rensburg was reflecting on what a busy night it had been for his officers.

He had spent the past few hours at the Mooikloof Ridge estate on Garsfontein Road in Pretoria East, around 15 kilometres from the Silver Woods estate and one of many similar upmarket security enclaves in the city, protecting the wealthy from the threat of industrious criminals. The Boschkop police station covers a large swathe east of the capital, much of which comprises such security estates.

The colonel had been on duty in Mooikloof with his team, investigating an armed robbery that had been reported. He had left the scene and driven back to the station to collect the medical registers because one of the suspects arrested in Mooikloof had been transported to hospital. Van Rensburg wanted to make an entry in the register and also check on the night shift at his station.

Perhaps it was fortuitous, perhaps rotten luck. But as the colonel walked into the Boschkop police station in the dead of the night, the telephone rang. It was a report of a shooting at the Silver Woods estate.

Van Rensburg had a problem, one that is all too characteristic of police stations in South Africa. He didn't have a car to send to the scene to follow up. One of his vehicles had transported the suspect arrested at Mooikloof to hospital while the other was still on the scene with other members of his team. Because his was the nearest motor vehicle to the scene, the responsibility fell on him to respond.

The station commander turned to a low-ranking constable in the charge office and asked her to accompany him. Constable Christelle Prinsloo told her commander she knew the location of the address they had been given and the two jumped into Van Rensburg's car and raced out to Silver Woods. They pulled up to the address at 3:55am – five minutes after Reeva Steenkamp had been declared dead.

The first observation the colonel made was that there was an ambulance parked outside with its rear doors open. He also noted a dark-coloured Mini Cooper and a white BMW as well as the security checkpoint the estate guards had set up, controlling access to the house.

Van Rensburg made his way through the checkpoint and into the house where, at the bottom of the flight of stairs, he saw a body covered in towels. As the police officers entered the foyer, a female paramedic approached them to inform them that the woman was dead on arrival. Together they removed the towels and the black bags that had been tied to the woman in haste, desperation and in vain. The paramedic pointed out the wounds to the head, the right side of the victim's hip and to her right arm, above the elbow, as well as to the left hand.

Once he had finished inspecting the corpse, Van Rensburg's next task was to establish the course of events that had led to the shooting. For this he needed to speak to the shooter and examine the scene.

He made his way further into the house, towards the kitchen, where Oscar was standing with Carice. A veteran police officer, Van Rensburg would have observed the pops of colour and evidence surrounding him as he took stock of the situation: the rectangular gift wrapped in striped red, silver and white paper; the pink heart-shaped sweets in clear cellophane resting atop the present; the white envelope addressed to 'Ozzy', underlined by a swirly line and two hearts; the dark-wood and chocolate-brown leather photo frames; an image of a man on a superbike; all would have stood out. So too would the orange and metallic-grey miniature Lamborghinis on the granite kitchen counter and a 9 mm Luger bullet, standing upright like a soldier on the roof of one of the toy cars.

Van Rensburg found Oscar emotional, in tears and vomiting. Because he was in civilian clothing and even though his colleague Constable Prinsloo was in full uniform, the policeman introduced himself by his official rank, Lieutenant-Colonel Schoombie van Rensburg from the Boschkop police station. He felt it was important that the man knew he was a police officer. Van Rensburg asked Oscar what had happened but the athlete was simply too emotional to talk, and there was no answer.

Carice was standing with Oscar, talking to him and consoling him. Van Rensburg questioned her about the plastic bags around the body because he was concerned why they had been placed there. Carice explained to him that Oscar had called her father asking for help and that when they arrived, they found him carrying Reeva down the stairs.

As Carice spoke, Oscar paced up and down around the centre island. Van Rensburg thought it best to ask him to stand on the furthest side of the kitchen, near the basin, as far away from the body as possible.

Realising the status of the accused, the high profile of the crime and the circumstances surrounding the shooting, Van Rensburg knew he would need to get the very best investigators on the scene, quickly. He immediately got on the phone and began making calls.

He gave orders and issued instructions for medical officers, fingerprint and forensic experts and photographers to get to the scene. Many of his staff had spent a large chunk of the night working the earlier case in Mooikloof so he had to be mindful of that. Fortunately, one of his best detectives, Captain Hilton Botha, had not been called out earlier so he was at home and available. Botha was one of the most experienced and knowledgeable detectives stationed at Boschkop. While Prinsloo made many of the calls issuing Van Rensburg's instructions, the commander thought it best to make personal contact with Captain Botha.

• • •

'Oscar's shot his girlfriend,' Hilton Botha turned and said to his wife Audrey after ending the call on his cellphone. His phone had rung just after 4am – it was his commander instructing him to go to the scene in Silver Woods to handle the case. With 24 years' experience in investigating murders, Botha was the man for the job.

Both Botha and his wife knew exactly who 'Oscar' was. It wasn't only because the captain had investigated a previous assault case involving the athlete – Oscar had achieved such fame, such prominence, that a surname wasn't required for him to be identified in South Africa.

It took only 15 minutes for Botha to reach Oscar's house and report to Van Rensburg. His first observation, with his detective's eye, was the amount of blood in the house and the body, covered in towels, lying at the foot of the staircase. He was quickly brought up to speed. He was told how Oscar carried Reeva down the stairs, how he gave her mouth-to-mouth resuscitation, how Oscar and Carice tried to stop the bleeding. Botha later recalled how a witness had told him that Reeva was 'still breathing, making a gurgling sound' and how a doctor had arrived on the scene and declared, 'There's head wounds – it's not going to help.'

Botha also later recalled, in an interview with *Vanity Fair*, his impressions of the superstar's home. 'It was a big house and very neat and tidy and you could see the money talking, with all the ornaments and portraits and paintings. There were shelves stacked with trophies. There was also one of those big box frames, with a picture of Mike Tyson, along with a signed boxing glove.'

Botha and Van Rensburg navigated their way around Reeva's body and made their way up the staircase, following the blood trail through the lounge, down the passage, into the bedroom and through to the primary crime scene in the bathroom. As they passed the open box of watches in the bedroom, Van Rensburg made a mental note: there was blood on the box and he knew that they were valuable and could be appealing to a cop with itchy fingers and a lack of morals.

Inside the bathroom they found the firearm, still cocked and with the safety latch in the 'fire' position, evidenced by the clearly identifiable red dot. They saw Reeva's metallic iPhone and initially thought it may be two phones, but it was just that the cover had slipped off the device. They checked the window in the bathroom and saw that it was open but there was no evidence of tampering and nothing to show that there might have been forced entry by a potential intruder. Van Rensburg also looked out the window to see if there was any way a suspect could climb up and gain entry, but there was none – although there was a ladder lying on the grass below, which had been left by workers responsible for carrying out renovations on the house.

The experienced policemen absorbed it all, allowing the information to percolate, and began to piece together the evidence. What had transpired behind that battered meranti door in the athlete's luxury home in the early morning hours of Valentine's Day? What story did the scene tell? The forensics, the ballistics, the blood spatters, the bullet casings, the cricket bat, the cellphones and what the neighbours heard – all contributed to formulating a version of events. But already the policemen's instincts had kicked in. After all, this was not their first murder scene. They already had a picture of how this had played out.

Van Rensburg walked back downstairs and straight into the kitchen. He had questions for Oscar. He wanted to know whether he and Reeva were alone in the house at the time of the shooting. They were, confirmed the athlete. The colonel told him that in light of what he had seen upstairs, he viewed him as a suspect at that stage and warned him of his rights, although he stopped short of arresting him. The officer felt there were still more leads he had to follow up first.

As news of the shooting spread and several more calls rang out across the city, activity at the scene of the crime began to escalate. More police officers arrived, including photographer Warrant Officer Bennie van Staden. Oscar's brother Carl also appeared, and it wasn't long before his lawyer, Kenny Oldwadge, walked in. Meanwhile, as the investigation gathered momentum, Oscar was moved from the kitchen to the garage of his home.

Van Rensburg and Botha walked the official photographer through the crime scene. The two men turned Reeva's body over so that Warrant Office Van Staden could take pictures. They gathered more and more evidence, enough for them to come to the conclusion that they had a prima facie case against Oscar.

'There is no way anything else could have happened,' Botha later told *Vanity Fair*. 'It was just them in the house and, according to the security registers, she had been staying there for two to three days, so he had to be used to her by that time … There was no forced entry. The only place there could have been entrance was the open bathroom window, and we did everything we could to see if anyone went through it, and it was impossible. So I thought it was an open-and-closed case. He shot her – that's it. I was convinced that it was murder, and I told my colonel, "You already read him his rights, so you have to arrest him."'

Oscar was sitting bare-chested on a gym bench in the garage. His shorts were bloody down the right side, exposing his battered and spattered prosthetic legs. His head was in his hands and he was crying. Botha noticed that his hands and chest had been washed clean. Despite attempts by a low-ranking constable to intervene, Van Rensburg had allowed Oscar to rid his body of crucial evidence.

'Do you remember me?' Botha asked Oscar, referring to the assault case he had investigated four years prior. Oscar confirmed he did.

'What happened?' Botha wanted to know.

'I thought it was a burglar,' said Oscar.

It can't be. It's impossible, Botha remembers thinking. The police were certain that Oscar's story about an intruder could not be true. In the presence of his lawyer, Lieutenant-Colonel Schoombie van Rensburg read Oscar Pistorius his rights and formally arrested him for the murder of his girlfriend, Reeva Steenkamp.

• • •

The phone on the bedside table vibrated and woke Justin Divaris from a deep slumber. It was 3:59am on Valentine's Day.

Justin rolled over, looked at the screen and mumbled to his girlfriend Samantha Greyvenstein, 'Oscar's phoning me.' He ignored the call, but when it rang for a second time Samantha urged him to answer it. 'Answer the phone, maybe it's something serious,' she said.

'Hi, Oz,' Samantha heard Justin say, followed by, 'Don't speak shit!'

Oscar had told his friend that he had shot Reeva.

'What are you talking about? I don't understand you,' Justin repeated.

'There has been a terrible accident – I shot Reeva.'

It was at that point that Carice had taken the phone from Oscar and continued the conversation with Justin. She told him it was true and that he should get to the house.

'Is she okay? Did the gun go off by accident?' Justin wanted to know.

'No. She's not okay. You need to get here.'

Samantha heard him say, 'I'm coming now, I'm coming now,' and he shot out of bed, turned on the lights and changed into a tracksuit.

'Is everything okay?' she asked Justin, who had turned a ghostly white.

'No,' he said. 'Oscar's shot Reeva.'

'*What?*'

'Get ready, we need to go.'

Samantha had heard a woman's voice on the other end of the phone and had assumed it was Reeva's. She thought the incident couldn't have been that serious and didn't think to question Justin further about the gravity of the situation. She thought it must have been an accidental discharge and that her friend had been wounded in the leg or somewhere like that and her life wouldn't be in any danger. Samantha had assumed that Oscar was just 'freaking out' unnecessarily. She wasn't overly panicked when she climbed into Justin's car.

But Justin was driving at speed in a McLaren and was still horribly pale. He hadn't said a word since taking the call.

'Is everything okay? What's wrong?' Samantha asked.

'I just hope she's okay,' Justin responded.

'What do you mean, you hope she's okay? She was on the phone to you now,' Samantha quizzed him, her voice increasingly anxious.

'No, Sam, that was the neighbour. Apparently it's not very good.'

It was then that Samantha started to panic.

'Oh my God, just get there. We just need to get there now!'

The 60-kilometre trip took Justin and Samantha just over a quarter of an hour, not entirely unlikely for a man who sells luxury sports cars. The couple barely said another word to one another for the rest of the journey as they lost themselves in their respective worries.

Samantha kept telling herself everything was going to be fine. 'As soon as the ambulance gets there, she will go to hospital and as soon as you get to hospital everything is fine, you know,' she convinced herself.

When they arrived at the gate to the estate security was reluctant to allow them in. 'No, it's fine, phone the house and they'll let us in,' Justin tried to explain to the security guard.

'I was hanging out the window saying, "Is the ambulance here yet? Have they come yet?"' recalls Samantha. 'Eventually the guy said to me, "The ambulance has come and left but they didn't take her with." I thought, ah well that must mean she's fine … They've patched her up and your mind tells you the best-case scenario all the time.'

It was still pitch dark when Justin and Samantha pulled up outside Oscar's house at 4:20am. The guards were trying to keep vehicles away but Samantha was already '*borrelling*' (tumbling) out the car before Justin had even brought it to a stop.

'I just wanted to get inside and go and see her but the neighbours came to Justin and said, "I don't think she should go in," and I said, "No! I'm going in!" The neighbour actually tried to hug me and I said to him, "Who are you? That's my best friend, I'm going in there!" Then Justin said, "Is she dead?" and they went, "Ja." And then I broke down and said, "Fuck all of you, I'm going inside."' But the police kept her away from the scene anyway.

· · ·

By the time Justin and Samantha were on the scene, a handful of police officers had also arrived. So too had Oscar's brother Carl. Justin and Samantha were barred from entering the house but they could see Reeva's covered body lying at the bottom of the stairs. The athlete was seated in the garage on a bench-press bench, dressed in a pair of bloody shorts.

'The minute we walked in and the minute he saw us, he just broke down, completely, uncontrollably. He was incomprehensible. You know when someone can't speak, they're dry retching on the floor,' recalls Samantha. 'I was just in so much shock. I just sat there. I was bawling my eyes out and then I'd stop and I'd just sit there. Her body was lying right there. She was covered by a blanket, but you could still see her hair and her hand. It was just completely surreal.'

Justin was allowed into the garage and sat down next to Oscar for a few minutes. The athlete was completely incoherent and repeated, 'My baba, I've killed my baba. God take me away.'

'Justin asked him what had happened. He kept saying, "I thought she was an intruder, I thought she was an intruder." And then he was saying, "God please take me now, I don't want to live,"' says Samantha. 'Eventually you can't actually speak to someone like that because you can't even understand what they're saying. Justin said, "Okay, just breathe," trying to console him. We didn't know what had happened.'

At that stage, Samantha and Justin could only think that there had been a terrible accident and questioned how on earth this could have happened.

'I was just thinking, "Oh my goodness, what a terrible accident!" One minute I'm crying for Reeva, one minute I'm trying to understand the whole thing, one minute I look fine and then the next minute I'm breaking down again. I think it's just too much shock, your brain can't actually deal with it in one day.'

Samantha ultimately chose not to go and look at her best friend's body although she had to fight the urge to do so. 'All I wanted to do was go up and pull the blanket off and give her a hug and say, "Get up, we're going." There was blood everywhere in the house. I think it was just a lot to take in. Justin and I were just in a *dwaal* [dazed, in a state of confusion] the rest of the day.'

Samantha sought refuge outside and sat down on the pavement, leaning against Oscar's white BMW. She sat there for what felt like half an hour, staring at the bricks, tuned out from the reality unfolding around her. Out of the corner of her eye she saw a flash and then another.

'I kept noticing a flash that caught my eye and that's when I looked up and that's when I saw … They were obviously taking photos.'

She also identified a problem that would become significant in court days later: 'I remember sitting there and I suppose I've watched enough *CSI* to know. It's a crime scene and I remember looking at all the other assistants, like the ladies, they were all wearing foot covers and gloves and I remember looking at Hilton Botha. He was wearing gloves but no foot covers and I thought, That's weird. I mean, of everything that's going on, that's what I think right there, Jeez, you're not wearing foot covers.'

It was Captain Hilton Botha who brought Reeva Steenkamp's iPhone out to Samantha in the hope that she might have the PIN code to help him unlock the handset. Botha wanted to get hold of the victim's next of kin. Earlier Samantha had said to officers on the scene that somebody had to contact Reeva's parents.

'I said to them, "Her parents need to know, somebody needs to tell them now." I said, "I'll phone them."'

No one had the Steenkamps' phone number so Samantha called a mutual friend. 'I need to get Barry Steenkamp's number,' she told him.

She was anxious that the news would break in the media before Reeva's parents had been told.

'No one should have to find out that their daughter has been killed on the

TV', says Samantha. Botha brought her Reeva's phone before she could get the number for the Steenkamps.

Samantha was reluctant to handle the device as it was clearly evidence in the case. 'He brought me the phone and it was a bag that he took it out of. He said to me, "Does anyone know the code? Can anyone unlock her phone?" and I said, "I can." There was blood on it and I said to him, "Are you sure I can touch that?" She had a black phone and I noticed there was a little bit of blood on it. And he said, "Ja, ja, ja, it's fine. Just put in the code."'

With the phone unlocked, Botha scrolled the contacts list and found the number saved under 'Mommy'. He punched the digits into his own phone and pressed the dial button, bracing himself for the incomprehensible job of delivering the tragic news to a mother – that her daughter had been killed.

. . .

It took nearly two hours from the time of the shooting for the news to make its way to Port Elizabeth, on South Africa's eastern coastline, where Reeva's parents June and Barry live. June answered her cellphone just after 5am and Captain Hilton Botha asked her if she had a daughter and what her name was.

'He said there had been an accident, someone had been shot, my Reeva was dead,' June later recalled. Botha told her he wanted to tell them personally so that they wouldn't hear the news on the radio. June immediately phoned her husband who was out at the time. She was so hysterical that Barry thought she was trying to tell him that their dog was dead. From that moment, she says, all the joy went out of their lives.

It took several more hours before the news of Reeva's death reached her Johannesburg family, the Myers, with whom she had been living in Sandringham. Gina Myers, Reeva's best friend, received a phone call from Samantha Greyvenstein at 7:45am.

'I could hear she was crying,' says Gina. 'She said, "Gi, are you sitting down?" and immediately I stood up and started screaming, "Where's Reeva? Where is she?" She said, "Gi, sit down, there's been an accident." She said to me, "Reeva's gone," and I started screaming and crying. I just lost all sense of what was really going on. My dad and my mom and my sister came running into the room. I had no idea. I didn't even really care. I just heard that Reeva is gone.'

And then, at 8.03 am on Thursday, Valentine's Day 2013, a tweet from the daily Afrikaans newspaper *Beeld* broke the news that would rock the world:

@Beeld_Nuus Oscar Pistorius skiet sy vriendin in sy huis dood omdat hy glo dink sy is 'n inbreker.*

@Beeld_Nuus Oscar Pistorius shoots his girlfriend dead in his house because he believed, thought she was a burglar.

A Lioness's Legacy

The two head-turning models lay sprawled across the carpet in the spare room of the home in the wealthy suburb of Atholl near Sandton, Johannesburg, nursing their cups of tea and contemplating their lives. One a gym-toned, striking brunette with carved features and intuitive eyes, the other a blonde with a warm, enveloping smile and laid-back demeanour. Both women, whilst foils of one another in appearance, had featured on the pages of *FHM* magazine, marking high points in their careers in the industry. But beyond their profession, the two had become best friends, sharing their lives with each other.

It was a Tuesday evening and Samantha Greyvenstein and Reeva Steenkamp were in their favourite spot. Stretched out on the carpet in Samantha's home, drinking tea and messing around on their laptops was a pastime they regularly shared together as one helped the other through a crisis. This particular Tuesday was Reeva's turn to support her friend through a meltdown.

'I was freaking out about something. I was having a nervous breakdown about my life and about work and I needed to talk to her. I met her there after work and it's quite sweet because she always used to get there before me and I'd walk in and she'd be sitting talking to our household staff. She's so chilled like that. She would have a long conversation with everyone and then I'd walk in and we'd make tea and then we'd go upstairs. I'd vent to her about my life and my problems and then she would come up with solutions. We'd lie on the carpet and we'd talk and we'd drink tea and we'd faff …' Samantha reminisces wistfully about the last time she saw Reeva alive. 'She was perfect.'

That evening in mid-February 2013 Reeva was effervescent as she spoke about the future and the potential it held. Her boyfriend of three months, Oscar Pistorius, had been talking to her about accompanying him on his travels around the world. 'She was very happy, and said, "He told me I must come overseas with him on his trips, so his agent sent me his itinerary and I've got to see if I can be away at the same time." He wanted her to go to Hawaii and Australia. I said, "Wow, that's awesome!" and she told me, "He's never taken a girl or a friend on any of his trips before." He goes to Italy for months and she was saying they were going to go to Italy together. That was when I said to her, "Are you really happy?" and she said, "If he asked me to marry him tomorrow, I think I'd say yes."'

Samantha believes that Reeva and Oscar had a future together. 'I definitely think they were in it for the long haul; I think they were very serious about each other. This was a proper relationship.' She wasn't shocked that her friend was considering marriage. 'After seeing how well they had been getting on and how they did everything together. They were besotted with each other like any other fresh new couple is, kisses and love and hugs and whatever when they were around us.'

Reeva and Samantha met 'out on the jol' around eight years before, through mutual friend Darren Fresco, at Cappello in Lonehill. Samantha remembers Reeva being 'awesome' and the two hit it off immediately. 'I didn't know Darren that well at that stage and he just called me out of the crowd and I went to go and say 'hi'. I met her and from there we were friends ever since. I liked her because she was so chilled.' Samantha laughs as she recalls what they discussed at the bar. 'She had just had her boobs done and she was a little bit sore and I was telling her that I wanted to get mine done and so we spoke about trivial stuff like that but she was awesome, very laid back. She was very humble; she didn't have any airs and graces whatsoever. She didn't care whether you were a street sweeper or the Queen of England; she was very down to earth.'

Reeva had only just moved to Johannesburg from her home in the coastal city of Port Elizabeth and she was not yet as extrovert as she would become. 'She was a little bit shyer in those days. She was very honest about the fact that she wanted to become someone, with the modelling, and so she worked hard at it, going to launches and any party that she got invited to, she needed to be seen out. But in those days she was a little bit less like that. She was also ten kilos heavier when I met her.'

Reeva had a relatively sheltered upbringing in Port Elizabeth where she attended a convent school, St Dominic's Priory. Teachers remember her as being vibrant, friendly and diligent, and she was a popular pupil, respected by her peers and authorities there.

Along with her schoolwork, she invested her energy into horse riding from a young age, a likely hobby as her father Barry was a racehorse trainer in the city.

She became accomplished in the sport and was decorated for her success. Reeva matriculated from St Dominic's in 2001 and completed her LLB at the Nelson Mandela Metropolitan University (NMMU) in 2005.

At age 14, Reeva took up modelling. But her real breakthrough came much later when she was already in university. In 2004 she was named as a finalist in the *Weekend Post* Faces of the Future competition. A year later she was also a finalist in *The Herald* Miss Port Elizabeth competition. It wasn't long before she was selected as the first South African Face of Avon, representing the international cosmetics company.

By then she knew real stardom did not lie in Port Elizabeth, but rather in Joburg. She moved to Gauteng in 2007, which is when she met Samantha.

Samantha was already a successful model and recalls taking Reeva with her to a shoot in 2009. 'I asked her to come along because it was kind of like a specialist thing. It was underwater modelling and the photographer was looking to put a team together that he could use. I said to her, "Come with," and she was so self-conscious in her bikini and she didn't want to do anything. If I look back at the photos, she was a bit heavier than she was when she died. It was funny because modelling was her whole life for the latter part of her life, but back then she didn't actually get that much work.'

At the time, Reeva was modelling for the Ice agency and was working with her boyfriend, Warren Lahoud, in his company. The Lebanese, with dark features, a boyish face and pristine smile, ran a successful fruit-and-vegetable supply business. Reeva had been applying to do articles at various law firms in Joburg. But because she had taken off several years to try to break into the modelling industry after university, she was repeatedly turned down for articles. She also attempted to do her pupillage to become an advocate but was unsuccessful. 'All the firms she had applied to, they all looked at her like she was some Barbie and told her you can't just pull in after eight years,' recalls Samantha.

In a 2011 interview with blog site The Bucket, Reeva spoke about her decision to move to Joburg from Port Elizabeth and weighing up a career in modelling versus the law:

> I landed a contract as the Face of Avon cosmetics and was flying to and from PE every other week ... and decided I needed to be based in a more metropolitan city with more contact in the industry. I made appointments with several agencies but Jayn from Ice called me up one day (I was having lunch at Moyo off Jan Smuts) and she refused to put the phone down until I walked into her Rosebank offices. So I paid the bill

and stayed on the line with her until I literally walked into Ice Models. The deal was sealed instantly and I made arrangements to move to Jhb.

During my final year of Law, I had a horse-riding accident and broke my back. After some time in hospital and with some rehabilitation, I returned to classes and made the decision to never let go of my dreams and aspirations. With this in mind, I attained my degree instead of taking a year off for rest and pursued my dreams of becoming a model in the big city. I could've been in a wheelchair but I was blessed to recover fully from the tragic experience.

I intend writing my bar exams next year whilst getting away once or twice a month to shoot local/international work. I want to be a qualified advocate before I'm 30 so it's important that I stay focused and academically diligent over the next year without a hectic modelling schedule.

From Reeva's application to do pupillage at the Johannesburg Bar, it's evident that she valued the principles of justice and was motivated to practise law, but she knew she would face challenges with her career:

I realise that a long period of time has lapsed between my graduating and making this application, but I am a fast learner and an eager student. I believe I have the ability to fall back into legal mind under the pressure of my will to succeed. I chose to alter my path after graduating after I broke my back in a horseriding accident and survived paralysis. I decided to travel the world and be a model whilst I was still young and healthy enough to do so. It is now, however, my intention to become a student of law once again.

Her application also contains her matric certificate and the results of various terms at NMMU as well as an invitation to join the prestigious non-profit honour society Golden Key. While her Grade 12 results were mediocre – she achieved Bs and Cs across the board – she regularly achieved distinctions at university.

In a 2012 interview with *Weekend Post* newspaper in Port Elizabeth, Reeva reflected on her decision to pursue modelling rather than be admitted to the Bar:

At the end of last year I made an application to the Bar. It was a nerve-wracking experience. As I walked out I got the call for the FHM shoot as well as two others. I made a decision to take the modelling shoots. I believe in destiny and faith.

Reeva's modelling success would come with time and weight loss, as fellow Port Elizabethan and then editor of *FHM* magazine Hagen Engler recalled in a column in the Daily Maverick days after she died:

Reeva had been an aspiring teen model when we met previously. I might have been judging her at a 'Faces of the future'-type model search in PE. In the end her break came when she was selected to represent Avon cosmetics.

After school, I lost track of her. By the time our paths crossed again in the casting room, she'd apparently studied law, and was running a fresh-produce business with her then-boyfriend.

Thrilled to see her, we weren't able to cast her that time. Though her personality sparkled like the night sky, she was carrying a bit of extra weight. Still sexy, though. She was a contender, but we didn't choose her for that particular calendar.

The next year, she was back, and in shape. She must have lost 10–15 kg at least, which is significant in the superficial world of bikini modelling. I don't think she made that calendar either. Something about too many blondes, or too pale. Like I say, it's a superficial world.

Undeterred, she came back the following year. And then. Then! That was the charm. She had trained herself to flawless super-fitness, was tanned and taut, but what set her apart was the attitude – that same knowing wink. She knew what this game was all about, and she was willing to play it. To train up, be flirtatious on video, bring that indefinable sexiness in the eyes, strike the awkward poses.

So there she was. On the calendar shoot for Bazaruto Island, Mozambique, where it was immediately clear she was one of the most beautiful models on the island. Her TV interviews were smart and sassy, striking just the right balance between one-of-the-guys humour and sassy coquettishness.

She didn't make the calendar cover, but we made a mental note to get her on the FHM cover as soon as possible.

That eventually happened in December 2011, where we shot at a hotel pool on the roof of Joburg. Reeva nailed it, and was fun to work with, if a little nervous about her first cover shoot.

> *We were impressed, and there was this vibe of, 'Wow, this girl deserves*
> *to be more famous!'*

Samantha laughs as she exclaims about all the attempts they made at cracking the *FHM* calendar over the years, knowing what it would mean for their careers.

'Reeva and I always had this joke that we had been to the *FHM* calendar casting eight times in the last eight years. We get told to go but every year we get told, "Your boobs are too big" or "You're too skinny," so we always thought, What's the point? But we ended up going anyway and the one year she got it, and that marked the start of her career. She then got the cover and from there she really worked hard. It wasn't just a case of doing shoots; it was a lot about creating this public persona for herself.'

Samantha says that while Reeva was committed to getting her body into shape, it certainly wasn't achieved through sweat and hours in the gym. 'I don't remember her losing the weight. She just started watching what she ate. She used to gym with me, but she used to do five little things and she'd be like, "Okay, I'm going to take a break now," so I always used to say to her, "Your body didn't come from gymming, it came from dieting." She was cute, she used to have a little routine: she would go to gym or she would skip at home or something – she wasn't the biggest die-hard gym fan.'

When Reeva featured on the *FHM* cover towards the end of 2011, she was still dating Warren. The two had been living together for around three and a half years but the distance between them had grown.

After Reeva and Warren broke up, she was a free agent but Samantha was already dating the successful entrepreneur Justin Divaris, owner of the luxury lifestyle company Daytona Group, which sells flashy high-end cars such as McLaren and Aston Martin. Samantha and Reeva spent a lot of their free time together, meeting for tea on Mondays at the Michelangelo Hotel in Sandton and going on adventures.

'She was very similar to me. I'm an only child. She was very much a *laat lammetjie* ["late lamb", born long after other children in a family]. She was kind of my go-to person for virtually anything, and vice versa. We used to see each other at least three times a week and have tea and a catch-up. Our weekly thing was to go to the Michelangelo and sit and have tea and scones and we had the same waiter all the time and the scones were heart-shaped and we used to sit there and be all proper.

'We would do the strangest stuff together,' says Samantha as she vividly remembers taking Reeva to get her first tattoo – tiny, stencilled initials on her wrist. It would be the first of three she would get on her body.

'She decided she wanted to get her first tattoo and I had just come back from modelling in Taiwan and I got my first tattoo on the back of my neck and she said, "No, I want to get it done."' The two had yet to meet legendary Parkhurst tattoo artist Pepe – who has inked Joburg's finest, from celebrities to hit men to sports stars – so they took a drive to a parlour in Festival Mall in Kempton Park.

'We trek out there and we've made an appointment and Reeva didn't have the strongest stomach. The minute she sees blood, she starts to go woozy. We walked into the tattoo parlour, and it had a very sterile smell and immediately when she walked in, she started ...' Samantha breathes deeply, mimicking her friend's exasperated reaction. 'I don't think she knew what she wanted and then eventually she decided on her grandfather's initials. The tattoo that she ended up getting was on her wrist and it was tiny. It was literally like pencil lines, three initials. I had to go and buy her Coke because she was feeling woozy and she sat looking away but it's quite funny because after that she became a bit obsessed with tattoos.'

Reeva's second tattoo was bold text across her back saying 'Only God can judge' in Italian, another nod to her grandfather who was of Italian heritage. The two tattoos illustrated her affection for her late grandfather, which was echoed in a tweet posted on 30 December 2012: 'Today I wish I could pick up the phone and call my grandfather. He had the answers to everything! Who would you call that you can't now?'

The third tattoo was on her left ankle – cursive script reading 'Lioness' to acknowledge her star sign, Leo. On Twitter she explained her choice with the hashtag #projectink. 'Abundance and power are yours, for you are the lioness' and 'The lionesses are the hunters for their pride and execute their skills with precision and complex teamwork', she tweeted.

Having broken up with Warren, with whom she had shared a flat, Reeva was looking for a new home. In mid-2011, she moved in with her close friend, make-up artist Gina Myers, and her family who live in a large facebrick and peach home in Sandringham. Gina had met Reeva six years previously while doing make-up for a fashion show at Fashion TV in Sandton. Reeva was interviewing her about her craft for FTV International. 'She then hired me for a job for the same company and later I saw her at a shoot where I did her make-up for her and it was inseparable from then.'

Gina's parents, Cecil and Desi, invited their daughter's friend to live with them. 'She had to move out of her apartment and she had a whole bunch of shoots and she was going to Cape Town for work and she wasn't here much and she was already so much a part of our family that my dad and my mom said to her, "Please, just move in with us, just for a couple of months. You're travelling so much you're hardly going to be at home anyway, we'd love you to come stay with us." It was so much fun. It was coffee together every single morning. Tea in bed every single night. It was really nice. It was a lot of fun.'

Reeva forged a tight bond with both Gina and her sister Kim, who affectionately referred to her as 'Alfie'. Gina giggles as she recounts why the name, a reference to a character from the classic comedy *The Little Rascals*, stuck: 'Whenever she put her hair in a pony, she had these little pieces of hair that kept sticking out, it's new hair growth, but they would never stay down. And the one night there was so much wind that all these pieces of hair were just flying everywhere, so I started calling her Alfalfa, and of course it shortened to Alfie and Alf.'

Gina's mother, Desi Myers, speaks highly of Reeva and lauded her for 'cooking for the family, always keeping her room spotless and always letting us know when she was coming home or not when she left the house, although she rarely stayed out overnight. Mostly Reeva stayed home, working on her computer, cleaning her room and bathroom. She went to various meetings during the day and a few events at night. I would say that other than the time she spent with Oscar – from January 2013 when we returned from our annual holiday – Reeva spent most nights at home watching TV and/or talking and laughing with Kim and Gina.'

Regardless of who one speaks to about Reeva, they are astonishingly complimentary, and not with the 'never speak ill of the dead' type of generosity. There appears to be a genuinely deep affection for her amongst her friends who describe her as 'beautiful' and 'special'.

'I love that when she felt so passionately about something and she loved it, and when she was really speaking from her heart, she used to put her hand on her heart and her eyes would look up and she would just be so ... and you knew that's exactly how she felt,' remembers Gina emotionally. 'Her hand gestures, the way she spoke. I think that's why she was always my person that I called. I could trust her to really tell me the truth and it was always going to come out sincere.'

Samantha has to stretch to find a flaw when asked. The only fault she can think of is Reeva's eyebrows – fortunately, Samantha owned her own beauty salon and has a talent for manicuring brows. 'I always used to sit there and look and she'd be like, "Oh my God, are you looking at my eyebrows again?" and I'd say, "Yes, please can we sort those out?"'

But when pushed, Samantha also concedes that Reeva could be pedantic and slothful. 'She would be like, "Oh my God, we've only got 25 kilometres to go, we need to fill up" and you could drive another whole day on that! And then she would freak out, "No, Sam, we have to fill up!" She was also a creature of habit. She'd come and sleep at my house and we would get up and have a piece of toast with peanut butter and a cup of tea. She liked to chill.' Samantha flips between present and past tense when describing her friend's idiosyncrasies.

'She doesn't like to be rushed in the morning. I think that's the one thing that irritated me sometimes is if I wanted to get up and go, if I wanted to go somewhere early, or "Let's get up and go for an early breakfast before work" – she would say, "No, no, no, no. Let's not do anything early."'

Reeva was passionate about women's rights and was particularly vocal about sexual abuse – so much so that after her death her parents announced they would be starting a foundation for abused women in her honour.

Reeva's own Twitter timeline reflected her compassion and concern for those who had suffered and made particular reference to the brutal rape and murder of 17-year-old Anene Booysen in Bredasdorp in the Western Cape. Four days before Reeva was killed she posted a graphic of a man's hand silencing a screaming woman on her Instagram feed:

> I woke up in a happy safe home this morning. Not everyone did. Speak
> out against the rape of individuals…

Reeva had had her own negative experience while living in Port Elizabeth, as she recounted to ZAlebs in her final interview:

> *I once had to get a restraining order against a guy. I went on one date with*
> *him and on the way home to drop me off, we had to 'pop by his place to let*
> *the dogs out' as he'd forgotten. He didn't own any pets and after I told him*
> *there wouldn't be a second date, he moved back home with his parents*
> *because 'his house smelled of my perfume'. Psycho.*

Fun and frivolous, Reeva wasn't looking for anything serious in her private life, having just come out of a five-year relationship with Warren. She was more focused on advancing her career – but it didn't hurt when she had a brief fling with professional rugby player and Blue Bulls heartthrob Francois Hougaard. She met the 24-year-old tattooed scrumhalf in early 2012 and the relationship didn't last long before fizzling out.

'I definitely think there was like a bit of a spark, but I know for a fact that she wasn't looking for anything. They saw each other for a few months and I think eventually they said, "Are we taking this to the next level or aren't we?"' explains Sam.

But iMessages between Reeva and a friend tell a slightly different story – one of a young woman confused and unsure of where she stood with the rugby star. On 30 October 2012 a friend said in an iMessage that she had asked Hougaard what was happening between him and Reeva: 'So he gave me a weird look and his reply was that you guys are only friends. He emphasised the friends part ... I think just from this response I can tell he doesn't want a committed relationship sister ... He told him if that is the case, then he MUST tell you. He cannot hold you on a line. It is not fair to you and I do not want to see either one of you hurt from this ... you are GOOD FRIENDS and should not loose each other.'

The state of affairs with Hougaard was weighing heavily on the model. 'This thing is making me ill. I just don't get why 2 people can't have fun together just cos of who we are it's fucked up and I don't care that he's 24,' she said as response in an iMessage.

Messages show that Reeva spoke to Hougaard on the evening of 30 October. She explained how she felt and how they should proceed with their relationship. She discussed this with her friend the next morning.

'We are just going to be the friends we started off being and that's amazing because right now we both need that! I had an amazing 4 months of romance and I told him if it wasn't for him I'd still be stuck in a loveless relationship,' she said.

Hougaard declined requests by us to be interviewed about his relationship with Reeva.

· · ·

In the meantime, Reeva was on the cusp of local stardom – and yet, according to her closest friend, Samantha, she never became arrogant or big-headed. In a country where being a television continuity presenter or featuring in magazines' gossip pages is equated with being 'famous', Reeva was edging towards her goal.

'She knew what she was capable of, but she was very, very down to earth. She worked really hard at it. She was always thinking about the next step and what she needed to do and where she wanted to be,' insists Samantha. 'It wasn't just like, "I want to get married and have kids." Once she started modelling, she realised she had a talent and she could actually go somewhere with it.'

Gina remembers how Reeva could sense that her future was about to change. A couple of weeks before Reeva's death, Gina received a message from her predicting a shift. 'She said to me, "Gi, our lives are about to change, I can feel it." She was excited about life, especially because there was so much that was about to happen for her and she could feel it. She had just joined new management and all she could talk about was how excited she was about the new things and the new adventures and the possibilities that were coming along with it. Huge things were happening for her and she was happy about it.'

Then, in November 2012, Reeva climbed a notch higher on the celebrity ladder when she was selected to feature in a local reality TV show called *Tropika Island of Treasure*. The series, filmed on location in Jamaica, sees celebrities and ordinary people compete in remote, exotic locations in a variety of daily challenges to win R1 million.

Samantha says this was the direction Reeva was looking towards. 'She was really keen on getting into TV presenting, I think *Top Billing* would have been a goal for her. Especially after she did *Tropika Island*. That was good exposure for her.'

Local celebrity guru Jennifer Su told *City Press* newspaper that the last time she saw Reeva, they had spoken about her plans for the future: 'I was having dinner with Reeva and Oz very recently after an event. I've never seen Oz look so happy like that night. Reeva is beautiful beyond words in a naturally sexy way – and she asked me about TV presenting. She was interested in branching out beyond *FHM* and modelling, and to do more TV work. We made a lunch date for next week where I was going to take her to the studio and make some introductions.'

It was at a Daytona Group corporate 'track day' at the Kyalami Race Track towards the last quarter of 2012, that Reeva met Oscar Pistorius properly. Reeva had been invited to the event by Samantha and the Paralympian was there as a guest of Sam's boyfriend, Justin. The two men share a passion for fast cars and Oscar was in the process of purchasing a McLaren from the Daytona Group. The car, valued at R3.5 million, was a gift to himself for Christmas following what he called a 'good year'. Samantha and Justin were both friendly with the athlete, who had been to their house for dinner and they saw each other socially. Samantha was impressed by how well-mannered and kind Oscar was, considering his fame and status. 'I thought he was great guy. I'd still say I'd never come across a guy who was so well-mannered in this day and age. Polite, considerate. I thought he was a lot of fun. I thought he was a great guy, that's why I hung out with him. I didn't see anything ... I was never in a situation where I thought to myself, you know, this guy is cooked.'

By the first week of November 2012, Oscar's relationship status was already complicated. He and his girlfriend Samantha Taylor had just returned from a weekend away at the Sun City resort. Taylor later testified in court that there was 'a lot of commotion' in the relationship at the time. She did not, however, consider what had transpired between them at Sun City to be a break-up. The true extent of the problems in the relationship would only be revealed to us after the trial had been completed.

Oscar opted not to take Samantha Taylor as his date to the South African Sports Awards. But he did need a date – and it was Justin who suggested he take Reeva. On the afternoon of the event, 4 November, Justin called up his girlfriend's friend and asked her if she would accompany Oscar to the awards. 'Justin phoned Reeva and asked, "Do you want to go to the Sports Awards tonight?" She said, "Uh … in like an hour's time? But okay." She scraped her hair back, put a dress on and went,' recalls Sam.

Much-publicised photographs of the couple on the red carpet belie the last-minute request and any accompanying awkwardness – Reeva, statuesque in a cascading tasselled peach dress with shoestring straps and her blonde hair pulled into a ponytail, beams as she glances up into the athlete's smiling eyes.

That night Reeva told *City Press* newspaper, 'We're just friends. I promise I'll tell you if there's anything more … It's just a coincidence that we're sitting at the same table and arrived in the same car.' She also told an interviewer on the red carpet: 'Oscar is a very, very sexy boy. He doesn't do it in an arrogant, obnoxious way. He does it in a very classy, understated way. He's a gentleman.'

'The next day,' says Sam, 'she was like, "Jeez, what an amazing guy." She said, "We sat and spoke for hours, we liked the same things, he seems like a lot of fun." I was very happy for her!' but Samantha adds that Reeva was worried about Oscar's youthfulness. 'She said, though, that he's very mature for his age. Obviously with what he's had to deal with and being in the public eye since he was so young. You know, achieving what he's achieved, he must be more mature for his age.'

Inconveniently, Oscar was friends with Reeva's ex-fling Francois Hougaard, and she had to tread carefully as she entered into this new relationship. Her dalliance with the rugby player had also prepared her for dating a celebrity. 'I think it might have been a little bit overwhelming in the beginning, but she had been with Francois before. I know she wasn't chasing the limelight but I think she quite liked it. She liked what he was well known for. He wasn't an actor or a model or something like that, he's achieved a lot.'

Hougaard soon found out about the Sports Awards, and the next day Reeva had to deal with the fallout, despite the pair calling it quits just days earlier. The model discussed her concerns with a friend in an iMessage: 'My gosh I'm trying to sort out so much shit now. Hougi is so fucken upset about yesterday with oz and it was so innocent I was just trying to help :(I don't know who told him in such a shit way he has such a big tour going on its not a joke and Oscar told him it was last minute and made sure it was ok! People are interfering and stupid.'

In another message, Reeva told a friend: 'I was a last option. I think after Tropika filming I'm giving up on this career I can't have this kind of negativity and games and people stabbing each other in the back.' Despite what Oscar had told Reeva, Taylor would later dispute this both in court and in an interview with us.

While the friend tried to be understanding, she offered a view from Hougaard's side and how he might have perceived the situation. 'Hmmmm….. Probably a huge misunderstanding but maybe you should have thought it through before agreeing to do it – even if you wanted to help him out. Also not sure why he asked you if he had Justin and all those boys that could attend or even his brother or sister. It was a massive event with people from the sports industry, with media present, nothing unfortunately will be a secret. I don't blame him [Hougaard] for being upset.'

But Reeva nevertheless asserted her independence and made it clear that she no longer had any attachment to the rugby player: 'I went. I had fun and I have no regrets! No one else could go! I can guarantee u he would've asked u if u were at track day that's how chilled it was. Hougi made a fool of me the last few weeks and has no claim over me! I'm 29 and I make my own decisions I won't let anyone make me feel like this!'

Samantha doesn't believe that Reeva began dating Oscar for the wrong reasons and she never felt any discomfort or had any qualms about his so-called disability and the fact that he wore prosthetics.

'I asked her and she said she doesn't even notice. I said to her, "Is it inhibiting in any way?" I mean, everyone is wondering it, it's just I asked it. She said no and that makes me feel like she really cared for him and she completely overlooked all of that. I think for other girls that were in it just for the fame, they would force themselves to be okay with it, but I know for a fact that it wasn't an issue for her at all.'

Samantha also rubbishes suggestions that emerged shortly after Reeva's death that she could have provoked Oscar into a rage after mocking him about his handicap. 'A lot of people heard rumours going around, "Ah, you know, she must have said to him, 'You're half a man,' or something like that"; it's absolute bull.'

She adds that Reeva was never cruel and, in fact, always tried to avoid confrontation, choosing to walk away from a fight to let tempers cool rather than see it escalate. 'Reeva was often more the silent-treatment kind of person. If they ever did get into an argument, she would say, "Come and talk to me when you're ready to talk." She wasn't an aggressive person at all.'

• • •

Despite the controversy and hearsay, however, the budding relationship quickly picked up steam and by all accounts it wasn't long before the couple were falling for each other.

Gina says the week after their first date, Oscar was at their house almost every day. 'We had our customary Sabbath Evening on the Friday night and Oscar also attended. Oscar braaied for us and brought us a cake. Oscar also made his speciality pap for us. We all got on with Oscar and he appeared gentlemanly and responsible. My whole family thought so.'

Reeva spent nights at his home in Pretoria but, as Samantha recalled, it was all a bit too fast and too intense for her.

'Oscar might have fallen for her really quickly where – obviously, because she had just come out of a relationship with Warren and then with Francois – I think she felt, "Okay, we need to take it slowly." I asked how things were going, she would say, "Ja, well, we're going slowly," like she wasn't in a rush or anything. She didn't want a serious relationship at that stage.

'He was quite clingy. If she got a message and she maybe read it and didn't write back straight away, he would write back, "Hi, what are you doing? Why didn't you write back?" and she was like, "Whoa, I can't deal with this." And I know at the beginning they had one or two big arguments on the phone. I remember I met her for tea and I said, "How are things going?" and she said, "Ag, we had the biggest blowout on the phone last night." She said, "I just put down the phone, I'm not interested in talking about it" but that then obviously makes him more mad and he tries to phone her back. They went through a phase where they did argue a lot but she honestly just put it down to new relationship squabbles. And she did say he was intense, but she never emphasised it was a problem. She would say to me, "Oh my God, he's so intense, but he's amazing." She said, "If I don't write back to his message within five minutes, then he's like, 'Where are you?'"'

Gina also details Oscar's obsessive nature and intensity in her statement.

'When their relationship began, Oscar ran after her and called her incessantly. Reeva did like him, but did not like the pressure that he exerted on her. She often told me that she wished that he would just calm down a little bit. He would call her many times in the space of a few minutes. Once, when we went to a party in December, he drove past. She told me that she suspected he might have been checking up on her. He said that he was just going to check out a Bentley with Justin. But she was convinced he was checking up on her as he wouldn't usually be in that area and it was 5 or 6pm on a Sunday.'

This wasn't the only incident that led to Reeva and the Myers sisters questioning Oscar's possessive nature, and Gina reveals they went as far as to joke about him stalking Reeva.

'One night, she went to the bathroom at home and returned to her room to find that there were a few missed calls from him. As a joke, when she eventually answered, my sister and I ran to the curtains to check whether he was outside. Thereafter, we referred to him as the "Stalker".'

Cecil and Desi Myers also picked up on Reeva's concerns about Oscar's intensity. Both mention this in their sworn affidavits.

'Oscar phoned Reeva constantly. I was very keen to meet the Paralympic/Olympic star and was introduced to him the following week when he arrived at my house to see Reeva. From that day on Oscar visited our house regularly and phoned Reeva constantly. Reeva was becoming overwhelmed and complaining about him making her feel claustrophobic, not giving her any space or allowing a relationship (if any) to take its natural course,' recalls Cecil. 'After numerous complaints from Reeva about Oscar's eagerness to hasten the relationship, I asked Reeva if she would like me to have a chat with Oscar. She was grateful and said, "Yes, please do." The perfect opportunity arose one afternoon when Reeva was delayed in getting home and Oscar arrived before she did. I privately spoke to Oscar telling him that if he liked Reeva, he should take it slowly as she had recently been in a long-term relationship. I do not recall my exact words to Oscar but I do remember politely telling him that Reeva was feeling smothered with his many phone calls and eagerness to see her daily. Oscar said that I was right and that he would take it easy.'

In her statement, Desi recalls conversations that she had with Reeva that increased her concerns about Oscar and the relationship.

'… About two weeks before her passing. We were sitting in the lounge. I was watching TV and she was looking at her cellphone.

'Reeva: Desi, what must I do about Oscar?

'Me: What do you mean?

'Reeva: I keep getting tweets about Oscar. About the fact that I do not know what he is really like and that he has girlfriends all over the world, one in Italy, one here, one there, etcetera.

'Me: It is obviously jealousy, Reeves.

'Reeva: I know what you're saying, but where there is smoke there is fire. What if it's all true?

'Me: You should approach Oscar and ask him honestly or you can spy on him [giggle], which would not make a very trustworthy relationship, or you can take a chance and trust him and if it is true that he is the womaniser they say he is, you'll find out sooner or later.

'We never discussed this topic again.'

Desi says she remembers Reeva telling her how moody Oscar was, but excused his behaviour by saying that he was training hard and was sick. 'On one occasion, Reeva told me that Oscar had screamed at her over something small – she never told me what it was – and that she had had enough. Her phone rang over and over again, and when I asked if it was Oscar trying to call her she said it was but she was not going to answer it. It was then that Reeva told me that when a person screams or shouts at her she shuts down.'

But, insists Samantha, towards the end of her life Reeva was smitten. 'By the end, I definitely think she had fallen in love with him. They were only together four months but I think she felt very deeply about him. She was super happy, slept over at his house all the time, were always doing things as a couple together.'

Reeva's Twitter account is littered with clues that give some insight into the altering state of their relationship. On 25 November, she posted: 'Wise words for an amazing person @OscarPistorius: The world breaks everyone and afterwards some are strong at the broken places.' On 6 December she tweeted, 'Wondering what my stalker is up to? Kinda miss him lurking around tonight ...' Five days later, she commented: 'Love comes from finding someone who makes you feel comfortable with yourself. Almost like finding the other part of yourself,' while on 30 January she put up an image reading: 'It's beautiful when you find someone that is in love with your mind. Someone that wants to undress your conscience and make love to your thoughts. Someone that wants to watch you slowly take down all the walls you've built up around your mind and let them inside.'

Her love for Oscar was clearly growing, so much so that she began publicly hinting at marriage. At a friend's engagement party on 15 December, she tweeted: 'Being around this bridal party makes me appreciate my friends & look forward to the day I get married to the man of my dreams.' Six weeks later, on 7 February, she posted a picture of a spectacular wedding dress, with a resplendent feathery, flowing white train and the words, 'I'm in LOVE!'

Samantha was never worried about Reeva and never considered that she may ever be at risk being with Oscar. He had never given her any cause for concern. 'No. People do crazy stuff and you hear stories about how they are with other people, but until you actually see or you hear from the other person that they are worried ... Ja, I can't ... I honestly can't say that I was worried for her at any stage because she never mentioned she was afraid. She never said to me, "Oh, I'm worried for my life."'

In an interview in the days following Reeva's death, Gina agreed that Reeva seemed to be happy and there were no flashing indicators to make her think otherwise. 'As far as her happiness goes, there was nothing ever that concerned me or made me think that there was something going on. She never spoke about anything like that and we spoke a lot. We did. There were no warning signs. None. She was happy. I think in every relationship there's ups and downs and there's stuff that you go through when it's a new relationship. Everything was normal.'

But while Gina publicly stated that she saw no obvious warning signs, in her sworn statement to the authorities she does mention several incidents that raised questions for her, revealing at least some inkling that things may not necessarily be as they seem at face value.

On one occasion in December 2012, the couple had a blow-up on the phone while Oscar was in Doha that led to Reeva breaking off the relationship with Oscar – although they later reconciled.

'Reeva and I attended a comedy evening that had been hosted by *Tropika*. They had an argument and Oscar had screamed at her over the phone. I could hear her talking and when she came out of her room, she was crying. I asked her what had happened. She replied that she had never been spoken to in such a disgusting manner in all her life. She also stated that she refused to be with someone who could talk to her like that. I think that was the fight that started because she sent him a photo that he said she had also sent to somebody else. When she joked about it, he went mad.

'Oscar tried to call her many times that night. He even tried to call me. He did this often. Whenever they fought and she did not want to speak to him, he would call me. She asked me not to answer his calls. That night, she sent Oscar a very sincere email in which she told him that it was too much for her and the way in which he spoke to her had really upset her and she would not stand for it. She told him that he was an amazing person and that she wanted him to be happy but that she needed a few months to just be by herself because as much as she liked him, it was not healthy to continue like that. He replied by saying that he would wait for her and that he was really sorry.'

On another occasion, Gina recalls that Oscar became upset because Reeva had eaten muesli and yoghurt for dinner. 'This was a major issue and she carried on about it the whole night. My sister and I could not understand why this was such an issue and why it had happened.' Over the following weeks, Oscar began visiting the Myers' house less frequently and Gina rarely heard from him. She found this strange because, at the start of the relationship, he had often called and messaged her.

In her statement handed to the prosecuting team, Gina's sister, Kim, also mentions several incidents that raised at least a suggestion of concern for Reeva.

One of these was when she, Gina, Reeva and Oscar visited the Nando's drive-through in Greenstone on 10 January 2013.

'As they ordered food I got out of the car to go take pictures of the sunset. They thought it would be funny if they locked the car doors and didn't let me back in. They were informed that the food may take a while so they drove around and came to park in the parking. Everyone then got out of the car and Oscar and Reeva then went to go sit on the pavement. My sister and I decided it would be funny to jump into Oscar's car and lock them out, which we did. I was in the driver's seat and my sister was in the passenger seat. We were laughing until Reeva motioned to us with her hands that there was a gun by my sister's feet. We looked down to find a silver gun (belonging to Oscar) lying on the floor of the passenger seat at which time we both got a fright and jumped out of the car. We both remarked how dangerous this was.'

Gina recalls how freaked out she was. 'Reeva was pointing her hand in the shape of a gun and trying to tell me something. She kept pointing and then pointing at her head. I then looked down by my feet on the passenger side of the car and saw Oscar's firearm lying on the floor of the car. I freaked out as if I had seen a spider and we both jumped out of the car.'

Later that same evening, another incident took place that upset Oscar and concerned Kim.

'After getting home and finishing our food, my sister left and it was just myself with Oscar and Reeva. Reeva mentioned that Tashas in Melrose Arch had just started to stock frozen yoghurt with various toppings. We all decided that we should go and get some but didn't feel like getting out of the car to go inside and eat it. I mentioned we should get takeaways and we all agreed. I then called Charles Nel, who is one of the managers at Tashas Melrose Arch, and asked if we could order three frozen yoghurts with toppings and if at all possible he could bring them out to us whilst waiting in the road so we did not have to get out the car. He agreed. I did not have my bag with me and Oscar did not have any cash so we stopped by the FNB ATM at around 8.05pm so that he could draw some money. I then messaged Charles to tell him I would be there in two minutes and we then met him at the roadside by Tashas. Upon giving us the three frozen yoghurts, Charles said we could have it "on the house". Oscar refused to accept that and straight away got out of the car to go after Charles and give him the money. I had joked with Reeva that if Charles thinks he can outrun Oscar Pistorius, he has a surprise coming … Oscar got back into the car fuming with anger, having been unsuccessful in paying Charles for the yoghurt ice creams. He said he was very angry and does not want anything for free … and that he does not want to owe anyone anything.

'I tried to reason with him, stating that Charles had done this as a favour for *me* as I was a very loyal customer and he did not even know that I was coming through with two other people. He continued saying that he does not ever want to go to that Tashas again. He was then silent for the remainder of the journey and refused to eat his yoghurt ice cream. When we arrived at my house, Reeva and I went inside and Oscar stayed outside. Reeva went to put both hers and Oscar's yoghurt ice cream in the freezer (I had finished mine). I looked at Reeva and she looked at me … I said to her, "Reeva, it's just yoghurt ice cream. Charles was doing *me* the favour, this is not normal behaviour!" She replied that she knows it is not normal, but Oscar is just stressed.'

Samantha reveals that Oscar's enthusiasm for firearms did not 'freak' Reeva out and she was actually proficient in handling a gun herself. Both women had been for training and regularly went to the shooting range. 'It's an interest we all have. For me, in this country, I feel like you need to actually go and learn how to handle a gun properly. And I'm not ashamed to say it. Justin and I both go for proper training with the best people that there are, because if you ever get into a situation that is violent I need to be able to use every single gun that falls in front of me and that's being responsible.

'Reeva liked it more from a sport point of view. She'd been shooting with Warren before, she'd also been for training.' In fact, months before her death, Reeva posted a photograph of herself on Instagram, grasping a 9 mm pistol with both hands, her arms stretched out and her head cocked. Muffs covered her ears and protective glasses, her eyes. She wrote: 'Shooting games this morning! I feel less stressed now :)'

In December 2012, Justin and Samantha invited Oscar and Reeva to holiday with them in Cape Town.

'I think they had maybe had a little fallout before Christmas and Oscar came to Cape Town and he stayed with us for a few days on his own over New Year's. We went for lunch one day and Oz was saying, "Why don't I get Reeva to come down and then we all go away for a day or two?"' So Reeva flew down to the Cape and the two couples went straight to the five-star luxury Arabella resort near Hermanus. 'It was awesome; we went and lay by the pool, we drank cocktails, we went for dinner.' They returned to Cape Town and Oscar and Reeva closed themselves off at a hotel in Green Point. 'I think they just wanted some time on their own.' According to Samantha, this appears to have been the turning point in their relationship. 'When they got back to reality, from there the relationship was awesome.'

Oscar was in the process of buying a house down the road from Justin and Samantha in Atholl and it was likely that Reeva would move in with him. 'She was pretty sure that would happen. She was running around getting him all the things he needed, like a wash basket, and so on. He was meant to move in a month after it happened,' Samantha says with a sense of melancholy, perhaps a sadness at what could have been.

But the relationship was not without its problems and a deeper reflection on events shows up its more turbulent, tumultuous characteristics.

One of the more significant rows was on 27 January 2013, the day of Reeva's close friend Darren Fresco's engagement party. Gina recalls that she had asked Reeva if she could catch a lift with her and Oscar, and when the couple arrived with British athlete Martyn Rooney, Oscar was already in a foul mood. 'They were running very late. I had gone to get flowers for them just before picking me up. When I got in the car I could sense there was tension. Reeva said they'd been running late the entire morning. I said thank you to Oscar for fetching me and he was very short in saying no problem. I could definitely sense something had happened. When we parked, Oscar and Reeva walked in front while Martyn and I walked behind them. At one point Reeva let go of Oscar's hand and came to walk with us. Oscar turned around and said something along the lines of, "Are you not going to walk with me?" in quite a stern voice. She walked forward and just said to me, "I'll tell you later." The engagement party was really nice, and at one point Reeva called me and said we were going. We got in the car, and clearly her and Oscar had just had a fight. She messaged me and said he had been like that the entire morning. When I asked what happened she said she'd tell me at home.

'He dropped us off and drove away. She said they had had a fight because they were walking back from getting food, and Oscar stopped walking with her when she said hello to a guy friend she had known for years. He was there with his wife and child and she was saying hi. When she turned around to introduce Oscar, he was standing a metre or so behind her. Oscar got annoyed apparently and said she was flirting with him.

'That day we had an afternoon nap. When I woke up I had missed calls from Oscar. She sent him a message about the whole thing and now he was trying to get hold of her. She said: "Gi, call back and tell him I'm sleeping."'

WhatsApp messages between the two would later emerge in court, giving a raw and real account of the state of the relationship. Most notable was the exchange between the two following the fight at the engagement party:

Reeva: *I'm not 100% sure why I'm sitting down to type you a message first. But perhaps it says a lot about what's going on here. Today was one of my best friends engagements and I wanted to stay longer I was enjoying myself but its over now. You have picked on me incessantly since you got back from CT and I understand that you are sick but it's nasty. Yesterday wasn't nice for either of us but we managed to pull thro and communicate well enough to show our care for each other is greater than the drama that attacked us. I was not flirting with anyone today. I feel sick that u suggested that and that u made a scene at the table and made us leave early. I'm terribly disappointed in how the day ended and how u left me. We are living in a double standard relationship where u can be mad about how I deal with stuff when u are very quick to act cold and offish when you're unhappy. Every 5 seconds I hear how u dated another chick you really have dated a lot of people yet you get upset if I mention ONE funny story with a long term boyfriend. I do everything to make u happy and to not say anything to rock the boat with u. You do everything to throw tantrums in front of people. I have been upset by you for 2 days now. I'm so upset I left Darren's party early. SO upset. I can't get that day back. I'm scared of u sometimes and how u snap at me and of how u will react to me. You make me happy 90% of the time and I think we are amazing together but I am not some other bitch you may know trying to kill your vibe. I am the girl who let go with u even when I was scared out of my mind to, I'm the girl who fell in love with u and wanted to tell u this weekend. But I'm also the girl that gets side stepped when you are in a shit mood. When I feel you think u have me so why try anymore. I get snapped at and told my accents and voices are annoying. I touch your neck to show u I care you tell me to stop. Stop chewing gum. Do this don't do that. You don't want to here stuff cut me off. Your endorsements your reputation your impression of something innocent blown out of proportion and fucked up a special day to me. I'm sorry if you truly felt I was hitting on my friend Sams husband and I'm sorry that u think that little of me. From the outside I think it looks like we are a struggle and maybe that's what we are. I just want to love and be loved. Be happy and make someone SO happy. Maybe we can't do that for each other. Cos right now I know u aren't happy and I am certainly very unhappy and sad.*

Oscar: *I want to talk to you, I want to sort this out.. I don't want to have*

anything less than amazing for you and I.. I'm sorry for the things I say
without thinking and for taking offense to some of your actions. The fact
that I'm tired and sick isn't an excuse. I was upset that you just left me
after we got food to go talk to a guy and I was standing tight behind you
watching you touch his arm and ignore me and when I spoke up you
introduced me which you could've done but when I left you just kept on
chatting to him when clearly I was upset. I asked Martin to put on that
kendrick lemar Album in the car and don't know it, granted that was a
shut song but you could've just lent forward and whispered in my ear to
change it scene I had to drive to pick up your friend. I was 30 min late
and I know you don't like it when I drive fast but then you should've
asked Gina to drive herself so that we wouldn't have to. When we left I
was starving, the only good I'd had was a tiny wrap and everyone was
leaving for lunch, I'm sorry I wanted to go but I was hungry and upset
and although you knew it it wasn't like you came to chat to me when
I left the table. I was upset when I left you cause I thought you were
coming to me. I'm sorry I asked you to stop taping my neck yesterday, I
know you were just trying to show me love.. I had a mad headache and
should've just spoken to you softly. In sorry for asking you not to put on
an accent last night.. Pretty much the same and didn't have the energy.

YOU magazine also published details about arguments that occurred while the couple was on holiday in the Cape, while the *Sunday Times* reported on how the duo argued in public, on their way to the parking lot, after the Virgin Active Sport Industry Awards at Emperors Palace on 7 February.

In her statement, Gina gives more insight into the events that took place that night.

'The night that Reeva attended the Virgin Active Awards with Oscar, I returned home from VIP at approximately 1.30am. I walked upstairs and started to lock up. Reeva's room is near the security door. I heard her talking in a slightly raised voice and repeatedly saying the word "but". I could not hear much else. I knocked on the door, but she did not respond so I left. I then sent her a message saying, "love you Alfi, come wake me up if you need anything." She responded immediately "omg" and then "omg you're awake. Im coming." I replied, "lol".

'I then walked into her room and saw that she was covered in the blanket with her hand on her face. She always fiddled with her eyebrows or something when she was frustrated. She appeared similar to the video footage of her when she drove into Oscar's complex as seen in the *Carte Blanche* programme. I cannot remember the exact details of the fight but she told me that Oscar just wanted her to be attached to his side the whole time and if she was not, he freaked out. This occurred that evening, when they were leaving and she walked around one side of the table and he walked the other way around. He was then annoyed because she was not next to him. When she walked ahead of him, he became angry and told her that people would say that they were fighting.

'He had a fight with her and dropped her off at home. He then called her and this was the reason why they were arguing over the phone. He eventually said he was going to sleep and they ended the conversation. She then said to me once again, "Gi, I cannot do this."'

Reeva's WhatsApp message to Oscar that night revealed just how upset she was about the fight:

> *I like to believe that I make u proud when I attend these kinds of functions with u. I present myself well and can converse with others whilst u are off busy chatting to fans/friends. I also knew people there tonight and whilst u were having one or 2 pics taken i was saying goodbye to people in my industry and Fix wanted a photo with me. I was just being cordial by saying goodbye whilst u were busy. I completely understood your desperation to leave and thought I would be helping u by getting to the exit before u because I can't rush in the heels I was wearing. I thought it would make a difference in us getting out without u being harassed anymore. I didn't think you would criticize me for doing that especially not so loudly so that others could hear. I might joke around and be all Tom boyish at times but I regard myself as a lady and I didn't feel like one tonight after the way u treated me when we left. I'm a person too and I appreciate that u invited me out tonight and I realise that u get harassed but I am trying my best to make u happy and I feel as tho u sometimes never are no matter the effort I put in. I can't be attacked by outsiders for dating u AND be attacked by you, the one person I deserve protection from.*

In an interview with *Heat* magazine a week before she died, Reeva spoke openly about how she worried that 'lies' could ruin her fledgling relationship with the athlete. She said that while she respected and admired him, she also feared that negative publicity could harm his career: 'We haven't been talking to the media because I don't want to get it tainted. I don't want anything coming in the way of his career. He's such an amazing athlete.' She added: 'You know what they do, they make things up, "Reeva cheats on Oscar" and rubbish like that. I wouldn't want lies about us jeopardising it. I'm trying to work on my modelling career and remove myself from the whole *FHM* stigma,' she said. 'I want to be seen as a classic model.'

Gina reveals that in the last few weeks of Reeva's life, she was incredibly stressed about her career, her finances and her relationship.

'For the last two weeks of Reeva's life, she complained on a daily basis that she felt sick. She was sick from anxiety, but said that she did not know what had caused it. She seemed really stressed. She told me that she was stressed about money for her parents and that she desperately needed to give them money but that she was also low on cash. She had so many plans for this year and they were only starting to materialise.'

Reeva's mother, June, regularly asked her daughter for money – a few hundred rand here, a thousand rand there, which Reeva duly deposited into her account.

Her death compounded the family's financial woes and left them without a source of financial assistance. On 29 June 2013, June Steenkamp told *The Daily Mail*: 'Our hearts just feel broken. But we have no choice but to sue. Pistorius has placed us in this position. We are struggling financially. Reeva was helping us. On the night she died, when she was on her way to Oscar's house, we talked about her sending us money to pay our cable television bill. I was fretting because I thought I was going to miss her first TV appearance. She told me not to worry, she would send money the next day. She regularly helped us with food and utility bills.'

Part of Reeva's stress was attributed to a new international television series, *Strike Back*, for which she had auditioned. She told Gina that as part of the role, she was required to kiss someone and she was concerned about how Oscar would react. Gina says that while Reeva knew the role would fast forward her career, she didn't know how she would tell her boyfriend.

'On the day that the filming of this series began, she still had not told Oscar. She just told him she was on set. On set, she was told that the part was far more intense and revealing than she had thought. The actor had come in and told her that it was more explicit and there was more nudity than she had been told. She called me and told me that she had refused to do so and was leaving. She left without doing the part. She also told me that she had subsequently told Oscar what had happened. She told me that Oscar had then told her never to be scared to tell him stuff, it was fine, she had left and should come through to Pretoria. She went through to Pretoria that night. The next day, she told me that he was not impressed with the whole thing but that he would get over it.'

One of the casting agents on the series, Steve Jordaan, remembered Reeva being in make-up, ready for the shoot, but walking off set because she was unhappy about the nudity. 'Reeva was going to play the raunchy little waitress in the opening scene with lead actor Sullivan Stapleton. She used the *Tropika* show as her excuse, saying the nudity wouldn't be good for her image, but talk on set was that she had a fight with Oscar after he found out it was a topless scene,' he said.

The scene involved the actress and Stapleton in a steamy state of undress – and Jordaan cast Nicolene Botha at the last minute. 'The director was fuming. In the casting video she was specifically told that she was auditioning for a nude scene, and she was okay with that. It was a complete surprise,' said Jordaan.

Gina states that whenever she asked Reeva whether she had told Oscar about her financial problems with her parents, Reeva said she did not want to because she did not want to make him feel as if he needed to give her money. Additionally, she stated that Oscar always made out as if his problems were bigger. 'She told me that she felt like it always had to be about him.'

On Sunday, 3 February 2013, while she was out for breakfast with a friend, Gina received a call from a distressed Reeva. 'She was crying and told me that she needed to sit down and talk to me about stuff. She repeated the money problems that she had with her parents and that she needed to help them. I told her to stop putting pressure on herself and to breathe. She was in her car on the way to lunch with Oscar, but she was alone. She repeated that she had a sick, horrible feeling and that we needed to sit down and make plans. I calmed her down.'

Gina was becoming increasingly sceptical about Oscar and his possessive nature, and yet, despite this, Reeva also told her that she was finally ready to tell Oscar that she loved him. On the face of it, the couple did seem more and more in love. In her sworn statement, Gina recounted the events of the last time she saw her best friend alive. It was Tuesday morning, 12 February, and she was sitting on Reeva's bed chatting about the day ahead. Gina elaborated further on their exchange in an interview with us: 'It was the last time that I saw her and it was just before she got ready for the day. We were sitting on her bed and she had her laptop. She asked if she could show me the pictures she was printing for Oscar for Valentine's Day. It was some pictures of them together and one picture of her alone and one picture of him alone. She turned around to me and showed me the picture of him. And she said, "Gi, does that not look like the face of a murderer?" We laughed because we called him the stalker. She was joking around. She definitely wasn't serious about it.'

Samantha repeatedly returns to that final Tuesday evening she spent lazing on the carpet with Reeva, 'faffing' and pondering the future. Reeva, a romantic with a penchant for celebrating special occasions, had big plans for Valentine's Day. So much so that the day before she posted this tweet:

> What do you have up your sleeve for your love tomorrow??? *#getexcited*
> *#ValentinesDay*

Samantha gives a rare insight into what Reeva had up her own sleeve for her love. 'She had planned this whole thing, she was so excited. She was like that, she liked special occasions,' Sam remembers. Reeva was plotting an elaborate breakfast picnic in the garden of Oscar's home, replete with heart-shaped biscuits.

'She had planned to make a whole breakfast. They were going to get up early and they were going to have a picnic in the garden. She would make heart-shaped biscuits and make a picnic. She had gone and got heart-shaped sweets, you know those little sherbet things that say, "I love you," and stuff all over them. She was planning on making him pancakes with Nutella. She was going to get up early, go and put the blanket out in the garden, put stuff around it at sunrise as a surprise ...' Samantha trails off. Reeva had also planned on giving her 'boo' a framed photograph of them, which she had wrapped.

In an interview she gave to ZAlebs just days before her death, Reeva spoke of how she planned on spending the day spreading love: 'I've realised that although Valentine's Day can be a cheesy money-making stint to most people, it's a day of expressing love across the world. It doesn't have to only be between lovers, but by telling a friend that you care, or even an old person that they are still appreciated.'

According to the *Mail & Guardian* newspaper, Reeva visited Party Box Goodies, a gift shop in the Hazeldean Square shopping centre up the road from Oscar's house on the afternoon before her death. She apparently told the shop assistant, 'My boyfriend really loves Valentine's Day' as she purchased wrapping paper for the gift:

> *She was there to buy 'Valentine's Day wrapping paper', according to the shop assistant who helped Steenkamp. The assistant, who asked not to be named, said that the blonde model appeared happy and in love. 'She was smiling and laughing when she arrived,' said the assistant. 'She walked out smiling, too ... I offered to wrap the gift for her. It was a photo frame and four photographs of the two of them [Pistorius and Steenkamp]. I told her that it's good for women to give Valentine's Day gifts instead of*

expecting presents from their boyfriends. She agreed, and added: 'This is a surprise for him. He loves surprises.'

Reeva was meant to meet Gina for coffee on the afternoon of Wednesday, 13 February, but because she was already in Pretoria, she decided not to.

'I finished my job at about two and she said she was going to come through to Joburg, and when I finished I messaged her and she just said, "My Gi, I'm still in Pretoria." She was so excited and she had planned all these new things and she told me about certain goals that she had and she was *really* excited that day and I even said to her, I said, "You know I'm here to support you for anything and I'm so happy to hear that and I'm so excited for you."'

• • •

At around 6pm, Reeva pulled up to the security access point at the Silver Woods estate, the window rolled down and her elbow resting on the door of her gun-metal-grey Mini Cooper. Her hair was tied up and she was wearing a simple black vest. Reeva smiled broadly as she exchanged a laugh and bantered with a guard at the boom before being waved through into the complex. Some ten minutes later, Oscar's white BMW pulled in to the estate. He had driven through from Johannesburg where he had been visiting Justin at the Daytona Group in Sandton. Samantha recalls the day vividly because she had tried to get Oscar to lure his girlfriend to Johannesburg so that she could go to a movie with her.

'I'd finished work at about three and I'd said to her I wanted to go to a movie that night. I was going to go to movies on my own. I'd sent her a message at about ten in the morning and she said, "Ja, okay, let me just see how my day goes, I'll message you." I went past the dealership just to say hi to Just, and Oscar was there. I was standing with him at reception and Justin was going out for dinner with two of his guy friends that night, so I said to him, "You go for dinner with Justin. Phone your girlfriend and tell her to come here to come to movies with me."

'Reeva had messaged Oscar earlier in the day indicating she might drive through to Joburg, but wanted to get a few things done at his house in Pretoria. "Baba I hope u don't mind but I came back to the house to work a bit and do some washing. It will help me a lot to get stuff done and relieve some stress. Ill go through to Jhb at like 3 xxx".

'So he phoned her while he was standing with me and it was so cute, "Boo Boo, don't you want to come here and bring me a change of clothes and then

I'll go to dinner with Justin and you go to a movie with Sam and then either we can sleep over there or we'll drive back after or something." I heard her saying, "Hmmm, I'm so tired, I'm already at your house and I don't want to drive from Pretoria now." She said, "Please just come home and let's snuggle. Just come over and let's like chill and make a veggie burger or something." That was their night in: veggie burgers. He got off the phone and he said, "Oooh, I better go home!" So I left it. I went to a movie on my own, Justin went to dinner. That was it.

'The last time I WhatsApped her was at six or seven. I think I sent her a message saying, "Fader." I think I might have actually taken a photo of the movie house going, "Here's me on my own with my popcorn and my slush and I hope you're enjoying yourself." She replied, "Oh, I love you, I'm tired, I'll see you tomorrow. Sorry." Just like she always is …'

Samantha can't help but wonder what would have been had she pushed harder for her friend to join her that night. 'I often think I wish I had forced her to come because I … I don't know. I don't know what happened that night, and I don't know if, if she had come and then gone back that the same thing would have happened. I can't help but think if I had just changed the series of events, maybe from earlier, then it wouldn't have happened but, ja, you can't …'

There was nothing in Oscar's behaviour that afternoon that struck Samantha as curious or out of character and there was no indication from her best friend that things were not as they should be. 'She didn't lose it with him or anything. As far as I know they chilled and watched a movie. The last time she was on the phone on WhatsApp was at 21:13.' At 20:42 Reeva had sent Gina's mother a message telling her she wouldn't be home: 'My Des!!!! I'm staying in PTA again it's soooooo far to drive I just decided to stay here today and work! See u for valentines day xxxxx.'

Samantha returned home after her movie and went to sleep. But she was startled awake at 4am when Justin's phone rang. It was Oscar.

The Bullet in the Chamber

He shook the hands of the competitors in the lanes alongside him, paced up and down the track, crouched into his stance and pressed his carbon blades against the starting blocks. A smile stretched across his face. Eighty thousand people hushed, awaiting the crack of the starter's gun. His grandmother was in the crowd, so too were other family members and close friends. It was 4 August 2012 and Oscar Pistorius, from Pretoria in South Africa, was about to become the first amputee in history to compete on the track, and the first double amputee to take part in the Olympic Games. For years, he had persistently, doggedly, fought for the right to be able to compete in able-bodied competition, insisting that he did not unfairly benefit from his prosthetic legs. Courtrooms full of men and women had argued and debated the merits of his case, determining his future. All the toil and the training had culminated in this moment – he was the real deal, a global icon, a respected superstar. And he was on top of the world.

Not only would he compete, but Oscar would coast through the first heat of the 400 metres race in a second place time of 45.44 seconds, reaching the semi-final the next day. He would finish last in that race but would go on to carry his country's flag at the Olympic Games closing ceremony days later – a celebrated hero.

'I've worked for six years to get my chance. I found myself smiling in the starting block, which is very rare in the 400 metres,' said the Blade Runner after the race. 'I didn't know if I should cry or be happy. It was such a mix of emotions.' He paid tribute to his late mother and recalled her advice: 'A loser isn't the person that gets involved and comes last, but the person who doesn't get involved in the first place.'

• • •

It was these words that Oscar's mother wrote to him in a letter when he was a baby, just before surgeons performed his bilateral amputation at the age of 11 months. She would keep the letter for him to read as an adult.

Oscar was born on 22 November 1986 at the Sandton Clinic in Johannesburg. He suffered from fibular hemimelia, the congenital absence of the fibula – the bone that extends from the ankle to the knee. His feet were also malformed. Each only had a big toe and an index toe and was missing the outer bones.

His parents Henke and Sheila set out on a 'pilgrimage' to seek medical opinions. In his book *Blade Runner*, authored with Gianni Merlo, Oscar recounts how they were insistent on researching alternatives that would allow him to lead the most 'normal' life possible: 'At the end of every consultation, my father would ask the surgeon one question: "If it was your child and you were unable to operate yourself, who would you turn to?" In this way, my parents were able to tap into a network of extraordinary surgeons and trusted hands.'

Their search led them to South African specialist Dr Gerry Versveld, who was convinced that if they took the bold decision to amputate both legs below the knee while Oscar was still young, he would be able to learn to walk with prostheses. 'I have a profound respect for them [my parents] because it cannot have been easy, but then again the Pistoriuses are a stubborn people,' says Oscar.

Six months after the double amputation, Oscar received his first pair of prosthetic legs at the age of 17 months. Made from plaster and mesh and with a flesh-coloured lycra 'skin', they gave him the mobility he craved to become a 'wild child', following his older brother Carl everywhere he adventured. Oscar believes that his personality and outlook on life were shaped around this time, when his family was instrumental in laying the foundation stones of his competitive nature. His parents pushed him forward, encouraging him to try every kind of physical activity, rather than playing into the label of being 'disabled'. As Carl, 18 months his elder, put on his shoes every morning, so Oscar would put on his prostheses. 'It was all the same to me,' he insists.

'This attitude is integral to how my family approaches life and their philosophy has made me the man I am today: "This is Oscar Pistorius, exactly as he should be. Perfect in himself." My brother, sister and I were brought up with one iron rule – no one was allowed to say: "I can't",' he explains in his book. In a letter written to him by Carl, his brother echoes this sentiment: 'Part and parcel of our family's approach to life is the lesson that if you lose your way in life, no one can find it for you, you have to do it yourself. Only you can help yourself. You must rely on yourself and find that way and stay true to that way.'

Oscar won his first sporting trophy when he was only six years old – for

Greco-Roman wrestling. At the age of nine, he took up boxing. He played tennis, rugby and cricket and even played provincial-level water polo. Oscar did not see himself as disabled and his competitiveness drove him. He says in his book, 'I won my first medal in wrestling. The first time you win an award is an unforgettable moment. You are enveloped in a warm buzz of emotions – pride, happiness, and the acute sense of recognition that comes with applause from your loved ones. It is addictive, almost like a drug – but a positive drug, pushing you forward to greater success.'

Oscar's life took a significant detour in 1993 when his parents parted ways, and the divorce impacted significantly on the family's financial welfare. Henke Pistorius came from hard-earned wealth. In 1944, his father, 'Oom Hendrik', started a limestone mine that still operates today as H. Pistorius & Co., 'the oldest supplier of the best quality agricultural lime in South Africa'. It would prove to be the foundation of a business empire that has expanded into various fields, most notably commercial property development.

Oom Hendrik's four sons, Theo, Arnold, Leo and Henke, all played a role within the family business, but Oscar's father has since been cast in the role of pariah, the black sheep of the flock. It is a tightly knit Afrikaner unit and many of the next generation of grandchildren and their spouses are also employed by the family business. According to company registers, the patriarch and the three sons own around 120 active companies in the country. Henke, meanwhile, has had less success in business and has invested his energy in a dolomite mine in the Eastern Cape.

In his book, Oscar recalled how he, his older brother Carl and little sister Aimee, had to watch their pennies, which taught them all financial responsibility. 'As small children we lived in an enormous house and were spoilt rotten, and so when my parents divorced and we were forced to downsize we had no understanding of real hardship. Fortunately there is always a constructive lesson to be drawn from these experiences.'

During his early years, Oscar's mother, 'an optimist with a bubbly personality' and a 'great sense of humour', didn't work but his father's bankruptcy and his parents' split put an end to the idyll. Sheila had to take a part-time job but still ensured that Oscar received the best care and specialist attention for his prostheses and benefited from latest technological advancements. 'I remember her baking a cake in honour of my first set of toes!' he recounts.

Although the children lived with their mother, their father was still very much a part of their lives and the relationship remained 'amicable' and 'mutually respectful'. Oscar writes about how his father spoilt them and ensured they never wanted for anything, buying his kids go-karts and boats. But over the years, the distance between Oscar and his father grew, as indicated in an interview conducted with *The Guardian*'s Donald McRae in 2011. 'My father wasn't around much when we grew up. I saw him seldom – and it's the same now. He lives and works very far from me on a dolomite mine.' When asked if he and his dad spoke on the phone, Pistorius replied: 'Mmmm, not much. We chat about once a month. He's a cool guy but he's more of a mate. He's not much of a parent. It's just life.'

When Oscar reached high-school age, his parents allowed him the choice of which institution to attend. Having been raised in Johannesburg, he decided he wanted a change and chose the highly regarded Pretoria Boys High School, an English-language boarding school. This was despite his father having attended the neighbouring Afrikaans school, Affies. The two schools were rivals on the sports fields and it would have been tradition for Oscar to follow in his father's footsteps – perhaps an early indication of his intentions to be his own man and distance himself from his dad. Oscar flourished at Pretoria Boys where sport was high on the priority list and he was taken by the facilities available to pupils. 'There was even a shooting range,' he would recall.

He remembers himself as a content boarder with many friends, who was both the perpetrator and subject of practical jokes. On one memorable occasion, his dorm mates managed to fill him with terror. They used lighter fuel to set fire to steel cupboards in his room in the middle of the night. When Oscar lurched for his prostheses, which he diligently left at the foot of his bed each night, he couldn't find them. He became panic-stricken and thought he would be left to die when suddenly the fire magically disappeared. The boys came running back into the room laughing and informed him that it was all a hilarious practical joke – their way of extending him a 'warm welcome'.

In his first year at Pretoria Boys, Oscar was a keen cricketer and tennis player, but as he grew in confidence he decided to pursue his ambition to play rugby and water polo. He excelled at rugby in particular and was assisted by new, lighter prostheses designed by his father's friend, aeronautical engineer Chris Hattingh. The legs were handcrafted, relatively short and shaped liked hooks, precursors to the 'blades' for which he would become universally known. While Oscar didn't participate in athletics, he did well in the occasional long-distance endurance race and running was an important component of his rugby training. Sport would prove to be the teenager's salvation when he was hit by the most devastating development in his short life.

Oscar's mother, Sheila, died on 6 March 2002. The athlete has since had the date tattooed alongside her birth date, in Roman numerals on the inside of his right arm. On his left shoulder is a Bible verse from 1 Corinthians: 'Therefore I do not run like someone running aimlessly; I do not fight like a boxer beating the air. No, I strike a blow to my body and make it my slave so that after I have preached to others, I myself will not be disqualified for the prize.'

Sheila had remarried a few months prior to falling sick with a viral illness that was initially misdiagnosed. She fell into a coma and Oscar was regularly summoned to the hospital after his mother had taken a turn for the worse. Despite these false alarms, Oscar vividly remembers the day he and Carl were rushed to the hospital for the last time. It has left an indelible mark on his memory, as he recounts: 'That day I was at school in a history lesson when the school principal interrupted the class to tell me I had ten minutes to collect my things; my father would be waiting for me at the school gate. Carl and I arrived at the gate just in time to witness my father driving his enormous Mercedes towards us at breakneck speed. It was clear that something was not right: he was shouting at us to hurry up and get in, and seemed to be on the verge of tears. Although my parents had been divorced for years they still felt great affection for one another. All of our closest friends and family were at the hospital, and it became increasingly obvious that this day was different and that my mother was very close to death. We were rushed into her room to be by her side, and ten minutes later she left us. It was a very distressing moment.' Oscar was only 15 years old at the time.

With their mother's passing, the Pistorius children became like 'rudderless boats', floating between boarding school, their aunt Diane's home and the houses of their friends. Oscar found solace in sport. 'Sport was my salvation, as it helped me get through this difficult time. My mother had been a strong woman, the centre of my world. Sporting activity was the only thing that could distract me from such a loss,' Oscar stated in his book.

But Oscar experienced another 'traumatic' and 'life-changing' event the following year when he suffered a significant rugby injury. He was tackled badly and broke his leg, preventing him from playing the sport again.

As part of his rehabilitation process, Oscar began physiotherapy at the Sports Science Institute and was instructed to start sprint training to regain functionality in his knee joint. It was then that he was put in touch with coach Ampie Louw, who remained with him throughout his career. The combination of the training regime and new, lighter 'Flex-Foot Cheetah' prosthetic legs meant Oscar developed a keen interest in running and realised his potential. In his first competitive race in January 2004 he broke the 100 metres world record, with a time of 11.72 seconds – 0.48 seconds faster than the previous record for double amputees. Within a month, Oscar had improved his time, broke the record again and competed in the South African Disabled Games. His participation introduced him to a new world of disabled sport that he had never delved into before – but he was still intent on returning to the rugby field with able-bodied competitors.

After only eight months of athletics, he had been chosen to compete in the Paralympics in Athens in 2004, aged a mere 17. Overcoming nerves, competing against sporting legends such as Marlon Shirley and Brian Frasure and four false starts, Oscar won the gold medal in the 200 metres race. He had tasted a new high.

Oscar had also discovered a new universe. 'It opened my eyes to a world that I had previously been disdainful of. I began to understand that by partici-pating solely in able-bodied sport, I was depriving myself; I had never before enjoyed similar levels of sporting camaraderie and sportsmanship. Disabled sport is equally competitive – after all, it is a competition between serious, dedi-cated athletes – but a unique atmosphere of profound mutual respect prevails. I came to regret having come to disabled sport so late, and in particular to races between amputee athletes.'

Overnight, Oscar became a sporting celebrity and was elevated to the level of superhero for disabled people worldwide. In his personal life, Oscar had also found young and tempestuous love for the first time with a youthful woman named Vicky Miles, whom he talks about as 'beautiful, charming and unusual'. In his book, Oscar talks about falling head over heels in love a total of four times by the age of 24. Many of these relationships were defined by passionate peaks and troughs, intense love and ugly arguments.

'Our relationship was very intense and, although this most probably con-tributed to our eventual separation, it meant that while we were together we approached every moment as though it was our most important, indeed our last. We had a very fiery relationship and often rowed,' he wrote about his time with Vicky, which came to an end after two years.

Oscar became a prefect in his final year of high school in 2005 and profes-sionally he continued to break through virtual ceilings. He competed in the able-bodied South African Championships and finished sixth in the 400 metres race. He also took part in a number of events recognised by the International Association of Athletics Federations (IAAF) and was invited to attend races internationally.

In 2006, Oscar enrolled at the University of Pretoria to study for a Bachelor of Commerce degree, specialising in Sport Science. He also continued to compete more seriously and changed his manager, from his father Henke to Peet van Zyl, a 'quasi-father figure'. The agent would be called upon numerous times not only to manage Oscar's skyrocketing public profile, but to rescue him from trouble, and would also testify for him in his murder trial.

One such incident from which Oscar did indeed need rescuing was in August 2006 when he landed up behind bars for the first time. Having already developed a keen interest in firearms, Oscar was at a shooting range with a friend when gunpowder rubbed off onto his prosthetic legs. A week later, he flew to Assen in the Netherlands for the Disabled World Championships where he won a gold medal and improved his times in all three of his chosen disciplines. But on the way home via Iceland, Oscar lost his airplane ticket and was interrogated and searched by airport security. When they discovered the gunpowder residue on his prosthetics, Oscar was immediately arrested and accused of terrorism.

He says, 'Then, again, without warning, an officer appeared with my belongings in tow, and told me that I was free to go as the security risk had been neutralized.' He finally managed to get on a flight home.

Back home and on the track, Oscar was training harder than ever before in the hope of qualifying for the Beijing Olympics in 2008. But as his times improved, so too did the controversy around him. Some began to suggest that his blades were giving him an unfair advantage and needed to be viewed with circumspection. This was the start of a more fundamental challenge for Oscar – not just to qualify to take part in the Olympic Games, but to prove that he was in fact entitled to participate in the competition.

Oscar had previously been invited to participate in the Helsinki Grand Prix but was unable to do so because of school commitments. In 2007, he finally felt that his qualifying times were good enough for him to be competing at such a high level internationally. Ironically, it so happened that in March 2007, the IAAF met in Mombasa in Kenya to adopt a rule that would for all intents and purposes impede his participation.

Rule 144-2 prohibited the use of 'any technical devices designed to improve performance' during a race. In short, it prevented the use of any device that would see one athlete benefit from technology over another. Some believed that the rule was adopted to target Oscar specifically and stop him from competing in events, but in June the IAAF issued a press release stating that the rule was not to be interpreted as concerning his sporting participation, at least until proper testing could be done on his prostheses. This meant that, despite the swirling controversy and negative press, Oscar could compete and did so in the 400 metres event at the Rome Golden Gala in July 2007. He came second in a time of 46.90 seconds – but more crucially, he had made history. It was the first time, at the Olympic stadium in Rome no less, that a disabled athlete had competed alongside able-bodied competitors at international level.

Of course, this meant that the media scrutiny and the criticism from naysayers would be ramped up. This was amplified by the British media who bombarded the runner with questions about the IAAF decision and whether his Cheetahs – his artificial blades – improperly benefited him on the track. Why should he want to take part in the Olympic Games when the Paralympics had been designed for people with just his kind of disability? Did he consider the Paralympic Games inferior?

'I believe the two games are not mutually exclusive. It is not because I am able to compete in the Olympics that I will not compete in the Paralympics. To me the Olympics are just another sporting avenue and like most other athletes I am eager to explore every possibility and to be present and competitive in all the top sporting arenas. I do not consider the Paralympics to be inferior, merely different, and it remains incontestable that the Olympics are the ultimate sporting event. I am not a Paralympic athlete, nor am I an Olympic athlete. I am simply an athlete and a sprinter,' Oscar explains in his book.

Oscar was becoming increasingly well known for his resilience and perseverance in his dogged attempt to compete. This was largely attributed to his attitude to life in general, as he sets out in his autobiography. 'If God were to ask me if I wanted my legs back, I would really have to think carefully about my answer. I do not feel remotely as if I have been short-changed by life. Had I been born with normal legs I would not be the man I am today. My less-than-ordinary life has helped my potential to shine through. I am not sure that I would have had the same motivation and determination to improve myself and become an athlete.'

With the 2007 racing season over, Oscar returned home to South Africa with a shadow hanging heavily over his career and his achievements. The IAAF had taken the decision to carry out tests in the November of that year to prove definitively whether or not his prostheses constituted a technical advantage. The tests would be conducted at the German Sport University Cologne, supervised by the renowned Professor of Biomechanics, Dr Gert-Peter Brüggemann. The IAAF had already begun studying Oscar's blades at the Golden Gala in Rome when high-resolution cameras were installed along the length of the track to measure his stride. Technicians at the University of Rome subsequently found that his stride was not longer than that of other athletes, but they did discover that Oscar's performance could be measured differently to other athletes. While most able-bodied athletes reach the peak of their race in the first 70 metres, he starts slowly and peaks at around 200 metres to 300 metres.

So it was that Oscar subjected himself to two days of tests in Germany that saw his performance being measured alongside five other able-bodied athletes who had run similar 400 metres times to him. 'The tests themselves were conducted in a circus-like atmosphere. I was at the centre of a throng made up of doctors, scientists, technicians and then the cameramen who were filming the procedure for the IAAF; the pressure on me was intense. This was the first time ever that the IAAF (or anyone else for that matter) had dedicated time and resources to researching the question of prosthetics.'

A month later a leaked copy of Professor Brüggemann's report was published by German newspaper *Die Welt*, days before Oscar had been sent a copy. The tests had found that over a distance of 400 metres, his prosthetic limbs gave him an unfair advantage, effectively banning him from competing in able-bodied competition. Professor Brüggemann found that the carbon-fibre prostheses constituted a mechanical advantage because the energy restored from the track to the athlete is over three times higher with a prosthetic limb. He also found that Oscar was able to run at the same speed as able-bodied athletes while expending 25 per cent less energy and this explained why he was so much faster towards the end of a 400 metres race.

Oscar had until 10 January to comment on the Brüggemann report – which didn't leave him much time. Together with Peet van Zyl, he discussed the findings with experts around the world, specifically the University of Miami's Professor Robert Gailey. Oscar's backers didn't disagree with the research and tests conducted in Cologne but did take issue with the interpretation of the data. In short, they argued that the analysis could not only be conducted on the final phase of a 400 metres race, but rather that each phase of the race should be studied. They also insisted that both the positive and negative implications of prosthetic limbs must be considered and not merely the benefits. As a result, Oscar responded to the IAAF by the deadline of 10 January, arguing that the tests were biased and were limited in scope and that the conclusions should be rejected. The IAAF responded by ratifying its ban, effectively barring Oscar from competing in able-bodied competition. His only choice was to appeal to the Court of Arbitration for Sport in Lausanne, Switzerland.

Oscar thus needed to put together a team of experts to run their own tests that would challenge those conducted in Germany. This team included Professor Hugh Herr from the Massachusetts Institute of Technology, himself a double amputee; Professor Rodger Kram from the University of Colorado; and Professor Peter Weyand from Rice University in Houston. Legally, Oscar was assisted by law firm Dewey & LeBoeuf, which had contacted him offering its services. It was agreed that the tests would be conducted in Houston in February, days after Oscar attended the Laureus Awards in St Petersburg in Russia.

'It was soon clear that the Houston results would differ from those charted in Cologne,' said Oscar in his book. 'This was a huge relief to me, as the IAAF had relied heavily on these specific tests results to demonstrate my technical advantage. Over a period of ten days I participated in many different tests; at times I thought that I was repeating the same experiment endlessly, but in reality there were slight but significant variations both in the focus and in what was required of me. My acceleration was studied in detail; my oxygen consumption was measured at different speeds at different points during the race, as was the conduct and handling of my individual prostheses. I learnt much over this period, and left Houston feeling resolved and confident that the process would prove that the tests in Cologne had been inconclusive.'

By March, Oscar's team had reached the conclusion that there was no way that his prostheses gave him a technical advantage over other athletes. 'When one considers all the hard work and emotional turmoil, all the controversy and speculation, it was immensely gratifying finally to be able to repudiate my critics and show that my achievements were mine alone and dependent on my commitment, training and talent and not my prosthetic limbs,' he reflected in his book.

As Oscar waited for the Court of Arbitration hearing scheduled for late April, he concentrated on life at home, his training schedule, a new love interest and a new house – in Silver Woods in Pretoria. The new girlfriend was Jenna Edkins, who Oscar describes in his book as 'a delightful, sweet-natured, beautiful' 18-year-old with blonde hair and 'sparkling eyes'. The new house was in an upmarket, green area of the capital in a secure housing estate, which Oscar found went a long way towards helping him feel 'more stable and rooted' in life. 'After my mother's passing and my years in boarding school I found that I was yearning for a space of my own that I could make my home. In truth the house is much larger than I need, but I wanted it to be somewhere I would be able to grow into and where all of my family and friends would be welcome to spend time or just drop in,' Oscar says in his book.

He had a 'substantial' wooden table made up for entertaining and fitted the house with several television screens, all with the intention that the airy, open-plan house would be a homely, hospitable spot for entertaining. Oscar wanted the house to be a venue where he, his family and his friends could 'make the most of being together and celebrate life'. His two dogs, Silo an American pit bull and Enzo, a bull terrier named after Enzo Ferrari, shared the house with him.

At the end of April, Oscar and his team flew to Lausanne for the hearings at the joint International Olympic Committee and the Court of Arbitration for Sport headquarters. His fate on the athletic track would be decided by a room full of officious lawyers – unforeseen preparation for what would come later in life on a far more intensive level when his fate would again be determined by the law. Oscar admits he found the pace intense and was 'absolutely gripped' by the proceedings, which he found 'fascinating'. The judges' mandate was only to examine the issue objectively because Oscar was not being accused of any wrongdoing as such. 'It was rather unusual to see everybody come together and debate and dissect the matter intelligently and dispassionately, without the adversarial climate that is often created when you have two opposing teams and a person in the dock who has allegedly committed some misdemeanour,' he wrote in his memoir. 'I also found the hearings psychologically very demanding. Not only was this my last chance, but my battle, which had started as a personal quest born out of personal frustration, had developed into a symbolic fight against discrimination. I felt that I had come to represent all people like me, both today and in the future, who play sport or anything else for that matter and who want to be treated as equals.'

The court returned a verdict in May, while Oscar was in Milan, waiting in the offices of his lawyers. It ruled to overturn the ban, having found that it was not possible to conclude that the prosthetic limbs gave him a technical advantage over other athletes. This was because at no time was it conclusively proven that the advantages of competing with the prostheses outweighed the disadvantages of competing with those same limbs.

Even the IAAF seemed pleased with the outcome of the appeal court, which effectively was a loss for them. A picture of Oscar racing around a track on his J-shaped blades was posted on the association's website and a statement was released by the IAAF's president Lamine Diack. 'Oscar will be welcomed wherever he competes this summer. He is an inspirational man, and we look forward to admiring his achievements in the future.'

By this point, however, there were just four months to go until the Olympics in Beijing and attention was now firmly fixed on whether he would qualify to compete. 'It's still going to be difficult. I've missed lots of races,' Oscar was quoted in *The Washington Post*. 'Now that the ban's been lifted, my focus is back on athletics. I'm psyched about that.'

To qualify for South Africa's Olympics team, the 21-year-old still needed to shave half a second off his personal best time in the 400 metres, from 46.56 seconds to 45.95 seconds. There was the possibility that South African officials could name him as a member of the country's 400 metres relay unit, but the national team was unlikely to be good enough to qualify for Beijing.

South African athletic officials went so far as to waive the requirement that Olympics-bound athletes compete in the national championships in March. They planned to accept any qualifying time from a sanctioned event, anywhere in the world. Oscar had several races already scheduled in Europe before South Africa had to announce its Olympic team in July. 'The young man is a fighter,' said Leonard Chuene, then president of Athletics South Africa. 'Let's give him opportunity and support, and I believe very strongly he will make it.'

Despite running a personal best 46.25 in the 400 metres at the Spitzen Leichtathletik meeting in Lucerne, Oscar failed to meet the Olympic 'A' standard qualifying time by 0.70 seconds. His ability to train had clearly been derailed by the ongoing scientific testing and court proceedings and he was forced to be realistic. Instead, his focus shifted to the Paralympics in Beijing where he wowed, overcoming disappointment by winning the sprint triple – the 100 metres, 200 metres and 400 metres races.

Oscar had tasted Paralympic Gold again and with the door open to him to compete in the able-bodied Olympics, his gaze was set on London in 2012. By this stage, his star had also been elevated and he had been launched as a global superstar. 'The fastest man with no legs', as he was endearingly labelled, was named in *Time* magazine's list of 100 most influential people, listed third in the 'Heroes and Pioneers' category. He became the face of international fashion brands such as Thierry Mugler, Oakley and Nike. He also developed an appetite for the fast life, driving luxury sports cars and indulging his passion for firearms.

But cracks also began to appear in the golden boy's public profile, and he occasionally made the headlines for the wrong reasons. And yet, despite this, the shine never quite tarnished – no one wanted to face up to the athlete's less inspirational qualities.

• • •

He realised the boat was filling with water. All he had heard was the splintering sound of the crash and knew he had to keep calm. He lifted his hand to his face and felt blood. He could also feel that much of his face was smashed in from the nose down.

As paramedics rushed to the scene of the accident at the Vaal River, so too did Oscar Pistorius's cousins. The group had been enjoying a Saturday out on the water on 21 February 2009. Some wanted to return to shore and Oscar suggested they travel with his cousin in another boat. The athlete and a friend, John, wanted to take a slow sunset cruise.

Oscar testified in his murder trial about the events leading up to the accident.

'We were on the water, I guess about just before six o' clock. We met some of my family and friends at another place on the water and on returning, there were a couple of people on my boat and some of them were in a rush to get back to the house to cook dinner and so my cousin was in another boat and I suggested that they go with him, as we were just taking a leisurely cruise up the river and it was just my friend John and I in the boat and at a point we were just chatting, sitting and chatting and at a point he stood up to, I think to light a cigarette or to make a phone call and at that point he shouted and I looked forward and I could not see anything.

'The Vaal river runs from east to west, and we were heading back west, so the sun was setting in front of us and I could only see the sun on the water, and a couple of seconds later, I just remember the sounds of the propeller, the boat, and I hit the steering wheel and the propeller went into the air. I remember the sound of the engine.'

The accident changed Oscar's life – he 'thought it was all over'. He was airlifted to Milpark Hospital in Johannesburg where he spent five days in intensive care, three of which were in a medically induced coma. He suffered serious head and facial injuries, a broken jaw, a smashed eye socket and broken ribs as a result of the impact.

While Oscar didn't go into detail about the crash in his autobiography, he did acknowledge that he needed to be more responsible. 'I love racing, speedboats, cars and bikes. My love of racing is something I need to keep in check; I can't afford the risk of getting hurt and disrupting my training. I guess I learnt that the hard way, with 180 stitches and several broken bones from a massive accident in 2009, when my speedboat hit a submerged pier. But, truth be told, I've been breaking bones all my life.'

Reports following the crash suggested that all was not as innocent as it seemed. Initially, it was reported that the boat had hit a submerged tree stump but then it was revealed that he had actually crashed into a jetty.

Bottles of alcohol had reportedly been found on the recovered boat and eyewitnesses told us that members of Oscar's party were 'rat-faced' drunk. At the time, a witness also told *The Times* newspaper that the runner had been at the Stonehaven River Pub before the accident 'watching rugby and having a few drinks'. Oscar's manager Peet van Zyl confirmed that he had been at the pub but denied the drinking. Oscar also denied being drunk during the incident when he testified in his murder trial years later.

Police confirmed that they were investigating the possibility that the consumption of alcohol had played a role in the accident and were considering a case of negligent driving.

Oscar's blood alcohol was not tested following the crash. The blood alcohol limit for operators of water-borne vessels is 0.05 grams alcohol per 100 milliltres blood – the same as for motorists. Two weeks after the incident the National Prosecuting Authority took a decision not to prosecute Oscar. 'There are not sufficient grounds,' then National Prosecuting Authority spokesperson Tlali Tlali confirmed.

However, after Oscar testified about the incident in court, the same eyewitness who had told us about the incident in 2009 came forward to the Daily Maverick and Eyewitness News alleging that the athlete had lied about the incident during his testimony. Michael Aitken, a property owner on the Vaal and MD of a telecommunications company, was on the scene of the accident, and took issue with Oscar's claim that the accident had happened at sunset because the setting sun was in his eyes.

'It's such an absolute fib. He says this thing scarred him. It would scar you if you crash into a stationary object in the middle of the night while tearing down the river in party mode.'

Aitken says he and 11 guests were eating dinner at his weekend home, after 8pm, when his butler came to inform him that there were people 'crying' in the river.

'I, together with a guest, Mr Markus Schorn, ran to my boat, which was moored in the river, and began to search for the people who were calling. As it was very dark, it took a few minutes to locate the people. We found two men standing chest deep in the water. The one was calling frantically and the other, standing hugging himself, appeared to be in shock. They seemed to be unaware that the river bank was only a metre or two behind them, and that they could have walked out of the water.'

Aitken says he didn't see any damage to Oscar's face and his boat had sunk without a trace. They were about to take the men aboard his boat when another barge approached at speed. 'The people on board called out to us to leave as the men in the river were "their people". Mr Schorn and I concurred in our opinion that the people on the barge appeared to be very drunk. This was made more apparent by the actions of a young woman on the barge who leapt into the water from the bow of the moving barge, narrowly avoiding injury.'

Aitken is adamant that the crash happened hours after the sun had set. 'In my mind it was round about nine o'clock at night. It was very dark and we had difficulty finding these guys in the dark.' Schorn has also confirmed Aitken's version of events.

Media reports in 2009 gave various times for the accident having taken place from 20:30 until 22:00, all well after sunset. The Daily Maverick quoted another individual, not part of Aitken's dining group, as saying that he had an altercation with Oscar on the river that same evening, which occurred 'long' after sunset – and before the accident.

After Oscar's testimony in court, a pleasure-boat operator at the Vaal made another revelation to us. He claims that he had a confrontation with the athlete after sunset on the night of the incident, that Oscar was drunk and that he showed him his gun.

The operator, who does not want to be named, says that around 30 people were having a party on the top deck of his boat, when Oscar and two friends pulled up wanting to buy drinks.

'His boat was full of booze, bottles, bottles, all over the place. They were pissed as farts. They called us a bunch of Engelsmanne [Englishmen], we told him he was a Dutchman and should fuck off. He said, "Do you know who I am? My name is Oscar Pistorius. I'm the Blade Runner." He lifted up his shirt and showed me his gun in his shorts. Then he put his shirt down, climbed into his boat and left. That was at about 7:30pm. The police came to me the next morning and asked if I want to lay a charge. I said no, there was no fight, he was just cheeky.'

We have not been able to confirm whether this incident took place, but Aitken, Schorn and the pleasure-boat operator all cast doubt on Oscar's version that his boating accident had occurred at sunset.

• • •

In the same year as the boating incident, the National Prosecuting Authority was again called upon to consider whether or not to prosecute Oscar Pistorius in a court of law. The golden boy, with a squeaky clean reputation, shocked many when he was arrested following an apparent assault at a house party at his Silver Woods home. He spent a night in the holding cells at the Boschkop police station after being charged with grievous bodily harm to student Cassidy Taylor-Memmory. The charge was downgraded and eventually dropped but Oscar's reputation was impacted by the publicity around the incident and the matter resulted in a messy civil dispute that dragged on for years.

Taylor-Memmory, a timid, young blogger from Pretoria, who runs a website called The Glam Green Girl, attended a party at Oscar's house on 12 September

2009. Her friend Melissa Rom was dating the athlete at the time and Taylor-Memmory had only met him once before. She and two other friends arrived late as they had been at their part-time student jobs. She claims she and her friends sat in the garden enjoying the party until Oscar and his girlfriend began to fight.

'This led to Oscar asking all of Melissa's friends to leave, using vulgar language. I had left my handbag in the garden where we all had been sitting and needed to get back into his property to fetch it. As I approached his large outside doors, Oscar was furiously trying to close them. He started to punch the door and that is when one of the top door panels fell and hit my left leg. Six weeks prior to the party my plaster cast had just come off after having reconstructive surgery on my left ankle. After this happened I went to tell Oscar that he had hurt me to which he replied, "Well, go call your fucking lawyer", recalls Taylor-Memmory.

'After the incident at Oscar's house I arrived home and was hysterically crying. Like any loving parents would do, my parents wanted to protect me and my mom and dad felt it was best to let the police deal with the matter and for them to decide what should be done. The police saw the cut on my leg and they thought it would be best to open a case of assault against Oscar,' she recounts. Taylor-Memmory's mother opened the case with the Boschkop police and investigating officer Hilton Botha was appointed to the case.

This was the first time the policeman met the athlete. Curiously, Taylor-Memmory's lawyer Ladine Botha told the *Mail & Guardian* that records at the police station did not show that Oscar was either processed or booked in there and that the cell's register book did not reflect his name. Hilton Botha also chose not to raise this prior arrest during Oscar's bail application following Reeva's death but was pushed into divulging the details by the enquiring magistrate.

At around 10pm on the Saturday night, the 22-year-old athlete was arrested on a charge of assault with intent to do grievous bodily harm. After being held in custody overnight, the charge was downgraded to assault. Oscar released a statement saying that he had asked Taylor-Memmory to leave the party and she reacted unhappily, kicking the door, which broke, injuring her. 'I categorically deny that I in any way assaulted the woman,' said Oscar. He also accused Taylor-Memmory of consuming alcohol and becoming abusive to other guests at the party. He claims he had asked her to leave because her 'abusive behaviour' was upsetting the guests. She was escorted out, he said, and he closed the door behind her.

Taylor-Memmory says Oscar's behaviour on the night shocked her because she had never experienced any volatile behaviour on his part before. She also categorically denies that she was drunk, despite Oscar's legal team suggesting photographs showed her downing shots of alcohol. 'I was most certainly not drunk! The police who interviewed me after the incident never asked to test me for alcohol,' she says.

After being released from custody, Oscar laid a R2.2-million civil claim against Taylor-Memmory for damages. He alleged he lost public appearance fees and he felt humiliated about being arrested. In return, she laid a counter claim against him demanding a public apology.

Taylor-Memmory claims that while Oscar dropped his case against her, she persisted with her claim for a further four years until it was settled in December 2013, just months before Oscar went on trial for murder.

Oscar's lawyer dealing with this incident, Gary Pritchard from Hogan Lovells, suggests Taylor-Memmory's version is a 'blatant untruth'. He says both claims were simultaneously withdrawn by the parties in December 2013 when the matter was settled.

The matter was due to go to trial in February 2013, just a week after Oscar shot Reeva. Pritchard says neither side was ready to proceed and the matter was removed from the roll so that settlement discussions could continue. 'The time-line and December 2013 settlement had absolutely nothing to do with the Reeva incident and would have had exactly the same result whether the incident on 14 February 2013 had happened or not,' insists Pritchard.

'All I wanted was an apology from Oscar and the settlement of the legal fees. I have never made a public appearance or even approached the media about it. It has ultimately been resolved through a settlement in December 2013,' the blogger recounted in an exclusive interview with us. 'Some days I wish I had never gone through with it all, but I stood up for myself, which was extremely difficult especially when you feel like the whole country is against you. But I'm proud of the fact that I never backed down and I learnt that you should always stand up for what is right, even when you stand alone. Oscar settled the legal fees but I did not receive an apology. I agreed to it because I was so tired of it weighing me down, I wanted to put this incident behind me.'

Taylor-Memmory has never spoken about the incident or the lawsuits that followed the incident and says she has been 'bombarded' and 'hounded' by media and journalists over the years. She says she remains traumatised by the experience and still finds it difficult to speak about it. 'I was utterly harassed. I was harassed by the media as well as the public. I received hate mail on a daily basis. People who didn't know me from a bar of soap were calling me the most horrific names. It became so difficult at a stage that I needed a bodyguard when I went out in public due to all the hate rants.'

While the National Prosecuting Authority took the decision not to proceed with the case against the athlete, some damage had been done to his public profile. After the global acclaim that followed his victory at the Court of Arbitration for Sport, and in the wake of his near-fatal boat accident and the controversy that accompanied it, Oscar could not afford to be in the media spotlight for the wrong reasons again.

• • •

On the track, Oscar set about trying to achieve the ultimate goal of competing in the 2012 Olympic Games in London. Having recovered from the injuries he sustained in the boating accident, he dropped 17 kilograms and was far leaner. The accident altered his lifestyle and strengthened his focus.

In January 2011, a trimmer Oscar won three International Paralympic Committee (IPC) Athletics World titles in New Zealand but was beaten for the first time in seven years in the 100 metres by American Jerome Singleton. Oscar subsequently won the T44 400 metres in 47.28 seconds and the 100 metres in 11.04 seconds at the BT Paralympic World Cup in May to reassert himself as the fastest Paralympic sprinter in the world.

He continued to compete in a number of able-bodied races in 2011 and posted three times under 46 seconds, but it was in Lignano, Italy, on 19 July that Oscar set a personal best of 45.07 seconds in the 400 metres, attaining the World Championships and Olympic Games 'A' standard qualification mark. On 8 August 2011 it was announced that Oscar had been included in the South African team for the IAAF World Championships in Daegu and was selected for the 400 metres and 4x400 metres relay squad. In the heats of the 400 metres, Oscar finished third in a time of 45.39 seconds, his second fastest time ever, to qualify for the semi-final.

In the heats of the 4x400 metres relay, Oscar ran the opening leg as the South African team made it to the finals with a national record time of 2 minutes 59.21 seconds. Controversially, Oscar was not selected for the team for the final but was nevertheless awarded a historic silver medal, having run in the heats, and so he became the first Paralympic athlete to win a World Championship medal.

His chances of qualifying for London were fast becoming a reality. But pressure from the media, particularly the UK press, was immense. So much so, that in September 2011, Oscar stormed out of a BBC interview following what he believed was an 'insulting' question.

The BBC interviewer, Rob Bonnet, asked: 'Some people regard you, no doubt, as an inspiration to Paralympic athletes, no question about that. But it might also be said that you're an inconvenient embarrassment to the South African authorities and the IAAF because, effectively, you're taking them into uncharted ethical waters here. What's your reaction to that?' Pistorius replied: 'I think that's an insult to me and I think this interview is over.' Bonnet insisted that his question had not been intended as an 'insult'.

In order to qualify for the Olympic Games, Oscar was required to race the Olympic qualification time of 45.30 seconds between January and June 2012. He achieved this at the Provincial Championships for Gauteng North in South Africa on 17 March, setting a time of 45.20 seconds. But that was not enough to book him a ticket to London. According to the South African Olympic body SASCOC's own rules, he was required to run at least 45.30 seconds twice in international competitions in order to qualify and needed to break that time at the African Athletics Championships in Benin in June. He missed the mark, hitting a time of 45.52 seconds.

'I am obviously disappointed that my time was just outside of the Olympic qualification time by two-tenths of a second,' Oscar said in a statement. 'I had felt very strong coming into this competition as my fitness and speed has been continually improving.'

Then, in a remarkable about-turn, the country's officials changed their decision just weeks before the games to allow him to compete. He was selected to compete for Team South Africa at the London 2012 Olympic Games in the individual 400 metres event plus the 4x400 metres relay.

Oscar was thrown the lifeline when SASCOC added 13 names to a provisional team in July 2012. He responded by tweeting:

> Today is really one of the happiest days of my life. Will be in London for both the Olympic and Paralympic Games!

Athletics South Africa board member and former sprinter Geraldine Pillay contentiously spoke out about Oscar's selection on investigative television show *Carte Blanche* after his arrest. 'There were things that we thought – let's just forget about that and move on because he was Oscar Pistorius. We were so obsessed with him, just winning medals; just being on every cover of every newspaper and magazines that we totally missed the plot.' SASCOC responded furiously and demanded that action be taken against Pillay.

'Oscar shouldn't have gone to the Olympic Games. Oscar wasn't going to be a contender. The times … he didn't qualify …' veteran broadcaster Graeme Joffe told

Carte Blanche about the selection. 'The selection criteria [are] steadfast, according to SASCOC, but they bend the rules to suit themselves.'

But Oscar Pistorius was South Africa's pride, the country's 'good thing' and sporting authorities did not want to miss out on an opportunity to parade him on the world stage and make history. It had the potential to be a marketing coup. And so it was that, despite Oscar not qualifying for the individual 400 metres race, the decision was taken that he would represent South Africa because he was going to be at the games in any event as part of the 4x400 metres relay team.

Oscar competed in a 400 metres heat of the Olympic Games and finished in second position in a time of 45.44 seconds. He qualified for the semi-final, but finished last in that race. Memorably, Grenada's Kirani James, who won the semi-final, rushed over to Oscar after the race, embraced him and asked to swap bib numbers with the Blade Runner, an indication of the high esteem in which he was held by fellow competitors. 'My hat's off to him, just coming out here and competing,' James told reporters. 'I just see him as another athlete, another competitor. What's more important is I see him as another person. He's someone I admire and respect.'

Having been knocked out of the individual category, Oscar still had the opportunity to compete in the 4x400 metres relay. The heat was eventful – the Kenyan team was disqualified from the competition after a collision with South Africa's Ofentse Mogawane, who was running the second leg of the race. As a result, Oscar, who was waiting in the third position, never received the baton and did not run. It was a massive anticlimax after the build-up to the event. After the South African management appealed, the squad was reinstated in the competition and given lane one out of nine lanes in the Olympic final.

The following evening Oscar and his teammates Shaun de Jager, LJ van Zyl and Willie de Beer competed with Oscar on the anchor leg. They finished in eighth place in the Olympic final.

Having rewritten the history books, Oscar was chosen to bear his country's flag at the closing ceremony of the Olympic Games. Just days later, he again carried the flag in London as he led the South African Paralympic team into the same stadium.

At the Paralympics, his focus shifted to winning medals. He opened strongly and set a new world record in the T43 200 metres race. In nine years of competition, Oscar had never lost over the distance. And then, all of a sudden, reality did not go according to the script.

In the final of the 200 metres, Oscar – astonishingly – did not win and finished second behind Brazilian athlete Alan Oliveira. The Brazilian came from behind with just 30 metres to go to chase down the favourite, sending gasps through the 80 000-strong crowd. A media storm erupted around Oscar as, just minutes after the race, he displayed a lack of dignity and humility by publicly questioning the legality of Oliveira's blade. The irony was monumental – here was an icon who had spent years fighting to ensure that his ability was not undermined by the apparent benefits gained from his prosthetic legs and now he was accusing a competitor of exactly the same thing.

'Not taking away from Alan's performance, he's a great athlete, but these guys are a lot taller and you can't compete [with the] stride length. You saw how far he came back. We aren't racing a fair race. I gave it my best,' Oscar said.

He insisted that he had been raising the issue with the IPC for several weeks, complaining that competitors were using blades that elevated their knees to four inches above their natural height and lengthened their strides and were running 'ridiculous' times as a result. 'I run just over 10 metres per second, I don't know how you can come back, watching the replay, from eight metres behind on the 100 to win. It's absolutely ridiculous.' However, Oscar's own world record set in the heats was faster than Oliveira's winning time in the final.

Oscar, who by the IAAF requirements could not alter the length of his blades if he wanted to continue to compete in able-bodied competition, felt that he was not competing on a level playing field. 'I've never seen a guy come back from eight metres (behind) on the 100 metres mark to overtake me on the finish line,' said the South African to *The Telegraph*. 'We've known [about the longer blades] for about a month. I've brought it up with the IPC but nothing's been done about it. I believe in the fairness of sport, I believe in running on the right length.'

The IPC responded by confirming that no rules had been broken. 'There is a rule in place regarding the length of the blades which is determined by a formula based on the height and dynamics of the athlete. All athletes were measured today prior to competition by a classifier and all were approved for competition,' said a spokesperson for the Committee.

The young Brazilian said he was 'disappointed' by the claims from Oscar. 'Pistorius is a great athlete. The interview when he said my blades were too big, he was bothered by the time I had in the semi-finals and wanted to get to me with this polemic. But it did not work. I don't know with whom he's picking a fight, it's not with me,' he said. 'For me he is a really great idol. And to hear that coming from a really great idol is difficult.'

British media were saturated with coverage of Oscar's comments and much of it was negative, with critics questioning his eruption in the face of a rare loss.

The morning after the race, Oscar published an apology – he was not sorry for what he said, but rather for the timing of his comments.

'I would never want to detract from another athlete's moment of triumph and I want to apologise for the timing of my comments after yesterday's race. I do believe that there is an issue here and I welcome the opportunity to discuss with the IPC but I accept that raising these concerns immediately as I stepped off the track was wrong. That was Alan's moment and I would like to put on record the respect I have for him. I am a proud Paralympian and believe in the fairness of sport. I am happy to work with the IPC who obviously share these aims.'

Oscar also tweeted his congratulations to Oliveira and thanked the crowd for their support:

> Congratulating Alan of Brazil for his 200m win.. The fastest last 80m I have ever seen to take it on the line. pic!

But a degree of damage had been done to Oscar's poster-boy image and a seed of doubt about his character had been planted in the minds of some.

'Pistorius had never lost a 200 metres race before, and he could not believe that it had happened. Modest as he may seem – at the start line he responded to the adoring applause of the 80 000 with a polite little bow – he has, like any champion, a sizeable temper and an ego to match,' wrote Andy Bull in *The Guardian* about the incident.

But Oscar was more determined than ever and wanted to reclaim his status as the premier Paralympic sprinter in the world. Motivated, he came out for the 4x100 metres relay with the South African team with the aim of not only taking the title but also breaking their own world record. Oscar anchored the team, which successfully achieved its goal, taking over seven-tenths of a second off their previous record.

. . .

The mixed zone at the Olympic Stadium in London was the one area where nothing was off the record. It's a vast area under the main grandstand, just beyond the finish line of the athletics track and where the Paralympic athletes faced the media for the first time after their competition. The mixed zone provided a more informal meeting place than an official news conference, though access was strictly controlled by team media officers, and a waist-high barrier separates journalist from athlete.

The evening of 6 September 2012 was hot and sticky, the atmosphere at the stadium even more charged than usual. The evening's penultimate race was the men's 100 metres for double- and single-leg amputees and it was won in a Games record time by one of the darlings of the British Paralympic movement, Jonnie Peacock. Oscar had finished fourth behind fellow South African and roommate Arnu Fourie.

Oscar had anticipated finishing outside the medals in this event, as he had long since stopped training for the shorter distance. It was the first time he had been in action since his criticism three days earlier of Brazilian sprinter Alan Oliveira's long running blades. The comments had cast something of a pall over the poster boy of the Paralympic Games, and Oscar knew he had to make amends.

He might have overdone his enthusiasm by saying the race was the best he had ever competed in, but his praise for Peacock and his genuine excitement for Fourie's bronze medal achievement was helping to restore his Paralympic image.

As usual that evening, Oscar was besieged by the media. He was always in high demand, but that evening the journalists were clamouring for a follow-up to the Oliveira controversy. And Oscar did not disappoint. He worked the media like the professional he had become – not turning down a single interview and making his way slowly through the various countries' TV crews, answering all their questions. Oscar always took a long time moving through the mixed zone.

While he was charming a global TV audience, Fourie – who was not in as much demand from the foreign journalists – had completed his interviews with the South African TV crews and had made his way to a group of five South African radio and print journalists.

He spoke to them excitedly about the race, and it wasn't long before some of the journalists went off to file their stories for the morning. Broadcaster David O'Sullivan was, however, keen to record an interview with both Fourie and Oscar, so O'Sullivan and Fourie remained in the mixed zone, continuing to talk while waiting for Oscar to finish his TV commitments.

O'Sullivan asked Fourie what it was like to be Oscar's roommate. He thought it was an innocuous question, aimed more at passing the time, but Fourie's response took him by surprise. Fourie let on that he had moved out of their tiny room in the Paralympic village because Oscar was always fighting with and shouting at people on the phone.

O'Sullivan was taken aback. He had expected to hear how they might motivate each other, sit and chat about their strategies – he certainly didn't expect to hear that Oscar was being distracted by fights and arguments with people on the other end of a telephone line.

Neither O'Sullivan nor Fourie pursued the conversation any further as Oscar arrived shortly afterwards and the discussion went back to the evening's earlier race. But Fourie's comment lingered with O'Sullivan and, as he travelled back to his hotel that night, he listened back to Fourie's almost throwaway remark on his recorder. It struck him as incongruous that, at the height of his fame, on his biggest stage, with so much glory beckoning, Oscar should be embroiled in arguments on the phone. Why does he allow himself to be so badly distracted? thought O'Sullivan. Surely he had bigger things to deal with?

Some 18 months later, O'Sullivan recalled the incident in an article he wrote for the *Sunday Telegraph* detailing his encounters with Pistorius over a period of almost nine years:

> *At the London Games, I was chatting to Oscar's roommate in the Athletes' Village, Arnu Fourie, who had just won the bronze medal in the 100 m, edging his good friend Oscar out of the medals. Oscar was genuinely elated at his mate's success. They were obviously very close and I asked Fourie what it was like rooming with Oscar. He told me he had been forced to move out, because Oscar was constantly screaming in anger at people on the phone. I thought Fourie was joking and waited for him to smile. But he was serious. I was taken aback. I had never thought of Oscar behaving like that. I realised he was more complex than I had thought.*

O'Sullivan first met Oscar in September 2004 while doing a broadcast for Talk Radio 702 to welcome home the South African Olympic swimmers who had won gold in Athens. 'Because I have a passion for the Paralympics, I asked if Fanie Lombard could also come along so that we could throw forward to the upcoming Athens Paralympic Games. Fanie couldn't make it, and the team's media officer suggested that she bring a newcomer along for the interview instead. I thought she said his name was Oscar Pretorius, and introduced him as such in a throw-forward to his interview.

'When he sat down during the ad break, he very politely corrected me. I didn't know what his disability was, and he pulled up his pants legs to show me his prosthetics. I remember him being a very quiet schoolboy with slight acne and braces on his teeth. He could have been mistaken for being shy, because he was quiet and unassuming, but as soon as the interview started, I realised he had confidence that belied his age. I liked him immediately.'

The broadcaster says that Oscar struck him as being very normal and humble in the early days of his career. 'After Oscar came back from the Paralympics with a couple of medals and world records, he started being noticed. He was in demand for motivational speaking and asked me to help him write a speech. I sat with him for a couple of days going through his family history. I heard none of the stuff that has been revealed in court. When I look back on my notes, he painted a picture of a very normal upbringing, enjoying school life, not ever experiencing disadvantages because of his disability. He told me stories that were so typical of your average Pretoria schoolboy, riding motorbikes, playing in the veld, getting up to mischief. Over the years, I watched Oscar grow in confidence and stature, but he always remained the same person towards me – unassuming, quiet, respectful.'

He saw no signs that Oscar was troubled or was destined to implode. 'I only ever heard stories – the motorboat crash, tantrums he would throw with SABC producers. He once phoned me from Beijing just before the 2008 Paralympic Games, complaining about their training kit. But I thought he was quite justified in moaning – the kit was late and he had work to do.'

Former CNN sports broadcaster Graeme Joffe says that warning signs did begin to appear, but no one wanted to acknowledge them.

'I met this incredible, humble kid, the drive, the positiveness. I was in awe of him. It was the real Oscar. Then, sadly over the years, I think, as fame and success and money came into his life, I saw a very different Oscar,' Joffe told a BBC television documentary in the weeks after Oscar's arrest. 'So many incidents have happened, and they've been well documented over the last five or six years … Here, I think, you had a troubled athlete. Not so much this incredible role model for the rest of the world – no question about that – but deep down, this was a troubled athlete,' Joffe elaborated to CNN. Joffe, like many others, had noticed Oscar beginning to change over the years.

With fame and the global stage, Oscar had developed a taste for the fast life, which *The New York Times* pointed out was not an uncommon attribute of successful, competitive athletes. Writer Michael Sokolove spent time with the Blade Runner at his Pretoria home:

> *Pistorius is, as well, blessed with an uncommon temperament – a fierce, even frenzied need to take on the world at maximum speed and with minimum caution. It is an athlete's disposition, that of a person who believes himself to be royalty of a certain kind – a prince of the physical world.*

In his article, Sokolove wrote about Oscar's erratic and high-speed driving, as well as his appetite for risk, mentioning that at one point the car's speedometer clocked 250 km/h while the athlete was at the wheel:

> *Hanging out with Pistorius can be a great deal of fun. You also quickly understand that he is more than a little crazy ... The people around Pistorius worry about his risk-taking, but there's only so much they can do. His manager, Peet van Zyl, shrugged when I asked him about it. 'It's the nature of the man,' he said. 'At least we did get the motorbike away from him.'*

Oscar's penchant for firearms and his acute awareness of his own security was clear for Sokolove:

> *As he put together lunch for all of us — fruit smoothies, breaded chicken fillets he pulled from the refrigerator — he mentioned that a security alarm in the house had gone off the previous night, and he had grabbed his gun and tiptoed downstairs. (It turned out to be nothing.)*
>
> *I asked what kind of gun he owned, which he seemed to take as an indication of my broader interest in firearms. I had to tell him I didn't own any. 'But you've shot one, right?' Actually, I hadn't. Suddenly, I felt like one of those characters in a movie who must be schooled on how to be more manly.*
>
> *'We should go to the range,' he said. He fetched his 9-millimeter hand-gun and two boxes of ammunition. We got back in the car and drove to a nearby firing range, where he instructed me on proper technique. Pistorius was a good coach. A couple of my shots got close to the bull's-eye, which delighted him. 'Maybe you should do this more,' he said. 'If you practised, I think you could be pretty deadly.' I asked him how often he came to the range. 'Just sometimes when I can't sleep,' he said.*

Jonathan McEvoy from *The Daily Mail* also visited Oscar at his home in the secure Silver Woods estate and noted his jumpiness at threats to his security:

> *In Oscar's bedroom lay one cricket bat and one baseball bat behind the door, a revolver by his bed and a machine gun by the window.*
>
> *In this vast and beautiful land of post-apartheid South Africa there is too often a gun at the end of their Rainbow.*

In 2011, the year I visited Oscar, there were 7,039 reported home inva-
sion robberies in the Gauteng Province alone – the area that covers
Johannesburg and Pretoria, the cities in which he was born and lived.

Yes, he is hidden away on the Silver Woods estate on the eastern
outskirts of Pretoria and is protected by armed guards round the clock,
but as he told me: 'The problem is when the guards are in on the crime. It's
usually safe in guarded estates like this until that happens.'

Like Sokolove, McEvoy also experienced Oscar's wild driving when he drove
him to the airport in his BMW 'fitted with all manner of go-faster gadgets' and
'tyres screeching as he rounded corners like a man possessed'.

Months after the Valentine's Day shooting, writer Jonny Steinberg recounted
another telling and little-known allegation involving Oscar and his gun in *The
Guardian* newspaper:

A couple of years ago, two journalist friends of mine spent an afternoon
with Oscar Pistorius. For much of the time, they recall, Oscar was quiet
and self-contained. And then, apropos of nothing, he told a story. He was
driving on the outskirts of a black township, he said, when a dog ran
under his wheels. In his rear-view mirror, he watched as it dragged itself
off the road by its front legs, its hind legs useless to it now. Its back was
clearly broken. He stopped and got out of his car to find that the dog's
owner had come out on to the street, shouting, cursing, gesticulating.
What to do? Oscar grabbed his gun, shot the dog through the back of the
head and drove off.

• • •

After the Olympic Games and the success of 2012, Oscar ordered himself a
R3.5-million McLaren MP4-12C Spider. Life was good. He had an estimated R17
million in endorsements from various global brands including Nike, Oakley,
Thierry Mugler and British telecommunications company BT. He was revelling
in the lifestyle that success had brought him.

In his personal life, Oscar was again involved in a passionate and turbulent
relationship with a blonde beauty. He had been seeing Johannesburg student
Samantha Taylor, whom he had met at a rugby game in 2010. The two had got to
know each other over time and began dating in September 2011. However, during the Olympics, while Oscar was in London, the couple broke up. But when

he returned to South Africa in September 2012, they reignited their relationship. 'Upon his return from London he begged me to go out with him again and said he would get a psychologist for us to make our relationship work,' claims Taylor in an affidavit deposed for the purposes of Oscar's murder trial. She would also go into extensive detail about their relationship in an interview with us.

In November 2012 the couple fell out again during a trip to Sun City. 'We were fighting about him being rude to me,' explained Taylor in the affidavit. They were meant to go to Durban together but didn't. While they were on a break, the marketing student said she realised the relationship was over when she saw her boyfriend at the South African Sports Awards with model Reeva Steenkamp.

In the affidavit signed by Taylor, she gave insight into her relationship with Oscar, his mood swings, drinking and enthusiasm for guns:

> He one night got intoxicated at home and fell hurting his lip. This was when we had a get together. When everyone left and we went to bed he became abusive saying 'You bitch' several times accusing me of hitting him. The next day he could not remember the incident. He often used alcohol and became intoxicated when in his 'off season'.
>
> He liked firearms and while in Las Vegas (2012) he told me that he was going to gunshops. This also happened when he was in London for the Olympics. I often went to the range with him (in Pretoria). He was a firearm enthusiast. Once after being stopped by traffic police he fired out the car because of anger. (this was in ±September 2012). He only fired one shot.
>
> He had many mood swings, turning from friendly to aggressive in an instant. He also cried a lot when he knew that he was wrong in our relationship. He was extremely jealous, possessive and obsessive about me.

After news of Reeva Steenkamp's death broke, Taylor's mother posted on Facebook: 'I am so glad that Sammy is safe and sound, and out of the clutches of that man. There were a few occasions where things could have gone wrong with her and his gun during the time they dated.'

It was over Samantha Taylor that Oscar became embroiled in a heated altercation with former professional soccer player Marc Batchelor.

With his peroxide hair, dubious friends and elaborate tattoos, Batchelor's reputation precedes him. 'Batch', as the ex-SuperSport presenter is known, moves in the same circles as well-known underworld figure and hired hit man Mikey Schultz – a circle that is not fond of Oscar Pistorius. Batchelor's friends also refer to him as 'The Sherriff' due to his eagerness to take care of their problems, at times with what appears to be a little too much enthusiasm.

So it was that Batchelor became embroiled in the dispute between his friend *Clifton Shores* producer and mining multimillionaire Quinton van der Burgh and the Blade Runner.

Batchelor had seen Oscar around at charity events but the two men had never got on. 'He was arrogant from then,' says Batchelor. 'He was always looking for accolades. And, you know, when the room is full of ex-sportsmen and there are celebs everywhere, I mean why must he always make an entrance?'

While Oscar was in London for the Olympics and he and Taylor had broken up, Samantha went on several dates as well as an overseas trip with Van der Burgh. Batchelor claimed Oscar was fuming when he found out and confronted Van der Burgh at a race day at the Kyalami track, while the millionaire was entertaining clients.

'Oscar runs right up to Quinton and says, "Hey, you fucking cunt! You fucking asshole! You fucking sleeping with my girl while I'm fucking running for my country!" all this "f-" and "f-" … "I'll fuck you up." This that and the next thing, "Who the fuck do you think you are?" Quinton says he stood there. He just didn't know what to do 'cause, first, he's with all his clients and this is like a multibillionaire. Oscar turned and said, "You better watch where you go, you better watch your back," as they left and then Quinton got hold of me and he said, "Listen, I'm nervous now." So I said, "Do you want me to sort it out?" and he said, "Please."'

Batchelor claims he tried to get hold of Francois Hougaard who was on tour with the Springboks in Ireland. He knew that Oscar and the rugby player were friends, so he left a message with the scrumhalf's roommate. '"Just tell Hougaard, tell him that," I said, "I'm looking to speak to him and I want to get hold of Oscar because Oscar is threatening people and if Hougaard wants to get involved in this shit then he must be very careful what he's dealing with because he must play rugby, he mustn't get involved with this."'

The message reached Oscar and when the runner bumped into a mutual friend of his and Batchelor's at a party at the Vaal Dam, the situation escalated.

'I was at a braai in the south with Mikey [Schultz] – and my friend was at this house party at the Vaal. I see on my phone he's phoning so I answered the phone and I say, "Hey, what's up?" and he says, "It's fucking Oscar, what's your fucking problem, boy?" So I said, "Listen, don't fucking call me boy," and he went off. No, he's going to break my legs and he's got bats and this and that … he was just screaming, for like 30 seconds about he's not scared who I am and who I know

... and I swore back at him, I said, "Now listen here, you cunt. Who the fuck do you think you're talking to?" So he says, "Hold on, Marc." Now he's quiet, hey. As long as he's in front of people, he's trying to show off. So he goes up into an area where it's quiet and he says, "Come on, can't we sort this out?" and "What's wrong?"'

The phone cut out but Batchelor says Oscar called back two minutes later. And it's "Fuck you! It's Oscar, you cunt. Who the fuck are you?" He went from screaming to "Please can we sort this out?" So I said, "Listen, you little cunt, where are you? I'll come there now and I'll fuck you up," and he says, "You can come here now and I'll fuck you up, I'm ready for you!" So Mikey actually heard the second part of the conversation. With the second call he came outside and was like "Jeez". I laughed it off. So we were laughing.'

Oscar took the matter to the police's special crime-fighting unit the Hawks and Batchelor was summoned to a meeting with three high-ranking police 'colonels'. The unit investigates serious, complex, organised crime, and some would argue that Oscar's course of action was an excessive show of force and influence for so minor an incident. Batchelor claims the meeting was only arranged because of Justin Divaris's connection with Gauteng Hawks head Shadrack Sibiya, a claim that Divaris has consistently denied.

Batchelor claimed that Oscar had a bad temper and that at the meeting with the police officials, he had a black eye because he had been involved in a fight.

'So I walk in there, and I say, "What's happening, guys?" and there's colonels and lieutenant-colonels and I'm taking pictures with the cops. Then Justin and Oscar walk in. Fuck. So I go, "You've got to be shitting me. I'm here for this?" and I got cross. So the one colonel said to me, "General Sibiya can't be here. We take these kind of threats in our society very high." So I said, "What do you okes do here?" so he said, "We do hits ... the organised crime, we do big drug deals, murder, robbery." So I said, "What is this that I have done? Or he's done or this one?" Oscar couldn't look at me, he was shaking. He had a black eye and he had stitches in his head from the party. He was so pissed, he fell and cut his head. He was dancing with his gun ... So he admitted to phoning me, swearing at me, he says, "I swore back at him."'

It emerged that Oscar had laid a charge of intimidation against Batchelor, who in turn charged the runner with defamation.

Hawks spokesperson Paul Ramoloko had to address questions raised by the media about the bizarre meeting at the police office. "We are not investigating any case, or anyone," said Ramoloko.

Oscar made no comment to the media at the time of the incident, but his version of events was different, as he alluded to in an interview with Afrikaans magazine *Sarie*, published in the February that Reeva died but which was conducted in November 2013. He intimated that the media had got him wrong. 'You can't – or won't – give your side of the story because you want to keep your private life private. Many of the details in the newspapers have been heartbreaking. You trust someone and then they go and do something very unexpected. You learn,' Oscar told the magazine.

'You are just never too sure in a relationship. You take a chance every time you meet someone. But you can't be too cynical about anything in life. All you can do is hope the person you're with has integrity. It is difficult to find the right person, one who is trustworthy, who will keep your private stuff private. It requires a very special person to be in a relationship with a sportsman. I know it. It is not an easy life. I travel so much. You need someone who can travel with you or who is super accommodating. Is it a challenge? Yes. I haven't found the right person yet, but it's okay.'

In the interview he spoke of how he dealt with negative publicity and the importance of humility in life.

'When I was younger, I wanted to call the journalist and get things off my chest. At the end of the day (he sighs) … If I comment on a story, it just becomes bigger. (He keeps quiet and thinks.) Fame isn't that great. Like anything in life, it has its pros and cons, its highlights and lowlights. The best thing you can do is not to let it go to your head when you achieve things. Because it is only a matter of time before you are cut down. Just live life and be nice to people.'

Oscar would be involved in two further incidents in late 2012 and early 2013 that ordinarily would have lit up the headlines. But he managed to keep them both hushed and they only emerged when all his dirty laundry and baggage were being up-ended after his arrest. In late September 2012, while driving back from the Vaal River about an hour from Johannesburg, Oscar was in a car with Taylor and his friend Darren Fresco when they were pulled over by a Metro police officer. The athlete got into a confrontation with the officer over his firearm. Later on during the journey, he allegedly fired his gun through the sunroof of the car in which they were travelling.

Then, in January 2013, Oscar accidentally discharged Fresco's Glock firearm while they were sitting at Tashas, a restaurant in Melrose Arch in Johannesburg. Remarkably, Oscar was successful in keeping both incidents out of the press at the time. In April 2014, the *Sunday Times* newspaper also revealed how the athlete successfully dissuaded it from running an article about another incident in which he was assaulted at a club in Sandton in December 2012. The paper claimed the athlete denied being assaulted in order to save his image as Mr Clean, and also lied about his love affair with Reeva.

'The athlete was so obsessed with maintaining his squeaky clean public image and lucrative sponsorship deals that he repeatedly lied to try to cover up an assault during December 2012, for which he had to receive medical attention. He also lied about his relationship with Reeva Steenkamp in an interview on January 14 last year, denying he was in a serious relationship.'

When *Sunday Times* reporter Gabi Mbele approached Pistorius with information related to the assault, he pleaded with her not to run the story because it could 'ruin' him. After speaking with her editors, the reporter informed Oscar of their decision in a text message on 26 January. 'Editors have decided they won't be running anything about this, we think these guys are making up stories just to try get to you. So rest assured we not going with this. Thanks 4 calling me back. Gabi.'

The athlete was grateful, but persisted with this version: 'Thank you Gabi. I appreciate you asking me and I'd like to have things that are positive and open with you instead of hearsay and rubbish. If you could let me know who it is that is spreading stories I'd appreciate it. Let me know if you need anything. Oz.'

Mbele was clearly taken in by Oscar's version of events. 'Was also worried about this but Werner [Swart – colleague] said someone has the wrong end of the stick here hence we called you too. Don't stress about it, we wouldn't run anything without letting you know. Now focus on the good forget this, we not buying into people's maliciousness! Gab.'

• • •

A different public image of Oscar Pistorius was lurking, waiting to emerge. There were hints of it in the reports around his boat accident, murmurs when he stormed out of the radio interview, suggestions of it when there were claims of his promiscuity, and real recognition of its potential following his outburst at the Paralympics. But his poster-boy image still remained intact. Perhaps the South African media chose to ignore the indicators, unwilling to be party to the tarnishing of something so wonderfully successful and patriotic.

Despite the rumblings of negativity, Oscar continued to do much good, reaffirming his public image. He was an ambassador for Laureus, a global charity that promotes social change through sport. He was also an ambassador for the Mineseeker Foundation, which distributes prosthetic limbs to victims of landmines in Africa. In addition, Oscar was on the verge of launching his own new charity foundation and, just two days before he was arrested, he tweeted about it: 'In a run up to the launch of my foundation in July, I will give at least 10 kids mobility!'

The future was rich with possibility. He was training hard for a new season of racing, hoping to gain on his success in London in 2012; he was midway through the process of buying a new house in Atholl and moving back to Johannesburg; and sponsorships and endorsements continued to roll in. He had been invited to appear on the Jay Leno show and the Piers Morgan show amongst others; he featured on the covers of various local and international magazines; and he was to be the face of M-Net's February Academy Awards campaign.

Oscar had also fallen madly in love, again. He was smitten and had great plans for the future with his new blonde girlfriend.

But his words to *Sarie* magazine proved to be prophetic. Fame *isn't* that great. It has highlights and lowlights and it was only a matter of time before he was cut down. And the Icarus-like fall was incalculable, devastating, beyond anyone's comprehension – including his own.

Breaking News – Barry Bateman

It was Valentine's Day and my wife had given me one of those cheesy cards. I was feeling ill and had a nasty cough and a stuffy nose. At about 6:30am I called the news desk at Eyewitness News to discuss my diary for the day with Lynne O'Connor who was reading bulletins that morning. I explained that I was ill and wasn't prepared to be out and about, but promised I'd work on a Tshwane Metro Police report I'd been sitting on for several weeks, so she pulled me off the diary for the day.

But I still had to get my daughter to school, so I continued getting her ready. It was shortly after 7am that I received a call from a police contact at the Cullinan police station.

'Are you in Silver Woods, at the scene there?' he asked.

'What scene?' I responded.

It quickly became evident that I should have known what was happening.

'Oscar has shot someone at his home. Oscar Pistorius.'

'Shot dead or shot injured?' I asked, needing clarity.

'No, he shot someone dead. Apparently before five this morning,' he said.

The policeman provided me with the name and number of a captain from the Boschkop police station who was on the scene.

Shit! I thought. I quickly told my wife about what had happened and immediately called the cop on the scene.

'Good morning, Captain, this is Barry Bateman from Eyewitness News. I understand that there's been a shooting at Oscar Pistorius's home. Can you confirm?' I needed facts fast.

She was clearly nervous. 'I can't say anything at this stage; the police are still investigating at the scene.'

'Captain, I understand there has been a shooting. Please confirm whether someone is dead or someone has been injured.'

Her response was ambiguous. 'I can't say; we're still investigating.'

I ended the call. Although the captain had provided no information she had made it clear that something was happening.

I called the news desk back and explained the situation to O'Connor. It was early, there was no confirmation and we didn't know who the victim was. I asked to speak to sports editor Cindy Poluta.

'No. Fucking. Ways!' she exclaimed when I broke the news to her. I needed contact numbers and she undertook to text me the cellphone number of Oscar's manager, Peet van Zyl.

Then it occurred to me that I did, in fact, have Oscar's phone number from a job I had done a few years earlier. From my landline I called his cellphone, but the user was unavailable. It was 7:19am.

· · ·

I rushed outside and loaded my daughter into the car – fatherly duties trump all others. My four-year-old was strapped in and ready when I received the text from Poluta. I immediately called Van Zyl, the athlete's manager. In my best diplomatic and professional 'please help me, I'm desperate' tone, I explained that I'd heard there'd been a shooting, could he confirm this?

'All I can confirm is that there has been an incident, but I don't have any details. I am being denied access to Oscar,' Van Zyl said.

It was a mad dash down Atterbury Road to the crèche. The traffic, as it usually is during rush hour, was not sympathetic to my emergency. Neither was the routine of dropping off a child at playschool. Within minutes of stopping at the school, I had unbuckled her car seat, signed her in and kissed my little girl goodbye.

From the school, it was on to the N1 highway and then on the N4 to avoid the traffic down Solomon Mahlangu Drive to the east. The office was still frantically tracking down details and as I navigated morning highway traffic my phone rang. It was O'Connor and she had information. Oscar had shot dead his girlfriend. What's her name?

I remembered seeing Oscar pictured with a woman on the front page of local magazine *Sarie*. As it turned out, the woman in the picture had been Oscar's sister, Aimee, but at the time I thought she was his girlfriend. I knew the man as an athlete but very little about his private life, his hobbies or love life.

A few minutes later O'Connor called back, this time to confirm that *Beeld* newspaper had just tweeted that Oscar had shot dead his girlfriend and that he was apparently telling the police he had mistaken her for a burglar.

O'Connor wanted to go live on air. Being just minutes from Oscar's house, I gave her the green light.

I was the first of the media to arrive at the luxury estate, which like most had two entrances: one for residents and another for visitors. I tried my luck and joined the queue of about three cars to get in.

A guard with a clipboard approached the car. 'Where are you going?' he asked.

I wasn't going to lie. 'I'm going to Oscar Pistorius's house.'

'Who are you?'

'I'm a reporter.'

The guard told me management wasn't allowing anyone except the police and authorised people into the complex. So I parked my car near the entrance, slid my driver's seat back to convert it into an office and started working. As I looked up I spotted *Beeld* reporter Fanie van Rooyen – who had minutes earlier broken the story with the tweet – and photographer Alet Pretorius. A polite wave and a smile were all time allowed as I started throwing together a few lines for the breaking news at the half-hour bulletin.

It was mere minutes before the studio called to do the live crossing, and while I was holding to cross into the bulletin, at 8.32am, I tweeted:

> #OscarPistorius paralympian Oscar Pistorius has allegedly shot dead his girlfriend at his Pretoria home. BB

Within minutes of going live, reporting that Oscar had apparently shot dead his girlfriend, my phone started ringing. Fellow hacks on their way to the scene wanted to confirm the address. Each call was a quick exchange of details, and it wasn't long before the entrance to the luxury estate was swarming with journalists from just about every South African publication.

'What have your contacts told you?' was the question being thrown around. 'The cops are saying fuck all,' was the most frequent response.

My silver Honda Jazz, parked closest to the entrance, had become a gathering point, the communal car to lean on and from which to listen to the radio. We waited. As the breaking news story gathered momentum, we needed official confirmation, a statement, a briefing – anything.

The Police Briefing

The boom at the exit of the terracotta, faux-rock Tuscan complex rose steadily to allow the white mortuary van to drive through. The van bore the distinctive yellow-and-blue reflector tape, with the stencilled lettering of the Gauteng Forensic Pathology Services running across its flank. In the back lay Reeva Steenkamp's body. It was close to 9am. Journalists were still gathering at the estate's main gate as the mortuary vehicle drove out, an indication of how late reporters were to get to the story. In South Africa, it is not uncommon for the dead to lie at a crime scene for hours as teams of forensic experts comb the area for clues, take pictures and document evidence.

Reporters milled around outside the estate, filing reports with the little information they had gathered from unofficial sources. Just before 11am, a large convoy of police and private vehicles sped out of the complex. Journalists scrambled to establish whether Oscar Pistorius was in one of the cars in the cavalcade and some gave chase, others remaining behind to await a briefing from the police.

Before long several police officers from the South African Police Service (SAPS) strode out to the waiting cameras and microphones to address the world's media. Responsibility for communication of this matter had been escalated from police station level – Boschkop – to Gauteng provincial level.

Brigadier Denise Beukes, her blonde hair neatly tucked away under a SAPS-issue cap and her lipstick pristine, led the briefing. She was composed and measured, selecting her words carefully as she delivered her statement:

> We can confirm that there was a shooting incident this morning at the home of the well-known Paralympic athlete Oscar Pistorius. At this stage we can confirm a young woman, a thirty-year-old woman, did die

on the scene of gunshot wounds. A 26-year-old male has been arrested
and charged with murder. At this stage he is on his way to a visit to the
district surgeon for a medical examination and will be appearing in the
Pretoria Magistrate's Court at two o'clock this afternoon. We have also
taken cognisance of media reports during the course of the morning of
an alleged break-in or that the young lady was allegedly mistaken to be
a burglar. We're not sure where this report came from; it definitely didn't
come from the South African Police Service. Our detectives have been
on the scene; our forensic investigators have been on the scene and the
investigation is ongoing.

Her comments took most journalists by surprise and, for the first time, the story began to shift. The only version until that point had been that Oscar had mistaken Reeva for an intruder and that the shooting had been a terrible mistake. Initial reports even suggested that Reeva had been sneaking into his house to surprise him for Valentine's Day. Now it appeared the scenario could be very different.

To the surprise of some reporters who had gathered, Beukes took questions. The first enquiry was whether or not she could identify the deceased?

'At this stage the challenge that we've got is that her family has not identified her and so until her family has identified her, we're not at liberty to give her name to the media, unfortunately,' Beukes explained, using her hands for extra emphasis.

Others wanted to know why Oscar was going to the district surgeon and whether he was receiving some kind of special treatment by appearing in court so swiftly after his arrest.

'Look, obviously when a person has been accused of a crime like murder they look at things like testing under the fingernails, taking a blood alcohol sample and other standard medical tests that are done,' Beukes said, insisting that there was no special treatment at all. 'If a person requests to be brought to court, then it is possible. The person was arrested this morning, he was taken to the police station like any other person who is detained and arrested. We will be opposing bail; he will be bringing a bail application this afternoon and we will be opposing bail.'

Then, without skipping a beat, Beukes dropped another soundbite that would fuel speculation surrounding a potential motive. She was asked whether or not eyewitnesses had been interviewed.

'There are witnesses that have been interviewed,' she confirmed. 'We're talking about neighbours that had heard things earlier in the evening and when the shooting took place. I can confirm that there has previously been incidents at the home of Oscar Pistorius. I'm not going to elaborate on that, just that there have been previous incidents … of allegations of a domestic nature.'

Could this illustrate a pattern of domestic altercations?

Beukes closed the impromptu briefing at the entrance to the Silver Woods estate by confirming that there were no signs of forced entry on the property and reiterating her earlier statement that initial media reports did not emanate from the police.

'The SAPS were just as surprised to hear over the radio that the allegations had been made that the deceased had been perceived to be a burglar. We were very surprised, and those allegations did not come from us,' she said.

• • •

Around 5 kilometres away, at the Boschkop police station, Oscar was just arriving. The police station is located amongst smallholdings in the far east of Pretoria. Except for the luxury estates close to the city, it serves mostly the semi-rural areas stretching to the border with Bronkhorstspruit. It was nearing midday when, despite the scorching summer sun high in the sky, the athlete, dressed in grey tracksuit pants and a grey hoodie, was escorted into the building amidst an entourage of police, family members and lawyers. Photographers were already waiting. Oscar's brother Carl covered Oscar's head with a tracksuit, shielding his face from the snapping lenses while their sister Aimee trailed behind. Within an hour, the paperwork had been filed and Oscar was moved to the Mamelodi Day Clinic where the district surgeon on duty would be responsible for drawing blood and taking urine samples. He would also make observations about the accused's physical appearance and carry out any other tests required.

As glass vials filled with Oscar's blood in Mamelodi, journalists who had been briefed by the police at his house sped off to their next location in anticipation of a bail application. Oscar was scheduled to appear at 2pm but no one was quite sure where. The athlete's lawyers wanted to bring the bail application that afternoon but, at such short notice, it was unlikely they would find an opening on the roll at the Pretoria Magistrate's Court. It then emerged that his lawyers wanted to try the court at the Pretoria Central Prison. A magistrate was alerted and assigned, and the media started gathering.

But as the day went on, it was clear Oscar wouldn't have time to apply for bail. The courts stop operating at 4pm. While the media's speculation turned to the possibility of a last-minute urgent application in the North Gauteng High Court, Oscar's lawyers and family were preparing him for his first night in jail at the Boschkop police station.

Fall from Grace – Mandy Wiener

We crowded around the flat-screen television in the newsroom, our necks craned to watch as Brigadier Denise Beukes's press conference was broadcast live. There was a sharp intake of breath and a chorus of exclamations as the policewoman disregarded reports that had been running all morning about the shooting being a mere accident. When she revealed that there had been previous incidents at Oscar's house of a domestic nature, we knew that the story had completely flipped.

I hammered on my keyboard as Beukes continued to speak, live-tweeting her statement to a public desperate for any new information about the incident. Details were, as we say in the industry, 'sketchy', and there had been little to no official confirmation of anything. For nearly three hours, there was only speculation and presumption feeding the media machine.

At first, I didn't quite comprehend the magnitude of the story we were dealing with but within minutes of the news breaking, it reverberated around the world. It took less than five minutes for my cellphone to ring – a major international news network looking for an interview, quickly.

Amidst the confusion and the chaos of an unfolding story, I raced into my Sandton office and began working the phones, managing the story from there while Barry was on the scene in Pretoria.

• • •

One of the initial major journalistic hurdles was to confirm the identity of the victim and to ensure that her relatives and friends had been informed before announcing her name on air. We knew that Oscar had been photographed with the glamorous, striking blonde reality television star Reeva Steenkamp over the previous weeks and their pictures had been published in the entertainment pages. The hashtag *#ReevaSteenkamp* was also trending on Twitter but we needed on-the-record confirmation.

A colleague gave me a number for Reeva's modelling agent, Sarit Tomlinson, and I immediately called her. When Sarit answered I could tell straight away that she was in pieces. Her job is to publicise the fabulous, not deal with this kind of crisis management on an incomprehensible global scale. Sarit had Reeva's parents on the other line and just didn't know what to tell them. She agreed on a brief, generic comment: 'Reeva's parents are in Port Elizabeth; we are all in shock and are in communication with people on the scene but we need to wait for official statements.'

A close friend of June Steenkamp, Samantha Sutton, also spoke about what was unfolding in Port Elizabeth: 'The parents are both in a bad way. We got medication from the family doctor to calm them down and are giving them tea. Her mother keeps saying "Reeva can't be dead" and she doesn't believe she is gone.'

As the morning passed, the story exploded and the full extent of the implications began to set in. Every radio station, TV network, news website and blog across the world wanted to speak to someone in South Africa and our newsroom phones lit up. Together with my colleagues, we did dozens of crossings. As we hung up, we would lift the handset again to do another. And as the news gathered momentum, we watched Oscar's fame, reputation and career unravel.

• • •

On Rivonia Road, the busiest street in Sandton, workmen in blue overalls and luminous yellow safety straps climbed a ladder to the summit of a billboard and began to pull down a massive poster bearing Oscar's face and the words 'Every Night is Oscar Night'. Television network M-Net had withdrawn its entire Academy Awards live coverage campaign featuring the athlete 'out of respect and sympathy to the bereaved'. The massive poster drooped down, Oscar's smiling face dangling upside down as it fell from grace. The image spoke volumes.

On Oscar's official website, the banner featured the sprinter in green-and-black racing gear exploding out of his starting blocks with the strapline 'I am the bullet in the chamber'. After some time and prodding from the public, the unfortunately timed banner was removed.

At the same time, there were intense deliberations about whether or not the reality series *Tropika Island of Treasure*, featuring Reeva, should continue premiering in a few days as planned. Samantha Moon, the executive producer and creator, confirmed that they had decided to go ahead with airing the show. She commented:

> *The more we thought about it, the more I felt quite strongly that right now the country and the world knows Reeva as a model with amazing images of this beautiful girl. But what we have is proof of how wonderful she was. For me, the fact that South Africa will get to know this girl that we love and feel the loss of very deeply, I feel that if we were not to air it, we would be in some way contributing to erasing her. I would like everyone to know her as an intelligent, fierce, fearless woman. She was exceptionally caring and generous and truly loving. One of the things the contestants often joked about was that you couldn't be in Reeva's company for five minutes without being afflicted by 'Reeva Fever'.*

Meanwhile, we waited for clarity on whether there would be a formal bail application in the afternoon. That night South African president Jacob Zuma delivered his annual state of the nation address in parliament. I cast my mind back to the previous year when Zuma had praised Oscar in his address. 'Our star performer, Oscar Pistorius, has set the standard for the year by winning the 2012 Laureus Award. Congratulations,' Zuma proudly boasted to the country. This year the Paralympian's shadow hung over the event like a cloud.

After my final live TV crossing for the night from the windy rooftop of a building in central Johannesburg, I took a moment to digest the unfathomable, surreal events of the day.

While I had fielded calls from radio and TV stations in the United Kingdom, Australia, Canada, Spain, the Czech Republic and other more remote countries, facts were regurgitated and so were the questions. They were mostly about Oscar.

At home, as South Africans, we struggled to come to terms with the news, not wanting to comprehend the truth of what might have occurred in Oscar's bathroom that night. We justified, contemplated hypotheses and drove speculation about why he would have shot and killed his girlfriend. The country had been rocked to its very core. Then, true to form, we began to joke. The reality was simply too much to bear. And in South Africa, reality is often stranger than fiction. South Africa repeatedly produces material that not even a best-selling crime writer could conceptualise. Perhaps that is why it is so difficult for us to deal with reality. It just seems, well, too unreal.

Oscar had brought us such pride on the world's stage and now the veneer had been stripped off, the gloss was horribly tarnished.

• • •

Five months earlier, I had been in London with the Paralympics in full swing and the Blade Runner riding the crest of a spectacular wave of popularity. He had been the first disabled athlete to run in the able-bodied Olympics and was the unofficial face of the Paralympic games.

I woke one morning in my hotel room to screaming headlines about a controversy. Oscar had been the man to beat in the 200 metres final but had come up short, and he had accused the winner, Brazilian Alan Fonteles Oliveira, of having an unfair advantage because his blades were too long. Oscar had spent years fighting claims that carbon-fibre prosthetics were an advantage compared to human legs.

That Monday morning, there was little sympathy for Oscar. It was the first indication I, and many others, had that the gloss of the golden boy might be tarnished. There was talk about how the outburst might have ruined his brand. He issued a statement apologising for the timing of his comments after the race but, in essence, he stayed true to his complaint. The damage had been done and the seed had been planted.

Watching the criticism build on television breakfast shows, I tweeted:

> #OscarPistorius Views here in UK are that 'Oscar can't have it all, he must choose' vs. sympathy that he's a victim of his own success. Sentiment definitely seems to be against him.

Now, less than 24 hours since the shooting at his house, stories began to emerge of a rather different Oscar. Of a petulant, hot-headed young man prone to flashes of anger. Rumours began to surface of the questionable circles he was moving in; so too did anecdotes about bad behaviour, a passion for fast cars and lethal firearms. I reflected on all of this and wondered why it had not been picked up sooner. Did we, the media, choose to ignore the leads and the stories because it was our hero Oscar?

On the Joburg rooftop I flicked through my phone and reread a litany of messages that had come through during the day amidst an overwhelming bombardment of calls. Some were from a mutual friend, one who was mourning a deep loss. It was one of those poignant, unique moments in which I had to pause and shift from the sometimes surreal frenzy of the news machine and allow reality to sink in. Until then it had been all Oscar, Oscar, Oscar: the Blade Runner, Paralympics golden boy, worldwide icon, PR machine.

I hadn't realised until that point that Reeva Steenkamp and I shared several mutual friends and yet had never met. In the messages left on my phone, they all spoke glowingly of her with genuine love and affection:

> Reeva loved tea. She thought it was a universal panacea and any problem could be solved with it. She also loved scones.

> She was a Leo and we were planning her 30th in Vegas. She would drop anything to come to you if you needed her or felt sad.

> She was mad about Oscar, completely in love with him, as he was about her.

> She wanted to be famous.

I realised that for Reeva Steenkamp's family, the reality of her absence would be unmistakable. For her friends, who were once afflicted by 'Reeva Fever', there would be no denying the reality of her bloody, tragic end. For Oscar, the incomprehensible reality of the nightmare he was in would only just be beginning to dawn.

The First Appearance

The Pretoria Magistrate's Court shares the same block as the Pretoria Central police station, sandwiched between Pretorius and Frances Baard streets and Bosman and Sophie de Bruyn streets. The older and original section of the court building, with its marbled facade and pillared entrance, was gutted by fire in 2010 and remains a burnt shell. The pavement overhang at the Schoeman Street entrance to the newer magistrate's court building is the overnight shelter for half a dozen city vagrants and the smell of stale urine and rotting rubbish permeate the air as you walk through the large steel doors into the court complex. Once you're through the ageing metal detectors and into the gloom of the officious facebrick corridors, the waft of oily hot potato chips from the canteen is overwhelming.

Chief Magistrate Desmond Nair's office is deep within the bowels of the building. It sits beyond a heavy metal door, a uniformed security guard and a clumsily taped-over intercom system, at the end of a rabbit warren of passageways on the ground floor. The labyrinth of corridors opens into a small waiting room with a bench and discarded wooden table holding a visitors' register, and then into a large spacious office featuring an impressive boardroom table with plush chairs and a royal ruby carpet. The office has no windows and is lined with wood panels and legal journals while brown cardboard folders are piled up on the floor, each one holding the contents of disciplinary cases against colleagues on which Nair is working.

The moustachioed lawman is small in stature, but large in presence. He's occupied this office since being appointed Chief Magistrate of the Pretoria region and its contents are testament to the years of familiarity. Well-worn legal handbooks are within an arm's reach for quick reference, his black-and-red robe is slung over a coat stand behind him and three separate images of Nelson Mandela hang on the walls. A toilet roll, a yellow-scented oil candle, teacups, piles of paper and stationery clutter the polished red-wood desk.

Nair had arrived at work on Thursday morning, 14 February 2013, and had taken his seat at his desk. He had not heard the news on the drive into work. Only once he was into the swing of the morning, was he told by the Acting Senior Magistrate at the court that he had received a message from prosecutors that Oscar Pistorius had been arrested.

The investigating officer Hilton Botha would have called the Magistrate's Court to let officials there know that he had a high high-profile case that needed to be allocated. Chief Prosecutor at the Pretoria Magistrate's Court, Matric Luphondo, discussed the matter with the Senior Public Prosecutor for the region, Sibongile Mzinyathi, and together they took the decision to allocate the case to Advocates Gerrie Nel and Andrea Johnson.

The initial plan was to take Oscar to court at the Pretoria Central Prison. The Prison Court is a branch of the Pretoria Court, which falls under Nair's jurisdiction. Nair was concerned from the outset that it would not be feasible for the matter to be held at the Prison Court due to space constraints and ordered that the case be brought to the Magistrate's Court. However, there was also confusion on a legal basis around which level of court should hear the bail application. According to legislation in South Africa, a crime considered to be a so-called Schedule 6 offence must be heard at the District Court unless the Director of Public Prosecutions issues a certificate or otherwise orders that it be heard in the Regional Court. As far as Nair was concerned, there was no reason why the case should not come before him.

While the legalities were being deliberated, police officers in charge of the investigation were also attempting to follow protocol. If a matter arose within a certain geographical jurisdiction in Pretoria, such as the Silver Lakes area in which the Silver Woods estate is situated, it would fall under a particular police station. Following the fire at the Magistrate's Court, certain police stations had been allocated to specific courts in order to speed up the work backlog. Ordinarily, Oscar's case would have been amongst those allocated to the Prison Court, but for Nair that made no logistical sense.

In agreement with the Chief Prosecutor, it was decided that Oscar would appear in the Magistrate's Court the following day to bring a formal bail application. Nair allocated the case to Court C, a room he regularly uses as it is conveniently close to his office and it would be able to cope with a large volume of people.

Nair went home that evening and, over dinner, told his wife Paddy and their three children that he would be presiding over Oscar's bail application the following day. News of the shooting had gripped the family in much the same way that it had caught the attention of the rest of the country. Fortunately Nair had experience with highly publicised cases involving celebrities and knew that the case was not up for discussion – not with his children or his wife.

Over the course of his career, Nair had been the presiding officer in several other cases featuring high-profile individuals. In 2008, he had convicted former middle-distance runner Sydney Maree on two counts of fraud and sentenced him to five years in jail. The athlete, who had competed for both South Africa and the United States, was found guilty of transferring funds from the National Empowerment Fund to his personal bank account while he was the acting chief executive. Nair also presided over the bail application of rugby player Jacobus 'Bees' Roux who had been arrested in August 2010 for allegedly beating a metro police officer to death. Nair granted bail of R100 000 – seen as exorbitant by the rugby player's legal team. Roux entered into a contentious plea bargain deal in the High Court a year later, for which he was given a five-year suspended jail sentence after pleading guilty to a charge of culpable homicide. Roux had said in court that the police officer, Sergeant Johannes Mogale, had wanted to rob him and he had acted in self-defence. As part of the agreement, the rugby player paid Mogale's family R750 000 as compensation. Another well-known rugby celebrity, Naas Botha, had appeared in Nair's courtroom as part of a maintenance matter, while radio personality Gareth Cliff also made an appearance before him for speeding.

The case that had garnered the most sustained media attention was that of Judge Nkola Motata. In 2007, the High Court judge had crashed his Jaguar into the wall of a residence in Hurlingham in Johannesburg and was video-recorded making racial slurs. Following a prolonged court case, Nair convicted the judge of drunk driving and gave him a R20 000 fine.

Nair had thus tasted the backlash of public and media attention before and was cognisant that there would be intense interest in this case too. However, neither Nair nor his family had any idea of the scale of the story and the sheer size of the media contingent that would face him when he walked into his courtroom the following day.

The Legal Teams

The drive into the Pretoria central business district before 6am is a breeze. The taxis are just starting their routes for the day and there are very few motorists. Court proceedings usually get underway at around 9am in the Magistrate's Court, but queues were expected on this Friday morning, so getting there early was vital.

At the crack of dawn, the vagrants outside the Frances Baard Street entrance to the courthouse make way for the newspaper vendors who carpet the stone tiles with broadsheets, tabloids and posters blaring headlines. Only one story was leading the papers on Friday, 15 February 2013:

'Bloody Valentine'
'Deadly Valentine'
'Blade Gunner'
'Valentine's Tragedy'
'Golden Boy Loses His Shine'

Various portfolio photographs of Reeva accompanied accompanied pictures of her lover leaving the Boschkop police station, his hands thrust deep into his pockets and head bowed.

The courtroom was full but finding a seat was not impossible. Photographers took up their places around the dock. They stood shoulder to shoulder, some of them crouched down, while others looked over their colleagues' heads. The benches to the right behind the dock were reserved for family members. Oscar's father Henke, his uncle Arnold, his brother Carl, and sister Aimee took their places in the front row behind the accused.

Speculation was rife about which prosecutors would handle the matter but it became clear fairly early on that advocates Gerrie Nel and Andrea Johnson had been tasked with the case. They were a crack team famous for putting the country's former police commissioner and head of Interpol Jackie Selebi in jail for corruption. Their handling of that case and of Operation Bad Guys – which centred on the murder of mining tycoon Brett Kebble – had seen them fall out of political favour with their bosses at the National Prosecuting Authority. They were viewed with suspicion and left to their own devices in a forgotten corner of the NPA's Silverton offices. But this was a massive case with international interest and their employers had clearly decided they were the most capable prosecutors for the job. Together, they had recently prosecuted the killers of young Pretoria mother Chanelle Henning, who had been shot dead shortly after dropping her young son at school.

Nel, a diminutive Afrikaans-speaking man with a hard, creased face and short white-blond hair is a relentless prosecutor with a fastidious obsession with detail. His wit is dry and sarcasm thick and he rarely shows emotion. The part-time wrestling coach is known for his patience in meticulously building cases and will carefully craft a conviction witness by witness until the full picture of his strategy emerges. While sitting in court he passes the time by doodling, drawing elaborate sketches in his notebook, yet always following proceedings intensely and quick to jump to his feet to object.

Nel grew up in the Limpopo platteland, in what was known as Potgietersrus and is now called Mokopane. He earned his stripes as a junior prosecutor for the state against former Conservative Party MP Clive Derby-Lewis and right-wing Polish immigrant Janus Walusz, who were convicted of assassinating South African Communist Party leader Chris Hani at his home in 1993. The murder was part of a plot to attempt to derail negotiations to end the apartheid regime.

In 2008 Nel was sensationally arrested by the SAPS in a pre-dawn raid on his Pretoria home on trumped-up charges as part of a bitter rivalry between the SAPS and the elite crime-fighting unit the Directorate of Special Operations, also known as the Scorpions. The unit was controversially disbanded by the ANC government after it investigated and prosecuted several high-ranking politicians, including President Jacob Zuma.

Nel was head of the Scorpions in Gauteng and his persistent prosecution of Selebi drew the ire of senior police officers – so much so that they dug up a reason to see him in handcuffs, but the charges against him did not stick. After his arrest, the National Prosecuting Authority was forced to issue a statement denying that the prosecutor had ever been part of any 'riot cases', as claimed in the media at the time. The organisation also denied he had ever been a member of the right-wing Afrikaner organisation, the Broederbond.

As a result of his relentless prosecution of Selebi, Nel made himself unpopular within the NPA, particularly with the former acting head of the organisation Nomgcobo Jiba, who also allegedly blamed Nel for the prosecution and conviction of her husband, ex-Scorpions member Booker Nhantsi. Nhantsi was convicted of the theft of trust funds totalling nearly R200 000 before Zuma granted him a presidential pardon.

Despite their success rate, however, Nel and his team were repeatedly subjected to in-house investigations and witch-hunts. The animosity also had its roots in the Selebi case and Nel's belief that Jiba had played a role in having him arrested on trumped-up charges. Jiba was indeed suspended from the NPA for her alleged role in the arrest, and during her Labour Court application against the prosecuting authority, produced extracts from Nel's diaries seized during a raid on his office. Jiba eventually settled her case with the NPA and returned to the organisation at the end of 2009.

Much to Jiba's chagrin, in 2012 Nel won the International Association of Prosecutors (IAP) Special Achievement Award for his work against the national police commissioner and his 'fierce pursuit of the vision of the National Prosecuting Authority's ideals to achieve justice in society'. The IAP lauded Nel's prosecuting skills and the approach he had taken to his cases. 'It bears mentioning that the IAP is proud to have recognised the exceptional qualities of integrity, independence and perseverance that Advocate Nel has displayed in the past,' it said.

'It is hardly surprising that the NPA has chosen Advocate Nel to lead the prosecution in another reportedly sensitive and difficult matter that would seem to require a prosecutor such as one with Advocate Nel's track record.'

A state advocate endearingly recalls how, when she first became a junior prosecutor in Johannesburg in the late 1990s, she was very curious about 'this funny, short man who would rush through the Director of Public Prosecution's office during tea time with his arms filled with files, his gown flapping behind him and a bevy of policemen trailing in his wake'. Nel was cutting his tea break short because he was claustrophobic and wouldn't catch the lifts in the building. He needed the time to run up the stairs to make it to court in time.

Nel is highly regarded amongst criminal defence attorneys who have come up against him in court. 'Gerrie is the one man in the National Prosecuting Authority who, if he is briefed in a matter, will do everything in his power to get a conviction. You have a specific place in the toolbox of the NPA for someone like Nel. If you want a conviction, you give him the case,' says one lawyer who has regularly come up against the prosecutor in court.

Andrea Johnson is a petite, fiery prosecutor, one who is regarded by her colleagues as highly principled. In her Durban Indian accent, she says it like it is, but will always ensure her actions are proper and that she is 'doing the right thing'. Johnson, who was schooled in the small KwaZulu-Natal town of Scottburgh, was fast-tracked through the echelons of the civil service. Her first job was prosecuting in Alberton before she did a short stint in the district courts where she was the first junior advocate to secure a life sentence at the time. She became a senior state advocate in the late 1990s, and in 1999 was amongst the first batch of prosecutors assigned to the Scorpions special unit. She has worked closely in tandem with Nel ever since.

Despite the public profile of the accused, Nel and Johnson were indifferent about being allocated the case. They were blasé about the unprecedented media interest in the matter and couldn't quite understand why it was receiving so much attention. With their experience in publicised cases, the legal team expected there to be some significant coverage, but were taken aback by what a frenzy it was. Both knew who the Blade Runner was, of course, but neither had a particularly keen interest in athletics and were not taken in by the massive celebrity of the man. Their view was simply that it was a case like any other and switched themselves off to the coverage and speculation that at the time was very much in sympathy with Oscar and the view that the shooting had been a terrible accident.

• • •

Sitting at the defence benches was one of the country's most prominent criminal advocates, senior counsel Barry Roux. In a country where defence advocates bill fees in the tens of thousands of rand a day and have achieved rock-star status for getting bad guys off, Roux was considered to be amongst the best. With his cheery grin, short greying hair and reading glasses perched on the tip of his nose, his demeanour can be deceiving. His high-pitched voice and Afrikaans accent can also take one by surprise. Bashful and meek outside the courtroom, Roux is a predator at the lectern and has earned a reputation for cutting cross-examination. Despite the high esteem in which he is held by his colleagues, he doesn't project the same narcissistic arrogance and self-indulgence that oozes off other senior advocates, although he does like to talk, a lot.

Roux was born in Mahikeng in the North West province and spent his first few years as a farm boy. His mother Margaret was well known in the district for her freshly baked bread, while his father was 'a soft guy, who could never kill a thing'. While he attended the Rooigrond farm school in his junior years, he was later sent to boarding school in Lichtenburg.

While Roux may not have had a 'calling' to study law, he made the decision to go into the field towards the end of his school career. He was conscripted to the army and joined the Department of Justice as a clerk and then as a prosecutor, while simultaneously studying for a BJuris through the University of South Africa. He quickly gained experience and by his second year at the Department was prosecuting cases, a young 19-year-old handling incidents of drunken driving and assault. In 1978, at just 22, he was appointed as a magistrate before going to the Justice Training College in Pretoria where he presented courses to his peers on the law of evidence.

But Roux wanted to go to the Bar and become an advocate, where he could learn from the likes of the esteemed Sir Sydney Kentridge and Constitutional Court Justice Johann Kriegler – and did so in 1982 when he did his pupillage. He focused on criminal law and particularly enjoyed medical negligence cases as he was intrigued by the explanations and detail shared by the doctors in these matters. He achieved silk in 2000 when he was made Senior Counsel.

In what is likely his longest-running case, Roux acted for so-called tax dodger businessman Dave King in a multibillion-rand, 11-year-long case with the South African Revenue Service (SARS). The former Rangers Football Club director finally settled the matter, agreeing to pay the taxman in excess of R700 million. Roux prosecuted another high-profile businessman, Roger Kebble, for fraud in what was known as the 'Skilled Labour Brokers' affair, in which Kebble was charged with siphoning off money paid to SLB while he was in control of the Durban Roodepoort Deep mining company. The case was struck off the roll in 2005. Roux also featured in the case surrounding the murder of Kebble's son Brett. He acted for Clinton Nassif, the Kebble's former head of security, who sold out the mining magnate's hired hit men in exchange for a deal with the Scorpions. Roux withdrew from the case after Glenn Agliotti claimed that Roger Kebble had paid Roux not to prosecute him. The allegations were never proven to be correct.

Barry Roux and Gerrie Nel dealt with each other during the Kebble investigation and have met in courtrooms on a number of other occasions. The most notable was in 1999, in the case of Kempton Park dentist, Dr Casper Greeff, accused of paying a handyman to kill his wife and make it appear to have been a robbery. Roux lost that round to Nel when Greeff was convicted and sentenced to life in prison. Roux and Nel dealt with each other on several other matters, particularly when the prosecutor was in charge of the Scorpions in Gauteng. Invariably, Roux would phone Nel to enquire about a case involving one of his clients.

'We respect Barry a lot. We were happy that it was him because we knew it would be someone who is open-minded, not petty, knows about process and procedures. He's extremely intelligent and open-minded. With Barry, it's a clean fight, it's a fair fight. Whenever there was a streak of unfairness, I say he was following instructions. It's not like him, he's not petty. He fights the case,' a member of the state's team told us.

Alongside Roux sat Kenny Oldwadge, another seasoned law man. Oldwadge, with his bulky frame and red cheeks, was the lawyer who had first addressed journalists outside Oscar's luxury estate.

A former police officer, Oldwadge was admitted to the Johannesburg Bar in 2002 and is described as 'tenacious', 'disciplined' and 'no-nonsense' by a senior colleague. Members of the police investigative team weren't quite so thrilled to see Oldwadge on the opposing benches. 'He was one of those policemen who pushed the boundaries and walked all over people. He's always very suspicious and pompous,' said one.

Sources say Oldwadge has angered many a cop and prosecutor. 'He fights with everyone. If he doesn't have anyone to fight with, then he'll fight with himself. He's unpopular amongst magistrates, judges and prosecutors. He brings out the horns in them. He just rubs them up the wrong way,' says one senior counsel.

Oldwadge has also featured in a number of high-profile cases. He successfully defended Sizwe Mankazana, who was charged with culpable homicide and drunk driving after the car he was driving crashed, killing Nelson Mandela's 13-year-old great-granddaughter Zenani.

Oldwadge acted, too, for Kaizer Chiefs boss Bobby Motaung in his R143-million case of fraud, corruption and forgery in the Nelspruit Regional Court. Motaung and his co-accused faced charges relating to the construction of the Mbombela Stadium for the 2010 FIFA World Cup. The charges were thrown out of court and the case struck from the roll in June 2013.

Oldwadge is no stranger to the Pistorius family and represented the Olympian's brother Carl during his own trial in the Vanderbijlpark Magistrate's Court, where he was charged after an accident in 2008 that led to the death of a female motorcyclist. Blood tests conducted by the police proved that he was not under the influence of alcohol at the time, while the court found that the motorcyclist was riding at excessive speed when she collided with the back of Carl's vehicle. Carl was acquitted of culpable homicide in May 2013.

It would later emerge that in the hours following the Valentine's Day shooting, there had been a mad scramble to secure legal representation for Oscar.

Early that Thursday morning, high-profile criminal attorney Ian Small-Smith received calls from both the sportsman's father and his agent, asking him to defend Oscar. Small-Smith's reputation precedes him and he would have been the first choice for many an accused finding themselves on the wrong side of the law. Although he's now largely retired, Small-Smith and his firm BDK, earned their reputation by successfully representing, amongst others, underworld figures, bad guys and dubious characters. He negotiated the sensational plea bargain deals for the three self-confessed hit men who killed mining tycoon Brett Kebble in an apparent assisted suicide in September 2005. In a curious set of circumstances, he also represented prosecutor Gerrie Nel when he was arrested.

Small-Smith selects the few cases he still takes on very carefully and, in any event, was too busy to rush to the police station to assist that morning. Instead, he offered to send a colleague from BDK to handle the case that day and he would then take it over when his time freed up. He also called top senior counsel Mike Hellens and asked him to be on brief for the matter.

Other attempts were also being made to secure the country's best counsel for Oscar. A call was put through to high-profile criminal defence attorney Ian Levitt who has acted in several publicised cases, asking him to act but he was overseas at the time. Another call went to Robbie Kanarek, who had successfully represented Glenn Agliotti in the Kebble case. Both attempts were made by friends close to Oscar.

Senior defence counsel Laurance Hodes, who had been briefed by Kanarek as Agliotti's advocate, was also lobbied to take the case and bail Oscar out. His success in getting Agliotti acquitted had received a great deal of media coverage and it was believed he could do the same for the runner.

It was rumoured that Oldwadge's mandate had been terminated – but that proved incorrect and he remained on brief.

Carl Pistorius had a history with Oldwadge and put his trust in him and Oldwadge was on the scene of the shooting in the early hours of 14 February. It was he who took the brief to Barry Roux. Surprisingly, the decision was also made to use Brian Webber – an attorney from the firm Ramsay Webber, who managed Oscar's commercial concerns – rather than an experienced criminal attorney. Having only acted in one criminal matter before, Webber had little experience in the dirty game of strategy and cunning associated with murder charges and plea bargain deals.

Roux was working at his chambers in Sandton on that Thursday when

Oldwadge phoned, asking him to assist with Oscar's bail application. Roux was told that bail would not be opposed and didn't think much of the matter. In fact, he hadn't heard any of the media coverage of the breaking news that morning because he had driven to the Planet Fitness gym in Sandton from his home in Kempton Park just after 5am – before the story broke – and had been at his office at the Village Chambers across the road from the gym since then. As a result, Roux was oblivious to the storm raging beyond his office walls, which are adorned with colourful caricature cars, wedding photographs and legal journals.

At one point during the day, Roux noticed a man he recognised as the clerk for the State Attorney arriving at his chambers to serve papers for the case. He only remembered the clerk's brief visit because of the extremely colourful shirts the man favoured. Roux left his office after 11pm that night, still unaware of the media storm swirling around his new client's case.

It was for this reason that Roux was flummoxed when he arrived at the Boschkop police station to consult with Oscar on the morning of the bail application. He had driven through to Pretoria with Oldwadge early in the morning and had anticipated that there might be a few media vehicles outside but instead was met by a bombardment of cameras, microphones and satellite trucks. At the courthouse, the scene was amplified and Roux battled to make his way through the hordes, but fortunately, the foreign correspondents in Pretoria weren't familiar with him and he managed to slip through the crowd. Realising the massive public interest in the case, Roux thought, Hell, I better speak to Gerrie, and quickly met with the prosecutor whom he had come to know well over the years.

Now both men were ready to proceed.

While reporters found their spots in the courtroom, photographers were still jostling for position around the dock, the activity prompting a court official to order that every photographer and camera operator vacate the courtroom so that an accreditation process could resume. Officials also wanted to lay down the law as to when pictures could be taken of the accused.

The media hype that had gathered momentum since the shooting more than 24 hours earlier was encroaching on the courtroom. A member of the state's team, whose identity we have kept confidential, said the attention puzzled them. 'I think the fact that it was just the two of them, and everyone in the media speculating about the kind of relationship they had, something must have just happened in those hours before she died and what else could have happened between a young couple other than a fight? We agreed it was pre-meditated; it could never have been an accident, absolutely not.'

Away from the humid, claustrophobic courtroom, behind the wooden door and thick steel gate, Oscar was preparing for his first court appearance. With the clang of keys on metal grabbing the attention of the entire courtroom, several individuals emerged from the holding cells to speak to the athlete's family. Bottles of water and food were handed over and returned to the cells. Proceedings were about to start.

• • •

Yvette van Schalkwyk has 24 years' experience as a court-appointed social worker and probation officer. In February 2013, she was working for the Department of Social Development, where she had been since 1989 after acquiring her Bachelor of Social Work degree.

On the morning of 15 February, the court orderly at the Pretoria Magistrate's Court approached Van Schalkwyk and asked her to assist with Oscar Pistorius. The court manager also put in a request for her to accompany him during the bail application. She didn't know why the request was sent to her, but she assumed it was for emotional support and to monitor Oscar's behaviour. At that stage, she knew nothing at all about the facts of the case.

So it was that the probation officer made her way to the holding cells in the court building where she found Oscar preparing for his court appearance, 'heartbroken' and 'emotional'.

'What I saw from the first time that I saw him, from the first second, was a man that was heartbroken about the loss. He cried, he was in mourning, he suffered emotionally. He was very sorry about the loss, especially for her parents. The suffering they are going through. That was the theme throughout the whole period that I saw him. It was mainly about Reeva, the loss. He loved her,' Van Schalkwyk would later recount to the trial court.

'He cried 80 per cent of the time. He talked to me about what they planned for the future. His future with her, the loss that he never is going to see her again. Her family, her mother and father, what they are going through. That is what I saw, I saw a heartbroken man that [was] suffering emotionally.'

Despite his fragility and apparent emotional distress, Oscar knew he would have to attempt to pull himself together to walk out into the courtroom, into the dock, and face the world.

• • •

Magistrate Desmond Nair pulled on his black-and-red robe and made his way from his office to Court C. It had already been an eventful morning, with a delegation of foreign and local media clogging the passageway to his chambers as they awaited clarity on whether or not they could photograph and film proceedings. Nair was beginning to realise the extent of the public interest in the case and, while he wasn't daunted by the scale of the coverage, he knew he would have to be on top of his game that morning.

When he arrived at the courtroom, he took in the scene – the swollen public gallery, the benches crammed with reporters – before turning to a security officer to inform him that he would not enter until the situation was under control.

Nair then took a moment to compose himself, aware that he would have to be very careful of every decision he made. He reminded himself to be conscious of the accused person's right to be respected and that he had to ensure that he received a fair bail hearing.

The courtroom finally settled and Nair adjusted his robe. He wanted to feel in command of his courtroom, but he didn't want to give the impression to the media and the public that they were subservient to him. He had to affirm the perception that he was in control and that the world could be reassured that he would take charge.

· · ·

11:28 AM Feb 15th
#OscarPistorius Chief Magistrate Desmond Nair enters. Nel calls for the accused. BB

Magistrate Desmond Nair swept into the courtroom in a dramatic manner, his robe billowing behind him, and took his seat. Nel, the prosecutor, rose as everyone else in the room sat down, and called for Oscar Pistorius to be brought in.

The once triumphant athlete who had graced the globe's tracks, often with his hands in the air celebrating triumph, entered briskly with his hands by his side and his head down. He was dressed in a dark suit and tie. Oscar positioned himself towards the centre of the dock and stared at the floor. His face was contorting, overcome with emotion and anguish. It was clear he had not had much sleep.

'The state versus Oscar Leonard Carl Pistorius,' said Nel, as he called the case. Nair's first task was to set the accused at ease:

> Court: *Alright let me then ask for some silence please. It is important*
> *people, the murmuring, the whispers, I want to hear a pin drop.*
> *Please give me your cooperation, it is important. Goeiemore Mnr*
> *Pistorius. Wees rustig – is u Afrikaanssprekend?*
> Accused: *English Sir.*
> Court: *English. Take it easy, be calm, you can take a seat, it's fine.*
> Accused: *Thank you Sir.*

The prosecutor proceeded by telling Nair that the state would apply to have the matter postponed for seven days for further investigation.

Oscar, who was by this time seated in the dock, broke down in uncontrollable sobs, his body heaving as he gasped for air. His father, Henke, who was in the first row of benches, leaned forward and placed his left hand on his son's back. It did little to calm the accused. Tears escaped Oscar's fingers as his hands cupped his face, and his leg was bouncing. It was evident for all to see that this was a broken man.

Nair ruled that no live recording would be allowed, but pictures and filming could take place when the court was not in session – a standard ruling with which many local reporters are familiar. The magistrate did, however, order that the audio of the closing argument and judgment in the bail application could be broadcast.

· · ·

Then the real business of the day began. As anticipated, the defence set about bringing an application for Oscar to be released on bail. However, there was a crease that had to be ironed out first – one that would result in the defence having to ask for a postponement before the formal bail application could be heard.

The state wanted the court to consider the case under the more serious crime of premeditated murder rather than of murder or culpable homicide and thus to deem it a Schedule 6 offence. Roux, on the other hand, wanted the matter dealt with in terms of Schedule 5, and asked that the bail application be postponed until the following Tuesday in order to allow the defence time to prepare.

Nair confirmed this stance in an exchange with the prosecutor.

'The bail proceedings – is the state saying premeditated murder?' asked Nair.

'We will argue it was premeditated murder,' said Nel.

According to South African law, a Schedule 6 offence is the most severe charge possible – a Schedule 5 is serious, but Schedule 6 is the same crime committed in a more aggravated manner. For example, if the Schedule 5 charge is murder, Schedule 6 would be the murder of a policeman, for example. If Schedule 5 is rape, Schedule 6 would be the rape of a minor or the rape of a mentally challenged individual. In other words, it is the same offence, but a more aggravated, severe form of the crime. In this particular instance, premeditated murder is listed in the Criminal Procedure Act as a Schedule 6 crime. The determination of which schedule the offence falls under has implications for bail and for sentencing. The standard required for an accused person to be granted bail is higher and the jail time the accused could face is extended. On a Schedule 6 offence, the accused would carry the onus to show that there are exceptional circumstances that should result in his being granted bail. He would have to satisfy the court – through giving evidence or by an affidavit – that exceptional circumstances exist that are in the interest of justice to permit his release. On a Schedule 5 offence, the accused only needs to show that it would be in the interest of justice to release him and he does not need to go the extra mile to show exceptional circumstances.

Roux also asked that Oscar be detained at the Brooklyn police station, and added that they had already obtained permission from the station commander Brigadier André Wiese.

Nair, however, wanted a valid reason why the accused would be held at a police station, considering that it is standard to be detained at the local prison. The magistrate wanted to ensure that Oscar did not receive any preferential treatment by virtue of the fact that he was a celebrity. The world was watching the case unfold, searching for any glitch in the system or preferential treatment for the celebrity accused.

'We have obtained permission from the station commander. The reason being that we have limited time, we need to do after-hour consultations … We need to deal with information as we receive it and take it up with the accused and in the normal prison situation you cannot do that after hours,' explained Roux, making the point that there were no visitation hours at Pretoria Central Prison. Nel supported the request.

> 12:09 PM Feb 15th
> #OscarPistorius Nair postpones the matter until Tuesday. Oscar is to [be]
> kept at Brooklyn police station. BB

As court was adjourned, Oscar stood up to leave. He glanced back over his right shoulder at his sister and father. Henke stretched out his hand to touch his son, but as he did so, Oscar flinched, turned his back on his father and walked out of the dock, back into the holding cells.

Shortly after the proceedings, the Pistorius family issued a statement disputing the charge of murder 'in the strongest terms':

> *Firstly, and most importantly, all our thoughts today must be with the family and friends of Reeva Steenkamp.*
>
> *Oscar Pistorius has appeared in court here in Pretoria this morning formally charged with the murder of Reeva Steenkamp. The alleged murder is disputed in the strongest terms. These are now live and active legal proceedings which must be allowed to take their course through the process of proper investigation by the police, evidence-gathering and through the local South African judicial system. In a short hearing lawyers representing the athlete asked for a postponement for a bail application until Tuesday next week to allow time for their own investigation into the circumstances of the tragedy, which was agreed by the Magistrate, who also agreed that Pistorius would be held in custody at a local police station. Oscar Pistorius has made history as an Olympic and Paralympic sportsman and has been an inspiration to others the world over. He has made it very clear that he would like to send his deepest sympathies to the family of Reeva. He would also like to express his thanks through us today for all the messages of support he has received – but as stated our thoughts and prayers today should be for Reeva and her family – regardless of the circumstances of this terrible, terrible tragedy. We will endeavour to issue other statements as matters develop but in these circumstances I am sure you appreciate it is very difficult to answer any more specific questions. Thank you very much for your attention.*

Oscar was transported to the Brooklyn police station where he would be held in a single cell for the weekend.

While the focus had been on the courtroom in Pretoria, Cecil Myers and his son were confronting the distressing task of identifying Reeva's body at the mortuary. Cecil had taken on the responsibility on behalf of her parents in Port Elizabeth.

Reeva's Last Photo Shoot

The thick white plastic body bag was wheeled into the autopsy room on a gurney. The red tag that clasped together two zips, making a tamper-proof seal, bore a printed ID number that corresponded with documents the police had provided to the mortuary services. The number identified the deceased. It was 24 hours after Oscar had killed Reeva and the model had now become, as indicated on the bag, 'Property of Gauteng Forensic Pathology Service'.

The pathologist tasked with conducting the autopsy, Professor Gert Saayman, and nine other pathology and police officials waited in the autopsy room for Reeva to arrive.

The staff donned their plastic aprons and red-soled gumboots. With them were police blood spatter expert Ian van der Nest and his crime scene photographer colleague Bennie van Staden, in their dark-blue SAPS-issued overalls, chevron reflectors on the short sleeves, the type worn by crime scene investigators. Investigating officer Hilton Botha was amongst the delegation of SAPS officials in attendance. He and some of the other visitors to the unit were given baby-blue disposable bibs with matching bootees, which covered their well-polished black leather shoes. It was this type of disposable bootees that would be the cause of much consternation for Botha a few days later when he took the stand in Oscar's bail application. All except Saayman wore the blue surgical gloves.

The professor wore a white lab coat, with his name and designation pinned over his chest, just above his heart. His black Bic pen etched notes onto a dozen pages held fast by a steel clamp biting down on an old clipboard. The top-right section of chipboard had seemingly been broken off some time ago.

Saayman is not only head of pathology services in the province, a position he's held since 1998, but also head of the Department of Forensic Medicine at the

University of Pretoria. A highly regarded expert in the field, he has conducted over 15 000 autopsies during his career and his process of preparation was a familiar one to him.

Also attending the postmortem was independent pathologist Dr Reggie Perumal. He would be listed as number 9 on the list of witnesses present in Saayman's official report. Perumal regularly testifies in court cases against the state. He featured in the case of the death of former South African cricketer Tertius Bosch, the trial of socialite Rajiv Narandas accused of murder, and is on brief for the Legal Resources Centre to investigate the Marikana miners' shooting in 2012. He was also hired by the Zimbabwean vice-president Joice Mujuru to help investigate the murder of her husband ZANU-PF heavyweight Solomon Mujuru. Perumal grew up in Chatsworth and studied medicine at the University of Durban-Westville. He worked at the district surgeon's office before going into the private sector in 1994, at the age of 39.

Oscar's hired expert had been dispatched from Durban at short notice on a watching brief to take notes and report back to Oldwadge and Roux. In a situation like this, the professor provides the audience with running commentary of his findings. In the event there is a major discrepancy in the findings, the pair could sort it out then and there by asking another pathologist for his or her opinion, or take tissue samples or photographic evidence to be discussed at a later stage. The parties have to come to consensus before the body is released to the family, however, because there is generally no opportunity to go back and reconduct the autopsy. It was likely that both men would be called as witnesses in a potential trial and their expert opinions weighed in opposition for the prosecution and defence.

The body bag seal was broken and the zips parted to reveal Reeva's naked body. Beside her inside the bag were the items of clothing she had been wearing when she had died – a light-grey pair of Nike shorts and a black sleeveless top.

The shorts were unfolded and held up in front of a photographer, revealing that the right side was stained crimson red. Closer inspection of the elastic waistband revealed a very small, round hole corresponding with the wound on Reeva's hip.

'This appearance is not inconsistent with having been caused by a projectile from a firearm,' said the professor, while recording his finding on the clipboard.

While Saayman constantly voiced his observations, the click of camera shutters echoed in the clinically clean autopsy room – these would be the last photos taken of the young model.

The black vest had several holes torn open on its right side and was covered

Oscar in his garage just hours after killing Reeva. He had already washed blood off his hands and chest. SAPS

Arrow stickers and blue Post-its mark the blood spatter trail and the spot where Reeva died at the foot of the staircase. SAPS

A view from the upstairs landing looking down to where Reeva's body is covered by a brown sheet. SAPS

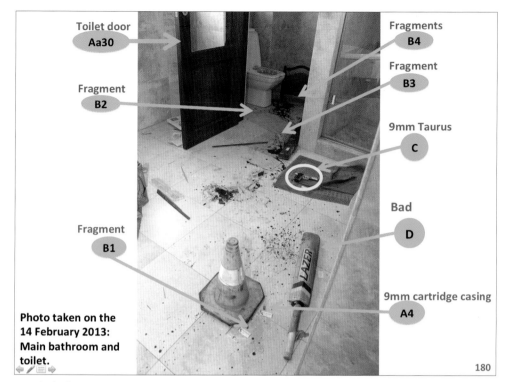

Toilet door
Aa30

Fragments
B4

Fragment
B3

Fragment
B2

9mm Taurus
C

Fragment
B1

Bad
D

**Photo taken on the
14 February 2013:
Main bathroom and
toilet.**

9mm cartridge casing
A4

180

The bathroom as it was presented in the court exhibit Album 2, which plotted key evidence at Oscar's house. SAPS

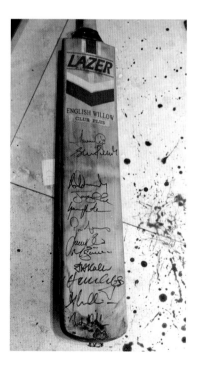

ABOVE: Oscar's 9 mm Taurus PT 917 cs handgun on the mat in the bathroom close to Reeva's iPhone. SAPS

LEFT: The face of the cricket bat in the bathroom revealed national cricket players' signatures. SAPS

The left side of the bed with Reeva's flip-flops and her overnight bag. The firearm holster was next to the bedside lamp. SAPS

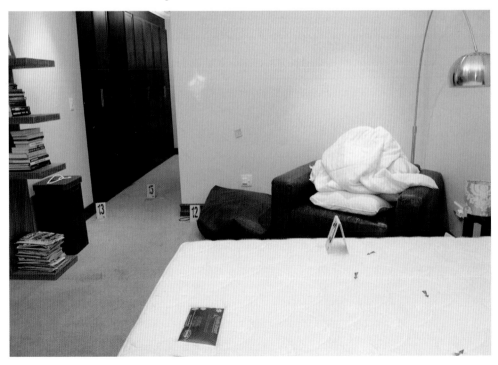

Numbered boards mark the locations of evidence in Oscar's bedroom. SAPS

BELOW: The blood-spattered watchcase in Oscar's bedroom. Two timepieces went missing during the police investigation of the scene. SAPS

ABOVE LEFT: The police's Photo 55 shows Oscar's bedroom with the fan in the doorway, the curtains partly drawn, the duvet on the floor and the jeans appear to be slightly on top of it. SAPS

ABOVE: The police's Photo 68 is a close-up of the duvet and a pair of jeans. Also visible is the smaller black fan, unplugged and to the right. SAPS

The inside of the toilet cubicle, showing the bowl that appears to have been flushed, the magazine rack and the pool of blood on the floor. SAPS

A close-up of the inside of the bowl shows clear signs that it was flushed at some point, washing away blood to create the clean white lines. Door splinters and spatter had also settled on the left side. SAPS

The toilet door with four bullet holes marked as it was reconstructed for demonstration purposes in court. The mark where Oscar claimed he kicked the door is visible above hole 'C'. The scratch marks in line with the handle were created when the loose panels were transported in a body bag.
ANTOINE DE RAS

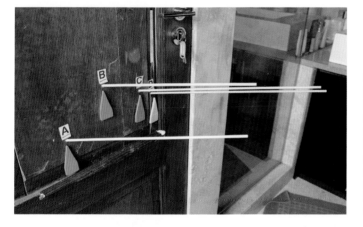

Probes placed through the bullet holes attempt to map the trajectory of the bullets. Also visible, to the left, are footprints believed to have been caused by police stepping on evidence, and the mark caused by Oscar kicking the door, above the 'C' sticker. SAPS

Photographer Bennie van Staden takes a picture while standing on the toilet. Probes through the bullet holes in the door map the projectile trajectories and indicate where Reeva might have been positioned. SAPS

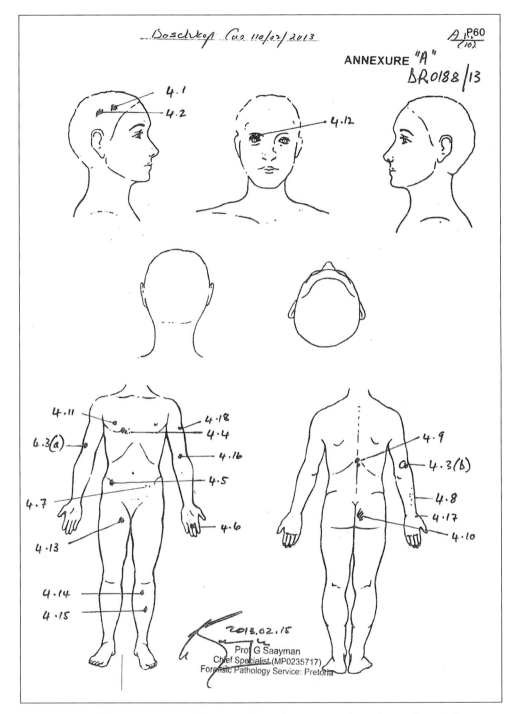

A diagram in pathologist Gert Saayman's report indicates the positions of Reeva's wounds marked out on a person in the anatomical position. Marks 4.1 and 4.2 depict the head entry and exit wounds respectively; 4.3(a) the arm entry wound; 4.3(b) the exit wound; 4.4 the wounds caused by fragments exiting 4.3(b); 4.5 the hip wound; and 4.6 the wounds between the webbing of the left hand. SAPS

ABOVE: Reeva's bloodied shorts as they were photographed during the postmortem. A bullet entry wound is visible along the waistband to the left. SAPS

LEFT: The bullet fragments removed from Reeva's skull during the postmortem. The picture depicts the lead core (bottom), and the copper jacket (top), with at least one of the exposed, jagged petals designed to slice through flesh. SAPS

Oscar's kitchen with the Valentine's Day gift Reeva had bought for the athlete. SAPS

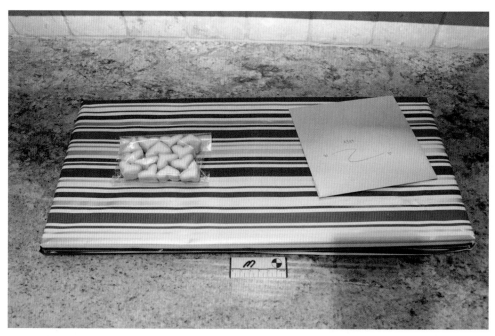

The Valentine's Day gift and card Reeva had bought for Oscar. It contained three framed pictures of the couple. SAPS

STANDER/VILJOEN

STIPP

NHLENGETHWA

OSCAR

MOTSHUANE

VAN DER MERWE

TOP: An aerial view of the Silver Woods estate. SAPS

MIDDLE: An aerial view of the balcony and door leading from Oscar's bedroom. SAPS

BOTTOM: The front door to Oscar's house was sealed on the first day after police had conducted their investigations. SAPS

The table (back left) at Tashas where Oscar, Kevin Lerena and Darren Fresco, as well as visiting athlete Martyn Rooney, were seated when Oscar negligently discharged Fresco's handgun. SAPS

Former investigating officer Hilton Botha prepares to give evidence at the bail application. ANTOINE DE RAS

Oscar's defence team at the bail hearing. BARRY BATEMAN

Oscar's relatives at the bail application. From left are uncles Arnold and Theo (in the background), Oscar's brother Carl and father Henke (seated). ANTOINE DE RAS

The first photograph to emerge of Oscar in
the dock shows him weeping. The picture
made the front pages of newspapers across
the world. ANTOINE DE RAS

A moment of reflection for the
accused during his bail application.
This image won photographer
Antoine de Ras international awards.
ANTOINE DE RAS

The holding cell at the Brooklyn police station where Oscar was detained during his bail application.

Oscar's uncle Arnold addresses the media at the Pretoria Magistrate's Court after his nephew was granted bail. ANTOINE DE RAS

with bits of human flesh and bone fragments. Found amongst the fibres and overlooked by investigators on the crime scene was a small piece of bullet shrapnel. An official handed it over to the evidence officer before it was sealed and labelled, along with the two items of clothing. The packet would be reopened several months later for the items to be photographed again but by then the blood on the shorts had dried to a dull brown.

Reeva's body was removed from the body bag and placed on her back on a cold stainless steel table. Her once finely manicured and pampered hands had been sealed inside clear police evidence bags to preserve any evidence investigators might harvest from under her nails. Two bracelets on her left wrist bore numbers linking the body to case files and other evidence – the plastic wristband, not unlike the ones worn in hospital, had the number 48 scratched on to it in black ink, while the cable tie held in place a larger tag – DR188/13. Reeva was just a number.

Her body was still caked in blood, and had to be documented in that state before the autopsy could proceed any further. The ECG stickers above and below her breasts were still in place. Measurement rulers were held up against her and the first pictures snapped included another identity tag: 15/2/13 R STEENKAMP.

The men used their surgical gloves to manoeuvre her head into position for the cameras. Her blonde hair, the exact shade of which she had spent hours agonising over, was now red, matted together with blood and brain matter. The plastic evidence bags were removed before she was rolled onto her side to reveal wounds on her back, which was now turning purple as the blood in her body settled; only where her skin was in contact with a surface did it retain its pallor complexion. It was only then that her body was cleaned. The blood and tissue were washed off, revealing hundreds of tiny light-brown freckles on Reeva's face. She wore no make-up, her finely plucked and sculpted eyebrows free of the fine spatter kicked up when she was struck by the bullets.

'In the right frontoparietal area in the hairy scalp is a penetrating wound with irregular shape and irregular edges,' muttered Saayman, jotting down his notes. He was referring to the top-right side of Reeva's head where she had been struck by a bullet. The full extent of the damage was not immediately clear. Although her hair had been rinsed, blood still covered most of the wound. A razor was used to shave away a palm-sized section of her hair, revealing two holes through her skull – an entrance gunshot wound, and the exit wound.

The professor moved on to Reeva's right arm. Just above the crease where the elbow bends was a small hole, identified as another gunshot entrance wound. Her arm was deformed and it was clear that the bullet struck the bone, shattering it.

Around the wound was a series of small cuts. The back of Reeva's arm presented an entirely different picture, revealing a gaping wound.

'There is extrusion of tissue from the wound. The wound edges are irregular in areas and partially serrated and torn,' said Saayman.

Measurement tabs were placed around the wound as photos were taken.

'The overall appearance of these two wounds is consistent with that of exit gunshots injury probably caused by a projectile or portions thereof, together with possible secondary projectile injury including possibly bone fragments.'

The professor was writing as he was speaking.

'Are you satisfied, Dr Perumal?' asked Saayman.

The hired expert said he was.

The outside of Reeva's forearm revealed many small cuts scattered over a relatively large area. 'The appearance is not inconsistent with multiple superficial secondary projectile or shrapnel injuries.'

Saayman believed the wounds to be caused by wooden splinters, which he would describe as secondary projectiles in his report.

Saayman also documented the abrasion under Reeva's right breast, towards her midline. Considering the bone and tissue fragments on Reeva's black top, the professor concluded that the wound was caused by the same bullet, which passed through her elbow and, having lost a lot of its momentum, was incapable of penetrating her chest. Smaller abrasions in the area were probably caused by bone from the arm picked up as secondary projectiles.

On Reeva's right hip was another small hole, akin to an entry wound, which was surrounded by significant discoloration and bruising. The wound lined up with the hole through the elastic of the grey casual shorts that accompanied the body.

The hip, head and arm wounds were all located on the right side of Reeva's body. Saayman walked around the gurney to the other side to inspect damage to the soft flesh between the index and middle finger of Reeva's left hand. While Saayman believed the injury was caused by a projectile travelling from the top of the hand towards the palm, the nature of the folds and skin creases on a human's hand make such determination difficult.

Reeva was then rolled on to her stomach. Two small bruises were immediately visible in the middle of her back. 'There is no perforation of the skin and the abrasions appear to overlie the bony prominences of the subjacent thoracic vertebrae,' said the professor.

The wounds were typical of blunt trauma, caused by banging oneself against the corner of a chair, or being hit by a projectile that had already spent much of its energy. The only blunt object in the cubicle with Reeva when she was shot that fitted this description was the small wooden magazine rack. This suggestion would be an issue of contention between the state and defence, with the latter arguing that it was indeed the furniture that caused these marks.

With the deceased now on her stomach, a bruise on her right inner buttock was visible. An official assisting with the postmortem, wearing gloves, pushed the skin around the area, manoeuvring to establish whether a bullet could be felt under the skin. Nothing was found. But the pathologist knew what he was looking at. The bruises were adjacent to the hip wound on Reeva's front. Had the bullet perhaps disintegrated on impact?

While Reeva's face appeared intact, her right eye was blue and swollen, as if it had been hit with a blunt object. It was clear that this was the result of internal damage caused by the gunshot wound – in other words, not the result of direct trauma to the eye, but rather internal damage caused by the shot to the head.

A study of Reeva's entire body revealed a number of other small bruises and scratches: a reddish discoloration of Reeva's right nipple, a bruise on the upper part of her thigh, bruises on her shin and a small scratch on her right thumb. Saayman would suggest they were of no significance to the injuries that led to death, or that they had been caused some time prior to Reeva's death.

The external exam was thus concluded and the team prepared to dissect the body. A study of the wounds would show that while some of the projectile that entered her head had exited Reeva's skull, a significant portion destroyed her brain. The bone was significantly damaged. 'There are multiple further irregular and linear cracks or fractures involving the right temporal and parietal bones.'

Cracks permeated from the site where the bullets had made holes in Reeva's head, making their way down to the base and over the top of her skull.

Her brain was removed. 'A deformed irregular and jagged projectile is found to be lodged within the inner table, in the base of the right occipital fossa,' remarked Saayman.

'This projectile has a predominantly black metal jacket with jagged sharp protrusions which partially surround and irregular lead core.' The pathologist recognised the bullet as Black Talon ammunition. In 15 000 autopsies, the professor has seen this all too often given the high instances of gun-related crime in South Africa, where nearly 50 people are killed each day. The ammunition used in this instance explained the damage to the young woman's body. The fragments were removed and handed over to the police as evidence.

The professor inspected Reeva's nasal area, mouth, tongue, neck and throat and found no tissue damage, a point he recorded in his notes. Despite bruises under the right breast of the deceased, Saayman found no deep injuries to the chest and no abnormalities to the airway and oesophagus.

There was, however, haemorrhaging within the inner wall of one of the chambers of the heart, but this is commonly seen in patients who have suffered severe head trauma or sudden major blood loss. Reeva's liver was pale – another sign of massive blood loss.

The team removed Reeva's stomach, placing it in a stainless steel dish. It spilt its contents – a light-green soup of dark green, orange and red chunks. 'Vegetables,' remarked the professor. The time-of-death entry on the certificate accompanying the body noted that Reeva had died some time after 3am. Saayman believed that the partially digested food in her stomach – which he could identify – could not have been consumed more than two hours prior to her death. This finding would be crucial to the state's case, and prompt the defence to call two expert witnesses to refute the pathologist's conclusion in this regard; however, Perumal, who was present at the autopsy, was not one of the experts called.

A study of her bladder showed that it contained no more than a few millilitres of urine.

A dissection of the hip wound revealed major damage. 'There is very extensive soft tissue haemorrhage and hematoma formation in the pelvic area.'

The pathologist switched to using a fluoroscope, a specially designed light used to highlight projectile particles, which revealed that the bullet had disintegrated after hitting Reeva's hipbone. Tiny pieces, varying from 1 mm to 3 mm, littered the hip region, where it shattered the bone and tore away flesh. As a result, Saayman decided it was impractical even to attempt to collect the bits of steel from the body.

The professor concluded, instructing officials to stitch up the body. Reeva would soon be released to her family.

A Weekend in Jail

The weekend newspapers had a field day. The Saturday papers dropped with an image of Oscar covering his face in court. The picture was thought to be a violation of the court order restricting photographs being taken while the court was in session. The lens man, Antoine de Ras from *The Star* newspaper, had snapped the image from outside the courtroom through a porthole-like window in the door and uploaded it before he had learnt of the order. More than a year later, De Ras won Journalist of the Year in the Sikuvile Journalism Awards for his picture titled, 'Oscar Weeps'. In his motivation for the entry, he said, 'I shot a frame of Pistorius in the moment he stood in the dock for the very first time, overcome by emotion. My photo was legitimate and righteous. Taken before the prohibition order and indeed before the court was in session, meaning I wasn't in danger of being in contempt.' There was, however, frustration amongst the journalists that they could be barred from court for violating the rules. Oscar's legal team was also considering legal action as a result of the pictures.

Oscar's father, Henke, whom he'd snubbed a day earlier, was interviewed by the London *Daily Telegraph*. It was one of several reports using him as a source before the family and their PR team stepped in and silenced him.

Oscar and his father shared a tumultuous relationship and were not close. Henke said the Pistorius family had zero doubt that Oscar shot dead Reeva thinking she was an intruder.

'When you are a sportsman, you act even more on instinct,' he told the newspaper. 'It's instinct – things happen and that's what you do.'

Controversially, he also blamed the country's high crime rate and the ANC government for his son's actions and to justify why the Pistorius family owned more than 55 guns.

'Some of the guns are for hunting and some are for protection, the handguns. It speaks to the ANC government, look at white crime levels, why protection is so poor in this country, it's an aspect of our society,' he said. 'You can't rely on the police, not because they are inefficient always but because crime is so rife.'

He said he personally had never had to use a gun in self-defence, but added: 'That doesn't mean I haven't been hijacked, attacked. As a family, we value life much too much to produce guns at every opportunity we can use them. I have been in positions where I can use a gun but we have been brought up in a way that we value the lives of others very highly.'

The Pistorius family swiftly issued a statement distancing Oscar from his father's comments and the ANC was similarly quick to respond, criticising the remarks.

In the meantime, the Steenkamp family was also being asked to comment on the court proceedings and the incident.

'We do not want to speculate about what happened,' Reeva's uncle Mike Steenkamp was quoted as saying to *Beeld* newspaper. 'We would rather pay attention to the criminal process which will take its course now. We are a religious family. And if you believe in God, then you know justice will be in his hand,' he said.

The gunshot-riddled door and the bloodied cricket bat featured prominently in the weekend papers. According to the *City Press* report, 'a source with inside knowledge of the case' confirmed that police were investigating three possible scenarios following the discovery of the cricket bat. The first was that Oscar used the bat to 'viciously assault' Reeva; the second was that Reeva used the bat to defend herself from her enraged lover; and the third scenario was that the bat was used to break down the toilet door, which Reeva had locked. The report also claimed that investigators had specifically requested that the athlete's blood be tested for drugs and steroids.

Rumours were also raging amongst journalists that investigators had found steroids in Oscar's room. A tip-off had come in that cops had found performance-enhancing drugs and syringes in a drawer in the bedroom.

The implications were huge. If this were indeed true, it would fit into the so-called roid-rage version of events being bandied about in the tabloid media: that the Blade Runner was pumped up on steroids and lost his temper. None of the rumours could be confirmed, though, and despite the pressure for a scoop, local journalists kept their distance from the rumour.

Monday morning, however, broke with a UK tabloid 'exclusive': 'Steroids found at Blade Runner's mansion – cops find bloodied cricket bat too' was the headline in *The Sun*.

According to the reporter's 'source close to the investigation', officers found banned steroid drugs in the athlete's home, as well as evidence of heavy drinking before the shooting. The report further claimed that police were now investigating the possibility that 'Pistorius may have blasted Reeva in an explosion caused by the performance-boosting steroids' – and they were investigating whether the murder suspect was 'in the grip of roid-rage', a side-effect of high doses of the outlawed drugs.

More theories as to what exactly had happened that morning emerged in media reports in the days leading up to the first court appearance. *The Sun* suggested that Oscar had first shot Reeva in the bedroom, that she fled to the toilet where she locked herself in and was then shot a further three times: 'Police now believe the first shot was fired at her in the master bedroom – hitting her hip as she fled to the bathroom. Wounds to the top of her head suggest that as she sat doubled up in pain on the toilet she was hit three more times by bullets that ripped through the door.'

The bloodied cricket bat also appeared in this version, but now with claims that Reeva had sustained 'skull crush injuries', suggesting that her head was smashed in with the bat.

By this time the rumour had also emerged that Reeva had apparently received a text message from Blue Bulls rugby player Francois Hougaard. The pair had previously dated before she started going out with Oscar. This text message was alleged to have angered Oscar, and was what started the fight that led to the shooting. There was, however, no official comment or evidence to back up this theory and phone records would later dispute it.

• • •

While speculation gathered momentum, Oscar was preparing for his bail application in his cell at the Brooklyn police station. As police stations go, Brooklyn is one of the better ones. It serves the affluent community of Waterkloof and the predominantly student-inhabited area of Hatfield. The station commander is the no-nonsense, old-guard Brigadier André Wiese.

Over the weekend a pastor – uninvited – visited the athlete, as did some family members. Oscar's manager Peet van Zyl also went to see him to offer his support and discuss his immediate racing future. Van Zyl had been Oscar's manager for seven years and they had a strong bond. The pair took the significant decision to cancel all races Oscar had been booked to compete in, including Brazil, the United States, the United Kingdom and Australia.

Van Zyl told reporters that Oscar's sponsors at that time supported his client, and that they were happy to let the legal process take its course before taking a decision on whether or not to retain him as a brand ambassador. But despite Van Zyl's apparent optimism about Oscar's potential future, it was becoming increasingly obvious that he would never be able to return to his former glory and things would never again be as they once were.

Saying Goodbye to Reeva

The black Mercedes-Benz hearse pulled up outside the white, weather-beaten chapel at the Victoria Park Crematorium in Port Elizabeth. Personnel from Doves Funeral Services took their positions on either side of the coffin holding Reeva Steenkamp's body and carried it through to a side entrance. It was draped in a cloth and an arrangement of white flowers was perched on top. Slight cloud gathered overhead as the so-called friendly city's ubiquitous wind whistled through the trees.

By request from family members, journalists retreated beyond a boundary wall, a distance from the tranquil setting of the memorial service. They watched as mourning friends, relatives and the occasional celebrity walked the path to the chapel. Reeva's parents were embraced as they moved slowly into the building. Not far behind them was Gina Myers, her sister and parents, Reeva's 'adopted' Johannesburg family.

Most notable amongst the celebrities was rugby player Francois Hougaard, in a dark suit and with sunglasses shielding his eyes. Hougaard's appearance caused a stir amongst media curious about weekend reports around the potential text message that might have ignited a row between Oscar and Reeva. Radio DJ Thato Sikwane, popularly known as DJ Fresh on 5FM, was amongst the mourners. The ANC Women's League was also present, and Nelson Mandela Bay deputy mayor and Women's League provincial secretary Nancy Sihlwayi came out to support the victim's family. 'The city is in grief, a little angel is no more,' she told reporters before controversially remarking that Oscar should not receive bail and that he 'must die in jail'.

Following the event, Reeva's uncle, Mike, and her half-brother, Adam, addressed reporters, saying that her death had left a void in the family. Her uncle struggled under the weight of the moment, breaking down in tears as he spoke about how his niece would be missed at family gatherings. 'Like the pastor said, we will keep Reeva in our hearts forever,' he said. He confirmed that Reeva's ashes would be scattered by her family at a private ceremony in the future.

• • •

Several months later, the Steenkamps gathered at a Port Elizabeth beach to carry out that final task. The moment was captured for posterity by a camera crew filming a documentary for the UK's Channel 5, entitled *Why Did Oscar Pistorius Kill Our Daughter?*

A clergyman, his cream cassock flapping in incessant gusts of Port Elizabeth wind, led the family and gathered friends in a brief ceremony. Reeva's mother June, her face drawn, clutched a bouquet of long-stemmed red, white and dusty pink roses, which were subsequently placed on an artists' easel below a black-and-white portfolio portrait of her dead daughter before being cast into the crashing waves. Reeva's father, the burly, bearded Barry, struggled to maintain his composure as he leaned on his son Adam, who had flown in from the UK to attend the ceremony. Reeva's half-sister Simone Cowburn had also made the trip. Around a dozen people were gathered on the beach, including Reeva's ex-boyfriend Warren Lahoud, her cousin Kim Martin and her uncle Mike.

The family had chosen to scatter her ashes in the Indian Ocean because they had done the same with her grandfather when he had died. According to her mother, Reeva also loved to swim, loved the beach and loved being with dolphins, as had been so visibly illustrated by footage of her from the *Tropika* reality show. June was sure that this would be an appropriate resting place for her daughter.

Adam, his pants rolled up to his knees, took several steps into the foaming waves, clutching a plain pine wooden box in one hand and supporting his father with the other. Barry hadn't bothered with pulling up his jeans, choosing instead to allow them to soak up the salt water. Together they reached into the pine box, drawing out fists full of ash and scattering Reeva's remains into the wind and the ocean. The pastor, holding his shoes in his hands, watched from the beach as each family member and friend took a moment to remember Reeva, savouring the salt of the sea and their tears.

The Bail Application

A thousand kilometres away from the poignant, moving memorial ceremony in Port Elizabeth, the circus of Oscar Pistorius's bail application had begun to play out. The date was 19 February, five days after Reeva's death.

The Department of Justice had warned journalists over the weekend that only 26 reporters would be allowed into the courtroom. The queue to get in started outside the court building as, initially, journalists were not allowed to enter. Only Oscar's lawyers and family were allowed to filter through and enter the court.

What had started off as a relatively organised affair, with journalists lining up in an orderly queue, quickly degenerated into a mass of shouting, swearing and angry individuals fighting to get into the courtroom. By 9am the majority of reporters had managed to get in, with Oscar's father, uncle and siblings already seated in the gallery. Around ten black leather office chairs had been positioned in front of the dock facing the magistrate. These were for the camera crews and their reporters. Chairs lined the sides of the courtroom, but reporters were taking up just about every available space, including the floor, and it was treacherous navigating the room.

Camera operators and photographers were taking pictures of the Pistorius family, while the athlete's legal team stacked up dozens of files on the defence bench, ready to launch the bail application.

Advocate Barry Roux sat directly behind the lectern, from where he would argue his case, while his co-counsel, Advocate Kenny Oldwadge, was to his immediate right. The pair leaned in to each other to overcome the bustle and noise in the courtroom as they paged through documents. Seated further to the right of the defence bench was hired forensic expert Reggie Perumal and ballistics expert Wollie Wolmarans.

At about 9:35am a court orderly asked that everyone quieten down as he placed a bottle of water on the magistrate's desk. Minutes later the cry of the orderly, 'Rise in court', signalled the magistrate's arrival. Court was in session.

The holding cell doors opened and Oscar walked into the dock. The first order of the day would be to establish whether the bail application would be heard as a Schedule 5 or a Schedule 6 offence.

State prosecutor Gerrie Nel introduced the case and its particulars before informing Nair that the state had drafted its charge sheet.

'In summary of the allegations and our case is that the applicant shot and killed an unarmed, innocent woman during the early hours of 14 February 2013. The incident took place in the residence of the applicant and we're confident that it will not be in dispute that the applicant fired four shots, three of which hit the deceased and caused her death, she was unarmed and inside the toilet with the door closed, the applicant fired shots from outside the closed door of the bathroom. The state argues that the applicant is charged with an offence referred to in Schedule 6 which is murder when it was preplanned or premeditated.'

The courtroom was hushed as Nel revealed a picture of what the state believe played out in Oscar's home in the early hours of Valentine's Day: 'We say there may have been an argument between the applicant and the deceased and the evidence might point in that way, we say the only reasonable inference is that the applicant armed himself, attached his prosthesis, walked … 7 metres to the bathroom and shot the deceased while she was in the toilet, he fired four times and aimed at the basin, that would be our argument.'

Nel insisted that even Oscar's own version – that he had believed he was shooting at an intruder – amounted to premeditated murder.

Central to Nel's argument was the contention that preplanning or premeditation did not require months of planning but rather that Oscar could have planned to shoot Reeva 'moments' before he did so. 'If I arm myself, ready myself and walk a distance with the intention to kill somebody, it is premeditated,' he explained.

Defence Advocate Roux countered, stating that the matter was not even a case of murder, let alone premeditated murder. He said the accused intended to take the court into his confidence and make a full disclosure of what had transpired on the morning in question. The tension and anxiety in the room was palpable.

Roux also challenged Nel to provide evidence that there was a problem in the relationship that could have led to the argument and pointed out that Oscar had offered a 'spontaneous defence' in that he thought he was shooting at a burglar.

'I will at the appropriate time, if necessary, put before you case after case after case reported when husbands by accident shot their wives, or the father the child through doors, believing that's a burglar, an intruder, that someone is going to harm them.'

He pointed out that Oscar broke down the door after the shooting. 'If you strip this and you scratch the veneer off, where's the premeditation? Where's the plan? Because you shoot through a door because you believe it's a burglar?

'What is there in the state's armoury, in the state's factual basis to say no, no, that is not so … that is a premeditated or preplanned murder? Nothing. The bag's empty,' he insisted.

As Roux concluded, Nel quickly rose to his feet.

'I must say that I'm now more convinced,' he exclaimed, arguing why this was indeed a case of premeditated murder. 'He got up from a bed, put on his prosthesis, armed himself, walked 7 metres. It's not "I wake up, there's somebody standing in front of my bed, I think it's a robber, I shoot." Of course that's not preplanned.

'We have a woman in the early hours of the morning in the house with her boyfriend going to a toilet, locking herself in, locking herself in early morning using the toilet. We say there are other inferences why somebody would do that.

'This deceased was in a 1.4-metre by 1.14-metre little room, she couldn't go anywhere, when those shots were fired it must have been horrific. You can go nowhere.

'There were two people in the house and he should have been worried about his girlfriend first before he took any other steps.'

Nel was becoming increasingly animated with his hands, occasionally glancing back towards the gallery and the accused. Oscar maintained a constant stare, his focus squarely on Nel.

After a few questions to Nel, Nair allowed Oscar to leave the courtroom before he adjourned and left himself. It was just before 11am.

A bustle returned to the courtroom as reporters grabbed the opportunity to compare notes, record stories and make phone calls. The brave – and desperate – left the courtroom to take a toilet break. About an hour after the proceedings adjourned, a court official asked those in the room to quieten down.

The Chief Magistrate began delivering his ruling on what schedule this case would be dealt as. Oscar broke down again, his head slumped forward as his brother Carl leaned forward from the bench behind him and placed his hand on his younger sibling's back. As he neared the conclusion, Nair made the significant ruling that, based on the evidence presented by the state, 'I cannot at this point in time completely exclude, if not premeditation, planning.'

Nair concluded that for the purposes of the bail hearing, the matter would be dealt with as a Schedule 6 offence. It was a punch to the gut for Oscar. Court adjourned.

• • •

At about 1:30pm proceedings resumed with the real business of the day: the formal bail application. Would Oscar present a version to the court? In his delicate emotional state, would he be able to take the witness stand or would he depose to an affidavit? Each of these options carried immense risk for his legal team.

His advocate stood and announced that his client would address the court by means of a statement. Oscar would present his version of events, his account of what had transpired at his house in the early hours of Valentine's Day, in a sworn affidavit. Whatever version he presented to this court, he would have to stand by it through any trial that might follow.

Roux began to read:

> I have been advised and I understand that I bear the burden to show that the interests of justice permit my release and that I am obliged to initiate this application. I fail to understand how I could be charged with murder, let alone premeditated murder, as I had no intention to kill my girlfriend, Reeva Steenkamp ('Reeva'). However, I will put factors before the Honourable Court to show that it is in the interests of justice to permit my release on bail.
>
> I state that the state will not be able to present any objective facts that I committed a planned or premeditated murder. For this reason I will hereunder deal with the events which occurred that evening. The objective facts will not refute my version as it is the truth.

The statement delved into the athlete's 'personal circumstances' to support why he should be granted bail:

> I am a professional athlete and reside at 286 Silverwoods Estate, Silverlakes Drive, Silverlakes, Pretoria ...
>
> My professional occupation currently provides me with an income of approximately R5.6 million per annum.
>
> I have cash investments in excess of R1 million at various banks within the RSA.

I have never been convicted of any criminal offences either in the RSA or elsewhere. There are no outstanding cases, other than the present, being investigated against me by the South African Police Services ('SAPS').

On the 13th of February 2013 Reeva would have gone out with her friends and I with my friends. Reeva then called me and asked that we rather spend the evening at home. I agreed and we were content to have a quiet dinner together at home. By about 22h00 on 13 February 2013 we were in our bedroom. She was doing her yoga exercises and I was in bed watching television. My prosthetic legs were off. We were deeply in love and I could not be happier. I know she felt the same way. She had given me a present for Valentine's Day but asked me only to open it the next day.

After Reeva finished her yoga exercises she got into bed and we both ...

Nair interrupted Roux as Oscar's sobbing escalated. 'Mr Oldwadge, can you check on your client please?'

Oscar was inconsolable. By this point, Carl was standing behind the dock, leaning forward and hugging his brother from behind. The accused was covering his face, but a few glances up showed that it was contorted, red, and tears were streaming down his cheeks.

Roux offered a rather cold response to the magistrate. 'That is a difficulty that we have to deal with. The fact is that we have a similar situation all the time, and it will be there right through the ...'

Nair interrupted; he was having none of it. 'You know, my compassion as a human being doesn't allow me to just sit here, you know?'

'I was unaware of that because my back was turned to him, but it is a difficulty we have encountered,' said Roux, now glancing over his shoulder towards his client.

Nair said he would adjourn the proceedings for two minutes to allow Oscar time to speak to his family and regain his composure. 'Mr Pistorius, you need to concentrate on the proceedings.'

Before adjourning, the magistrate ordered that no photographs be taken, even when he left the courtroom. The Pistorius family huddled around Oscar who remained in the dock. Five minutes later Nair returned and Roux continued reading the statement, delivering his client's version of the events that led to the shooting. The courtroom was hushed in anticipation:

After Reeva finished her yoga exercises she got into bed and we both fell asleep.

I am acutely aware of violent crime being committed by intruders entering homes with a view to commit crime, including violent crime. I have received death threats before. I have also been a victim of violence and of burglaries before. For that reason I kept my firearm, a 9 mm Parabellum, underneath my bed when I went to bed at night.

During the early morning hours of 14 February 2013, I woke up, went onto the balcony to bring the fan in and closed the sliding doors, the blinds and the curtains. I heard a noise in the bathroom and realised that someone was in the bathroom.

I felt a sense of terror rushing over me. There are no burglar bars across the bathroom window and I knew that contractors who worked at my house had left the ladders outside. Although I did not have my prosthetic legs on I have mobility on my stumps.

I believed that someone had entered my house. I was too scared to switch a light on.

I grabbed my 9 mm pistol from underneath my bed. On my way to the bathroom I screamed words to the effect for him/them to get out of my house and for Reeva to phone the police. It was pitch dark in the bedroom and I thought Reeva was in bed.

I noticed that the bathroom window was open. I realised that the intruder/s was/were in the toilet because the toilet door was closed and I did not see anyone in the bathroom. I heard movement inside the toilet. The toilet is inside the bathroom and has a separate door.

It filled me with horror and fear of an intruder or intruders being inside the toilet.

I thought he or they must have entered through the unprotected window. As I did not have my prosthetic legs on and felt extremely vulnerable, I knew I had to protect Reeva and myself. I believed that when the intruder/s came out of the toilet we would be in grave danger. I felt trapped as my bedroom door was locked and I have limited mobility on my stumps.

I fired shots at the toilet door and shouted to Reeva to phone the police. She did not respond and I moved backwards out of the bathroom, keeping my eyes on the bathroom entrance. Everything was pitch dark in the bedroom and I was still too scared to switch on a light. Reeva was not responding.

When I reached the bed, I realised that Reeva was not in bed. That is when it dawned on me that it could have been Reeva who was in the toilet. I returned to the bathroom calling her name. I tried to open the toilet door but it was locked. I rushed back into the bedroom and opened the sliding door exiting onto the balcony and screamed for help.

I put on my prosthetic legs, ran back to the bathroom and tried to kick the toilet door open. I think I must then have turned on the lights. I went back into the bedroom and grabbed my cricket bat to bash open the toilet door. A panel or panels broke off and I found the key on the floor and unlocked and opened the door. Reeva was slumped over but alive.

I battled to get her out of the toilet and pulled her into the bathroom. I phoned Johan Stander ('Stander') who was involved in the administration of the estate and asked him to phone the ambulance. I phoned Netcare and asked for help. I went downstairs to open the front door.

I returned to the bathroom and picked Reeva up as I had been told not to wait for the paramedics, but to take her to hospital. I carried her downstairs in order to take her to the hospital. On my way down Stander arrived. A doctor who lives in the complex also arrived. Downstairs, I tried to render the assistance to Reeva that I could, but she died in my arms.

I am absolutely mortified by the events and the devastating loss of my beloved Reeva. With the benefit of hindsight I believe that Reeva went to the toilet when I went out on the balcony to bring the fan in. I cannot bear to think of the suffering I have caused her and her family, knowing how much she was loved. I also know that the events of that tragic night were as I have described them and that in due course I have no doubt the police and expert investigators will bear this out.

Everyone in the room exhaled, almost collectively.

Roux concluded reading the affidavit by placing the standard requirements into the record – that the accused was not a flight risk and would not interfere with the investigation or with the witnesses. Pistorius then confirmed the content of the statement to the court. Roux read three more affidavits into the record: from Oscar's friend Alex Pilakoutas, from Justin Divaris and from Justin's girlfriend Samantha Greyvenstein. These were character statements in defence of the sportsman.

Pilakoutas stated that he considers Oscar one of his closest friends and they see each other several times a week. He recalled how Oscar had told him in

November that he had a met a woman, Reeva, whom he intended taking to the sports awards.

'Oscar told me that his relationship with Reeva was not like any of his previous relationships. Oscar had really fallen for Reeva and he wasn't afraid to express it. Even though it was still early days in the relationship, Oscar and Reeva were very comfortable around each other and they were happy,' he said.

Divaris told the court that he and Oscar had a mutual love of cars and often spoke to each other on the phone. He had introduced the couple at a track day he had hosted at Kyalami race track and the two had hit it off. Oscar invited Reeva to attend the South African Sports Awards with him and their relationship blossomed, but they were 'taking things slow'. In December 2012, the couple joined Divaris and his girlfriend, Greyvenstein, on holiday in Cape Town and the relationship became increasingly serious. 'Oscar would often tell me how much he loved Reeva and that she was a fantastic person who understood him. He said he loved spending time with her and that she could be "the one". Apart from seeing and speaking to Oscar almost on a daily basis, as a couple my girlfriend Sam and I saw Oscar and Reeva together almost twice a week. They were always happy and you could see that they enjoyed each other's company immensely. The only issue in the relationship that I was made aware of was that Reeva sometimes thought Oscar was moving a little fast. However this did not derogate from the fact that they really truly loved each other. Oscar often told me that Reeva could be the girl he would one day marry.'

Divaris's girlfriend Greyvenstein expressed equally fond words about the accused in her sworn statement. 'I got on well with Oscar immediately, I found him to be an extremely polite, well-mannered, humble man. He was the epitome of a true gentleman,' she stated.

The statements portrayed Oscar as a loving boyfriend and depicted the relationship with Reeva as one of happiness. The final affidavit to be presented by the defence was that of Oscar's first cousin Graham Binge. The two had spoken on the phone on the evening of 13 February from around 20:25 until 20:45. Oscar was looking at buying his sister Aimee a new car and was seeking advice. They chatted about vehicle theft syndicates and a house Oscar had recently bought in Johannesburg.

Roux concluded his presentation and, with just over an hour left of the court day, Nel asked that the matter be postponed until the following day. The defence did not object. Captain Hilton Botha, the detective in charge of the case, was bracing himself for his time on the witness stand.

Bumbling Botha

Hilton Botha is a short man, fairly well built, with broad shoulders and an olive complexion, evident of someone who spends a lot of time outdoors. A career policeman, Botha spent 24 years in the police service, 16 of those as a detective. He strode into the courtroom, a brown police file tucked under his arm and a black suit jacket slung over his shoulder. With his jaw locked tightly, he took his seat in the witness stand. He would be the state's main witness in this bail application and its case would stand or fall by his testimony. The pressure was immense.

Inside the courtroom Oscar's family took up their spots directly behind where the accused would sit. In preparation, the defence team had already set out their files and other documentation on the row of desks in front of them, and several members of the team huddled over what appeared to be the floor plan of Oscar's house – likely to be used to plot movement on the morning in question.

Prosecutor Gerrie Nel stood, adjusted his black robe, and began guiding the policeman through his evidence.

Botha had arrived at Oscar's house at about 4:15am that Valentine's Day after receiving a call from his station commander. He found Reeva's body at the bottom of the stairs, bloodied and covered in towels. She had been shot three times and had been declared dead by paramedics.

Nel asked Botha to describe what he found when he entered the home, and the policeman took the court through a virtual tour of the accused's home through a clumsy description of left and right turns. He explained that he had gone through the main door, passed the deceased's body, up the stairs and into the main bedroom where he found a king-size bed, book cases, cupboards and a couch. An overnight bag was on the couch to the left of the bed and a woman's slippers were found on the same side. He had then walked through a passageway lined with cupboards into the bathroom.

> Nel: *Now what did you find in the bathroom?*
> Botha: *In the bathroom I saw a part of the door, the toilet door lying in the bathroom itself, cartridges, there was a cartridge at the entrance but still in the hallway.*
> Nel: *In the passageway?*
> Botha: *In the passageway there was one cartridge.*
> Nel: *Yes?*
> Botha: *9 mm. And there were three in the bathroom.*
> Nel: *And did you see any firearm?*
> Botha: *There was a firearm on a shower mat in front of the shower on your right-hand side.*

This was the first vivid first-hand account of the crime scene and those in the gallery hung on to every word, anticipating descriptions of a bloody cricket bat and bullet-riddled door. Nel continued to guide Botha through the scene.

> Nel: *How big is this toilet?*
> Botha: *The toilet is exactly 1.4x1.14 metres in diameter.*
> Nel: *Let's get back to the firearm. You saw a firearm which was where?*
> Botha: *In front of the shower, on the shower mat, there was a silver coloured Taurus 9 mm firearm.*
> Nel: *That's not all that was there?*
> Botha: *No, there was also two cellphones, one iPhone 4 and one iPhone 5 that was lying next to the firearm on the mat. The one iPhone 4 was a bit under the mat but you could see it.*

Botha explained that he had also found two BlackBerry phones on a cupboard in the bedroom. He had checked to see if any of the four phones had been used that morning and had established they had not. No one had called an ambulance and no one had called the police from any of those devices.

Nel then turned his attention to the bullet-riddled toilet door. Botha described that the top part of the door had been broken, and four shots had been fired through it. Botha stated that Oscar had used a cricket bat to break through the door.

Botha confirmed that he had found a cricket bat on the scene, lying on the floor, and that the bat had likely been used to break down the door. However, that would only be confirmed once 'tool markings' had been established by ballistics experts. Nel wanted to know from his witness where the shooter was likely to have been standing, whether the distance the shots had been fired at could be determined and whether the trajectory of the bullets had been established. This would prove to be a crucial exchange and a position that the state would later have to do an about-turn on.

According to his preliminary investigations, the detective believed that the shooter would have to have been standing inside the bathroom, with his back to the basins, when he fired the shots directly at the toilet bowl.

> Nel: *You were able to, with the people on the scene, form an idea of how far the shooter must have been from the door when he fired the shots, is that correct?*
> Botha: *That's correct. 1.5 metres.*
> Nel: *And where would he have been?*
> Botha: *He would have had to stand next to the shower with his back against the washing basins.*

As a disclaimer, Botha told the court that the ballistics and forensics tests still needed to be completed, but from his analysis it appeared that the bullet trajectory was from the top down, suggesting that Oscar was wearing his prosthetic legs at the time of the shooting.

> Nel: *The accused's version is that he was, he never had his prosthesis on when he was standing over there shooting or wherever he was standing shooting. I say the version of the accused is he went to the bathroom with his gun, without his prosthesis on and he then fired, so one will have to know, check the angle and if the bullet was fired up or down to indicate if that was correct. But you were there, you saw it?*
> Botha: *Yes.*
> Nel: *Now just seeing it for yourself, what was the angle of that bullet, up or down?*
> Botha: *It seemed to me that it was down, down. It was fired down.*
> Nel: *So, from the top down?*
> Botha: *Yes.*
> Nel: *And you measured it against whom?*

> Botha: *I measured it against myself; if I would have drawn my firearm and*
> *I would have shot normal stance it would have been down.*

After a query from the magistrate, it was agreed that plans of the house would be projected onto a big screen to make it easier to illustrate the events. The defence team hooked a laptop up to the projector, and a floor plan in blue ink was soon visible on a white screen behind the prosecution team. The diagram showed the upper level of Oscar's home – with his bedroom, balcony, passage and bathroom marked out on the plan.

Pointing to the diagram, the officer explained how there was just one small window in the toilet cubicle and no other way of escaping the room. Botha then took the court back to Oscar's bedroom and described how a person walking from the balcony – where Oscar said he had retrieved a fan before hearing noises in the bathroom – would have had to pass the bed where Oscar believed Reeva was sleeping.

Nel moved on, enquiring what else the police had found in Oscar's bedroom. 'On the cabinet below the TV we found two boxes of steroids and …' said Botha. Gasps rippled through the stuffy courtroom. Nel quickly interrupted his witness.

'Steroids or testosterone?'

'Testosterone,' clarified Botha. 'Testosterone and needles and injections. It's not anabolic.'

Oldwadge quickly looked up from taking notes and squinted at Botha, a look of utter disbelief on his face. It was a significant revelation, and one that would support the so-called roid-rage version as previously reported.

Nel then read from Oscar's affidavit in which he claimed he was worried about crime in South Africa and had fallen victim to crime on several occasions. Botha testified that despite these claims, there was no police record of Oscar ever opening a case in which he was the victim of crime.

The prosecution shifted focus to an incident at Tashas restaurant, a popular and trendy eatery at the Melrose Arch shopping complex in Johannesburg. Nel was attempting to create an image of a volatile young man who was prone to violent outbursts, trigger-happy and overly enthusiastic about firearms.

It had emerged that Oscar and a group of friends, including training partner UK athlete Martyn Rooney, professional boxer Kevin Lerena and Darren Fresco were sitting at a table at the restaurant when Fresco handed Oscar his firearm. Oscar was handling the weapon under the table when it accidentally went off, the bullet fortuitously lodging in the floor. Botha said the Paralympian feared bad publicity as a result of the incident and convinced Fresco to take responsibility for the accident.

Nel asked Botha about why someone who slept with a firearm under his bed and was apparently fearful of crime would fall asleep with a sliding door to the bedroom left wide open.

Botha said he found the holster for the firearm on the same side of the bed on which he had found Reeva's overnight bag and slippers. It seemed that the prosecution was now exploring the implausibilities of Oscar's version of events. How, then, did he not see that Reeva was not in the bed at the time he unholstered his weapon?

'I would have tried to find out where my girlfriend was because he was on her side of the bed, and tried to get her behind me and maybe leave the room …' testified Botha.

Nel then guided the investigating office to statements taken by witnesses in the housing complex and what the neighbours saw and heard. Some claimed to have heard the couple fighting in the hours leading up to the gunshots ringing out.

Botha confirmed that a neighbour claimed to have heard what sounded like fighting and loud talking between 2am and 3am, before hearing gunshots. Crucially, Botha claimed a witness saw lights on at the athlete's home prior to the shots. Nel, it seemed, was reaching a crescendo.

> Nel: *Mr Botha, the accused's version of self-defence and protecting himself, do you believe that?*
> Botha: *No, it can't be believed. There's no way that that could have happened that way.*
> Nel: *What do you believe?*
> Botha: *I believe that he knew that she was in the bathroom and that he shot four shots through the door and killed her.*

• • •

The state had built its case against bail and, by all accounts, it was looking solid. But as is so often the case with the drama of legal argument, only one side had been presented and an alternate picture was still to emerge. Doubt would be cast on Hilton Botha's interpretation of the evidence and his own credibility would also be called into question.

With the skill and ease of an experienced criminal advocate, Barry Roux began to dismantle Botha's testimony, block by block. Why did he testify that Oscar had not given him a version on the scene? How did he know how far the bullets travelled? Had he tested the visibility in the bedroom at night? Did the witnesses say they specifically heard Oscar or Reeva's voices?

Oldwadge was grinning from ear to ear, staring smugly at the investigating officer as he was forced to make one concession after the other to Roux. Just minutes earlier, Botha had been confident, easily providing Nel with answers without hesitation. Now he was stuttering, his grasp of the English language failing him as he battled to find answers to Roux's questions. Botha confirmed that the athlete did provide the version of the burglar at the scene that morning. Roux then put it to Botha that the trajectory the bullet had to follow to hit the toilet bowl was consistent with his client's version, and once again the seasoned investigator couldn't dispute this. Botha had earlier testified that the shooter was standing in front of the basin in the bathroom, but Roux pushed him to concede that the location of the cartridge was more consistent with a person standing in the doorway, where Oscar in fact claims to have been.

The advocate then moved to question the neighbours' statements. He took issue with the allegations that one of the neighbours saw a light in Oscar's house prior to the shooting, and also questioned the number of shots fired.

> Roux: As a matter of interest, have you tested the visibility at any point in the evening, of course, inside that bedroom where the curtains are drawn and the blinds are closed?
>
> Botha: No, I haven't.
>
> Roux: We have and I can tell you it's pitch dark. Do you have any reason to say that statement made to you now could not be true and, if so, why?
>
> Botha: The statement we have says that the lights were on in the house when [Oscar] said the lights were off.
>
> Roux: Before or after the shooting? You said it in evidence, after the shooting.
>
> Botha: There was shots heard, [the neighbour] went out, he looked, he saw the lights were on.
>
> Roux: Yes, after the shots he saw that the lights were on.

Nel quickly bounced to his feet and complained that Roux was interrupting his witness. Roux apologised but immediately went on to gain even more ground against the state. He confirmed that the witness claimed to have heard as many as eight shots – two to three shots in two volleys – yet Botha agreed that only four shots had been fired. Roux also undermined the claim by a neighbour who alleged to have heard arguing for an hour before the shooting. He confirmed that the woman could not say for sure that she had heard Reeva's voice and could not be certain that the talking had come from the home of the accused. Roux asked the policeman to explain how far away the neighbours lived from Oscar's house. It was at this point that Botha's evidence was reduced to a farce.

'Six hundred metres,' proposed Botha. Some in the gallery gasped in disbelief, realising the impossibility of this.

'Silence!' barked Nair, settling the courtroom.

Oldwadge was shaking his head as Roux moved in for the next line of questioning. Why had Botha not taken steps to find out Oscar's cellphone number? Why, when the defence had been so willing to comply and assist the police with their investigation, didn't he ask the accused or his brother for any outstanding cellphones?

Botha was floundering.

Roux moved to discredit his evidence around the testosterone that had caused such a stir a short time earlier. He asked Botha for the exact name of the substance he had found in the bedroom. The officer couldn't say. Botha conceded that he never took a picture of it or noted down the name in his pocket book.

'It's a herbal remedy,' said Roux, explaining that it was actually Testocompasutium co-enzyme. 'He can use it and used it before and many athletes use it, it's not a steroid and it's not a banned substance. Have you taken any steps to establish that?' Botha had not. He accused the investigating officer of failing to verify information, choosing instead to introduce untested evidence to the court.

Roux asked whether Botha agreed that if a person went to the bathroom at 3am, their bladder would be empty. Would that be consistent with going to the toilet?

Botha agreed. The postmortem on Reeva showed that her bladder was empty, which Roux said was consistent with the version that she went to the bathroom to relieve herself. Botha further conceded that, according to Oscar's version, had Reeva gone to the toilet, he would have heard noises emanating from the bathroom. The advocate added that the autopsy showed that Reeva had sustained no defensive wounds or signs of an assault.

The defence advocate zeroed in on phone calls made to and from Oscar's phone in the moments after the shooting. Why hadn't Botha phoned Netcare to confirm whether the accused had made an emergency call to the ambulance service? Why would Oscar have been crying on the phone when speaking to a security guard? Could that possibly have been part of the premeditated plan, to purposefully not switch off the phone and then cry? All of this was leading to Roux's argument that Botha took the approach to 'discard anything that could be consistent with a defence and only to focus on any possible thing that could be inconsistent'. Roux wanted to know from the cop if he could find any evidence inconsistent with Oscar's version of events. Botha could not.

It was 1pm when Nair adjourned for lunch.

• • •

Oscar's bail hearing was proving to be a master class in cross-examination and Botha was struggling. He used the 30-minute lunch break to compose himself and, when he returned, Roux asked the policeman whether he still stood by what he had said when led through his evidence. Botha gave an assurance that he did.

Roux then put it to him that at the house on the morning of the shooting Botha had told several of Oscar's relatives, as well as Oldwadge, that he felt bail should not be opposed. The officer admitted that he had said this. Roux then asked about the .38 Special ammunition found in the safe. Botha said it had been wrongfully handed over to Oldwadge, but the next day when he requested it back, it was returned. Botha again conceded that no attempt was made to establish who the rightful owner of the ammunition was. The advocate placed it on record that the bullets belonged to Oscar's father Henke and he was storing them for him.

Then Roux revealed another explosive piece of information. The defence's forensic expert had found a spent bullet projectile inside the toilet bowl but, astonishingly, it had been missed by police forensics teams. The advocate called into question Botha's testimony about the trajectory as well as the distance of the shots fired, as ballistic and forensic analysis had yet to be completed. Botha also acknowledged that he had no facts or evidence to show that Oscar had attached his prostheses before the shooting.

The lawyer then explained that, usually, Oscar would sleep on the right-hand side of the bed but on the night of the shooting, he had slept on the left as he was struggling with a painful shoulder. Once again, Botha could not dispute this.

The advocate skilfully worked through each of the claims made by the investigating officer and countered them with his own. Finally, to close off his questioning, Roux asked Botha whether he had entered the house on the morning of the shooting with protective covering on his shoes.

> *Roux:* When access was given to the ballistic person acting on behalf of the
>   applicant you were in the house without protective shoes, yes or no?
> *Botha:* It happened, yes.
> *Roux:* Yes. It should not happen that way, you agree?
> *Botha:* I agree.
> *Roux:* Because it compromised the scene in all fairness. I'm not talking
>   about deliberate actions Mr Botha, factual.
> *Botha:* Yes, it was not deliberate but there was no more feet covers left.

By making this admission, the experienced investigator opened the door for
the defence to claim that the crime scene had been contaminated and that evidence found on the scene could have been compromised and could thus not be
relied upon. This is a classic defence strategy and Roux would be looking for
any oversight made by officers on the scene. Any error on the part of forensic
experts would be fodder to cast doubt down the line. The admission that protective bootees were not worn by the main investigating officer was a gift for Roux.
Anyone with any knowledge of criminal trials and police work would have let
out a deep sigh and shaken their heads at the concession. Had the police bungled the crime scene? It was a narrative all too common in South Africa where
public confidence in the cops is doubtful at best.

With that question mark hanging, Roux concluded his cross-examination.
Botha had collapsed spectacularly. But still some within the prosecuting team
put on a brave face, downplaying the importance of Botha's admission, stating
they didn't think this was a problem as they had achieved their goal with the bail
application anyway. By going for a Schedule 6 premeditation charge, they had
forced Oscar and his legal team to put a version on record – a move that would
repeatedly come back to haunt them.

Advocate Nel was quickly back on his feet and set about trying to regain
ground lost to Roux. He questioned why a 'vulnerable' person would have
rushed towards the danger in the bathroom. He also clarified whether Botha
believed that Oscar's version could be true. Nel also sought clarity on just how
far the neighbours who had given statements were from the crime scene. Botha
reconsidered this potentially embarrassing testimony, stating that it was more
likely 300 metres, rather than 600, as he initially testified.

Before Botha was released from the stand, Magistrate Nair had a set of
his own questions. He asked the captain about his prior dealings with Oscar
and his investigations into previous violent incidents involving the accused.
Botha recalled the occasion when Oscar was arrested for assault following an

altercation with a woman at his home. He was referring to the Cassidy Taylor-Memmory incident, for which Botha was the investigating officer. Nair wanted to know why the matter hadn't been explored during the questioning and Nel told the court that the matter was subsequently withdrawn and was the subject of a civil claim.

'The accused before court is an international athlete, he's a Paralympic athlete, he uses prosthesis on both limbs. I'm sure that we would all agree that his face is widely recognisable internationally. Do you subjectively believe that he would take the option, being who he is, using prostheses to get around, familiar as he is, to flee South Africa if he were granted bail?' asked Nair, gesturing to Botha. The witness insisted he believed Oscar could flee.

Nair pushed the issue. 'Do you think it probable that a person who has won Olympic Gold would want to forsake his career whilst he may have the option to prove his innocence in a court of law?' he questioned, doubting Botha's sincerity.

'Your Worship, I only say it's possible. It's possible. Lifetime imprisonment is not a joke. I know everything he does, he's a great sportsman, but anything in that direction is possible. I've heard about people fleeing the country for five years' sentence, but that's all I can say. It's possible.'

At 2:40pm, a defeated Hilton Botha stepped off the witness stand. He had been through the mill and his evidence was riddled with holes. His reputation was on the line. Little did he know that worse was still to come.

From Investigating Officer to Accused

A n email dropped into Eyewitness News reporter Alex Eliseev's inbox. It was from journalist and author Laurie A Claase. From his Sandton office, Eliseev had been following Hilton Botha's evidence to the court in Pretoria throughout the morning and could tell how the scene would play out. He had covered enough criminal trials in his time as a court reporter to know.

'Is the investigating officer in the Pistorius case the same Hilton Botha that is out on bail for allegedly shooting at a minibus taxi carrying passengers on the R568 road between KwaMhlanga and Ekangala? The minibus taxi was apparently riddled with bullet holes.' Claase had seen an article from *The New Age* newspaper that detailed how Botha and two other warrant officers from the Boschkop police station were arrested in 2011 after they allegedly shot at a minibus taxi carrying seven passengers, while they were drunk, on duty and in a police vehicle. The three officers were charged with seven counts of attempted murder, possession of firearms under the influence of alcohol and malicious damage to property. They were out on bail of R2 000 each. Charges had been provisionally withdrawn but the case was referred to the Director of Public Prosecutions who took the decision to reinstate the charges in early February 2013, less than two weeks before Reeva Steenkamp was killed.

Eliseev spent hours working the phones trying to get confirmation from police spokespeople, prosecutors and court officials. It was only late that night that he received the phone call he was waiting for. Confirmation.

The following morning, as the prosecution and the defence were preparing to present closing argument in the bail application, the country woke to an Eyewitness News exclusive that would rock the bail application. While newspaper headlines slammed Botha's collapse on the stand the previous day, there was now fresh fodder for him to worry about.

'When the Hilton Botha story broke, we had not yet had a full taste of the global appetite for this case,' explained Eliseev. 'But news that the lead detective was facing his own criminal charges, which he denied, detonated a news bomb.

'International organisations immediately jumped to cover the twist, and giants like the BBC used Skype to get the latest from our newsroom. Throughout the day, reaction poured in, debate raged about the impact this would have on the case and what it said about the police service. Within hours, a briefing was called by police commissioner Riah Phiyega and Botha was pulled off the case.'

Members of the prosecuting team were driving to court when they heard Eliseev's report on the radio. It was the first they had heard about the charges. Before long, their phones began to light up as reporters from other news organisations looked to confirm the story and get a comment. They had nothing to say – they knew nothing about the case.

While they were taken by surprise, the state's team did have its suspicions about the sudden re-emergence of the case against Botha. The timing was too coincidental. But how would this development affect the state's bid to prevent bail? It would have to be raised by either one of the legal teams for it to have any impact. As court resumed for the day at 11am, the pressing issue was whether or not it would come up.

Shortly after Magistrate Nair entered the courtroom, prosecutor Gerrie Nel told the court that there were three issues he wanted to address before proceedings started.

The first concerned an unidentified woman – known only as 'Annamarie' – who wanted to bring an application and requested that she be allowed to address the court. Both Nel and defence advocate Barry Roux told Nair that they didn't think the court should entertain the matter.

It would emerge that the woman was previously married to the runner's orthopaedic surgeon, Dr Gerald Versfeld. She was concerned about Oscar's state of mind and wanted him to be examined by a psychiatrist for 60 days. Magistrate Nair dismissed the application, but did invite her to launch an application in the High Court down the road. The woman said she would do just that before storming out of court. It was not the last time Annamarie would make an appearance in the matter.

Nel then placed it on the record that the prosecution team had only learnt the previous day that investigating officer Hilton Botha was facing seven counts of attempted murder. It was apparent that Nel could not ignore the morning's developments in the media. Nair was concerned that his plans for the day had been thwarted, and ordered that Botha appear before him. Court adjourned while Botha was tracked down to make an appearance in the courtroom.

Speculation was rife that the magistrate wanted to question Botha on the pending case against him and why he had not disclosed it to Nel and his team. After about 45 minutes, proceedings resumed with Botha once again in the dock.

Nair posed questions around the previous arrest of the accused, the Cassidy Taylor-Memmory incident and the argument involving Marc Batchelor. He also wanted to know whether the officer had obtained detailed billing records of the phones seized at the scene. Botha said he was trying to obtain such records.

After only a few minutes on the stand, Botha was excused. Nair had not asked about his pending attempted murder case. It was never even mentioned.

Nel then moved on to the third item he needed to address before Roux could start delivering his closing argument. He explained that Botha had told him about an article in the *Sarie* magazine in which Pistorius apparently disclosed that he had property in Italy.

Nel then read the article in Afrikaans to the court, and provided a translation: 'I spend about four months in a year in South Africa. The past two years I had a house in Gamona, Italy, and I spend four months in a year there. My house there is between the mountains and it's really quiet and tranquil.'

Roux assured the court that his client had no property abroad.

With the table cleared, Roux began to deliver his closing argument. He immediately dealt with perhaps the most serious potential criticism of his case – that Oscar had not given what is referred to as viva voce evidence. He had chosen to testify by an affidavit rather than take the witness stand. Roux, however, argued that the weight of the evidence should not be discounted, because the state did not dispute the version given by the accused.

Roux then hit straight at the integrity and reliability of Botha.

'The investigating officer in his evidence further admitted that the contents of the supporting affidavits dealing with a loving relationship between Reeva and the applicant, thereby negating any positive motive to kill Reeva, are consistent with his investigations relevant to the relationship.'

Roux said the evidence submitted by the state supported his client's version that he did not commit a planned or premeditated murder, and requested that the court not find that the matter was a Schedule 6 offence. 'The poor quality of the evidence of the investigating officer Botha further exposed an endeavour on the part of the state to avoid disastrous shortcomings in the state's case,' he said.

He then dealt with the individual allegations levelled by the prosecution team, disputing Botha's testimony point by point, and concluded with: 'We say Your Worship, and we say it with great deference, that Botha's evidence can be aptly summarised as extremely poor and patently designed to bolster the state's case as the contentions, submissions and grounds for opposition at the close of the state's case equalled a monumental collapse. There was just nothing and he did nothing.

'He is well known, he is a professional, he's an international athlete, he's an icon, he represents so many things. Is there any, any acceptable, reasonable possibility that a person disclosing his defence comprehensively, sitting here in court, waiting for the police to come to his house, that that person will not stand his trial? Common sense will dictate that it borders on close as it can be on impossibility,' he said.

• • •

It was the turn of the prosecution. Gerrie Nel went straight to the heart of the law. Had the accused shown that there were exceptional circumstances, in terms of Schedule 6 in the Criminal Procedure Act, that in the interest of justice he should be released on bail?

'I have not heard an argument saying that this in itself is an exceptional circumstance. I think what the argument is, is the fact that the state doesn't have a strong case, or that because it's not a murder it's an exceptional circumstance. Or, "I'm Oscar Pistorius. I am a world-renowned athlete." That in itself is not special. It cannot be, not in a court,' contended Nel, his submission animated and laced with contempt.

Nel then raised a crucial legal principle – that even according to Oscar's own version to the court, he had planned to kill a person. He suggested that if the court accepts the applicant's version of events, then all that would remain is that Oscar planned to kill an intruder. 'Everything he did up until the time he shot was planned. So on his version, "I didn't plan to shoot Reeva, but I planned to shoot that intruder", it's planned,' he exclaimed. Nel argued that no court would accept that Oscar had acted in self-defence on the version that he had provided. There were two people in the house, and only one survived to provide a version.

Nel stated that it was highly improbable that Oscar felt vulnerable, considering he stormed at the supposed intruder in the bathroom. He said that it was also highly improbable that Oscar would have fired the shots without first establishing whether there was indeed a threat.

Nel explained that even in Oscar's own version of events, he had the intention to kill. He asked rhetorically, for effect, why Oscar would have wanted to shoot.

'There's a question that we ask, why did he shoot? Did he want to kill the intruder, not Reeva? Let us give him the benefit of the doubt. "I've never wanted to kill Reeva but I wanted to kill the intruder" on his own version. It's not my version. He must say that otherwise why did he fire? Did he just fire to scare? He fired four shots through a door 1.4x1.14. "I know, it's my house", just to scare someone, at a height that can hit you or could he fire into the bath or anywhere? He must say: "I fired to kill" because I struggle to see if it's not murder preplanned or with *dolus directus* then it must at least be murder *dolus eventualis*. "I fired, I thought there might be somebody in, there was a risk but I took the risk and I fired," I don't think so. It cannot be his version. His version must be: I wanted to kill someone in that cubicle because that's why, I felt threatened.'

Nel was at the climax of his closing argument. He argued that there was only one person who could provide insight into the incident and he was sitting in court – but he had elected to give an affidavit and not take the stand. It would have been so much better for Oscar to take the court into his confidence, concluded Nel.

Judgment in the Bail Hearing

B y the last day of the bail hearing the Justice Department finally appeared to have come up with an access system that worked. The media interest had been unprecedented. Even when the country's President Jacob Zuma and National Police Commissioner Jackie Selebi had made appearances in court, there had not been the same number of reporters attempting to gain access to a courtroom. For the Oscar Pistorius case reporters had arrived from across the globe and, in the corridors outside the courtroom, journalists could be heard filing stories in a variety of languages.

That Friday morning Oscar's coach Ampie Louw was passing the time chatting to journalists in his relaxed, down-to-earth manner. He said it was heartbreaking seeing the youngster whom he'd trained for nine years standing in the dock. 'If he gets bail I want him back on the track as soon as possible,' he said. Louw confirmed that all Oscar's competition commitments had been cancelled, but he still wanted him back on a training plan.

The day's proceedings began with Nel making a few final arguments against bail being granted. He was unemotional and ruthless as he contended that Oscar's tears throughout the week's proceedings were likely the result of his realising that his career was in tatters after the shooting. The athlete's sister Aimee raised her hand to her mouth, visibly shocked at the way Nel was referring to her brother, whose head was again bowed.

The prosecutor referred to President Zuma's recent state of the nation address during which he made a call for crimes against women to be prioritised. 'The degree of violence present in this case is horrific. You're stuck in a cubicle where someone fires blindly into it, not one, not two, but four shots,' he emphasised.

The magistrate enquired as to what kind of life the accused would lead if he were to flee – after all, he was recognisable throughout the world.

'A life of freedom,' insisted Nel.

But Nair went further, asking how his prostheses would affect his life on the run. Nel argued that the athlete could not be treated any differently as an accused simply because he was physically disabled.

Nair had heard enough, and retired to his chambers to prepare his ruling. Judgment would be delivered at 2:30pm.

• • •

For the duration of the third week in February 2013, South Africa endured what Editor-in-Chief of Eyewitness News Katy Katopodis described as the five stages of grief outlined by the Kübler-Ross model: Denial, Anger, Bargaining, Depression and Acceptance in varying orders.

The Valentine's Day shooting and the deep emotion that accompanied the tragedy shocked the country to its core. Oscar Pistorius had been South Africa's 'good thing', a celebration of achievement in the face of adversity, a unifying character proudly paraded on the world stage. For there to have been such a dramatic fall from grace, a collapse of Shakespearean proportions, was simply incomprehensible.

The nation was raw and the tragedy was virtually the only thing that anyone could talk about. It was as if every individual took personal ownership of the incident. From each hairdressing salon to coffee shop to corner café and water cooler, the merits of the case were debated and versions dissected. The upshot was that regular laypeople became better educated about the criminal justice system and processes that were followed. But the downside was that every citizen was now a 'legal expert' and believed their understanding to be the correct one.

As information emerged from the Pretoria courtroom, emotions and attitudes shifted. The pendulum of public opinion swung. When Hilton Botha was on song, being led through his evidence by Gerrie Nel, popular consensus was that Oscar Pistorius was absolutely, without doubt, guilty. Later in the day, as the captain was forced into several awkward concessions and it was then revealed that he too was facing criminal charges, there was an about-turn on Twitter and on radio talk shows. The overwhelming view was that the police were incompetent and it was all just a terrible, unfortunate accident. Emotions vacillated from one end of the spectrum to the other.

The full attention of the country was focused on the courtroom in central Pretoria and the decision of the Chief Magistrate.

• • •

By the time Barry Roux and Gerrie Nel had finished presenting their closing arguments to the court, Magistrate Desmond Nair already knew that he was going to grant Oscar Pistorius bail. The lawyers had presumed that Nair would want the weekend to prepare his judgment and Nel suggested they look at Monday morning to set a time for it to be delivered. But Nair assured them that it would be delivered that afternoon. The magistrate took the view that if he was going to fix bail, it would have been another 48 hours of unnecessary detention for the accused.

Nair returned to his office and took refuge in his vices of caffeine and nicotine as he prepared his 'extemporary' judgment. His assistants busied themselves around him, acting on requests for case law and varying authorities on matters such as exceptional circumstances and the weight of affidavits.

The Chief Magistrate had made copious handwritten notes while sitting on the bench, which he handed over to them to type during the tea and lunch breaks, and they helped him slot these various pieces of paper and case law into the correct order. The result was that there was no comprehensive typed-up judgment that went from paragraph one to the end, but rather that Nair would compose the wording of his ruling as he went along.

• • •

Long, fat, black cables slithered across the carpeted floor of the courtroom between laptops, discarded bags, crouching reporters and the other detritus of four days of bail application. The judgment would be transmitted live by all the major international news outlets and technicians were making sure everything worked. Magistrate Nair had agreed that the audio of the judgment could be broadcast, but live visuals would not be allowed. Space in the stuffy room was at a premium. An American doing a stand-up to camera told his audience: 'You thought Superbowl seats were hard to find; try this courtroom!'

Across town, Oscar's uncle Arnold had designated two of his sons-in-law to draw R1 million in cash to pay for bail if it were to be granted. In a country where it is not uncommon for citizens to be followed from a bank teller or a bank machine, held up at gunpoint and robbed, this was no easy feat. Several banks declined the request from the young men and they knew they would be under pressure to deliver. The world was watching and it was likely that judgment would only come through late in the afternoon when the cashier at the court could be closed for business.

Eventually, the men found a sympathetic bank manager and emerged with a bag full of banknotes. Although they were relieved that their mission had been accomplished, they still faced several hours of hanging on to the money, waiting for the magistrate to deliver his ruling. Much to their frustration – and to those watching blank screens on television while listening to the judgment – Nair took far longer than anticipated. The men drove round and round the court for hours as Nair spoke on and on.

Nair opened with a summary of the evidence put before him, including the affidavits presented by the defence and the testimony of Hilton Botha. He referred to vast case law around the purpose of bail and background on how it is governed by the South African legal system.

In ruling on the decision to view the case as a Schedule 5 or 6 offence, Nair said he was not as convinced then as he was before of the state's contention that this was a case of premeditated murder.

'At this point I have to look at the facts the state has to give me. I must rely on the bona fides of the senior counsel who is presenting the state's case, and what he has in his possession at this point is nothing more than circumstantial evidence. But that does not prevent the matter falling under the category of Schedule 6 and I'm going to approach in that vein from here onwards,' he said.

Nair had chosen to treat the offence as a Schedule 6 crime – this meant the bar would be far higher for Oscar to be granted bail. Nair explained that if the defence had succeeded in showing that the state had a weak case, then that would be considered an exceptional circumstance, which would permit release on bail.

Nair zoomed in on the performance of Hilton Botha on the stand. He found that the policeman had made several concessions and errors during his cross-examination and the magistrate made his way through a litany of these. Nair said that while there were many concessions made by Botha, he alone did not constitute the state's case.

Nair appeared to be favouring the defence's case, but then in an instant, he shifted position. He had found numerous improbabilities in Oscar's version of events: 'I have difficulty in appreciating why the accused did not ascertain the whereabouts of his girlfriend when he got out of bed. I have difficulty in also coming to terms with the fact that the accused did not seek to verify who exactly was in the toilet when he could have asked. I also have difficulty in appreciating why the deceased would not have screamed back from the toilet. I have difficulty understanding why the deceased and the accused would not of like mind in those circumstances have escaped through the bedroom door than venture into the toilet. I have a problem also, as to why the accused would further venture into danger knowing full well that the intruder was in the toilet, leaving himself open to being attacked even before he shot.'

Nair said these improbabilities needed to be explored and would probably only be determined if the accused gave evidence under oath and submitted himself to cross-examination. He stated that it was on these points that the defence had failed to show that the state did indeed have a weak case – at least to the point that it could constitute an exceptional circumstance to their benefit.

Despite all this, he found that the state had been unable to show that it had such a watertight case that it would compel the accused to attempt to flee his trial.

'The issue before me is whether this accused, being who he is, and with the assets he has in the country, would possibly seek to duck and dive all over the world when, even by the state's own concession, he may at the worst case scenario face culpable homicide. I cannot find that it has been established that the accused is a flight risk.'

The magistrate spoke for over two hours. During this time, international networks had been displaying images of black screens while carrying the audio of Nair's ruling. Reporters tweeted every minute detail of colour and atmosphere from inside the room in order to portray some picture to accompany the audio.

The tension was tangible as Nair crept ever so slowly towards finality. Some journalists had two typed-out versions of tweets ready to copy and paste into their profiles and hit 'send'. Oscar's cousins circled the block for the umpteenth time with his bail money.

After a long pause, Nair continued: 'I have come to the conclusion that the accused has made a case to be released on bail.'

A shout of 'Yes!' boomed out from the public gallery as celebrity businessman and self-proclaimed 'friend' Kenny Kunene punched the air. Smiles rushed over the faces of the Pistorius family, while Oscar dropped his head in relief.

Nel quickly rose. 'As the court pleases,' he said, before moving onto discussions on the bail conditions.

Nair said he was grateful for the time counsel had taken to discuss the terms of bail, but made it clear that the decisions surrounding bail would be up to the court.

'Bail is fixed at an amount of one million rand,' he announced.

Nair went on to list a slew of travel and movement restrictions, and also imposed the condition of a correctional officer who would be able to monitor Oscar at any time of the day.

• • •

Usually, in matters of this nature, the prosecution and defence would agree on the conditions and the amount at which bail would be set. One of the two parties would write up an order for the court to approve. This had happened in this case and the state and Oscar's lawyers were satisfied with the agreed terms and conditions. However, Nair surprised both sides when he dismissed their agreement and took it upon himself to impose stringent, little-heard-of conditions that would be roundly dismissed by an appeal judge a month later.

After a week in jail, the Blade Runner would be released from custody. The bag men made their way into the court building in a rush to pay the cash bond before officials knocked off for the weekend. And eventually a silver Land Rover was allowed into the court precinct through the tunnel that leads to the holding cell entrance.

The Sophie de Bruyn driveway was jammed with a pack of camera operators, some on motorbikes ready to give chase as the vehicle made its way towards Waterkloof. The 4-metre-high brown gates opened as the 4x4 approached it. The vehicle passed through as lenses pressed up against the glass windows. As photographers hastily downloaded their images showing the international superstar seated in the middle of the back seat of the car, the vehicle sped away.

Oscar was free, for now.

• • •

Magistrate Nair drove out the court complex through the phalanx of video cameras just as dusk was beginning to set late on the Friday afternoon. As he made his way down Schoeman Street out of the city centre, he felt a great sense of relief that the weight of the week and the case had been lifted. He had spent most of the preceding nights awake, working through his notes on the application. The magistrate had always believed that the easiest mistake a presiding officer can make is to not review the arguments put before him before returning to court the following day. He was exhausted.

But his relief was short-lived. That Sunday his family was struck by a tragedy of enormous magnitude. The bodies of his first cousin and her two sons were found at their Johannesburg home by her ex-husband. It was believed she had poisoned her children before taking her own life. At the end of a week so overwhelmingly dominated by death, Nair felt the desolation of the loss. This wasn't a case to be assessed by stark facts and finite law, but rather to be mourned on a human level. A reminder of the true value of life and loss.

Meet the Magistrate

Magistrate Desmond Nair loves the law. He speaks with great passion and conviction of the peculiarities and nuances of legal proceedings, more so when he's delving into his favoured field of bail. It is for this reason that he agreed to a rare interview about a matter that he has presided over. It is highly unusual in the South African legal system for a magistrate or judge to sit down with a journalist to discuss a case that has come before them. It's February 2014 and the country is gearing up for Oscar Pistorius's trial to get underway. Technically, Nair is allowed to speak about the case because he has disposed of the matter. It has been moved from the Magistrate's Court to the High Court and a trial judge has been appointed.

Nair was central to the Olympian's initial court proceedings as it was his voice that was carried live on global news networks while delivering his judgment in the bail application. While he downplays the so-called fame he achieved, it is no secret in Pretoria's legal circles that Nair has a tendency for pageantry and would have enjoyed the show of the event playing out on the world's stage.

Nair began his career as a magistrate in the small town of Dundee in KwaZulu-Natal on South Africa's eastern flank. He had grown up in the province – he was born in Dannhauser near Newcastle and studied at the University of Durban-Westville (now a campus of the University of KwaZulu-Natal) for his BA Law and LLB. He prosecuted in Dundee for two years before taking up a post on the bench. In 1995 he was appointed as a magistrate in Johannesburg before spending time in the Specialised Commercial Crimes Court (SCCC) in Pretoria. He is now the Chief Magistrate in Pretoria.

As a boy, his was a disciplined home and while he can't profess to having been a victim of apartheid or having been heavily involved in the struggle for liberation, he was certainly aware of the principles of justice and equality. While at school, young Desmond discovered an ability to debate and speak publicly. 'The teachers at school saw the potential when it came to public speaking and then I would be debating all the time. I was chosen to represent the school at what was known as the Jan Hofmeyr Speech Contest, and that was with all the schools, across the colour line, in Dundee. I spoke about justice and fairness and equity. I think that is where some of the teachers realised, you know what? This guy is a talker.'

It was this realisation that set Nair on the path to a law career. But still he chose to go to the bench rather than the more lucrative option of private practice. 'I don't think I was as much comfortable wanting to fight and take instructions to fight. I find myself more at ease being a judicial officer. Being an umpire. But I get involved in the matters as well. I don't believe, like I'm told, that in civil matters it's the parties who bring the matter to court and if they err or they don't call a witness, you should be very careful before you jump in. I'm still very active as a judicial officer.'

The 45-year-old father of three was only 25 when he was first appointed as a magistrate. His head of office in Dundee had gone on leave over the December holidays in 1994 and he was picked as the stand-in. 'I took to it immediately. I enjoyed it from day one and I found the interpretation, the application of the law, to be enjoyable. I was so dedicated,' he says pointing at the shelves full of books lining his office walls. 'Those law reports, behind you now, I would pick them up like a novel, just to read. And I would read them non-stop!' he exclaims. He even has a photograph, taken by a colleague, of himself as a young magistrate pouring over volumes of reports.

Nair's time on the bench at the SCCC and as Chief Magistrate in Pretoria prepared him well for the intensity of the world's focus and the Oscar Pistorius case. At the SCCC, he became used to the calibre of argument, and of advocate, that feature in High Court trials. 'It was there already that I was sentencing guys to 15 years, 10 years for white-collar crime, mostly, complicated fraud matters and most of the accused would employ senior counsel. I had already had the experience of the SCs before me, so I wasn't really daunted by the quality of counsel that some of the accused persons have had representing them,' he explains.

It was the drunk-driving case of Judge Nkola Motata that truly tested Nair and taught him about the intricacies of dealing with the scrutiny of a trial run through the media.

'The matter involving Judge Motata was a lengthy one. It took us more than 18 months to finalise and I would say I cut my teeth there in dealing with matters of that magnitude. It was a full trial. Although it was a drunken-driving matter, we got involved in 19 interlocutory applications wherein I had to give judgments and, during the course of that trial, two or three times the matter landed up in the High Court,' Nair reminisces. 'One had to be very, very careful. You had to mete out justice. And you also had to deal with the fact that there would be this great public pressure to see whether he's going to get off with a lighter sentence.'

But, Nair admits, nothing could really have sufficiently prepared him for the unprecedented level of interest that Oscar's appearance drew. 'You couldn't compare the Pistorius matter to any other matter, including Judge Motata, simply because I had never experienced the surrounds of the courtroom with the international media. I remember on the first day, when the bail application started, there were about 40 or 50 people who were waiting outside here who wanted to speak with me before the matter started to see how we were going to work out the logistics,' he says, referring to the media's persistence in wanting to broadcast the appearance live. 'I had to appoint a task team within this office to deal with the media so that I didn't engage them and then, of course, I had to deal with the fact that when I got into the courtroom – even though I had made certain rulings in terms of law – you still found people breaching those rulings.' Nair, of course, had to balance Oscar's rights with the public interest in the case and the media's desperation to get the story.

'You want to appear to be firm, but polite at the same time … One must remember that our case law, when it comes to televising proceedings, also talks about the dangers of being drawn into this whole media frenzy and not focusing on your job because it does affect your concentration. If you're new to it, you can get fazed by it.'

Nair was annoyed that his ruling about the accused being photographed or videoed while court was in session appeared to have been violated and a picture of the athlete in the dock was wired around the world, appearing on the front pages of newspapers. In that instance, the editor visited Nair in his chambers to provide an explanation and apologise. 'I was very, very taken aback by the fact that I had made a ruling – and you don't expect it. They put an explanation on the table in terms of how it happened. I think they all realised that you would not want to let the South African media be the cause of a banning order in terms of media in the courtroom. Rather let it be somebody else, but not the South African media houses. I saw a tremendous amount of respect for me, for the rulings I made. They were always very careful.'

Nair strokes his moustache as he casts his mind back to that day in February 2013, when he first realised that the world-famous Paralympic athlete and icon would be appearing before him in court as an accused. He was first told the news of Oscar's arrest by the Acting Senior Magistrate. He was shocked. 'As a person, shock, you know, because you've heard and read about him. But I had to remind myself from the first minute, you may just be presiding on the matter so you're going to just have to focus yourself on the person as an accused person.'

The matter did indeed come before him and he had to steel himself before walking into Court C on that Friday, 15 February.

'It was very daunting, because in as much as I had met many of the international media in this very office before we went to court that day, when I got into the courtroom and for a split second saw this crowd standing all around him, I had to ask the security personnel, "Look, I'm not going to enter until you clear them out." The gallery was packed, so you've got to up your game. And it comes naturally, you know, because you realise now that it's at another level. Not only am I being judged as a judicial officer, but the country's criminal justice system is now being crystallised into one point of focus for the entire world. You've got to be very careful with everything you do, everything you say, how you say it.'

Nair, who regularly interrupted proceedings to enquire of Oscar whether he was all right, adds that he was also mindful of how that bombardment of media attention could overwhelm the accused. 'I'm alive to the fact that it would have been an equally daunting experience for Mr Pistorius himself, like any accused person. I think there was a part of me that spared a thought for what it must feel like to have all those persons around you flashing cameras, and at one point I went so far as to say, even in my judgment, to surround a person as if you are seeing somebody who is an alien, it doesn't run well with me. His rights as an accused person have to be respected. It doesn't take away the fact that I could have ruled that he be kept in custody, that was not going to affect it. It was just to make sure that he got a fair bail hearing.'

The magistrate agrees that Oscar was among the more emotional accused ever to have appeared before him. 'But it was not new to me. White-collar criminals just by virtue of the fact that they were accountants, they were doctors, they were lawyers, they were senior people in government and all of a sudden you are sitting there in a box, in the dock. But with Mr Pistorius, I agree, he was particularly emotional. It was a constant concern for me to make sure that he understood what was going on. It very often happens in criminal matters involving rape, robbery, murder where you find witnesses breaking down and it's always been my habit if a person starts crying to spend another minute or second assessing whether they are in a position to continue or not. Humanity dictates that you do what is right and even though his counsel were saying, "It's fine, continue," for me it wasn't their call ultimately to make.'

Nair adds that it was important for Oscar to be aware of what was going on during proceedings because he would have had to make critical decisions, such as whether or not to testify during the application. 'It is very easy in that state of emotion to kind of not focus on anything that is being said and you, as the accused, are the one that must give your counsel instructions. I kept asking him, "Are you okay? Do you understand what is happening?" because it is for him to tell his counsel which way he wants this matter to go. The very decision to bring the bail application on affidavit rather than testifying is something that he would have been the only person to make that call in consultation with his advocates and assuming, for whatever reason, he said, "No, I want to take the stand now," that bail application would maybe have continued for three weeks.'

Oscar took the decision to offer a version of events via an affidavit during his bail application and Nair found that he did meet the requirements of what was expected of him, despite choosing not to take the stand.

One of the praises of Nair's handling of this case, and many others, is how careful he always is to ensure that laypeople understand the law. He shepherds the accused, complainants and witnesses through what media like to refer to as the 'legalese' and takes time to lay out the implications of any legislation. For many who were unfamiliar with the justice system in South Africa and were now studiously following the court proceedings, hungry for an understanding of what was going on, Nair's careful explanations were welcomed. Nair realised early on that, in the interests of justice, he had to explain to the public what was going on.

Many followers, mostly those from outside the country, struggled to under-stand why so much evidence was being led at such an early stage when the trial had yet to start. Nair says this was not a peculiarity and it is often neces-sary for such a large amount of detail to come out during a bail application. 'Unfortunately, the magistrate or judge presiding in a bail application is expected to watch a trailer of a movie in order to get a sense of what the full movie is going to be like. So you are asked to formulate a picture of the trial in your mind,' he explains.

His judgment took over two hours to deliver because he spent a large portion of that time explaining to the rest of the world how the bail system works in South Africa. 'It dawned on me that, on that level, with the amount of interna-tional interest, my judgment must explain not only to the South African public, but internationally, what our bail regime looks like, where's it coming from and how it operates.'

He also doesn't think he was at all rattled by the fact that his entire judgment was carried live on international networks such as CNN and Sky. 'If you're going to allow the thought of your being on international or national radio or TV to come to the fore, you are going to become conscious of it. You are going to watch what you say, how you say it and so on and so on forth. I think I was alive to the fact that this is beaming out, but I blocked it out. For me, at that point in time, I was with you guys [the media].'

During the bail application, global media interest was at a premium and while every development within the courtroom was amplified, one of the biggest news stories came when court was not in session. The explosive revelation about the charges against investigating officer Hilton Botha could well have derailed the bail application. The news came once Botha had finalised his testimony and there were expectations that Nair could recall him to the stand. Although the state did formally inform the court of the charges, the defence did not push the issue. And Nair did ask the policeman to come back to court and resume his testimony – but did not broach the subject of his own case with him, to the surprise of many. The magistrate has to tread carefully now about just how much he knew about the charges against Botha that morning and why he didn't quiz him about the revelation.

'No, I didn't need to ask him at that point in time. I had the urge to make sure that I get a complete picture from him on every issue that I needed, but I had taken a conscious decision not to pay attention to the media during that period, so whatever was happening outside, if it came to my ears by mistake I just ignored it because it hadn't been formally brought to my attention. If, on the other hand, the defence team took issue with that themselves, they would have opened the door for me to take issue with it. For me the case was about Mr Pistorius.'

Of course, it would have been nearly impossible for Nair to entirely ignore the media coverage of the global sports star's court appearance. Newspaper posters stuck on poles lining the streets of the city displayed bold headlines and radio and TV news bulletins carried little else. Yet he insists he made every effort not to be influenced.

'In the car I listen to my own type of music. I love Hindi music, especially the older '60s, '70s, '80s and I hardly listen to the news in the car. When I got home during that period I would watch the cooking channel or BBC Lifestyle, which I love to watch, so one thing I knew I should not do and try my best to avoid unless I walked in and the thing was on, the kids were watching, I would probably walk out.'

He says the billboards on the streets were more difficult to avoid. 'You can't help but take notice of that, but what do you do? You look at it and just think, oh. And I must tell you, they are rather distracting, because in some instances they are talking about you. So you see it, you read it, you play it back in your head for a second or two, even later that day, but when you walk into the courtroom, you know that if you are going to pay any attention to that you will err.'

It is not unusual in South Africa for court proceedings to be tweeted live by journalists. There are few rules and little precedent regulating the Twitter coverage of trials and this was highlighted during the Pistorius case when the public's appetite for news was met by reporters on the platform. Nair, like other presiding officers in courts in the country, had to navigate this new territory with little to guide him along the way.

'I've heard my kids talk about Twitter, I've heard my staff talk about Twitter, but I didn't, up to now, take time to go and meticulously read about it,' he admits, but adds that he's not worried about its impact on his work. 'The nation can pretty much work out second for second what is happening in that courtroom, but it's not interfering with me, it's not interfering with counsel and you are allowing access to justice. The problem I have is what's going out in terms of the accuracy because it's in the third person.'

As a result of the subjective nature of the reporting on the platform, he would urge reporters to be more responsible when tweeting about his cases. Beyond the realm of the reporters, Nair's conduct and decisions would have been open to the general Twittersphere for comment but he didn't fuss about this. 'My daughter would, from time to time, say to me, "Daddy, do you know what they are saying about you on Twitter?" and I replied, "Okay, just leave it." And she would say, "I'm so angry with this person, I'm so angry with that person," and I would say, "You know what, just forget about it."'

Nair's three children and his wife were all taken with the idea that he was involved in the case – like most South Africans, they quickly developed a fascination with the events playing out in his courtroom. 'They were quite fascinated, each one in their own way. The twin boys were 11 and my daughter was 14, so they are at an age where they have heard about Mr Pistorius, they have seen him on TV, although their sport is cricket and mine is boxing. I didn't take a serious interest in athletics, but for the kids it was, like, awesome! That's the word they would use: "It's awesome, Dad," but I had to draw their attention to the fact that the pupils at school will obviously hear that I am dealing with the matter and we should be careful about it. For most of my matters, I work at home and my kids respect my privacy. You will never find them going through my stuff or going through the notes. They're not at an age, in any event, where they would understand the legal jargon and the good thing about my wife is that she respects my work, she would never peer into an affidavit unless she said, "Can I take a look at that?" She has never known of the judgment I am about to give in any matter, ever. And she's never prodded me at, like five o'clock in the morning, "What are you going to do? Have you decided what you are going to do?" I think I even heard her, at some point, say to me that her friends were enquiring from her – which is human nature – what's going to be the outcome and she simply told them, "Just trust me guys, Des won't talk about this.'"

Nair is adamant that he was not influenced in any way, although he did seek out different viewpoints on contentious issues of law. 'Not about whether he should get bail or not. About the law, yes. "What is your feeling about this? Do you think it was premeditated murder? What is your view on that?" I would even spend time with my wife Paddy explaining the difference between pre-meditated murder, *dolus eventualis* and *dolus directus*, legal terms that I learnt as a prosecutor, which I had to refresh.'

A year on from the frenzy of that week in February 2013, the magistrate has had time to reflect on his performance. Has he spent many hours in his office in the bowels of the court, neurotically dissecting every word of a ruling that was beamed around the globe?

'With hindsight, you know, you always want to make it better, always. You know, when I read the judgment, which I do, sometimes I think to myself, "Maybe I should have done it differently." I'll come to the same conclusion, but the way in which I structured the judgment should have been different. I've criticised myself, not on the ruling, but on the structure of the judgment and I could have structured it differently, slightly, here and there. But I think at that time, at that moment, you do things at that time.'

He uses tennis and boxing analogies to better explain his point. 'I mean, Maria Sharapova lost now, before the quarter-final and if you go back and probably ask her, "Why? How?" and she will say to you, "I should not have done this," or, "I should not have done that," but the fact of the matter is even Gerrie Coetzee would like another shot at the world title. But what he did wrong in 1981 with Mike Weaver only he knows!'

Despite his self-flagellation, Nair seems comfortable with the inevitability that he will forever be associated with this one case and his performance in it. 'It does come back every now and then in terms of it being so exceptional in my career for the public interest in the matter, for the application of the law and for the immense pressure I was put under to deliver at that level. I'm sure if one is hypertensive your blood pressure will definitely be running higher than normal on every day of that matter because, you know, there are so many little things: you get there, the court is not ready; the recording system is not working; the operator is not ready; you've got to worry about time, and, of course, as the presiding magistrate or judge, you don't know what's coming next. You can't predict whether the defence is going to call the accused, whether after all the affidavits have been handed in, the defence stands up and says, "Your Worship, we wish to reopen the case and call the accused," you don't know. What is Mr Nel going to do next? What is Mr Roux going to do next?

'When I look back, I often think about the emotions on the counsels' faces at different times during that bail application. Counsel are watching you all the time. When you interject to ask questions, especially during argument, and you remember I took both prosecution and state to great lengths to explain why they were arguing a, b, c and d … it's then that counsel don't really know. They start to guess which way this one is going. So by the time you step into court to give your judgment, they are playing back, "Why did he ask me that? Why was he asking about this …?" I've heard afterwards that the judgment was something of a pendulum: at some point looking like it was going this way, at some point looking like it was going that way, but that's again my personal style of giving a judgment.'

Nair also believes that the focus of the world's attention on his courtroom bodes well for the public's perception of the country's criminal justice system. As a result of the interest in the application, more people have learned about how the system works in reality and the merits and flaws of its ability to mete out justice.

'I think it's very positive that fate would have it that the South African criminal justice system, more specifically the bail operations in a courtroom have come to the fore. We had the opportunity to show how you do a bail application in a country that has a remarkable Constitution and everything in the Criminal Procedure Act is so married to the Constitution. I personally think that at any level – at bail level, at trial level, at appeal level – any international jurist would be proud. I know I gave it my best and I've got no reason to believe that, apart from the bail conditions that were overturned in some respects, the law was incorrectly applied.'

Ultimately, Nair chose to set bail at R1 million, considerably higher than the R250 000 Oscar offered to post. The magistrate has been known, such as in the case of Chanelle Henning, to set bail high, reaching up to R5 million, and with his international deals and success, the Paralympian could have been considered lucky not to have his bond set higher.

'I was satisfied with R1 million,' Nair says sternly and hints at the possibility that he had considered a higher amount. 'In the thought process up to the fixing of the amount, one thinks about various options when it comes to the amount of bail and the conditions. It's part of the decision-making process. I'm a firm believer that bail must be fixed at an amount which you certainly would be able to afford, but you will feel the pinch if you lost that amount of money. You must remember that a substantial portion of the bail was made up by guarantee and bond, so for me it's never about taking blood for stone. You can't fix bail at an amount that is clearly impossible for an accused to pay.'

A month after Nair delivered his judgment, Oscar took the decision on appeal in the High Court in Pretoria. Judge Bert Bam presided over that appeal and overturned some of the conditions imposed by Nair. These included that he surrender his passport to the magistrate's office, that he refrain from applying for a passport or travel documents until the case against him is concluded, that he refrain from entering the international departure hall of any airport, that he submit himself to the supervision of a probation officer, that he not be charged with an offence relating to violence against women while on bail, and that he refrain from consuming alcohol or a banned substance.

Bam stated that the conditions that Oscar report to the Brooklyn police station twice a week, and that he not go to his home at the Silver Woods estate, also be disregarded because they were not in Magistrate Nair's order. The judge also found that his court had the right to hear the appeal, because the Criminal Procedure Act did not limit it to the magistrate's court where the bail application was heard.

Bam was scathing of Nair in his ruling, finding that he had 'misguided himself', was 'patently wrong' and had imposed 'punitive' conditions on the accused. He also warned that bail should not be used as a tool to inflict an 'anticipatory punishment'.

'I think he's capable and competent but in this matter he was overwhelmed and overreaching. I think he just got caught up in the excitement. I think his judgment touched on things that were absolutely unnecessary. And I was shocked about the bail conditions, because half of those things I didn't even know you could actually do. Why he appointed a probation officer, who knows? Obviously some or other judge was going to change it. [Nair] opened the door and I think he gave [Bam] sufficient opportunity to criticise him,' says one public prosecutor who watched the case closely.

The defence's decision to appeal Nair's ruling – and to go to the High Court rather than return to him – clearly touched a nerve.

'It took me by surprise because my personal view was that you ought to have come back to me and said, "We've got an issue with this, this and this." But I respect the fact that they have a right to go on appeal and I respect the judgment by Judge Bam,' says Nair. He's diplomatic when asked about Bam's harsh choice of words. 'It's not unusual to hear those sentiments or comments when a matter is taken on appeal. I've also acted for a term now in the South Gauteng High Court and I've had appeals against refusal of bail where I have had to evaluate the judgments of my friends who are magistrates – and Regional Court magistrates in some instances – and overturn their decision.'

In the wake of Bam's ruling, there had been hushed rumblings in Pretoria's legal circles that the criticism of Nair's decision had its roots in a previous stand-off between the two men, a legacy of a long-fought legal scrap. Nair had presided over the case of Olympic athlete Sydney Maree and convicted him. Bam was the senior counsel representing Maree. Does Nair believe this was payback? No, he assures.

'Well, factually you are correct, I presided over the Sydney Maree matter and then Judge Bam was the senior counsel who represented Mr Maree. And we have worked together in the past. I would want to respect Judge Bam as being the gentlemen that he is and somebody who would not allow previous legal battles to be at the forefront when he is presiding over a legal matter.'

Nair still has unanswered questions about the incident and the version put forward by Oscar. It was these questions, which he included in his judgment, that the defence would have to answer in the trial.

'At the time that I raised those questions in my judgment, it wasn't calculated to influence anybody else in the future. It's just my style from the time I started on the bench to write a judgment into probabilities and improbabilities by asking questions in the judgment because that is how you test probability and improbability. But I think you may well hear those questions again in future.'

Now that he has disposed of the case, will Nair be watching the trial as it plays out down the road at the High Court, like the rest of the country?

'I think I will,' he smiles, his moustache stretching across his cheeks. 'There's no impediment to me following it now at all.' But will he be watching it for the sensation or for the law? 'For the law,' he says predictably, a reminder of just how deep his love for the law runs. 'Because you can't help but put yourself in the position of the trial judge. I often said during the hearing, "I'm not the trial judge," when I qualified some things, but if I were hearing the matter, what would it be like in terms of the law? Purely in the law.' He can't help but wonder.

Life Carries On

O ver the period of a year, from February 2013 until March 2014, both the prosecution and the defence prepared for what inevitably became known as 'the trial of the century'. The state's legal team of Gerrie Nel, Andrea Johnson, Captain Mike van Aardt and a contingent of top police investigators busied themselves securing affidavits, consulting with witnesses, conducting extensive forensic tests and carefully constructing their legal argument.

The same scenario was playing out in Barry Roux's chambers in Sandton, which inconveniently were undergoing a large-scale renovation. A trip to the defence's 'war room' involved a hazardous walk around building rubble and under scaffolding. Files labelled 'State vs Pistorius' began to stack high in Roux's office, with some having to occupy space on the carpeted floor.

But it wasn't only the lawyers who were furiously working: Oscar's PR machine also found themselves busy putting out fires as his name constantly reappeared in media reports. The appetite for stories about the fallen superstar was insatiable; every move he made and every development around him was publicised.

In March 2013, reports surfaced that Oscar was on the verge of suicide, that he was a broken man and that he was struggling to pay for spiralling legal fees. The reports emanated from a BBC3 documentary, featuring an interview with Oscar's friend Mike Azzie. 'He just always seems to mention Reeva and to ask us to pray for her and her family,' said Mike. 'But most of all, you've got to understand that we are there for him and we will always be his friend. He has no confidence in his tone of voice and he is just a man that is almost like someone that is walking around in circles and doesn't know where he is going. I would say that, just speaking to him, that he is a broken man and that I would go as far to say that he would be on the verge of suicide. It really worries me.'

The Pistorius family quickly moved to quell the rumour and shut down the suspicions:

> Oscar Pistorius is in deep mourning but despite the tragic circumstances he is certainly not suicidal, as has been rumoured.
>
> The family's spokesperson, Oscar's uncle, Arnold Pistorius, says Oscar has an excellent support structure in his family.
>
> 'From the moment we were first informed about the dreadful event of the early morning of 14 February 2013, we have worked hard to come to terms with the sad news of Reeva Steenkamp's death and Oscar's role in it.
>
> 'As a family it drew us closer together, supporting and encouraging each other, praying for Oscar – whom we love and who remains our son, brother and nephew.'

One dilemma facing Oscar in the year that followed was whether or not he should resume training. Running was what defined him before the shooting and how he had achieved fame and glory. He had not been on the track since Valentine's Day. His last competitive race had been his victory in the 400 metre final at the Paralympics the previous September. He had visited his training track at the University of Pretoria in March, but he had not chased the stopwatch as normal, settling instead for a short jog. That visit to the training ground had been captured by a schoolgirl on her cellphone and sparked rumours of his return to racing.

In early April 2013, his agent Peet van Zyl stated publicly that Oscar wanted to get back to training, but that he was not 'mentally ready' to compete.

'From our meeting, it was clear and evident it's going to take some time for him to be ready to compete. He's trying to process this whole ordeal,' said Van Zyl.

Oscar's family and his long-time coach Ampie Louw were keen for him to get back into training and into some kind of routine, but on 4 April his family issued a statement:

> Oscar is not back on any official training programme. This may change in future, but this will be a decision taken by Oscar, and Oscar alone. At this point Oscar is still in an extremely traumatised state and has made it clear to all of us that he is not able or willing to even contemplate this issue at this stage.

Three months later, Oscar made a formal return to his regular track routine, an event that was marked by the release of a two-minute video by his family. In the clip, Oscar was bearded and had lost a lot of weight. He was clearly emotional as he pulled on his carbon-fibre running blades. Dressed in a blue hooded Nike sweatshirt, he slowly made his way around the track in his first formal session in five months.

Back in April 2013, the family chose to issue another statement – this time in response to vitriolic and opinionated comments on Twitter and other social media platforms. They indirectly rebuked the group that had come to be known in the media as the 'Pistorians', fiercely loyal women who had banded together on Twitter, posting derogatory and offensive comments about Reeva, changing their avatars to images of Oscar and rabidly defending him against detractors at any opportunity:

> *Oscar, and the Pistorius family, are deeply disturbed by the tone of a number of recent reports in the South African tabloid press as well as commentary on various social media platforms.*
>
> *The disregard that is being shown by some – specifically those commenting via social media – for the profound pain that Reeva's family and friends are going through is very troubling.*
>
> *There is not a moment in the day that Oscar does not mourn for his girlfriend and Reeva's family, and all those who were close to her, are in his thoughts constantly ...*
>
> *It is a great sadness for Oscar that, in the short period that he and Reeva were together, the opportunity never arose for him to meet her family as she did his. He remembers that she always spoke with great love of her family.*
>
> *Although their relationship was young, she had become an intimate member of the Pistorius family. 'She touched all of us with her generosity of spirit and constant affection and will always remain in our hearts.'*

But Oscar couldn't keep his name out of the headlines. Out on bail, he had spent the time since the Valentine's Day shooting largely holed up at his uncle's Waterkloof mansion in Pretoria, apparently reading the Bible and watching television.

But he did venture out. On the heels of the family's statement in April, the *Sunday Times* reported on how he had enjoyed a few drinks on a night out at the Kitchen Bar restaurant in the Design Quarter in Fourways with tow-truck baron Craig Lipschitz. The Pistorius family public relations consultant Anneliese Burgess was quick to deny the claims as they appeared in the *Sunday Times*, which followed up its initial report with a further article:

The family statement criticised social media users for insensitive remarks and said Oscar's grieving process was 'incredibly overwhelming'.

This is at odds with an account given by a woman at Saturday's party, who said: 'He was drinking shooters and he was flirtatious. He didn't seem like someone [who had] lost the love of his life.'

Five people who said they saw a 'relaxed-looking' Pistorius said his arrival at the venue's private dining area, after 9pm, was frowned upon by some guests.

'One moment we are all talking and laughing and the next in walks Oscar,' one said.

'He's the last person we expected to see ... I can't believe he showed his face in public, carrying on as if nothing's happened.'

Pistorius, sporting a beard, is said to have flirted with several women. 'He was greeting a couple and then gave the woman a little pat on her backside. It was just so inappropriate,' said the guest.

Burgess told the Sunday Times yesterday that Pistorius 'strenuously and vigorously denies any inappropriate behaviour towards any people or women present, or "partying it up" with shooters'.

It would later emerge that earlier on the day of the Kitchen Bar incident, Oscar also attended a private party in Illovo. According to the *Sunday Times*, he was awkward at first but after several drinks began hitting on a Reeva lookalike, FHM model and lawyer Kesiah Frank:

But once he had knocked back a few drinks and shooters, Pistorius bounced back, according to guests who watched him. He then targeted Frank.

Pistorius took to the dance floor and kept asking the blonde beauty to accompany him to another party, several guests said this week.

He grabbed her hand to dance and flirted, giving up only after all his advances were rejected.

Also in attendance at the private party was former Brett Kebble murder accused and convicted drug peddler Glenn Agliotti. A guest at the party tells us that Agliotti made a point of welcoming Oscar to the event: 'Glenn did the braaing and Oscar came with his friend Craig Lipshitz. A model was there, two of Nelson Mandela's granddaughters were there. It was a *jol*, hey. Okes were a little bit nervous at first when Oscar arrived and we weren't quite sure what the vibe was going to be. But then Glenn made a little welcoming speech. He said, "Oscar, come here. No one's going to do anything. You're amongst friends here. We support you." There was a horse race that everyone had to watch because the guy whose birthday it was had a horse. It came third,' says the guest.

Agliotti confirms he was at the braai and that he welcomed Oscar. 'I didn't recognise him; he was sporting a beard. Craig introduced me and then I just welcomed him to the braai. I just said to him he must stay strong and hold his head up high. After what I had been through, I knew. A lot of people felt sympathetic towards him before the case started. He was very quiet, very reserved, stuck to himself. He didn't say two words to me.'

More recently, in July 2014, in the run-up to closing arguments in the murder trial, Oscar was allegedly involved in an altercation with businessman Jared Mortimer at the VIP Room in Sandton.

Mortimer told us that Oscar was in the company of former bouncer Guil Yahav, who had been previously acquitted of a murder charge. Yahav introduced Mortimer to Oscar. Mortimer is a close friend of former footballer Marc Batchelor, who had had his own run-in with Oscar previously, as well as self-confessed hit man Mikey Schultz. Oscar was moving in controversial circles at a time when he could ill afford to do so.

Yahav says Oscar called him earlier that afternoon to ask if he was keen to go out for a few drinks. 'He doesn't have many friends left in Joburg, so he probably wanted me to look after him that night,' Yahav says. The pair go back many years – Yahav attended Oscar's 21st birthday party at Hartbeespoort Dam.

It was also not unusual for Oscar to call Yahav looking for protection. 'He often got into trouble. He used to call me from Pretoria at 3am, crying, drunk and emotional, saying he has problems. He could get a bit out of hand.'

The athlete met Yahav at the Marco Polo lounge in Sandton. 'When he first saw me he had a sorry face, but that changed quickly. He said his legal fees were costing him a fortune and running into millions. He was chatting to other girls,' adds Yahav.

The ex-bouncer says that by the time they decided to head over to the VIP Room, Oscar was 'well on his way'. En route to the club, they bumped into the athlete's cousin and her friend, who joined them.

Mortimer claims Oscar was drunk and aggressive and was slagging off his friends Justin Divaris and Darren Fresco for selling him out. He was also allegedly bragging about how influential his family was and pulled out his phone to show off pictures of army vehicles and allegedly said, 'My family owns SANDF. I'll piss on Zuma.'

If it is true, it wouldn't have been the first time Oscar had shown contempt for the president. In January 2013, as the African Union's peace torchbearer during the African Cup of Nations tournament, he was scheduled to appear at a children's football match with Zuma in the Alexandra township in Johannesburg.

The previous night, 16 January, Oscar and Reeva were exchanging messages and making plans for the following day. 'Want to come. Meet zuma?' he asked at 10:49pm in a WhatsApp message.

'ill kick his nuts,' responded Reeva.

'He is a runt. Rather have a chilled day,' said the athlete.

Oscar's apparent claim that his family 'owns' the defence force in South Africa may have been a reference to a company, owned by his uncle Theo, that builds and supplies armoured cars. N4 Trucks 're-manufactures' armoured military vehicles that are used for guarding and peace-keeping efforts.

At the VIP Room in Sandton, the discussion between Oscar and Mortimer became heated. Yahav said he couldn't hear what was being discussed, but Oscar leaned over to him and said that he wanted to sort Jared out. 'I said he'll do nothing of the sort and told him to sit down and behave.' The argument escalated to the point that the pair pushed each other around until Oscar fell backwards onto a chair. Bouncers then stepped in.

Yahav says he was disappointed at how 'arrogant' Oscar was.

Oscar's version of events was vastly different from that of Mortimer and Yahav. His PR agent issued a statement saying he was provoked:

> We can confirm that Oscar was at a night club with one of his cousins. They sat in a quiet area of the private VIP section when they were approached by the individual identified as Mr Mortimer. The individual in question, according to our client, started to aggressively engage him on matters relating to the trial. An argument ensued during which our client asked to be left alone. Oscar left soon thereafter with his cousin. Our client regrets the decision to go into a public place and thereby inviting unwelcome attention.

Oscar's uncle Leo also issued a statement that gave some insight into the athlete's state of mind at the time:

> Whilst Oscar venturing out into a public space with his cousin, in the current climate and whilst his court case is still underway was unwise, those of us closest to him have been witness to his escalating sense of loneliness and alienation. This, we believe, is underlying some of his

*self-harming behaviour. As a family we are counselling Oscar to find
ways of dealing with his feelings of isolation.*

Leo also acknowledged that Oscar may have made a mistake by going to the
club:

*Being in a public space such as this, and thereby putting himself in a
place where this kind of confrontation could take place, was ill-consid-
ered. We do however believe that Oscar is grappling with an extreme
level of emotional pain that is manifesting itself in some of his recent
unwise actions and choices.*

It was evident that Oscar was finding it difficult to handle the immense pressure
of being at the centre of such intense public scrutiny and was overwhelmed by
the months of standing trial for his girlfriend's murder.

• • •

In late May 2013, Sky News broke an exclusive. It had managed to secure photographs of the bloody bathroom after the shooting, and images showing the
bullet-riddled door and pools of blood in the toilet cubicle were featured in the
network's news bulletins. It was suspected that the photographs had been leaked
by the police.

A few weeks earlier, the former lead investigator in the case, Hilton Botha,
reportedly stated that media houses had offered to pay officers for exclusive pictures of Oscar after he had been arrested. A foreign media house even apparently
offered a police officer R458 000 for a photograph of the toilet door.

As a result, the cellphones of 45 officers working on the case were confiscated
and an official investigation was launched.

'We wanted to get the original photograph that was sent to Sky to see if we
can't access the background information on the photograph to see what camera
was used but no one wanted to help us,' reveals a police officer close to the case,
who doesn't want to be named.

'There was an official enquiry at the head office. All the police officials on
the crime scene, all the cellphones were examined and downloaded. It was an
instruction from the national commissioner. There was a big meeting at head
office in the boardroom. Everyone who was on the crime scene had to report
there, and when they walked in they said, "Instruction from the National

Commissioner, hand over your phone. Hand over." And they did the extractions there. All the cameras as well. Because those photos are not from the crime scene album, they're different. They also took all the cameras and examined them as well. And nothing,' says the officer.

'There's one or two cops that were on the crime scene who resigned. Their phones weren't examined. And then there was one or two guys that, when their phones were seized, it wasn't the phones that were used the day of the crime.'

In the end, no one was caught – but it is likely that a police officer made a lot of money selling those photographs, although Sky News has denied ever paying for them.

The leak came just days before Oscar was due to make another appearance in court on 4 June 2013. His routine appearance before acting Magistrate Daniel Thulare was, however, brief as the prosecution asked for a postponement to allow the police to conduct further investigations relevant to the case.

But Thulare used the opportunity to send a warning to the media. Although he didn't mention the Sky News photos directly, the insinuation was clear. Thulare expressed concern over a potential 'trial by media' and told the state to investigate how information related to the case was being released into the public domain. During that routine court appearance, the case was postponed for two months. On the next day in court, the trial date would be set, the docket handed over to the defence, the indictment served and the witness list confirmed. This appearance inadvertently fell on what would have been Reeva Steenkamp's 30th birthday on 19 August 2013.

⸏ • •

Just days before Oscar was set to appear in court in August 2013, Gina Myers, her sister Kim, mother Desi and attorney Ian Levitt sat at a table on the roof terrace of a Hyde Park hotel. Their large dark glasses served a dual purpose, shielding the glare of the winter sun and discreetly hiding their red-rimmed eyes. The raw wound of Reeva's death was far from healing.

Gina reflected on the time they had spent with Reeva on her 29th birthday and how Gina would mark the occasion this time around. 'I think back to her birthday last year; we all went to Mimo's. That's where she wanted to go for her birthday and she had a sparkler! It's very surreal and it still doesn't feel real. The other day it was six months and that's just mind-boggling on another level. So the fact that it's her birthday and she's not here …' she tails off.

'We always usually have cake and we sat down for cupcakes all the time and now instead of having it with her, we are now going to have cupcakes for her, which is a little bit of a surreal thought and I think it can make us cry at any point, but we have to try and remember her and we have to try celebrate her, as hard as it is going to be. I think we will try our best to celebrate her.'

How would Reeva have spent her 30th birthday? Gina says her 'Alfie' had big plans. 'She was going to Vegas for her 30th. One of our friends was getting married there and it was going to be, it going to be a big year,' she says excitedly. 'You know, life carries on and you can get swept away and then you get those real moments when you realise that she's not coming back and you are going to have to spend her birthday without her.'

There was an underlying frustration for the Myers family that Reeva's birthday could be overshadowed by Oscar's court appearance, but Gina stressed that it didn't have to be that way.

'I think it's a choice. I think that if you want it to be about Reeva it will be. I know that every single person who loved her and cared for her and every single person she had an impact on; she gave talks to schools, she was becoming a big celebrity and she was doing well in her own career. And everybody she came into contact with, they will be remembering her and for us – we will be celebrating her. And for a lot of people it will be about her. It's a choice.'

Gina spent part of Reeva's 30th birthday in the public gallery of a court, a location she could never have predicted. Gina, Kim and Desi sat in the front row, an arm's length from Oscar and just a few seats from his sister Aimee. Dressed in funereal black, they stared as Oscar, Aimee and Carl silently held one another's hands and prayed as the commotion of photographers played out around them.

Reeva's boyfriend stood in the dock as the accused, wiping away tears and blowing his nose as he was formally served with an indictment containing the most severe count: the charge of murder for killing Reeva Steenkamp.

With the packed courtroom hushed, Magistrate Nair set down the trial to run from 3 March until 20 March 2014 at the High Court in Pretoria. When asked by Nair if he was well, Oscar quietly replied, 'Under the circumstances, Your Honour' – but as proceedings were postponed, the BBC's Andrew Harding tweeted that he had shaken the athlete's hand and asked how he was. Oscar apparently shook his head and mouthed, 'Not good.'

Less than an hour after the hearing ended, Carl Pistorius tweeted a photograph of Oscar and Reeva along with the words:

Remembered like yesterday. My life was impacted by u @reevasteenkamp & the lady u were! Always close to our hearts.

Facing the Law

With the release of the charge sheet and the witness list, the strength and strategy of the state's case was revealed. When he went on trial on 3 March 2014 in Pretoria, Oscar Leonard Carl Pistorius was to face four charges: murder and three separate counts on the contravention of the Firearms Control Act. Signed by the Deputy Director of Public Prosecutions for Gauteng North, Advocate GD Baloyi, the sheet contained details of the charges against Oscar and alternative charges on which he could be convicted:

COUNT 1: MURDER – READ WITH THE PROVISIONS OF SECTION 51(1) OF ACT 105 OF 1997

In that upon or about 14 February 2013 and at or near 286 Bushwillow Street, Silverwoods Country Estate, Silver Lakes in the District of Pretoria the accused did unlawfully and intentionally kill a person, to wit, REEVA STEENKAMP, a 29 year old female.

COUNT 2: CONTRAVENTIONS OF SECTION 120(7) OF THE FIREARMS CONTROL ACT NO. 60 OF 2000

In that on or about 30 September 2010 and whilst travelling in a vehicle with other passengers, on a public road at or near Modderfontein, in the district of Kempton Park the accused did unlawfully discharge a firearm without good reason to do so, by firing a shot with his own 9 mm pistol through the open sunroof of the car they were travelling in.

COUNT 3: CONTRAVENTION OF SECTION 120(7) OF THE FIREARMS CONTROL ACT NO. 60 OF 2000

In that during January 2013 and at Tashas Restaurant, Melrose Arch in the district of Johannesburg the accused unlawfully discharged a firearm to wit, a Glock 27 pistol, without any good reason to do so. Tashas Restaurant is a public place.

COUNT 4: CONTRAVENTION OF SECTION 9 OF THE FIREARMS CONTROL ACT NO. 60 OF 2000
In that on or about 16 February 2013 and at or near 286 Bushwillow Street, Silverwoods Country Estate, Silver Lakes in the District of Pretoria the accused did unlawfully have in his possession ammunition, to wit 38x38 rounds without being the holder of (a) a licence in respect of a firearm capable of discharging that ammunition, (b) a permit to possess ammunition, (c) a dealer's licence, manufacturer's licence, gunsmith's licence, import, export or in-transit permit or transporter's permit issued in terms of this Act (d) or is otherwise authorized to do so.

The indictment also contained seven points listed under a summary of substantial facts, which outlined the essence of the state's case:

1. *The accused was involved in a relationship with the deceased. The deceased chose to spend the night with the accused at his private residence. They were the only occupants of that residence at the time.*
2. *The deceased, a 29 year old woman, was shot and killed in the home of the accused just after 03:00am on the 14th of February 2013.*
3. *The deceased had locked herself into the toilet cubicle, situated adjacent to the main bedroom. The accused armed himself with his 9 mm pistol and through the locked door, fired four shots at the deceased. The deceased was wounded and died on the scene. The cause of death is given in the post mortem report as 'multiple gunshot wounds'.*
4. *Some of the state witnesses heard a woman scream, followed by moments of silence, then heard gunshots and then more screaming.*
5. *The accused said to witnesses on the scene that he thought she was an intruder. Even then, the accused shot with the direct intention to kill a person. An error in persona will not affect the intention to kill a human being.*

6. *On a separate occasion on 20 September 2010 the accused, who is the licensed owner of a 9 mm pistol, fired a shot through the sun-roof of the car whilst travelling on a public road. There were other passengers in that car.*

7. *In January 2013, the accused whilst having lunch with friends at a restaurant in Melrose Arch in Johannesburg, handled the firearm of one of his friends and a shot was discharged. This shot narrowly missed his friend and hit the floor of the restaurant.*

Attached to the indictment was a list of 107 state witnesses who the prosecution could potentially call to give evidence during the trial. Only once the prosecution had closed its case, could the defence legal team consult with those witnesses who had not been called and potentially secure them as their witnesses.

This list contained a litany of Oscar's neighbours from the Silver Woods estate, a large contingent of police officers and forensic experts, several of Oscar's friends and ex-girlfriends, Reeva's friends and some colourful characters with whom Oscar had previously had run-ins. These included footballer Marc Batchelor, several members of the Myers family, boxer Kevin Lerena, ex-girlfriends Melissa Rom and Samantha Taylor, and Samantha's mother Trish, Justin Divaris and Samantha Greyvenstein as well as numerous members of Oscar's own family.

Now that the defence was aware who the state intended calling and the strategy it would be adopting, it could retain the services of its own expert witnesses. The defence also hired The Evidence Room, an American forensic animation firm based in Cleveland, Ohio, that specialises in recreating crime scenes. Founded by 43-year-old CEO Scott Roder in 2003, the company reportedly works on 100 cases a year and can charge as much as US$10 000 per video. In the run-up to the trial, Roder spoke to *Time* magazine, with the magazine describing the videos as 'Pixar meets murder trial: illustrating car crashes and murders with faceless cartoons of people in jagged geometric landscapes.

'We don't give opinions, we don't say "this is how it happened", we describe the scene,' Roder told *Time*. 'That's our job: to help people understand the bigger picture.'

The defence continued to work with University of Pretoria forensic geologist Roger Dixon and firearms and ballistics expert Thomas 'Wollie' Wolmarans. Forensic pathologist Reggie Perumal, who was retained by Oscar's team on the day of the shooting, was believed to still be working with the defence. *Time* also reported that a US forensic scientist famous for testifying in the OJ Simpson murder trial was asked to join the team, but this was never confirmed by the defence.

But as much as the legal teams were preparing for the forensic battle that lay ahead, the broader belief was that the trial would turn on technical legal arguments. Researcher and author Antony Altbeker, who has written numerous books about policing and criminal trials in South Africa, believed that the outcome of the case would come down to the law. 'The big point about Oscar's matter is that we know who did it, we have his version and there's no mystery about who killed Reeva. So the big questions are ultimately going to be legal questions. I don't think the forensics will matter an enormous amount. The only way the forensics will *really* count in this trial, I think, is if there's any part of them that undermine his credibility, where he has said x and the forensics show y,' said Altbeker before the trial started.

Johannesburg-based criminal attorney Tyrone Maseko shares Altbeker's view on the weight of the forensics versus the importance of the law in this trial. 'In murder cases forensics can be very important; however, in this case I do not believe that they are determinative for the reason that Oscar admitted killing Reeva. Therefore the central questions become factual and legal. Insofar as some of the questions being factual, the forensics can be of assistance to the court in the sense that the court still needs to enquire into the reasonable possibility of the accused's version of events,' says Maseko.

With a selection of the most brilliant and highly respected lawyers in the country set to spar against one another on such a publicised stage, it was inevitable that the law would be the battlefield on which they would cross swords.

Judge vs jury

South Africa has a legal system as diverse and textured as its population. It is a meld of the customary law system inherited from indigenous African cultures, a civil law Roman-Dutch system from the original Dutch settlers who arrived at the Cape of Good Hope in the seventeenth century and a common-law system from the British who colonised a chunk of the country from 1910 to 1961, when it was known as the Union of South Africa before becoming a republic. In 1994, at the end of apartheid, South Africa adopted a groundbreaking interim constitution that was formalised in 1997. While the law is hybrid, and the Roman-Dutch system is the bedrock, broadly speaking the law governing criminal acts follows the English model.

The court system in South Africa is organised in a hierarchy from the Magistrates' Courts at the bottom to the High Courts in each division of the country, a Supreme Court of Appeal in Bloemfontein and the Constitutional Court in Braamfontein, Johannesburg, which is the highest authority in both constitutional and non-constitutional matters.

Criminal trials are officiated over by a presiding officer, such as a magistrate or a judge. South Africa no longer has a jury system after it was abolished in 1969.

When South Africa abandoned the jury system, the jury was replaced with a system of assessors. The judge can request to be joined by one or two assessors who, like a jury, help in deciding questions of fact, leaving questions of law to the judge. Assessors are usually either experts in a particular field under scrutiny in a case or advocates, magistrates or legal academics. In this way, specialist cases are dealt with by specialists in a particular area.

Legal experts are of the opinion that a judge is unlikely to be manipulated and/or corrupted in some way. As a result, the concept of a 'mistrial' does not exist in South African law. It is the judge's responsibility to apply the law of the land and follow due process, as well as to ensure that the accused is given a fair trial. The decision of a magistrate or judge is open to a review process, which could see a case travelling up the hierarchy of courts over a period of time as lawyers seek to establish whether or not an alternative presiding officer would find the same result.

South Africa also subscribes to what is known as an 'adversarial system' or an 'accusatorial model' of criminal procedure, which sees lawyers for both the prosecution and the defence being allowed the opportunity to cross-examine a witness while the presiding officer remains impartial, playing the role of referee or arbiter.

Wits criminal law associate professor James Grant describes how this works. 'An adversarial system is characterised by an impartial passive adjudicator who decides on the case put before him or her by the two parties to a dispute. The role of lawyers in this system is to make the best case possible for his or her client. In an inquisitorial system [a modern example of which is France], the adjudicator remains impartial, but adopts an active truth-finding role. Lawyers in this system assist the adjudicator in finding the truth. In South Africa, while our system is primarily adversarial, our judges are allowed to ask questions of witnesses for clarification, and may even go so far as calling their own witnesses.'

Judges don't get involved in assisting either side and it is up to both parties to prove their case. 'They do not "descend into the arena" and ask questions or procure evidence that is designed to assist any party in the proceedings. The parties themselves bear the onus of making their case or defence to the presiding officer and he or she merely arrives at a decision at the end of the proceedings,' adds Maseko.

He explains that cross-examination in a criminal trial such as the Oscar Pistorius case sees lawyers interrogating the evidence of any witness called by the opposing side, with the view of discrediting the evidence presented by the witness. 'This can be done in one of two ways, either by demonstrating to the court that the witness's evidence cannot be relied on because it is factually inaccurate. This can be done by getting the witness to concede that their recollection of events is not good or accurate and/or presenting to the witness evidence, documentary or otherwise, which is more reliable and which evidence contradicts the witness's testimony before court and asking the court to draw the necessary inference. Another way in which counsel can discredit a witness is by subjecting them to intense cross-examination with a view to exposing them as a liar. This is dangerous for any witness to do as he or she can be charged with perjury.'

Professor Grant explains that the thinking is that it is exceedingly difficult to persist with an untrue version of events when your story is examined from different angles. 'This is because lies offer an alternative version of events – of reality – they shift one into a hypothetical world. To succeed with a false version, one must have an excellent memory (to recall and not deviate from false statements you have already made) and a brilliant mind – to think every aspect of your lie through. Cross-examination tends to reveal inconsistencies in a false version where an accused loses track of the lies he or she has already told, or has not thought his or her lie through completely.'

In this model, cross-examination can be intense and lawyers can be aggressive and combative, which is why the judge's role is often to act as a referee. But Grant believes this style is not entirely necessary. 'It is famously said that the art of cross-examination is not to examine crossly. Ideally cross-examination will quietly and calmly extract concessions from a witness without the witness realising that he or she is making any sort of concession. However, witnesses can often be obstinate. Regrettably, both lawyers and witnesses are humans who are discussing something over which they inevitably disagree. It is almost inevitable tempers may flare.'

Ultimately, it is up to the judge presiding over the matter to reach a determination on guilt or innocence. 'The court' – as the judge is often referred to – has to decide whether the doubts about the guilt of the accused are reasonable or not. In this instance, on the murder charge, the judge has to make a call on whether it is a reasonable possibility that Oscar really thought he was entitled to kill whoever was behind the door. If the defence is able to prove that any possible doubt is reasonable, he would be acquitted of murder.

Murder, premeditated murder and culpable homicide

The prosecution in this case took the bold approach of charging Oscar with the most extreme Schedule 6 charge of 'premeditated murder', as well as with three firearm-related offences. While some believe this approach was taken merely to force the defence into putting a version of events on record at the bail application, it is likely that the prosecutors made an informed decision as to what might have happened on the morning of Valentine's Day 2013.

'They believe the facts fit the charge,' explains Maseko. 'The prosecution is also keenly aware that having charged Pistorius with premeditated murder, murder and culpable homicide are competent verdicts on that charge and they do not have to allege these separately. Therefore they have nothing to lose by charging Oscar with premeditated murder instead of murder or culpable homicide.'

The fact that the prosecution charged Oscar with 'premeditated' murder in reality only has an impact on how easy or difficult it was for him to be released on bail and on what kind of sentence he could theoretically receive. In substantive criminal law, there is no distinction between degrees of murder (unlike in the US where there is first-degree and second-degree murder, for example). In other words, for the purpose of the judge's verdict, murder is murder.

As Professor Grant explains, the concept of 'premeditation' 'is quite irrelevant to a charge of murder. It is, instead, only relevant to bail and sentencing. It places a charge into Schedule 6 of the Criminal Procedure Act, and therefore into a category for which a release on bail is extremely difficult to secure. Beyond bail, its effect will be that, if convicted of premeditated murder, the default minimum sentence is life imprisonment, unless an accused can show "substantial and compelling circumstances", which would justify a court imposing a lesser sentence. The concept of premeditation is very poorly defined in our law. It usually refers to some extent of planning.

'In the US, premeditation is identified where an accused laid in wait for his victim. This is the basis on which we conventionally distinguish between a killing in the "heat of passion" versus a "cold-blooded killing". Conventionally a "hot-blooded" passion killing is regarded as less culpable, but the opposite intuitions are triggered in respect of deliberate, calculated, cold-blooded killings.

Presumably part of the reason is that the time available to someone planning a cold-blooded killing presents the person with opportunities to reconsider and yet they recommit themselves to their evil purpose throughout this period.'

In Oscar's case, the prosecution argues that he only needed a couple of moments to plan the murder, which goes against the conventional understanding of premeditation in which you take hours, days or months to plot a killing.

This alternative conception of premeditation was introduced locally, in part due to outrage by the public in certain matters where shockingly low sentences were handed down to criminals for very serious crimes.

So, if Oscar were to be found guilty of premeditated murder, the minimum sentence would be life imprisonment (with a minimum of 25 years before he qualified for parole) unless he could prove substantial and compelling circumstances that would allow the judge to consider a term less than the minimum sentence.

If Oscar were to be found guilty of murder (not premeditated), the minimum sentence would be 15 years' imprisonment because he is a first offender.

If Oscar were to be found guilty of culpable homicide, he might well have a custodial sentence imposed on him because of the involvement of a firearm in the killing – this could see him jailed, receive a fine or have to do community service. The judge has no obligation to impose a particular sentence and she has discretion.

· · ·

So what does the prosecution have to prove in order to convict Oscar of murder?

The legal definition of murder is 'the unlawful and intentional killing of another person'. The intentional killing is not 'unlawful', however, if an accused has a recognised defence and the 'intent' is assessed subjectively – in other words, we have to ask the question, 'What was the accused actually thinking?', not 'What should the accused have been thinking?'

Murder is a common-law crime, which in layperson's terms means it is not a crime that has come into existence simply because of a piece of legislation. It has always been reprehensible to kill another human being where there has been an intent to do so and without an acceptable reason for the killing. 'From a legal perspective, in order to convict a person for the killing of another human being the state has to prove its case beyond reasonable doubt. To secure a conviction for murder, the state is required to prove all of the following elements: (1) unlawfulness, (2) killing, (3) person [that a human being died] and (4) intention,' says Maseko.

Often the most fertile ground for differences between the state and the defence in a criminal trial is around the issue of 'intention', as Maseko elaborates: 'The theory behind "intention" as a requirement for most offences in our law is that we are not a primitive society that condemns people for actions for which they do not have a guilty mind – that is to say, they have not deliberately and conscientiously caused harm to another while having all their mental faculties intact.'

While it could be a difficult concept for the average person to wrap his or her head around, the issue of 'intention' is central to the Oscar case.

Intention is assessed subjectively and it is up to the judge to reach a decision about the accused's state of mind when the offence was committed. Depending on whether or not Oscar had a 'guilty mind' would determine the crime on which he would be convicted, if any, and the amount of time he would spend in prison.

There are three different kinds of 'intention': *dolus directus*, *dolus indirectus* and *dolus eventualis*.

Dolus directus is what we commonly associate with the word 'intention'. It is a direct intention to commit a crime, where an accused deliberately acts in a way that is meant to bring about an unlawful consequence. His or her aim and object is to kill that person and he or she knows it's wrong but goes ahead and does it anyway. An example of this is if you decide to rob a corner café and the owner refuses to open the safe, at which point you shoot and kill him. You thus have a direct intention to kill. The assassin acts with *dolus directus* in respect of his or her 'mark'.

Dolus indirectus exists where, although it is not the accused's aim and object, he or she foresees the unlawful act or consequence as certain or as virtually certain. As an example, if your aim is to kill a person inside a car by throwing a hand grenade, which detonates, into the vehicle, you have a direct intention to kill the person but an indirect intention to cause malicious damage to the car.

Another example is a scenario in which you want to burn down your competitor's store in order to boost your own business. You know a homeless man sleeps in the store at night, which would be difficult to escape in the case of a fire as the lights would be off and the store is crowded with stock. Your aim and object is not to kill the man but to destroy the store, although you realise the man will almost certainly die in the fire. You therefore have indirect intention to kill the man.

Dolus eventualis exists where the accused's aim and object is not to bring about the unlawful consequence that follows from his or her actions, but he or she foresees the possibility of the consequence and goes ahead with his or her action anyway. The accused accepts that there is a risk of a crime being committed, and he or she proceeds nevertheless and the risk materialises. This form of intention is often referred to as 'legal intention'. The tricky part about *dolus eventualis* is that the accused must be shown to have foreseen the outcome.

A classic example of acting with *dolus eventualis* is when you go duck hunting. If you find ducks on a lake and take aim at a duck, but, as you are about to fire, you notice that there are children playing on the opposite side of the lake. You realise that if you fire at the duck, you may miss, and the bullet could strike and kill one of the children. You really don't want to kill a child, but you really want to kill a duck. You then accept the risk of killing the child – shrugging it off as only a remote possibility. After all, you reassure yourself, you are an excellent shot. You pull the trigger, miss the duck, and strike and kill a child. On a charge of murder, you are liable for the murder of the child on the basis that you had intention in the form of *dolus eventualis*.

Another example of *dolus eventualis* is where you steal copper cable at a railway line, which results in trains colliding and commuters are injured or die. If you foresaw that tampering with the railway cabling may affect signalling and trains may collide with a tragic outcome but proceeded to tamper with the cabling, then you had *dolus eventualis*.

Another example is where you are in a bar when you see someone flirting with your girlfriend. You want to teach the guy a lesson so that he will never flirt with your girlfriend again and so you beat him up. You pick up a glass from the bar and smash it with full force into the side of the man's head. You know that a person can die if hit with force in the temple but you proceed to smash the man in the head anyway. Your aim and object is to assault the man, not to kill him, but you foresee the possibility of the man dying and proceed with the assault. The man falls to the ground unconscious and later dies of the head injury. You fulfil the definition of *dolus eventualis* – the law considers that you had intent to kill.

The presence of *dolus directus* or *dolus indirectus* or *dolus eventualis* can prove intent and would see the accused being convicted of murder – unless, of course, the accused has a defence that could show that he or she did not have intention to kill.

'For the purposes of the law, the concept of intention has two components: (1) the accused's state of mind must fulfil the definition of a legally recognised form of intent (*dolus*) and (2) the accused must have knowledge of unlawfulness (in other words, put colloquially, ignorance of the law *is* a defence),' explains Kelly Phelps, a senior lecturer in the Public Law Department at the University of Cape Town. 'If either 1 or 2 is missing there will be no intent to kill. In Pistorius's case the defence he is raising is called putative private defence (mistaken belief in private defence) – in other words, he contends that he genuinely lacked knowledge of unlawfulness and therefore did not have intent to kill as defined by the law.'

For Oscar Pistorius to be convicted of murder, the state would have to prove that one of these types of *dolus* existed and that he had a 'guilty mind', known by the Latin term *mens rea*, with an intention to kill.

However, he could be convicted of the lesser charge of culpable homicide. For this, the state would have to prove *culpe* – that Oscar was negligent or careless. This would mean that Oscar was 'blameworthy' and, while he did not have the intention to cause anyone's death, the death nevertheless resulted from his negligent action.

The only distinction between culpable homicide and murder is what the accused was thinking at the time of the crime. The legal definition of culpable homicide is the 'unlawful and negligent killing of another human being'. So, murder requires 'intention' whereas culpable homicide requires 'negligence'.

Maseko explains: 'The test that is applied by our courts to determine whether negligence existed on the part of the accused is to measure their conduct against the standard of care that society expects of fellow human beings to preserve the life of another or, conversely, not to act in a manner that may result in the endangering of another human being's life and possibly causing their death albeit unintentionally.'

To prove culpable homicide, the state's case would have to pass all three legs of the test:

1. Would a reasonable person, in the same circumstances as the accused, have foreseen the reasonable possibility of this consequence and that it is unlawful?
2. Would a reasonable person have taken steps to guard against that possibility?
3. Did the accused fail to take steps that he should reasonably have taken to guard against it?

If all three questions are answered in the positive, then Oscar's conduct could be regarded as negligent and he could be convicted of culpable homicide.

'If the fictional reasonable person would have foreseen the death and would have taken steps to guard against it, and the accused failed to take such steps, then the accused is held to be negligent. Like intention, it is not sufficient that the accused meets the definition of negligence; the accused must also have knowledge of unlawfulness. For a putative defence to remove negligence, the accused's mistaken belief that he was acting in self-defence must not only be genuine (to exclude intention) but also a reasonable mistake in the circumstances (to exclude negligence); says Phelps.

'Reasonable person'

For the court to decide whether or not Oscar should be convicted of 'culpable homicide', it has to apply what is known as the 'reasonable man' or 'reasonable person' test. If the action the accused took or the mistake he made was one that reasonable people would make in the same circumstances, and they didn't know something at the time that they know now, then their actions would be held to the same standard as this 'reasonable man'.

Negligence is determined by referring to the standard of the reasonable person in the circumstances of the accused, explains Professor Grant. 'If an accused acted in a manner contrary to what the reasonable person, in the same circumstances, would have done, the accused was negligent. At its core, this is a test that compares the conduct of the accused with what is to be expected of a reasonable person in the same circumstances as the accused. Any "gap" between what the accused did and what the reasonable person, in the circumstances of the accused, would have done represents negligence on the part of the accused.

'Immediately one may recognise that the identity of the "reasonable person" is all-important. The reasonable person is a hypothetical person, constructed by a court to judge whether an accused acted with sufficient care. The more like the accused the reasonable person is "constructed" to be, the less any "gap" between the conduct of the accused and that of the reasonable person will be. The accused will argue that all of the characteristics and attributes of the accused must be attributed to the reasonable person, including, of course, an impediment or disability that the accused has.'

But this reasonable person test is a vexed and convoluted question in law. How do you define the reasonable person to allow the test to be applied across the board? And could Oscar be held to the same standard as this 'reasonable person', with his disability and life experience?

'In applying this test to the facts before the court, the court needs to determine who this reasonable person is, what qualities they possess,' says Phelps. 'Both the defence and the prosecution will need to assist the judge in closing arguments in determining what qualities this reasonable person should possess in this case. In order to do this, they will rely on settled case law as well as areas of the law that are less settled and open to interpretation. The reasonable person as envisaged in South African law is not a bastion of perfection or a quivering wreck sitting on the couch wrapped in cotton wool lest anything bad should happen as a result of his or her actions.'

The notional reasonable person was clearly described in the well-known delict case *Herschel v Mrupe*: '[the reasonable person is] not … a timorous faint-heart always in trepidation lest he or others suffer some injury; on the contrary, he ventures out in the world, engages in affairs and takes reasonable chances'. In other words, the test is not calibrated to eliminate all risk-taking, only unreasonable risk-taking.

The reasonable person test was actually featured in a South African movie called *A Reasonable Man*, based on the classic case testing this notion. In the 1930s, Mbombela, a young man of around 20, lived in a rural village in the former South African homeland of the Transkei. He wasn't educated, and believed in the existence of evil spirits called 'tokoloshes'. It was widely believed then, and still is today, that a tokoloshe could take the form of a little old man with small feet. Mbombela also believed that to look the evil spirit in the face would be fatal.

One day a group of children who had been playing outside a village hut they believed was empty came running in terror to Mbombela to report that they had seen a figure that had two small feet, like those of a human, inside the hut. Mbombela concluded that this must be a tokoloshe and went off to fetch his hatchet.

In the dim light of the hut's interior, he lashed out at what he believed to be the tokoloshe, striking it several times with the hatchet. But moments later when he investigated 'the victim', he discovered it was in fact his nine-year-old nephew.

Mbombela was convicted of murder and sentenced to death. The court took a purely objective test to the construction of the reasonable man, refusing to take Mbombela's belief in the tokoloshe into account. The Appeal Court, however, dismissed the charge of murder, but convicted him of culpable homicide and sentenced him to 12 months' hard labour.

'In other words, the court found the accused lacked intention for a murder charge but possessed negligence for the culpable homicide charge. The court refused to take into account in the determination of reasonableness the "race or the idiosyncrasies, or the superstitions, or the intelligence of the person of the accused", despite the recognition by the court that belief in the fatal powers of the tokoloshe was widespread amongst the community of which the accused was a part. This case has been heavily criticised over the years for leading to unfairness in the context of a multicultural society like South Africa,' says Phelps.

While it might seem fair that the law should take each individual's attributes – including religious and superstitious and traditional beliefs as well as disabilities and vulnerabilities – into account, if that were to happen it would effectively result in the collapse of any standard. There would be no point to the reasonable person test.

That is why in Oscar's case, technically, the test cannot be 'lowered' to take into account his disability, as Professor Grant explains. 'For this reason, the law has, to date, refused to take account of any characteristic, attribute, impediment or disability of an accused. To use the conventional language, the law is not prepared to "lower" the standard by taking account of personal attributes of an accused. Our courts are only prepared to "lower" the standard by taking account of the immediate external circumstances in which he, the accused, acted – such as, for instance, driving a car where the brakes have failed, or being in the dark at night. By doing this, the law is "lowering" the standard to take account of the context in which the accused acted. On the contrary, though, our courts do "raise" the standard to take account of a special skill that a person ought to have if he or she engages in an activity that requires that skill. Thus, any person who performs a surgical procedure on another person will be judged against a standard of the reasonable surgeon. Our courts are likely to regard using a firearm as requiring special skill. Therefore, on a charge of culpable homicide, and on the law as it stands, Oscar Pistorius can expect the court to compare his conduct to that of a reasonable gun-owner, in the circumstances that prevailed at the time, without taking any account of any impediment, disorder, or disability on his part.'

Phelps considers whether Oscar's disability should be taken into account by the judge: 'Arguably, it must be taken into account – that is, the reasonable double amputee – as it would be absurd to expect a man with no legs to have the physical ability of a man with legs. So if the disability is taken to be "the circumstances of the accused" then where does the court draw the line? Surely it goes without saying that a severe physical disability has a significant impact on a person's personality and emotional and/or psychological make-up. Such factors are internal characteristics and routinely not considered by the court. But then surely the court is treating a disabled person as if they didn't have that disability, which would render the law artificial and potentially unfair. This is the sort of debate that the legal teams will need to engage in with the judge.'

Putative private defence

Antonio de Oliveira – a businessman and white, illiterate, immigrant from Madeira – lived in the Johannesburg suburb of Rewlatch with his partner, Mrs Cordeiro. An employee, Vusi Nyandeni, also lived on his property. Robberies and housebreakings in Rewlatch were common and, as a result, De Oliveira armed himself.

One Sunday afternoon in 1988, the couple were asleep in their bedroom when Cordeiro was awoken by dogs barking. She saw black men she didn't recognise outside and heard glass breaking. She screamed at Antonio, who calmed her down, took his gun and fired six shots at the 'intruders'.

In his statement to the police, De Oliveira explained what had happened: 'I told my wife not to worry. I would sort it out. I then took my pistol from the table next to my bed and I fired six or seven shots and these blacks ran away. I saw afterward that two black males were lying on the ground. I was not thinking about anything at the time as I was half asleep when I shot these shots.'

The men he had shot at were not intruders. They were his long-time employee Vusi Nyandeni, his brother Paul and two friends. The shots killed Nyandeni's brother, wounded Nyandeni himself and just missed one of his friends.

Nyandeni testified against his employer in court, stating that when they had arrived at the property, the door to the servants' quarters was locked and so he rang the front door bell. He claimed that De Oliveira and Cordeiro appeared at the bedroom window demanding to know what was going on. According to Nyandeni, De Oliveira threatened him that if he ever brought strangers to the house he would shoot them. De Oliveira went off, fetched his gun and began shooting.

In his trial, De Oliveira used a defence called 'putative private defence' – although he was not entitled to fire at the victims, he mistakenly believed he was.

Private defence is the technical name for self-defence – and it is wider in definition than self-defence. Private defence includes one's right to resort to reasonable force in defence of any legally protected interest, such as your body, your life or those of another person.

'So society accepts that while killing another human being is wrong, undesirable and therefore unlawful, it also accepts that there are limited circumstances under which it is acceptable to kill another. One of those circumstances is when another person wants or attempts to take your life, then you are allowed to choose your life over his or hers; that is self-defence, and if you raise the defence successfully then your actions are not unlawful in those circumstances.

So, self-defence negates unlawfulness because it makes your actions lawful,' describes Maseko.

For this defence to work, a person needs to actually be under attack. De Oliveira, like Oscar Pistorius, was not in reality under attack so the argument of self-defence would not be open to them. The question then is, how does the law deal with this 'honest' mistake? Should you go to jail because you believed that you were entitled to act in self-defence but later learn that you were actually grossly mistaken?

'Putative' means 'mistaken'. So putative private defence means a supposed or mistaken defence, where the accused relies on his or her mistake that he or she was entitled to act in private defence.

'Colloquially, this means "mistaken belief in self-defence", says Phelps. 'In other words, he mistakenly believed that he was acting in self-defence. Self-defence is a defence that eliminates the unlawfulness of a killing. A putative defence eliminates the *mens rea* (intention or negligence) of the killing, in that he lacked knowledge of the unlawfulness of his conduct.

'The putative defence works as follows: in order to successfully defend a charge of murder, the mistaken belief must be a genuine one. In other words, the court must determine what he was actually thinking, not what he should have been thinking. Did he genuinely, though wrongly, believe he was acting in self-defence? If the answer is "yes", he is acquitted on murder for lacking intention to kill. Next, to successfully defend the culpable homicide charge, the genuine mistaken belief must also be reasonable in the circumstances. If the mistake is considered reasonable in the circumstances, he will be acquitted for culpable homicide too,' says Phelps.

Professor Grant illustrates how this works in reality: 'So, if X runs at you with a knife with the intention of stabbing you to death, if you have no alternative you may resort to lethal force in response. Private defence is judged objectively, by reference to reality. If you resort to lethal force against someone who is not, in objective reality, attacking you, you may not rely on this defence of private defence. However, if you are not actually under attack, but you mistakenly think you are, and you do resort to lethal force and kill the perceived attacker, you may rely upon the defence of "putative private defence" if you also believe that you had no alternatives and that you are entitled to use lethal force.'

In De Oliveira's trial, the court rejected his defence and he was convicted of murder. He appealed the decision and the ruling by Judge Smalberger set out the principles of putative private defence – the defence that Oscar Pistorius is likely to rely on too:

The impression gained from the appellant's plea explanation at the com-mencement of the trial, and what was initially put to certain of the State witnesses under cross-examination, was that that he sought to justify his conduct on the basis that he had acted in defence of his life and/or prop-erty, that is, private defence ... It subsequently transpired that the defence was rather one of putative private defence ('putatiewe noodweer'). From a juristic point of view the difference between these two defences is sig-nificant. A person who acts in private defence acts lawfully, provided his conduct satisfies the requirements laid down for such a defence and does not exceed its limits. The test for private defence is objective – would a reasonable man in the position of the accused have acted in the same way (S v Ntuli 1975 [1] SA 429 [A] at 436E). In putative private defence it is not lawfulness that is in issue but culpability ('skuld').

If an accused honestly believes his life or property to be in danger, but objectively viewed they are not, the defensive steps he takes cannot constitute private defence. If in those circumstances he kills someone his conduct is unlawful. His erroneous belief that his life or property was in danger may well (depending upon the precise circumstances) exclude dolus in which case liability for the person's death based on intention will also be excluded; at worst for him he can then be convicted of cul-pable homicide.

On appeal the unlawfulness of the appellant's conduct was not in issue. Accordingly the only issue was whether the State had proved beyond all reasonable doubt that the appellant subjectively had the nec-essary intent to commit the crimes of which he was convicted, in other words, that he did not entertain an honest belief that he was entitled to act in private defence. Any argument based on the reasonableness of the appellant's belief and conduct was not persisted in, and rightly so.

The case of former Springbok rugby player Rudi 'Vleis' Visagie is potentially a perfect example of putative private defence.

Early on a Sunday morning in 2004, Visagie and his wife Frieda were asleep at home on their plot in Maggiesdal, outside Nelspruit, when his wife woke up and shouted that someone was stealing their daughter Marle's car. The vehicle was being driven out the gate.

Visagie took his gun and shot at the car, hitting the 'thief' in the head. But then, on further investigation, the Visagies were horrified to discover that the apparent thief was actually their daughter. She had been driving her own vehicle and was on her way to surprise her boyfriend for his birthday. Marle was rushed to the Nelspruit Mediclinic with a head wound but was declared dead on arrival.

'There appears no basis on which to suspect that Visagie knew, or had the slightest idea, that it was his daughter driving the car. As such, this appears to be a perfect example of putative private defence being a valid defence to a charge of murdering his own daughter. Although Visagie was not entitled to resort to lethal force in the circumstances, he mistakenly believed that he was entitled to do so. Thus he intended to act lawfully, and could not be convicted of murder,' explains Professor Grant. 'It is arguable whether his conduct was reasonable and it is possible that he may have been convicted of culpable homicide. Nevertheless, the NPA [National Prosecuting Authority] declined to prosecute, taking into account the gravity of the tragedy and that living with what he had done would be its own punishment.'

In 2012, Glenn Boshoff of Centurion shot his eight-year-old daughter through a closed bedroom door, thinking she was an intruder. When burglars broke into the family's home in a secure complex, Boshoff was awoken by his dogs barking and went to investigate. He apparently saw an armed intruder at the bottom of the stairs and another climbing through a window. Boshoff grabbed his revolver out of the safe. In the meantime, eight-year-old Edith had woken up and made her way to her parents' bedroom. As she turned the handle of the door, Boshoff fired a shot, thinking she was an intruder trying to get in. It was only when he opened the door that he discovered his daughter. The six intruders fled the scene and Edith was rushed to hospital in a critical condition where she died.

Other similar cases have been reported in the media over the past few years and if Oscar's version of events is indeed true, he is not the first person to suffer such a tragedy.

In Oscar's case, assuming the state does have a case strong enough to prove murder, he would have to raise a believable defence of 'putative private defence'.

'What putative self-defence says is that, simply put, the law will not punish you if you made a genuine mistake of verily believing that you were entitled to a defence excluding unlawfulness, but actually in reality you were not entitled to that defence because in reality there was no threat to your life. But if all the surrounding circumstances of the killing are looked at, it is clear that your mistake is one that is reasonable, then you lack "intention" and you cannot be convicted of murder, but also your actions were not negligent because your apprehension of imminent danger and your actions to ward it off were reasonable in those circumstances,' explains Maseko.

In 2010, Goodness Mchunu and two accomplices were charged with murder, attempted murder and arson after she attempted to set fire to her boyfriend's shack in revenge for him having a wandering eye. Goodness, a resident of Lidgetton in KwaZulu-Natal, set fire to the shack but her boyfriend wasn't there at the time. She fled when she realised she had 'burnt the wrong people', those inside the residence at the time of the incident. One man was killed and another escaped with burn wounds. Neither of these was her boyfriend – the target of the arson attack arrived home to find his shack in flames.

In this case, it was her aim and object to kill her boyfriend so there is direct intention (*dolus directus*) regarding the murder charge. There is indirect intention on the arson charge (*dolus indirectus*) – her aim and object was to kill her boyfriend, but by setting fire to his dwelling she foresaw the destruction of his dwelling by fire as a substantially certain outcome of pursuing her aim and object to kill.

'This case is also an example of the rule of law "*error in objecto*" (mistaken identity), which is the state's alternative argument in the Pistorius matter. That is, a mistake as to the identity of the occupant of the shack will not be a defence to a murder charge – when she set fire to the shack she intended to kill the person inside the shack, though she was mistaken as to the identity of the person,' explains Phelps. 'The major difference between this case and Pistorius's is the putative defence. He is not arguing mistaken identity but mistaken belief in self-defence. This is what the judge will need to reconcile and the parties will need to argue.'

The problem Oscar faced with putative private defence is that the court has to be convinced that he genuinely believed his life, and or that of Reeva, was in danger. That is why the state dedicated a great deal of time leading evidence to show that it was unlikely and improbable that Oscar could have genuinely believed that it was an intruder behind the door.

'As to the question of whether, on Oscar's own version, he believed it was an intruder behind the door and he fired shots because he believed his and Reeva's lives were in danger, assuming that it was an intruder behind the door, would it have been reasonable for him to fire four shots at someone he didn't know was armed, that is, he hadn't assessed the extent of the danger (if any) to himself or Reeva. Is that a reasonable reaction? Can it be said that the action taken to ward off the attack was commensurate with the attack? These are questions that will be argued by both counsels to different ends and the court will ultimately have to pronounce on these questions,' describes Maseko.

In essence what the defence is saying is that Oscar genuinely believed that Reeva was in bed when he approached the toilet door and that he was convinced someone – an intruder whose motives he couldn't have known – was inside the house and in the toilet. He was fearful because it was dark and he couldn't have known what the next action of the intruder would have been. He approached the door to investigate and when he saw that it was closed and heard a noise, he fired, because – presumably – if he hadn't he could have been fired at.

'It is not a bad argument except that the factual basis of that defence had to be laid by Oscar himself,' says Maseko. For this reason, Oscar was left with little choice but to testify. His defence would also be at pains to show how vulnerable and fearful Oscar is and just how aware of security he is.

The judge will decide

In order for the state to prove its case of premeditated murder, it has to show that Oscar Pistorius planned the murder of Reeva Steenkamp. It has to prove that he planned intentionally and unlawfully to kill another human being. For premeditated murder, the state has to present the court with a motive for the murder. It would be difficult to prove premeditation without establishing a motive and showing the court what might have driven Oscar to set in motion the deliberate actions that led to the killing.

'If the court is of the opinion that the state has not proven beyond reasonable doubt that the act of killing the deceased is one that the accused considered and had the opportunity to bail out of, but did not, then if all the elements of murder are proven beyond a reasonable doubt, the accused will be found guilty of murder,' explains Maseko. 'If the court finds that the state has failed to prove murder either because it accepts the accused's version that he lacked intent in that he genuinely believed that it was an intruder in the bathroom, the court will have to go a step further and determine whether his actions were not negligent, that is, would a reasonable man in the shoes of Oscar Pistorius faced with the same circumstances have reasonably foreseen that it may be Reeva in the toilet and not fired? This entails looking at all the surrounding circumstances, such as the time of the night, the interaction between the accused and deceased prior to the shooting, the duration of the whole thing, the sounds the accused allegedly heard, security at the estate, and all the other actions that the accused could have taken such as to flee, etc.'

Against a charge of murder, the defence must show that Oscar was genuinely mistaken in respect of every requirement of private defence. On a charge of murder, the defence is judged subjectively – by what the accused was actually thinking. To escape a conviction of culpable homicide, Oscar has to show that his mistake was reasonable, that he genuinely believed he was under threat, and this will be judged by the reasonable person test.

'Remember, the defence doesn't technically have to *prove* anything; it simply needs to raise reasonable doubt,' emphasises Phelps. 'The burden to prove its case rests on the state in all criminal trials. To lay a foundation for the putative defence, Pistorius's team needs the judge to believe that he genuinely thought his life was in danger and that he was responding to protect himself and his girlfriend. Evidence of his fear of crime/objective safety issues provides an air of plausibility to his version of events. In other words, if the court accepts that he was genuinely fearful of crime/for his safety then it could assist the court in accepting that he genuinely, though mistakenly, believed there was an intruder in the house on the night in question.'

The judge has many decisions to make. Some of these will turn on the her opinion on the credibility of Oscar's testimony. The judge also has to make a judgment call on the gun-related counts, in addition to the murder charge.

There will inevitably be doubts as to the guilt of the accused on any of the charges, but it is up to the court to decide whether or not these doubts are reasonable. The judge will decide whether the state has met its burden of proof and proved its case for each of the charges beyond a reasonable doubt.

The State vs OLC Pistorius

After weeks of sweltering heat in the capital city, the rain swept in and fell relentlessly, at times in violent sheets, at others in a persistent drizzle. Like the hundreds of journalists who had flown in from around the world to claim their seats in the courtroom, the storm parked itself at Madiba Street and didn't leave for at least the first week of the trial.

Taxis barrelling down the road outside the High Court in Pretoria threw up waves of water on to the pavements where rows of outside broadcast vans had been stationed, satellites on their roofs at the ready. Presenters dressed in suits and jackets hoodwinked their viewers, their legs below the camera shot comically wrapped in plastic bags to keep them dry.

Across from the Palace of Justice, on Palace Street, metro police officials kept a close eye on the traffic. Newspaper vendors peddled their broadsheets previewing the trial, with the headline of the local *Pretoria News* reading 'Oscar's Date with Destiny'. The mezzanine veranda at the post office facility across the road from the courthouse had been hired out to eager broadcasters looking for an elevated position, and it was jam packed with gazebos, camp chairs and camera tripods. The media pack, both local and foreign, had just emerged from arguably the biggest breaking news story in the history of the new South Africa, the death of former President Nelson Mandela. Some had even hung around in the country in anticipation of the next big story: the Oscar trial.

Dodging raindrops, a lone drone buzzed in the sky, its operator searching for the perfect shot of the accused arriving at the courthouse. It was 3 March 2014 and Day One of the Oscar Pistorius murder trial.

No one knew with any certainty how things were going to roll. The media were anxious; standing in knots outside the entrance, photographers speculated about whether Oscar would get special treatment and be brought into the court-house through a back entrance, avoiding their glare. Security had been ramped up and anyone wanting access to the courtroom, including the families of the accused and the deceased, was required to be accredited, with tags of varying colours hanging on lanyards.

What would Oscar look like? Would he still have the beard he was spotted sporting over the past few months? Who would he arrive with and how?

There was also a concern that the media circus could turn out to be nothing but a damp squib and the trial would not run at all. Weekend media reports had suggested that the defence could bring an application for a postponement, requesting further particulars from the prosecution. The state's legal team insisted it was prepared and ready to run. It was all up to the defence.

The gauntlet of reporters and public jammed the main entrance to the large brick building, standing inside the tall wrought-iron gates, in front of the impos-ing rust-coloured pillars. Beyond the heavy wooden doors and the glass arch, those journalists who had accreditation for the main courtroom (GD) loitered on the black-and-beige chessboard tiles, their bags filled with laptops, cables and recording equipment. Others filled the hard wooden benches, below posters advertising free legal services.

Investigating officer Captain Mike van Aardt marched his way through the crowd, holding a black A4 notepad binder. Trailing behind him was the national head of detectives, General Vineshkumar Moonoo. Their special red tags allowed them immediate access past the security guards, clad in luminous bibs, manning the doors.

Outside photographers waited in the rain at the side entrance to the court-house, where Oscar's brother and sister had entered a short while earlier. They anticipated that he would follow suit and use the same door. But they were wrong; surrounded by a bevy of 'bodyguards', the husbands of his uncle Arnold's four daughters, Oscar walked into the building through the main entrance. For the duration of the trial, these same 'bodyguards' – Dieter Kruger, Reinecke Janse van Rensburg, Johan van Wyk and Johan Visagie – would accompany the runner each time he walked in and out of the building, escorting him to a wait-ing Land Rover or down the road to his lawyers' chambers or to the Tribeca restaurant for a quick meal.

As the Blade Runner walked in an onlooker shouted, 'It's Oscar!' and the photographers turned around and saw his entourage enter. The athlete passed through the security checkpoint and metal detectors before turning back and shaking his head at those wielding their cameras. One of the 'bodyguards' chuckled and a photographer mumbled, 'I can't believe he duped us all. We were waiting like idiots in the rain.'

A court orderly escorted Oscar into courtroom GD, guiding him to his seat in the dock. He passed Reeva's mother, June Steenkamp, but turned his face away and avoided eye contact. The officer swung open the little wooden door and showed Oscar in. He turned and waved to his relatives in the public gallery before taking his seat.

The room is about 20 metres wide, with six rows of seats in the public gallery. For the case of *The State vs OLC Pistorius*, the first row was reserved for family – it was split down the middle, the right side for Reeva's relatives and the left for Oscar's. Two rows behind the family were allocated to the media and the remainder for the public.

On every day of the trial, Oscar was supported by members of his tight-knit and extremely protective family, led by the wealthy, confident and erudite Uncle Arnold, and including his brother and sister, his other two uncles and their wives, as well as his various aunts and cousins.

June Steenkamp sat just a few arms' lengths away from Oscar's family, supported by members of the ANC Women's League in their green uniforms, a friend, her cousin Kim Martin or the couple's advocate Dup de Bruyn SC. June watched as detailed evidence of her daughter's death was matter-of-factly and unemotionally presented to the court and she responded stoically, rarely shedding a tear.

Oscar only greeted June once, the gesture coming, perhaps coincidentally, after she had complained in a magazine interview about his careful avoidance of any kind of eye contact with her.

Gina Myers, her sister Kim and their mother Desi also regularly occupied the front row, glamorously dressed in funereal black with their sunglasses on standby.

Court GD is one of only four courtrooms on the ground floor of the High Court and is the furthest room to the right. It's the closest one to the main exit and side entrance and it is for this reason that it usually hosts the most high-profile cases and those that require the most intense security measures. Logistically, it is the easiest courtroom to isolate and officers can bring accused into the room securely. For a decade, it was used for the infamous Boeremag treason trial in which a group of white supremacists stood trial for ten years under high security, accused of trying to overthrow the African National Congress-led government in 2002, and were convicted in late 2013.

Court staff had prepared the room for the world's spotlight. The wooden benches were polished to a high sheen and the fluorescent lights on the ceiling cascaded light down the wooden wall panels. The two high-back burgundy leather chairs, with wooden embellishments, at the head of the room, awaiting the two assessors, were also gleaming. Between them, a smaller high-back black chair was positioned, its more supportive structure preferred by the slightly built Judge Thokozile Masipa. To the right of the chairs stood the drooping national flag.

Eight flat-screen monitors had been set up in the courtroom, their yellow wallpaper announcing the details of the case in green and white text:

Gauteng North High Court
Case Number CC 113/13
Boschkop Cas 110/02/2013

A coat of arms sat at the top of the screen, the star of the police logo on the bottom left and the lady justice emblem of the National Prosecuting Authority on the bottom right, with a South African flag in the middle. There was a screen for the judge, another for the accused, two on either end of the room for the media and the public and two on both sides for the legal teams.

A large air-conditioning unit on a swivel stand had been wheeled into the room for the trial and three cameras on tripods had been set up to broadcast proceedings to the 'overflow' courtroom next door, which accommodated additional journalists and curious members of the public. Over time that room began to resemble a movie theatre, with the lights dimmed and viewers resting their feet up on the seats in front of them, exclaiming their reactions at the big screen and snacking away, much to the dismay of the security guards trying to keep some kind of order.

Smaller cameras had also been fitted in the main courtroom for the live televised broadcast of the trial. This was a first in South African legal history. Following an application by several media houses a week before the trial commenced, Judge President Dunstan Mlambo granted permission for the hi-tech cameras to be installed.

Mlambo stated that the media houses were allowed to broadcast audiovisual images of sections of the trial, including evidence of all state experts and the evidence of police and former police officers about the crime scene. Closing arguments by the state and defence legal teams, delivery of the judgment or sentencing, if applicable, could also be broadcast.

Although Oscar's legal team had opposed the application, arguing it would result in an unfair trial, in his ruling Mlambo said, 'It is … in the public interest that, within allowance limits, the goings on during the trial be covered … to ensure a greater number of people in the community who are unable to attend the proceedings are able to follow wherever they may be.'

Between the public gallery and the burgundy chairs of the judicial officers is the arena in which the action would take place. In front of the public gallery is the stairwell to the holding cells below, then the dock for the accused, and in front the seats for the legal teams alongside their lecterns. The defence sat to the left: Kenny Oldwadge closest to the middle and Barry Roux next to him. Behind them were attorney Brian Webber and his two candidate attorneys, Roxanne Adams and Rohan Kruger. Ballistics expert Wollie Wolmarans sat alongside them.

To the right was Advocate Gerrie Nel, his junior Andrea Johnson, Investigating Officer Mike van Aardt and an empty chair for whichever expert witness Nel needed to consult with during evidence. In a string in the row behind them sat the police's investigative team: Gerhard Vermeulen, Chris Mangena, Gerhard Labuschagne, Ian van der Nest, Bennie van Staden and Francois Moller. For the brief period when Labuschagne was away attending a conference, his underling Major Bronwyn Stollarz took his place. As the trial progressed, investigator Andrew Leask, who had spent years working with Nel and Johnson, joined this row.

Facing the legal teams, in the seats below the judge's platform, sat her registrar Suzette Naudé, the official court stenographer Ria Davel in front of her machine, and the private transcriber, Barry Kagan, hired by the defence legal team.

As Oscar waited for the judge and her two assessors to enter the courtroom, he spoke with his lawyers. He leaned in as Roux motioned towards him, and stood in a huddle whispering, their arms crossed over their bodies. Using his left hand Oscar tapped Roux three times on his right forearm, ending the conversation. Oscar turned away and again took up his position as the orderly instructed the room to rise.

My Lady

With her red-and-white robe, neatly braided hair, angular features and round glasses, Judge Thokozile Matilda Masipa is the image of quiet authority, despite her occasionally fragile appearance when she has difficulty walking and needs to be supported by an orderly. Masipa, who qualified as a lawyer in her forties, spent 15 years on the bench before being routinely allocated *The State vs OLC Pistorius*. Prior to studying law, she was a social worker and journalist.

Masipa was born in 1947 in the Orlando East neighbourhood of Soweto. It was the year before the National Party came to power and the influence of its apartheid policy played a significant role in her life and, by implication, on her outlook.

She was one of ten siblings, five of whom died at a young age, leaving her as the eldest of the five surviving brothers and sisters. One of her deceased brothers was stabbed to death by unknown perpetrators when he was just 21 years old. Her father was a travelling salesman who later worked as a chauffeur and her mother was a teacher by training.

In a profile on her life featured in the 2007 documentary *Courting Justice*, directed by Jane Thandi Lipman and produced by Ruth Cowan, Masipa recalled what her upbringing was like:

> When we had visitors, I had to make a makeshift bed under the table and cover it with curtains. My dad made [our home] look like a three-roomed house – he built a partition between the bigger room … They slept in the bedroom, but the bigger room was a dining room and a kitchen. So I would sleep in the kitchen if visitors were around. When there were no visitors, I would sleep in the dining room.

When we grew up, Orlando East was an area, a very poor area, where people really did not have recreational facilities. A lot of young children didn't have role models, because all they saw at weekends was where people were getting drunk and people getting stabbed, because crime was rife even then – it's just that now it's different, people use firearms. But then people used to stab one another; they would go to a shebeen, get drunk and then start fighting and then stabbings would go on. So young children saw that happening and most of them didn't really go to school with an aim that they want to do something, they just went to school because someone said, 'You have to go to school.' They didn't have plans, they didn't say, 'This is what I want to be,' because they just didn't have any role models. That is why it means a lot for me that I was able to be something.

Masipa went to school at St John Berchmans in Soweto, run by Roman Catholic nuns, until Standard 5 (Grade 7). In the documentary, she recalled:

The classrooms were very crowded, and because it's a school not for privileged children, like any other school in the township, you find that those kinds of problems – the schools are crowded, some of the teachers are not really well-qualified. So it was really, it just shows that if you're lucky enough to just, to hold on and persevere, you become something …

When I grew up, in the '50s, there was this legalisation of apartheid; I can remember that quite well. We were very young, but very perceptive, because before the apartheid era, we used to at school, for example, we used to learn through the English medium, but suddenly when Bantu Education was introduced, we were taught things like arithmetic. We started finding ourselves with things called isibalo, and we never knew why it was that then we had to be taught in, you know, in Zulu or Sotho. And I also remember the, you know, teachers starting to resign from schools, so we had that problem as well. And when [then Prime Minister] Strydom died [in 1958] – I can remember, it's quite bizarre, but I can remember now that people were dancing in the street, being happy that he was, he was gone.

She spent one year at school in Natal and three more at St Theresa's Girls High School in Manzini. Masipa travelled by bus or taxi between her parents' home near Johannesburg and her school in Swaziland. Despite being just a teenager,

Masipa was interrogated during her attempts to reach Swaziland, a popular exit route for freedom fighters opposing apartheid at the time. Authorities wanted to know if she was a threat with any kind of political association. She would have returned to Swaziland for her two final years of schooling, but she broke her shoulder in a bus accident and was forced to finish her education in Alexandra township in 1966.

After she finished matric, Masipa went off to work for two years because her parents couldn't afford for her to study further, and found herself in a state of flux, moving from job to job. She says this in the documentary:

> So during those two years I had a real experience of what life was like when you were black and you were not educated. Because I had thought if you had matric, you're quite educated, because I'd seen these white, you know, girls working in the offices, typing, doing all kinds of things, and I couldn't do that. You were employed as a clerk; I remember I was employed as a clerk. But I did all kinds of things; I was a messenger, I was a tea-girl, and I just thought to myself, you know, this can't be life. And I think that is what motivated me to go to university.

After those two years she decided that, whether or not there was money to be made, she had to go back to study and, on her mother's recommendation, registered for a Bachelor of Arts (BA) in Social Work and Psychology.

By then she had met her husband, who was working in construction at the time. He had not finished his schooling, but harboured ambitions of becoming an accountant. After her first year at university, Masipa continued her studies via correspondence through the University of South Africa, returning to Johannesburg to marry her man. They had two children in quick succession in 1971 and 1972 and during that time she completed her BA. Her husband, who is now a tax consultant, also studied through correspondence at the University of the Witwatersrand.

Masipa then began searching for a job as a social worker but when she failed to find one she became increasingly disillusioned. She did some practical work at the Bantu Affairs Commission and was extremely disheartened by perpetuating the stereotypes of black women. She spent much of her time there trying to trace the parents of lost children or filling out forms for pensioners – hardly the challenging work she was looking for.

It was around this time that she saw an advertisement for junior reporters at *The World* newspaper. She called and expressed interest, went for an interview and was hired. Masipa was stationed in Soweto in 1976, both a volatile and exciting period in the country's history. It was the time of the Soweto uprising, the school boycotts, when the township was combusting. *The World* was at the centre of this all – editor Percy Qoboza was arrested and photographer Sam Nzima snapped the iconic image of dying schoolboy Hector Pieterson being carried by Mbuyisa Makhubo, with his crying sister Antoinette Sithole running alongside them.

Quiet and reserved, Masipa found the job tough and soon discovered that as a journalist it's not enough only to be a good writer. You have to have a knack for speaking to people. The mentor who trained her took her from one drinking hole to another, explaining to her that it was in the shebeens of the township that she would find her stories. She learnt quickly to come out of her shell so that she could succeed as a reporter working primarily on crime stories.

In October 1977, *The World* was banned by Justice Minister Jimmy Kruger and the staff detained. A profile on Masipa in *The New York Times* gives further insight into her experiences at this time:

> One day in 1977, after their male editors were arrested, Judge Masipa, by then married with two sons, and four other female reporters organized a demonstration in downtown Johannesburg.
>
> The women were arrested and spent one night in jail, recalled one, Pearl Luthuli, now 60. Inside their cell, they used the newspapers they were carrying as sheets and blankets.
>
> The next morning, the white wardens ordered them to clean their cell before releasing them for a court appearance.
>
> 'There was a toilet in the corner there that I cannot bear to think about even up to today,' Ms. Luthuli said. 'The next day, we had not used the toilet, but they expected us to clean it. We refused.' The wardens eventually relented, she said.
>
> Ms. Masipa was already moving on. She began using her Zulu name, Thokozile, dropping Matilda, or Tilly, as everyone called her.

Masipa and other employees who remained moved on to the *Post*, which was launched in 1978. When the *Post* was closed down in 1980, the staff then migrated to *The Sowetan*, which is still published today. While at the *Post*, Masipa launched a supplement called *Post Women*, which she headed.

After a while, however, she became disillusioned with journalism and spent a stint in the advertising industry as a copywriter. But four years later she returned to the media world when she took a job at *Pace* magazine in 1988. At the same time she made the decision to start studying for her LLB. She and her family were living in Tembisa, a township to the east of Johannesburg. Although the family had an old car, they only used it on weekends, and during the week she caught the train to the city and her husband and children waited on the side of the road for her return. Her husband cooked supper as she worked on her assignments, often staying up all night to meet a deadline.

Once she had completed her LLB, she began to look to doing her articles. She was already over 40, an anomaly in the legal fraternity. As a result, she went straight to do pupillage at the Johannesburg Bar to become an advocate. She spent three months working under a Master, a practising advocate, and then wrote her bar exams – and failed.

Masipa was devastated. She had never failed at anything in her life. She seriously contemplated leaving her job because, as a pupil, you don't earn any money and she had a family at home that she needed to feed. But Advocate Max Labe SC, chairperson of the Johannesburg Bar at the time, got wind that she wanted to leave and summoned her to see him. Labe impressed on her the need for people of colour at the bar and convinced her to remain. She had failed Criminal Law, so her Master referred her to a new Master who specialised in this section and she passed comfortably on her second attempt.

Defence counsel Mannie Witz remembers receiving the phone call from Labe, asking him to take Masipa on as a pupil.

'He said will I take this lady as a pupil and I didn't know she was actually older than me. I thought it's like going to be a youngster. He brought Matilda to see me. I said fine, no problem. She was already in her early fifties. I didn't know she was already going to be earmarked to become a future judge. I still said to her, "At this age in your life, what do you want to come and do pupillage for?" She said this is her interest and her passion.

'We had some very good, lekker, liberal guys in our group. She spent time with me but she moved around with all the different advocates. Lovely person, very quiet, very reserved,' recalls Witz.

He describes her as very hard-working and diligent, and was shocked at the hours that she put in. 'She did very well, she passed with flying colours.'

Masipa was admitted as an advocate in 1991, one of only three black women at the Johannesburg Bar at the time, along with Kgomotso Moroka and Lucy Mailula. Her appointment was so unusual that she once received a call from an opponent wanting to set up an appointment, and he asked to speak to 'Mr Masipa'. It never occurred to him that she might be a woman. New on the scene, she recalled in the documentary that she was mostly occupied by criminal or unopposed divorce matters:

> *During that time I started working as, helping as an assessor in crimi-*
> *nal work. I sat with different judges. And after that I became an acting*
> *judge, I did that I think for six weeks, and then people started pressuris-*
> *ing me to come to the bench. At the time I felt really, I wasn't ready, but*
> *people said, 'You know, you learn when you are on the bench,' and that's*
> *exactly what I did.*

In 1998 she was appointed as a judge in what was then the Transvaal Provincial Division of the High Court of South Africa, only the second black woman to be appointed to the bench after Mailula. Masipa had been at the bar for only seven years, relatively 'young' in terms of experience, but had been recommended by a colleague during a time when the focus was on transformation.

She learnt from the likes of Bob Nugent who went on to become a Supreme Court of Appeal judge but was also eager to learn from other colleagues at the bench. She also established early on that she prefers to sit with assessors, to assist her in looking at the facts of the case. In one of the first cases she presided over, she sat with two assessors who had legal backgrounds and found the experience 'beautiful'.

Judge Masipa spent time out of Johannesburg presiding over circuit courts and discovered a trend that saddened her – young children coming to court facing charges of serious crimes such as murder and robbery.

Masipa acknowledges that she has a special interest in the rehabilitation of offenders. There have been instances in which teenagers accused of serious crimes have come before her in court and she has been reluctant to send them to prison. She felt that they deserve a second chance and recommended correctional supervision instead. As she described in *Courting Justice*:

> *There was this horrible case of three youngsters who raped a 14-year-old*
> *girl, who was also at a shebeen; they raped her and then killed her. These*
> *are terrible cases. You just don't know whether to, you don't know what*
> *to do with these young people, because they are young; if you send them*
> *to prison, obviously they're going to come back worse, if you don't send*
> *them to prison, people are not safe or people don't even trust the justice*
> *system any more, which is even worse. You know, they start to take law*
> *into their own hands. So you, it's quite a big challenge, you've got to see,*
> *you know, balance – and that's a very, you know, it's a very tricky thing.*

In the documentary, Masipa acknowledged that her upbringing in Orlando East had an impact on the way she rules:

> *It does, it does a lot because I sort of can identify with what these young-sters are going through. Because a lot of youngsters appear before me in criminal matters and I do understand, because this is where I come from. And I think it does impact on my judgments. I'm not saying that I'm a lot lenient, but I'm more understanding; understanding where a person comes from really makes you, I think, it balances your judg-ment. It does make me a lot more compassionate. I am compassionate by nature, but coming from this area, I think does make me a lot more compassionate. I'm able to – even outside court – I'm able to communi-cate with youngsters that I see might be tempted into getting into crime.*

Masipa also explained how being a woman might impact on some of her rulings:

> *If you sit with a male colleague, for example on a rape case, you can see that there's a, you know, there's a difference between the way a woman sees rape and the, you know, the way a man sees rape, although we're all judges. So women judges do make a difference. You know men will ask you, the first question … 'What was she wearing?', you know, if a woman was raped, or 'Where did she come from?' It doesn't matter where she came from, you know, it doesn't matter what she was wearing. But, you know, it's, these are the, you know, things that we're trying to break as women, and I'm sure we are making a difference.*

Despite her preference for rehabilitation over incarceration, when it comes to youths Masipa has not been opposed to harsh maximum sentences when she has deemed it necessary, particularly in incidents of violence against women.

In May 2013, for example, she handed down a 252-year sentence against the 'Axe Man' Shepherd Moyo, a serial rapist. Masipa gave him 15 years for each of his 11 counts of robbery, 12 years for attempted murder and life sentences for three rape charges.

She said in her judgment that the three rape victims of the man who carried out a spate of house robberies in northern Johannesburg had been left traumatised for life and his lack of remorse made it unlikely that he could be rehabilitated.

'The worst, in my view, is that he attacked and raped the victims in the sanc-tity of their own homes where they thought they were safe,' she said.

In 2009, Masipa handed down a life sentence to a policeman, Freddy Mashamba, who shot and killed his former wife after a row over their divorce settlement. 'No one is above the law. You deserve to go to jail for life because you are not a protector. You are a killer,' Masipa told him.

She has also presided over other high-profile matters that have featured in the media spotlight. She heard the case involving the dismissal of Eskom chief executive Jacob Maroga and his claim for R85 million in compensation, where she ruled in favour of Eskom and the Department of Public Enterprises. In her judgment, she commented on the government's powers in relation to state-owned enterprises, saying: 'A shareholder does not have the right to inter-fere in the decision-making of the board in respect to the company's internal affairs.'

Masipa also ruled in a landmark judgment in the case of the *Blue Moonlight Properties 39 v Occupiers Saratoga Avenue and the City of Johannesburg*, where she found that the city had failed to fulfil its obligations to find alternative accommodation for squatters threatened with eviction from old warehouses in Berea. 'It is clear that the city is trying to distance itself from the problems of the unlawful occupiers in this matter,' she ruled.

Being one of the few black female judges in the country currently on the bench, she says in *Courting Justice* that she hopes her presence encourages more people to seek out justice:

> *What is most challenging is the fact that when black people in particular see you sitting there, you know that they expect a lot from you, and you just have to live up to that. Sometimes it's not that easy, sometimes the woman comes before your court and she's saying to herself, 'Well she's black, she's a woman, she must understand this.' But you still have to look at what the law says. You will look at it with different eyes because you're compassionate, you might make things, you might make things easier for her by explaining things and not being too hard on her. But not everyone understands that.*

While Masipa is a driver for transformation and change in the legal fraternity, she takes issue with the pace at which it occurs. She's critical of the lack of sup-port there is for female judges who have to take care of children and their fami-lies. She lists this as one of the reasons there are so few female judges.

Judge Masipa and her husband live in Midrand, between Kyalami and Leeuwkop. Both her parents have passed away; her dad died just after she qualified as a lawyer and her mom soon after she had been appointed to the bench. She has also lost one of her two sons, who died from a stroke when he was 21. Her surviving son is married with three children and she dotes on her grandchildren, even though she struggles to fit time with them into her schedule. She also financially supports a crèche and a women's beading project run by her sister.

Unassuming, quiet and reserved, Judge Thokozile Masipa was thrust into the media spotlight in a way almost no other judge had been in the history of the country's courts. Her every move was under intense scrutiny and her resolve would be tested as the former crime reporter and social worker made a determination on whether or not the country's one-time golden boy had committed murder.

A Plea of Not Guilty

Following the court orderly's instructions, all those in court rose. Judge Masipa slowly and stiffly made her way to her chair, followed by her two assessors. Advocates Nel and Roux each took turns to stand and introduce themselves and their teams, before Masipa dealt with housekeeping issues. The first of these was to swear in her two assessors.

Janette Henzen-du Toit became an advocate in 1998 and was admitted to the Pretoria bar and the bar in the North West province. She has worked for the Legal Aid Board and as the High Court unit manager at the Johannesburg Legal Resources Centre. She first sat as an assessor in 2005 and also has experience as an acting judge. She is studying for her doctorate in criminal law, criminal prosecution, law of evidence and constitutional interpretation.

Less is known about Themba Mazibuko, who was admitted as an advocate in July 2012. In the Afrikaans newspaper *Rapport*, Herman Scholtz reported that Mazibuko is considered a rookie in the legal fraternity. Before being admitted as an advocate, he owned a construction company as well as a hair salon in Soweto. In an earlier interview, Mazibuko's mother Pretty told Scholtz that after school her son studied engineering but dropped out, becoming a labourer and ultimately setting up his own business. Years later his career turned to law, and less than two years after being admitted, he was assisting on the most high-profile case in the country. Judge Masipa had appointed Mazibuko as an assessor in the matter she presided over before Oscar's murder trial, so she has worked with him previously.

It is the judge's discretion to appoint assessors and they are generally experts in a particular field into which the case delves. They can only assist with matters of fact and not law. For instance, if there is a dispute over the colour of a getaway car, they could overrule her, but they could not overrule her on interpretation of the law. Criminal law lecturer Kelly Phelps explains: 'The judge can request to be joined by two assessors who, like a jury, help in deciding questions of fact, leaving questions of law to the judge. Assessors are usually either experts in a particular field that is under scrutiny in a case (for example, a fisheries experts in a case dealing with the fisheries industry) or advocates, magistrates or legal academics. In this way specialist cases are being dealt with by specialists in that area.'

Once the assessors had been sworn in, Nel was up on his feet again and read aloud the four counts that Oscar Pistorius would have to answer to in the trial. Oscar stood as they were read out and four times the judge asked him to plead. The exchange was exactly the same each time:

> Court: *Do you understand the charge?*
> Accused: *I do, My Lady.*
> Court: *How do you plead?*
> Accused: *Not guilty, My Lady.*
> Court: *Thank you.*

Then defence advocate Kenny Oldwadge stood and read Oscar's plea explanation into the record:

> *In the High Court of South Africa, Gauteng Division, Pretoria. Case CC113/13.*
> *In the matter between the State and Oscar Leonard Carl Pistorius, the accused.*
> *Explanation of plea in terms of Section 115 of Act 51 of 1977.*
> *I, the undersigned, Oscar Leonard Carl Pistorius hereby furnish the following explanation of plea with reference to the charges to which I plead not guilty.*

First, Oscar – via Oldwadge – addressed the murder charge, offering his explanation of what led to the Valentine's Day shooting. Oscar went into far greater detail than was expected and gave far more information than he did during his bail application just over a year earlier. Some lawyers argued that this was to his detriment – and the prosecution argued this too. They questioned why he had not put this detail into his initial statement and asked whether he was doing this to tailor his version of events. However, the defence approach was that Oscar had nothing to hide and by putting a detailed version before the court so early on would boost its credibility in the eyes of the judge:

1. *In its formulation of this count, the State has contended that I unlawfully and intentionally killed Reeva Steenkamp, hereinafter referred to as Reeva.*

2. *This allegation is denied in the strongest terms. In fact, at the time of the tragic accident which led to Reeva's death, we were in a loving relationship.*

3. *Whilst I admit that I inflicted the fatal gunshot wounds to Reeva, this occurrence was indeed an accident in that I had mistakenly believed that an intruder or intruders had entered my home and posed an imminent threat to Reeva and me.*

4. *In my application for bail, I concisely dealt with the events of 14 February 2013. I am advised that I will have an opportunity to deal with a comprehensive version of the events when I testify. For purposes of my plea explanation, I emphasise the following:*

4.1. *During the early hours of the morning I brought two fans in from the balcony. I had shortly before spoken to Reeva who was in bed beside me.*

4.2. *Unbeknown to me, Reeva must have gone to the toilet in the bathroom, at the time when I brought in the fans, closed the sliding doors and drew the blinds and the curtains.*

4.3. *I heard the bathroom window sliding open. I believe that an intruder or intruders had entered the bathroom through the bathroom window which was not fitted with burglar bars.*

4.4. *I approached the bathroom, armed with my firearm so as to defend Reeva and I. At that time, I believed Reeva was still in the bed.*

4.5. *The discharging of my firearm was precipitated by a noise in the toilet which I, in my fearful state, knowing that I was on my stumps, unable to run away or properly defend myself physically, believed to be the intruder or intruders, coming out of the toilet to attack Reeva and me.*

Oscar then moved from a defensive stance into attack mode:

5. *I respectfully believe that the State has no basis whatsoever for alleging that I wanted to take Reeva's life. I will demonstrate hereunder*

that notwithstanding the fact that all the objective evidence will
corroborate my version of the events, the State has embarked on a
strategy to rely on unsubstantiated allegations in an endeavour to
prove that I wanted to kill Reeva.

6. *The strategy was also employed at my bail application. I will here-*
under concisely deal with some of the material aspects to support
my contention herein.

7. *At my bail application the State inter alia contended that I had*
deliberately shot Reeva whilst I was positioned at a distance of about
1.5 metres from the toilet door and whilst I was standing on my pros-
theses. The allegation with reference to 1.5 metres and me wearing
my prostheses was clearly designed to suggest that I had pursued
Reeva to the toilet and that I therefore knew that Reeva was in the
toilet. Thus, that I did not entertain any fear at the time when it is
alleged that I entered the bathroom.

Oscar then went after the state's use of neighbours' testimony, which was likely
to be the backbone of its case.

8. *The State has also by means of the evidence of the then investigat-*
ing officer, Hilton Botha, sought to rely on a statement by a witness
who I am told is a certain Estelle Van der Merwe, who claims to
have heard what sounded like a woman's voice prior to the shoot-
ing, talking nonstop, like fighting. The witness did not say that the
alleged talking came from Reeva, nor that the sounds so mentioned
emanated from my house.

9. *The statement, it would appear, offers an opportunity for the State*
to contend at the bail hearing, that 'there may …' – and this is a
quote, My Lady – '… there may have been an argument between
the applicant and the deceased and the evidence might point in that
way'.
This witness has since deposed to a further statement which materi-
ally contradicts her first statement. In the further and better par-
ticulars, the State disavows reliance on the first statement. The State
has also conceded in the further and better particulars, that they
are not aware of any of the detail regarding (the alleged) argument
and that it may become clear during the trial.

10. *Van der Merwe's house is located approximately 105 metres from*

my bedroom, with my bedroom and bathroom windows facing in the opposite direction to Van der Merwe's house. It would not have been possible for Van der Merwe to have heard anyone talking from my bedroom, in their bedroom. The State is furthermore in possession of statements by a number of witnesses, including witnesses resident in either the estate where I reside, or in an adjacent estate. None of these witnesses claim to have heard any argument between Reeva and I, nor any woman's voice talking prior to the shooting. Notwithstanding the fact that two of the witnesses (who live in closer proximity to my house than Van der Merwe) were awake at the time when Van der Merwe alleged that she had heard a woman's voice.

Oscar insisted that there was no motive for him to shoot Reeva and dismissed suggestions that – as the prosecution alleged – a fight had led to the shooting:

11. *I refer to the above, as the State now alleges in the further particulars provided, that there was in fact an argument between Reeva and I and that I killed Reeva 'because of the argument'. I am unable to comprehend on what basis the State (at the bail application) could only rely on a possibility of an argument between Reeva and I and now with even less available evidence (by disavowing Van der Merwe's first statement) allege that there was in fact an argument and that I shot Reeva 'because of the argument'.*

12. *I deny this allegation and reiterate that there is no justification whether legally or factually for this unfair and incorrect allegation to have been made. The aforesaid allegation is also not supported by any of the statements disclosed to me by the State.*

13. *Furthermore contrary to what was contended for by the State during the bail application, the State has now conceded that it cannot be contended as a fact that I was about 1.5 metres from the toilet door and that I had my prostheses attached at the time when I discharged the firearm anymore.*

Oscar then disclosed his hand and revealed that his legal team would be looking to scrutinise the police's handling of the crime scene:

14. *The unfair approach adopted by the State is further evident from the evidence given by Hilton Botha at the bail application whose*

evidence will be demonstrated to have been false in material respects. More particularly, that it was designed to falsely incriminate me on an allegation of premeditated murder. It will also be demonstrated during this trial, whilst Botha was the investigating officer and tasked with preserving the scene, that the scene was contaminated, disturbed and tampered with. This feature of the State's case will be dealt with when Botha, amongst others, gives evidence.

Oscar had taken the highly irregular approach of attacking the prosecution's case even before the first witness had been called. It was a bold, high-risk move that could readily backfire. He also pre-empted the state's tactics, warning against the introduction of any evidence that could tarnish his character. Introduction of such character evidence is not allowed in South African law:

15. *I have been led to understand that it is unusual to challenge the State's case in my plea explanation to the extent that I do herein. However, I am left with no alternative but to explain my innocence with reference to the allegations levelled against me. The aforegoing will be exposed by having regard to the State's intended approach in this trial. This approach is to not only seek to unfairly draw inferences from purported statements of fact, which are not supported by the objective facts, but also by virtue of the statements disclosed to me by the State, to seek to introduce any admissible character evidence, under the guise that such inadmissible evidence would be admissible, similar fact evidence. To demonstrate that there was an alleged nexus between the (inadmissible) character evidence and the (non-existing) argument which allegedly led to me killing Reeva.*

16. *I am furthermore advised that as the State is aware of the fact that it has no evidence to prove an alleged argument and in particular in view of the fact that the State has conceded that it does not know what the feature or import of such alleged argument would have been, the only intended purpose of an attempt to introduce inadmissible character evidence would be to engineer and bring about an inadmissible attempted assassination of my character. I am advised that during the conduct of the trial, my legal representatives will object to the introduction of such inadmissible character evidence, on the basis as stated above.*

17. *I respectfully state that no truthful evidence can ever be tendered*

*that I fired the shots 'because of the argument'. I deny this allegation
in the strongest terms because there was no argument.*

18. *The allegation that I wanted to shoot (or kill) Reeva, cannot be further from the truth.*

Oscar finished his plea explanation by answering to the gun-related charges:

19. *I admit that whilst I was in possession of the firearm as alleged, a shot went off. Save as aforesaid, the remaining allegations as contained in this count, are denied.*

20. *I admit that at all times relevant to this count, I had not been issued with a licence to possess .38 calibre rounds of ammunition. Save as aforesaid, the remaining allegations as contained in this count, are denied.*

For the duration of the reading of the plea explanation, Oscar stood in the dock, his hands clasped in front of him. Oldwadge carefully enunciated each sentence, regularly clutching his robes with both hands in front of his chest and adjusting them.

Judge Masipa asked Oscar to confirm the explanation, referring to him as 'Mr Pistorius'. He leaned forward, placing his mouth close to the tall microphone in front of him and answered, 'I do, My Lady.'

Gerrie Nel then proceeded to read several 'admissions' into the record – issues not disputed by the defence, such as Oscar's blood tests taken on the day of the shooting and the photographs taken by the police photographer.

And then, with the formalities out of the way, the prosecution called its first witness, Michelle Burger. The so-called trial of the century was underway.

What the Neighbours Heard

The radio in the car was tuned to a news station as the couple headed off on a much-needed weekend away. The young professionals, he an IT project manager at Citadel Investment Services, and she a lecturer in Construction Economics at the University of Pretoria, were driving to the small town of Sabie in Mpumalanga in the east of the country, where he was to compete in a mountain-bike race. Like so many others in South Africa, the couple had been following the proceedings in the Pretoria Magistrate's Court where Oscar Pistorius's bail application was being heard. But unlike others, they had a vested interest in developments and were listening to the radio with a careful ear.

Michelle Burger and her husband Charl Johnson live 177 metres away from the Olympic athlete's house, in an adjoining estate called Silver Stream, and had been awoken by screams on the morning of the Valentine's Day shooting. But, media shy and assuming others who lived closer to the scene would prove to be more beneficial witnesses, the couple had not approached the authorities. But during that drive to Mpumalanga what they heard on the radio forced them into action. During the bail testimony it was claimed that only one person shouted that morning – Burger and Johnson believed they had very clearly heard two people. Investigating officer Hilton Botha spoke of witnesses being up to 600 metres away – Burger and Johnson were so much closer. The couple felt obliged to act.

On TV they had seen aerial photos of the two estates and realised they lived a lot closer and would be in a better position to assist the police. Ironically, as it would emerge, they would be the witnesses farthest from the scene. Burger contacted an attorney friend and an advocate, Nicky Maritz, who advised them to write down whatever it was they could remember from that night into statements to be handed to the police. The couple was, however, hesitant to give affidavits at a local police station because of the media attention that it would draw; they wanted to do this privately. Burger and Johnson wrote down their statements – but before they accompanied Maritz to a police station, investigators came knocking at their door.

• • •

As they prepared for trial, Gerrie Nel and his prosecuting team looked at the evidence that had been collected over the course of a year's investigation. Together with his junior Andrea Johnson and the investigating officer Mike van Aardt, Nel had been consulting with Oscar Pistorius's neighbours who had heard screams and gunshots on the morning of 14 February 2013. Since the bail application the previous year, two key witnesses had come forward to strengthen the state's contention that an argument, a fierce fight, had led to Oscar killing his girlfriend intentionally.

Like other luxury residential complexes in the area, the Silver Stream estate on which Burger and Johnson live featured high walls topped with electrified fences, 24-hour security patrols and a guarded, access-controlled entrance. These enclaves for the new-rich and privileged provided sanctuary from crime as well as added privacy. A neighbour's house, an electric security fence, a scattering of poplar trees and open stands separate them from Oscar's dwelling and they have direct line of sight of his house. The prosecuting team believed the witnesses would be crucial pillars in their case, a strong opening hand to play. Only two people were present when Oscar shot Reeva. One of them was dead and only one person's version existed, that of the accused.

Of the dozens of houses dotted around the crime scene, in the same plush estate as well as in neighbouring complexes, the state relied on only five people to testify. Their testimony challenged Oscar's claim of mistaken identity, and submitted to the court the story of a fight that started at least two hours before the athlete used his firearm to shoot and kill his girlfriend.

The two men and three women were the closest Nel had to eyewitnesses – they could provide timelines and a recollection of the noises that roused them from their sleep. While one couple attests to the noises at 177 metres from the crime scene, neighbours who live right next door to Oscar, whom the state did not call to testify, were unable to support their claims. Burger and Johnson, the couple who live in a neighbouring estate; Dr Johan Stipp and his wife Annette who live in Silver Woods, with their bedroom overlooking the back of Oscar's house where his bathroom windows are located; and Estelle van der Merwe, who lives with her husband diagonally across the road from the athlete, and was woken up two hours before the shooting to the sounds of a woman arguing.

From the evidence of these five witnesses, the state built a timeline of events that it believed reaffirmed the claim of an argument leading up to the shooting. This was, however, contested by the defence, casting doubt on, firstly, the order of the events that morning and, secondly, the interpretation of the sounds heard by the neighbours.

• • •

Michelle Burger was given the unenviable task of opening the state's case as its first witness – media attention was peaking, the public gallery packed. In the chronology of events on the morning of the shooting, she wasn't the first person to hear something suspicious, but on her strength of character and conviction, she was Nel's strongest witness. Burger is a petite woman who arrived at court in an all-black outfit, with her brown hair neatly pinned back. Fastidious and well-prepared, the lecturer at the University of Pretoria had visited the court-room a week earlier to familiarise herself with the surroundings. Like all the other neighbours who testified, she opted not to have footage of herself testify-ing broadcast – the world only heard her voice.

Burger described to the court being wrenched from her sleep by the distinct blood-curdling screams of a woman in desperate distress, which wafted across the open stands and through the wide open windows of her house, 177 metres from the crime scene. The same noises roused her husband, Charl Johnson, who immediately rushed to the balcony to better hear the commotion in the dis-tance. In the still of the early morning, Burger could hear not only the screams of a woman calling for help, but then also a man calling for assistance, which immediately brought her to the conclusion that there was an armed robbery underway. Nel used this claim to argue that this was, in fact, Reeva calling out for help as she fled from her enraged boyfriend, who was pursuing her with his firearm.

In her scramble to summon help, Burger incorrectly called the security of the estate where she had previously lived, before handing the phone to her husband. The call was made at 3:16am and lasted 58 seconds. Johnson realised his wife's mistake and cut the call. He returned to the balcony where the screams contin-ued, but were soon snuffed out by what Burger described as the distinct cracks of four gunshots. As the shots came to an end, so did the woman's screams.

Feeling helpless, but believing neighbours closer to the source of the incident would help, the couple went back to bed but had a restless night.

Burger told the court that it was only days later that they decided to approach the police and offer their story because they had heard Oscar's claim in the bail application that he had mistaken Reeva for an intruder. This did not correlate with their experience. Burger sobbed in court when Nel asked her about how she felt giving that statement to Van Aardt. 'It was quite raw still. It was awful to hear her shout before the shots. It's very difficult for me. When I'm in the shower I relive her shouts,' she said emotionally.

Burger's evidence showed that, crucially, there were screams before the gunshots. She had heard a female and a male before the four shots were fired – a claim that buttressed the state's suggestion of a fight before the shooting.

Like an opening batsman to face a new bowler, Burger was the first to experience Barry Roux's cross-examination. She proved to be resilient and firm on the stand, refusing to concede under intense questioning from the defence advocate. It was crucial for Roux to cast doubt on Burger's version of what she had heard and the order in which she had heard it. The defence needed to show that what Burger and her husband thought were gunshots were, in fact, the sounds of Oscar breaking down the door with a cricket bat.

So it was that Roux introduced the court to the defence's explanation for what witnesses had heard that morning. There had been two sets of sounds – the first volley being the gunshots, followed by a pause and screaming, and then the second set of noises being the cricket bat as it struck the wooden door. What Burger had thought to be gunshots were in fact the cricket bat.

Not surprisingly, Roux's suggestion immediately sparked public debate: could the sound of a cricket bat striking a door be as loud as and so similar to a gunshot that the sounds could be confused? The state was dealing with witnesses woken up in the dead night in a panic, who claimed to have heard shots, but could they have been mistaken?

'Could there have been four shots when you were still asleep and you heard the screaming afterwards?' asked Roux, as he proposed this new timeline to the witness – that it was the gunshots that, unbeknown to her, had roused her. Burger maintained that what she had heard was screams.

On the face of it, Roux's timeline seemed to make sense – it would later explain how some witnesses heard two sets of bangs – but could he convincingly explain how a cricket bat striking a door could be confused for a gunshot?

Roux's focus turned to what Burger had heard. She had claimed that the woman was screaming during the four shots and that the voice faded away after the final shot. Could this have been Reeva inside the toilet cubicle, wounded and in pain from the first shot to her hip before being killed by the final three shots? Burger said that the last she heard of the petrified woman's screams that woke her was briefly after the final shot rang out. The defence, however, worked at dismantling this claim by making yet another startling revelation: the screams were not Reeva's – rather they were the accused's.

'If Mr Pistorius is really anxious and he screams,' said Roux, 'it sounds like a woman.'

He was suggesting that the noises the neighbours had heard that morning were not Reeva screaming for help, but Oscar shouting in desperation as he attempted to break down the door to get to his girlfriend. This would become a point of ridicule in the public debate of the trial – Oscar screamed like a girl.

Roux continued: 'He was beyond himself, he was screaming after that [the shots], higher and lower and that is why you hear what you, that time of the morning, associate with a very anxious woman screaming and a man screaming, you heard both,' said Roux. 'It was the same person.'

The defence advocate also went on to question how the witness could testify with such certainty about the facts – at 177 metres away from the house, with a man who sounded like a woman when he was anxious, not hearing the voices simultaneously, and the cricket bat striking a door from inside the bathroom. Burger's only experience with firearms was hearing shots on the odd occasion at night, and visiting a shooting range twice in her life when she personally shot a firearm. Roux referred to the statements made by neighbours who lived considerably closer to his client who had heard only the sounds of a man crying – Burger did not hear these. The advocate was determined to drive home the point: there were at least four more witnesses that the state did not include in its case who do not corroborate what a witness living in a neighbouring estate claimed to have heard. It was the probability of her claims that he was testing.

While Burger could not say what an English willow bat striking a meranti door sounded like, she was adamant that what she had heard that morning were gunshots. Roux was trying to show the court that Burger was unable to rule out this possibility because she was unfamiliar with the sound of the bat striking the door. But Michelle Burger wasn't biting.

Burger also could not confirm or deny the claim that Oscar screams like a woman when he is anxious, and yet persisted with her evidence that it was a woman she had heard screaming that morning. She further denied the suggestion that it was the gunshots, on Oscar's version of events, that could have woken her up.

Roux also suggested that it would make no sense for a man who is about to shoot his girlfriend to have called for help – hearing the man scream for help is inconsistent with the version of a man about to kill his girlfriend. Roux, of course, was pushing for the concession but Burger remained resilient, refusing to budge.

She remained convinced that what she heard were the desperate screams of a woman shortly before her death. No matter how many times Roux put it to her that what she had heard was Oscar shouting and a cricket bat hammering the door, there was no persuading her that anything other than her own version was the truth. Burger would not make even the slightest of concessions to Roux. So moved was she by the sound of the blood-curdling screams that what she heard that morning still haunts her. The trauma of the experience seeped through on the stand when her guard dropped momentarily, and she cried as she spoke of how the screams have stayed with her.

The prosecution was satisfied that it had played a strong opening hand with Burger testifying first. The evidence of her husband Charl Johnson and other neighbours would, they hoped, cement this.

· · ·

Charl Johnson picked up his camera fitted with a zoom lens, fetched a step ladder and made the precarious ascent to the roof of his double-storey house in the Silver Stream estate. It offered him an unobscured, 360-degree view of the houses and gardens of the people living around him, but more importantly, he could see over the tops of his neighbour's poplar trees to the grey-coloured house where Oscar had shot and killed his girlfriend – the source of the screams that had woken him up barely 12 hours earlier.

Johnson had told friends and colleagues of the horror he and his wife experienced, and had seen aerial footage on 24-hour news channels of the neighbouring estate. Still believing that what he had heard was an armed robbery – contrary to what was emerging as a case of Oscar mistaking Reeva for an intruder – he had to check for himself how close he was to the crime scene. Once he was finished on the roof, Johnson used a measuring tool on Google Maps to establish that he was about 150 metres from Oscar's house. It all became clear to him – he believed it was Reeva's last screams that woke him.

The IT project manager is a soft-spoken man. Unlike his wife, who exudes confidence and asserted her position in the witness box, he appeared timid and very uncomfortable on the stand. In the opening minutes of his evidence, he was asked to speak up several times by Nel, Roux and even the judge. Johnson recalled the events of 14 February as his wife did: waking up to the screams of a woman, standing on the balcony hearing both a man and woman calling for help, a failed attempt at calling security, and then hearing gunshots that brought the screaming to an end.

But there was one major difference between his evidence and that of his wife: Johnson remembers hearing about five or six gunshots. Nel had told the court early on in the trial that he would deal with discrepancies in witness statements – this was one of them. But for Nel, Johnson's second set of ears simply confirmed what Burger had heard and thus bolstered his case that there had been a fight before Oscar shot Reeva.

The main thrust of Roux's cross-examination was, by contrast, that this was not in fact a corroboration of the facts, but rather collusion between the couple in order to incriminate his client. Johnson said he had done his utmost to ensure he was not exposed to any reporting or information about the trial prior to his testimony, even telling friends that once the trial started, he would only speak to them after he had testified. He also told the court that he had not read the statement his wife had given to the police, nor had she seen his; they'd spoken to each other about the incident after the fact as a means of supporting each other, he said; and that he had avoided media reports, TV and newspapers in order to block out the trial while Burger was testifying.

Roux argued that the couple had discussed Burger's evidence, and that it was just too remarkable for it to be mere coincidence for there to be so many similarities. Johnson was shaking his head in disapproval of the advocate's claims, but also in apparent disbelief that Roux would accuse him of being part of such an elaborate plan to frame his client.

But Roux came down hard on Johnson, stating that the court deserved witnesses who were uncontaminated and could provide independent versions of events to allow the court to make a decision.

'Witnesses are not always reliable,' said Roux, sounding genuinely affronted that the witness would mislead the court. 'Sometimes they are not lying, but many times, many times the only way to satisfy yourself about reliability is to maintain a strong independence in versions.

'You have not favoured the court with that, Mr Johnson. You and your wife. I am sorry, I put it to you. You could just as well [have] stood together in the witness box.'

Here the judge intervened before Johnson could respond. 'Are you not going a bit too far, Mr Roux?' asked Masipa. The advocate withdrew his question.

Roux then introduced the defence team's timeline to Johnson, suggesting again that the sounds he heard were in fact Oscar hitting the cricket bat against the door. Using as reference points the 3:16am call Johnson made to security shortly before hearing what he believed were gunshots and Oscar's 3:19am call to Johan Stander, Roux stated that the only sound Johnson could have heard was the cricket bat striking the door because it perfectly coincides. But like his wife, Johnson wasn't moved: he was adamant that the sounds he heard were gunshots – later adding that he owned a firearm himself, had shot at firing ranges and was familiar with the sound of a handgun discharging.

The advocate finally narrowed his argument down to three main facts that he felt did not fit in to Johnson's version: the man screaming for help; the timeline, which according to Roux, indicates that the noises Johnson heard could only have been the cricket bat striking the door; and that Johnson did not hear the bashing of a door after the shots.

Johnson, however, dismissed Roux's suggestion that the voices he had heard were only of Oscar, adding that it had been easy for him to distinguish the male from the female voice that morning. He also challenged the claim that what he believed were gunshots were the bat hitting the door because of how quickly the shots were in succession, far quicker than someone was able to wield a bat.

Wrapping up his questioning, Roux stated that with Reeva locked in the toilet cubicle with the window closed, there was no way Johnson could have heard her screams, even if he was closer to the house. Johnson disagreed, and explained how it could have been possible. 'One of the, let us call it scars that my wife and I have after witnessing this incident is, often we hear jackal calls from the veld in Farm Inn – a neighbouring small wildlife reserve – and it reminds us of the screams that we heard.

'So it also reminds us how far and how clearly the sound travels in our area, and when it is deathly quiet at three o'clock in the morning, I do believe that I heard a lady screaming and that it is possible for the sound to travel that far,' said Johnson.

The state would have been satisfied with Charl Johnson's performance in the witness box. Despite Roux's best efforts to force concessions on the timeline of events and the possibility that the screams he had heard were those of his client, the witness held out and supported his understanding of what had happened with rational arguments.

· · ·

The last place Estelle van der Merwe wanted to be was in court, in front of the packed gallery and the world's cameras. She'd dressed for the occasion in a brown jacket and matching top, and sported white highlights down the length of her long brown hair. Van der Merwe had waited anxiously in the witness holding room for her turn, even being allowed to testify earlier than planned – ahead of Johnson. In the first few minutes she was asked several times to slow down and relax. Her nerves were showing.

Van der Merwe lives diagonally across the road from Oscar and her balcony, as measured by the police, is 98 metres from the house. She told the court about waking up just before 2am on the morning of Valentine's Day to a woman's voice. It sounded as if the person was having an argument, she said – the only witness to have heard what sounded like a person having a fight, her testimony thus bolstered the state's case, especially when weighed up against other evidence. Annoyed at the disturbance, she said she looked out of the windows to see if she could see anything, but eventually went back to bed without having identified the source.

This was crucial for Gerrie Nel. The state pathologist would testify that the food found in Reeva's stomach was consumed no more than two hours prior to her death shortly after 3am, which put her up and awake and eating from about 1am – within the timeframe and contrary to Oscar's contention that the couple was in bed sleeping.

Van der Merwe said she eventually fell asleep again, but this wasn't to be for long – just after 3am she was woken by what she believed were four gunshots, followed by what sounded like someone crying. After several minutes of listening in the dark and wondering what was going on, she and her husband peered out of the window at Oscar's house – several vehicles, including the ambulance, had arrived.

Oscar's neighbour also told the court about being woken up in the early hours of the morning about a year after the shooting by what sounded like two men having an argument. She noticed some activity at Oscar's house, but had gone back to bed.

So it was that Roux started his cross-examination by explaining that on the morning of 21 February 2014, the defence team was at Oscar's house to conduct a sound test – a man and a woman screamed as loudly as they could to establish how far the sound would travel. While the Van der Merwes' bedroom balcony faces Oscar's house, the athlete's balcony and bedroom were on the opposite side of the house, and the advocate suggested that it would be highly improbable that the voice Estelle van der Merwe heard was in fact emanating from his client's house.

Roux questioned Van der Merwe's recollection of the talking she had heard that night – the pauses between voices, that it was barely recognisable, that no language could be discerned, and the fact that she believed it was emanating from the Farm Inn side of her house – which is the opposite side to the direction of Oscar's house – because that is where she checked first. Van der Merwe was, however, adamant that the voice she heard was that of a woman.

She further confirmed that despite hearing what she believed to be an argument, when her husband established later in the morning that the noises had in fact been gunshots, she did not tell him about the argument and the voice she had heard. Roux argued that if Van der Merwe really believed there was a connection between the woman's voice and the shooting she would have immediately raised this with her partner. But Nel addressed this point in his re-examination of the witness, and Van der Merwe said she had made the connection and told her husband of this after she had learnt that it was their neighbour Oscar who had shot his girlfriend.

Van der Merwe wrapped up her evidence in under two hours. While there was no disputing she had heard something at that odd hour, there was no certainty either that it emanated from Oscar's house or that it was, in fact, the voice of someone having a fight. It's the inferences that the state drew from her evidence that the defence challenged.

• • •

Dr Johan Stipp is a radiologist based at the Jakaranda private hospital in Sunnyside, Pretoria. He lives in a house behind Oscar's, that at the time was across a vacant stand on which houses have now been built, a distance of exactly 155 metres from the athlete's bathroom window. Stipp's bedroom looks on to the back of Oscar's house where the bathroom and toilet windows are visible – with a direct line of sight to where the shooting took place. Despite his bland grey suit, the doctor spoke as confidently as he would when wearing a white coat in front of a lightbox, and later even referred to his profession when his memory was questioned. 'So you must remember, I am a radiologist, so I look at an image. While I am looking at that image, I am talking, I am talking, I am looking, I am seeing. It all happens at once. I am trained to do that,' he said.

The doctor described being woken up by three bangs, which he believed to be gunshots, before walking on to the balcony to establish what was happening. From here he saw a house in which the bathroom lights were on, as well as lights at the neighbouring house, belonging to Mike and Rontle Nhlengethwa. Oscar would tell the court that he only switched on the bathroom lights some time after shooting at the door. Stipp described the time it took him to get to the balcony from when he heard the shots as mere 'moments'.

While outside on the balcony, Stipp said he heard a woman scream about three times. 'The screams were very loud,' said Stipp. 'She sounded extremely fearful. I would imagine those would be the type of screams you would hear if someone was in fear of his or her life.

'There were repeated screams, like I said, three or four times and yes, she sounded in severe emotional anguish, scared, almost scared out of her mind I would say.'

Just like Burger and Johnson, Stipp was adamant that the person screaming hysterically was a woman.

He said he went back inside and tried to call estate security, but there was no answer. Stipp said that while he was calling the police, he heard another three bangs, which he believed was a gunman opening fire again. When he eventually got through to security he explained what had happened and asked them to send someone immediately. He walked back on to the balcony to look again at Oscar's house, which was when he heard a man calling for help three times. When the security guard arrived he told them where the shooting had come from. After directing security, he said he looked at the windows of Oscar's house and saw someone was moving in the bathroom, from right to left.

The problem for the prosecution was to explain the two sets of bangs – did this not fit with the defence version that the first set was the gunshots, and the second set the cricket bat striking the door? Nel said consistently throughout the trial that he would deal with this in his closing argument, and yet when it came to that his focus was instead on the suggestion that witnesses aren't perfect rather than providing an explanation for the first set of sounds. In fact, his argument centred around the second set of sounds, which he said was preceded by screams.

After a brief discussion with his wife, Stipp decided to go to the house because he feared this was a family murder and that there might be children involved. When he arrived he found Oscar kneeling over Reeva, trying to stop her bleeding from the hip wound and clearing her airway.

For the first time in the trial the court and the public was hearing a first-hand account of what was happening in Oscar's house on the morning of the shooting. Stipp was amongst the first people to arrive on the scene and provided a detailed description of what he saw and heard. The doctor distinctly remembers Oscar's first words to him: 'I shot her, I thought she was a burglar and I shot her.' The doctor immediately assessed Reeva's vital signs, and once he realised she was mortally wounded, went back outside to where another neighbour, Johan Stander, was standing. It was then that Stander called an emergency service number before handing his phone to Stipp. While waiting for the ambulance to arrive, Stipp said Oscar went upstairs and returned a few minutes later. Despite Stipp's claim, however, Nel never questioned Oscar about it when he was in the witness box, but it would emerge that the accused had gone upstairs to collect Reeva's identity document for the paramedics after she was declared dead.

Stipp confirmed to the court that he was confident that the bangs he had heard were gunshots, that the screaming started moments after the first shots, that the person screaming was a woman and that the bathroom lights were on when he looked over at the house. And when Nel asked about the time difference between the second set of bangs, the doctor stated that they were right on top of each other, in quick succession. It became clear that Nel would argue that this set of noises, which took place after the screaming, were the gunshots that killed Reeva and not the sound of a cricket bat striking a door.

Dr Stipp appeared to be a valuable state witness for the defence because Roux believed that the radiologist's version of events supported the timeline offered by his client – hearing two sets of noises was consistent with the first set being the gunshots and the second being the bat striking the door. But, as would soon become clear under cross-examination, the state had a different interpretation of the noises Stipp claims to have heard.

Roux questioned the doctor's depiction of time lapses, suggesting that it could not have been 'moments' after the shots that Stipp heard the screams and saw the lights on in the bathroom. The advocate used Stipp's testimony about a conversation he had with his wife to prove that it must have been a longer period than simply moments. This was important for Roux because, according to Oscar, he fired the shots in the dark, first retreated, tried to find Reeva and only once realising that it could have been her in the bathroom did he start calling for help and later switched on the light in the bathroom.

Roux turned his attention to what would be the focus of his criticism of Stipp in closing argument: the doctor's timeline when set against the objective facts. Stipp said that he heard the cries for help after he attempted to call security, but there had been no answer. He then, he claimed, tried to call the police, before calling security for a second time – at which point he finally connected and spoke to the guards. Roux, however, showed that the security call log proved that Stipp did in fact connect to and talk to security at 3:15:51am for 16 seconds, and that it was the second call that went unanswered at 3:27am. This accorded with other evidence that put the three bangs – the cricket bat sounds – at about 3:16am, and that Stipp was already with Stander outside Oscar's house when the 3:28am call was made to an ambulance service. According to Roux, this proved the witness was tailoring his evidence, and that this – in the larger context of his evidence – cast doubt on his perceptions of time.

In further revealing evidence, Stipp agreed with Roux that Reeva sustained mortal wounds, including a devastating head wound that would have rendered her non-responsive and unable to scream. So, for the witness to accept that a person was unable to yell after sustaining those wounds, it must then follow that it could not have been Reeva screaming, and the only other person who could have been making a noise was Oscar. And yet, despite his concession on Reeva's wounds, Stipp remained adamant that the screams he had heard sounded like those of a woman.

Roux said that decibel tests had been conducted and an expert witness would testify that when Oscar is anxious, he screams like a woman. In fact, no such testimony was actually ever led by the defence.

While Stipp's testimony appeared to support Oscar's version of events, the duel between counsel during cross-examination saw the state disclose exactly how it would argue the events unfolded – the second set of noises, which Roux said was the bat striking the door, was, according to the state, the gunshots that killed Reeva. And the screams that the defence said were from Oscar, the state argued were in fact the last screams of a desperate woman fearing for her life.

But again the problem Nel faced was having to reconcile the two sets of sounds on the timeline, which appeared to be in favour of the accused. The state still did not, and would never have an explanation for the first set of sounds.

But perhaps a greater concern for the state was the apparent incompatibility of the witnesses' timeline against the available facts. While Stipp appeared confident throughout his testimony, the questions the defence posed surrounding his version, as set out in his evidence against the call logs, raised questions about his reliability. The defence would invest an extraordinary amount of time and energy focusing on Stipp and his version. They would build a timeline for the events of that morning and show the court how what Stipp said simply did not fit in with it. They would argue that when tested against the 'objective facts', Stipp's account could not possibly be accurate. The timelines were all out of kilter and what Stipp believed to have occurred, could not have.

This would, of course, raise significant questions about Johan Stipp's credibility as a witness, his version of events and his perceptions of time.

• • •

Annette Stipp, an occupational therapist by profession, was witness 19 out of the total of 21 state witnesses called, and she reflected on events as they occurred for both herself and her radiologist husband. Despite the uncomfortable position in which she found herself, she addressed the court with confidence.

Stipp remembered feeling ill that night and was suffering from a nasty cough that woke her up. She testified that she checked the clock – it was 3:02am – shortly before hearing three bangs which she believed to be gunshots. She also noted that this clock usually ran a few minutes fast. She immediately asked her husband whether he also heard the noises and whether he knew what they were. Stipp said that from the bed she could see out her balcony window, with its curtains pinned back, and the lights on at two houses in the distance – one of them Oscar's bathroom light and the other at Mike Nhlengethwa's house.

This was the second witness to testify about the bathroom light being on shortly after the first set of noises, which was then followed by screaming.

Four weeks into the trial, the defence decided on a change and put junior counsel Kenny Oldwadge in to conduct the cross-examination of Annette Stipp – a move that surprised many. People watching the live feed of the trial immediately started speculating what the reason for the change could be, but at the lunch break Oscar's attorney Brian Webber explained that they were merely 'spreading the load'.

With Oldwadge, the court was introduced to a new style of delivery. When he delivers his questions he starts off in a rather low pitch that steadily creeps up to a crescendo when he makes his point or concludes. When the witness answered a question the way he wanted it answered, he simply said, 'Wonderful', before continuing. Commentary on social media focused on how pompous and erudite Oldwadge was in his presentation, using verbose language and tucking his thumbs into his gown for effect.

Right from the outset of his cross-examination, Oldwadge focused on issues related to her version of events: the period between hearing the gunshots, whether she would indeed be able to see Oscar's house from her bed and, not surprisingly, the source of the screams she claimed to have heard.

The advocate also suggested to Stipp that from her bed she did not have a clear line of sight to Oscar's house. She disagreed, but Oldwadge pointed out that in the police photos of the Stipps' bedroom, contained in Album 11, the right-hand curtain was held in place with a tie-back, but the left curtain was being pulled back by her hand. 'Is it not to provide you with a clearer view of our client's home, madam? Is that not perhaps what it is?' he said, grilling the witness.

'I think for the photograph, yes,' agreed Stipp. 'But I must say, I think, if you lie in my bed, you have a very, very clear view of both the houses on the opposite side.'

Stipp was adamant, like the previous witnesses, that the screams she had heard were those of a woman, and the shouting she heard was at an entirely different pitch, so she believed the latter to be a man. She was also convinced that the two sets of noises she heard were gunshots. In her first statement to the police Stipp had claimed that she saw a man walking in the bathroom at Oscar's house – but she had testified that she did not see the man. She explained that she later corrected her statement with the police – she had not seen a man walking behind the window. Oldwadge was not appeased. Why would she have signed the affidavit if it was not correct?

She explained that in hindsight, and after careful thought about what transpired, she could not in fact recall seeing the man walking behind the windows. And for Oldwadge, this was the proof he needed to show that Stipp did not have a clear and accurate recollection of what transpired that night. So, although she insisted she had a good recollection of the events, Annette Stipp agreed that on this particular score there had been a lapse of memory.

While Stipp left the stand with that concession, the state believed she had further cemented its case. Like witnesses before her, she was in no way persuaded that what she heard could have been Oscar in a heightened state of anxiety, as suggested by the defence team. And the sounds she heard? Stipp was adamant that they were identical, which again posed a hurdle for the prosecution to explain the source of the sounds that had woken this couple.

· · ·

It was security guard Pieter Baba who welcomed Reeva to the Silver Woods estate for the last time. With a smile and a quick chat, he opened the boom gate and allowed the model to enter in her Mini Cooper. He testified confidently wearing a bright-red collared shirt, and was the only other layperson witness, besides Kevin Lerena, not to object to visuals of himself giving testimony being broadcast.

While Baba isn't a neighbour and doesn't live at the estate, he was amongst the first to be alerted to the unfolding drama. The shift leader had been working at the estate for about two years and was on night shift with four of his colleagues on 13 February. While he managed the team, he was based at the gate with another colleague, and there was a supervisor and another two guards to deal with issues inside the estate, including patrols.

Many middle-class South Africans are familiar with the duties Baba would have performed: when visitors enter the estate, he takes down the vehicle's registration number and the driver's personal particulars, including an identity number. Then he contacts the person they intend visiting to confirm that they are expecting the visitor. This security procedure is fairly standard at such gated complexes, but Baba said Reeva was exempted from such paperwork:

> *M'Lady, say for instance if the owner's visitor had been there at the owner's place during the day, maybe drive out of the premises and it so happens that this person tends to have forgotten something, that person will inform the security officers about that, then we would, we will grant that person permission to go into the premises again. Like from what I learned from other people, it was alleged that Reeva had some laundry in her car during that day, when she drove out of the premises and she then came back at a later stage.*

In his testimony, Baba said Oscar arrived a short while after his girlfriend. He spoke to him, but the athlete was on his phone. Baba didn't know Oscar personally, but he recognised him as the international sports star, 'a person who was always on the TV since I was young' and regarded him as one of his company's clients.

That night, at about 8pm when the front gate of the complex is closed, the guards were doing their rounds. Baba said it was shortly before 3am that a colleague told him he had heard what he believed to be gunshots, and after that he received a call from Johan Stipp who reported that he too had heard gunshots. He said he also received a call from another neighbour, Mike Nhlengethwa. With another guard, Baba sped over to Stipp's house where they found the doctor standing on the balcony. He said Stipp pointed him towards a house across from his where lights were on – he was pointing at Oscar's house.

The security guard said that when he arrived at the house he made a call to Oscar's phone, a claim that was tackled by the defence team.

> *Baba: I then spoke to Mr Pistorius that is when Mr Pistorius said to me: 'Security, everything is fine'. That is when I realised that Mr Pistorius was crying. That is when I said to Jacobs not everything was in order as Mr Pistorius was telling me. I then tried to speak to Mr Pistorius.*
> *Interpreter: So that he can do what?*

> *Baba:* So that he could come down M'Lady, just to make, so that I
> can make sure that everything was fine and that is where our
> conversation ended.
>
> *Nel:* And what happened after that?
>
> *Baba:* Mr Pistorius called me back, maybe he was not sure about
> calling me back. He just started crying over the phone, that is
> when the line went off again, M'Lady.

Baba stated that when Johan Stander and his daughter Carice Viljoen arrived at the house, he and two colleagues followed them to the front door where they spotted Oscar carrying Reeva down the stairs. He said he never went in to the house, and merely observed the unfolding drama from outside.

Roux questioned Baba about a guard-tracking system installed at the estate that monitors their movement on shift. At specific locations around the estate are clock-in points that a guard has to swipe past every hour. One of these devices is located right outside Oscar's house.

Roux presented to the court the guard-track records, which showed that at 2:20am the device outside Oscar's house was activated. This accorded with Baba's statement that he and colleague Nyiko Maluleke were in the vicinity at that time.

> *Roux:* And if I look at the statements, well I have to look at Mr Malulek[e]'s
> statement, that there was no noise or no disturbance at that time?
>
> *Baba:* Your Worship when we went past that place, everything was normal.
>
> *Roux:* As I understand Mr Malulek[e]'s statement and maybe you can tell
> me if it is true or not, is that the garage, the outside light was on,
> but not the inside light?
>
> *Baba:* Everything was normal as it is always the situation at Mr Pistorius's
> house every night.

Baba's evidence, however, contradicted the testimony of Estelle van der Merwe, who said she woke up to what sounded like a woman having an argument at around 2am. And the state, of course, was relying on her evidence to suggest that Oscar and Reeva had had an argument. But, according to Baba, the lights were off and everything appeared normal.

Roux moved on to another vital piece of evidence for the defence, the call record of the security telephone. It showed that Stipp called the number at 3:15:51am. Baba said Stipp told him that he had heard gunshots coming from a neighbour's house. This was the call that Johan Stipp claimed had not connected.

The next entry in the log showed that neighbour Mike Nhlengethwa called security at 3:16:36am, and he also reported hearing shots to the security guard.

Baba testified in his evidence-in-chief that he called Oscar first, before the athlete returned his call. Roux referred the witness to Oscar's phone records, which showed the sequence of events was, in fact, the other way around: it was Oscar who called security at 3:21:33am and Baba who returned the call at 3:22:05am. Despite this indisputable evidence, Baba insisted he was correct. 'M'Lady, I phoned Mr Pistorius first. Mr Pistorius then called me back afterwards and that is true. It is true, M'Lady, that Mr Pistorius had been crying,' he said. Roux presented other records collected by the state to show that the security was indeed wrong, but no amount of evidence was going to change Baba's mind. Roux eventually withdrew on the matter, confident that the court would make a finding in his client's favour based on the available evidence.

The next debate was around what exactly Oscar said to Baba. The witness said the accused told him, 'Security, everything is fine', but Roux referred to the security guard's initial statement to the former investigating officer in which he said Oscar had told him that 'he is okay'. Roux was challenging the inference that the accused attempted to downplay the situation at his house, and show that what Oscar was actually telling security was that he was unharmed.

The security's guard's evidence did not prove to be particularly helpful for the state, but it did assist the defence in setting out its timeline of events. The calls to the security phone and Baba's movements would be compared against the statements of neighbours, particularly the Stipps. The security guards further confirmed that about an hour before the shooting, all was quiet at the Pistorius household – suggesting that testimony from other witnesses who claimed there had been sounds of an argument in the early hours of the morning was inaccurate.

• • •

The neighbours called by Nel to testify in the state's case were not the only people who heard something that deadly night, and they weren't the only 'earwitnesses' consulted by the state in the months leading up to the trial. When the prosecution closed its case, these witnesses became available to the defence to be called to testify.

For weeks the court had heard of Johan Stander – the first person Oscar called after discovering Reeva in the toilet cubicle and amongst the first to arrive on the scene – but he was not called as a state witness. Many of us sitting on the media benches in the public gallery wondered why. Was it because what he had to say did not correlate with the state's version of events?

Stander is a middle-aged man with grey, spiky hair and a weathered face with reading glasses perched on top of a sharp nose. He considers himself more than simply Oscar's friend, but rather a confidant, mentor and father figure. When Stander moved in to the estate in 2009, Oscar offered to help move the Standers' furniture in for them. The friendship grew, with Oscar regularly dropping by for coffee, and Stander caring for the athlete's dogs when he was competing over-seas. Oscar also befriended Stander's daughter Carice over the years.

Stander had provided the police with a statement the day after the shooting and then deposed a second affidavit later in 2013 when Mike van Aardt had taken over the investigation. He had also consulted with the prosecuting team and was under the impression he was a state witness, expecting to be called, albeit reluctantly, to testify against his friend and neighbour. One of these con-sultations with Nel took place as recently as January 2014 when he was told that only he or his daughter would be called to give evidence. But once the state's case had been closed, neither of them had been called to the High Court in Pretoria. This left the door open for Oscar's legal team to use Stander and Viljoen to bol-ster the defence's case. Stander was the defence's fourth witness and his testi-mony was stirring and vivid.

Stander testified about how he was a member of the estate's management committee until January 2013 and recalled several incidents of crime, which he had relayed to Oscar. He remembered an incident in Milkwood Way where intruders scaled the electric fence and tied up a woman before stealing items from the house. In a second incident, intruders used a ladder to gain access to the house. This was important for Oscar's defence because it planted the seed of possibility – and fear – that a ladder could be used to gain entry to a house. Stander further recalled a house being burgled and a robbery in his street where the home-owner was locked up while items were stolen. The evidence was to show the court that, as a friend of Oscar, and former member of the estate man-agement, the subject of crime would have come up and been in Oscar's mind. Stander stated that the incidents were recorded in the estate's incident book and were discussed at minuted estate management meetings. He said that when Oscar returned from events abroad he would pop in for a cup of coffee where he would be informed of incidents at the complex.

Stander had met Reeva for the first time in the December before the shooting when Oscar visited his home before leaving for Cape Town on holiday. When the athlete asked his neighbour to look after his dogs, Reeva said it wouldn't be necessary because she would stay at the house and feed the animals.

Shifting the court's attention to the shooting, Stander testified that he had received a call from Oscar at about 3:19am – he remembers it clearly: 'Oom [Uncle] Johan, please, please, please come to my house. Please. I shot Reeva. I thought she was an intruder. Please, please come quickly.'

He jumped out of bed, waking his wife in the process, and walked out of their room into the passage where he found Carice, who told him she had heard someone screaming for help. Together they sped across the estate to Oscar's house where they found his front door slightly ajar. When Carice pushed it open Oscar was coming down the stairs with Reeva in his arms.

Stander said Oscar was relieved to see them and pleaded with them to help take her to the hospital before placing her on the floor at the foot of the staircase. He described Oscar as being in a state of panic as the pair tried to calm him down, but just as he was about to call an ambulance, Dr Stipp arrived at the scene. While the radiologist assessed Reeva, Stander called emergency services. Paramedics arrived about 20 minutes later, only to declare her dead. Stipp and Stander then exchanged numbers before the doctor left. During their brief conversation, Stipp had explained to Stander that he had heard four shots, screaming, followed by another four shots.

Stander told the court that he had remained at the scene where he saw Oscar go upstairs to collect Reeva's ID for the paramedics, and was there when the first police officer – Lieutenant-Colonel Schoombie van Rensburg – arrived on the scene. He said several vehicles had parked outside the house, with officers both in uniform and civilian clothes. From where he was standing outside, 'one could see how the people were moving up and down the stairs'. It was a claim that would be seen to support the defence's contention that the crime scene had been contaminated and tampered with.

Stander explained in detail, often coming close to tears himself, how he first set eyes on Oscar that morning, that he was 'broken, desperate, pleading', how remorseful he believed Oscar was for the killing – the type of comments the defence needed and had been asking previous state witnesses about.

In his cross-examination, Nel questioned Stander about the security in the estate and the breaches about which he had earlier told the court. He believed the incident in which the woman had been tied up had happened some time in 2011 or 2012, but said he could not disagree with Nel if the police records showed that it was actually in 2009. Stander said the incident involving the ladder took place also between 2011 and 2012, but could not say whether it had been reported to the police – in fact, it had not been.

As per estate regulations, Stander's property was also not secured with burglar bars – in fact, his daughter went to bed on the night of 13 February with her balcony door open. Nel had thus made his point: there were few incidents of crime in the estate and the Standers felt comfortable enough to sleep with doors wide open. Stander also confirmed to Nel that when Reeva stayed at Oscar's house alone for a week while he was in Cape Town, there was no real concern for her safety, although they did communicate via SMS.

Nel pressed the witness on whether he had discussed with Oscar how many shots he had fired and why he had opened fire. 'He never said to you it was an accident?' asked Nel.

'When he phoned me he said: "I made a mistake",' explained Stander.

That was exactly what the prosecutor wanted to hear. It was precisely what Oscar would say during Nel's opening salvo – 'I made a mistake' – which he repeated three times before Nel asked him what mistake he had made. It also spoke to Oscar's 'intention', which was a crucial element the state needed to prove in the case.

And now here was Oscar's friend offering the same version of his defence – that it was an accident. But then Stander apologised, saying that he himself had just made a mistake and it was the inference he had drawn from the conversation that morning.

But Nel wasn't convinced, and interpreted the comment as Stander showing his support for the accused by introducing a claim to support his defence.

After a brief re-examination by Oldwadge, the assessor Henzen-Du Toit asked Stander several questions about the alarm system and whether Reeva knew how to operate it – as she had similarly asked Oscar. The neighbour was confident that Reeva did know how the system operated and which buttons to press on the remote control to activate and deactivate the alarm. It was unclear why the assessor sought to establish this, but she might have been testing the possibility that Reeva might have at some stage during the night left the bedroom and gone downstairs to eat. This would explain pathologist Gert Saayman's findings related to the contents of Reeva's stomach. Stander's evidence provided the defence with another timeline to work from and it also confirmed Stipp being outside Oscar's house at 3:28am when the call was made to an ambulance service.

• • •

Carice Viljoen is Stander's daughter, who has married since the incident. At the time, she lived with her parents in the Silver Woods estate and was also friends with Oscar. Viljoen was clearly nervous when she took the stand, at times speaking so fast that Roux was forced to interject and ask her to slow down. And yet, despite coming close to tears on several occasions, she insisted that she be allowed to continue.

On the witness stand, she described being woken up by the barks of her dog on the morning of Valentine's Day. Her balcony door was open and in the distance she could hear a man screaming for help; there were three screams, she said. She stated that after closing the sliding door to her room and climbing back into bed, where she contemplated taking some action, she saw the lights switch on in her parents' bedroom. As she left her room she encountered her parents and her mother explained that Oscar had just called saying he had shot Reeva. Viljoen and her father arrived at Oscar's house minutes later.

Viljoen said when she pushed open the front door to Oscar's house she saw the frantic athlete carrying Reeva down the stairs. The witness started crying as the tempo of her testimony picked up. She described how she told Oscar to put Reeva down on the floor, dismissing his request to help take Reeva to a hospital. Viljoen said she was kneeling on one side of Reeva with Oscar on the other where together they tried to assess her. Viljoen then ran upstairs to collect towels from a linen cupboard to try to stop the bleeding, but it was all in vain. She remembered Dr Johan Stipp arriving, but he was inside only briefly before going back out, and later the paramedics prompted her and Oscar to step back from Reeva to allow them to work on her.

Viljoen testified that when Oscar went to fetch Reeva's ID upstairs, she went after him to call him back, fearing that he would shoot himself. A short while later, at about 3:55am, she saw Oscar trying to place a call, but he was not making any sense. She took the phone from him and told the person on the other end of the line – his friend Justin Divaris – what was happening before helping him call two more people: his brother Carl and agent Peet van Zyl.

Viljoen remembered Colonel van Rensburg being the first police officer on the scene, and seeing two additional officers in plain clothes inside the house. She told Roux that besides those three police officers, she saw no others inside the house until later in the morning when more arrived. She said that only after Carl arrived did Van Rensburg properly secure the scene and control who entered and exited the area. Viljoen said while she was with Oscar in the kitchen, trying to comfort him, she remembered seeing people going up and down the stairs, but she could not identify them.

Viljoen testified that she later accompanied Aimee upstairs to fetch clothes and a few personal items for Oscar. After collecting the items and sitting in a car, she said Aimee decided she would take Reeva's handbag from the crime scene. 'She went into the house and walked past the policemen standing there and took the bag. I left the bag on the kitchen counter, the table, after I took the licence out and I left it there and she just went and fetched it because we wanted to keep it safe for her mother,' said Viljoen.

This testimony was to provide another example of how the police failed to secure the crime scene properly; that someone could simply walk into the house and exit with an item without it being checked or documented was not correct procedure. Oscar's second cellphone was another item removed from the scene, but police would only make this discovery days later.

Viljoen did remember, however, that when she joined Aimee upstairs to collect clothes and a watch for Oscar, a policeman – who she pointed out in court – accompanied the pair. The same police officer did not allow them to go into the bathroom, the primary crime scene.

'This is Warrant Officer Van Staden, Bennie van Staden, photographer,' said Nel.

'It is kind of burned into my mind for the rest of my life,' she said, indicating the magnitude of the trauma experienced that morning.

'Unfortunately … his face,' quipped Nel, before he continued. 'Now can I also just show you a photograph? There is an album in front of you. If you open that red one over here.'

'Is this going to be a photo that is going to make me cry?' asked the witness, fearing it could be a graphic image from the crime scene.

'No, it will not,' said the prosecutor, to hushed laughs from the gallery.

The photo depicted the upstairs linen cupboard with one of its double doors opened and a blue towel crumpled on the floor in front of it. It was exactly as Viljoen had left it; she clearly recalled dropping the towel there in her haste to attend to Reeva downstairs.

This proved two things for Nel: the crime scene upstairs was being preserved and the police didn't allow unaccompanied people to wander around the bedroom; and that an item like the towel had not been moved. This was contrary to Oscar's claims of at least six items being moved by cops after the shooting.

Nel questioned Viljoen about her understanding of Oscar's state of mind that morning. She confirmed that he was able to tell her that the towels were upstairs when she asked, and that he specifically asked her to keep her fingers in Reeva's mouth while he fetched black bags.

'He is the one that constantly asked when the ambulance would arrive, so he was following what is going on?' asked Nel.

'Well, he asked questions, but he was … everything was in a frantic state, My Lady, so I would not know if he was following what was happening.'

'But if you gave him an instruction, he would follow it?'

'Yes, he would, My Lady,' she said.

In the meantime, the defence was slowly constructing the timeline of events that would form the backbone of its case when it came to closing argument. Viljoen's evidence would prove to be crucial in this construction.

Her evidence supported the timeline as set out by her father. Stander received the call from Oscar at about 3:19am and, according to Viljoen's evidence, it took them about three minutes to get to the house. The defence used this to estimate the time that the first witnesses arrived on the scene at about 3:22am. The defence would also look to Viljoen's testimony about the time that she heard the three calls for help, to corroborate the testimony of other neighbours who had heard the same calls. They matched up, slotting another block of the overarching timeline in place. And while Roux continued to build the timeline, he believed that Stipp's version – and with it the state's case – would crumble.

• • •

Michael Nhlengethwa, a self-employed civil engineer, lived next to Oscar on the other side of a shared wall. If you were to face the athlete's house, Nhlengethwa's home would be to the left in the same street. He shares the house with his wife Rontle, who also testified, and his children.

Nhlengethwa met Oscar in 2009 when he was considering buying the house – the developer introduced them to each other so he could inspect the athlete's house to get an idea of the types of finishes intended for his own home. Oscar was also the first person to welcome the new resident to the estate, and they struck up a neighbourly relationship. Oscar usually made the effort to get out of his car, come over and greet him properly, but they did not socialise together.

It was during one of their impromptu sidewalk encounters that Oscar introduced Reeva to his neighbour as his fiancé – a moment Nhlengethwa said he would never forget. 'When she came towards me, I raised my hand to greet her and she just opened her arms, she just came and hugged me.

'I could see the person that she was because, you know, when a person brings you closer to her, that means something,' he said.

So impressed was Nhlengethwa with Reeva, he told Oscar, 'This one is for keeps.' The athlete told his neighbour that he would soon be moving out of the estate to a house in Joburg because he wanted to be closer to Reeva.

For Roux, this demonstrated the loving relationship between his client and Reeva. It showed that Oscar was a friendly, courteous neighbour who was well liked by those around him. But it also exposed a potential lie: Oscar later told a psychiatrist that the reason he wanted to move to Joburg was because he was scared for his safety at Silver Woods.

On 14 February Nhlengethwa recalled being woken by his wife who said that she had heard a bang, which she thought could have been inside their house. He got out of bed to check on his daughter in a neighbouring bedroom, and then walked around the house checking doors and windows for anything suspicious, before returning to the bedroom. It's then, he testified, that he could hear a man crying very loudly, as if he needed desperate help, and realised something was wrong.

He said the noise was very high pitched. Roux had told state witnesses that when his client is anxious, his screams sound like those of a woman – and this neighbour confirmed that it was a man's voice – albeit high pitched – that he had heard.

This was an absolutely critical statement from the witness. Here was a neighbour, who lived considerably closer to Oscar than any of the witnesses who had been called to testify. While the others had claimed to have heard what sounded like a woman screaming, Nhlengethwa believed it to be a man. It was a clincher for the defence. They would later argue that they did not believe it necessary to call an expert to prove that Oscar sounds like a woman when he screams because Nhlengethwa, and others, had testified to this. This statement also questioned why, perhaps, the state had not called Nhlengethwa – because his testimony would have undermined their case.

Roux referred Nhlengethwa to the security phone records that showed he called security twice at about 3:16am when he told security that there was an emergency and someone urgently needed help. He said that as the crying continued, he peeked out of his window waiting for the guards to arrive. While his wife, Rontle, would testify to hearing a man call for help three times, Nhlengethwa said he did not hear this, possibly because he was on the phone at the time.

Nhlengethwa watched as the security vehicle briefly stopped outside the Stipps' house, before speeding off and a car from that same house speeding away a short while later. He saw them all come to a stop outside Oscar's house. It was then Nhlengethwa went outside to offer assistance and he stayed until the paramedics left, when he realised there wasn't much he could do. Nhlengethwa said he looked inside the house from the front door and saw Oscar kneeling over the dying woman, but never ventured into the house. 'I could not take watching what I saw in that point in time,' he said.

Under cross-examination Nhlengethwa admitted to Nel that he had followed every word of the trial as it happened in court from day one, but he was satisfied that his statement to the police was accurate. He admitted, too, that he found it hard to believe the testimony of the Stipps and Burger and Johnson. They lived much further away from the crime scene than he and yet claimed to have heard so much more, but he conceded that he might well have slept through the commotion.

Nhlengethwa said he did not hear any shots or loud bangs, and clarified that he and his wife did not hear anything that sounded like a door being broken down with a cricket bat. This immediately called into question the value of this witness, because even on Oscar's own version, he first shot at the door before hitting it with the bat – and this witness hadn't heard a thing.

'You never heard anybody scream?' asked Nel.

'I heard a man that was crying,' Nhlengethwa said, adding that he also could not establish exactly where it was coming from.

· · ·

Rontle Nhlengethwa was one of two of Oscar's neighbours who re-enacted the screams as they heard them on the morning of the shooting. She said she was woken up on the morning of 14 February by a 'bang', which is the only way she was able describe the loud noise. She didn't know what it was or where it came from, but it was enough to startle her and prompt her to wake up her husband. Rontle's recollection of events mirrored her husband's, except for the point where he left her in the room to inspect the house when she heard what sounded like a man calling for help three times very loudly. She then heard a man crying, which she described as sounding as if the person was hurt and needed urgent help.

Roux asked Rontle to demonstrate to the court what she had heard. She composed herself, taking a few seconds and clearing her throat, before she let out a loud, long wail in the courtroom. 'But in a voice of a man,' she was quick to qualify. The court sat silent, imagining this scream breaking the silence in the dead of night.

But why hadn't Roux asked the previous witness, a man, to demonstrate what he had heard? Rontle did, however, state that the crying was high pitched, as had her husband.

'It is interesting that more people heard: "Help! Help! Help!"' said Nel to Rontle in cross-examination. 'Stipp,' he continued, 'heard: "Help! Help! Help!" after the second of the shots he heard.'

It was now clear that the state would argue that these witnesses' versions of events followed the second set of noises heard by other neighbours, which would explain why the Nhlengethwas only heard Oscar crying and no screaming.

> Nel: *Now you never left your room?*
> Rontle: *Not at all, M'Lady.*
> Nel: *And you never heard further 'bang' shots?*
> Rontle: *No, only those that I told the court about. If I would have heard such sounds, I would have informed the court about that.*
> Nel: *If one takes into account Dr Stipp's evidence, about when he heard 'Help! Help! Help!', the bang sound you heard was the last bang sound you heard.*
> Rontle: *Well that is the only sound I heard.*

The question thus remained: could a bang loud enough to wake a neighbour have been the cricket bat, as argued by the defence, or a gunshot as contended by the state?

• • •

Another neighbour who shared a wall with Oscar is Rika Motshuane, who lived to the right of the athlete's house. She woke up on the morning of 14 February hearing a man crying, and subsequently roused her husband. 'The crying was very loud and it was very close,' she said.

Just as he had done with Rontle Nhlengethwa, Roux asked the witness to demonstrate to the court what she had heard. Motshuane let out two long wails, which she said were continuous on the morning in question. Roux had now asked two female witnesses to demonstrate the crying they had heard – again, why had he not asked the male witness who had also heard it?

Motshuane, she says, peeked out of her window towards Oscar's house when she heard a commotion from that direction. Her husband called security, who explained that whatever was happening at Oscar's house was being taken care of.

The witness told Nel in cross-examination that in her statement to police, she had estimated that she heard the crying at about 3:20am – this was squarely after the second set of noises that the state believed were the gunshots. Motshuane didn't hear any gunshots.

• • •

In early May 2014, while Oscar's closest neighbours were testifying for the defence, a sideshow erupted in court, drawing attention away from the content of the witness testimony, much to the defence legal team's frustration.

Oscar was accused of trying to intimidate Kim Myers by going up to her in the public gallery and asking, 'How can you sleep at night?' The exchange was reportedly heard by those around her, including a warrant officer who reported the incident to prosecutor Gerrie Nel. Myers, through her attorney Ian Levitt, also lodged a complaint with the National Prosecuting Authority.

In a statement, Levitt suggested that Oscar may have been upset by comments made by the Myers family in media interviews. 'My client, Kim Myers, was approached by Oscar Pistorius in court today and in a very sinister tone was asked, "How can you sleep at night?" My client views this unwelcome approach as extremely disturbing and I have been in communication with the National Prosecuting Authorities as well as the Investigating Officer. All other parties have also been informed. My client however will remain focused on the trial and will continue to attend court in support of Reeva.'

But when reporters in court questioned Oscar about the claim, he replied: 'No, I haven't spoken to her.' He insisted: 'I haven't spoken to them for a year and a half. I walk past them in the corridors and hold doors open for them but they don't look me in the eye.'

Oscar's attorney Brian Webber dismissed the allegation as 'grossly untrue'. A source within the defence team told us that they were annoyed that on a day when their witnesses had made significant strides in countering the state's neighbours' testimony, the media focus was only on the alleged incident between Myers and Oscar. There was very little reporting on what the neighbours had told the court.

· · ·

Ten neighbours – five for the state and another five for the defence – testified in total. Add to this the evidence of the guard who was in charge of security at the estate on the morning of the shooting.

The opposing sides in the murder trial had presented starkly contrasting versions of events. On the one hand, there was the evidence of what sounded like an argument, then the blood-curdling screams of a woman, the image of a man walking in Oscar's bathroom, the light on in his house and then bangs. The state believed that the terrifying screams before the shots could only have been Reeva fleeing her boyfriend in the moments before she was killed and that it was compelling testimony of an argument between Oscar and Reeva, which led to him shooting her intentionally in a fit of rage.

On the other hand, there was the evidence of a man screaming not a woman – claims from neighbours living far closer to Oscar's home. There was also the testimony of those who arrived first on the scene, who told of the athlete's distress and insistence that he had believed his girlfriend to be an intruder. Crucially, the defence had now also collected all the building blocks of its timeline, which it would construct to show that the state's version, particularly that of Dr Stipp, was simply impossible.

Both sides were saddled with significant problems – holes poked during cross-examination. The greatest difficulty for the state was to explain the two sets of noises heard at about 3:12am and at about 3:17am – even by the state's own witnesses. According to the defence's version, the first set of noises was, in fact, the gunshots and the second sounds were the cricket bat – this appeared to undermine the state's version, particularly as it failed to explain the first sounds.

Roux was, however, left with the challenge of proving that his client's screams could have been mistaken for Reeva's, an issue that the last three neighbours he called addressed in their testimony. While these people heard screaming, they were adamant it was a man in a high pitch. This would support the claim that the shouts were from Oscar as he desperately tried to break down the bathroom door with his cricket bat in order to save his girlfriend.

It would, however, be left to Judge Masipa and her assessors to decide whether the state's witnesses had convinced them of their version of events beyond a reasonable doubt. If they found that the defence's witnesses gave a version that was reasonably possibly true, it would be difficult to convict Oscar of murder.

The Last Meal

Nel's first expert witness, the lanky, wire-haired state pathologist Gert Saayman, presented something of a change in tone after the first week of testimony from neighbours, friends and security guards. Professor Saayman had been listening in on testimony for the first week, sitting amongst the ballistics, forensic and blood spatter analysts behind the prosecution team.

Going in to the trial it was well known that the cause of Reeva's death was several gunshots, but the specifics and the finer details of her last moments remained unknown because the postmortem was one aspect of the investigation that had been kept well under wraps.

A pathologist's job is to study the deceased – both externally and internally, by means of dissection – and describe to the court the nature of the wounds, what impact such wounds would have had on the subject while still alive, and offer an explanation of what might have caused the wound. A study of the organs also provides insight into other factors that may have affected the deceased; in the case of Reeva, a study of her stomach's contents was to prove useful for the state.

A pathologist's report and testimony is by its nature graphic, and includes descriptions of wounds and procedures that leave nothing to the imagination. So when Nel called the professor, he told the judge that there was an objection from the witness to his testimony being broadcast, which was an exception to the order that all state expert witnesses should be televised: 'He has an ethical issue that he would want to raise about the evidence he is about to give,' said Nel. 'M'Lady, he will give evidence in graphic detail about the postmortem on the deceased.'

While a temporary blackout had no real bearing on the trial itself, there was however a battle of public opinion worldwide. On one hand, the public who supported the deceased wanted to know how Reeva had died, while those siding with the accused agreed that such testimony would be an affront to her dignity, and do nothing but fuel the voyeuristic appetite the trial had cultivated.

Reeva's mother hadn't been in court for the last week, but the doctor's concerns went beyond the courtroom to where the world was watching. 'I believe that by such public and contemporaneous streaming of information of this nature,' said the professor, 'it is almost inevitable that we will impinge upon, or harm the rights of remaining relatives and friends of the deceased.'

While there was considerable debate as to the merits of this compromise, Judge Mapisa eventually ordered that there would be no live broadcast of Saayman's testimony; a package of Saayman's testimony was to be compiled by the media team and submitted to the prosecution and defence legal teams to approve prior to broadcast.

The judge also provided clarity on her prohibition of social media, showing how unfamiliar she was to this new phenomenon in courtrooms. 'Someone was kind enough to give me more information about blogging and tweeting. As a result of that, in respect of this witness, blogging and tweeting is allowed.'

· · ·

'I hold concurrent appointments as Head of the Department of Forensic Medicine at the University of Pretoria,' started Professor Saayman. 'That is an academic and teaching appointment, and concurrently as the Chief Specialist or Head of Forensic Pathology Services in the Gauteng Department of Health in Pretoria.'

The professor, who has more than 30 years' experience and has conducted thousands of postmortems, has held that position since 1998 – he's responsible for wide-ranging investigations of death, whether natural, unnatural, unexplained or sudden and was no stranger to high-profile cases and the glare of the media. In the trial of Fred van der Vyfer – accused of murdering his girlfriend Inge Lotz and controversially acquitted – Saayman testified that it was highly unlikely that an ornamental hammer caused the extensive injuries to the woman's head, neck and chest, as contended by the state. He also testified for the state in the case of Pretoria mother Chanelle Henning, who was shot dead in 2011 by gunmen moments after dropping her son off at school.

Experienced court reporter Zelda Venter says that in the 20-odd years she's been covering the High Court in Pretoria, Saayman has been a regular feature in the biggest cases. 'He's a no-nonsense professional and very highly regarded.

I can't remember a case where his evidence has been rejected. The professor is respected by the legal fraternity, and counsel very rarely questions his evidence; they tend to accept his findings,' she said.

Saayman conducted the postmortem on Reeva the day after Oscar killed her, before compiling his report, which was signed off on 1 July 2013.

'M'Lady, I concluded that the deceased had died as a result of multiple gunshot wounds.'

Nel flicked through the professor's report, asking him to confirm what each section entailed – the report was a mere 12 pages, but set out in great detail the types and extent of injuries Reeva sustained.

And then, as the doctor was describing the injuries observed on the corpse, switching between medical jargon and layperson explanations, the sound of someone gagging became audible in the court. Oscar was heaving forward with his head in his hands.

'My Lady, may I just have a moment?' said Nel, looking back at where the accused was seated. 'I get a report from there that … My Lady, I understand that the accused got sick in court. May I ask for a short adjournment?' The judge granted the request.

Oscar was inconsolable. Aimee and Carl immediately went to support their brother. Aimee sat down next to him, to his right, and with her left arm over Oscar's shoulder she leaned in to whisper in his ear. When she pulled back, a solitary tear could be seen trickling down the bridge of her nose.

Carl was standing upright on the other side of the wooden barrier, his right hand stroking Oscar's back. There was little they could do, and it was going to get worse as the graphic details of his girlfriend's injuries were read into the court record. A court orderly fetched a bucket from outside the courtroom, probably from the cleaners' storeroom, and placed it on the floor between the athlete's legs. His cheeks and ears were bright red, while beads of sweat stood out on his brow and trickled down his temple to mingle with his tears. Members of the public in the gallery as well as journalists were stunned – more than a year after the incident, these detailed descriptions conjured up raw memories of what Oscar had done to another human being. His reaction appeared sincere, but outside the court his detractors were not convinced, with some critics dismissing the vomiting as part of a stage-managed show to win hearts and minds. It was difficult to watch.

After seven minutes, Oscar was again alone in the dock. Judge Masipa and her assessors re-entered the court. 'Is your client fine for now?' she asked Roux.

'My Lady, he is not fine, but it is not going to be fine. So it is a difficulty and I think we should continue.'

'But what does he say?' Masipa showed concern for the accused. 'Would he proceed? Can you please find out?'

Roux had been faced with a similar situation during the bail application when Nair questioned the well-being of Oscar, who had broken down when his version of events was read into the record.

The advocate told the magistrate that this was an issue they had become accustomed to, and that the situation was not going to change. It was agreed, after he briefly consulted with Oscar, that the advocate would keep an eye on his client, and that the trial should proceed.

Court was on several occasions interrupted by the retching sounds of Oscar with the bucket gripped between his legs, his body heaving, as Saayman explored in graphic detail how Reeva's body was damaged.

Masipa was at pains to be reassured that the accused was in a position to understand proceedings. Her concern, experienced by some as an indication of 'softness' towards the accused, was actually more orientated to ensuring he was following what was happening in court.

Having dealt with the external injuries, Saayman turned to his findings upon dissecting the body, starting with the head. He described the type of wound caused by the bullet to the head, which indicated that it hit at a very shallow angle of entry, but further there was a large area of the right side of her skull that was cracked, including on the bone sutures.

'The base of the skull also had fractures and this is purely because of the explosive nature of the projectile as it enters the skull with a lot of kinetic energy being released and there being energy waves which disbursed through the skull causing fractures in the skull at a point distant from where the bullet had entered the skull.

'So there were multiple fractures involving virtually the whole skull, both the dome part and the base of the skull.'

Saayman commented that when Reeva's brain was removed from the cranial cavity, the cause of this devastating damage became apparent. He found a jagged piece of projectile lodged into the bone at the base of the skull – Ranger or Black Talon ammunition. The pathologist and prosecutor used the two names interchangeably to refer to hollow-point ammunition. While the particular variety was an issue of contention amongst the ballistics experts later in the trial, we studied crime scene photographs that revealed the headstamp on a spent copper cartridge in the bathroom to bear the lettering 'WCC +P+', while the bullets in Oscar's pistol magazine showed that the projectiles were black-tipped. Firearm enthusiast websites, mostly in the United States, identify the rounds as

Winchester SXT, a 127-grain hollow-point. The Black Talon round is identified by its nickel-plated cartridge and is a heavier 147-grain bullet.

The pathologist explained that Black Talon was first produced by the US company Winchester, and was later removed from the market but was subsequently replaced and marketed under the brand name Ranger.

'Have you had experience with this Ranger type ammunition?' asked Nel.

'It is something which unfortunately we, as forensic pathologists in South Africa,' said Saayman, 'get to deal with gunshot injuries on a more regular basis I think than most and yes, I have had a number of previous cases where the victim has suffered injury as a result of so-called "Black Talon ammunition".'

He said manufacturers develop specific kinds of ammunition to perform different purposes – some are built to have a high penetrating value, while others are designed to break up and destroy human tissue. 'This particular kind of projectile is referred to as an expanding bullet,' the pathologist explained, taking care to note that he was not a wound ballistics expert. 'It is designed to open up, or to flatten out, or to mushroom upon striking tissue, such as human tissue and in the process, it becomes markedly deformed and larger in frontal or cross-section diameter.

'So it is a projectile that is designed to cause maximal tissue damage,' he said.

Saayman referred the court to a picture in the album of Reeva's skull cavity with her brain removed, to a section showing where part of the bullet had become lodged in the bone. The next page in the album showed the lead core and jagged slivers of the metal jacket recovered from Reeva's skull.

'The fundamental feature of this projectile is that as it strikes tissue, the usual result is that it folds out like the petals of a flower; it opens up and in that way presents a much broader front or presenting face to the tissue, which therefore facilitates the transmission of kinetic energy.

'These "petals" that fold out were furthermore specifically designed by the manufacturer to have very sharp jagged edges and this causes even more tissue damage as the bullet tumbles in the tissue.'

It had become clear that Oscar had armed himself with killer ammunition, designed to cause as much damage to the target as possible.

Saayman described his findings related to other parts of Reeva's internal organs, with nothing significant or out of the ordinary – until he arrived at the stomach.

'The stomach contains approximately 200 ml of partially digested food residue with the appearance of primarily vegetable matter and with a slightly green and grey colour, in which whitish cheese-like particles may be seen,' he said.

This was a significant finding for the prosecution team, and its importance soon became clear. Saayman took some time to explain to the court that digestion periods vary from person to person and depend on the type and volume of food consumed. 'It is likely that the food we see in the stomach of the deceased had been introduced within approximately two hours of her death, or less,' said Saayman, pausing briefly before clarifying his finding. 'In other words, two hours prior to her death, she probably ingested this food.'

It was common cause that Oscar had killed Reeva just after 3am. The food in her stomach and Saayman's conclusion puts her up, awake and eating at about 1am. According to Oscar, the couple was asleep at that time. He believed she must have got up to go to the toilet, and that was when he had mistaken her for an intruder.

Only a few millilitres of urine were discovered in Reeva's bladder – no more than a teaspoonful. Could this be the result of her urinating moments before being shot? Oscar stated in his bail application that in hindsight he believed that Reeva must have gone to the bathroom, and it was argued by Roux that this finding related to the bladder supported the claim.

Nel asked Saayman to discuss the presence of private pathologist Dr Reggie Perumal at the postmortem. Saayman acknowledged him being there as nothing unusual, and that Perumal had been given a watching brief by Oscar's legal team. He explained that in such a situation, Saayman would verbalise his observations, providing running commentary as he conducted the autopsy to ensure there was no misunderstanding as to what the findings represented:

Saayman: *So at the time really all I asked of Dr Perumal was, 'Are you satisfied? Are you happy? Is there anything more to be done and is this how you also interpret the findings?'*

Nel: *And he said what?*

Saayman: *To the best of my recollection, he was in agreement with what I had, obviously at that time not yet reported, but I had indicated to him how I interpreted these findings and he agreed that that was essentially correct.*

The court was thus surprised several weeks later when another pathologist took Perumal's place in the stand to testify for the defence. It was first prize for any legal team to have its own expert present to witness the postmortem, so why would Roux not call the man dispatched on a watching brief?

Oscar's legal team later issued a statement saying that Perumal's absence was the result of his lack of availability and that he remained a member of their expert team. When contacted, Perumal was not prepared to divulge why he did not testify.

One source in the defence team told us that Perumal was kicked out because he had spoken to the media, but another suggested that while this was a concern for the lawyers, it wasn't the main reason he wasn't called.

'With Perumal, he was there to see if Gert Saayman was correct in his post-mortem. He confirmed the correctness of the postmortem. It was never disputed by the defence so there was never a need to call Perumal to the stand. Yes, the defence legal team was frustrated that Perumal had spoken to the media but that wasn't the reason he wasn't called. The reason was simply that the postmortem was not in dispute and Perumal's evidence was just to confirm Saayman,' said the source.

Nel then turned to explore the effect the various wounds would have had, had they been sustained individually – starting with the hip wound.

Saayman said that the hip wound would have caused almost immediate instability or loss of stability related to the limb – the person would collapse, and it would be very unlikely that the person would be able to get back up on their own.

The pathologist told the court that the injury to the right arm would be a particularly devastating injury – breaking and shattering the right upper arm. 'There would, for all practical purposes, have been no functionality retained in that arm after the injury.'

And the head wound? 'Probably almost instantly fatal, M'Lady,' he said.

Saayman further added that the injuries to the hip and arm individually could also have been fatal – adding that people routinely die of similar injuries.

The state's first expert witness had thus provided the court with a graphic account of how the deadly projectiles ripped through Reeva's body, and how each of these shards of high-velocity steel would have affected the target. Several other expert witnesses, including those for Oscar's defence, relied on this information to compile their reports and plot Reeva's likely movement as the bullets pierced the wooden door. But perhaps one of the most important findings for the state was the content of the dead woman's stomach, which the defence would call two witnesses to refute.

• • •

The focus of Roux's cross-examination was mostly on the issue of gastric emptying because if the court trusted Professor Saayman's findings in this regard, it would put Reeya up and awake at about 1am, two hours prior to her death, and coincide

with a neighbour's testimony that she heard what sounded like a woman arguing coming from Oscar's house at about 2am. This was contrary to Roux's client's
version of events that they were both in bed and asleep, as well as the security
guards' assertion that all was quiet and peaceful while doing their patrol at about
the same time. But the defence advocate's experience in medical malpractice litigation meant he was in familiar territory when dealing with medical literature.

However, he started by questioning the effect the rapid succession of shots
striking the body would have on cognitive function and what response could
be expected from the victim. Saayman responded that the head wound would
cause immediate incapacity, but the trauma of the other wounds could impact
cognitive ability for a few seconds. Roux was trying to rule out the possibility
that Reeva could have screamed – to allege that after the first shot Reeva was
so shocked that she couldn't think clearly, and the remaining shots followed so
quickly that she died before she regained any cognitive ability.

Turning to gastric emptying, the advocate listed several medical journal articles and asked whether Saayman had consulted a specific one. Saayman had not;
rather, he had consulted several articles and textbooks, and relied on a 'synthesis
of my own experience, own observations and reading the literature'. Roux asked
to see the articles Saayman had relied upon, asking for a brief adjournment.

When the session resumed, Roux asked Saayman to read into the record the
titles of five medical journal articles related to how food is digested and passed
through the body. This was clearly going to be an academic argument in which
the defence fought its case with the literature while the witness who had conducted the postmortem relied on literature as well as decades of experience to
reach his findings. Roux noted that the professor was at great pains in his evidence to point out that the time it took food to pass through the stomach varied
from person to person and depended on the type and volume of food consumed.

Saayman agreed, adding that he tried to be balanced when presenting the
evidence. But Roux questioned whether the pathologist had examined Reeva's
small intestine, to see how much food had been passed through. He hadn't. The
advocate said that according to the literature this step was necessary to establish
a more probable time the food was ingested prior to death.

By this point, despite the continued graphic reference to Reeva's internal
organs and discussions related to body function, Oscar had recovered from the
inconsolable state seen earlier, although his bucket remained within reach and
he occasionally buried his head in his hands with his fingers to block his ears.

Roux referred to *The Forensic Medicine: Clinical and Pathological Aspects*, and
Saayman directed the court's attention to a particular paragraph: 'The following

gastric emptying times are given in the literature. One to three hours for a light, small-volume meal. Three to five hours for a medium-sized meal. Five to eight hours for a large meal.'

The professor read further, noting clarity in the article that despite these findings, quite often a four-hour period would ensure that a stomach was empty.

Roux referred Saayman to a table in the same publication, which explained that the volume of meal would have to be known prior to the food being consumed to make a time determination based on the amount found in the stomach. Almost as the professor stopped reading, Roux hit home his point. 'Now in this case, what is the percentage of the volume of the last meal that you found in the stomach?'

'I would not know, M'Lady.'

The advocate was not only trying to show that gastric emptying as a means to determine time of death was an imprecise science, but also that the professor had not conducted an examination of the entire digestive system in order to make a conclusive finding.

Roux quickly snapped to other well-known literature in this regard to make the point that there would be great variations from meal to meal, person to person and day to day in the same person. The defence was hitting straight at the reliability of the pathologist's claim that he believed Reeva had eaten a meal no more than two hours prior to death. What had started out as riveting evidence was now more like a debate on medicine in a university lecture hall.

But Saayman stood his ground, confidently providing an elaborate explanation for how science and studies worked, and used an analogy of firing a shotgun at a wall and how some pellets might stray, but most would be concentrated in a narrowly distributed area.

'I must stress that it is proper scientific methodology to say that we tend to abide in the first instance, by that which science and literature and repeated research has shown us, to be the probable values and on that very basis every single day, thousands of endoscopies and gastroscopies are done, because gastroenterologists know that after four to six hours, after a meal, the stomach is for practical purposes empty.'

'I understand that,' said Roux. 'Thank you, M'Lady. I have no further questions.'

Saayman had remained firm despite the defence advocate's attempts to undermine his findings, but Roux would call two witnesses in an attempt to cast doubt on the professor's evidence.

• • •

Nel explored only three aspects in his re-examination of Professor Saayman, starting with cognitive function after being shot – it was the state's case that Reeva was screaming up until the last shot to the head killed her. He referred to Saayman's answers to the question from Roux about a stress response after being shot – the fight-or-flight mode. 'Now cognitive function … I just wanted to know, would that include screaming? Would screaming be possible?' asked Nel.

'Yes, screaming would of course be possible and that is a voluntary action and probably an expression of fear or anguish,' said Saayman.

'And the wound on the arm …?' Nel explored a potential reaction from someone who had sustained such a wound.

'I would think it would be somewhat abnormal if one does not scream when you sustain a wound of this nature, or wounds of this nature,' Saayman said. This, of course, opened the door to the probability that Reeva would have screamed after being struck first in the hip and then in the arm, before the final shot to the head rendered her unconscious. Those screams would tie in with the evidence of neighbours, who testified they heard the terrified high-pitched calls of a woman in distress up until the last shot was fired; the suggestion also raised the question that, if Reeva was screaming, why did Oscar keep shooting at the door?

The prosecutor moved on to his second issue – the bladder and the fact that it was virtually empty. He wanted to know whether the state or the amount of urine in the bladder would have been any different had Reeva been awake and emptied it two hours prior to her death.

'If she voided her bladder half an hour or an hour before her death,' explained Saayman, 'it could also have been virtually empty, because it may well be that at that time there was no further substantive urine production.' This meant that it might be possible that Reeva could have emptied her bladder when she was eating, prior to her death, and disputed the defence team's claim that her bladder was empty because she had emptied it shortly before death – it was Oscar who claimed that Reeva went to the toilet while he was collecting the fans.

On the issue of gastric emptying, the pathologist reiterated that estimating the time it takes food to pass through the stomach was not an exact science, but that it did not mean a determination could not be made. 'The best I can offer the court,' he said, 'as a summation of my entire experience in this field and my reading of the literature and my own anecdotal observations, given the nature of the meal, the appearance thereof in the stomach, was that I would suggest that we are dealing with a period of approximately two hours.'

Nel concluded, and Saayman was excused, but he would return to court later in the trial when the defence team's pathologist testified. Then Saayman listened to the evidence provided and consulted with Nel to guide him in terms of the testimony provided.

. . .

Dr Jan Botha was the first witness called by the defence team, despite it being usual practice for the accused to take the stand first. In this instance, an arrangement had been made with the state that Botha be called first because he had a genuine family emergency – his wife was ill – and Nel did not oppose the request.

Botha, who was called to stand in for Dr Reggie Perumal, obtained his medical degree from the University of Cape Town in 1969 and later his Master of Medicine in Anatomical Pathology from the same institution, and has been registered as a specialist pathologist since 1975.

Like Saayman, Botha has decades of experience and had been the chief state pathologist in the Free State until his retirement in 2010, but he had also worked in the private sector. In that period he said he'd presented evidence in court on thousands of occasions, and conducted as many as 25 000 postmortems.

When Saayman entered the court, he put down his bag and a few files before greeting Botha, who had stood up to shake his counterpart's hand. The pair engaged briefly in conversation, before Saayman took up a seat to Nel's right, from where he would consult with the prosecutor as Botha testified.

As in his cross-examination of Professor Saayman, Roux's evidence-in-chief of the defence pathologist focused on the issue of gastric emptying. Before Roux asked his witness to refer to academic articles pertaining to the subject, he asked what the doctor's position was on the matter. 'The modern consensus is that it is a highly controversial and inexact science, if one wants to call it that,' said Botha. 'All the books virtually, warn of the dangers and the variations not only from person to person, but in the same person from day to day.'

Botha referred to the 'landmark' Truscott case in Canada that tested the value of using gastric emptying as a determining time of death. Canadian Steven Murray Truscott was sentenced to death by hanging in 1959 at the age of 14 for the murder of his classmate, 12-year-old Lynne Harper. His sentence was commuted in 1960 to life in prison, but was finally parolled in 1969.

But nearly 50 years after the incident, in 2007, Truscott was acquitted on appeal in which it was found that his murder conviction had been a miscarriage of justice. Evidence from experts was presented, who concurred that 'an estimate of the time of death based on the volume of stomach contents and state of digestion should never be used as probative evidence', and the use of gastric emptying to ascertain time of death 'cannot withstand scientific scrutiny'.

Roux led his witness through questions related to the amount of food, the time of the last meal, the medication the deceased was taking, the psychological state of the deceased as well as other factors – information, he said, a pathologist would not ordinarily be privy to – telling the court that these factors would be relevant if it became necessary to call another expert witness to testify in this regard. Dr Botha believed that Saayman could not make a finding on the time of death based on analysis of the stomach contents.

Botha also studied Saayman's report with regard to the location of the wounds on Reeva's body, the location of the bullet holes through the door, the damage to the toilet cubicle walls, as well as police ballistics expert Captain Chris Mangena's report and made a finding on the sequence of the wounds. Botha echoed Mangena's finding that the first shot struck Reeva in the hip, but unlike the police expert's finding, he said that the victim was probably leaning forward at the time it struck her because of the shape and detail of the entry wound – the collar of abrasion. 'The hip wound would have caused immediate instability and she would have fallen,' he said. 'I'm not sure how much pain she felt. Certainly shock and instability.'

The witness said the second shot, which Mangena said missed its target, struck Reeva in the right arm. Botha couldn't say for certain, but he believed that the third shot struck Reeva between the fingers on her left hand and then ricocheted off the back wall.

'I think by this time she had dropped considerably ... she then fell down. She fell against the magazine rack. She certainly didn't fall on top of the magazine rack,' said Botha. 'And it was on this position, while falling against ... as she was going down against the magazine rack, she incurred the last shot to the right side of the head.'

Botha dismissed Mangena's claim, saying he was 'absolutely confident' that the two wounds on Reeva's back were not caused by a bullet that had ricocheted off the back wall, but were in fact caused by the edges of the magazine rack when she fell against it.

This was different to Mangena's finding in two key respects: that the shots to the arm and the head took place when Reeva was seated on top of the magazine rack. Botha disputed this by first noting that one would then have expected blood spatter on the wall above the magazine rack, and secondly claiming that there was no blood on the magazine rack or on the magazines. Botha said the splinter wounds to Reeva's right forearm could not have occurred if she was far away from the door – she must have been closer, not further back where Mangena claimed she was. The defence version was that Reeva sustained the wounds quickly while still close to the door as Oscar pulled the trigger in rapid succession, but on the state's version, there was time – time for Reeva to fall backwards onto the magazine rack, time when one of the bullets missed her, and importantly, time to scream.

Several neighbours told the court they heard screaming during and up until the last shot was fired – could that have been Reeva? But Botha also ruled out the possibility that the deceased could have screamed after being shot. 'I think a combination of shock, panic, fear and possibly pain, I think before she would be in a position to react to that, the remaining bullets would have struck her.'

Lastly, Botha said the teaspoon of urine in Reeva's bladder indicated that it had been emptied shortly before her death, which further supported Oscar's claim that he believed Reeva had got out of bed and gone to the bathroom to relieve herself.

· · ·

The question of Reggie Perumal and his notable absence was first for Gerrie Nel. Did Botha read his fellow defence pathologist's report and how much of it did he use or discard before coming to his findings? Botha responded that while he had read Perumal's report, he did not use it, and relied on Saayman's report to reach his findings because it was far more detailed. This was a significant admission for the state because it raised serious questions over the contents of Perumal's report. It made no sense to hire an expert of that pathologist's calibre, have him in Pretoria to attend the postmortem in person, and then for fellow defence experts not even to consider it.

Nel slowly made his way through the various issues emanating from Saayman's testimony, in particular the angle of the bullet through the door and the wound it would inflict and, of course, the reliability of gastric emptying as an indication of time lapse. Was Saayman's finding that the food was consumed approximately two hours prior to death wrong? he asked Botha.

'I said he might be right, he might be wrong,' explained Botha. 'I cannot say that it was two hours, or think it was five hours.'

Nel was satisfied. 'Good. So you are not saying he is wrong ... He is saying, "I used my experience, I used what I saw, my view is two hours." You say, you do not know if he is wrong, but he could be?' Botha agreed with Nel's summary, which was a boon for the state because it meant Saayman's evidence trumped the defence pathologist.

Nel moved on to the sequence of shots and wounds about which the doctor gave evidence by referring him to the letters marked 'A' to 'D' on the wooden door mounted in court. Botha revealed, to Nel's astonishment, that he had not established which of the lettered holes corresponded to the wounds on Reeva's body because he had not even considered the door. 'But, professor, if you want to give the court your expert opinion on the sequence of wounds, why do you leave out the most important piece of the puzzle?' asked the prosecutor.

'Because, it's obvious,' explained Botha, 'I am not a ballistician. I am a pathologist, I base my opinion on wound ballistics.'

For Nel, it was another tick for his case, but Botha continued, saying that he based his findings on the locations of the wounds on the body – that the hip was the lowest, the arm wound in the middle and the head the highest wound, which showed the sequence of shots being fired at roughly the same height while the body collapsed towards the ground.

'That is if she is in the anatomical position?' Nel was quick in with the question. Botha confirmed that that is how he made his determinations. The standard anatomical position for a human being is standing upright, with the arms to the side and palms of the hands facing forward.

'But not in the toilet, you cannot say that in the toilet, can you?' Botha couldn't. There was no way he could, with the body moving and falling around, that one could make an accurate finding if the anatomical position of the body was assumed when making any findings.

Nel had struck another blow in this evidence. But this did not deter him from pushing just as hard on other issues raised as evidence by other witnesses: Mangena's findings related to the holes in the toilet door, the possible location of Reeva's head and the matter of the blood spatter on the back wall. The latter proved a particular point of interest when Botha was forced to concede that there had indeed been blood on the wall.

This posed another problem for the defence: its expert was giving evidence without properly studying the crime scene photographs. If a judge has to choose which expert's findings carry the most weight, the balance would likely tip in favour of the witness who had taken into account all the available evidence, rather than an expert who had not studied all the available evidence.

But that would not be the end of it. Nel persevered, challenging Botha on a number of issues until he either conceded or at least admitted some uncertainty on his part. This included how the small track-like wounds on Reeva's back came to be inflicted and by what; and the likelihood that the screams came from a wounded Reeva; as well as the sequence and timing of the shots. The doctor accepted Nel's proposition that if Reeva had fled to the toilet and was hiding in fear, she would have been primed and ready and would have screamed when the shots went off.

The prosecutor questioned Botha on his understanding of a double-tap – discharging a firearm twice in quick succession – because it was understood that Oscar had fired two sets of double-taps. Botha confirmed that he was aware that this was part of Oscar's explanation of what happened that night – Roux had put it to previous witnesses.

But when Roux started his re-examination he told the court that while he did ask Mangena about double-tapping, he was told soon after that that was not Oscar's contention, but that he had rather fired in quick succession. 'It was incorrectly put by me,' said Roux. 'So let me correct that.'

How was it possible that an advocate of Roux's calibre would submit as evidence something he had not heard from his client? The fact that this correction had come so late in the trial might suggest that Oscar could have tailored his evidence when faced with the facts presented by the state, which absolutely ruled out his version of a double-tap. Nel raised this issue when the accused took the stand.

The cross-examination of Botha called into question many of the defence expert's findings, which appeared to swing this witness in favour of the prosecution team. When pressed, Botha could not dispute some of the major findings of Saayman, such as the evidence on gastric emptying. This was significant, as the court could accept the state's witness testimony that Reeva was eating at least two hours prior to her death, the time the accused claimed she was in bed next to him. It wasn't the strong start the defence would have wanted, but the anaesthetist who subsequently addressed this issue further for the defence was adamant that no absolute timelines were possible.

• • •

Professor Christina Lundgren is considered a leading expert in the field of anaesthesia, with more than 30 years of experience and hundreds of published journal articles. She was called by the defence to cast doubt on Saayman's findings related to Reeva's last meal.

The professor wore a neat black jacket with a white blouse, her greying hair cut so short it barely touched the garment's collar and she was quietly confident in her delivery. Lundgren explained that an anaesthetist must have a wide-ranging understanding of various physiological and pharmacological factors that might affect patients' health while they are unconscious, so as to ensure their safety. And one of the most important aspects is to establish whether a patient has any food in his or her stomach because one of the most dangerous complications that can occur is for food to be regurgitated and inhaled into the lungs, 'which is an absolute disaster for the patient, hence we are experts in gastric emptying'.

She stated that there are general guidelines – related to clear fluids and solid food – adopted by anaesthetists to reduce the risk of a patient's stomach containing solid food at the time they are put under. Clear fluids can be consumed up to two hours before an operation and it will be expected to have passed through the stomach. 'When it comes to solid foods, the studies are very difficult to perform,' she said, as she listed a host of factors that affect the rate at which food is digested and passed through the stomach.

But there is, however, an accepted guideline. 'We have always felt that four to six hours after a buttered slice of toast and a cup of tea is acceptable time for you to come to theatre and have an empty stomach but, in fact, the anaesthetic literature has not been able to prove that there is no solid food in the stomach after four hours, hence the consensus amongst anaesthesiologists is a minimum of six hours after any solid food, so to ensure and in the hopes that the stomach is empty after that six hour period.'

Lundgren recalled, anecdotally, a patient who had fasted in hospital for at least eight hours prior to a procedure but regurgitated green stomach contents as she was putting the woman to sleep. 'She still had not emptied her stomach and had no good reason not to have emptied her stomach after eight hours, and if I chat to colleagues, they have all had similar experiences. So it is not an exact science, unfortunately,' said the professor, echoing what Botha had said in his evidence.

Roux had provided the expert with Oscar's version – that Reeva had consumed a meal of chicken stir-fry between 7pm and 8pm the evening before she was killed – and asked her to study the contents of Reeva's stomach from the autopsy photographs and offer the court her opinion. 'After six hours of fasting, after this meal, her stomach should probably have been empty but there are so many unknowns about possible factors that could have delayed gastric emptying that one cannot state it as being a fact and I would say it would be purely speculative.' Like Botha, she could not provide a hard-and-fast answer.

Nel was very polite to Lundgren, setting out firstly that he found her evidence balanced and that he did not have many differences of opinion. 'Understand that

I am not fighting with you, I just think that we will have to go through certain things.'

Lundgren had listed numerous factors that might have delayed gastric emptying, from the types of medication a person was taking and whether they smoked cigarettes to underlying medical conditions and their exercise and sleep routine. But she conceded that on the facts before her, related to Reeva, she did not know that any of them existed except that the patient was pre-menopausal.

Lundgren was a tough witness for Nel and was not going to be pushed into conceding on the possibilities presented by the prosecutor that any accurate determination on the time of the last meal could be made by studying the stomach contents. When the prosecutor looked at Oscar's timeline – around eight hours from the time the couple ate between 7 and 8pm and until when she died at about 3am – and the resulting improbability any food would have remained in the stomach, Lundgren offered that the insoluble fibre in the vegetables might have delayed gastric emptying.

But Nel continued to push the witness, referring to Saayman's evidence that even in death the enzymes in the stomach would continue to break down substances. So how was the pathologist able to recognise food if it had been in the stomach for so long? 'I am a clinician, I deal with live patients and I have immense respect for Professor Saayman, who is a forensic pathologist and his patients are deceased. So I am not a forensic pathologist and I do not wish to comment,' Lundgren said.

Saayman had inserted a disclaimer in his report when he acknowledged that gastric emptying is an inexact science, noting on his finding that 'if there is any substantive evidence to the contrary, that must be weighed up by the court and ultimately, it will be the prerogative of the court to make that decision'.

'Do you agree with that?' asked Nel, attempting to force the witness into a confrontational stance with the state's witness. 'Is there anything that you see that would say the court should not take that into account?'

But Lundgren wasn't biting, opting for a diplomatic course of action and referring the court to the forensic pathology literature already submitted that questions the reliability of using gastric emptying as a measure. 'I am not prepared to comment on what Professor Saayman's opinion is. It is as it stands, however, I have been given forensic pathology evidence to read and there it states quite categorically that it is not a good idea to judge the time of the last meal from the stomach contents.'

The cross-examination came full circle when Nel referred back to Lundgren's own report in which she stated, based on the available evidence that included the meal of chicken stir-fry, that 'in the ideal world, after six hours of fasting, after this meal her stomach should probably have been empty'. With Lundgren unable to identify any of the factors she listed as affecting gastric emptying being present in this case, Nel was satisfied he had done enough with this witness to ensure Saayman's evidence remained persuasive.

It would be up to Judge Masipa to decide whether to accept the expert witnesses' testimony on gastric emptying – this could be a crucial element in deciding whether or not Oscar and Reeva were awake in the hours before the shooting and whether an argument between the couple possibly led to the incident or not.

The Door

Exactly three weeks after the shooting, on 7 March 2013, a white body bag arrived at the office of police ballistics expert Chris Mangena. It had been dispatched by the Case Administration Section of the Forensic Science Laboratory in Pretoria. Mangena, a captain attached to the Ballistics Unit since 1995, has worked on nearly 6000 cases over the past two decades.

Mangena broke the red seal marked '30002', pulling apart the two zippers to reveal the item to be studied. It contained 'One damaged 227x79 cm Wooden Door' – the meranti door from Oscar Pistorius's bathroom through which the athlete had shot and killed Reeva Steenkamp.

The door had taken an interesting journey from the Paralympic superstar's house in Silver Woods to Mangena's office – one that would cause some consternation and raise many eyebrows. It also, arguably, led to the resignation of Colonel Schoombie van Rensburg, the station commander at the Boschkop police station (a claim he denies), which was handling the murder investigation. It is the type of incident that occurs occasionally in South Africa, where the quality and standard of police forensics can be dubious as a result of high case loads and substantial backlogs.

On the day after the shooting, Colonel Van Rensburg returned to Oscar's house. The atmosphere was far calmer than the previous morning when he had been the first police officer to arrive following the shooting. He had already had to deal with a watch being stolen from the crime scene and now Van Rensburg had been informed that, amid the media frenzy, some newspapers were willing to pay up to R60 000 for a photograph of the door. He knew that the door had to be removed from the scene immediately.

'We decided to take it down,' Van Rensburg told the trial court a year later. 'The door is the most valuable evidence, exhibit on the scene, because it indicated the shooting holes. The deceased was behind this door when she was shot. So that was the main reason … it had to be seized. But when we received the information on the Friday, we decided we would do it immediately.'

In a scene out of a keystone cop sitcom, the officers set about trying to find packaging, and a form of transport that would be big enough to hold the door. 'It is a very big … big door, as you see,' explained the station commander. 'So we made arrangements that we take body bags. Now I personally drive to Bronkhorstspruit and got body bags, different sizes of the body bags and then only the biggest body bag the door could fit in.'

Lieutenant-Colonel Frans van der Merwe from Forensic Services and police photographer Warrant Officer Bennie van Staden set about taking down the door. There might have been a concern about whether or not the officers would have been able to reconstruct the exhibit once it had been removed, but Van Rensburg was confident it would be easy to reassemble with a screwdriver. They took down the door and sealed it in the body bag with official seals.

Once they had carried the bag outside the house, the next problem was trying to fit the door into a police car. The men had to call in a long-wheel-base vehicle to fit the door into the back, but then they encountered another concern. The loose panels of the door had shifted and the officers were concerned they would rip the body bag, which would mean that the evidence could be contaminated. Securing this crucial piece of evidence was proving to be a real headache for Van Rensburg.

A police constable drove the door to the Boschkop police station where it was handed in to what is known as the SAP13, where exhibits for all investigations are booked and held. Usual practice at Boschkop is for the bigger exhibits to be kept in the charge office, which is a temporary facility. However, on that Friday afternoon, the officers could not fit the exhibit in and decided to leave it standing in the passage of the charge office. When the station commander arrived back at his office, he found the door, still sealed, leaning against the wall in the passage. According to 'Standing Orders', it is the responsibility of the station commander to safeguard the property and the exhibits. So Van Rensburg signed for the door and took the unusual step of choosing to keep it in his office. He was quizzed about this decision when on the stand during the murder trial.

'Now I know someone will ask the question, why do you take it to your office. The first thing about the office is it is secured. There is security … I am the only person that had a key to the room … It was kept there in my office the whole weekend.'

The arrangement was that on the Monday, Warrant Officer Van Staden and Lieutenant-Colonel van der Merwe would collect the exhibit and hand it in at Forensic Services. But the investigating team got caught up in the bail application and before they realised, more than two weeks had passed.

'Now during this period this door was kept in my office. I was the only person in control of that office. No meeting was held during that period in that office. If someone come and see me I close the door, I lock the door and I went to another office and have a conversation with that person. Also … there was only two faxes on the station. One fax is in my office. Sometimes the people come and they want to fax something. I took that faxes and I fax it myself. So nobody else did tamper with that evidence …' explained Van Rensburg to the court.

However, the body bag did not stay sealed the entire time it sat in the office. On 18 February, the defence forensic team requested to see the door. Private ballistics expert Wollie Wolmarans arrived at Boschkop along with a photographer, and in the presence of the investigating officer Hilton Botha, the station commander broke open the seal and drew back the body bag to allow them to see the exhibit. Says Van Rensburg:

> We open and we let it … the door stand upright and we open as far as possible that they can see it. There was splinters, small splinters that was falling out at one corner. So I picked that splinters up with hand gloves and I put it back on the body bag and then they started taking photos. Then the request was that we have to take it out, because they want to see the height of the bullets … ag, what the holes is and I said: 'No, I am not going to take out this thing.'
>
> Actually they was agitated with me, they said then there is no use that they come here and see this thing. So I say, sorry that is the only allowance that I am going to make for him, to see the door and then we sealed the door … ag we sealed the bag again and we sealed it with another seal … and then it was taken back into my office, and again lie in front of my desk.

Van Rensburg kept the door until he handed it over to the photographer Warrant Officer Van Staden. The station commander resigned from the police service several months later, leading to media speculation he had been pushed out because of the bungling of the crime scene and the decision to keep this crucial piece of evidence in his office. However, Van Rensburg insisted both to the press and in court that he had left to follow his passion, coaching sport.

The door was held at Forensic Services after it had been collected, along with the Lazer cricket bat, by Van Staden. He photographed the exhibits before sending them off for analysis.

• • •

And so it came to be that the body bag containing the meranti wood arrived at Captain Mangena's office.

Having broken the seal on the body bag, the captain noticed that the door was in pieces, the panels knocked out by Oscar using the cricket bat were loose inside the bag, along with the shards and splinters collected from the crime scene. The package had arrived with an instruction to investigate (1) the bullet trajectory; and (2) terminal ballistics.

Standing the outer frame of the door against a gun safe in his office, Mangena slid the panels into position – only a narrow sliver of wood broken from the far right panel was missing. There was still blood on the door, as well as what appeared to be footprints, believed to be from a police officer's boot. These footprints were a focus during the cross-examination of several state witnesses as the defence attempted to prove that the crime scene had been contaminated.

Mangena took the measurements of the door: 227x79 centimetres. He then inspected it for spent propellant powder particles – burnt gunpowder – but couldn't find any. This could have provided clarity on how close the shooter was to the door when he pulled the trigger.

Vertically, the door was divided by a single horizontal wooden beam at its bottom third. The handle was situated to the right and located about halfway between the top and bottom of the structure. Four bullet holes peppered the horizontal region between the door handle and the wooden dividing bar – Mangena marked them from left, 'A', 'B', 'C' and 'D', and measured their distance from the floor, before noting them down for his report:

A – 93.5cm
B – 104.3cm
C – 99.4cm
D – 97.3cm

The front of the door, which would have been facing Oscar, displayed clean entry marks – near-perfect little round holes. The inside of the holes appeared to be scorched, perhaps darkened by the transfer of particles from the bullets fired through it. The other side of the door, facing inside the cubicle where Reeva was positioned, presented an entirely different pattern – irregular splintered sections of wood were missing, up to three times bigger than the holes on the front. Fine splinters from these holes were picked up by the projectile passing through the wood and had become imbedded in Reeva's skin, as noted in the pathologist's report.

This was as much as could be done in the office. The real work for Mangena would be at the crime scene. The following day Mangena met photographer Bennie van Staden at the house to take him through the crime scene and assist him with photographs, as requested by the investigating officer Mike van Aardt. They weren't alone – Oscar's private forensics experts Wollie Wolmarans and Jannie 'Wessie' van der Westhuizen were there to monitor the investigation for the defence. Other members of the investigating team, blood spatter expert Colonel Ian van der Nest and forensics expert Colonel Gerhard Vermeulen, were also present.

Mangena and Van Staden carried the door inside the house and up the stairs following the blood spatter trail on the floor, into Oscar's bedroom, down the cupboard-lined passage and into the bathroom. The sticky bright red spatter and pools of blood of three weeks earlier had turned a dark red, almost black in places, and had coagulated, bonding with the tiles and seeping into the grouting. The pile of bloodstained towels and the cricket bat were gone – packed into evidence bags weeks earlier. The two officers had with them the piece of evidence that had separated Oscar from Reeva, and now they had to put it back in place. Vermeulen helped the men, using the same screws that originally held the door in position.

'The first time the door was hung out of position on the first attempt and the door couldn't close. A millimetre that way or that way and that trajectory won't be right again. Why was this door removed? They say it's for security purposes, but I've got my doubts. They don't want us to see it,' a member of the defence team told us.

Mangena then began the process of meticulously marking out the scene, starting with the four bullet holes through the door, and again measuring their height from the floor. Van Staden followed his every move with a click of the camera to document the process. With the door hinged and open, peering into the small cubicle Mangena noticed marks in the far right corner. Ricochet marks, he thought. From left to right, he marked them 'E' and 'F', which he believed were corresponding marks.

In court, Mangena explained his finding: 'The bullet ricocheted on the first wall marked "E", he said. 'And it deflected to another wall on that side. So creating both holes.' He also noted down the heights of each mark:

E – 89cm
F – 87.5cm

Another mark on the wall, which Mangena tagged as 'G', bore traces of lead – as if the projectile had fractured after hitting an object and losing a lot of its momentum. 'It did not break the tile. It only left traces of it on the tile,' the ballistics expert explained to the court.

With the bullet holes and ricochet locations marked out, Mangena pushed yellow steel rods with a near-perfect 9 mm diameter through the holes in the door – the path of the bullets were thus mapped in 3D. Inside the cubicle, the four rods projected towards the toilet bowl leaving very little place to hide. By extending the rod through hole marked 'B', Mangena matched the trajectory to the ricochet mark 'E' on the wall – the only bullet that missed its target. Using his trusty EVI-PAQ level and angle finder – an industry standard in forensic circles – Mangena determined that the bullets travelled at a downward 5- to 6-degree angle. Next he turned to his laser, mounted on a sturdy Manfrotto Tripod. By lining up the beam of red light with the mark 'E', through mark 'B', and adjusting the position and height of the laser, Mangena placed the shooter at the entrance to the bathroom – 220 centimetres from the door. With the blinds and door closed, Van Staden stood on the toilet seat to take a photograph looking down – the thin beam of light passed through the door, striking the point where Mangena believed a bullet ricocheted.

Having gathered all the information he could from the crime scene, Mangena and the other officers removed the door from its hinges, packed it back into the body bag and took it to the laboratory for further examinations.

Meanwhile, Mangena had also been sent a disk containing all of the crime scene photos and pictures from the postmortem that had been captured by Van Staden. He gave special attention to images of the spent cartridge cases and bullet fragments and of Reeva's vest showing the holes where bullets had struck her. He needed to understand what the crime scene looked like when it was fresh, as he would explain to the trial court.

'When you are reconstructing the crime scene, you have to get the idea of the whole crime scene, how the crime scene was positioned,' he said. 'If there are any chairs, if there is any furniture, anything that can be moved in the crime scene which might have a role in reconstructing the crime scene.'

Absent from the crime scene on the day of the investigation was the small wooden magazine rack, located to the right of the toilet bowl when facing it. The captain analysed pictures of the locations of the spent cartridges – three in the bathroom, one in the passage – and the position of bullet fragments inside the cubicle.

Key to reconstructing the scene is knowing the location of the injuries sustained by the deceased – Mangena pored over the autopsy photos. He noted the tissue and bone fragments on Reeva's black top, the bruises on her back and chest, as well as the height from her heel and location of the hip, head, elbow and finger wounds. He then gathered the measurements taken of Oscar at Ergonomics Technologies, and was ready to put it all together to create the scene.

Using his 19 years of experience in the Ballistics Unit of the police, Mangena ruled out the possibility that Reeva was sitting on the toilet when the first shot was fired – the holes through the door were too low for them to have struck her in the hip. Reeva was standing upright and against the door, facing it, when the first bullet – in a downward trajectory – passed through point 'A' on the door, 93.5 centimetres high, and struck her on the right hip, 93 centimetres from her heel. The match-up of hole to wound meant this had to be the first shot – it entered her pelvic area and shattered the hipbone, making it impossible to stand.

She fell backwards, but not on to the floor – the height of the remaining holes through the door could not account for the wound to Reeva's elbow; instead, she collapsed on to the magazine rack in a seated position.

Oscar fired the second shot, the bullet passing through point 'B' on the door, missing Reeva but striking points 'E' and 'F' on the wall above her head, breaking into fragments before striking the critically wounded woman on her back and causing the bruises noted in the autopsy. From there, the lead core bounced off her back and into the toilet bowl.

He pulled the trigger for a third time. Mangena could not establish whether this marked point 'C' or 'D' on the door, but was confident it caused the wound to Reeva's right elbow. In the seated position on the magazine rack, he believed Reeva had her arms up covering her head in a defensive position – the height of her elbows in this position corresponded with the height of the bullets through the door at a downward trajectory. During his testimony in court, Mangena vividly demonstrated how Reeva would have been holding her arms wrapped over her head, cowering away from the shots piercing holes through the door as she sat slumped down on the magazine rack.

The third bullet passed through the door, then through Reeva's upper arm, where it shattered the bone, exited the underside of the upper arm and spattered tissue and bone fragments on to her vest. The shards of steel that ripped though her flesh had spent a significant amount of their energy and were left with only enough momentum to cause the bruises below her right breast.

Oscar then pulled the trigger for the last time. Mangena believed that with the devastating wound to her right arm, making the limb unusable, Reeva just had her left arm and hand to try to protect herself. With her left hand on top of her head and cowering with her head in a forward position, the last bullet tore through the soft tissue between her index and middle finger, which was up against her head, before striking the skull. The projectile fragmented, sending part of it into her brain while another piece exited a few centimetres further back, before hitting the wall, mark 'G'.

In Mangena's view, that last shot caused the victim to collapse – her head coming to rest on the toilet bowl and her body wedged between the toilet and magazine rack. The pool of blood on the floor must have been caused by her hip and elbow wounds, and bloodstains on the toilet seat and inside the bowl confirmed this.

This sequence of events was important for the state. After sustaining the first wound to her hip, and as she collapsed backwards and the second bullet was fired and missed, did Reeva scream? The pathologist, Professor Saayman, testified that after sustaining a wound of this nature, it would be abnormal not to scream. And if Reeva did scream, why did Oscar continue firing? Is this the screaming neighbours heard when they woke up in the dead of night?

Mangena bought three replica doors to test fire the 9 mm Black Talon ammunition as he understood that this was the ammunition used by the athlete.

Mangena wanted to establish just how far Oscar was standing from the door when he opened fire and he knew that the evidence would tell him. When a firearm is discharged, not all gunpowder particles inside the cartridge are ignited. The partially burnt and unburnt particles travel down the barrel of the gun and exit the muzzle at high speed, embedding on items within a certain range.

Starting at a distance of 10 centimetres, the captain fired shots at test sheets of paper and worked his way back to 60 centimetres – in all instances, propellant particles were discovered on the paper. He then moved back to 1 metre away – and no particles could be detected. This put Oscar no closer than 60 centimetres to the door when he pulled the trigger – the furthest he could go back was against the wall at the entrance to the bathroom. Mangena could make no finding on the location of the spent cartridges – test firing with this ammunition and Oscar's firearm provided such varying results there was nothing conclusive to be drawn. During a deflection test – to see how much the bullet's trajectory changes when fired through the door – the captain found that the most deflection was 3 degrees, which is very little. Referring to his notes and the findings of the laser trajectory test at the crime scene, and comparing them to Oscar's measurements, particularly his shoulder height without his prosthetic legs fitted, Mangena concluded that Oscar was on his stumps when he pulled the trigger.

Having completed his investigation, Mangena wrote his report, coming to this conclusion as 'the best possible and probable explanation':

> *The deceased was initially upright behind the closed door inside the toilet area. She sustained a penetrating wound to the right side of her hip. She then assumed an intermediate seated/semi seated position where she then received further wounds and then assumed the position next to the toilet seat. The shooter was most likely not wearing his prosthetic legs and fired from a distance greater than 60 cm from the toilet door.*

Captain Mangena was the 16th witness to take the stand for the prosecution, giving his testimony on 18 March 2014. He had attended every day of the proceedings and sat amongst the rest of the experts behind the prosecution team. His shaved head gleamed light off it and he sported a neatly trimmed moustache. On the day he took the stand, he wore his regular dark suit, a light-blue shirt and white tie. His testimony was crucial for the state's case.

The door was what separated Reeva from Oscar. It was what prevented the shooter from identifying his target. A study of the bullet holes by an expert such as Mangena would provide the state with the location of the shooter as well as where the victim was positioned as the bullets passed through the timber. This evidence would present a timeline of Reeva's last moments – from which bullet struck her first, to the one that ultimately led to her death. Prosecutor Gerrie Nel led the expert through his evidence, taking the court back to 7 March 2013 when he received the door and the instruction to investigate.

Over 12 court days, Barry Roux had established himself as a fierce cross-examiner with each state witness before Mangena experiencing the sharp end of his skill. But the ballistics expert was ready for Roux and remained resolute and firm in the face of a barrage of questions. He refused to be sucked in to the silk's game and repeatedly responded with a firm 'I disagree' to Roux's 'I put it to you'.

Roux fired off questions at the ballistics expert on whether he understood the term 'douple-tap' – a process whereby a shooter fires two shots in quick succession. Of course Mangena knew what this meant; he shoots at competition level and is able to shoot at this speed himself. Roux suggested that this was what Oscar claimed to have done. 'That is the version of the accused. It was two double-taps,' said Roux, revealing an element of his case yet to be made public.

There was a frown from the officer in the dock. 'I tend to disagree with that.' He had just spent the last hour explaining how Reeva was shot in the hip, and how she fell back before being struck by two more bullets. If the shooter had in fact fired a double-tap, Reeva would have been struck twice in the hip area with the holes closer together. Mangena was having none of it. He explained himself once again to the court.

The advocate was quick to refer to Dr Stipp's evidence, saying that this supported the notion of a double-tap. Mangena did not dispute this, but was again adamant that because of the different locations of the wounds, there had been a break – although he couldn't say how long – between the first and second shots. This tied in with Michelle Burger's evidence of hearing a bang followed by three further bangs: Bang. Bang, bang, bang. Rather than Bang, bang. Bang, bang.

In a dramatic turn later in the trial, when Nel was cross-examining the defence team's first witness, Roux surprisingly withdrew the claim that Oscar had fired two double-taps. He said that his client had corrected him, but this was never put to the court. The question Nel raised with the accused during his own testimony was where Roux had come up with the term 'double-tap', if his client did not provide it to him?

> Nel: *It was definitely not two double-taps?*
> Accused: *That is correct, M'Lady.*
> Nel: *Why would Mr Roux think and put to Captain Mangena that you fired two double-taps?*
> Accused: *I am not sure, M'Lady. But that is what he put to Mr Mangena and in the first break I corrected him and said to him that it was not a double-tap.*

Roux moved on to the angle at which the bullet hit the hip wound, referring to the shape of the wound, and suggested that that was not a straight-on wound, but rather at an angle. Again, Mangena disagreed, adding that the shape of the wound could have been caused by a misshapen bullet having passed through the door.

Mangena did, however, admit to not testing the magazine rack against the wounds on Reeva's back. Roux said defence experts – Roger Dixon and Wollie Wolmarans – would testify that she fell against it, causing the bruises on her back. Mangena also did not conduct a proximity test to establish exactly how far the victim's arm was from the door when it was perforated by the splinters, nor a test to establish the spread of the splinters. But he remained confident that such tests were irrelevant to his findings.

Roux pressed the witness on this. 'I have not done the tests,' said Roux. 'It will be the evidence of the ballistic experts that the right arm was in close proximity of the door.' The defence wanted to show that it was the right side of Reeva's body that was angled towards the door. This would allow them to suggest that she was walking out of the toilet when Oscar began shooting, rather than hiding away in the cubicle. Barely two weeks after Roux told the court this, the defence team dispatched its own expert, Wolmarans, to conduct this very test.

Once the trial was concluded, Wolmarans would highlight that he felt this was the biggest mistake of Mangena's evidence. 'The splinter test is in my opinion very essential in giving an opinion on what the position in the toilet was at the time of the shooting. He just ignored it. He had one year to do it and all the exhibits was in his possession all the time. Including the firearm in question,' Wolmarans told us.

'Roux cross-examined him on the splinters and he testified that it is his experience. He never conducted the test but he disagreed. Even with all the experience in the world you will conduct test to confirm your findings. Every case is unique and you cannot depend on your experience. The Black Talon is a unique type of ammunition and the door is solid meranti wood, and the shot was fired through the door at an angle. How he can be so sure that she was not near the door without proper testing? It is totally unacceptable,' argued Wolmarans.

However, Mangena did address this during his time on the stand: 'In that position I am of the opinion it was more than one shot. Those splinters are not only here, if you can look at the arm also, there is also some marks on the splinters. Now these ones on the lower arm, where do they come from if she was in this position and the bullet came … then does it mean she was in the position but the palm has to be in front of the body, when this splinters … and the closer you get to that, the more groupings of those splinters will be there. The further away you move from the door, they more spreading, they start to open up,' said the state ballistic expert.

The defence counsel also zeroed in on why the state had claimed at the bail hearing that Oscar had fired the shots while standing 1.5 metres from the door and was wearing his prosthetics at the time. The state had done a complete about-turn on this evidence and Roux wanted to know why. He suggested that this evidence had been cooked up during the bail application in order to bolster a case of premeditated murder. Mangena, however, could shed no light on this as he said he didn't know. Roux also worked to try to force Mangena to confirm that a cricket bat hitting wood sounds like gunshots, but Mangena wouldn't be drawn on this, insisting that he was not a sound expert.

There was a confidence to Mangena not seen in any of the other witnesses. And, despite Roux's efforts, he refused to budge. The advocate put his version to the witness, further proposing that the officer's interpretation of events could be wrong.

'I will not change my theory,' said Mangena. 'That is how I could determine the shots.'

The Bat

On the morning the state's second expert witness was expected to testify, word reached the court's corridors that the prosecution team had a little surprise planned for the day. Once the courtroom doors were opened, it immediately became clear what this was: a 1:1 scale model of the toilet cubicle where Reeva was shot had been constructed inside the courtroom. The claustrophobic 1.14x1.4 metre dimensions accurately demonstrated how she had no place to hide. White chipboard frames made up the walls, which extended around the doorframe – the actual door from the crime scene had been erected in the frame. A light-coloured wooden brace on the inside of the door held in place the shattered panels, smashed out a year earlier by the accused. A toilet, similar to the one at Oscar's house, had been placed inside the cubicle, as well as a magazine rack.

The exhibit certainly caught Oscar's attention – he spent some time before proceedings started inspecting it closely, leaning forward with his head close to the bullet holes, peering on the inside and then outside as if he were tracking the projectile's trajectories.

The cricket bat also made its first appearance in the courtroom several days before it was formally submitted as an exhibit. Usually carried by the investigating officer Mike van Aardt, it was wrapped in a large clear, blue-printed police forensics bag. It caused whispers in the gallery amongst journalists who for the first time got sight of the object they'd all heard about.

The sporting implement emerged in some reports after the shooting, with allegations that Oscar had apparently used the bat not only to bash down the toilet door, but also to beat Reeva. Some British tabloid press reported that Reeva's family had been told her skull had been fractured after being struck by the bat.

But pathologist Gert Saayman confirmed during his testimony that it had been the bullet that struck her head that had caused the skull fracturing, and there were no signs of blunt force trauma, rubbishing these initial speculative reports.

The English willow Lazer cricket bat was found face down in the bathroom with drops of blood and spatter across its spine. It was positioned to the right of where Reeva would have been lying – if one entered the bathroom – and was close to the basins and cupboards. While crime scene photos showed it had a perished yellow rubber handle fitted to it, in police investigation photos and in court, this grip was no longer present. The wooden face displayed the signatures of 12 cricketers – when it was presented in court, former Proteas batsman Herschelle Gibbs remarked on Twitter that he'd identified his own signature:

> Just saw my signature on the bat used by the accused on oscar trial… lol
> #neveradullmoment

Oscar's own name was written in black marker on the top-left side of the bat. The bat hadn't appeared to have seen much cricket action, and was probably used with a tennis ball or solely as an ornamental piece for its signatures. Oscar explained that he used it to bolster security in his room because he placed it between the sunglasses rack and his door as a stop if someone was able to break the door lock, which he locked every night.

The police's expert in this field of analysis, Colonel Gerhard Vermeulen, focused on three main marks – one on the bat itself and another two on the door, which he believed illustrated that Oscar was on his stumps at the time he struck the door with the bat. The mark on the bat, if looking at its face, was on the bottom right-hand corner: a set of etched-in lines starting in the midline of the bottom of the bat and going up at a 45-degree angle towards the right side of the bat. The mark on the door was about 150 centimetres from the ground, while the other was an actual hole through the door where the bat pierced through.

The defence did not dispute that the door was struck with the bat, but argued that their client was on his prosthetic legs when he did the hitting. This was the major discrepancy around the bat – the defence argued Oscar had already put his prostheses on when he hit the door, but the state insisted he was still on his stumps. This was important as it spoke to the timeline of Oscar's version of events and whether he would have indeed had time to put on his prosthetic legs. What did the evidence say?

Three weeks after the shooting, on 7 March 2013, Vermeulen received the instruction from his commander to investigate the Oscar case, and a day later he was at the crime scene, together with Mangena, Van der Nest and Van Aardt. The defence's firearms expert Wollie Wolmarans was also there. Vermeulen, the commander of the Material Analysis subsection at the police's Forensic Science Laboratory in Pretoria, with nearly 30 years' experience, was tasked to investigate the bat and the door as well as the steel plate covering the inspection hole on the bath. On 26 April the metal plate and the bat arrived at Vermeulen's office in sealed plastic evidence bags.

Although Vermeulen was tasked with studying the steel plate soon after the shooting, its existence astonishingly remained out of media reports until the trial. Information and pictures of the steel plate came as a shock to the court – it had become public knowledge that police discovered the broken door and the cricket bat in the bathroom, but not this plate. The shiny square piece of metal, measuring about 30 centimetres on each side, is used to cover a hole in the tiled brick structure that supports the bath and gives a plumber access to the drainpipes. If one were standing close to the toilet door, facing it, the plate would be located to the back and left at about ankle height. It appeared as if the plate had been kicked, but after Vermeulen's evidence it didn't feature again, with no explanation from Oscar's team, nor Nel asking for one. Vermeulen found that the steel plate had been bent after being struck by a blunt object, or a blunt object falling against it – and hard enough to have caused a faint vertical scratch – but he could not determine the type of object used.

On 30 April 2013 Vermeulen received a call from Mangena asking him to join him at the Forensic Science Lab to inspect the door. Taking a closer look, he identified two distinct marks – the compressed wood at an angle above the door handle, and a mark that was more like a hole through the door. Photographs were taken of this process and, during the trial, the album marked 'Exhibit Y' contained 16 photos, mostly of Vermeulen conducting tests in what appeared to be a storeroom, where numerous shelves and items in boxes could be seen packed neatly away. The panels in the door were being crudely held in place with clear tape, and while Vermeulen wielded the bat, Mangena's hand could be seen holding up a measuring tape for the record.

Nearly a year after conducting these tests, while giving his evidence to the trial court, the investigator asked Judge Masipa if he could take off his jacket in court to demonstrate. Vermeulen wanted to replicate the April tests, as depicted in the photos taken at the Forensic Science Lab. He wanted to demonstrate how he matched up the various marks. 'The investigation revealed that the cricket bat actually made a physical match with the marks, which is of undisputable confirmation that the bat was used to bash the door,' said Vermeulen. It was, however, never in dispute that Oscar had used the bat to break down the door.

Incongruously dressed in his suit pants and tie, Vermeulen stood in front of the wooden panels, slightly to the right so as not to obscure the judge's view, holding the bat with both his hands against the door. It was a match. He then grabbed the bat by the handle and positioned himself where the person wielding it – and made the mark – would have been located, his left shoulder close to the door, but his arms slightly lowered. When Nel asked him to perform a mock swing at the door, it was clear from the demonstration that the bat would have struck the door a lot higher, approximately 1.85 metres high, but the mark on the door was about 1.53 metres high. The state would argue that for Oscar to have made that mark on the door, he would have had to have been on his stumps.

Nel asked the officer to position the bat against the mark, and questioned him about his body position and posture. 'I would have been in an uncomfortable position, not a natural position,' said Vermeulen. 'Even if I stood further away from the door, it would have been in a very uncomfortable and unnatural position for me.'

Vermeulen then pulled out a small stool, and balanced on it with his knees. This put him at approximately the same shoulder height as the accused on his stumps, and he swung the bat again. This time it matched up with the first mark on the door.

The second mark on the door saw the bat break through the wood, smashing out a large splinter, and becoming wedged between the panels – scratch marks on either side of the bat's toe confirmed this. He compared the marks and the way the bat fitted into the door to a nail being driven into a piece of wood – if you pull that nail out of the wood, it's difficult to merely just push it back in because the force of the hammer actually displaces and expands the wood. Vermeulen suggested that the bat was jammed through the door in this way.

But he insisted that for a person to have caused such damage to the bat and door, he would have been in a different position. Vermeulen once again gripped the bat by its handle with its face to his left, but this time stood in front of the door and facing it. He pulled his arms up over his right shoulder and whipped them forward as if he were attacking – the wooden corner of the improvised ram slotted snugly into the gaping crack in the door. Another match, but, like before, he said he had to be in an unnatural position to make the mark, except when he was lowered to about Oscar's shoulder height.

Vermeulen believed that while the bat was slotted through the crack, it was twisted to break the panels away. This would have allowed Oscar to pull away the other panels and peer inside to where Reeva was lying.

It was important for Vermeulen to demonstrate that a person in two different positions caused the two marks, and he further believed that whoever had caused them had a significantly lower shoulder height – like the accused without his prosthetic legs fitted.

Vermeulen told the court that apart from the two marks about which he had testified, there was only one other mark that drew his attention. That mark was located just below the door handle, but he could not confirm that the cricket bat or any other item had caused it. 'It seems like it is a kind of a shaving or a mark that was caused by an object going kind of in line with the door, as opposed to a perpendicular direction. It is very difficult to confirm that it is in fact one hundred per cent what happened there. The other characteristic of that mark is that it is quite low, low down on the door, which is not a normal position where I would suspect a mark to be caused by a cricket bat, if someone wanted to break open the door,' he said.

This remark would come back to haunt the policeman during cross-examination.

• • •

During the adjournment, Advocate Barry Roux picked up the bat and, while surrounded by his own expert Wollie Wolmarans, attorney Brian Webber and Oscar, he swung it at the door but from various positions and different angles. Oscar was guiding his advocate, explaining how he wielded the bat that morning when he attacked the door, while Wolmarans directed the meeting's attention to a mark on the door, higher than those on which Vermeulen had concentrated. Oscar had been taking notes throughout the morning as Vermeulen was testifying. At one point he was seen folding a piece of paper that had a stick figure drawn on it, which appeared to be holding a bat standing in front of a door.

Roux wasted no time going for the credibility of the witness and the reliability of his tests. 'Colonel, are you a certified tool mark examiner?'

Vermeulen revealed he was not, but said he had used a technique to obtain the match between the bat and the marks on the door as a tool mark examiner would.

'Have you done microscopic imaging of the mark on the door?'

He had not.

Roux quickly turned to the experiments he had been conducting during the adjournment, putting it to Vermeulen that he could replicate the mark on the door by standing in different body positions, using different shoulder turns and at varying distances from the door. The point Roux was making was that a person did not have to be in this 'natural' or 'comfortable' position – as described by the police officer – in order to replicate the mark on the door.

Roux asked Vermeulen once again to take the bat and wield it in front of the door as he had done earlier, but this time he should be down on his knees. The expert obliged. 'Now do me a favour and lift your feet,' instructed Roux.

Down on his knees with the bat in his hands, Vermeulen lifted his feet, which were behind him, as if to precariously balance solely on his kneecaps. He immediately lost his balance and had to return his feet to the floor. Roux had attempted to demonstrate his client's inability to maintain his balance when on his stumps.

'Could you hit the door with the bat?' he asked, seemingly satisfied his demonstration went well to prove his point.

Vermeulen wasn't biting. 'Well, I do not know whether I would be able to do it if I grew up without legs.'

'Would you want to try again?' urged Roux.

'The other argument is also valid, M'Lady, if he had enough balance to fire a firearm, then I would suspect that he would have enough balance to hit a door with a cricket bat.'

Vermeulen declined to replicate the experiment proposed by the defence advocate, insisting that he was not used to walking on his knees; whereas the accused had spent a lifetime on his stumps. (Oscar later testified that when he fired the shots his back was against the bathroom wall, which would have provided him with stability.)

Roux interrogated Vermeulen's description and findings based on the assumption that the person hitting the door was in a 'natural position', or in the 'expected position', and to demonstrate his point, positioned the officer in front of the door in various positions. The policeman thus spent the morning taking the three or four steps between the witness box and door, wielding the bat on instruction from the defence advocate as he interrogated his findings.

In the varying positions – with his knees slightly bent, or his back bent forward – he had to concede that the bat did in fact match up to the mark, but he would always insist that this was in an unnatural position. But it raised the question – an unnatural position for whom? Could he speak for Oscar? Roux pointed out that with the policeman's additional weight and shortness, he had a different physique to the accused.

The state forensic analyst agreed with the defence that the door had been intact when it was shot – the bullets first, then the bat – which he confirmed by analysis of the damage. This is explained by a crack down one of the panels through bullet hole 'D'. The crack enters the hole at the top to the right and continues out the bottom left. Vermeulen explained that the crack would have carried on in a straight line down the grain of the wood if the hole had not been there. Wolmarans also later supported this theory.

This confirmed the defence's sequence of events – that Oscar first fired the shots through the door before bashing it down with the cricket bat.

True to form, Roux went on to direct his attack to police process, an age-old tactic of defence advocates. Invariably, questions will be raised during a criminal trial about whether or not police acted according to protocol; did they retain the integrity of the crime scene and properly preserve the exhibits?

Roux then asked about the door, telling the court that he would produce photographs that showed additional marks on the door that were not present on the day of the shooting, like the shoe prints. The unmistakable tread of boots – like those worn by police officers – had been trampled along the two centre panels of the door. It appeared as if these were caused by the fine dust kicked up from the tile grouting when the tiles fell off the back wall. The boots had perhaps transferred the dust on to the meranti wood. This would in all likelihood have happened on the crime scene when the panels were still lying around the bathroom. This suggested yet again carelessness and unprofessionalism on the part of the police, and Roux made a meal of it.

The defence advocate attacked every detail of Vermeulen's investigation in an attempt to establish any kind of reasonable doubt, such as the slight angle at which the door was leaned up against a cabinet in the labs on the test day could have altered the findings, and that Vermeulen did not compare photos of the door on the day of the shooting to the door when he was studying it.

The expert could not explain where the large splinters from the section broken out by the cricket bat had disappeared to. Vermeulen believed they were unaccounted for, possibly not collected at the scene. He explained that he did not seize the door at the crime scene on the day of the shooting; he was only handed the case weeks later, but he conceded that he never asked about the splinters because they were not relevant to his investigation. Roux presented a statement and photos to the court from a lieutenant-colonel at the Forensic Science Lab's trace analysis section who had, in fact, studied and compiled a report on the splinters that Vermeulen claimed he could not locate. Vermeulen insisted that the first time he had seen the splinters was in court.

To illustrate his point, Roux referred to the photos of Vermeulen and Mangena conducting the tests on the door – photo 480 in the albums – and asked the man to describe what he saw. The screens in the courtrooms came to life and showed a picture of Vermeulen's arm holding the bat against the door, while Mangena, wearing blue gloves, held a tape measure against it.

But there was something else of significance. 'Oh,' exclaimed Vermeulen, 'there are some pieces of wood next to that ...'

And there they were, in plain sight. The large splinters from the crack in the door had been removed from the body bag in which the door was being kept, and placed on top of the crumpled-up bag as the men inspected the door. For Roux it was all about testing the competencies of the experts and the thoroughness of their investigation in order to show the court that there could be doubt about their findings. Vermeulen accepted that this was an oversight on his part.

Another oversight, it emerged, was that he did not study a mark just below and to the left of the door's brass handle because he had focused solely on matching up the bat to the door. He could find no other marks that matched up to the bat. 'We will present evidence that that mark was caused by the prosthesis kicking the door or making contact with that door and the fabric of the sock was in fact still embedded [in the door] and varnish of the door [was found] on the prosthesis,' said Roux. This was another important aspect of Oscar's timeline – that he first tried to kick the door before fetching the bat.

How and why did Vermeulen overlook this? 'I could not link it to the cricket bat so that is why I only elaborated on the first two marks that we spoke about,' he said, before suggesting that the mark could have been caused by Oscar possibly tripping over or stepping on the piece of wood after it was knocked from the panel.

Roux appeared incensed, arguing that it was impossible for the sock fibres to become embedded in the wood of the door and the varnish on the prosthesis without significant force being applied – like a kick. 'The fabric was tested, the wood was tested, the prosthesis was tested, they all match,' he insisted.

Despite these assuring claims from the defence team, it later emerged that the tests had been conducted by Roger Dixon, and by the time he stepped off the stand Dixon's credibility was questioned by many.

But for now the focus was still on the state and the fact that it had not tested the prosthetic legs and the sock fibres against the mark on the door, despite Oscar telling the bail court a year earlier that he had kicked the door with his prosthetic legs.

Vermeulen admitted that he did have the prosthetic leg in his possession, but he was only requested to examine damage to the plastic covering on the shin. He had not used his initiative to carry out any kind of tests outside the ambit of his instructions. He also accepted that if a study of the mark on the door proved to be a match to the prosthetic foot – although he was not convinced of it – it would indicate that Oscar was wearing the prosthetic legs at the time.

Roux presented a photograph to the court of the prosthetic leg where a sample of the plastic covering had been removed 'in order to do the comparison and the markings in the microscopic testing in relation to the mark on the door' – he was referring to the tests conducted by Dixon. Vermeulen said he knew Dixon; he had been his commander before he left the police's forensic laboratory, and he had experienced him as a competent person.

In wrapping up his cross-examination, Roux asked Vermeulen whether he had seen the YouTube video of a man conducting the bat vs gun sound test. The video had been posted online and had gone viral. It showed an American expert, Alexander Jason, conducting an experiment to determine if a bat strike on a wooden door could produce a sound similar to a gunshot when heard at a distance. It wasn't an attempt to replicate Oscar's door, his bat or the technique used but despite this, it seemed to suggest that the sounds were similar.

Vermeulen had not seen the video.

'I do not know how scientific, but it was done with a microphone 180 metres away and the person taking a bat and hitting a door and then after that, firing a 9 mm to compare the significant resemblance of the shot and the bat,' Roux told him. 'Did you do any test when you heard about the version that there was, of the accused, there was first a shooting and the hitting of the door, to understand the resemblance between that?' asked Roux.

Vermeulen had not conducted such a test, but neither had the defence team, and it was only after this video emerged that Roux dispatched Wolmarans and Dixon to the shooting range to conduct a similar test.

• • •

When he re-examined Vermeulen, Nel wanted to deal with nine items, and posed them as fairly straightforward questions. While Vermeulen provided some explanation to support his answers, it was clear what his answers were:

1. The fact that pieces were missing and you could not locate them at the time of your investigation; did it affect your findings?
    No.
2. If the bat had hit the door anywhere above Mark 2, you would have expected to see the indentation in the wood?
    Yes.

3. For you to hit the door with the bat at Mark 2, you would be in an unnatural position, and to hit even lower than that you'd be at an even more unnatural position?

Yes.

4. Is there any damage to the door handle?

No.

5. Do you still stand by your findings in relation to the angle and position of the bat when it struck the door, even after the demonstrations from Mr Roux?

Yes.

6. The bat being wedged through the door would have placed the accused in an unnatural position if he was wearing his prosthetic legs?

Yes.

7. You testified that the bullet hole was caused before the panel was broken – but are you able to say whether Mark 1 caused by the bat against the door was before the shots?

No.

8. For you to establish at what angle the bat hit the door, was a microscopic investigation necessary?

No.

9. If the mark pointed out by the defence team is in fact a kick mark, can you say whether it was caused before or after the shots?

No.

Nel paused here and asked Vermeulen to speculate, as he had been asked to do by Roux. It was earlier put to the witness that the only reason why the accused would have kicked the door was to open it because it was locked. 'Could there be other reasons?' asked Nel. 'Let us speculate. You were asked to speculate. Could it be to scare someone? Is it possible? Just to make a noise? That is possible.'

Vermeulen agreed that was indeed a possibility.

The Blood and the Bowl

Colonel Ian van der Nest has seen his fair share of bloodied crime scenes and mutilated victims. For 20 years he's been investigating the circumstances of unnatural deaths, first at the Biology Unit, and then at the Victim Identification Centre of the police's Forensic Science Laboratory, where he is highly regarded amongst his peers. Van der Nest has been directly responsible for over 1 300 investigations, excluding those where he has assisted colleagues.

His blood spatter analysis played a major role in the investigation of the 2010 murder of right-wing Afrikaner leader Eugene Terre'Blanche. The accused in the matter, Chris Mahlangu, had bragged to friends that he and an accomplice beat their victim to death during a scuffle over unpaid wages. But Van der Nest's study of the blood spatter pattern and the body disputed that claim. Mahlangu was convicted of the murder, while the court acquitted his co-accused.

Van der Nest was instructed late on Valentine's Day to attend Reeva's post-mortem scheduled for the following morning. At the autopsy he made his own observations, took notes and also helped other officials take measurements and photos of the body. Later that day he went to the crime scene. Van der Nest testified that he was asked specifically to investigate what appeared to be blunt force trauma to Reeva's right eye, the blood spatter around the house, as well as the cricket bat. Investigators had to rule out that Oscar had at some stage attacked Reeva with the bat.

Album 5 presented in evidence included pictures of Van der Nest's investigations in the house. He identified areas by letters of the alphabet, like 'AA', 'BB' and 'CC', which were written on small blue Post-its and stuck on a surface near the particular spatter to be photographed. Area 'AA' was the spots of blood that came to rest on the couch in a small lounge located beneath the staircase. 'BB' was the blood between that lounge and the kitchen, while 'CC' marked out the area where Oscar had placed Reeva's body at the foot of the staircase. The blue Post-its tracked the blood trail up the stairs, down the passage through the TV room, into Oscar's room and through into the bathroom.

Van der Nest said he soon ruled out the spatter patterns as being the result of blunt force trauma:

> I could see no area of origin and these stains were not radiating from a specific source which one normally associates with a sort of blunt force trauma. To me this was an artefact from the arterial spurt that had arisen from above and 'from above', I mean the landing between the stairwell between the upper and ground level.

The walls down the sides of the staircase showed dozens of fine drops of blood. One particular pattern was in a distinct vertical line, caused by the arterial spurt from one of Reeva's wounds. 'If one follows my progression of the alphabetised markings, even upstairs and you will see that there is a commonality in all of this in that they have a serpentine or an S-shape and that is typically what you would expect in an arterial type of spurting pattern,' he said.

Van der Nest used various terms to describe the blood spatters on the scene: 'contact staining', 'drip trails', 'passive drip staining' and 'arterial spurt'. He explained that the shorts Reeva was wearing had become saturated with blood emanating from her hip wound, which contributed to the drip trail from the bathroom down the stairs. And Reeva's long blonde hair had also become soaked with blood and acted like a paintbrush when coming in to contact with items such as the staircase rail and the tiles in the bathroom.

Van der Nest's study of the bathroom confirmed what was already known: 'The deceased sustained wounds while being in the toilet. These wounds were consistent with gunshot wounds from my observations at the postmortem and that three of these wounds, which the deceased sustained could have resulted in severe bleeding,' he said, referring to the head, hip and arm wound. Van der Nest said the spurting could have occurred from the head wound or the elbow wound.

The scene marked 'UU' dealt with the toilet itself, with close-up photos of the toilet bowl, its lid and the seat that showed up very fine spatter, broken pieces of hair together with particulate consisting of human tissue debris. Van der Nest found this to be consistent with the damage caused to Reeva's head, which meant that her head was in close proximity to the toilet seat lid when the bullet struck it. He further explained that the bloodstains on the seat indicated that after the incident that caused the particulate spatter, Reeva's head came to rest on the toilet.

'The head was in the surrounds of the toilet because the pieces of broken hair and particulate and bone matter would follow in the direction of the projectile because that is the kernel direction of the force. So she must have sustained or received the wound somewhere in front of the lid of the toilet,' he said.

The two main pools of blood – on the toilet seat and flowing into the bowl, and the large pool on the floor – were caused by the head and the arm wound, and then the hip wound respectively.

Van der Nest agreed with ballistic expert Captain Mangena's reconstruction of what happened behind the door. After the shooting, Reeva was retrieved from the cubicle using a combination of drag-lifting movements that created the patterns on the floor. Van der Nest said that the evidence and the spatter throughout the house showed that she was picked up from the floor and carried into Oscar's bedroom, then in to the TV room, down the passage, down the stairs and placed at the bottom of the staircase.

• • •

Roux's cross-examination of Van der Nest was concluded in less than five minutes because there was nothing to dispute. He referred to the expert's report where he was quoted as referring to paragraphs in Oscar's bail application statement. 'The version of events as set out in paragraph 16.13 to 16.17 in the aforementioned statement are consistent with the observed bloodstained patterns,' said Van der Nest in his report. In the particular paragraphs Oscar stated how he broke down the door panels, moved Reeva out of the toilet cubicle, picked her up off the floor and carried her downstairs.

'Do you still stand by that?' asked Roux.

'I do,' said Van der Nest.

And with that, the expert was thanked and excused from proceedings.

• • •

Perhaps most interesting was what Van der Nest did not testify about – whether or not the toilet had been flushed. Intriguingly, it is this piece of evidence that private forensic experts thought most crucial before the trial began in March 2014.

Former senior policeman and author of numerous books on forensics, Hennie van Vuuren, stated that the analysis of the toilet bowl would be critical. 'I would like to know whether the contents of the toilet has been analysed because that will tell us a story. What was the reason why Reeva was sitting in the toilet. Has the contents been analysed? Oscar never mentioned anything about hearing the toilet being flushed. So what was happening really? Physical evidence will tell us that story. If proper, complete, accurate analysis of all evidence has been made.'

Van der Nest did not make a finding in this regard in his report, so was not led on this from the state's side and there was no questioning on it from the defence. A cursory layperson's study of a photograph of the inside of the toilet bowl shows clear white sections of porcelain separating the 'columns' of blood, like vertical stripes on a candy cane. The white stripes marked where water appeared to have washed away the blood.

A source in the investigating team said they'd established that at some point the toilet was flushed. The source said blood flow had in some areas been replenished, which meant that the water was flowing from the cistern, or at least partially, at the time Reeva's head was still over the toilet bowl.

It was thought that Reeva had already bled into the bowl, and when Oscar broke down the door and entered the cubicle, he might have inadvertently leaned on the flushing mechanism. But this cistern has a partially recessed button, with options for heavy and light flow, so whoever flushed the toilet must have done so purposefully. Did the accused literally attempt to flush evidence down the toilet? Or had Reeva been shot moments after having flushed the toilet herself?

Private forensic investigator Cobus Steyl believes that the latter is indeed possible. 'Reeva could have flushed the toilet and that was the sound that caused Oscar to shoot. She fell in such a way that her head was bleeding over the bowl with some of the water still flowing towards the end of the flush. The initial shot to the head would cause the blood to gush out like a shaken bottle of Coke, but then it stops because she is bleeding from the wounds lower on her body,' he said.

Steyl stated that the flow pattern of the toilet water could easily be established by putting a dye in the water and test flushing it. He said it appeared that towards the end of the flush, after the valve had closed, there was still some water in the pipe, but that this tapered off.

He believes that while this fact may have been irrelevant to each side's case, it should still have been presented to the court. 'You never know whether it could play a vital role towards the end of the case when all the information is put together. It is for the court to decide what is important or not,' he said.

Speaking after the closing arguments had concluded, defence forensic scientist

Roger Dixon was insistent that this was an absolutely crucial piece of evidence that should have been introduced to the court.

'The toilet had been flushed! She sat and flushed. That trickle takes maybe thirty seconds to taper down. She flushed, he yelled, she slammed the door, she fell down and the last trickle of the toilet after the flush cut those runnels through the blood. The water ran over the blood. The blood didn't happen afterwards. She flushed the toilet. If she had been so scared and frightened she would have peed in her pants. Her bladder was almost empty,' said Dixon.

'We didn't find very much urine in the bowl. It had been tested,' he revealed.

'This was the third startle. It destroys the state's case totally. With the third startle, his worst fears are confirmed. That's the crux of the case. It destroys the "I'm going to chase you and kill you because I don't like you any more" idea. It shows that she went to the toilet with her cellphone, under her own steam, no hurry, no rush. When he yelled, she reacted by locking the door.'

Dixon said this wasn't part of his remit and it was something he only discovered after he had concluded his testimony.

A member of the prosecution team said Nel didn't introduce this evidence because there were simply too many possibilities to consider. 'There was no realistic conclusion to reach based on the available evidence, we would have just been guessing.' The National Prosecuting Authority did not comment on questions sent to it about this.

Roux didn't touch on this either – flushing the toilet was not in his client's timeline and if Roux believed a police officer on the scene had inadvertently flushed the toilet he almost certainly would have pounced on it.

But the evidence appears to show that at some point the toilet was flushed. As Hennie van Vuuren said before the trial had even begun, this evidence would tell a story – a story that both sides have chosen to ignore.

In any event, the weight of the forensic evidence and how it slotted in to the version being offered by either party would ultimately have to be decided on by Judge Masipa.

ContraDixon

Roger Dixon speaks with the authority and confidence you would expect from an expert witness with a Master's degree and nearly 20 years of experience in the police's Forensic Science Laboratory. A middle-aged man, neatly dressed in a grey suit and matching tie, with a grey beard and moustache, he stood upright in the witness box with his hands on the desk in front of him, one folded over the other. He rocked back and forth as he addressed the court, and tapped out the syllables of the words he spoke, enunciating clearly for all to hear what he had to say. Following each question his hands invariably left their resting position, taking flight in the space in front of his chest, with his fingers flexing and assuming all manner of positions to animate and emphasise what he was trying to convey to the court. Dixon liked to talk and often ventured off on a tangent before being reined in by Roux. This habit landed Dixon in trouble when Nel took over the questioning for cross-examination.

And yet, despite his confident and assuring demeanour, Dixon broke two cardinal rules of expert testimony in a court of law: don't testify on a subject you are not an expert in and don't talk more than is necessary.

He was the first witness to testify after Oscar stepped off the stand. On the morning of Dixon's testimony, Johannesburg daily newspaper *The Star* featured a headline reading 'Oscar trial: Now for damage control'. There was an expectation that he would bring with him redemption.

Dixon was introduced to the court as a forensic geologist with degrees in Chemistry and Geology, who had previously headed up the Materials Analysis subsection at the SAPS, now being managed by Vermeulen. In his career in the police, he had obtained qualifications and attended numerous courses offered by local and internal organisations, including the FBI. He was responsible for 'all types of trace evidence, forensic geology, fibres, all types of organic pollutants, crime scene investigations which were varied, such as industrial accidents or theft, or break-ins and break-outs … it is a very wide generalist area'.

In this case, as Roux led him, Dixon testified on an incredibly wide variety of subjects, including ballistics, wound ballistics, pathology, sound and light levels and other fields, but in cross-examination he conceded he was not an expert on these subjects, but a layperson. An irresistible cliché crept into the headlines as it became apparent that Dixon was a 'jack of all trades, master of none'. It also emerged that this was the first trial he had testified in as a private, independent expert and that he had not even ventured into this field in several years since leaving the police.

At first, Dixon gave evidence that seemed to support the case for the defence. He testified about how Oscar's bedroom was pitch dark when the lights were not on and that he would not have been able to see Reeva getting up and going to the bathroom. He also believed it would not have been possible for Oscar's neighbours, the Stipps, to have seen him through his bathroom window without his prosthetic legs on. Johan Stipp had testified he had seen a man without a shirt walking past the window. In addition, Dixon testified that a mark on Oscar's prosthetic leg was consistent with attempts to break down the toilet door while wearing his prostheses.

The geologist also attempted to bolster the defence's version about the bruises on Reeva's back and what had caused them. The prosecution's witnesses claimed that the bruises on her back came from a projectile but Dixon believed the abrasions were caused by the magazine rack in the cubicle. He believed they were consistent with horizontal abrasions as if she had fallen back onto the rack.

The state's witnesses had contended that Reeva was facing the door and talking to Oscar when she was shot. Dixon, however, contested this, claiming that she was standing at an angle to the door with her right arm slightly raised. This supported the defence's version that she was about to leave the cubicle and was reaching for the handle.

When Dixon moved onto ballistics evidence, it surprised many watching the developments in the courtroom. Experienced expert Wollie Wolmarans was expected to take care of this realm of evidence, but it became clear that Dixon and Wolmarans had worked on the case together and this seemed to prompt the geologist to step beyond the area of his own expertise and into Wolmarans's field.

Dixon and Wolmarans were at the crime scene together in March 2013, when Mangena and his colleagues rehung the door for them to inspect it *in loco* and a week later they visited the Forensic Science Lab for further inspection of the exhibits. Dixon identified the various marks on the door, as well as a critical third mark higher up on the door, which he said was one of the three marks made when the bat struck the door. Vermeulen, however, had discussed only two marks and did not include the third one in his report.

Dixon took an identical door from Oscar's house – the pantry door, made of the same meranti wood – and conducted tests in which the door was struck with the cricket bat, as well as fired bullets through it, in order to replicate the effects that would arise when it is hit, damaged and abused, 'in the fashion which is evident on the door'. He was responsible for hitting the door, and while testifying complained that he still had pain in his left forearm from the exercise – indicative of how recently the test had been conducted. 'It takes a lot of force to break that door,' he said.

The defence forensics team conducted the tests at a shooting range at night. In a scene reminiscent of the YouTube video discussed during Vermeulen's testimony, microphones and recording stations were placed at 60 metres and 180 metres from the door.

With Dixon in the witness box, the recording made at the 60-metre spot was played to the courtroom. Oscar plugged his ears with his index fingers and leaned forward with his elbows on his knees, looking down at the ground. After some awkward technical difficulties trying to get the sound clip to play on the laptop, three banging sounds were heard first, followed by four similar sounds in quick succession. They did seem to sound like gunshots, but what was also clear in the clips were the sounds of crickets or frogs chirping in the background.

Dixon explained that the first three strikes of the cricket bat were done by pulling the blade over his shoulder, but for the four shots in rapid succession he wielded the bat as if he were in the classical cricket batsman posture, striking at the bottom end of the door.

These clips were played again in court the following day, as were the gunshots clips, first at the 60-metre point and then at 180 metres. They sounded very similar to the bat striking the door, but what was notably different was the sounds of the bugs in the background, which were much less pronounced.

'Does that accord with the test that you attended?' asked Roux.

'The first ones were the cricket bat, at 60 and 180 and the second ones were the gunshots at 60 and 180,' said Dixon – an answer he came to regret in cross-examination.

Dixon's analysis of bullet hole 'D' mirrored what Vermeulen had told the court weeks earlier – that the cracks on opposite ends – at the top and the bottom – of the hole indicated that the bullet pierced the wood before the bat striking it caused the crack. The defence experts had conducted tests of their own; they first cracked the replica door and then fired a shot through the crack to prove that, if the crack came first, it would form a continuous line through the bullet hole.

Dixon's study of the mark in line with the door lock showed that the varnish had been abraded and, on closer inspection, white fibres were embedded into the door – a close-up photograph of the mark was shown to the court. 'In reconstructing the sequence of events, the only material which is consistent with this white fibre, is the white socks worn over the prosthesis of Mr Pistorius,' said Dixon. It appeared the defence team had done its homework. This seemed to prove what Roux had put to previous witnesses: the mark corresponded with Oscar's version that he had kicked the door before taking the cricket bat to it.

The next photo showed the sole of Oscar's right prosthetic foot, on which Dixon pointed out dark vertical lines near the toe, which he said was varnish that had become embedded in the rubber covering. This photo had been taken by the police, so why hadn't Vermeulen or any of the state experts linked this evidence to the door? Dixon further rubbished Vermeulen's suggestion that the mark on the wooden panel could have been caused by Oscar kicking it on the floor after the panel had been knocked out of its frame because a significant amount of force – like a kick – would need to be applied for the transfer of materials to take place.

Dixon identified and explained the remaining two marks. He also presented photographs to the court of the bat and explained that these marks corresponded to those on the door. He further explained that the tiles that had come loose from the wall to the left of the door were probably caused by the first blow against the frame of the door, which would have sent shock waves through the outer frame and into the wall. These vibrations could have been strong enough to cause the tiles to fall off.

The former police expert took a swipe at the conduct of the SAPS officials on the way they handled the scene, describing it as most unprofessional:

> If a photographer needs to go around before anything has been marked or moved, there is a lane which you sacrifice, you choose what is the least likely way of getting around the crime scene in order to minimise compromising it.
>
> Walking over panels, it is in my experience at crime scenes, it is unfortunate. People walk all over the place.

This type of criticism was being echoed in the streets outside the court. It wouldn't be the first case bungled by police incompetence or negligence, and if the police behaved in this manner at one of the most high-profile cases in the world, what was the average person experiencing at everyday crime scenes across the country? However, in this extraordinarily high-profile case, the police had made use of their very best forensic experts and those with the most experience.

· · ·

Speaking to members of the prosecution team as well as police investigators, it was clear that Nel was going to give Dixon a lambasting when it came to cross-examination. The prosecutor was itching to tear a strip off the former police-man. It all came down to the role of an expert witness in a trial and the scope to which that person can competently testify. The qualified geologist was employed at the University of Pretoria's Department of Geology where he was responsible for analysing 'soils and all sorts of things', but he wasn't affiliated to any forensic body and did not conduct regular proficiency tests in his fields of expertise, like the police do. Yet he felt competent enough to provide expert evidence on forensics.

'You understand what the difference is between a normal general witness and a expert witness?' asked Nel in his opening line of enquiry.

'The difference is that the layman has not got specific knowledge in the area in which they are doing their examination,' explained Dixon. 'And an expert would be somebody who has got experience in applying their training to the matter at hand.'

The prosecutor questioned whether, as an expert witness, he would have to explain to the court the processes undertaken to reach the final conclusion. Dixon started his answer by listing the items he had studied, and then pointed out that while he is not a ballistics expert he did apply logic to reach his conclu-sions, before using an analogy of a geological map that plotted out bedrock to infer that similar principles applied to crime scene investigation.

It was tedious. Nel was swinging his spectacles in his right hand, put his leg up on his chair and at times talked to his colleague Andrea Johnson as the witness rambled on. This was to be a hallmark of Dixon's testimony.

Nel cut to the chase. 'You gave evidence on sound,' he asked, referring to the tests of the bat being struck against the door compared to gunshots. 'Are you a sound expert? Just answer that question.'

'I would hope that my evidence that I present is sound, yes,' said Dixon, being facetious.

While Bennie van Staden, the official photographer, sitting amongst the state's experts behind the prosecutor, could barely contain his laughter, the answer annoyed the prosecutor. 'Are you a sound expert, sir?'

'No.'

Nel continued to clarify his question to avoid further games from the witness:

> Nel: *Have you received training in decibels and sound?*
> Dixon: *The tests that I undertook, where I wielded the cricket bat, was*
> *purely to determine whether the sound made by the bat striking the*
> *door could in any way be confused with a sound made by a gun*
> *being fired.*
> Nel: *You need to be an expert to do that. What expert skills did you use?*
> *Wielding a bat?*
> Dixon: *I made a sound.*

The tests were done at the shooting range where guests are required to wear ear protection when discharging firearms. But Dixon didn't wear protection when he struck the door with the bat. 'I know what the sound of a gunshot at close range is. It is a very loud crack and it can damage the ears. A cricket bat hitting an object does not generate that very loud crack at close range.'

Dixon also conceded that he had not used the actual cricket bat used by Oscar when conducting the experiments.

Once the prosecuting team had had an opportunity to listen to the recording, Nel tackled Dixon on possible manipulation of the tests. 'I listened to the sounds and on listening to it, I formed the idea that the bat sounds were amplified,' he said. The background noises of the crickets or frogs had been the giveaway. Nel was referring to the bat sound where the background noises were clearly audible, but this was not the case on the recordings of the gunshots. Did the defence team have the bat recordings amplified to sound as loud as the gunshots? Nel certainly believed so.

Dixon did not testify from a report, nor did the defence provide one to the state when the witness took the stand. Instead, Dixon said he compiled several reports on various subjects and tests that he submitted to counsel. When questioned on this, Roux offered to provide Nel with the various reports Dixon had compiled, but this was an afterthought and in response to questions. Several of these reports were later handed over to the state.

Nel wasn't satisfied that Dixon would simply come to court – and play the clips – and still not provide a report or any other information to support what had been presented. 'As far as a scientific expert is concerned, that is enough? The court does not know where you were. The court does not know what recording equipment was used. The court does not know how the door was set up.' Dixon had not divulged any of this, although Wolmarans presented the court with all these details in his report, which curiously was compiled after Dixon's testimony.

Unbeknown to the defence team, Nel had got wind that a second round of shooting tests had been conducted at the range. But Dixon did not state this in his evidence-in-chief, and he was forced to reveal to the court that he was not present when the second set of tests was conducted – although Wolmarans was, along with most of the other people at the first test. At the first test the brand-new firearm was jamming, so the shots in quick succession could not be recorded, only single shots.

'So what was played to court did not happen on one day?' asked Nel, stunned by what he had just heard. 'You identified the gun ... but you were not present when it was done?' The prosecutor was now agitated:

> Nel: *It goes towards integrity of a witness and I am putting it to you, the question is about integrity and nothing else. You identified gunshots and you were not present when they were made. Why would you do that?*
> Dixon: *Because I have heard gunshots.*
> Nel: *No, you cannot get away with that, Mr Dixon. You have been a policeman for many years, you have testified in various courts. Mr Dixon, it is a serious issue for an expert to identify things and he was not present. I am putting it to you, Mr Dixon.*

Dixon confirmed that after the failed first test with the firearm he had suggested that the recordings could be digitally edited so that the single shots could be grouped to sound like they were firing in quick succession. It was Wolmarans who decided to conduct the test again, so as to present to the court an unedited sound clip. Of course, this raised questions over the integrity of the witness: why would he even consider submitting as evidence altered audio recordings? Dixon also confirmed that the two men recording the gunshots and bat strikes were not audio specialists, but sound engineers.

Nel was relentless and forced Dixon into what was arguably the most embarrassing and memorable concession of his testimony. The geologist admitted that 'the instrument' he had used to test the visibility in Oscar's bedroom was 'my eyes'. He attempted to explain that his intention was to see what was visible when he was only using his eyes simply because this was the most relevant aspect to this case.

Nel insisted that this was subjective and Dixon conceded that the ability of a person to see would be subject to conditions such as the state of his or her eyes and whether or not the person was used to being in the dark. In fact, Dixon went as far as to concede that with the curtains open and a full moon in the sky, there was 'quite a lot of light' in the athlete's bedroom. Dixon also didn't know that, according to the state's version, Oscar's balcony light was on and the curtains were open.

During his evidence-in-chief, Dixon had used photographs he had taken during his investigations, with a model posing on his knees in Oscar's bathroom. By this he had wanted to establish whether or not the Stipps would have been able to see Oscar through the window if he was wearing his prosthetic legs. Under cross-examination Nel established that the man in the photographs would have been 20 centimetres shorter than Oscar when he was on his stumps.

'It is something I omitted,' Dixon acknowledged.

Dixon had also looked from the street outside the Stipps' house, rather than from their actual balcony when he was attempting to establish what the couple could have seen from their home on the morning of the shooting.

And yet, despite the barrage from Nel, Dixon remained confident. In fact, he was so self-assured that he challenged the ballistics evidence of Captain Mangena and the forensic evidence of pathologist Gert Saayman.

Dixon said that according to his calculations, none of the four bullets Oscar had fired had failed to hit Reeva. He also claimed he had managed to detect tiny splinters around Reeva's hip that Saayman had missed during the autopsy. Dixon had only attended three autopsies in his life, compared to the nearly 15 000 of Saayman, and Dixon had not been present at Reeva's.

Nel zeroed in on Dixon's earlier claim that the marks on Reeva's back had been caused by the magazine rack and not shrapnel. The geologist had suggested that the 'kinetic energy' of being hit by a bullet in her hip would have caused Reeva to move backwards, like in movies the prosecutor suggested. But Nel challenged him to try to find any literature to support the theory that a bullet could move someone backwards. Dixon believed that by studying photographs he had identified a bruise on Reeva's back that Saayman had not picked up.

Nel argued that Saayman had extensively detailed the bruises in his report and, on the back foot, Dixon admitted that his 'layman's impression' was different. He had been snared by Nel's trap as he acknowledged he was a layperson and not an expert in the field in which he was testifying.

During his testimony Dixon had also claimed that when carrying out the ballistics tests, they were forced to use a different type of ammunition because the so-called Black Talon bullets that Oscar had apparently used were hard to come by. Oscar, however, had disagreed, saying on the stand that he used Black Talons simply because it was the type of ammunition required for his firearm.

In response to this, Sky News correspondent Alex Crawford tweeted: 'Sky did a test with Black Talon bullets and we were supplied with them within a day.'

While on the stand Dixon told the court that he did not want his testimony to be affected by any external factors, so he had avoided following the trial. He claimed he had no television or radio at his home and he did not read newspapers. But it wasn't difficult for journalists to unearth his Twitter account. And it was clear from his account that he had been following the first few days of the state's case, retweeting posts of interest.

Also, on numerous occasions Nel had to repeat his questions because Dixon seemed to be avoiding answering. The prosecutor rephrased his questions to extract a simple yes or no answer, but still the response from the witness was long-winded and often unrelated. Their exchange even became heated, prompting the judge to step in:

> Nel: *You know I am going to be rude because you do not listen to … the question was, is an expert …*
> Court: Mr Nel!
> Nel: *Yes, My Lady.*
> Court: Please restrain yourself.
> Nel: *I will, My Lady. May I then through the court, just ask the witness to respond to the question.*
> Court: Yes.
> Nel: *And just the question. Did you hear that, Mr Dixon?*

Roux had made quite a deal about the need for microscopic analysis of exhibits in order to identify materials positively and match trace evidence collected from different items. The defence advocate had put it to the state witnesses that their own defence experts had conducted such tests, but now Nel challenged these tests.

Dixon said the only fibres he looked at under a microscope were those on the sample cut from the bottom of Oscar's prosthetic foot:

> *I compared my physical observation of the fibres that were trapped in the varnish on the door with an examination of the fibres which were stuck on the underneath of the right sole prosthesis.*

I did not examine the socks. I did not have them. I saw photographs of those socks being worn on the prosthesis, at the scene.

This wasn't even close to the scientific rigour Roux had sold to the court several weeks earlier. While Dixon may have observed the fibres on the foot at a microscopic level, the same was not done for the other samples to make the finding.

And there was more. Included in one of Dixon's reports, which had by now been handed over to the state, were two photographs taken of the door in court several weeks earlier. 'The lighting in the court when we came to examine the door afterwards, the lighting showed it up very nicely. On previous examinations it did not appear as visible. I could see the fibres. We did not have good pictures. So this was very nice and it was well lit. It shows them up very clearly,' said Dixon, before admitting he had taken no previous close-up photos of the mark apparently showing the fibres embedded in it.

'But remember,' said Nel, 'when you came into court on 13th of March, there were people cleaning the door? The ladies that clean the court were busy cleaning the door. You were upset. You said how can they clean it, remember?' The door by that time was no longer a forensic exhibit, and was in the public domain, but Dixon argued that in his experience, often long after the crime, 'there is always something left over'. His testimony was now bordering on laughable.

'And you exclude that that could be fibres of a mutton cloth used in cleaning this door?' Nel was hitting straight at the processes and admissibility of Dixon's evidence. His tactic was cross-examination 101 – undermine the credibility of the expert witness so that his or her evidence would be inadmissible.

'My Lady, I did not observe the cleaners putting an excessive amount of energy into cleaning the door, because that is caused by a strong blow ... So I stay by my conclusion that those fibres were caused by the sock that was worn on the prosthesis, and not by a cleaner with a mutton cloth,' he said.

Dixon, of course, hadn't taken a sample to rule this out.

The geologist was presented with Oscar's prosthetic leg, the one the athlete wore on the night of the shooting. Nel had asked Roux whether it was appropriate, seeing as it may appear insensitive, but there was no objection. Awkwardly wielding the leg about and peeling off a sock, he pointed out where the sample plastic covering had been cut from its sole. This was the first time the expert had seen the prosthesis in real life. The scene was farcical.

It seems that the only test Dixon conducted that did appear to be sound was a chemical analysis of the varnish removed from the prosthetic leg and the varnish on the door that showed that they were a match. He used a gas-chromatograph at the university's lab. But did he test the varnish on any of the other wooden doors in the house to exclude that the transfer took place on another door? Dixon had not. Varnish could also have been transferred to the sock, but he didn't test that either.

Dixon had felt the ignominy of searing cross-examination. He was wounded, fragile and scampering. He had been vociferously ridiculed on social media earning the title 'ContraDixon'.

'I was police forensics for 18 years. If you're an expert witness and you go to court, and our court system is adversarial, that's one of the things you must expect. I've had a lot of support from friends. I said, "Once more unto the breach, dear friends,"' Dixon told *The Guardian* after he stepped off the witness stand:

> *It's over. I'm not going to dissect it. If you have regrets, it means you did something wrong. If you're pleased, it means you beat somebody and that's not what it's about. I am aware there has been quite a lot of commentary. These were all highly influenced by other factors. I'm not worried about it. I'm being honest. I'm working accurately to the facts. The world could see this: I wasn't against being televised. I was accused of not having integrity. That's Mr Nel's opinion. He was trying to get to me. You know what they say: all's fair in love and war.*

On the morning of his last day under Nel's scrutiny, Dixon took the unorthodox step of posting in jest about his experience on Facebook: 'Third day in court today. Let's see how much of my credibility, integrity and professional reputation is destroyed. It is difficult to get belief in those who will not listen because it is not what they want to hear. After that, beer!'

Clearly a fan of the social media site, his account reveals he is a man of varied musical tastes. He likes Beethoven, heavy metal, harp music and Meat Loaf. And that Friday evening, once the trial had been adjourned and he had been dismissed, Dixon stayed true to his word. He drank a beer at the International Police Association bar in Pretoria. Sharing a beer with him was Wollie Wolmarans, the ballistics expert who was yet to testify.

Jack of All Trades, Master of 'Nine'

Roger Dixon eagerly opens the plastic container, its bright-red handles and 'Jolly' sticker belying the significance of its contents. Inside is a slice of Oscar Pistorius's prosthetic leg. It's just a slither really, with a few spots of dried black blood and a streak of varnish. Dixon points to it and explains its significance. He quickly closes that container and opens another that holds a police-issue evidence bag and a chip of tile from Oscar's bathroom.

We're inside Dixon's pokey office in the understated Stoneman Laboratory at the University of Pretoria, nestled between a parking lot and a lush botanical garden. The room is cluttered with large, covered microscopes, pieces of rock, graduated sieves and other paraphernalia you would expect to find in a researcher's retreat. Incongruously, a De'Longhi coffee machine is switching itself on and off on a side table.

Dixon had a rough ride in the trial. He was savaged on social media, with memes ridiculing him doing the rounds and jokes made at his expense. We want to know from him how he feels about this and whether his pride and reputation remain intact.

'Well, I've been trying to collect all the pictures and images about me because some of them are quite funny and I want to have a page on my Facebook page which has got all of them there: my brief moment of glory, if you can put it that way,' he says with a laugh. He is hilariously self-deprecating and sarcastic. It's a necessary trait when one has been humiliated on live television and yet, despite his upbeat demeanour, it is clear he has been bruised.

'People are suddenly absolute experts, they know what the answer is, and anybody who differs from their opinion is evil, is incompetent, is a liar ... just my Twitter account, I had Twitter to follow the news, because I don't have radio and TV at home so I can check up, what's the news headlines. I jumped from 13 followers to 600. It was an overnight sort of stardom and the messages that I started receiving there, some of them were extremely bad. So I stopped watching Twitter because it actually made me feel bad.

'I came out feeling fine. And then I got upset when I read what other people's opinions were and are based on the fact that what I said didn't fit "their" story. And the way people said things was sometimes extremely … it's libellous, some of these Twitter things I got and messages and email I received, I can take the people to court and I can sue them. Because people say things and they type things down just like that. But would you sit down and write a letter saying those things and post it to somebody? Would you say it to their face? No!' says Dixon bitterly.

He believes the massive media hype and live video coverage of the trial had a significant impact. Over the course of several months, the broadcast turned witnesses into pseudo-celebrities and created heroes from villains, but Dixon isn't pointing any fingers.

'Normally when you go to court and you testify and there are people who don't like what you are saying, and they get aggressive and you can get accused of lying, it's within a court. Yes, it's open, there's journalists there, but a journalist then has to listen and understand and write a report and then it's published. Now you've got this direct, international feed all over the place. People are seeing it live, they are hearing it, they are immediately making judgements.

'You're moving from the world of a small area which is dull and boring – the law – to celebrity. We're going from the Roger Dixons of this world, giving dull and boring evidence, to the Kim Kardashians of the world whose every move, no matter how inconsequential is reported on ad nauseam and they make money out of it. There's no ways that you can actually equate the two, and having public broadcasting directly there compromised the trial, as far as I am concerned.'

Dixon, who elected to give televised evidence, echoes what many critics of the live broadcast have claimed: that it has resulted in an unfair trial because witnesses might have been scared away or could have tailored their versions.

'Our legal system actually has been all these years that the witnesses must be unaware of what the other witnesses are saying, so your evidence that you present is much less influenced by outside events around the case. As a scientist doing an investigation before the case, yes, I consult with people. You are a team, you consult, that is not a problem, but what about eyewitnesses?'

Or in this case 'earwitnesses'.

'They see how the first person and the second person gets attacked and grilled and, all of a sudden, my opinion and from what I know is that they suddenly become unwilling to testify, or from what we see, they suddenly think, "I can become a movie star," and they start saying things which fail to be credible and I think that's the influence of this instant TV fame. I mean it's much better than *Big Brother* or your local soap. And it's for free!' says Dixon, his humour never far away.

The sense one gets from talking to Roger Dixon is that he's bitter and frustrated that Gerrie Nel was elevated to a popular, crime-fighting character and anyone who dared to differ was cast as 'evil', being from 'the dark side'.

Dixon claims not to care what the court of public opinion decides about him. That is opinion, not fact, and scientists only deal in fact, he reminds us. 'They were not my audience, all right. To be honest, my dear, I don't give a "blank",' says the scientist in his best imitation voice. 'I'm quoting somebody,' he adds, in case his joke was missed.

'See, if you are professional, your court is the audience. And the assessors. The accused. The victim and the legal people. That is your audience. It is not that ... you know, the peanut gallery outside.'

But deep down it does hurt. 'At the end of the day, I do care, but I'm not going to let it worry me because, you know, most of them are totally wrong. It's irrelevant and whether they're saying it because it will sell a story to a newspaper, or whether it will buy them an extra round of drinks in the pub – I notice that was taken up,' he sniggers, a reference to the Facebook post he wrote on the last day of his evidence. 'I mean, really, if people can seriously believe that I was worried with my integrity ... that thing that I wrote in Facebook, was successful. It was taken up by somebody and totally misinterpreted.'

Dixon is not a fan of the adversarial court system in South Africa, which sees two sides competing to 'win'. It is this approach that he believes has seen the prosecution make compromises by only leading evidence that favours the state's case. It's also brought out the ugliness of personal point scoring.

'That has unfortunately got to the state where the two sides, especially the side that has got all the evidence and got all the stuff, doesn't want to share it. This is a problem. It's something I have encountered throughout my career, because it becomes an object of "I must beat the other person" – I'm not talking specifically about this case. But if the shoe fits ... basically it comes down to: this was a competition between two sides represented by two people and somebody is going to win. At times it felt to me that is the way it was.

'Many statements were made by Mr Nel which immediately became facts and news headlines all over the world. "My integrity was destroyed", this, that and the other thing. That is a standard tactic in court. If you can make the expert witness doubt themselves, if you can make them stumble, if you can make them feel that perhaps they aren't properly qualified, this that. And you can fail them on their ability to present well, then the evidence also is diminished, so I've experienced that quite a lot in court, because many of the cases where I've testified on are not straightforward, normal things.'

After he stepped off the stand, Dixon said about Nel's conduct that 'all is fair in love and war' but it is evident that he didn't approve of the prosecutor's behaviour.

'I would have liked that he had a little more sound basis for some of his statements. I would also have liked that he kept to the facts. Everybody has their own style or conduct. I note that I was found to be "boring", "monotonous," etc. and my Twitter site was "boring" and this and that. The facts have to be presented in an unemotional way, because they are the facts. People mustn't see me getting really emotional about something. If I need emotion when presenting my evidence, that means I lack evidence and doing the emotional stunt and attacking the person means you're actually doing that because you actually can't attack the facts.'

Dixon won't go so far as to say that this case was a travesty of justice, but he will say that he believes it was compromised – in many ways – most significantly, by what he calls the 'deliberate manipulation of the facts'.

'It is a fact that because we are adversarial, the parties have two strongly opposing sides. You will not lead evidence which is not supportive of your main premise. So, any evidence which weakened your case, you will leave out, won't you? I think everybody who participates in the court case has an obligation. However, it is my experience that that is often not the case. It could be that the prosecutor is going on the evidence that is presented by the investigating officer, I have known investigating officers to manipulate physical evidence in order to secure a conviction. I have testified against those people.'

During his time at the SAPS, there were a number of occasions when Dixon was called upon to watch the watchmen – to do tests that ultimately revealed that officers had manipulated evidence. The most notable of these is the role he played in the investigation into the murder of Stellenbosch student Inge Lotz. He did the tests on the infamous fingerprint 'folien', which showed that the police had lifted prints off a drinking glass rather than a DVD case. This was seen as critical to acquitting Lotz's boyfriend Fred van der Vyfer.

Dixon left the police at the end of 2012, after 18 years of service, the majority of time as a colonel. He left the service because of the way the Forensic Science Lab was being run. 'I had one instrument there that after 18 months I still couldn't get an order number to have it repaired because the whole process was so poorly managed and incompetent. I was totally frustrated fixing up other people's mistakes. I wasn't able to do what I wanted to do and what I was employed to do, which was to be a forensic scientist.'

When he joined the University of Pretoria in January 2013, he had no intention of ever working as a private forensic scientist. He was a divorcee with two adult children and a new career and new life. That all changed when Oscar shot Reeva.

'I was sitting having lunch at the restaurant on campus, under the trees, nice and pleasantly relaxed in work attire – shorts and sandals,' Dixon remembers wistfully, 'and I got a phone call on the same afternoon as the bail hearing judgment and I was asked if I was prepared to get involved.'

The call came from private ballistics expert Wollie Wolmarans.

'He was the main forensic person who was organising that and I was asked if I would be prepared to be part of it because there were things that needed investigation that they weren't expert on. I must admit, just that got my heart racing and I felt that frisson of excitement,' he says animatedly. 'It is one of the reasons why being a forensic analyst and going to crime scenes and whatever … it's changing all the time, the investigations are not years of research and whatever. It's different and it's exciting. So I thought about it …'

Within hours Dixon found himself sitting in his car outside Oscar's house at Silver Woods, listening to Magistrate Nair delivering his judgment on the car's radio. He was waiting for the investigating team to arrive and to have his first look at the scene.

Together he and Wolmarans, working initially with private ballistics specialist Wessie van der Westhuizen, carried out their investigations. Dixon occasionally met with Oscar during consultations with his legal team in counsel's chambers. 'He was very tense. Very nervous. Sort of … very down. Not a happy chappy,' says Dixon candidly.

With the stakes so high in this trial, was there a point when he thought the state might resort to dubious tactics?

'Suspicious, maybe, maybe not … because sometimes things would appear in public which can only be attributed to a certain person or event and there were no outside witnesses to it. So, yes, maybe it's just pure coincidence,' he hints. 'As a precautionary measure, because the matter had been raised – I don't know who came up with it – we tended to switch off our phones or leave them in the car or whatever when we had meetings and discussions. The possibility is always there. It's really unfortunate, though, that one has to do this, because that implies that nobody is trustworthy. And that's bad, our society today is rather sick.'

Following the investigations, Dixon's role was to 'pull it all together', which is why he was the first defence expert to testify. 'I presented an overview of the sequence of events in the bathroom. I put it all together. I did the interpretation of the crime scene. I'm looking at a logical sequence of events based on physical or chemical properties. As I said, I am not an expert in this specific thing ... however, what I do is I interpret the crime scene, I interpret the interaction based on scientific principles. All right, wood breaks. Who's an expert in the breaking of wood? Show me one. No. You're a scientist. You do research. You look at the literature. You take wood of the same thing and you test it. You recreate the situation, you have to ... you know, apples with apples, which in the Oscar Pistorius case with the door, for instance, the police did not use the same door for their tests; they used another door. A different ammunition.

'Now all of a sudden, what I am doing by grabbing a cricket bat and hitting a door, I'm not qualified to do that. Excuse me? I'm not a professional cricketer, no. How many professional cricketers – by the adulation from the TV public, they must be qualified – how many of them go around hitting doors with a cricket bat? How many people have actually heard a door being hit by a cricket bat? Now a door of a specific type in a specific situation? You show me please where you have a qualified expert in that?'

Dixon gets a little worked up at this point – after all, this was one of the key criticisms of his testimony, that he was a 'jack of all trades, master of none'. He finds a joke to counter this, saying he's a 'jack of all trades, master of nine'. He's also quick to respond to the 'I used my eyes to measure the light' mockery.

'In today's day and age, people think that machines and instruments are the be-all and the end-all. What instrument analyses a crime scene?'

But what about his assertion that he works on fact alone, and not on interpretation?

'I interpret the facts, to come up with an expert opinion, which is my interpretation of the events – but it is all based on facts. The interpretation is the end result of considering the facts,' he insists.

'Fact,' he continues with emphasis. 'If I see something move, it moved. That's not interpretation. It moved. That's a fact. I cannot say how fast it moved unless there was a mark and another mark and I know the distance and I've got my watch out and I clock it. Therefore I saw it move, and I saw it move at that speed because I have recorded it. Now, if I am looking with my eyes, what am I doing? I am recording a scene and I am interpreting the signal via my brain. Now if I have a lens on my camera and I have a recording medium and a memory card, what is the difference? The difference is that the eye is far more powerful than a camera lens. A camera lens is limited. With the eye you see more.'

While Dixon defends his own abilities with conviction, he's critical of the conduct of the police investigators. 'The first thing you do on a crime scene is you don't touch it. You record everything properly first, then you examine and you work out what you are going to do. That is a crime scene. You can preserve it intact. There is no reason to take a door off and take it somewhere else. There might be some test you need to do in the pristine state and now it's no longer in the pristine state, and how do you know that will have an effect? You never know. The only evidence we had of the original state was from the earliest photographs which the police took, which I only saw later on in the case.

'If I had still been in the Forensic Science Laboratory and I had been involved, and I had to examine the stuff, I would have given the same story that I have given now. My story was quite contradictory of some of the evidence presented by one of the witnesses for the state.'

Dixon won't name the witness, but it's obvious that his biggest gripe is with the ballistics. Captain Chris Mangena was the state witness who dealt with that. It's a recurring theme when speaking to those on the defence team.

But Dixon remains confident, despite his experience on the stand. Prior to the judgment, he's impervious to what the judge's finding might be on his credibility (and ultimately Masipa did not mention him) and is self-assured enough not to doubt his credentials despite the public mauling. He says he'll be back to testify another day.

'Why not? I'm not scared. That was my job. If you are scared of something like that, you don't do it. However, I do know that there are plenty of forensic scientists who would not testify on things like that. In fact, a lot of people would rather put a finding of "undetermined" than make a statement which could lead them to go to court.

'If the police employed me and paid me for 18 years and when there was a problem people came to me because if nobody could solve it I might have a chance because of my particular skills and expertise, why must I doubt now because I am outside the police? I went to the dark side and now everything I do is suspect because I'm siding with the evil forces,' he jokes, his sense of humour showing itself again.

While he gives an assurance that he hasn't been scared off, one can't help but suspect that he might seek refuge here, in his inconspicuous office hidden in the botanical gardens, surrounded by his rocks and soil and microscopes. For a while, he might busy himself with editing the *South African Clivia Yearbook* again or doing analysis for groundbreaking research – until that 'frisson' of excitement courses through his veins once more and he's lured back to another crime scene.

The Gunshots

Thomas 'Wollie' Wolmarans is tall and grey haired, with a moustache to match. He has bucketloads of experience, spending 20 of his 60 years working in the South African Police (SAP) force but now operating as a private ballistics expert. He works out of a shooting range in Pretoria and is occasionally known to invite journalists over to demonstrate his opinions on a case, followed by a sit-down in the quaint coffee shop next door. There's no mistaking his passion for his craft.

Over the course of his lengthy career, Wolmarans has conducted more than 10 000 forensics investigations and has testified in over 500 cases in South Africa and neighbouring countries. He has almost unrivalled experience with firearms, which he accumulated in the South African Defence Force, in the Forfeited and Confiscated Firearms Section of the SAP, at the South African Criminal Bureau and during time spent seconded by the police's Ballistics Unit to Zimbabwe (Rhodesia at the time). Since 1977, he has given expert evidence in various fields, including ballistics, microscopic identification of fired bullets and cartridge cases, photomicrography (the examination of firearms), and the photography and reconstruction of crime scenes. He retired from the SAP in 1992 and has since practised as a private and independent forensic consultant. In 2000 he was employed by the United Nations as a crime scene officer for the International Criminal Tribunal for the former Yugoslavia. Countless hours firing weapons have damaged his ears and left him with tinnitus, making communication with him challenging at times.

Wolmarans had been sitting in on the trial since day one. Through Roux's cross-examinations it was evident he would be called to challenge many of the state's findings, particularly those of Captain Mangena. Wolmarans and Mangena shared a respectful and collegial relationship, with the elder man saying that Mangena referred to him as 'Oom', the Afrikaans moniker for 'Uncle', while he used the term of endearment 'my seun' ('my son') when talking to Mangena.

The witness had with him his report, dated 23 April, which meant it was compiled and submitted to Oscar's defence team after the accused himself had testified, and after fellow expert witness Roger Dixon had spent time in the box. The timeline caused problems for both Wolmarans and the defence – why had Wolmarans compiled this report so late, and did it mean he was tailoring it according to the evidence that had gone before? In addition, was this why he and Dixon had shared a beer once the geologist had finalised his testimony?

Oscar's defence team hired Wolmarans on the day he killed Reeva – Thursday – but he only had access to the crime scene on the Sunday at around 3:30pm after the police had concluded their investigation and relinquished control over the house.

The house had been secured by a company called Platinum Risk Solutions and the key was handed to the ballistics expert. Wolmarans's first task was to do a walk-through of the house, wearing protective clothing and taking photographs as he went. Colleagues from CSI Africa, a private forensics company, arrived a couple of hours later and began doing a fingerprint investigation of the scene. Wolmarans noted that the main bathroom door, through which Oscar had shot Reeva, had been removed.

The following day Wolmarans returned to the house. As part of his routine, he inspected the bloody toilet bowl. The private expert donned a pair of surgical gloves and fished around with his hand to find any evidence the police might have overlooked. To his surprise, he discovered a piece of the lead core of a bullet. While feeling around in the toilet bowl he also recovered a small piece of tile that was missed by the police's forensic investigators. A mere visual inspection of the bowl would not have turned up anything because it was filled with blood.

This discovery was used in the bail application to cast additional doubt over the police's handling of the crime scene, and asked questions about the state's case in light of the fact that items had been overlooked. On the Tuesday, Wolmarans handed the bullet fragment to then investigating officer Captain Hilton Botha at the Pretoria Magistrate's Court.

Wolmarans again returned to the crime scene on 8 March 2013, the same day that Captain Mangena and the other officers reinstalled the toilet door for their own tests. The private ballistics expert merely observed and took a few pictures as the policemen took control of the situation, although Wolmarans requested a sample fragment of the meranti door. The piece was handed to him by Captain Mike van Aardt and placed in a sealed evidence bag with the number PA60011432811 marked 'Boschkop 110/2012'. Wolmarans later handed the piece over to his fellow defence witness, Roger Dixon.

Wolmarans drove out to the Silver Woods estate one further time, in November 2013, as the defence team was preparing for trial. The toilet door was rehung in the bathroom by two police officers, in the presence of Van Aardt, Dixon and members of the legal team. A week later, Dixon and Wolmarans visited the Forensic Science Laboratory in Silverton to examine exhibits that had been collected from the crime scene, such as the gun, bullets, Reeva's clothing, the cricket bat and the toilet door.

When Wolmarans was first hired by the defence on Valentine's Day in 2013, two major disputes between the state and the defence showed up in the bail application: firstly, that Oscar was allegedly on his prosthetic legs when he shot Reeva; and secondly, whether he stood about 1.5 metres from the toilet door when he fired the shots. These two issues were no longer in dispute when Wolmarans was called to take the stand in May 2014. In fact, Mangena in his own evidence pointed to the fact that that these had been resolved.

Wolmarans wanted to explain to the court how a firearm worked, and asked Mangena, while gesturing towards him from the witness box, whether he could use his gun. 'I do not know if it is permitted, My Lady. I will make it safe and I can explain the gun to you how it works.'

Nel appeared as bemused as Mangena and the rest of the experts, who looked at each other, shrugging their shoulders. 'We've got a crack team,' said the prosecutor, 'but we do not have any guns, My Lady.'

Masipa appeared relieved. 'You do not have any? It is a good thing.'

'My Lady, then I will explain it with photos,' said Wolmarans, his show-and-tell cut short.

'I would prefer that,' said the judge.

The expert explained to the court how a semi-automatic handgun operated – and that it would fire as quickly as the user could pull his finger – before explaining the dynamics of hollow-point ammunition.

Wolmarans said the ammunition used by his client was not Black Talon, but rather Ranger ammunition – also manufactured by the Winchester company, but of a lighter grain. This was contrary to what Oscar had confirmed to Nel under cross-examination: 'Who fired at her with Black Talon ammunition?' asked Nel. 'I did,' Oscar said in response.

It was unclear why the expert had not discussed this type of ammunition loaded into the handgun with his client prior to drafting his report.

The defence expert read through his report, often referring to photos taken by Mangena and a Captain Motha and explained that he took measurements of his own of the door and related marks inside the toilet cubicle. But he believed it was unlikely that the door would have been reconstructed with absolute accuracy, which would in turn influence the authenticity in determining the bullet trajectories. Wolmarans was thus undermining Mangena's findings, telling the court that while the state's expert came to certain conclusions, there were no certainties, and added that the angle at which the projectiles struck the door would have caused substantial deflection and the bullets would have strayed from a direct path.

Based on this, Wolmarans stated that any of the shots – 'A', 'B', 'C' or 'D' through the door – could have caused ricochet 'Mark E' and subsequently deflected to 'Mark F'. 'Captain Mangena used a laser to connect B and E,' explained Wolmarans. 'The difficulty with that is that the straight connection between B and E ignores a possible deflection.'

'If there was deflection, would that have been possible?' asked Roux.

'No, My Lady, as I said then it would have been on another place. So it was totally ignored.'

On 26 March, more than three weeks into the trial, after Mangena had testified and been cross-examined – and also after defence witness Dixon had taken the stand – Wolmarans conducted live-firing tests on the pantry door taken from Oscar's house. The test was conducted to establish the spread of wood splinters and bullet fragmentation. Wolmarans handed in the witness boards – the large pieces of cardboard placed behind the door to pick up secondary projectiles – to the court as an exhibit, and Masipa and her assessors studied them for several minutes as Wolmarans explained what he had established. The boards were marked 'Black Talon' because at the stage the tests were conducted, the expert was still under the impression that those were the rounds Oscar had used.

Wolmarans said his tests proved that Reeva's right upper arm must have been between 6 centimetres and 20 centimetres from the door when the bullet that struck her perforated it.

Contrary to Mangena's findings on the probable position of Reeva behind the door when she was shot, Wolmarans felt 'it is not possible to determine with accuracy the sequence of the shots and the body position of the deceased'. He referred to a photo taken during the postmortem that showed a probe inserted into the hip wound on Reeva's body. It appeared to show that the probe entered at an upwards trajectory, which appeared to support his theory of deflection. A study of the entry hole to the door and the entry wound by Mangena, however, found that the bullet was travelling in a downward trajectory. Wolmarans found that 'Hole B' resulted in the wounds to Reeva's upper arm; that the head wound could have been caused by the bullet passing through holes 'C' or 'D' and that she was not in a standing position when they struck her. Further he argued that 'C' or 'D' could have been the projectile that damaged the webbing on Reeva's left hand and that it was unlikely her hand was on her head at the time it was shot, as Mangena had so vividly re-enacted.

Wolmarans studied Reeva's black vest and agreed with the findings by pathologist Professor Saayman that the damage to the top and wounds below the deceased's right breast were caused by a piece of fragmented bullet. But he found no damage to the back of the vest, or evidence that it had been struck by a projectile, as claimed by the state. Wolmarans said a bullet ricocheting off the wall would have spent all its energy, and would thus not be moving fast enough to have caused the two abrasions on Reeva's back. He believed that the projectile that hit those two points was, in fact, the core he found in the toilet bowl along with a piece of tile.

'The only reasonable manner in which the injuries to the back of the deceased could have been caused, was when the deceased was falling, probably during the firing of the shots and her back came in contact with a hard surface, which could only have been the magazine rack,' he said. This reinforced Dixon's version of events.

Crucially, Wolmarans believed that Reeva fell back after being struck on the hip and was hit by other bullets in such close succession that she had no chance to scream.

Notably absent in the evidence provided by Wolmarans was anything related to the alleged tampering of the crime scene. Oscar had told Nel during cross-examination that Wolmarans was amongst his expert witnesses who would testify about things being moved on the crime scene, but there was no mention of this. It illustrated the strength of the state's witnesses in this regard, that perhaps Roux no longer believed that the allegations would stand.

• • •

On the morning Nel was to start cross-examining Wolmarans, Captain Mangena arrived at court with a large brown cardboard box tucked under his arm and a nylon zipper bag slung over his shoulder. Before his cross-examination, Nel asked for a short adjournment to allow the state's expert to 'reconstruct something' around the door exhibit in the courtroom. Mangena unpacked his box and bag to reveal a tripod, metal probes and various other pieces of equipment. He spent the next 30 minutes erecting the tripod, affixing a clamp holding a laser beam to it and moving it into position in front of the door. After much trial and error, he had lined up hole 'B' through the door with mark 'E' on the back of the mock-up toilet cubicle. When court resumed Nel invited Masipa and her assessors to view the reconstruction up close. As the judge walked around the door and the cubicle, aided by a court orderly, Mangena sprayed a fine mist from an aerosol can that was illuminated as the microscopic particles floated in front of the red laser beam, tracking the trajectory of the bullet that missed Reeva.

Nel's point of departure was to question the timeline of events in relation to defence witness testimony and the various tests conducted by the defence expert. Dixon had concluded his testimony on 16 April, but Wolmarans submitted his report to the defence team on 23 April – a report he claimed was in development since he was hired a year earlier. 'In most cases I give a verbal report to the legal team and as it goes on and I got more information and things, I amended my report,' he said, adding that he would on occasion send notes to the team, but they were not full reports. He conceded that he had not once prior to 23 April – nearly two months into the trial – furnished the defence team with a completed report.

'So, are you telling me that before this trial started, you did not have a report that you furnished the defence?' asked a gobsmacked Nel.

When we contacted Wolmarans in the weeks before the trial started, in February 2014, he said he hadn't consulted with the defence team in some time as he had undergone a back operation and wasn't certain whether he would be required to testify. 'That's the million-dollar question. It all depends what happens with the trial. Sometimes in a trial you think you're going to testify and then it happens that you don't.'

Nel clearly had Wolmarans on the back foot. The ballistics expert changed his response to say that there had been a previous report and that the most recent one was drafted so the legal team could assist him with his English. He also admitted that he did not keep a filing system of all his reports at his office, but rather had reports on his computer.

The defence's forensic experts appeared to be patching holes in their own case rather than punching holes in the state's case.

Wolmarans said he had met the accused only once, nearly a year earlier, when he took a few measurements, but he had never consulted with Oscar and never questioned him about what happened on the morning he shot Reeva. He said the athlete was, however, present at some of the consultations he had with the legal team, but the first he heard about how the shots were fired and the events as they transpired that morning was when Oscar had taken the stand.

Wolmarans said his findings were largely in keeping with those of Mangena about the sequence of the shots, their trajectories through the door and the way they were fired by the athlete. But he disagreed with Mangena about Reeva's position in the cubicle when she was struck.

Wolmarans also did not dispute Mangena's findings on the approximate location of Oscar in the bathroom when he fired the shots, and said he believed that it was hole 'C' or 'D' that caused mark 'E'.

He stated that after shot 'A' hit Reeva she collapsed, but it was difficult to say how and where she collapsed. The expert asked Judge Masipa if he could enter the cubicle exhibit and, despite a recent major back operation, would try to explain the movement 'in slow motion'. And so the witness removed his jacket and entered the cubicle. When he closed the door he was no longer visible to the court, but the judge and her assessors still had sight of him.

By bending over and painfully flexing his stiff body, Wolmarans explained that as Reeva was falling she would probably have lifted her hands to protect her face – in the defensive position as illustrated by Mangena – and the bullet through hole 'B' would have struck her in the right arm.

Nel said the difficulty Wolmarans had with the demonstration was that if a person were to line up the wound with hole 'B' at less than 20 centimetres from the door, there would be no place for Reeva's head because the entire body would be too close to the wall. Nel believed that this location of the body was impossible. But the expert disagreed.

Wolmarans often added a caveat to his comments, citing probabilities before asserting that knowing what really happened behind the door was impossible.

'We know there were four shots fired through the door. Four cartridge cases were retrieved,' he said. 'I'm no doctor but it makes sense to me was that she collapsed. What happened behind that door, we will never know.'

As the court discussed the possible scenarios and positions Reeva could have been in behind the door as bullets ripped through her body, Oscar assumed his usual position during such testimony. He leaned forward with his elbows on his knees and the palms of his hands on his cheeks in a way that allowed him to block his ears with his index fingers.

Wolmarans also referred to the version that the accused fired in rapid succession, but he could not say for sure what Oscar's exact firing ability was. He admitted he had not asked Oscar how quickly he had fired and he had never been present when Oscar explained how he had shot his gun. This, of course, raised further questions about his investigation: the expert had access to the accused, so why was he never asked to demonstrate, either by merely handling a gun and pulling the trigger as fast as he could, or at a shooting range? It would be the obvious test to conduct if it formed part of the defence's case.

Wolmarans testified, too, that he agreed with Dixon on the location of the magazine rack in the first album of the crime scene – that it had not been moved and was in that specific spot when Reeva was bleeding there:

> Nel: So it was there when she bled there?
> Wolmarans: She was there when she bleed, and I mean that is common sense.
> Nel: Although it is common sense, it is not the accused version.
> Wolmarans: Well, I do not know what ... that is what I am saying. That magazine rack was there when she started bleeding.
> Nel: Ja. So then the accused must be wrong?
> Wolmarans: He might be wrong.

It was not encouraging for the defence team when its expert witness testified that Oscar could be wrong on any aspect of its evidence.

The magazine rack was of particular importance to the defence's case – this would later emerge when psychologists and a sports scientist were called to testify about Oscar's heightened anxiety and elevated startle response. Oscar testified that the sound he heard that caused him to open fire was the magazine rack moving, 'it sounded like ... wood moving', which at the time he said he interpreted to be the door opening. But with the magazine rack against the back wall next to the toilet – in the location agreed to by all the experts – it could not have been the magazine rack that made a noise.

Nel questioned the ballistics expert about the mechanics and firing mechanism of Oscar's Taurus 9 mm pistol – what would need to be done for the weapon to discharge? This told the court what Oscar would have had to have done to prepare the weapon before storming the perceived threat.

Wolmarans said, firstly, that there would need to have been a bullet in the chamber. Oscar had indicated he often carried his weapon 'one-up', with one bullet in the chamber, so on the night in question this was probably the case. Secondly, said the expert, if the hammer was forward, and not cocked, the trigger would have to be pulled harder for the handgun to fire; however, if it was already cocked and the hammer in the back position, lighter pressure was required to release the trigger.

Oscar testified that he approached the bathroom with the safety mechanism off, but did not say that he had cocked the weapon – this meant he would have had to have applied significant pressure to the trigger for it to fire. And to fire four times, the trigger would have to have been pulled four separate times.

Nel clearly had something up his sleeve when he started asking Wolmarans about meetings he might have had with Dixon after he had been excused from the witness box. Rumours had begun circulating amongst some of the journalists covering the case that there was an audio clip of Wolmarans and Dixon having a conversation at the International Police Association bar on the Friday evening after Dixon's testimony. The clip was even uploaded onto YouTube. Nel was fishing.

Wolmarans confirmed he had met Dixon at the bar and on another occasion when he dropped by his house to say hello. He said it was highly improbable that the pair did not discuss matters related to the case, but Nel wanted to know whether he had altered anything in his report based on what had emerged in Dixon's testimony and cross-examination. Wolmarans said it was a possibility, but unlikely. 'M'Lady, Mr Dixon is not a ballistic expert so I will not even take his advice to change my report,' said Wolmarans. It was a reckless remark on which Nel was quick to capitalise:

> Nel: *That is an interesting comment. So you would not take Mr Dixon's advice on ballistics at all?*
> Wolmarans: *No, I will not take his advice.*
> Nel: *And the court should do the same?*
> Wolmarans: *He is not a ballistic expert.*

Nel had successfully managed to cast doubt on the conduct of the defence team and raise questions about when certain tests had been conducted and when Wolmarans's final report was handed in.

Wolmarans and Dixon were sent to the shooting range in late March 2014 – after Gerhard Vermeulen and Chris Mangena had both testified – with a mandate to establish whether a bat striking a meranti door could sound as loud as and similar to a gunshot. That night, the firearm was jamming so they were unable to record the handgun firing in quick succession. Wolmarans thus returned to the shooting range on 9 April to conduct the tests. 'Although I am not a sound expert,' explained Wolmarans, 'I can state that as a ballistic expert, the sounds caused by the cricket bat hitting the door resembled the sound made by the firearm, although not as loud.'

But, once again, there was a disclaimer from the expert: 'I must point out, M'Lady, that I have tinnitus. Tinnitus is a ringing in the ears all the time due to a lot of shootings during the course of my career.' This was hardly reassuring testimony from the expert.

Wolmarans confirmed that the first sound test – to establish whether the sound of a bat striking a door is as loud as and similar to a gunshot – was only conducted as a response to a similar test being conducted and posted on YouTube. He did, however, recall a decibel sound test conducted in about January 2014 at Arnold Pistorius's Waterkloof house, but it was a failure because when the bat struck the door the door had moved. 'The whole exercise was a mishap,' said Wolmarans. Oscar and Arnold were both present at the test, and it was the accused who had struck the door with the bat. Wolmarans said he had seen the test results, but he was unable to interpret them because he is not a sound expert.

The highly experienced ballistics expert left the court with as many answers as questions. Why had he taken part in sound tests when he acknowledged that he could barely hear? Why had he left his own tests for so late, only conducting them once other witnesses had testified? Invariably, this would lead to suggestions that he and Dixon had colluded to dovetail their evidence. And their drink together at the International Police Association bar mid-trial only reinforced that perception.

While this may have mattered in the court of public perception, would it have any sway with Judge Masipa, who might or might not choose to scrutinise any of the forensic testimony in her judgment?

The Sound and the Fury

When it emerged that an acoustics engineer was to be called, the assumption was that he had been brought in to confirm the claim that Oscar sounds like a woman when he is anxious or to back up the argument that a bat hitting a door could be mistaken for gunshots. There was also the possibility he could testify to the dynamics of sound waves as they travel through the air. There was speculation there might be another landmark moment in the case – when audio recordings of Oscar screaming would be played to an expectant courtroom.

Roux's witness was Ivan Lin, a director at a Joburg-based company of consulting engineers who provide services to broadcasting facilities. Lin studies how sound waves interact and are transmitted in an environment, as well as how human beings perceive sound waves. He was called by the defence to cast doubt over the reliability of the state's witnesses – the Stipps, Burger and Johnson – who claimed they heard the terrified screams of a woman on the morning Oscar killed Reeva.

Lin arrived at court with the answers to two questions: 'Can one reliably differentiate between a male and female scream at about 80 metres and 177 metres away respectively?' and 'Can one reliably discern the emotion of a scream from about 80 metres and 177 metres away respectively?'

He explained that hearing is a 'passive psychological process' in which sound is simply received by the ears, while listening is a complex process influenced by an individual's personal experiences and memories that affect how a heard sound is interpreted and perceived. As a result of this interpretation, and depending on a variety of factors, the interpretation is not always an accurate representation of what was actually heard.

'Does it mean in simple terms that two persons can listen to the same noise over a distance and have different views about the noise?' asked Roux.

'That is correct.'

Lin further explained how a variety of factors affect how sound is transmitted, such as physical barriers, air temperature, ambient noise levels, line-of-sight issues and factors related to the source of the sound.

In short, this meant that the neighbours called by the state to testify could not be absolutely certain about what they had heard on the morning of the shooting. However, Lin did not entirely exclude the possibility they had actually heard what they thought they had heard.

There were no absolutes. 'Typically one can differentiate a male and female scream, but one cannot say reliably without exception one can always say it is a male or female scream,' he said, adding that he could find no reliable studies or evidence to support the assumption that 'all male/female screams sound the same' and that without exception a 'female scream can sound like a male scream, and vice versa'.

The defence was trying to cast doubt on the reliability of the neighbours' claims, who were quite adamant, and expressed such certainty, about what they had heard – the blood-curdling screams of a woman in distress. Roux was trying to prove that such certainty is scientifically not possible, and when referenced to the defence's timeline of events that it had been Oscar screaming, then their version – as opposed to the state's version – became the most probable scenario.

Lin produced scientific models that took into account various factors on the night in question. Firstly, the source: inside the locked toilet cubicle with the window closed; in the bathroom with the window open; and on the balcony. He also varied the distances of the listener – 80 metres and 177 metres – as well as the location of the listener, from indoors with an open window and outdoors on a balcony.

It was a long process in court, with Lin meticulously reading through his findings. There was no questioning his credentials; he was clearly an expert in the field in which he specialised. But was he an expert fit for the court? State pathologist Professor Gert Saayman has testified in court cases for decades and it is evident in the way he presents his evidence. This was not Lin's forte – he struggled to make his facts and figures easily interpretable for the court, which is partly what an expert witness is expected to do. As a result, it was difficult to follow exactly what Lin was saying.

Roux had to assist the witness in making his evidence understandable. What Lin found was that the listener might have heard a scream at 80 metres away from the source, irrespective of whether the person screaming was in the toilet or bathroom or on the balcony. But at 177 metres away, if the scream was coming from inside the toilet cubicle, it was very unlikely that the listener could hear it, let alone interpret the source reliably. If the scream emanated from either the bathroom or the balcony, the chances of hearing and interpreting the scream improved, but not by much.

On the issue of whether a person could reliably discern emotions and differentiate between a male and female scream, Lin was not willing to venture an opinion, but stated that he offered scientific models merely to illustrate what could be audible and intelligible at the distances provided.

• • •

Just as he had done with previous defence expert witnesses, Nel sought to establish a timeline – when was Lin commissioned to compile his report? The expert told the court he had completed his report the week before, and had been commissioned by the defence team to write the report barely two weeks earlier. This was now more than a month after Dixon and Wolmarans had finished giving their evidence.

Lin said that defence attorney Brian Webber provided him with the variables for his equations – such as the locations of the noise and the listeners – and he also visited the estate to view the area for himself. He acknowledged that since the shooting there had been developments in the suburb and the topography had changed. He also conceded that it was very difficult to replicate the conditions of the morning of the shooting exactly because the smallest difference, even the length of the grass in the estate, could affect how the sound travels.

Lin said he was not provided with specific details related to the source and listener locations; for example, he was not told that at 177 metres the window was wide open. He further relied on the aerial photographs of the estate.

Lin based his calculations using an average scream level of 110 decibels, but Nel reminded the court that there was nothing normal about the night in question. 'On the state's version the deceased screamed because she feared for her life. That is an abnormal scream,' he commented.

'If somebody screams in absolute fear, would you not put it closer to 120 than 110?' asked Nel. Neighbours had described hearing the terrified screams of a woman, going as far as to describe them as sounding as though they came from someone who believed their life was in danger.

Lin was careful not to confirm Nel's suggestion outright. 'I think one needs to appreciate what 120 means. 120 dB is extremely loud, it is almost hearing a jet taking off at a 100 metres away and that is not … it is a very slight possibility but it is a possibility.'

Nel suggested that the hard tiles in the bathroom would have 'amplified' the sound, a claim Lin could not agree with. It appeared the prosecutor was using the incorrect terminology, but Lin tried to explain that the energy – the scream level – could not be increased; however, the reflective properties could allow the energy to be transferred from the enclosure, as opposed to being absorbed.

Frustration emerged at times, as Nel grappled with unfamiliar and complex terminology and concepts. 'I think we are all trying to understand this very complicated science of yours,' said Nel.

Nel wasn't aways satisfied with Lin's responses. Lin had been called as an expert witness and he would push on certain questions. 'It is commonly known that woman has high-pitch voice and it is a common perception,' said the witness.

The state's argument on this score was that a voice with a particular tonal characteristic would stand out and be more noticeable above ambient noise. In this instance, the terrified screams of a woman whose life was threatened would be unmistakeable.

Nel said four people identified the voice of a woman – with no exceptions – that everybody who heard that sound at that time identified it as a woman's voice. Lin was not aware of this fact.

Roux objected, suggesting the state should clarify that it was the prosecution witnesses who made the claim, not everybody. To avoid an argument, Nel changed the proposition to include only the state witnesses:

Nel: *Two were at 80 and two were at 177, they do not know each other, they have not spoken to each other. It happened independently.*

Lin: *My Lady, I cannot say they did not hear the sound. I do believe they heard a sound, but I cannot say they were correct or were they incorrect. It is not for me to interpret that.*

Nel: *No, no you are right. But they did. So as a scientist, that must indicate to you that they all heard … independent people heard a female screaming. So it is possible that what they heard at least was a female.*

Lin: *I can still cannot say whether they are correct or incorrect.*

Nel: *But it is possible, you are not excluding the fact that somebody at 177 metres in the bathroom … in the bedroom, would have heard the noise and made intelligible findings about it. Because that is what the*

> *witnesses testified. You are not saying the witnesses are lying.*
> Lin: *I have never ... I am not saying they are lying at all. I am saying*
> *they could hear, but I am not saying what they could was correct or*
> *incorrect.*
> Nel: *And so credibility finding, that is in the domain of the court, you will*
> *not say that they are lying, that they could not have heard.*
> Lin: *Not at all.*

The witness could thus not rule out the evidence of the state's witnesses. Even after all the calculations and possibilities considered, it was still very possible for human ears to hear and make out a woman screaming that morning. Roux had nevertheless cast some doubt. But would it be enough to dispel the claims that the blood-curdling screams of a woman pierced the early morning that Valentine's day?

Lin had not been asked to testify at all about the comparison between a cricket bat hitting a wooden door and the sound of gunshots. The only evidence that had been led to bolster this claim was that of a largely discredited Roger Dixon and Wollie Wolmarans, who by his own admission, is partially deaf.

Critically, no audio of Oscar screaming had been played. During the course of the trial, Oscar had told the court he was made to scream when he was anxious. But these recordings were never presented, leaving the claim that when anxious and screaming he sounds like a woman unsupported, except for the testimony of those immediate neighbours who had testified for the defence.

Despite this, Judge Masipa would have to come to her own conclusions about whether or not the defence had thrown enough doubt over the state witnesses' claims that they had heard a woman screaming that Valentine's Day morning. The onus lay on the state to prove its case beyond reasonable doubt, not on the defence to prove its case. If there was enough reasonable doubt in the judge's mind, then Oscar's lawyers would have done enough.

Pasta, with a Side of Gunfire

It was early afternoon at the tail end of the summer holidays. The piazza in Melrose Arch, lined with trendy eateries, was teeming with people returned from the country's beaches. Oscar Pistorius had also been to the coast with the new love in his life for part of the holidays and was catching up with friends at Tashas, the trendiest restaurant of them all.

Oscar took a guest visiting from the UK, fellow athlete Martyn Rooney, to meet up with his friend Darren Fresco and professional boxer Kevin Lerena. In an attempt to remain inconspicuous, the men chose a table in the far left corner inside the restaurant, close to the wooden tables heaped high with confectionary.

The patrons against the wall sat on plush cushioned couches, while on the opposite side of the table were two wooden chairs. Oscar sat in the corner, with a wall at his back and to his left. Lerena was opposite him, while Rooney was to the athlete's right and Fresco diagonally across from him, next to the boxer. It was lunchtime and the restaurant was packed as usual, with at least 200 people both inside and outside under a canopy of umbrellas to shield them from the scorching January sunshine. A queue of would-be patrons stood out in the piazza, holding tags and waiting for their numbers to be called.

Between the talk of nutrition, kilojoules and body mass, Oscar asked Fresco if he could see his firearm. The athlete had his eye on a Glock 27 and wanted to inspect his friend's handgun. This particular variant of the US-made weapon is a .40 calibre, described by the manufacturer as 'small, light, accurate, powerful … and popular with police both on and off duty'. Unique to this handgun is its trademarked 'Safe Action' system – it has no hammer and the trigger must be pulled for the weapon to discharge.

Fresco believed Oscar to be a competent firearm owner – they'd spent time at the shooting range together – and didn't question why he wanted to see the weapon. As Fresco leaned forward, with Oscar leaning in towards him to take the firearm, he allegedly warned the athlete: 'There is one-up.'

The buzz of multiple conversations was suddenly interrupted by the deafening crack of a single gunshot.

After the bang rang out a silence fell over the place. White noise filled the ears of the men around the table. 'Is everybody okay? asked Oscar.

Fresco was shocked. 'Just carry on as if nothing has happened.'

Oscar continued, 'I don't know what happened, how the gun went off. I'm sorry, it was a mistake. Are you okay?'

Lerena looked down and saw a hole in the tiles next to his foot. His toe had been hit by shrapnel and was bleeding. Fresco thought that their close proximity to the kitchen might lead some patrons to believe that the noise had been a gas explosion.

Owner of the franchise Jason Loupis and his wife Maria were working the lunchtime rush when they heard the bang. Jason's immediate thought was that it was a firearm – but he wanted to believe it was a balloon popping.

As he later testified:

> I went in the direction of the noise where Kevin and Oscar and them were sitting and I asked the guys, I said: 'Guys, what happened here?' And they all looked at me and then I said: 'No, seriously, guys, what happened here?' and Mr Fresco said to me: 'Sorry, Jason, my gun fell out my tracksuit pants'. And then I said: 'Are you guys being serious because this is, this is not a joke?' Because I thought someone could get hurt.

Jason couldn't believe what he was hearing. He turned around and walked back to his wife, checking to see whether anyone had been hurt.

'Can you believe that was a gun?' Jason asked Maria, who was still in the outside area. She also went to have a word with the men – Fresco told her the same story he had given her husband just moments earlier. 'But what is the first rule of owning a gun, "Safety First"'? asked Maria.

As Fresco answered yes, she slapped him over the head and walked off.

The group wanted to get out of there as quickly as possible. Oscar paid the bill. Lerena said he never again spoke of the incident, agreeing with everyone at the table that it should be kept under wraps. Fresco agreed. But by 2pm, Oscar had told Reeva and, in a message, pleaded with her to keep quiet about it:

Angel please don't say a thing to any one.. Darren told everyone it was his fault. I can't afford for that to come out. The guys promised not to say a thing.

Reeva agreed to play along:

I have no idea what you talking about ☺

A second message followed 20 seconds later:

But thank u for telling me I appreciate it x

• • •

In court, more than a year later, the hefty boxer in a black suit and red tie waited to be sworn in. He stood with his hands crossed in front of his waist with his shoulders back and his head high – easily mistaken for a bouncer outside a nightclub. He was to testify about the first of the firearm-related charges against Oscar, the incident at Tashas. Later the state would call the athlete's ex-girlfriend, Samantha Taylor, to tell the court about an incident in April 2012, when Oscar allegedly fired a gun out of the sunroof of a car. And then Fresco – allegedly present at both incidents – would be called by the prosecution to tie it all together.

In the days after the Valentine's Day shooting and before the formal bail application, the police busied themselves trying to find as much 'dirt' on Oscar as possible. As part of this process, former Scorpions investigator Andrew Leask, who is currently based at the Special Investigating Unit under the National Prosecuting Authority, paid his own visit to Tashas in Melrose Arch. He met with Marc Batchelor and his circle of friends, who had reason to feed information about Oscar to the authorities. Through 'Batch' and his mates, Leask was directed to Fresco, Taylor and Lerena, from whom he learnt about the Tashas shooting and the sunroof incident.

The additional firearm-related charges – counts two and three on the indictment – were only added to the charge sheet in late 2013 after attempts by the defence to have these excluded. While they have no direct link to the shooting on 14 February, the state used them to paint a specific picture about the accused: of a person who was reckless with firearms, who showed scant regard for the laws surrounding the use of guns, and who, when in trouble, refused to take responsibility for his actions. The charges were the mechanism to introduce character evidence, which is exactly what the defence believed the state was doing.

The official reasoning given by the state at the time of adding the gun charges was for convenience – the prosecutor argued that the gun charges dealt with many of the same witnesses thus it made sense to deal with the matters in one court in one trial from a pragmatic perspective.

'Arguably this is a thinly veiled argument. It is quite clear that the state has relied on the gun charges as a means to enter much more character evidence than they would otherwise have been permitted to do,' explains law lecturer Kelly Phelps. 'The gun charges set a backdrop implication of Pistorius having a bad character, which essentially forced Pistorius to put evidence of his good character on record to address the perception created. Once an accused puts evidence of his good character on record the state is permitted to cross-examine him on evidence of bad character.'

Professor James Grant largely agrees. 'These are clearly legitimate charges in themselves and it is perfectly legitimate for the prosecution to have coupled them with the murder charge. However, a more critical view would be to recognise that coupling these charges was more strategic than coincidence. The firearm charges relate to the reckless or negligent use of firearms. These charges will draw attention to the character of Pistorius, and the evidence led to prove the charges will invariably tend to show that Pistorius has a "bad character".'

As a general rule in South African courts, evidence about someone's character or their general reputation is only admissible in exceptional circumstances.

'By bringing the firearm charges at the same time as the murder charge, both "similar fact" evidence (evidence of prior bad acts), and bad character evidence will be admitted, albeit, on different charges. The effect of this is that, although and unless similar fact evidence and character evidence is deemed admissible in respect of the murder charge, it may, at least, operate at a subconscious level on the court,' explains Grant. 'Beyond this, evidence of the reckless use of a firearm may be argued to show something about Pistorius – in the sense that would make the character evidence and similar fact evidence admissible in its own right.'

The runner's lawyers made representation to the National Prosecuting Authority in September 2013 arguing why the charges should not be added, stating that they would unfairly prejudice their client:

> *The charges have no relevance to discharging a firearm to cause any possible harm to any person ...*
> *... the attempted consolidation is not to consolidate all the charges in*

the interests of justice, but patently to attempt an irrelevant and uncon-
scionable character assassination of our client ...

The alleged offences are not only removed in time and jurisdiction,
but have no relevance to the shooting incident on 14 February 2013 other
than to unlawfully seek to introduce inadmissible evidence to attack the
character of our client.

The North Gauteng Director of Public Prosecutions, Advocate Sibongile Mzinyathi, disagreed, stating that it is 'to the advantage of the state and relevant to the murder charge to expose the accused's reckless nature regarding firearms'.

In his plea explanation, Oscar denied both the firearm charges as well as the fourth charge for possession of the .38 calibre ammunition found in his safe. Many commentators believed this decision to plead not guilty was a major error, arguing that had Oscar taken the hit and pleaded guilty, he would have avoided character evidence being introduced. However, it was clear that Oscar maintained his innocence and thought the gamble was one worth taking.

• • •

The Knock-Out Kid, Kevin Lerena, was the first witness in the box to testify on the gun-related charges. He had updated his Facebook page days earlier, responding to questions about whose side he was on. 'There are no sides. Two lives and families have been affected by this,' said Lerena. 'So I'm on no side. I have been called to court, not to slate Oscar or the state, but to answer simple questions.'

Lerena consented to having his face shown in the live broadcast feed of the trial. He was the first witness in the trial to do so, which meant that he inadvertently made history as the first witness in a criminal trial to be broadcast live in South Africa.

In days past, the budding boxer had looked up to Oscar, regarding him as a sporting icon. The pair met at a Daytona Group track day at Kyalami Race Track in Midrand. Lerena used to date Gina Myers and was familiar with the circle of friends. Amongst the group at the event was Daytona owner Justin Divaris and Darren Fresco.

Lerena grew up in an athletic family and is no stranger to professional sport. His two cousins, Gavin and Brandon Lerena, are top jockeys in South Africa, and his parents were involved in horse racing. As a young boy, he was headed on the same equine career path, but in high school he started playing rugby and went on to represent the Lions in the Under-19 Currie Cup. Lerena's single mother couldn't support that career, so he started bouncing at nightclubs to earn an income, and this is where he was spotted by boxing promoters.

In Oscar, Lerena found a potential mentor. He was looking to someone he admired to help him advance in his sporting career. 'He is an icon and a legend in sport and athletics, you know, for me as a young sportsman to get help from a guy like him was very important,' Lerena testified in court. 'So I was rubbing shoulders with him and he was going to help me with a diet and a little bit of running.'

Lerena was preparing for a fight on 16 February and wanted to meet Oscar to discuss a plan to reduce his body weight. 'I fight in the cruiserweight division and Oscar knew how to, you know ...' he said, briefly pausing before clarifying in his flat Joburg accent why he'd seek the athlete's guidance. '... obviously being an athlete, how to like get in tip-top shape.'

During lunch at Tashas on 11 January 2013, the boxer ordered a pasta, while the three others at the table had soft drinks. Lerena testified that he was sitting opposite Oscar and next to Fresco, and told the court he heard Fresco warn the athlete that there was a bullet in the chamber:

> Nel: *Was anything being said whilst the gun was handed over? Whilst the gun was passed to Oscar?*
>
> Lerena: *Yes, from what I remember correctly, Darren said: I am one-up. There is a bullet in the cham ... there is ... I am one-up. I then believe Oscar removed that bullet out of the [intervened]*
>
> Nel: *You believe or did you see it?*
>
> Lerena: *I did not see that happen.*
>
> Nel: *You did not see it?*
>
> Lerena: *No.*
>
> Nel: *But let us just explain to the court exactly what you saw and what you heard. You saw the gun being passed under the table?*
>
> Lerena: *Well, the movements, the actions. I did not see the gun.*
>
> Nel: *And you heard what Mr Fresco said?*
>
> Lerena: *I am one-up. Yes.*
>
> Nel: *One-up. What do you understand by one-up?*
>
> Lerena: *That there is one loaded into the chamber. That people who carry guns, I suppose carry one-up.*
>
> Nel: *And what happened next?*
>
> Lerena: *A shot went off.*

Lerena testified that when he looked down he saw a hole in the floor. He also noticed there were 'grains' on his toe and he wondered whether it was from the marble tiles or the shrapnel. He was scratched from the shrapnel and there was blood on his toe. The boxer got up from the table and went to the bathroom to wipe it.

He was in shock from the incident. 'I have never been in a confined area, where a gunshot has gone off by accident, you know. There could have been a fatality, so for me, I was very shocked. I do not think it sunk in until three, four days after that, because when it happened I was not … I was shocked but it happens you know. I did not expect it. I did not understand it.'

During his testimony, Lerena was insistent that Oscar took responsibility for the incident, but asked his friend Fresco to take the blame:

Lerena: *Well the shot went off and I do remember Oscar very clearly saying, apologising: Is everybody okay? Is everything okay? I apologise. I do not know what happened, how the gun went off. But he did apologise and say: I am so sorry, it was a mistake. He said: Are you okay? Is everybody okay. We all said … I remember, I was fine. I was just obviously shocked by the gun, the bang of the shot that was very loud.*

    Nel: *What else was said?*

Lerena: *What else was said before, anybody came to the table, I do remember Oscar saying: Please. To Darren: Just say it was you. I do not want any tension around me. Just say it was you. And then once that was said, the people from the restaurant came to the table and then that is when Darren said it was him.*

According to Lerena, the men paid the bill, left and never spoke of the event again. Just over a month later, on the Sunday after Reeva was killed, the incident at Tashas resurfaced:

I fought on the 16th, when I woke up the Sunday morning after my fight, I had over 100 missed calls on my cell phone from countries around the world, the newspapers here saying about the Tashas incident. So I never discussed anything after this. For me, after I got up from that table, I never repeated it to anyone. I did not say what had happened, I just got woken up to calls that the story had been told and basically what it was saying in the stories, was Oscar had shot me in the leg. That was when

> *I stood up for myself and I went back to the media to protect my career*
> *and I said, that is nonsense, because I was not shot.*

As Advocate Roux stepped out of his corner for cross-examination, he ventured a joke with the judge. 'I may ask Mr Oldwadge to do the cross-examination, because I do not know if I want to cross-examine a boxer, My Lady,' he quipped.

Roux pressed home three points with Lerena, giving an indication of what Oscar's version of events might be. He said that Oscar was firstly angry with Fresco for giving him a weapon that was 'one-up' with a bullet in the chamber; secondly, he was concerned that someone could have been hurt; and, thirdly, that Oscar had asked Fresco if he understood what would happen if this incident reached the media.

There was no denial that Oscar had requested to see the firearm, nor that he had handled the firearm inside the restaurant – which would emerge in his own testimony as an inadmissible defence. Rather, the approach of the defence was an attempt to show that he did not hear the warning that the firearm had a bullet in the chamber. Roux told the court that his client would testify that it was in the process of opening the firearm breech that the shot accidentally went off.

The defence counsel stressed that his client was very apologetic and had checked to see whether any one had been hurt. Lerena countered that he could not definitively say what emotion Oscar was feeling and couldn't recall if he had been angry or not.

Roux had lined up the next section of his cross-examination – to put it on the record that Oscar never asked anyone to take the blame for the incident. Instead, Roux said, it was Fresco of his own volition who said he would take responsibility for the incident.

The advocate read excerpts from the statement made by Martyn Rooney, the British athlete who was the fourth man at the table. Rooney supported Oscar's version of events. 'Darren kept on telling Oscar not to talk because he was apologetic all the time and apologising and I said to him: "Just keep quiet, do not talk."'

Roux said Oscar also apologised to the owners and offered to pay for damages – another claim Lerena could not confirm. Lerena could not recall the verbatim exchange between Rooney, Fresco and Oscar, but could remember Fresco taking responsibility. Fresco would have to come and tell the court himself what went down that day.

• • •

Darren Fresco met Oscar on a breakfast run – a bunch of friends, fast cars and the open road. They shared a passion for speed and Fresco spent considerable time helping out at mutual friend Justin Divaris's Daytona car showroom. In addition to their enthusiasm for fast cars, Oscar and Fresco liked handguns and would on occasion meet up at the shooting range to fire off a few rounds together.

Fresco had known Reeva much longer than Oscar, having met her when she moved to Joburg about seven years earlier. Once Reeva had died, there was no question as to where Fresco's loyalty lay. He appeared as a state witness in the second week of the trial to testify against his former friend on the two gun-related charges.

With his shoulder-length brown hair, high forehead, scar running across his right cheek and a Twitter bio that reads 'If It's got Wheels or a Skirt, it's Gonna Cost You Money', Fresco became a target of ridicule by the public, especially for the 'selective amnesia' that seemed to characterise his evidence. His testimony did, however, give further insight into the two gun-related incidents and also provided a much clearer picture of the circles in which Oscar moved, the kinds of friends he kept whilst buoyed by fame and the reckless, wild, expensive life-style he indulged in.

Oscar glared at Fresco for much of his testimony and laughed when his advocate caught out his former buddy during cross-examination. Despite their seemingly unsalvageable friendship, Oscar still made an attempt to greet Fresco's new wife, Beatrix Leopold, on the day of Fresco's evidence. She and Reeva had been close, and she rebuffed Oscar's awkward overture. Speaking to Fresco in the corridors of the courthouse, it was blatantly clear that he no longer wanted anything to do with the athlete.

Before Fresco was sworn in, Nel told the court that Fresco had been offered a 'Section 204' indemnity. According to Section 204 of the Criminal Procedure Act, he was offered indemnity for prosecution in any crime he might have committed and in exchange he undertook to testify truthfully to the court. Ultimately it would be up to the judge to decide if he should be granted the '204' based on whether or not she thinks he told the truth.

Fresco said Oscar called him in January 2013 because he wanted him to meet his overseas guest, Martyn Rooney. Fresco was at work, but could easily stop in for lunch.

Fresco told the court that during that lunch Oscar had asked to see his Glock 27 and he handed it to him:

I had thought him being competent, I would not have to worry about
why he had asked me to see my gun ... within a second or so I had taken
the weapon out from my carry position and passed it to him under the
table ... We had been to the shooting range before and I knew he had a
big love for weapons and having been around him for a long time, my
assumption was that he had competency with it.

Crucially, Fresco corroborated Lerena's testimony, insisting he had told Oscar that the gun was 'one-up'. 'Having met halfway, M'Lady, at the table, while the gun still ... as soon as his hands had touched the weapon whilst leaning forward, I said to him: "There is one-up."'

Fresco told the court that having warned Oscar there was a bullet in the chamber, he never indicated that he had taken the magazine out of the firearm. 'Now, having obviously still been watching him, I saw ... I cannot say I saw what was done under the table, because I cannot see through tables, but I had seen a shoulder gesture which I had assumed was cycling the existing bullet out of the chamber.'

The Glock is an unusual weapon in that it does not load or fire in the same way most other handguns do. This detail is important because it could show that Oscar had to have made an intentional effort in order for the gun to go off, as Fresco explained: 'M'Lady, on that weapon there is no specific safety clip. As there is no hammer on the weapon. On the specific trigger itself, in the middle, there is a hairline trigger that you have to decompress and then pull through for the weapon to fire.' Advocate Nel assured Fresco that the state would lead expert evidence to prove what Fresco was saying.

Indeed, when the police's firearms expert Chris Mangena took the stand, he testified about the Glock handgun and its unique safety and firing mechanism. 'If you do not pull the trigger there on the trigger safety, the firing pin lock will remain there and the firing pin safety at the back will keep the firing pin at the back,' Captain Mangena told the court. 'So, if you do not pull the trigger, this firearm will not be able to fire a shot or discharge ammunition.' He further explained that the handgun was also not able to discharge accidentally if it was cocked, even if the user's finger was on the trigger – after being cocked, the trigger must be released and pulled for the weapon to fire. The defence never questioned this testimony, leaving the evidence open to be accepted by the court.

Fresco continued his testimony, leading the court through what happened after he handed Oscar the gun. 'After him having [taken] the weapon and having cycled one out, what I do not think he had realised at the time that he had cycled another bullet into the chamber of the gun and at that specific moment, he had pulled the trigger to, at the time supposedly make it safe. Almost instantly, My Lady, there was deafening hush you have ever heard [*sic*].'

Fresco hoped that other patrons in the restaurant would think a gas canister had exploded. Immediately, Oscar passed the gun back to him. 'Instantly he had passed the weapon back to me under the table and he said: Please there is too much media hype around me at the moment, please can we take the rap for it. Being a friend, I said: I would with pleasure, M'Lady.'

He again confirmed what Lerena had said – that Oscar had asked his friend to take the fall. 'The sounds in the restaurant returned back to normal as, basically as if nothing had happened,' Fresco continued. 'Then the owner's wife had come to me and said: What just happened? To which I replied: I am really sorry, my gun had gone off unintentionally. A little while after that the owner had come to our table ... And I had said again, I had just repeatedly apologised for what had just happened, M'Lady. I just said my gun had fallen out of my shorts and it had gone off.'

According to Fresco, Oscar never gave him an explanation and they never discussed the incident again. Fresco told the court that he personally had offered to pay for the damage, specifically stating to the owners that because it was his fault, he would happily reimburse them.

Although Fresco had consulted some of the most high-profile criminal lawyers in town, Advocate Mannie Witz and attorney Cliffie Alexander, he had still left crucial elements out of his affidavit. And there's nothing a defence counsel loves more than inconsistencies between versions.

Roux referred Fresco directly to the statement he provided to the police, which he had written with the help of a lawyer, 'specifically to make sure that I was not going to put myself in any line of trouble'. But the advocate pointed out that his testified version that Oscar had in fact asked him to take the fall for the shooting incident was not included in that statement. 'You go to an advocate and you tell them the truth,' said Roux. 'You want to protect yourself and I think it is just fair to say that you would share all the bad and the good facts with them, to make sure that you can get your protection.' While Fresco agreed with the advocate, he could not explain this omission. Roux also pointed out that Fresco did not include his story about the firearm falling out his pants in his statement – a second crucial aspect to his testimony.

And then Fresco slipped up yet again, revealing how he had been following the trial on a variety of media platforms, including Twitter. He had seen and heard what Lerena had told the court a week earlier, and of course Roux was suspicious about whether Fresco was tailoring his version to tie in with that of the boxer. Fresco had told the court that he was wearing shorts on the day of the Tashas incident, but Loupis had testified that he thought Fresco was wearing tracksuit pants. Fresco's response was, 'I saw that.'

The advocate turned to Fresco's testimony about the proximity of his head to Oscar's head when the firearm was passed to him – another piece of information not mentioned in his initial statement. Roux suggested that the witness had tendered this evidence so Oscar could not hide behind the fact that he did not hear the warning because it was too noisy in the restaurant, implying that Fresco had been told that this would be the defence of the accused. Roux added that another piece of Fresco's testimony – about the magazine in the firearm – was heard during Lerena's testimony when Roux put it to him that one of the reasons Oscar was upset was because the firearm was handed to him with a magazine in it.

It was clear from Roux's stance that Oscar's version was that he was entirely unaware that he had been passed a loaded gun. Time and again, he pressed Fresco about just how close his head was to Oscar's when he allegedly told him that the gun was loaded. Evidently, Oscar would tell the court that he had not heard Fresco's warning above the din in the restaurant.

Despite the holes punched in Fresco's evidence about the Tashas incident, he for the most part corroborated Lerena's version of events. There were only two other men at the table that day – Martyn Rooney had provided a statement and was unlikely to present himself to give evidence, so it would be Oscar's word against the other two.

The state, however, called two further witnesses to testify about this issue: the couple who own the franchise, Jason and Maria Loupis. This was done to close the circle of evidence, ensuring no gaps were left open. The only new information emerged on re-examination when Maria Loupis revealed that there was a child seated a short distance away from where the firearm had gone off.

. . .

Sipping chilled cocktails, the vibrant young couple takes the television presenter and her camera into their confidence, telling the viewers why they have fallen in love with each other. 'We have something special,' says Oscar, giggling endearingly, and looking adoringly at his girlfriend of a year and a half, Samantha Taylor. She speaks of how they share a common love for the outdoors, but also enjoy simply watching a movie together and going to the gym.

'He's lots of fun and has so much energy,' she giggles when quizzed by the show's presenter. 'I can't keep up with him,' says the exuberant young marketing student. In the next insert, they are the picture of happiness – he in a salmon shirt and khaki baggies, she in an emerald-green sundress. The backdrop is a tropical paradise, a golden beach with waves crashing.

It was October 2012, shortly after the London Olympics. Television show *Top Billing* had flown the couple to the Seychelles as part of the feature. Despite appearances, however, what is not revealed is that the couple had split weeks earlier when Taylor had discovered Oscar had gone on a date with model Anastassia Khozissova.

After returning from the Seychelles, they spent a few days at Sun City and then broke up – this time permanently. Just over a year later, Taylor told the High Court in Pretoria why their relationship had ended. 'Because he cheated on me with Reeva Steenkamp,' Taylor revealed. As far as Taylor believed, she and the athlete were still together when he appeared at the South African Sports Awards with Reeva on 4 November 2012. While she acknowledged there was a 'commotion' in their relationship, she did not consider it over. However, Oscar believed they had broken up.

Samantha Taylor was called in the first week of the trial to give insight into her relationship with Oscar and to provide the kind of detail only she or Reeva could have known. She had spent nights at Oscar's Silver Woods home. She knew his habits, where he left his firearm at night, how dark it was in his room, what he sounded like when he shouted. But primarily, she was in court to give her account of the time her boyfriend allegedly shot his gun through the sunroof of a moving car.

Taylor was only 16 when she met Oscar in 2010. They began dating in 2011 and she would spend up to four nights a week at the athlete's Pretoria home. But their relationship wasn't always picture-perfect. Taylor spoke of how he would lose his temper and shout at her, her sister and her best friend.

From Taylor's testimony, a picture emerged that showed Oscar as one who toted his firearm wherever he went and who was quick to rage. She told the court how he kept his gun on him 'all the time', even when he went to visit friends. He would place his firearm on his bedside table at night when he slept and his prosthetic legs would be alongside him on the floor. She also confirmed that he had two cellphones and that he often spent a significant amount of time sending messages.

Taylor was able to give the court an account of what the accused sounds like when he screams to counter the defence's argument that he sounds like a woman.

> *Nel: Now have you heard him scream?*
> *Taylor: Yes.*
> *Nel: Once or more?*
> *Taylor: A few times, M'Lady.*
> *Nel: But I think they would say that only when he is really anxious.*
> *When he screamed, did you see him being anxious?*
> *Taylor: I have seen him being very anxious.*
> *Nel: And he would shout at whom?*
> *Taylor: At myself.*
> *Nel: And did it sound like the shouts or screams of a woman?*
> *Taylor: It sounded like a man, M'Lady.*

Nel told Taylor that Oscar would claim that on the morning of the shooting he was anxious, and that he has had it tested that when he is in such a state his screams sound like those of a woman. 'That is not true. He sounds like a man,' Taylor responded.

Nel was trying to establish a pattern of behaviour as observed by someone who had prior, intimate knowledge of the accused.

Crucially, under cross-examination, Taylor was forced to make a telling concession about the screaming she had heard from Oscar:

> *Roux: So when you heard him screaming, it was out of anger but not in*
> *situations where he perceived his life to be threatened?*
> *Taylor: No, M'Lady.*
> *Roux: Is that a fair statement that I make to you when you said: 'no' ...*
> *[intervenes]*
> *Taylor: Yes.*
> *Roux: I think I understand what you mean. It means that you have not*
> *heard him screaming when he perceived his life to be threatened.*
> *Taylor: No, M'Lady.*

Taylor recounted how on 30 September 2012 she had travelled to the Vaal River with Oscar and Darren Fresco to visit some friends. Justin Divaris and Samantha Greyvenstein had travelled in another car.

On the way home, with Fresco at the wheel, the car was stopped by police officials because they were speeding. Taylor recalled that the officer asked the men to step out of the car and Oscar left his gun on the seat:

So Oscar had left his gun on the seat of the car and when the police had a look, he saw the gun was on the seat and he said to Oscar that the gun could not just be left, just be left on the seat there. So the policeman cocked the gun and the bullets flew out of the, out of the gun into the car and then Oscar got very angry and eventually they gathered the bullets, they found all the bullets and they put the gun back together and we drove away.

Taylor elaborated on her ex-boyfriend's anger:

He shouted at the policeman because he said that he was not allowed to touch his gun. After we left there, Oscar and Darren were pretty anxious and a little bit irritated with the policeman and so they laughed and they said that they wanted to shoot a robot [traffic light] and then Oscar shot a bullet out the sunroof.

She told the court that while she was sitting in the back seat, she saw Oscar take his gun and shoot out of the car. She heard 'a very, very loud sound' and both men then laughed.

She claimed that they didn't talk about the incident and carried on driving. They went to sign papers at the home of a friend of Oscar, but she couldn't recall where. Then they went to dinner in Sandton.

The pressure of being in the witness box under the world's gaze was at times too much for Taylor to bear. On two occasions, when asked how she felt about how her relationship with Oscar ended and his infidelity, she burst into tears, prompting the court to be stopped. Taylor was a shaky witness, lacking in confidence. Inevitably, her testimony was met with public scepticism and an assumption that she was a woman scorned, and hell hath no fury like one.

Roux's line of questioning suggested that the defence team believed her evidence was seated in a desire to get back at Oscar. Under cross-examination, Taylor conceded that after the couple's first break-up, she had a relationship with mining millionaire and TV producer Quinton van der Burgh while the athlete was at the London Olympics.

• • •

In her testimony in court, Taylor couldn't remember exactly where the sunroof shooting happened. She also couldn't say whether it was on a highway or suburban road – just that it took place about 15 minutes after the police had stopped their vehicle for speeding. She also couldn't recall the location of the friend's house where Oscar had apparently signed firearm-related papers. And she couldn't remember the name of the Sandton restaurant the trio went to, only that it was a burger joint at Atholl Square. She further couldn't recall whether Oscar took her home or whether she slept at his house that night.

Taylor's only real recollection of the events was that they had been at the Vaal River with friends and at some point on the way home Oscar fired a shot. Was this enough?

Roux questioned Taylor about his client's emotions at the time of the alleged shooting incident – was he angry, irritated or laughing? Taylor said he displayed all three emotions at different stages: 'So after we left the cops, he was angry. Before he fired the shots, he was obviously irritated from being stopped. He then joked around to fire shots and after he fired the shots, he laughed about it.'

The advocate was dismantling Taylor's evidence, casting doubt over her recollection of events. There were simply too many discrepancies and too many details she couldn't remember.

Roux put it to her that Oscar would testify that the only time he ever signed firearm-related documents in her presence was in Pretoria, and not in Johannesburg as she had testified. He would also claim that he did not fire a shot through the sunroof of the car, as she had told the court. It would be a flat denial.

'I can clearly say that he shot through the [sun]roof of a car,' reiterated Taylor, but by this point Roux was done. This meant it would be Taylor's shaky recollection pitted against Oscar's blatant dismissal of the allegation. Only Darren Fresco could sway the court.

• • •

'Are you fucking mad?' Darren Fresco allegedly asked Oscar after he fired his gun through the sunroof of a speeding car. At least, that was the version Fresco presented to the court.

Fresco met Samantha Taylor through Oscar Pistorius while they were dating. The network engineer took the stand after Taylor and while he agreed with her that Oscar had fired a shot through the sunroof, there were many discrepancies in their versions.

Fresco recounted to the court how he was driving home from the Vaal with Oscar and Taylor in the car, when he was pulled over twice – first for not having number plates on the vehicle he was driving, and then several kilometres down the road, for speeding. On both occasions, the officers issued him with fines. Fresco said the runner had his 9 mm pistol between his legs on the seat of the car, which ultimately led to the altercation with the officers on the second time they were stopped:

> *After the Grasmere toll plaza and just thereafter we had been pulled over by some Metro police for speeding. At this stage the policeman had come to my window and asked for my licence and asked me to please step out of the vehicle, which I had done. He was busy asking me questions and it was taking a bit longer and shortly, shortly after that the accused had come out of the vehicle to see what was taking so long.*
>
> *He had come round to my side, the front right of the vehicle to see what was going on and shortly thereafter there was another Metro police person who had gone round to where the accused had been sitting and had picked up his gun off his seat. Then there was an altercation, a verbal altercation between the accused and the Metro police officer. The officer had picked up the accused's weapon off the passenger seat, to which the accused had replied: 'You cannot just touch another man's gun.'*

Fresco explained that the officer had picked up the weapon and had 'cleared' it, causing the bullet that was one-up in the chamber to be ejected into the vehicle.

> Nel: So when the policeman cleared the firearm and ejected the one bullet, what happened? What did the accused do?
>
> Fresco: He started telling the officer: Now your fingerprints are all over my gun, so if something happens you are then going to be liable for anything that had happened.
>
> Nel: So now the bullet is ejected. What happened?
>
> Fresco: Then in the interim his licence, his firearm licence had been given to the Metro police officer to which he asked him a question: Mr Pretorius ... and he said: well, actually if you could read it, it would state Mr Pistorius.

Fresco scrambled around the car searching for the bullet and eventually found it after moving the seat. He seemed to remember Oscar putting the bullet back into the magazine of the gun.

As a further indication of how fast Fresco had been driving, shortly after that incident, another set of metro police officers arrived on the scene, telling the men they had been chasing them since the toll plaza. They were issued with a speeding fine and allowed to continue. Fresco says Oscar was furious that someone had touched his gun:

> Fresco: I was driving, the accused was in the passenger seat. Sam Taylor was in the back of the car and then without prior warning he shot out the sunroof. Instinctively I had literally just moved over to the right-hand side of the vehicle. Once I had flinched over to the right-hand side of the vehicle, having ducked down, I had seen the weapon being brought back in, through the sunroof.
>
> Nel: Did you say anything?
>
> Fresco: Apologies for my language M'Lady, but I asked him if he is fucking mad.
>
> Nel: What did he say?
>
> Fresco: He just laughed, M'Lady. By that stage it literally felt as if my ear was bleeding. I had a constant ringing in my left ear.
>
> Nel: Did you enquire from him why? What was he doing, after the shot was fired?
>
> Fresco: He just laughed about what had just happened.
>
> Nel: Did you discuss this incident with him at all?
>
> Fresco: No, after that basically we just carried on driving.

If true, it was remarkably reminiscent of the Tashas incident account: a gun discharged with reckless abandon and never a word spoken about it.

While Fresco had pointed out the location of the alleged incident to Investigating Officer Mike van Aardt, he conceded under cross-examination that they did have to drive up and down four times before finding the spot he remembered. There were pictures to prove it, marked with a little blue label in file HI. Fresco told the court the incident had occurred somewhere near Modderfontein, but Taylor could not pinpoint the location.

Like Taylor, Fresco remembered they had accompanied Oscar to a house to sort out some kind of administration related to a firearm. However, unlike Taylor, he could remember the restaurant they then went to: the Gourmet Garage at Atholl Square.

To undermine Fresco's credibility, Roux picked at fine details. The only things in common between Fresco and Taylor's testimony was that they were together with Oscar, returning from the Vaal River, when the athlete apparently fired a single shot out of the sunroof. The two witnesses did not corroborate their location or the exact circumstances that led to the shot being fired.

Taylor had told the court that Fresco and Oscar had been angry after they were pulled over by the police and that they were then joking about shooting out traffic lights. Fresco denied this, insisting that he was angry and that it was the accused who had found the incident funny.

Fresco admitted he had received the fines and then crumpled them up and thrown them in the car. He couldn't answer what happened to the tickets subsequently, but assumed Justin Divaris had taken care of them as the car was from his dealership.

In his evidence-in-chief, Fresco had told the court that when returning from the Vaal, Oscar had his gun between his legs and that he had had no issue with Fresco's speed. He also claimed that when Oscar was driving the vehicle on the way to the river, Fresco had taken a photograph of the speedometer at 200 km/h.

But Roux was in fine form. Awkwardly for Fresco, the defence counsel produced a photograph taken by Fresco at 4:41pm – when Fresco was driving home. The speedometer read 260 km/h and it was obvious the photo had been taken when Fresco was at the wheel:

> Roux: *Anything that you want to say, Mr Fresco? [No audible answer]*
> Roux: *I see there is silence.*
> Fresco: *If you have got the photo that I have sent in, then it must have been me driving at the time … [intervenes]*
> Roux: *Why …?*
> Fresco: *I do not remember this.*
> Roux: *No, it is more than that. It is you coming back after giving evidence the previous night and come with evidence under oath, (a), incorrectly saying who was driving the vehicle to the Vaal and (b), engineering evidence that it was in the morning.*

While the defence poked holes in Fresco's recollection of events and created a degree of doubt about the incident, it could also be argued that Oscar's reputation and image were tarnished by his testimony. A portrait of reckless, fast-living young men was presented to the court.

However, it was a very different Oscar who took the stand in his own defence to answer to these firearm charges and to challenge the evidence of his former friends and girlfriend. It was his word against theirs.

• • •

348 ONE TRAGIC NIGHT

Oscar pleaded not guilty to all of the firearm-related charges and argued with Advocate Nel as to why he was innocent of these crimes. But the charges opened the door for the prosecutor to explore several examples of Oscar's irresponsible regard for firearm safety and ultimately benefited the state in its attempt to portray the accused in that light. Had Oscar pleaded guilty, this would not have been allowed to happen.

In his evidence-in-chief, Oscar first dealt with the alleged sunroof shooting, then moved on to the Tashas incident and finally addressed the .38 Special ammunition in his safe at home.

The trip to the Vaal River with Taylor and Fresco was a relaxing day spent out on the water where the trio and other friends had lunch. They decided to head back to Joburg mid-afternoon because the athlete needed to catch a flight to Scotland that night for a golfing event. He confirmed that Fresco was driving the car, Taylor was sitting behind the driver and that they were stopped twice by the police, when on one occasion a police officer handled his firearm.

Oscar explained that when the police officers were questioning Fresco, he left his handgun in the car because he did not want to approach the police while he was armed. He said a policeman, in an aggressive and unprofessional manner, asked who owned the weapon before making the gun safe by ejecting the magazine and a bullet, both of which fell into the car.

'I was agitated, I was angry that he had handled my firearm. After he had helped me get the round back, I think at that point he did not want to engage in a conversation anymore,' Oscar said.

He testified that the three of them left the scene for Divaris's house, where they'd left their cars, and had dinner somewhere close to his house before he jetted off to Scotland. But Oscar said he did not actually remember flying out to Scotland that evening – he was told this by his legal team who checked his travel dates.

He further disputed the two witnesses' claims that he filled in paperwork related to firearms that night. 'The only paperwork that I can remember doing was in October. I do not remember filing any paperwork in September. I do not remember going to a house on that day. I do not recall that.'

And the shooting incident?

'That never happened,' said Oscar.

John Beare was the vice chairman of the Lowveld Firearm Collectors Association who helped Oscar obtain his firearm collectors' licence – the documentation that would facilitate his acquisition of up to 30 firearms.

'Now did you not go to his place that day?' asked Nel, referring to the meeting the two witnesses remembered him attending to sign firearm-related papers:

> Accused: *I do not know, M'Lady. I do not remember going to his house on that day.*
>
> Nel: *If he has a photograph of you on that day with his daughter, did you take photographs with his daughter?*
>
> Accused: *I have … I do not know Mr Bear[e] well, but on an occasion that I have … on one of the occasions that I have met with him, I took a photo with his daughter and his wife.*
>
> Nel: *Then it is possible that you were there?*

'Yes, M'Lady,' conceded the accused. Oscar could not remember the date he met Beare at his home, and he could not even remember exactly where Beare lived – so it was fair, then, that Taylor couldn't be criticised for not remembering the exact location of this meeting either, contested Nel.

Oscar quickly turned to attack the witnesses, Taylor in particular. There was clearly no love lost between the two.

'She lied in her statement and she lied when she was up here,' testified the accused. And yet, despite his accusatory tone, Oscar could not dispute Taylor's statement because he conceded that he could not remember either:

> Nel: *Then both of them indicate that you fired through the sunroof. That is definitely a lie?*
>
> Accused: *That is a lie, M'Lady.*
>
> Nel: *Both of them, independently will tell that lie?*
>
> Accused: *They both took the stand, they both had different stories as to why it happened, as to where it happened, as to how it happened, as to the reaction. That story was fabricated, M'Lady. It never happened. It was not the truth.*

Just two days earlier it was Taylor calling Oscar the liar. During his evidence-in-chief, which she was evidently watching, the former girlfriend tweeted: 'Last lies you get to tell … You better make it worth your while.' The tweet was soon deleted, but not before being retweeted hundreds of times.

Oscar claimed Taylor and Fresco had been in contact with each other and had been seen at the same events together; he was suggesting that they had colluded with one another to frame him.

But why didn't Roux challenge the witnesses on this allegation when they were in the box? Oscar couldn't say. And who told the accused about the two witnesses communicating with each other? Oscar couldn't remember.

Oscar agreed with Nel he should never have left his firearm in the car when he approached Fresco and the police officers after being stopped for speeding, and further agreed that the police officer in question was well within his rights to handle the firearm that had been left unattended. Nel walked the accused through the sequence of events: the officer picked up the handgun, dropped the magazine out and cleared the breach, which ejected a bullet, making the firearm safe:

> Nel: *Which means? The gun, the firearm was one-up?*
> Accused: *That is correct.*
> Nel: *So you carried that gun on the boat and at the function, one-up?*

'I think that would be correct,' said Oscar, before further confirming his earlier testimony that he was agitated and upset at the way the officer had handled his weapon.

Nel questioned why Oscar would carry his firearm with him to a social get-together at the river, and even when he went on a boat. Oscar explained he carried his firearm wherever he went, and his alternative was to leave it in his car. When he swam, he wrapped it in a towel and left it on the boat – which he initially did not see as negligent, despite Nel's insistence. Once the prosecutor suggested to the court that this was yet another example of the accused being unwilling to accept responsibility, Oscar changed his mind and agreed that leaving his firearm unattended is, in fact, negligent. This was a theme the prosecution took great pains to drive home throughout its argument: that Oscar was irresponsible, with little regard for standard safety procedures.

· · ·

'It was probably the scariest, scariest thing I have ever had to do in my whole life,' says Taylor, weeks after her testimony in court. 'You've got the judge and her assessors, you've got a prosecution team, you've got policemen, you've got lawyers, his defence team, you've got the ANC Women's League, and then you've got someone who you loved and someone who is like a stranger to you. That's your ex-boyfriend that's on a trial and you have to face him and you have to face his family and his friends who were once your friends as well.'

Taylor is aware of how she came across to the world and puts this down to being overcome by the moment. She calmed her nerves before stepping up to the witness box, but once she was sworn in she found it incredibly difficult.

'Before court, you calm yourself down and you say, "Just go up and it will be fine," and you go up there and I think you feel that you're on trial. It was so scary.'

She had resolved not to look at Oscar while she was on the stand but to rather keep her eyes fixed on her sister who had come along to support her.

'For some reason I just couldn't look at my sister and Oscar and I, we just … we stared at each other the whole time and I think that's why I got so emotional because it's such a frustrating thing to go through.'

What did she think was going through his mind as she was testifying?

'He probably thought, Why would you do this to me?' But, she reveals, she wasn't there by choice, as the jilted lover wanting to get her revenge on her promiscuous ex-boyfriend. 'I was subpoenaed to court, I didn't have a choice to go to court or not. The policemen, after the incident happened, they came to me in Cape Town and they took my statement and if they ask you a question, you've got to answer that question. I wasn't there to be the vindictive girlfriend. I wasn't there to get revenge on him how all the little Twitter trolls say. I was there to tell my truth and, unfortunately, we had problems in our relationship, so my truth wasn't necessarily so … nice and happy.'

Taylor is also clearly concerned at the perception that she came across as shaky and forgetful on the stand.

'You go up there and you remember everything and as soon as you get on the stand, you don't remember anything. So obviously after, when I had time to think about what went on, I could recall a lot more.'

She also dismisses what some have suggested on social media – that alcohol had impaired their memories on the day of the sunroof incident. 'I don't think any of us really drank, I know Darren Fresco doesn't really drink, Oscar had probably a few glasses of wine or a gin and tonic or whatever, I'd probably had a glass of wine, I'm not a big drinker either.

'The reason why I didn't know where we were and how we got there and how we got back is because I never go to the Vaal. I only just got my licence. I don't travel outside of Joburg. I grew up in Dainfern and I didn't really need to leave Dainfern. I didn't have a need to recognise signs or areas we were in. I would probably forget that and again that's why we have technology these days. I obviously use my GPS wherever I go. So I know people say they were all drunk and how I've got a bad memory of where I was, but I don't go to the Vaal often and I don't plan on going there often in the future, so I had no need to remember where we were.'

However, once off the stand, Taylor has a surprisingly detailed recollection of the house they visited later in the afternoon where Oscar allegedly went to sign gun papers.

'I can tell you the house was a brick house, they had the garden and garage and their cars were fairly nice, I think it was like an Audi and a Pathfinder. The house was an old middle-class house, they had a guard dog, an Alsatian, and the wife and the daughter were there,' says Taylor. 'In court you don't think of these things and it's really scary. I remember a lot. I remember the house. I remember the dog, I know that we went to the burger joint after, I don't know the name of the burger joint because I never go there and I'll probably never go there again. I know in court I said that I couldn't recall where we went after the burger joint, but I can now confirm everything, I was very nervous in court and I didn't think properly.'

She is also at pains to clear up an allegation made in court by her ex-boyfriend – that she and Darren Fresco conspired against him about the sunroof shooting.

'I would just like to say that the last time I ever spoke to Darren Fresco was when he threatened me over the phone to never come in their space again – when he threatened me was when Oscar and I had broken up the last time. He threatened me not to come back to Joburg, I had never been so badly spoken to by a man. It was so degrading. The first time after Oscar and I had ended that I saw Darren was in the witness room where he came to apologise to me about the way he spoke to me over the phone. The first time I saw him after the incident was in the courtroom. He had come to apologise to me in front of my lawyer. And you know what? If his defence team wants to put it on us that we had colluded, I would like them to please show me proof of phone calls and meetings.' Fresco declined to comment about Taylor's claim that he threatened her over the phone on Oscar's behalf or that he apologised to her in court.

Taylor also has a response to Oscar's claim that she had created a fake profile on Twitter to attack Reeva. 'In court Oscar made a comment about me creating a fake profile on Twitter to say nasty things to Reeva, which made her feel insecure. Again I would like them to show me proof and provide a track record. Any comments I have made in the past have come from my own account. We have managed to track the main member of "Pistorians" down, but took no further action on her as she doesn't seem to be any type of threat to me,' says Taylor, referring to the group on Twitter who rabidly defend the athlete.

Taylor wasn't entirely surprised by Oscar's emotional outbursts while on the stand. 'He is a very emotional person. I know when we used to fight, he used to cry all the time, but I think he played his role quite well, you know, when there's something sad, you're sad and when there's something that's good for you then you're okay with it.'

Once she had heard Oscar's testimony on the stand, Taylor revealed in an interview more about her take on the room and the events of that night. Does she believe it could be plausible? That the events could possibly have occurred as he stated?

> *There were many things that didn't make sense to me … Because I've been in that house for … you know, I was there a lot. The one thing I know that to have gone to the bathroom … often Oscar, while he was in training season, he would leave the curtain open a little bit because the natural sunlight came in at five o'clock in the morning which meant that we had to get up and go to train, so I don't know if he was training at the time, I don't know if his curtain would've been lightly open, but he often did keep his curtain slightly open so I know there was some sort of light coming in at three o'clock in the morning. The bathroom was definitely very dark, because that was a whole different side of the bedroom. There's a wall and there's … a long passageway and the passageway is very dark, so to be in the bathroom you needed to have put the light on to go to the loo or to at least see what you are doing. I know that if Reeva had gone to the bathroom, she would've put the light on because I definitely wouldn't go to the bathroom and leave the light off. If the cubicle light was broken, I definitely wouldn't close the door, especially at my boyfriend's house at three o'clock in the morning. I would … I don't know, I find that kind of weird. I definitely wouldn't close the door, especially if it's not even connected to the bedroom. The bathroom and toilet are separate to the bedroom, so I don't know … It definitely didn't make sense to me. I don't know why someone would lock the door even if they are at their boyfriend's house.*

• • •

Oscar's denials continued as he faced a quizzing on 'Count 3', the Tashas accidental discharge. Oscar recalled, as Lerena and Fresco had earlier, the lunchtime meeting at the restaurant to discuss the boxer's diet, as well as the athlete's eagerness to purchase a new firearm similar to Fresco's.

'It was stupid of me,' he acknowledged, 'and I asked if I can see his firearm.' Oscar did not dispute that he asked to see Fresco's gun, nor that he had handled it under the table in the busy eatery. He said he wanted to make sure that the weapon was safe – that it did not have a round in the chamber – and in the process of sliding the mechanism back he said a bullet was ejected from the weapon.

'… And the next thing I knew, a round went off.'

Oscar said he was angry at Fresco for passing him a loaded weapon that had a magazine in it, but was also relieved that no one had been hurt. He quickly returned the firearm to its owner under the table.

But, contrary to previous witness testimony, Oscar said it was Fresco who volunteered to take responsibility for the shooting by explaining that if anyone should ask, his firearm had accidentally gone off because it had fallen on the floor.

'I believed at that point that we both were to blame – I made a mistake for asking for a firearm in a restaurant and he made a mistake of giving me a firearm which was loaded and carrying one up. He told me not to say anything,' said Oscar, while conceding that he was concerned about the implications of news about the incident reaching the media.

The athlete said while Fresco told restaurant owner Loupis the fabricated story about the handgun being caught on his pants, he then owned up and told him that it was his fault before offering to pay for the damages and settling the bill.

For Nel, though, this was not responsibility enough. During cross-examination, he pushed the line he had followed throughout the process – that Oscar never believed he was responsible for anything and always shirked guilt.

'Talking about faults and taking responsibility, let us deal with the Tashas incident. Can you please explain to me why you pleaded not guilty,' asked Nel.

Oscar said he did so because he did not discharge the firearm. He was adamant.

'I physically did not discharge the firearm, My Lady, the firearm went off when it was in my possession but I did not have my finger … and I do not remember having my finger on the trigger,' he said.

The main attack on Oscar's defence in this regard was Mangena's testimony about the Glock's safety mechanism – that it is impossible for the Glock to discharge without someone actively pulling the trigger. Roux did not challenge Mangena on his evidence and the defence's ballistic expert Wollie Wolmarans would not contest it either. 'Then will you not accept that your finger was on the trigger, because that gun cannot discharge if your finger was not on the trigger,' said Nel, but the accused would not accept the proposition.

If it was always Oscar's version that his finger was not on the trigger when the firearm went off, why did his senior counsel not question the expert witness about this? The accused could certainly not explain it. 'If Mr Roux did not put that question to Mr Mangena, My Lady, then I am sure he has got a good reason for not doing so,' said Oscar. He was shifting responsibility to his legal team – but this was not the first or last time they were 'thrown under the bus' during cross-examination.

Nel, however, refused to accept the explanation; he knew Roux too well. The advocates had been adversaries for years and the prosecutor was sure that the senior counsel would not have slipped up like this. Nel told the court he believed Roux would never make such a mistake, and rather the reason he hadn't challenged Mangena was because it was never Oscar's version.

> Nel: *Let us look at it. You had it in your hand. Am I right?*
> Accused: *That is correct, My Lady.*
> Nel: *You ejected the one bullet.*
> Accused: *That is correct, My Lady.*
> Nel: *Nobody else touched that gun.*
> Accused: *That is correct, My Lady.*
> Nel: *But a shot went off.*
> Accused: *That is correct, My Lady.*
> Nel: *If that firearm is incapable of firing a shot without somebody pulling the trigger, who pulled the trigger?*
> Accused: *I am not sure, My Lady, what I am saying is that I did not have my finger on the trigger.*

It was Nel's relentless questioning on this that eventually pushed the accused to make the admission that the state needed. 'The firearm went off whilst it was in my possession, I take responsibility for the firearm going off when it was in my possession,' Oscar told the court, 'but I cannot say my finger was on the trigger when it was not on the trigger.'

Oscar explained as he was clearing the firearm the shot went off and 'I didn't have time to think'. This was the exact phrase he had used a day earlier when Nel was asking him about the four shots he fired through the door when he shot Reeva after claiming to have heard a noise. It's a phrase he'd repeat numerous times throughout his cross-examination.

'I did not have time to think,' said Nel, dismissively, antagonising the accused. 'We had that yesterday as well. So that is one of your defences. "I did not have time to think. I am a gun enthusiast, I did not have time to think."'

• • •

The fourth firearm-related charge was as a result of ammunition found in Oscar's safe on the morning of the shooting. When investigators started sifting through Oscar's house and cataloguing the evidence they came across a beige electronic safe, similar to those found in hotel rooms, in his bedroom cupboard. It was hidden behind a neatly stacked pile of T-shirts and in it Oscar stored medals from the Paralympic Games in 2004 (Athens), 2008 (Beijing) and 2012 (London), as well as a krugerrand amongst other items. Also in the safe was a blue box of 50 PMP, 158-grain .38 Special rounds. Oscar said he understood the charge, but he had never owned a .38 calibre firearm nor had he ever purchased .38 calibre ammunition.

'That ammunition was my father's for a firearm that he had registered or has registered in his name and he simply had it at my house for safekeeping. It was not mine, it was not in my possession. My understanding of the law is, you are allowed to give your ammunition to somebody for safekeeping. It does not have to be in your safe,' he said.

Oscar told Nel that he had two safes in his house: one downstairs to which he had sole access and a safe in his bedroom, which several people had access to via a combination lock. The prosecutor first took issue with the fact that Oscar claimed to keep ammunition in a safe to which several people had access, but he said he didn't keep his own ammunition there – he had a spare magazine in his bedside table and kept his firearm-cleaning kit in the safe downstairs.

Oscar testified that his father had asked if he could keep his ammunition in the upstairs safe, and that Henke had placed it in the safe on his own when his son was not there. Oscar could not say when it was placed there, only that it had been in the safe for quite some time.

Then Nel played what he thought to be his trump card. Henke Pistorius had refused to make a statement admitting that the ammunition in the safe was his. The assumption was that this was because of a breakdown in their relationship that saw Henke effectively ostracised from the Pistorius family. The accused, however, was unaware of his father's refusal to assist. 'My father and I have not had communication between the two of us, for many years. I have spoken to him, but there has not been a relationship,' admitted Oscar. 'He would sometimes come up to Pretoria or Johannesburg. He asked me if he could keep the ammunition in my safe. I said that he is more than welcome to and I let him do so.'

Nel then turned to Oscar's firearm competency tests in which he correctly answered that you may possess a particular type of ammunition only if you have a licence for that particular firearm or you are a firearm dealer. Oscar said that after consulting with Roux about his understanding of the law, the advocate confirmed his thoughts on it.

'No, it cannot be. Mr Roux would not do that,' said Nel, frustrated at the explanation. Again, Oscar was sacrificing the reputation of his defence counsel in order to save himself. 'Mr Roux would not have said to you, that it is in order for you to keep your father's ammunition in your safe. He would not have done that. I put it to you,' said Nel.

For Nel, this was another example of the accused not willing to take responsibility – why else would he not plead guilty to such a blatantly obvious transgression of the law? But Oscar continued to claim that while it was in his safe, he was technically not in possession of the ammunition.

Nel questioned the accused on why he kept a spare magazine in his bedside drawer, and – once again – his understanding of the law. After first admitting that he left the magazine in his bedside drawer at all times, Oscar said that he in fact put it in the safe whenever he left the house. 'At times I carry that extra magazine with me. At times I put it in my bedside table. If I went away, I locked it in my safe,' he said. But then less than a minute later he added: 'I am sure there was a couple of occasions that I forgot to lock it away, M'Lady. I cannot say and I cannot stand here and lie. There would have been occasions, but this is not related to the charge of the .38 ammunition in the safe.'

But it was indeed relevant for Nel as he attempted to show the court that the accused was a negligent firearm owner.

• • •

Besides Oscar's evidence disputing the testimony of his former friends and girlfriend related to the firearm charges, the defence team led no further evidence related to these charges. This came as a surprise to many.

Ballistics expert Wollie Wolmarans – Mangena's equivalent on the defence team – did not challenge the police witness's testimony about the Glock's safety mechanism; neither did he suggest possibilities and case studies showing how this particular firearm could go off without the trigger being pulled. He also did not testify about the laws related to ammunition being stored in order to confirm his client's understanding of the legislation.

On the two shooting incidents, all the court had to go on from the defence's side was Oscar's version. Nothing more. Either the defence thought that Oscar's version was sufficient to stand up to scrutiny or they had accepted a guilty ruling on these additional charges. The risks were high.

The Secrets of the Missing Apple

Captain Francois Moller's job as a cellphone analyst for the South African Police Service (SAPS) is to look backwards and connect the dots, primarily those that have left an elaborate trail on Steve Jobs's creations. Moller is stationed at the Technological Investigation Support Centre at the head office of Detective Services under commanding officer Colonel Mike Sales.

Moller's friendliness and jolly demeanour are underlined by his genuine smile. His apparent lack of jadedness and cynicism, which so often characterise career policemen, belies his credentials and experience as a cop. He spent five years in the early 2000s at the murder and robbery unit in Pretoria until it was shut down by then Police Commissioner Jackie Selebi. Moller then spent several months at the provincial head office assisting detectives with high-profile cases such as the kidnapping and murder of Sheldean Human before getting a promotion to the high-tech unit under now-retired Major-General Sharon Schutte. He was then moved to the specialist police unit, the Hawks, officially referred to as the DPCI (Directorate for Priority Crime Investigation).

Moller has regularly testified in high-profile court matters for which he analyses phone records to assist with the prosecution. Some of these cases include the Chanelle Henning murder, the Griekwastad family killings and the shooting of boxer Corrie Sanders.

In the trial of two men accused (and later convicted) of murdering young mother Chanelle Henning, Moller was responsible for a first in South African courts: he used Geotag data retrieved from the photos of one of the accused's BlackBerry handsets to analyse his movements during the planning stages of the murder. Moller plotted this movement on Google Maps and during his testimony in court would switch to Street View to show the judge key locations in respect of crime scene photos. The judge acknowledged the policeman's good work in his ruling.

Moller and Mike Sales were responsible for analysing the cellphones, iPads and computers belonging to Oscar and Reeva that were on the scene of the shooting. All in all, these included three iPhones, two BlackBerries, two iPads and one MacBook computer. The devices and their contents featured prominently in the investigation and court case and have to a large degree been shrouded in intrigue. They fuelled public speculation as to a motive for a potential murder and many believed in the run-up to the trial that the answer to the question of what might have led to a possible argument in the dead of night lay in the data and text on the cellphones.

Did Reeva receive a text message from an ex-boyfriend that sent Oscar into a blind rage? Or perhaps Oscar was surfing porn and Reeva stumbled upon this, sparking a fierce fight?

But it was not only the devices and their contents that were the focus of attention and the subject of scrutiny. Rather, it was the attempts, which were fraught with difficulties and became increasingly desperate, by Moller and Sales to gain access to these handsets that were particularly intriguing. Their endeavours even led them to Apple's headquarters in California in a mad scramble as the trial was already underway.

On the morning of Valentine's Day 2013, police officers at Oscar's home, led by investigating officer Hilton Botha, seized several devices in the house bar one iPhone 5. Reeva's black, scratched iPhone 4S with a metallic cover and dried blood specks on the front and back was found on the tiles in the bathroom, partially obscured by the charcoal bathmat, near a pool of blood and just centimetres from Oscar's silver 9 mm firearm. The athlete's white iPhone 5 was also discovered in the bathroom on the bloody tiles face up next to a smear of red. Two BlackBerries, which had not been used for several months, were stacked in the bedroom near the amplifier while his and her iPads were found on the carpet next to the bed, closest to the sliding door leading on to the balcony.

Botha handed the phones to Moller who had the responsibility of analysing the contents. All he had was the PIN code for Reeva's phone and he did not know the PIN for Oscar's phone, nor the numbers for either line. Early on the morning of the shooting Reeva's friend Samantha Greyvenstein had given Botha the PIN code for the phone in order for him to find a number for her next of kin.

Samantha keyed in the PIN code and Botha called Reeva's mother. But he neglected to write down the PIN and so later that afternoon, when Kim Myers and her father and brother arrived at the house, he asked them for the code.

Once Kim had phoned Samantha to get the password, Botha took the phone from the bag of evidence and allowed Kim to charge it in her brother's car. Together with the investigating officer, Kim and her brother checked Reeva's last messages before Botha took the phone back into evidence. He later gave the code to Moller so that he could access the device.

When Moller analysed the two phones originally sent to him, he was unaware that Oscar owned two phones – one a 'work' phone (with a number ending in 4949), the other for 'personal' calls (ending in 0020). The device Moller had in his possession was the athlete's work phone, while the other was unaccounted for.

Under Section 205 of the Criminal Procedure Act, the police may approach a court for an order giving them access to certain information, including a phone company's call records. The phone company has to hand these records over once the court issues this order. It was once Moller had this data that he discovered that Oscar had a second phone because his particulars were linked to two numbers. Oscar had replaced the two BlackBerries when he had done a SIM swap the previous year, so the data received by Moller was for Reeva's phone and Oscar's work and personal handsets. The data also ruled out any need to investigate the BlackBerries seized at the scene as evidence because they were no longer in use.

According to the data retrieved from the phone in the police's possession – the number ending with 4949 – no calls had been made by the athlete in the wake of the shooting. This was why when Hilton Botha took the stand during the bail application, he confidently told the magistrate that Oscar's phone showed no record of any calls being made on the morning of 14 February. It appeared that the athlete had not phoned the police or the paramedics. And yet Oscar's lawyers were adamant that the calls had indeed been made.

But where was the other handset with the second number? This was an issue Nel would have to raise in the bail application. 'We know that you seized two phones in the house?' asked Nel, leading Botha through his evidence in the bail application:

> Nel: Did you seize any other phones in that house?
> Botha: The two BlackBerries that were in the bedroom, yes.
> Nel: If the accused phoned; that phone you never received?
> Botha: I did not receive a phone, if he phoned. The phones that I received shows nothing that was happening that morning from those two units.

Then Nel made the revelation in court – a phone was missing from the scene and the defence had not handed it over to investigators. The defence responded by insisting that they were never asked for the phone. An arrangement was made for it to be given to the investigating team.

This handset was crucial to the investigation – the 0020 number was Oscar's personal number and the device he used most. The majority of his communication with Reeva and with his friends was done via this iPhone and if there were any clues as to what had occurred in the early hours of Valentine's Day, this phone would hold them.

The phone was collected from the defence a full 12 days after Reeva was shot – but little did investigators know they would face months of frustration and difficulty in trying to gain access to the contents of 0020.

Reports emerged in June 2013 that police had still not managed to analyse Oscar's phone, apparently because he had forgotten the password. His lawyer's, however, dismissed the reports, stating that they had provided the police with all the required information to access the phone.

Then in the second week of February 2014, just weeks before the trial was to start, we established that the police had still not managed to gain access. It was revealed at the time that red tape had hindered an application for international mutual legal assistance – Moller and his team were trying to get the phone to Apple in California where its manufacturers could analyse it, but had to go through the US authorities based at their embassy in Pretoria. The SAPS had been told to approach Apple directly in order to resolve the problem of access to the phone's data.

But this is where the process had hit a horrible wobble. The official application lay on someone's desk, somewhere between the National Prosecuting Authority and the SAPS, for several months. From May 2013 until December that year, the process stalled. It was only towards the end of the year, with the trial just months away, that top police management realised there was a problem and reignited the search for answers.

Why hadn't they been able to access the phone? Sources claim that the password Oscar had provided did not unlock the device, and the software Moller and his team were using was unable to bypass it.

In January 2014, the cops scrambled to get the paperwork in order and went knocking on the door of Pretoria Chief Magistrate Desmond Nair. The required affidavits were secured and a certificate was finally issued by the National Director of Public Prosecutions. Local representatives of American security institutions were also contacted. The way was finally paved for the trip to Apple in America.

All of this took time, and lots of it. The investigators were running out of this precious commodity with the trial now mere days away. They could not afford to be the reason that the matter be postponed, or even worse, struck off the roll due to lack of preparation.

By this stage the National Commissioner and the Minister of Police Nathi Mthethwa were apparently raging at the lack of answers and were angry that the process had not been done more efficiently.

While this was playing out in February 2014, local television network eNCA reported that it had gained exclusive access to Oscar's iTunes account using the username and password he had provided to the police. But it wasn't the iTunes account the police needed – it was much more complex than that. The password the police needed was one that was created when the phone was synced with a computer. It appeared that this particular password had been changed after the shooting when it was last synchronised with a computer. 'If you set up your iPhone, you have to create an iTunes account. Now on that account, if you log onto your computer, it will ask you in the set-up on your computer where you can decide to encrypt the data on your phone, whether you want to password protect it. That's the password that gave the problem,' explains a member of the state's team.

The policemen wanted access to Oscar's contact lists, call logs, Internet history, photographs, videos and all back-ups that could help with the investigation. While they could scroll through the phone, they could not download any of the information and use it as evidence in court. They also could not install their software to 'jailbreak' the phone – an approved and legal method to disable the security feature on the device to install third-party apps in order to download deleted information. They had done this on Reeva's phone and also on Oscar's work phone, which had been seized at the crime scene. The SAPS use two different products to analyse data: one is a Swedish product XRY and the other is made by the Israelis, called Cellebrite. Neither of these could access the device.

It was the second-last week of February and the trial was ten days away – due to begin on Monday, 3 March – when Moller, Sales and the police's head of detectives General Vineshkumar Moonoo received the green light to take the phone to Apple headquarters in California. On Thursday, 20 February, the US officials authorised the warrant and Moller and Sales were instructed to be at a meeting at Apple in San Francisco a week later, on Thursday, 27 February. And so, just a week before the trial was scheduled to start, the team jetted off to the United States.

They arrived at the tech giant's offices at 1 Infinite Loop in Cupertino with high expectations, but were soon disappointed as their fears were confirmed – the missing password was between the device and the computer it had been synchronised with, not the network. This meant that the Apple technicians could not help them.

The problem was that only one computer had been seized from the crime scene – Reeva's. None of Oscar's computers had been taken as evidence and yet crime scene photographs show a workstation in the runner's upstairs lounge and at least one MacBook laptop in the house. Some on the scene attest to there being as many as three laptops lying around the house, none of which was seized. Without the computer on which the account had been created, it was highly unlikely the police would be able to gain access to the phone.

They returned from the United States empty-handed, except for a back-up of the phone data on a hard-drive. Despite their best efforts, they could not unlock the secrets held by the iPhone. This meant that all they had going in to court was the data retrieved from Oscar's work phone and the contents of Reeva's phone.

· · ·

So what did the investigating team believe could be on Oscar's personal phone that they were so determined to access it? And what do they believe was done in an attempt to prevent them from accessing it?

During the course of the investigation, one of the SAPS software providers had, in fact, found a way to get into the iPhone.

Executives from Cyanre, The Computer Forensic Lab, South Africa's leading private digital and computer forensic company, had heard on the radio that the police were struggling to get into the device. They knew they had the technology the police needed so they called them up, as managing director Danny Myburgh explains. 'We supplied the software and the hardware to the police to do the forensics. When we heard over the radio that they were unable to decrypt Oscar's phone, we approached them and said we can make our equipment available to them. We set it all up for them and supplied it to them and we enabled them to access Oscar's phone. We didn't have a mandate from the SAPS to assist them with the analysis, so unfortunately we could not get involved or conduct the analysis for them.

'We know what type of information they could access from similar actions we've done in the past. We could typically decrypt about 80 to 90 per cent of the data. What could be extracted was calendar items, chats, contacts, limited amounts of locations and quite a lot of SMS messages. We concluded that the main reason why they went to Apple was to get that other 10 per cent that couldn't be decrypted. They went to extract that other 10 per cent because they didn't know what they could get,' explains Myburgh.

He says the police would have been in a perfect situation to see if any data had been deleted or if content on the phone had been wiped off. 'They could tell if there were large chunks of emails or messages that were missing. From what is there, it would have been easy for them to determine what is not there and what had been deleted.'

What the police did establish through this exercise was that at some point the cellphone was synchronised with a MacBook – one named 'Titanium Hulk'.

Only one person close to the accused has a fascination with the lumbering green Marvel Comics hero. It featured in his Twitter feed as quotes from comic strips; he wore green bandanas bearing the eyes of the behemoth; he edited pictures of himself to colour his own skin green; and one friend even remarked on social media, 'You truly are the Titanium Hulk.' Carl Pistorius. His Gmail address contains that very name.

So this was what had put a spanner in the works – it was suspected that when the phone was last synchronised a new password had been created, so relying on Oscar's old password would obviously not have worked. To confirm their suspicions, a source said police were able to track the phone over the time it had been missing and compared it to data linked to Carl's phone, which showed a potential overlap. Both phones followed the same route over a period of days.

The most intriguing piece of information to be gathered from the partial extraction of data had more to do with what *wasn't* on the phone than with what was. Our study of the data, compared to the extraction from the personal phone, shows that the entire call history had been deleted, the entire WhatsApp record and all its messages had been wiped out, and specific text messages had been deleted. Some of these messages were received on the device while Oscar was in the Brooklyn holding cells and while the device was unaccounted for. This would have to have meant that the device had been switched on, and allowed to download messages from the network to the handset, before they were deleted. This appeared to have occurred days after the shooting.

Moller was set to begin his evidence on Monday, 24 March – the third week of the trial. The weekend prior, there was a strong rumour amongst the media that Carl Pistorius was about to be arrested. Some had got wind that the Blade Runner's brother might be charged with defeating the ends of justice for allegedly removing the phone from the crime scene and tampering with it.

But it wasn't to be – Carl was not arrested, nor was he charged.

That Monday morning court started 11 minutes late and prosecutor Nel made an unexpected announcement to the court. Nel apologised to the court for starting a little late because the state had been 'engaging with the defence in terms of certain admissions'. Once Masipa was in her chair, Nel read the admissions into the record from a handwritten note, which he said had been drafted earlier that morning. It had clearly been done in haste and at the last minute:

> *Admission in terms of section 220 of the Criminal Procedure Act*
> 1. *That the two iPhones seized in the bathroom ... the two Blackberry phones, as well as two iPads seized from the bedroom on 14 February 2013 were handed to Captain Moller.*
> 2. *That Colonel Sales and Captain Moller downloaded the data on the iPhones and iPads and investigated these devices.*
> 3. *That the data received from Vodacom is correct and a true reflection of the data pertaining to the devices.*
> 4. *That on 25 February 2013, the accused handed over his personal iPhone to the South African Police Service. This phone was removed from the scene on 14 February 2013. This phone was also analysed and the data downloaded by Captain Moller.*
>
> *That will be the admissions, M'Lady, in terms of section 220. I beg leave to hand that up.*

Included in these admissions was the authenticity of the cellphone data from the service providers – this would mean that the prosecution would not have to call a representative from Vodacom to confirm the data, which is a run-of-the-mill occurrence in criminal trials. The second admission was that the defence would not dispute the chain of evidence around the phones – they would not dispute that the phones and iPads were seized on the crime scene, bagged and tagged, put in evidence bags and taken by Hilton Botha to Captain Moller who carried out the extractions and analysis.

What had led to this unanticipated announcement of admissions being made by the defence related to the phones? One might have expected that Oscar's counsel would have fought tooth and nail against the contents of the phone being admitted to a trial court with such ease. It was also expected that the defence team would challenge each and every step taken by the police investigators in securing information and maintaining the integrity of the 'chain of evidence', as is so often the case in criminal courts in the country. This was even more pressing in this trial, where the defence had blatantly accused the police of tampering and contaminating the crime scene. It all seemed too easy.

Did anything happen behind the scenes while the prosecution 'engaged with the defence' on the admissions?

It also appeared that the defence may have made a strategic error. What they did not realise was that by making the admissions the prosecution would not have to call former investigating officer Hilton Botha to testify. The only reason the state needed Botha on the witness stand was to confirm the chain of evidence regarding the phones and iPads – and that had now been mutually 'resolved'. Putting Botha on the stand would be high risk for the state as Roux would repeat what happened at the bail hearing and tear him apart over his handling of the crime scene, allegations that the scene was contaminated and his initial interactions with witnesses. It would have been a field day for the senior defence counsel.

However, a source close to the defence legal team said there was no oversight and they did not miss a trick. Rather, the situation was far more complex.

These questions around the unexpected admissions were echoed by experts in the industry watching the trial unfold. The way both the prosecution and the defence dealt with the digital evidence raised serious concerns for Myburgh and his team from Cyanre. As experienced forensic investigators, they found the conduct of the legal teams very strange.

'It is normal for them to challenge the chain of evidence. We didn't see that the defence tested the expert or the evidence. There was no question regarding the authenticity of the messages. It was watered down. We were expecting a lot more in terms of this. We were hoping that the forensics would open up this case and prove it beyond reasonable doubt. We expected the state to make a lot more of the digital evidence and for the defence to test it more vigorously. We're sitting in cases where we are under cross-examination for up to two years over this kind of evidence. So in a case of this nature, to have a person under cross-examination so fast, it was a bit weird,' explains Myburgh.

He also doesn't understand why the prosecution didn't make a big noise about deletions on the handset if any. 'There was no evidence to say, "We saw that he deleted this." Why not? Why not? If we had this situation in OJ Simpson, if this was in America, they would have stayed on this point for four days, showing exactly what was not on the phone. In this case, the phone was mentioned briefly and then nothing else. This points to why are you cleaning out this phone? What attempts did the police do to find backups? Did they go to the cloud? They would have been able to see if it was synchronised to his brother's computer – did they get a search warrant for his brother's computer? If not, what led them to decide not to do that?'

Later that Monday, once Oscar's neighbour Annette Stipp had completed her testimony, Moller took the stand armed with a litany of explosive and emotionally laden WhatsApp messages. The courtroom and the world were afforded rare insight into the reality of the relationship between Oscar and Reeva. At times it was uneasy and awkward but the prosecution believed it a necessary discomfort for this was the only way they could 'hear' Reeva's voice. Her words were being heard from the grave through the messages she had typed.

· · ·

The calling of Captain Moller to the witness box came with significant expectations from the media and the public over the lingering question of Oscar's iPhone and the missing password. In the weeks leading up to the trial, Eyewitness News radio reports had revealed the battle investigators were having to access data on the phone because the athlete had claimed that he'd forgotten his password.

Nel had worked closely with Moller on a previous high-profile case – the murder of Chanelle Henning – where data analysis of cellphone and bank accounts had proved critical to establishing a timeline and the movement of the accused. From a public perspective, a similar hope had been attached to Moller in this case. Moller's expertise is not only about deciphering some or other code or cracking a password to reveal the intimate secrets of an accused or the victim, but also about putting that data into context. He has a knack for weaving a narrative from the numbers, dates and times to help the court understand how the information matches real-world events.

Moller testified as to how he received the two iPhones and two BlackBerries as well as the MacBook and iPads from Botha, how he set about identifying whose number was whose, and the urgency of it all because he had to leave the city to testify in another case. He summarised how he ruled out the use of the BlackBerries and reached the conclusion that there was one phone missing. Moller told the court that the software he uses is designed to extract the data from the devices in an unaltered state. While it might seem obvious, it's important for technical witnesses to put this information on the record, to assure the judge and counsel of the integrity of the data being testified about. The first and basic data report extracted from Reeva's phone made up 2 688 pages, but a later and more rigorous analysis of the devices retrieved 35 654 pages of call logs, contacts, and 2 731 text and WhatsApp messages.

The LCD screen in the court flickered to life when Moller was asked to go into detail in terms of what he had found. He started with the basics of what the extraction files contained – case file information, his own details, details of the phone's owner – before Nel referred him to the first of the WhatsApp messages. The prosecutor asked Moller to read into the record a message Oscar sent to Reeva about a month before he killed her:

> **2013/01/11 – 13:03:37 UTC:** Angel please do not say a thing to anyone. Darren told everyone it was his fault. I cannot afford for that to come out. The guys promised not to say a thing.

He then read the follow-up message Reeva sent to Oscar:

> **2013/01/11 – 15:04:43** I have no idea what you are talking about☺

Unlike Reeva's facetious response, which ended with a smiley face emoticon, the court knew exactly what Oscar was referring to – the Tashas shooting incident. This was part of the state's evidence to show that the athlete acknowledged that he was responsible for the shooting, but that his friend Fresco had volunteered to take the fall.

Nel continued to lead Moller through the messages, asking him to read out those he wanted on the record. These included an argument about Reeva apparently smoking marijuana while on her Jamaican reality TV show. 'I do not know how many times you took or if you took other things or what you did when you were on them,' said Oscar in the message, seemingly concerned by what had been revealed to him. Moller read one of the most contentious messages Reeva sent to her lover, which would form the basis for the state's argument that the accused was abusive, possessive and prone to violence. Part of the 518-word message, sent on a Sunday afternoon 18 days before her life ended, read:

> *you have picked on me incessantly since you got back from CT and I understand that you are sick but it's nasty ... I was not flirting with anyone today ... I feel sick that you suggested that and made a scene at the table ... you do everything to throw tantrums in front of people ... I am scared of you sometimes and how you snap at me and of how you will react to me ... I am not some other bitch you may know, trying to kill your vibe ... I get snapped at ... Stop chewing gum. Do this, do not do that ... your endorsements, your reputation ...*

Those in the court were stunned. A badly controlled temper and the possibility of alleged abuse of some kind had been hinted at, rumoured and reported on from anonymous sources since the day of the shooting, but never supported. Here in court and in her own words, Reeva said she was at times scared of Oscar; it appeared to show his jealousy and temper.

Moller was asked to read Oscar's response:

> *I want to talk to you. I want to sort this out ... I am sorry for the things I say without thinking ... I was upset ... I was upset when I left you ... I am sorry ... I had a mad headache ...*

Moller read another WhatsApp message into the record in which Reeva recalled an incident on 7 February when she felt her boyfriend had mistreated her. In addition, Nel asked the witness to refer to other messages that were of a loving nature. 'I downloaded more than a thousand communications between the deceased and the accused person, of which I would reckon 90% were normal conversations and loving conversations,' said Moller.

Nel turned to deal with Oscar's phone seized at the house and handed to Moller on the Friday after the shooting – the number ending with 4949 – and the device delivered to him on 26 February, the number ending with 0020. As with the earlier data, Moller explained how he had used it to make certain findings. In this particular case, he described how the handset connected to named and identified cellphone towers, which could then be used to plot the movement of the device. He also explained how data connections – using Twitter, WhatsApp or the Internet – would be registered on the service provider's records as a GPRS connection.

Moller created two timelines using the data linked to both of Oscar's phones – the work and private handsets – one for 13 February, the other for the day of the shooting. The communication and movement analysis started at about 5:30pm on the Wednesday when he was driving through Midrand, south of Pretoria, on his way home. The connections Oscar's phone made along the highway plotted his route. The information confirmed the calls to and from Reeva's phone. The records show that at about 8:25pm Oscar called his cousin, a call that lasted nearly 30 minutes – the last call on this phone before the shooting. Moller said four more Internet connections were made on one of Oscar's handsets on 13 February.

The data shows that the athlete's 0020 handset connected to the Internet on the morning of the shooting at 01:48:45 for 309 seconds. Did this show that Oscar was indeed up and awake at the time he claims he was sleeping? The information appeared significant and appeared to coincide with the testimony of the pathologist that the food in Reeva's stomach put her up and awake about two hours prior to the shooting. Was this thus further proof?

The next data connection was at 03:18:45 and lasted for 75 seconds, while at 03:19:03 the first voice communication is made from the device to Oscar's neighbour, Johan Stander. That call lasted 24 seconds and thereafter several calls were logged in the following minutes:

- 03:20:02 – call to Netcare – 61s
- 03:21:33 – call to estate security
- 03:21:47 – call to Voicemail – 7s
- 03:22:05 – Security called back
- 03:55:91 – call to friend Justin Divaris – 123s
- 04:01:38 – call to brother Carl Pistorius – 34s
- 04:09:03 – call to agent Peet van Zyl

Moller stated that the call to Van Zyl was the last made from the device, and he further confirmed that this was the device handed to the police on 25 February, 11 days after the shooting.

Besides the handful of messages that the state used to show that Reeva's and Oscar's relationship wasn't the perfect, loving and caring romance the accused would have the court believe, the captain's evidence was clinical, composed of indisputable numbers and streams of data. His evidence left some people in the court wanting, if not outright disappointed. Since the shooting the phones and their contents had been touted as possibly holding the answers to what might have happened that night, but there was very little in the way of answers. Equally surprising was that the phone that underwent analysis at the Apple offices in the United States did not feature at all, and without a public explanation for what had happened in the preceding weeks, including Carl's alleged involvement, the police and investigators appeared to have made no significant headway with this line of investigation.

• • •

Moller testified over two days, the first day primarily dealing with the basics of his investigation and the text messages he retrieved in which Reeva told Oscar how she was scared of him and hinted at an abusive relationship. The second morning, a new face appeared in the public gallery – with his short bleached-blond hair gelled and styled to a bird's nest of spiky peaks, former footballer Marc Batchelor squeezed his broad-shouldered frame into a black suit for court. Batchelor was listed as number 35 on the state's witness list, but his presence in court indicated that they had no intention of calling him. As would become evident in Oscar's later testimony, there was no love lost between the burly former national soccer player and the Paralympian. A member of the investigating team said Batchelor was called to 'rattle' the accused, 'make him feel uncomfortable'. He sat in the row directly behind the dock next to Kim and Gina Myers. Oscar avoided any eye contact as he took his seat that morning. Aimee gave Oscar a book in the dock – *Breakthrough Prayer: The Power of Connecting with the Heart of God*. An open page revealed parts that had been underlined.

When Nel concluded leading Moller through his evidence-in-chief, Judge Masipa had barely left the courtroom before Barry Roux jumped up and took the handful of brisk strides back to his client in the dock, gesturing for him to lean closer as he approached. Attorney Brian Webber and his candidate attorney Roxanne Adams soon joined them and they paged through documents containing tables and information. The legal team was confirming dates and times on the phone records before the cross-examination started.

Oscar's athletics coach had also made a rare appearance in court. Ampie Louw is a tall, aged man with a kind face and a smile to match, generous with conversation but mindful of his responsibilities to Oscar. The pair met with a warm embrace, separated by the dock. Oscar's spectacles were pushed skew on his face as his friend and mentor buried the young man's face in his neck and slapped him reassuringly on the back.

With Moller back on the stand, Roux started by asking him to explain the functioning of handsets in relation to how they access the Internet. He referred specifically to one of the data connections on Reeva's device that showed she had been on the Internet for more than 11 hours – beyond the time she had been shot and killed. Moller said if a user had not closed an application after using it, it might keep the data connection open while running in the background. There are also push functions of different applications, such as email and other notifications that activate without the user's input. This was important for the defence – it explained that the data connection in the early hours of the morning did not necessarily mean that the accused was awake and using his phone.

In order to place on the record the specific times of events that evening, Roux referred to the estate security landline: the records showed that Stipp first called security, followed by neighbour Mike Nhlengethwa, then Oscar. Security then returned Oscar's call, as confirmed by the records and contrary to Baba's evidence. Moller also explained away the peculiar call to Oscar's voicemail minutes after the shooting. He didn't have an iPhone, he said, but he'd made enquiries with colleagues.

'The voice call button and the other buttons are very close,' he said. 'So my personal opinion about this call was that it was not an intentional call. That was during the time that Mr Pistorius was on the phone, he accidently pushed that button.'

Roux accepted the assumption. He read several more items to Moller for him to confirm, which he did. On the calls to Van Zyl, Moller conceded that his analysis couldn't say who made those calls, only that they were made from Oscar's handset.

Roux then turned his attention to the four messages Moller had read to the court that the state believed showed that Oscar was abusive. The captain said he had read through more than 1 700 messages:

Roux: What was your approach in determining relevance?
Moller: If one reads through these conversations and one thousand seven
                 hundred and something entries that there was, one can immediately
                 identify certain messages that stood out. By standing out I would
                 mean that it is not the ordinary or normal conversations, something
                 else that is happening here.
Roux: I can ask you many questions. Let us get straight to the point. You
                 found four relevant to arguing between them?
Moller: That is correct, M'Lady.
Roux: That is what you are looking at?
Moller: That is correct, M'Lady.
Roux: It is not that they are standing out. You were looking at messages
                 showing some argument between the two?
Moller: That is correct.
Roux: Yes, and out of that more than 1 700 you found four?
Moller: That is correct, conversations not ... because some of them were
                 more than only one message but yes, conversations.

For Roux it was about context and perspective. The vast majority of the communication between Oscar and Reeva was normal conversation, and yet the state had chosen to focus on the four examples of unhappiness and distress in the relationship that the messages appeared to reveal.

The advocate read Moller the message his client sent to Reeva about the

Tashas shooting incident, where he said, 'Darren told everyone it was his fault.'

'One thing that is not there,' said Roux, 'is that him saying to Reeva that he asked Mr Fresco to take the blame. It is not there?'

Moller agreed.

Roux spent the next several hours going through hundreds of messages between the couple. From the mundane good mornings and good nights, to the romantic and the fun. Messages ended with little Xs to denote kisses. Oscar checked up on Reeva to ensure she was safe at night. They shared dieting tips, supported each other when they were down. They spoke about cars, dreams and money.

Roux didn't venture on to the more intimate messages between the couple, but our study of the data report shows that the couple spoke about sex, and Reeva sent Oscar topless photos of herself, to one of which he responded: 'You so cute.. I love that … You've just made me feel really naughty..'

What also emerged was their fondness of pet names for each other: 'my boo', 'my baba', 'my baby', 'bub', 'boobi', 'my angel'. The defence had collected its own list of hundreds of messages that were compiled into an exhibit and submitted to the court.

After brief argument between Roux and Nel, the defence was allowed to screen in court surveillance footage filmed on 4 February at a filling station's convenience store. It shows the couple touching, hugging and kissing as they scan a fridge for snacks.

Roux referred back to the WhatsApp messages showing love and affection. Moller agreed that the messages accorded with the behaviour witnessed in the footage. Roux made the point that after these argumentative messages to which the captain had referred, the interaction between the two returned to normal, that it was not ongoing bickering and unhappiness, but rather moments of tension between a normal couple that were quickly resolved through open and honest communication. Just days before the shooting, Reeva offered to cook a Valentine's Day meal.

Two days before she died, Reeva met with her former boyfriend Warren Lahoud. She had considered postponing the meeting, but Oscar insisted in a message that she see him because he had a dentist appointment. It was hardly an example of the possessive and jealous boyfriend the state was trying to portray.

However, in interviews after Reeva's death, Lahoud spoke about how Oscar repeatedly called Reeva during their short coffee meeting and he thought the sportsman's behaviour was odd.

Later that same day Oscar referred to a physiotherapist appointment where he was to have his shoulder looked at. Oscar had claimed that he slept on the left side of the bed because his right shoulder was hurt – for Roux, this was evidence of the injury.

Moller was asked to read the messages right up to the last one in which Oscar told Reeva he would be home at about 6pm that evening: 'Please stay and do whatever it was you were going to do ☺'.

Roux had shown the court there was far more to the messages than merely the arguments on which the state had relied. Those arguments made up a minuscule number amongst the hundreds of messages the couple sent each other daily over the brief period they dated. Yes, the advocate pointed out, there were instances of unhappiness and arguments. But is this unusual for a couple? He didn't believe so.

In re-examination Nel looked at what was not in the messages – the state and the defence had both identified specific messages to argue a particular point, but what was missing? Almost all the communication was short messages. The only long messages in their entire collection were the unhappy, angry ones.

• • •

The evidence of Captain Moller set out two things for both the state and the defence. Firstly, it provided a timeline of events. Logged calls and data are indisputable and they tracked the movements and actions of the parties involved. Secondly, it provided insight into the relationship. Most importantly, it provided the prosecution team with statements from a dead woman in which she described in her own words the concerns she had about the behaviour of her boyfriend. Reeva's 'I'm scared of u sometimes' were the powerful words abused women related to, and in some people's eyes nullified every 'I'm sorry, but …' excuse provided by an abusive partner. It didn't matter how many loving words the couple exchanged in the months they dated, as laboured by the defence; it was the instances of apparent fear and belittlement that the state believed characterised the relationship.

• • •

Moller's boss Colonel Mike Sales was called to testify about the iPads the police seized at Oscar's house. In the weeks before the trial this evidence had caused some controversy, with reports suggesting that Internet browser history showed that someone had been visiting pornographic websites while Oscar claimed to be spending a relaxing evening with his girlfriend. The articles – their accuracy untested – spurred public debate on whether a man viewing porn amounted to infidelity, and further speculation that perhaps the couple were viewing porn together.

Sales used the same forensic diagnostic software his subordinate had employed on the iPhones to extract the data from the devices. The web browser history analysed started at about 6:30pm and ended at 9:20pm on the evening of 13 February. It showed the user browsed websites related to used car sales, Aston Martin, Ford Ranger and free mobile porn. The term 'youjizz' featured amongst the Google search words.

Sales found commonalities between the two devices he studied – similar web pages accessed on different dates across the devices. It suggested the couple used each other's iPads interchangeably.

In cross-examination all Roux wanted to know from Sales was whether or not he was able to establish who was using the device at the time a particular website was being accessed. It was obvious – he couldn't say. For the defence, this meant that the state couldn't claim their client's 'website activities from the time that he got home [were] in direct contrast to that of a loving couple spending time together', as stated in a request for further particulars prior to the commencement of the trial.

From the testimony of both Moller and Sales, a richer picture was painted of what went on in the hours and days before Reeva was shot. There was a better understanding of the relationship the couple shared, with details of their pet names and their disagreements being aired.

• • •

Perhaps the greatest mystery lingering after the phone experts left the witness stand was 'What was on the iPhone?' Almost everyone wanted to know why no evidence was led about the phone taken to Apple in the United States and why the police had not bothered cracking the code. For many, it seemed obvious that the answer to the question of motive lay hidden between the metal and glass of the handset.

For Danny Myburgh and his forensic experts at Cyanre, the way the phone evidence was handled in court left more questions than answers. 'They didn't explore Oscar's phone sufficiently. One thing that stood out for me – Moller was not very clear at all times on what device he was testifying from. No questions were asked. If you look at the evidence that was led – it was very one-sided. They looked at Reeva's phone and led evidence from there. They predominantly used Reeva's phone and there was little to no supporting evidence stating that the information was found on both phones. If you find messages on "A's" phone, but didn't find it on "B's" phone, you have to conclude that it was deleted. You can therefore prove validity and completeness by checking "A" against "B". It looked like they were just accepting the information without testing or validating it. If I was Barry I would have asked these questions. I would have asked them, "Well, did you find it on Oscar's phone?" Can you place Oscar behind the phone? It was as if … certain areas were "don't touch, don't ask, don't smell".'

A source close to the defence legal team gives some insight into just why Roux was so willing to make the admissions on the cellphones and appeared so passive in challenging the chain of evidence regarding the phones.

'The overall view of the electronic evidence, the WhatsApps was overwhelmingly in favour of Oscar. So the defence chose to make the admissions as 99 per cent of the WhatsApp messages supported Oscar's version and they decided it would be more prudent to deal with and explain the 1 per cent.'

As the contents of that phone were largely wiped, it was difficult for investigators to establish conclusively what activity took place via that phone. However, they did have the phone records from Vodacom, which formed part of the exhibits in the case. This meant they could see who Oscar had been talking to or exchanging messages with but they could not see the contents of those messages or know what the conversations were about. Inexplicably, the prosecution team and the investigators chose not to lead any of this evidence in court.

We analysed the Vodacom phone records by checking the service provider call records against the data extracted from Oscar's phone. This allowed us to plot Oscar's movements and who he was in contact with on the day before he killed Reeva. This was crucial as it set out a day in the life of the athlete and provided insight into exactly how normal, or not, circumstances were in the hours leading up to the shooting. We juxtaposed this against Oscar's own version of events in an attempt to finally answer one of the great mysteries lingering after the case.

Oscar told the court he woke up early in his Pretoria home on 13 February because he had several meetings to attend:

> I had woken up in my house in Pretoria. Reeva had slept over. I had to leave Pretoria early to skip the traffic. I couldn't be late for this meeting, there were many people involved. I got to Johannesburg, I guess about an

*hour before my meeting and I met up with a friend in Melrose Arch. We
met for a short time. We had a cup of coffee and then I had to be at my
meeting. I was there until about midday, about twelve o'clock.*

What was the meeting about and who had he met for coffee?

Oscar's first call that day was incoming, at 8:31am, and lasted a mere 12 seconds.
The number ended in '622'. Searching Oscar's contacts database identified the corresponding number: Ryan from Firzt realtors. This corresponded with Oscar's evidence that he met his estate agent and it was probably a quick call to confirm the
meeting. The data showed that Oscar's phone made the connection via the Silver
Lakes 3G tower, the one closest to his home.

Once Oscar was on the road to Johannesburg he made several calls. He
phoned his manager Peet, and then tried to make contact with a banker from
Rand Merchant Bank (RMB) at 9:40am. Coming through Midrand at about
10:20am, he called someone listed on his phone as 'Vayvay' and spent 24 seconds
on the call. He connected to the Vodaworld 3G tower for that call.

Running a consumer search on the number linked it to sports journalist
Vaylen Kirtley. She had contacted the athlete three days earlier, on Monday 11
February, eager to meet him. Oscar called her on Tuesday, speaking for about
three minutes, and they met on Wednesday 13 February for breakfast at a restaurant in Melrose Arch.

Kirtley says the meeting was a catch-up of old friends. 'Oscar and I met
when he started competing with disabled athletes in early 2004 and we became
friends and were friends since.' She adds that they had not seen each other for
a few months. 'We chatted about our families and his plans for the year. He
showed me pictures of a house he intended buying and pictures of Reeva – his
girlfriend. When I returned home I saw my mother and told her I had caught
up with Oz who sent his love and I told her he had this lovely new girlfriend
who, I thought, if anyone, he would marry one day. I assumed this by the tone
Oscar used when he spoke about his girlfriend. What happened after was truly
tragic.'

Earlier that morning, at 8:31am, Oscar had received an SMS confirming the
meeting he was to attend at a law firm. On his way from Melrose Arch to the
meeting a few blocks away, Oscar called the banker from RMB. The athlete had
had his R4-million bond approved for his new home in Atholl a week earlier.
The call to the banker lasted 532 seconds, or nine minutes. After this he received
a very short call from David at Nike, one of his primary sponsors.

As Oscar explained in his testimony, he then went to meet his estate agent:

> *I did not have any plans for the afternoon but I wasn't going to train because I had a shoulder injury. I thought that Reeva was going to come back to Johannesburg. I thought maybe after my meeting I would give her a call and see if she was doing anything. When my meeting ended at twelve, I phoned the estate agents that was brokering the purchase of my home. I met briefly with him, I am not sure for what reason, if it was to get house plans or photos or to sign papers. I can remember that from the message I sent Reeva, saying I was with Ryan.*

What Oscar did not mention in his testimony were the phone calls he made between his meeting at the law firm and his appointment with the property man.

At 12:57pm he chatted to his friend Justin Divaris. And then at 12:58pm he spent four minutes on the phone with a model, whose name is known to us. In fact, phone records show that since 1 January 2013 Oscar had called the model at least once a week. He had also been in contact with her on the Monday, making this the second call to the young woman that week.

Oscar went on to have his meeting with Ryan from Firzt realtors, and after that he went to Divaris's shop on Rivonia Road. He recounted what happened that afternoon in his evidence-in-chief:

> *From there I went to see my friend Mr Divaris. I was chatting with him for a while. He was still at work. I was asking him what his plans were for the rest of the day and he suggested, or he said to me that he was meeting another mutual friend of ours for dinner and asked me, if I wanted to join him. At some point his girlfriend, Mr Divaris's girlfriend arrived. Ms Samantha Greyvenstein. She is a very close friend of Reeva's and she asked what I was up to for the rest of the day and we informed her about possibly having dinner. The boys having a dinner, she said she was in a mood to watch a movie in Johannesburg. She said that she would phone Reeva or text Reeva and ask her if she wanted to come through and we were just chatting informally at Mr Divaris's work. I phoned Reeva, and there were texts that went back and forth between us. She said to me that she just going to finish her washing and then she would come. She was planning on coming back to Johannesburg. She asked me after my day, if I wanted to spend some time with my sister at home. I cannot remember the exact words in the messages, but I said to her that I do not mind ... what her plans ... if she wants to stay, she can stay. I do mind if she wants to come back. We could do something there. When*

I spoke to her on the phone, she told me that … I was aware that Sam had asked her if she wanted to watch a movie in Johannesburg. Sam told me that Reeva had said to her, that she did not want to come back. She was thinking of staying the night again at my house in Pretoria. And then I decided to … that I was too tired, that I did not want to stay in Johannesburg and go for dinner with Justin and his … and our mutual friend. That I would rather return home and in that process Reeva asked me if I would like to … if she like me to cook us dinner.

Oscar's call to Reeva was made at 3:54pm and was his last call before he got back onto the highway to head home.

On the way he spoke to his siblings Carl and Aimee, for about five minutes each. At 5:25pm he chatted to Aimee, referred to as 'M' in his contact list, for around 300 seconds before Carl then returned an earlier call that Oscar had made to him. Reeva had popped out of the estate to go to buy food for dinner and called her boyfriend at 5:44pm. They chatted for just two minutes before Oscar called his friend Alex Pilakoutas and then rugby player Wynand Olivier. Pilakoutas said in a statement read at the bail application that he and Oscar were close friends; they trusted each unconditionally and spoke to each other at least twice a week. 'Oscar would often confide in me with regard [to] his relationships. He always used to tell me how he felt about a girl.'

Pilakoutas also confirmed this last call to the court. 'As usual I asked how he was doing and Reeva, and Oscar told me that everything was fine and that he was doing well and that he would see me on Friday for Carl's surprise birthday dinner.'

At 6:07pm, while connected to the Wapadrand cellphone tower, which is located close to his home, Oscar made one more call from his car and spoke to the person for nine minutes. Estate security guard Pieter Baba testified in the murder trial that Reeva arrived at the estate at about 6pm. Surveillance footage shows her arriving in her Mini Cooper, smiling and having a brief chat with the guard. Baba said Oscar arrived a few minutes later. 'I greeted Mr Pistorius and he was on his cellphone, M'Lady.'

Who was Oscar talking to? He was never asked.

We cross-referenced the digits on the service provider report with the athlete's contact book. It turned up a single name: 'Babyshoes'.

Who was Babyshoes? There was no associated email address or other particulars that could help identify the contact.

Had Oscar contacted the person before? Looking back at the service provider report, searching for this number turned up more than a dozen text messages and phone calls between Oscar and Babyshoes since 1 January 2013.

The first text message to Babyshoes in this timeframe was sent on New Year's Day at 3:38am. On 11 January, the day Oscar discharged Fresco's firearm in the Tashas restaurant, seven SMSes were sent that evening from Oscar to Babyshoes.

On the afternoon of 12 January, Reeva sent Oscar a message telling him that she was feeling genuinely low, to which he responded that he believed he had a 'beautiful connection' with her. At about 20 minutes past midnight on the following morning, Oscar sent three text messages to Babyshoes.

The data showed that all contact with Babyshoes was outgoing: sent messages, not received. Searching the text messages wasn't helpful because many were deleted when the handset was unaccounted for. And, in addition, every single WhatsApp message was also wiped.

Then came a change in the contact pattern. At 1:57pm on 27 January, Oscar called Babyshoes and chatted for 400 seconds. A study of the phone records shows that the athlete doesn't tend to spend a lot of time on the phone talking to people. While he calls many people, most of the calls are short, from less than a minute to about two or three minutes. A seven-minute conversation is an anomaly.

Two hours after this call, Reeva sent Oscar the WhatsApp message in which she says, 'I'm scared of u sometimes'. The day that Oscar had an argument with his girlfriend, he had a long conversation with Babyshoes. Then that night Oscar called Reeva and they spoke for nearly an hour.

The next contact visible via the records available between Oscar and Babyshoes came on 6 February at just after 7.00am. The previous evening Reeva had sent Oscar a message saying she was worried that she cramped the athlete's style. He was dismissive, saying he had work to get through that night and had an early start the next day. Amongst the first calls on that day was to Babyshoes.

Two days later, on 8 February, at 10:39am, Oscar's phone connected once again to Babyshoes – and this time the pair spoke for 12 minutes. According to the records, apart from his calls with Reeva, it was one of the longest conversations Oscar had had on his phone.

What was significant about the day? Reeva's phone reveals that barely 11 hours earlier, she had sent Oscar a message about the fight the couple had had at the Virgin Active Awards, in which she said, 'I regard myself as a lady and I didn't feel like one tonight after the way u treated me when we left.'

It appeared that when Oscar had a fight with his girlfriend and there was unhappiness, he picked up the phone and had contact, sometimes at length, with Babyshoes. He had called this person before arriving at home on 13 February, and was still on the phone to Babyshoes when he entered the Silver Woods estate, although there is no evidence that Oscar and Reeva had argued that day.

• • •

Investigations revealed that the phone number listed as Babyshoes in Oscar's contacts was registered to a man in his sixties. His surname? Edkins. And he has three children – one of them named Jenna. This particular number was used by her.

Jenna Edkins was Oscar's girlfriend from 2008 until 2011. In his biography, the Blade Runner described the special presence in his life:

> At the beginning of 2008, I had started going out with Jenna, a delight-ful, sweet-natured, beautiful girl with blonde hair and sparkling blue eyes. She was eighteen. We had been honest with one another from the outset and I had explained to her that I was still not entirely ready for another serious relationship. On some level I still missed Vicky [his ex-girlfriend] terribly, and although our relationship was over I still had to come to terms with the hurt I felt. I was of the opinion that it was impor-tant not to rush into things, and I feel that we have a beautiful relation-ship because we took the time to get to know one another, and because our relationship developed from a strong and meaningful relationship.

Oscar and Jenna had broken up three years later, but she maintained a signifi-cant presence in his life. Samantha Taylor names her as being at the centre of her own break-up with Oscar, just weeks before he met Reeva and took her to the sports awards.

Jenna had vehemently defended the athlete on social media a day after the shooting and was the only ex-girlfriend to be interviewed by the panel when Oscar was later referred to Weskoppies Psychiatric Hospital.

On the day after Reeva's death, Jenna posted a series of comments on Twitter:

> People must stop jumping on the bandwagon with such hurtful allega-tions. Os is the loving , amazing inspirational person we know him to be..

> You have all my familys love and support #loveandsupportoscar

> All I am saying is let him speak, let his side be heard without jumping to conclusions.. Love and thoughts to Reevas famiy..

> I would just like to say , I have dated Oscar on off for 5 YEARS, NOT ONCE
> has he EVER lifted a finger to me , made me fear for my life..

Jenna was not questioned by the police, nor was a statement taken from her. And Oscar made no mention of their conversation lasting 522 seconds on the evening of 13 February 2013 in his evidence-in-chief – although he was never asked to detail all his telephone calls. The focus of his testimony was the near-30-minute conversation he had had later that evening with his cousin, Graham Binge, in Port Elizabeth.

The unavoidable question is why the state never pursued the possible relevance of this phone call and the other communications with Jenna.

The independent digital forensic expert says the police should certainly have followed up this lead. 'They had to very seriously analyse his movements and every activity of that day and they trace it to a person and then they just ignore it. This was one of the last calls on his phone. I know that the police would look at the 24 hours before the shooting, they scanned the whole phone but for me the crucial period would have been from the previous morning when he woke up through to the next morning.'

It is understood that Hawks cellphone expert Captain Francois Moller had provided investigators with a list of the identities of the numbers on the service provider list, but no one had made the connection between Jenna's father's name and Oscar. The prosecuting authority declined to comment on questions we sent to them about this revelation.

'It would be wrong to infer that the state erred in not leading that info,' a member of the state's team suggested. 'It would deal with character evidence which the state is not entitled to lead. If there is no SMS or WhatsApp communication, how do we infer from the phone calls where we don't know the content that something untoward was taking place. I don't think it's a big piece of evidence. Let's say we did pick it up – we can only pick up phone calls but who would tell us what they're talking about?'

A source close to the defence team is also at pains to explain that this is no great revelation, that Oscar's lawyers always knew about Edkins and had consulted with her, and this is certainly not the 'smoking gun' the public and the media have so desperately been searching for.

'There is a very good, friendly relationship between them now. He often called her. Reeva was well aware of the friendship. It became a genuine friendship. Previously it was romantic but there was no romantic connotation at all. It's not the smoking gun. The defence was well aware of the phone call to her and had in fact consulted with her and confirmed the friendship and not a romantic relationship. It was never raised by the state. If it was raised by the state as a smoking gun, the defence would have called Jenna and she was willing to testify,' insists the source.

Evidence of the continued contact and friendly relationship between Oscar and Jenna was also found in Oscar's house. In Police Album 10, which documents amongst other things, 'photos of portraits and photos in the house', there is evidence that the athlete kept reminders of his special bond with Jenna.

In the upstairs TV lounge the police took photographs of an A2 framed canvas picture collage featuring about 40 black-and-white pictures of Oscar and Jenna. Dozens of photos of the couple together, sometimes kissing and being playful, surround an A4 picture of the blonde and the athlete staring into each other's eyes. On the reverse side is an intimate and affectionate message written in black pen from Jenna to Oscar in celebration of their relationship and his 22nd birthday:

To My Baby

Happy Birthday ⊍ You are so precious to me and 22 years ago on this day the most Special Person in my life was born!! I am always here for you and as time goes on I hope to add many more Happy Memories to this board (the most amazing memories⊍... even tho a lot of them consist of you biting me♡ my starfish who poo in pants! Babyshoes have a wonderful day!

'What can I give you, my Sweet, my Lover, you who have given the world to me, showed me the light and the joy that cover, the wild sweet earth and the restless sea...'
♡ Jen xxx
(BabyPop)
22! Yay!

Oscar turned 22 in 2008, the year of the Beijing Paralympics. The games had taken place in September, two months before his birthday. The athlete took gold in the 100 metres, 200 metres and 400 metres sprints, setting Paralympic and world records in each race.

Four years later and another Olympic Games was on. Oscar was dating a different blonde – Samantha Taylor. By July 2012 the relationship was collapsing when the athlete sent an email not only to Taylor, but to her mother as well, addressing the document to 'Sam and the Taylor Family'.

Babyshoes featured prominently in this email. Gerrie Nel referred to the email in the murder trial when he questioned Oscar's manager Peet van Zyl about plans to take Taylor along to the London Games. However, the full contents of the email were not read out in court.

In his outpouring of emotion to his then current girlfriend, he revealed his deep-seated feelings towards Jenna Edkins and the powerful history that they shared:

> *Everyone has their darkness, yet everyone has a burning desire to need to find that one person that understands them. There thoughts without saying a word. There emotion without a flinch. Jenna and I started dating when I was 20, I met her and fell for her pretty quickly. I had grown up with her cousins and on the weekends that my brother sister and I were able to see my dad, my mom being friend with Jennas mom and aunt would take Jenna to church. It was [surprising] that we had only met some years after my mom had passed but this immediately drew me closer to her. I don't talk about my mom and my dad to anyone as it wasn't a pretty picture, not the one that I became accustomed to portraying as a kid anyway. The fact that my mom had known Jenna [meant] a lot to me and was one of the base notes of our relationship, which maybe kept it together long after it [should've] ended. Jenna and I started dating and in the [beginning] everything seemed like it was perfect. She understood me and was willing to support me no matter what.*

When Oscar returned from Beijing in 2008, he and Edkins began having problems and the relationship ended:

> *I found myself struggling to make sense of the things around me. Some of it went to my head and looking back, I regret a lot of the decisions I ended up making ... I had to deal with a lot of traveling and found myself wondering away from her. I met a girl later that year and in my mind I made myself believe that this is what I had been looking for. I fell quickly and I fell fast for this girl but within a couple of weeks I realised that I had been so desperate to chase something that wasn't there that I had made myself believe it was. Jenna and I got back together. After months of trying to make it work I realised I had broken her trust and*

called things off. A couple of weeks later I found what I thought I had been looking for but it didn't take me long to realise that it was my desperation and loneliness coming back to get me. I had all the money a 23 year old could spend and as fast as I was making it I was spending it. Trying to buy happiness, surrounded by fake friends, who although as time went on I knew were just there for the good made me feel better about myself.

It was then, in 2009, that Oscar crashed his boat on the Vaal dam and the situation with Edkins changed again:

I ended up in a coma for 6days after being airlifted. It breaks my heart when people joke about it and me being pissed because I can't remember everything about that night like it just happened and I thought I was going to die … I called my brother and sister and thanked them for always staying by my side and called Jenna even though we hadn't spoken in weeks to apologise for being a lost [dumb] fuck and playing with her heart. It wasn't my intention to hurt her but like I have so many times by being selfish done so. When I woke up in Milpark Jenna had slept next to my bed for 6days, she was in the middle of varsity exams and had her books all over the room.

When he recovered, he thought he had been blessed with a second chance. But months later when Oscar went to Europe for the athletics seasons, the relationship with Edkins fell apart again.

It was evident from the email to Taylor that while the athlete realised the relationship with Edkins was apparently over, he still wanted to be friends with her because 'she had been there with me through a lot'. 'At times I wanted it to be still there, Sam. I'm sorry, as I know you're hurting. I don't want to tell you what I think it is you want to hear, but the truth.'

Taylor would also reveal to us the full extent of her 'problems' with Edkins during the course of her time with Oscar.

So, while Oscar's relationship with Taylor had ended and he had moved on to Reeva, who he would claim to have fallen in love with, he still maintained contact with another ex-girlfriend: Babyshoes.

While there is no evidence to suggest that their relationship was anything other than friendship, it is nevertheless noteworthy that Oscar kept in touch with Edkins, made contact with her on occasions when he and Reeva appeared to have disagreements, and called her the day before that fateful Valentine's day.

Edkins declined to do an interview with us. In a brief response to questions sent to her about the nature of her ongoing relationship with Oscar, she commented: 'I do not wish to respond to mere allegations, for example, the allegations of Oscar calling me when he and Reeva had a fight or the statement given by Samantha are untrue. It is common knowledge that Oscar and I have remained friends over the years and I do not wish to be involved in any media hype around this terrible situation.'

The only mention of Edkins in Oscar's SMS or WhatsApp conversations with Reeva came on 15 January 2013:

> Reeva: Boo
> Reeva: Was it Jenna edkins or [Jenna] Dover that asked if we together?
> Reeva: Cos Dover is standing right behind me for this movie …
> Oscar: Edkins.
> Oscar: Xx
> Reeva: Haha
> Reeva: Juuuuust checkinggggg
> Oscar: ;)
> Oscar: Don't really chat to dover much

On the eve of Valentine's Day, Oscar arrived home to Reeva while still on the phone to Jenna Edkins. It is a conversation the police did not identify and Oscar did not speak about in his evidence – but whatever its substance, Oscar had been in contact with Edkins when he arrived home on the evening of 13 February.

Who was to say what relevance or consequence this could have had to the state's case or if it would have swayed Masipa at all if the police investigations had unearthed it?

Taking the Stand

With the closing of the state's case, the key question was whether Oscar would take the stand in his own defence. His lawyer Barry Roux had told the court in passing that his client would indeed testify, but there was still some doubt that it would happen. Oscar had been extremely emotional in court over the weeks of the state's case, crying and vomiting as evidence was led, and there was doubt as to whether he would be able to maintain his composure for the duration of intense cross-examination.

In reality, Oscar had no choice but to testify and take the court into his confidence. There were only two people on the scene at the time of the shooting – Reeva and Oscar – and he was the only one remaining, the only one who could give the court an account of the events of that morning. It was also crucial that he explain his state of mind to back up his defence of putative private defence. It was up to him to convince the court of what he was thinking, how he felt he was genuinely under threat and why he took the actions he did. If he failed to take the stand, it would amount to an admission to the charges against him.

University of Cape Town law expert Kelly Phelps agreed it was crucial that Oscar take the stand. 'Officially, no accused person has to testify (there is always a right to remain silent) but pragmatically he had no choice but to testify. This is because of the defence he has raised – putative private defence. This defence is assessed subjectively by the court – in other words, what that particular accused was actually thinking on the night in question, rather than what he should have or could have thought.'

Phelps adds that in the case of Antonio de Oliveira, the immigrant who shot at his employer and his guests (mentioned in a previous chapter), the courts made it clear that the only real way for the court to know subjectively what the accused was thinking is to hear from that person.

Professor James Grant agrees it wasn't really an option for Oscar to exercise his constitutional right to silence. 'Some have commented, rightly in my view, that one may remain silent at one's peril. This means that, while one has the right to remain silent, it is not always in one's best interests … There are situations in which, by virtue of the evidence against you, or by virtue of the nature of your own defence, you would be well-advised to testify. Oscar's (original) defence of putative private defence is one, which places in issue what the accused was thinking at the time of the incident. By its nature, his subjective mental state is all-important and he is the best person to explain what he was thinking,' says Grant.

Comparisons were incorrectly drawn between Oscar's potential decision and that of US football star OJ Simpson, who had chosen not to testify in his trial for the murder of his ex-wife Nicole Brown Simpson and had been acquitted. Phelps believes the cases are not comparable, other than for dramatic effect.

'In OJ's case there was an established track record of violence (as opposed to allegations of one in this case, with little or no evidence to back up the claim) and an abusive relationship between he and the deceased (as opposed to allegations of one with little or no evidence to back up the claim). There was also evidence that OJ planned to murder the deceased in a jealous rage in reaction to her moving on with another romantic partner. The case was not won or lost because he didn't testify – most accused persons will not testify if they can help it because a good cross-examiner can unnerve a saint on the stand and make them look guilty or suspicious,' says Phelps. 'Another key difference between the cases is that OJ tried to evade justice from the outset – Pistorius handed himself over willingly and never denied shooting Steenkamp; it is his explanation of why that differs from the states version.'

And so it was that on 7 April, after defence pathologist Jan Botha had completed his testimony, that Barry Roux announced to the court: 'I call Mr Pistorius.' It was what the vast majority of the people in the gallery – reporters – wanted to hear. Like a headline act at a show, the accused was the main attraction and had drawn the crowds. The main courtroom was packed to capacity and so was the overflow facility next door. The world was waiting to hear Oscar's version in Oscar's voice. He appeared tense, experiencing a retching episode during the pathologist's testimony, and was given a little time to compose himself.

Oscar packed away several items into a small bag that he left in the dock, clasped his spectacles and a packet of tissues in his right hand and opened the little wooden swing door of the dock as Aimee mouthed words of support. Steadying himself with his left hand on the dock, he made his way past his bullet-riddled bathroom door towards the witness box in the front right of the courtroom. His gaze was fixed forward, not once glancing over to the gallery where June Steenkamp and her entourage sat. He had chosen not to have his face televised during his evidence so only his quivering voice was audible as he was sworn in. But what the television viewers couldn't see was Oscar trembling, as he raised his right hand and declared, 'So help me God.'

Before leading Oscar through his version of events around the shooting, Roux invited Oscar to make the opening remarks he had requested to begin with. He wore a black suit, white shirt and black tie that day; sombre attire as an expression of his grief. The athlete tendered a deeply emotional apology directed at Reeva's parents. Her mother, sitting in the public gallery, stared stoically ahead, her jaw tightly clenched, guarding against any emotion. Next to her, her advocate Dup de Bruyn watched as Oscar crumbled. Aimee and Carl were less composed as the tears streaked down their faces while other Pistorius relatives watched on. Judge Masipa listened attentively, her chin resting on her fist as she focused on the accused:

> *I would like to take this opportunity to apologise to … Mrs and Mr …*
> *Mr and Mrs Steenkamp, to Reeva's family, to those of you who knew her,*
> *who are here today, family and friends …*

Oscar trailed off. He was overcome with emotion, his voice barely audible, so that Judge Masipa was forced to intervene. 'Mr Pistorius, I do not like doing this to you, but I can hardly hear you—'

Oscar continued:

> *I … I … I beg your pardon, My Lady, I will speak up. I would like to*
> *apologise and say that there is a lot of moments and there has not been*
> *a moment since … since this tragedy happened that I have not thought*
> *about your family. I wake up every morning and you are the first people*
> *I think of, the first people I pray for. I cannot imagine the pain and the*
> *sorrow and the emptiness that I have caused you and your family. I was*
> *simply trying to protect Reeva. I can promise that when she went to bed*
> *that night, she felt loved. I have tried to put my words on paper many,*
> *many times to write to you, but no words would ever suffice …*

As Oscar fumbled on, Barry Roux stepped in, reminding him that although he wanted to look at Reeva's mother while he apologised, he had to face the judge so that the microphone could pick up his voice. Roux was speaking softly, compassionately to his client, as if empathising with him in this solemn moment. But the awkward apology had ended and Roux began leading his client through his evidence.

Day one of Oscar on the stand ended early because, said Roux, his client was exhausted. As the judge left the courtroom at the close of proceedings, Oscar slumped back into the chair, leaned his head on his hand and started crying. With Carl and Aimee consoling their sibling, attempts were made to usher him outside, but he sat down on the step leading to the witness box and continued to cry. His psychologist sat beside him, her arm over his shoulder as she whispered into his ear. Pistorius family members formed a huddle around the pair, using their legs to shield the accused from the eyes of the prying media.

This was the start of seven days on the stand for the Blade Runner, with the world hanging onto his every word.

Oscar's Version

Oscar had already given a written version of events at the bail application. He then gave another written version during his plea explanation. On the stand as a witness, he spoke in far more detail. Speaking quietly but rapidly, his advocate led him through the events of 13 February and then on to the fatal Valentine's Day morning:

> From the time I arrived home, Reeva was preparing dinner. I was talking to her, and on the iPad I was surfing the net. I was looking at cars that I had wanted to get around to during the day. To have a look at and when I went upstairs as I ... as I was drawing the bath, I was on my iPad. I lay on my bed and took off my suit. I then sat in the bath for a while, I cannot remember if I was on it then. And then as I got out of bed, for a short time thereafter I was on it. We went down to dinner, I stopped using it. We were sitting and chatting.

Roux explained that an exhibit would be submitted to show that there was a gap in the website activity from 7:10pm until 8pm. Oscar confirmed this was right.

> I started dinner ... we started dinner shortly after seven, M'Lady. After dinner we sat ... at the dining room table for a while and we chatted about my day and we chatted about Reeva's contract that she was in the process of signing with a new management company ... I went through the contract and I made some changes for her on things that I did not think were applicable or things which could be binding for her in a negative way. And then usually after dinner we would have watched TV

downstairs, but I think we both had a taxing day, so we decided to go upstairs. I helped her with the plates. Whilst we were taking the plates off the … from the table, Reeva asked me if I would like anything to drink. Anything warm to drink, I cannot remember if I asked her for coffee or tea or what it was, but I said yes and I went back upstairs and she joined me a short time afterwards. A couple of minutes later.

It must have been around, just before eight or eight o' clock, I came into my room and I … I put the … open the balcony doors. It was a very humid evening. They had been working on my house for some time and the air-conditioning was one of the things that they needed to fix. There was some fault with it. So at the time the air-conditioning was not working.

Judge Masipa intervened to establish which room Oscar was referring to and he confirmed it was located on the first floor. He then picked up where he left off, opening the doors.

From my main room there is a small balcony. I opened the sliding doors onto the balcony. I placed … there is two fans. There is a steel tripod stand fan and there is a small plastic fan. A floor fan. I placed the tripod fan a bit further back with one of the legs on the balcony and the other two legs inside the sliding door. I placed the small fan pretty much between the legs of the larger fan, the tripod standing fan. I then closed the doors [till] they [were] more or less in line with the fans because at night, there is a light on the balcony that attracts insects and they come into my room. So I was trying to get most of the humid warm air out of the room, by having the fans there, they pulled the cool air from outside into the room. I drew the blinds and the curtains so that no bugs could come in from the outside and I had them more or less draped around the side of the standing fan.

Oscar went into great detail about the level of light in the bedroom – this was critical in explaining how he did not see Reeva getting up and going to the bathroom.

When I put curtains up in my home when I moved in, in 2008 I got all the curtains and blinds done. But in my room I got blackouts done on my curtains because of the hours that I travel, I am sometimes home for a day and a half or half a day, and the hours I sleep are not always usual, so I sometimes sleep during the day. So I got the curtains with this material, this fabric. If the curtains are drawn, you cannot see anything in the room. During the day you can barely see, if they are drawn, what you can see is along the walls, you can see the ... not along the walls, I beg your pardon ... along the top of the rail, you can see a bit of light coming in. But it is ... it is virtually pitch black, even in the day if the curtains are drawn.

I then drew the curtains which were around the fans. I do not think ... I do not think at that time I probably just left the blinds where they were, but I drew the curtain to hang over the ... over the fans so that not ... no insects could come in. You could see a bit of light through where the top fan was, but very little in the room. At that point the bedside lamp, bedside table lamp was ... light was on. Or one of the lights in the room was on, I do not recall if it was the bedside lamp, but one of the lights in the room was on.

It was at this point that Reeva came into the room, and he took his drink from her and put it down on the bedside table. He also emphasised his security awareness, by explaining the measures he took to secure the two of them.

I walked behind Reeva where she came in the room and I closed the bedroom door and I lock the bedroom door, as I do every night and I put the cricket bat between the sunglasses cabinets and the door. If you lay the bat down in that gap, the bat is about ... is about two centimetre short of being at the door. And the reason I put it there was because the lock mechanism on the door was not very strong. The doors were made, in house of a ... of a wood that was very hard but very brittle and I had problems with some of the latches and locks before. So it was a concern of mine that just locking the door, with the heat the gaps between the doors increased and the lock barely caught the door. So I put the cricket bat down on the floor inside the bedroom, so that if you ... if something happen that a person will not be able to come into the bedroom. That the door would be blocked by the cricket bat. That is something I did every night when I stayed at home.

Roux led Oscar to explain whether the house had an alarm system and whether it had been activated that night.

The house does have an alarm system, M'Lady. When I moved in I spent quite a bit of money putting up an alarm system. I put inside and outside beams on. The alarm system does not have any door monitors, but the outside sensors are battery operated. They are not, they do not work with wiring. So when they had painted the house in 2010, they had taken all the eyes off the outside walls and they painted the home and they were in the process of repainting now, so there were troubles with the alarm. If you take one of the outside sensors off the wall, before you activate it, it does not have a memory to remember what ... what was in its scope the previous time it was activated. But I did have an alarm, I put it on every night. It activated with a remote which was on my house keys. So after I put the cricket bat at the door, I just push a button and the alarm would make a noise to indicate that it was activated.

Oscar then continued with the series of events for the evening. He came back into the bedroom and sat on the bed.

If you are facing the bed on the bottom right hand side of the bed, I took my prosthetic legs off. I took them off so that they could get some air. I had been dressed the entire day in a suit and I was ... my legs needed to air, so I put them as close to the door as I could, next to the bed. I climbed onto the bed and Reeva jumped onto the bed, or got onto the bed as well and we sat chatting. The TV was on. I was texting my cousin in Port Elizabeth. Reeva was on her phone busy on ... I think it was on social network or an application. She was showing me pictures every now and again on ... a photo application which ... of cars and of interior decorating things that she liked. At a point I was texting my cousin back and forth and I thought maybe I should just phone him and I called him.

Oscar spent some time on the phone with his cousin Graham Binge, the son of his mother's sister. They had grown up together and Binge was travelling from Port Elizabeth to Gauteng for business.

Whilst I was on the phone, Reeva got out of bed and she started doing stretches and yoga on the floor. Like yoga exercises on the floor, at the foot of the bed. I had the phone on speaker phone and I was chatting to my cousin. Every now and again Reeva would sit up, or you know stretch and she would give me a kiss and we chatted for, I think roughly a half an hour. As I was saying good night, or the conversation was coming to an end, Reeva got up and she walked to the bathroom.

When I finished the phone call she called me to come brush my teeth. So I walked to the … I walked to the bathroom without my prosthetic legs on and I brushed my teeth. Whilst I was busy brushing my teeth she went back to the bedroom. When I came back to the room, she was lying in the middle of the bed and I walked to the closest side of the bed and if you look at the bed, on the left, earlier on in the evening when I got home I had … when I got upstairs I had taken my firearm and I placed it next to the … under the bed next to the pedestal. So that kind of … the bed has got … the bed base is a … is a furniture base and it has got four legs and the bedside table touches the floor along its entirety on its base, so I put it around the corner under the bed. So when I came back to bed I climbed onto the left hand side of the bed. It was not usual for me to sleep on the left, because … because of my shoulder injury I could not lie on my right shoulder, so for a couple of weeks I have been sleeping on and off on the left hand side of the bed. It was not long after that I started falling asleep and getting tired. It was still extremely warm inside the room and Reeva was still sitting up in bed. She was lying with her back against the headboard and I was lying with my head on her stomach, watching something on TV. I do not remember what it was and she would show me photos every now and again and [indistinct] and she would say 'baba, what do you think of this' or 'do you like this car' and she showed me a picture of a car she really liked and we had a short conversation about it and I was getting increasingly tired. I said to her, do you want me to close the doors or would you close them when you come … when you fall asleep. Will you bring in the fans and close the curtains, and lock the door when you fall asleep and she said … you know, she said to me that she would. Then I fell asleep.

Roux interrupted the sequence of events to clarify whether Oscar had plans for Valentine's Day, which was the next morning. This would be important to buttress the claim that the couple shared a loving relationship:

I have bought Reeva a bracelet from a designer that she liked earlier in the year. And I had not made plans for the 14th. I had not made any plans on the 14th. I had a dentist appointment on the 14th in the morning. Reeva was not going to stay at my house, so our plans were

*that I meet her in Johannesburg at this jewellery store that I got her the
bracelet from and the bracelet had a couple of trinkets or charms on it,
there were two bracelets I bought her and so, I said to her we both kind
of made a thing about not making a big thing out of Valentine's day. We
were just going to have dinner. I think for us that was a nice evening. Just
being alone and being at home, making dinner.*

Oscar explained that Reeva had bought him a gift – the red-and-white wrapped
parcel that remained on the kitchen counter in the hours after the shooting.

*I made as if I was going to open it. It had red and white and pink wrapping
paper and Reeva told me: You are only allowed to open it the next day.
So I did not open it and on the 8th August last year, on Reeva's birthday
I opened her Valentine's gift to me and it was a photo frame that she got
made that has four photos of her and I and the card that she wrote.*

Oscar seemed to have inadvertently got the date of Reeva's birthday wrong.

The courtroom was hushed as he led them through his version. Finally, adding to the tension, Roux called for an adjournment so that Oscar could change
in order to demonstrate to the court his height in relation to the toilet door.
Dressed in a pair of shorts, Oscar stood next to his toilet door wearing his prosthetics. Then in a poignant, breathtaking moment, he took off his prosthetics
and stood next to the door on his stumps.

It was the first time the world-renowned athlete had been on public display
without his prosthetics.

Once the height comparison had been made, Oscar replaced his prosthetics
but remained in his shorts as he resumed his testimony, stating that he fell asleep
between 9 and 10pm.

*I woke up, M'Lady in the early hours of the 14th February. It was
extremely warm in my room. I sat up in bed. I noticed that the fans were
still running and that the door was still open. Although the lights had
been switched off, Reeva was still awake or she was obviously not sleeping, she rolled over to me and she said: Can you not sleep my baba? And
I said: No, I cannot and I got out on my side of the bed.*

Eyebrows were raised. Surprisingly, Oscar had not recounted this early-morning
conversation in any of his previous versions.

I walked around the bed, the foot of the bed. I was holding onto the foot of the bed with my left hand. I got to the fans, where the fans were. I took the small fan, the floor fan, I placed it pretty much just inside the room and I took the bigger tripod fan and I took it by the part just underneath the fan and I placed it in the bedroom. The fans were still running. They were still running at the time and I then proceeded to close the sliding doors and lock them. I then drew the curtains.

Roux wanted to know if Oscar closed both the blinds and the curtains.

I just grabbed and closed. It was fairly dark at the time and I probably closed both of them, but I remember closing … closing the curtains. I came into the room, at this point the only bit of light that was in the room was a little LED light on the amplifier where the TV cabinet was. It was a little blue LED light and I could see a pair of jeans that were on the floor, of Reeva's jeans. I picked the jeans up and was going to cover, just place them over the amplifier, over the light.

And, he testified, this was when everything changed.

It was at this point that I heard a window open in the bathroom. It sounded like the window sliding open and then I could hear the window hit the frame as if it had slipped to a point where it cannot slide anymore.

> Roux: *Is it a wooden frame window?*
> Accused: *It is wood, all the frames in my house and doors are wooden frames, M'Lady.*
> Roux: *That is the window referred to in the evidence of the photographer?*
> Accused: *That is correct, M'Lady.*
> Roux: *What did you think at the time, Mr Pistorius?*
> Accused: *M'Lady, that is the moment that everything changed.*

His voice wavering, Oscar continued:

I thought that there was a burglar gaining entry into my home. I was … I was on the side of the room where you first have to cross the passage which leads to the … which leads to the bathroom. I think initially I just froze. I did not really know what to do. I had heard this noise, I interpreted it as being somebody who was climbing into the bathroom. There is no door between the bathroom and my room. It is all one. There is a passageway but there is no door. There is a toilet door, but there is no barrier between me and the bathroom. It is one ... one room. I immediately thought that somebody, if they were at the window to where the passage, entrance of the passage was, could be four, three four metres, they could be there at any moment and the first ... the first thing that ran through my mind was that I needed to arm myself, that I needed to protect Reeva and I and that I needed to get my gun. I then ... I was looking down the passage. I was scared that the person was going to come out, or people were going to come out at that point. I rushed as quick as I could. I could not see anything in the room, so I ran with my hand out in front of me, at times touching the floor and then when I got to my bed I made my way along the side of my bed. I grabbed my firearm from underneath the bed and it had a canvas holster on it. I immediately took it out the holster. At that point I wanted just to put myself between ... get back to where the passage was, so that I could put myself between the person that had gained access to my house and Reeva. When I got just before the passage wall, I remember slowing down because I was scared that at that point, this person, during the time that I had got from ... that I had left the ... to where I got my firearm, could have possibly already been in the passage, in the closet passage. So I slowed down and I had my firearm extended in front of me ...

Just as I ... just as I left my bed, I whispered for Reeva to get down and phone the police. I ... as I entered where the passa ... passage is, where the closet is to the ... where I entered the passage where the closet is to the bathroom, it was at that point that I was just overcome with fear and I started screaming and shouting for the burglar or the intruders to get out of my house. I shouted for Reeva to get down on the floor. I shouted for her to phone the police. I screamed at the people, the persons to get out. I was ... I slowly made my way down the passage, constantly aware that this threat, these people or persons could come at me at any time. I did not have my legs on and just before I got to the wall of the ... like where the tiles start in the bathroom, I stopped shouting, because I was worried that if I shout, the person would know exactly where I was. If I put my head around the corner, then I could get [a] shot. Just before I got to the ... just before I got to the passage of the bathroom, I heard *a door slam which could only been the toilet door. I could not see into the bathroom at this point, but I could hear the door slam and for me it confirmed that there was a person or people inside the toilet or inside the bathroom at that time.*

Roux interrupted Oscar at this point and asked the court to display the photograph showing the entrance to the bathroom as viewed down the passage. As had happened on previous occasions, when the police officer scrolled through the album he inadvertently stopped on a photo showing Reeva's bloodied and pale face.

June Steenkamp, like the court, was caught by surprise and sunk her forehead onto her hand as De Bruyn rubbed her back. Oscar moved backwards in his chair and put his head below the table as he started to gag. As Roux scowled at the computer operator, a court orderly fetched the sick bucket from the dock and gave it to the accused in the witness box.

After a few moments, Oscar continued, confirming photographs Roux presented to him as he went.

I got to the entrance of the bathroom, at the end of the passage, where I stopped screaming. At this point I was certain that the intruder or intruders were there …

At that point that I was entering the bathroom, I was not shouting or screaming, I was … at that point I thought that the intruder or intruders were going to come out or were around the corner or were in the bathroom at that time.

I approached this point of the entrance to the bathroom. I was walking with my left hand against the cabinet, against the closet, as far away from the entrance of the bathroom as I possibly could be. When I got the point at the bottom right hand side of the photo, I peered, I had my right, my pistol in my right hand and I peered into the bathroom. I then made my way pretty much to where the carpet and the tile meet on the left hand side, where the arrow is. The surface changed and where I can walk more comfortably on the carpet, I was not able to walk as … have as much mobility on the tile surfaces. I kept my left hand behind me and my shoulder against the wall and I had my pistol raised to my eye, to the corner of the entrance of the bathroom, over this point here.

Oscar pointed to the photograph. To assist him, a red ring was moved on to the image on the flat screen monitors to show where he was pointing.

There was no light in the bathroom. I could see, as I slowly peered into the bathroom, I could see that the window was opened indeed. I was pretty much on my ... back against the wall with my hand up against the wall to just balance. I was leaning with my back, slowly scuffling along the left hand side wall. I was not sure if there were people, or intruders were in the toilet or if they were on a ladder that they would have used to gain access to the first floor, or if they were around the corner at that point. I still had my firearm pointed in front of me and I peered around the corner to look where the shower was, which was around in the bathroom, in line with ... in line with the toilet.

I peered around this corner, which is in the bottom right hand side of the frame. At that point I saw that there was no one in the bathroom. The door was closed of the toilet and the window was open. Once I saw that there was not anybody around the corner wanting to attack me, I retreated a little bit, maybe a step or two back, still with my hand against the wall. I still had my back and my shoulder to help me balance. At this point I started screaming again for Reeva to phone the police.

His testimony was reaching a crescendo and, as he continued, Oscar became increasingly emotional. Reeva's mother, who had earlier leaned forward and bent her head down, her right hand covering her face, now stared directly at him. A small black-and-white portrait photograph of Reeva was pinned to the lapel of her white jacket.

A few seats away, Oscar's sister Aimee quietly cried, desperation etched on her face. She wiped away tears as her brother continued, his voice increasing in pitch and thick with emotion.

I was not sure where to point the firearm. I had it pointed at the toilet but my eyes were going between the window and the toilet. I stood there for some time, I am not sure how long. I was not sure if someone was going to come out of the toilet to attack me. I was not sure if someone was going to come up the ladder and point a firearm in the house and start shooting, so I just stayed where I was and kept on screaming ... and then I heard a noise from inside the toilet what I perceived to be somebody coming out of the toilet. Before I knew it, I had fired four shots at the door ... My ears were ringing.

I could not hear anything, so I shouted, I kept on shouting for Reeva to phone the police. I was still scared to retreat because I was not sure if there was somebody on the ladder. I was not sure if there was somebody in the toilet … [Pause] … I do not know.

Oscar worked to regain his composure. Roux stood upright with his head intently forward. He asked no questions, but allowed the extended silence to prompt the accused to continue telling his story.

I do not know how long [I] stood there for. I shouted for Reeva. At some point I decided to walk back to the room because I could not hear anything, my ears were ringing, I could not hear if there was a response or not. I did not have a phone on me. I walked … I walked with my hand out on the left hand cupboards with my pistol still raised. I kept on shouting for Reeva. I did not hear anything. At this point it had not occurred to me yet that it could be Reeva in the bathroom. I still thought that there would be intruders that were possibly in the toilet or on the ladder outside the house. I retreated back to a point where I got to the corner of the bed, with my hand out on the bed and I tried to lift myself up. I was talking to Reeva. There was nobody, no one responded to me. At that point I lifted myself up onto the bed and I placed my hand back to the right hand side of the bed and I looked, I felt if Reeva was there and I could not feel anything and at that point the first thing I thought was maybe that she had got down onto the floor like I told her to, maybe she was just scared.

Speaking at an accelerated pace and with his voice again breaking, Oscar finally gave his account of the moment reality first hit.

So I said … I cannot remember what I said, I was trying to talk out to her and I kept my firearm the whole time I moved along the bed backwards, I kept my firearm at the passage, there was not much light coming out but I did not want to even keep my … take my eyes off the … off the … where the closet was. I then … I think it was at that point, M'Lady, that the … that it first dawned upon me that it could be Reeva that was in the … in the bathroom or in the toilet.
I jumped out off the other side of the bed and I ran my hand along the curtains to see that she was not hiding behind the curtain. I could not see much in the room but I could see where the passage was and I … I … I felt around and made my way back up the passage, I still had

*my firearm in front of me. At this point I was mixed with emotions.
I did not know if ... I did not want to believe that it could be Reeva
inside the toilet. I was still scared that maybe somebody was coming
in to attack me, or us. I made my way back to ... inside the, inside the
bathroom and I walked up to the, up to the bathroom door. I tried to
grab the handle and rip open the door, I pushed the door open and
it was locked. I then took ... for the first time I turned around, with
my back facing the bathroom I ran back to the room. I opened the
curtains. I shouted from the balcony. I opened the doors and I shouted
from the balcony for help. I screamed: 'Help! Help! Help!' I screamed
for somebody to help me and then ...*

Oscar sobbed as he gave his version and then paused for some time.

*I ... I put my prosthetic ... I put my prosthetic legs on. I ran as fast as I
could back to the bathroom. I ran into the door. It did not move at all. I
leant back and I tried to kick the door and nothing happened. I was ... I
was ... just panicked at this point, I did not really know what to make or
what to do. I ran back to the bedroom where the cricket bat was between
the cabinet and the door.*

With Oscar deeply emotional, Roux stepped in to guide him along. 'Were you
screaming at that stage?' asked the defence counsel.

*I was screaming and shouting the whole time and crying out. I was ...
I do not think I can ... I do not think I have ever screamed like that or
cried like that or screamed or ... I was crying out for the Lord to help me.
I was crying out for Reeva. I was screaming ... [Pause] ... I ... I did not
know what to do. I ran back to ... I ran straight back to the bathroom
door and I placed my fire ... I do not remember but I must have placed
my firearm on the carpet in the bathroom.*

'Do you know if the light was on or off at that stage in the bathroom?' Roux
prompted again.

*The light was on at that stage, M'Lady. I do not remember switching it
on. I remember it being on when I kicked the door. I ran straight up to
the door and I started hitting it. I think I hit it three times. The first time*

I hit it I remember hitting, I hit the frame of the door and the shock in my hands and I swung again. There was a small piece open and at that point all I wanted to do was just look inside to see if it was Reeva. I then … I then hit the door. I think I hit the door three times and there was a big plank, I grabbed it with my hands and I threw it out into the bathroom. I leant over the middle partition. I tried to open the door from the inside but there was no key in the door and I leant over the middle partition of the door and I saw the key was on the floor. At that point all I wanted to do was just climb into the toilet over the middle part of the door. Whilst I leant over the partition to get in, I saw the key, so I took it and I unlocked the door and I flung the door open and I threw it open and I sat over Reeva and I cried and I do not know …

By this point Oscar was hysterical and began to heave, sobbing uncontrollably. His family, particularly Aimee, were equally emotional in the gallery. His uncle Arnold later said this was the first time they had heard the entire version of events, from start to finish, because every time Oscar tried to recall what had happened he would break down. On the Steenkamp side of the courtroom, the model's friend Gina Myers battled to contain her emotions as her best friend's boyfriend described finding her bloodied body inside the cubicle. Reeva's mother, however, maintained her steady glare at the witness.

I do not know how long … I do not know how long I was there for. She wasn't breathing!

Before Oscar had finished talking, Judge Masipa had dropped her pen and looked over at Roux, as if to prompt him to request for an adjournment. As she left the room, Oscar's sobs followed her. As court decorum dictates, he had to stand as she left. And he did, his chin on his chest as if trying to escape the gaze of the public gallery, grimacing and heaving as he kept in his emotions. With Masipa gone, he turned his back to the room, letting out sorrowful wailing. Aimee and Carl rushed to his side.

An uneasy silence fell over the courtroom and there was none of the usual conversation that quickly picked up in the gallery. We had witnessed the very personal and intense emotional collapse of a global icon, and there wasn't much to say. The sincerity of Oscar's grief was tangible and made indelible impressions on many inside the courtroom.

He was so distraught that his advocate asked for a postponement. Oscar returned to the stand the following morning and continued where he had left off.

> M'Lady, after I entered the toilet I knelt down over Reeva. She was sitting with her weight on top of the toilet bowl. I checked to see if she was breathing and she was not and I put my arms underneath her shoulders and I pulled her weight onto me and I sat there, crying for a … for some time. I had her … I had her head on my left shoulder and I could … I could feel the blood was running down on me. At a point she … I heard her breathing so I immediately put her weight on top of me and I swivelled around. I sat back with my … with my bum against the floor and my back up against the wall, where the door is on the left hand side of the door and I pulled her weight on me, and I turned around. So that I could get her to the … to the door of the toilet so that I could pick her up. I could see that her arm was … I could see that her arm was broken. I placed her in the … I could not pick her up, but I was kind of … I was on my knees and on one of my feet and I was pulling her into the bathroom. I placed her down and I pulled one of the bathroom carpets closer and I placed her head down softly on the carpet. I saw that her cellphone was in the toilet, so I grabbed her cellphone and I tried to phone off it, but it had a pass code on it that I could not access. I ran back to my bedroom, where my phone was. Next to the left hand side of the bed and … both my phones were there. I picked them up and I ran back to Reeva. I then phoned Mr Stander … Mr Johan Stander, who is a gentleman who lived in the estates. Somebody that I become a friend with. I phoned him, to ask him for help, to help me … come and help. I could not pick Reeva up. I was struggling to pick her up.

Phone records reveal that this call was made at 3:19:03.

> I was trying to pick Reeva up but I could not. I could not pick her up. I was scared that I hurt her more, so I put her on … I pulled her over onto … onto [my] body and I was trying to pick her up.

Roux interrupted his client to point out that the next phone calls were at 3:20:05 to Netcare 911 and at 3:21:33 to security.

> I did not really know what to do. I could see that she was breathing.

She was struggling to breath[e] … [crying] … I phoned … I phoned 911, Netcare 911. I do not recall speaking to the operator, but I remember him telling me that I needed to get Reeva to the hospital, that I must not wait for him.

I do not remember phoning the security though, but from the phone records, I see that there was a call made from my cell phone to the security. The … after I got off the phone with the … with the Netcare 911 call centre, I ran down downstairs to open the front door. I could barely pick Reeva up, I would not have been able to open the door and carry her. So I ran, I open my bedroom door and I open the front door. I then ran back up to my room and on the way into my room I tried to force the door open. There is … there is two … two doors to my bedroom, M'Lady. The one I use, just locks with a key and then the other one, has got a latch at the top and at the bottom. So I ran into the door and it did not break open and I unlatched the bottom latch and when I unlatch the bottom latch, the door opened. The house … all the doors at the bottom of the house, and much of the doors at the top are double doors. The one door is open, you can walk through it. I have got the doors made so that the house is wheelchair friendly, so the … if you want to have a wider passage, you have to open both the doors.

Oscar rushed back upstairs into the bathroom, picked Reeva up and carried her down the stairs. It was at this point that Johan Stander and his daughter Carice Viljoen arrived.

I do not recall carrying her some of the way, but I remember getting to the second flight of stairs and Mr Stander and his daughter Ms Stander [Carice Viljoen] arrived. At that point, I was shouting and screaming for him to help me get her to the hospital. When I got down to the bottom of the flight of stairs, either Mr Stander or Carice Stander told me to put Reeva down. They said: That the ambulance was on its way. Before I put her down, I said to them: That we need to get to the hospital … we need to get to the hospital. They said: Just put her down, the ambulance is on its way. And then, I just sat there with her and I waited for the ambulance to arrive and … I felt helpless. I wanted to take her to the hospital and it was … I had my fingers in her mouth to help her try breath[e]. I had my hand on her hip, I was trying to stop the bleeding.

Oscar breathed deeply and audibly and then explained how they tried to stop the bleeding with towels and black bags.

> *I was trying to hold Reeva's hip with my hand to put pressure on it so that ... so that it stop bleeding as much. Ms Stander asked me if I had any tape or any rope or anything like that, so the she could ... so that she could tie on Reeva's ... tie her arms in order not to bleed as much. I do not remember ... I do not remember if I went to collect the ... the ... there is a cabinet in my pantry, that has got all the type of utility things one would use in a house, like tape and bags and things. I do not know if I went and fetch them or if Ms Stander went and fetch them.*

Advocate Roux proceeded to lead Oscar through the next few moments as he remembered them, crying throughout his testimony.

'Did the paramedics arrive at the scene? Or first Dr Stipp?' asked Roux.

> *There was a ... there was a person that arrived at the house. Carice came in and she said to me that there is a Doctor and I immediately felt relieved. I looked up and I saw a person walking into my house. He was later ... I later found out it was Doctor Stipp. I still do not remember his face or what he looked like. Once he came into the house, I remember me crying for him to help me, to help Reeva. He did not seem like he knew what he was doing. He did not seem like he ... he seemed to be over-whelmed by the ... by the situation. Everything he told me to do, I was already doing. I was already trying to stop the bleeding, I was already trying help Reeva breath[e]. He kneeled down on her ... on her right hand side for a couple of minutes I think and then ... I do not remember seeing him again. He walked outside and he was outside. I was shouting for him to come back into the house and help me. But ... the paramedics then arrived. They asked for some space to work, so I stood up.*

'Did you still remain there or did you go somewhere else? Can you remember going to the kitchen?' enquired Roux. Oscar's answer followed a long pause.

> *Reeva ... Reeva had already died whilst I was holding her. Before the ambulance arrived, so I knew there was nothing that they could do for her.*

'Did you at some stage go to the kitchen?' Roux tried again.

> *I am … I stood back when they arrived and I stood a couple of metres away from them. It is a open plan home so I stood at the … couple of metres away, where the dining room and the kitchen kind of meet and then the lady paramedic came to me and she said to me: That she would like to inform me that Reeva has passed. The paramedic asked me for identification, if there was some form of ID. So I went and I got Reeva's handbag in my … it was in my … in my bedroom. I did not go through her handbag I just simply picked it up, walked into the room and got her handbag and brought it out. Ms Stander was waiting there on the first floor outside my room and I gave her … I gave the handbag to her. I then went with Ms Stander downstairs to … where the paramedics were. I sat in the kitchen on the floor, crying. Against the … there [is] a island in the kitchen, serving counter and I sat there and then I do not know how much time passed. But at that point a police, or some police officers arrive shortly thereafter.*

'Do you know who it was?' Roux pressed.

> *There were two officers. They were not dressed in police clothing. They were dressed in civilian clothing. I think the one officer had shorts on and the other one … the were just both casually dressed and then, it was Colonel Van Rensburg who arrived, I think at more or less the same time. He came up to me and he introduced himself. I was at that point unable to speak with him. I was just sitting on the floor crying. Some time had passed then he … a police officer asked me to just stay in the kitchen. I saw the one police officer was standing nearby at the bottom of the stairs. Another police officer asked me if there was anybody else in the house and I just motioned to him that there was not. He proceeded to check the bottom of the home. He then went upstairs and then he came downstairs. I did not have my head up much and I was not in sight of the staircase but at times I could not sit.*

With Reeva dead, Oscar remained in the kitchen, throwing up from time to time, as more people arrived on the scene.

> *Every time I looked up, there were more people in the house. There were*

*more policemen. There were people going up and down the stairs. I was
standing in the kitchen against the … where the far side of the kitchen
is, away from the dining room where there is prep bowl small sink and
I asked a policeman if I may wash my hands. Because the smell of the
blood was making [me] throw up and he said he would ask and Mr
Van Rensburg, Colonel Van Rensburg came back to me and he said
[to] me, I may wash my hands. I do not remember washing my chest. I
just remember washing my hands and washing my face. At that point
I was still standing in the kitchen and I saw Mr Hilton … Hilton Botha
arrived. He came in straight from the front door up to me. He asked me
if I remember him. He immediately from where I was, he went upstairs.
He came downstairs some time later. At the time I was in the kitchen, I
could not look around the corner. Because every time I saw Reeva, I got
sick. So I stayed … stayed more inside the kitchen and at a time … and
a time I went and sat in the pantry against the washing machine.*

'Can you remember the photographer that arriv[ed]?' Roux guided him.

*I was … I was still in the kitchen. It was some time and Mr Botha came
downstairs, when he went up the second time Mr Van Re … Colonel
Van Rensburg came up to me and he said to me that, he put his hand on
my shoulder and he said to me that I do not have to speak to anyone but
I need to go to the garage. They would like to take some photos. There
will be a police photographer. I think the same officer that was standing
at the bottom of the staircases … staircase, he followed me with Mr Van
Rensburg to the … to the garage. There was a police officer that stayed
in the garage the whole time. I think it was the same gentleman who was
at the bottom of the staircase and I was in the garage for several hours.
I asked the police photographer if he could just please take all the photos
he needed so I could take my clothes off because they were also stained.*

'And from the garage, where did you go to?' asked Roux.

*From the garage I was taken to the foyer of the reception area of my
home and a police officer, surname Labuschagne, came up to me. He
introduced himself. He told me he was a friend of a family member of
mine and that I did not have anything to worry about. I must just …
he was there to look after me. It was at that point that Colonel Van*

*Rensburg said to me that because I was the only person in the house,
that they are going to charge me. He charged me at the time, he said to
me that I was under arrest.*

Roux then began to build the timeline around Oscar's version that would be so
crucial to the defence case. Through Oscar's evidence, he laid the foundation.

> Roux: *In relation to time, if I may take you through times that we could
> establish by virtue of the telephone records. We know there was
> a time 03:17 where witnesses, there is a variation but where … if
> I look at Doctor Stipp's evidence and Ms Stipp's evidence, where
> they heard the sound … three sounds, doef, doef, doef. Which
> to them resembled firearm shots and then we know at 03:19,
> approximately two minutes later, you made a call to Mr Stander.
> Do you have any idea, on your version, the three sounds, what
> would that represent by 03:17?*
>
> Accused: *M'Lady, I … the three sounds would have been the cricket bat
> hitting the door.*
>
> Roux: *But if the 03:17 you say, were you walking in the bathroom shortly
> before you hit the cricket bat?*
>
> Accused: *Yes, M'Lady. I was walking … I was walking through the
> bathroom when I went to go and kick the door, when I went to
> go and fetch the cricket bat, I was walking through the bath …
> through the bathroom with my prosthetic legs on.*
>
> Roux: *Doctor Stipp and Ms Stipp also gave evidence about prior shots.
> You hear that in court?*
>
> Accused: *I did, M'Lady.*
>
> Roux: *What would that have been?*
>
> Accused: *That would have been firing my pistol, Ma'am. M'Lady.*

Oscar had walked the court and the world through those dramatic moments
and had recounted in extraordinary detail the moment he shot and killed Reeva
Steenkamp. With his full version now before the court, his testimony would
have to withstand the extreme test of cross-examination.

Trapped in a Secret

Samantha Taylor woke up and looked at her phone. There were multiple missed calls and messages piling up on the screen.

'Rest in peace,' she read, to her horror. Over and over again.

It was Valentine's Day and news had broken early that morning that Oscar Pistorius had shot dead his girlfriend. Taylor had dated the runner until November the previous year and, in the confusion, many assumed it was she who was the 'blonde victim'.

She was horrified by the news. Her immediate thought was that it was Jenna Edkins, another of Oscar's ex-girlfriends. It was only when she switched on the TV that she discovered it was Reeva.

'My first impression … I didn't think it was Reeva. I thought it was Jenna and when I phoned my mom I said to her, "I didn't actually know he was still with Reeva."'

The soft-spoken 20-year-old, who put her marketing studies on hold to become a life coach following the trauma of the shooting, cast her mind back to that February morning in an interview with us.

'My first thought was everybody has a gun for a reason, and that reason is to eventually use the gun. So I was thinking, "Oh my goodness, he's used his gun on a human." When they said it was an intruder, I mean, I can't say what happened that night. I don't think the truth – the real truth – would ever come out because there are three sides to every story, so unfortunately, I don't know what happened that night, but I can only tell from my experience.'

Taylor's experience was dramatic. And explosive.

She met Oscar in 2010 at a Springbok rugby game at Loftus Versveld Stadium when she was only 16 years old. 'It was a bit of a random meeting because the electricity had just gone out and we were just waiting in the cafeteria to get drinks and food and, you know, you end up making conversation with everyone around you. I thought he was very good looking, but I didn't actually know who he was. He was very vibrant, very charming. And he had quite a good sense of humour.' After someone pointed out his celebrity status, she Googled him to find out more details.

They were both in relationships at the time – Oscar was still dating Edkins. Around a year later, Taylor received a Facebook invite from him.

'We started chatting a lot over Facebook and he had ended his relationship and coincidentally I had also ended my relationship. He was overseas at the time, doing season training and we started talking on the phone a lot and it was like we almost became best friends,' she recalled. When he arrived home, he went to visit her and the relationship blossomed.

Taylor's mother, Trish, was charmed by Oscar. 'When they first started dating, I was absolutely fine with it. He and I got on really well and … he was very, very nice. I found him very well-mannered, very softly spoken. He would often just sit and we would chat about stuff. Like when he went on an overseas trip he would come back and show me all his photographs. He had a good sense of humour, so we really welcomed him into our family, I must say, quite quickly.'

Taylor and Oscar were together for the next year and a half. During this time the couple grew close and Taylor spent up to four nights a week at his Silver Woods home. Oscar stayed over in Dainfern, too, and in this period Taylor got to know his family fairly well.

'Do you know, Arnold said in an interview that he had never met any of Oscar's previous girlfriends, but I had actually gone to Arnold's house many times before,' insisted Taylor. 'We used to go there after gym in the morning and have egg and toast either with his cousins or with his aunt. Arnold was often there. He showed me around the house so I know exactly what the house looks like. He used to take me down to the pond at the bottom where they had some swans. I know he earns a lot of money. He's got a very big house, he's got nice cars so he's definitely very wealthy and I'm sure whatever business he has I'm sure he's a very powerful man.'

But she said Oscar and his uncle Arnold weren't close. 'They didn't seem to have a great relationship, but I know he got along with his cousins quite well. His sister and him had a very good relationship, they loved each other so much and she was such a good support for him. She's very quiet and very soft, so he was very gentle with his sister. Him and his brother also had a good relationship but I think they clashed quite a bit. I think they were doing a bit of business together and there was, you know, a bit of a rocky relationship as well, but they were quite close. Him and his father, he never spoke about his father, he told me they never had a good relationship. I don't know anything about his father.'

Taylor said Oscar spoke about his mother often, describing her as his rock. 'I actually joined him and his brother and his sister on his mother's birthday and we had a dinner in the garden and just prayed in remembrance of her. He loved his mom very much. He said she was such a strong woman, she used to empower all of them, so I think that definitely affected the family a lot.'

It was an idyllic picture, but under the surface, the Taylors experienced a different Oscar. Taylor's mother became suspicious.

'Something inside me often worried and early on I could see he was lying about where he was or what he was doing. That didn't sit well with me. I used to get a knot in my stomach,' said Trish.

She suspected he was cheating on her daughter. 'In the beginning I gave him the benefit of the doubt. One of my other daughter's friends was at the house early in the relationship and she said, "Oh no, Samantha's got to be careful, he's such a cheat. He cheats on all his girlfriends," and I still said, "I'm sure he'd never, he's so mad about Samantha, he'd never cheat on her,"' she said.

Taylor didn't need prompting to reveal what she euphemistically referred to as 'problems' experienced by the couple. 'Our relationship in general was really amazing, we both loved each other a lot, but like every relationship, there were problems and our problems grew over time. There were quite a lot. He's got quite a short temper and he gets irritated very easily, so it was always like walking on eggshells. I didn't know what to do or where to go in case he didn't agree with it,' said Taylor. She carefully selected her next words.

'I think it was … I don't know how to describe that … I think it was very … almost possessive. It was a bit obsessive.' She said she could 'definitely' relate to Reeva's emotions in the messages she sent to Oscar, which were read out in court, saying he scared her at times.

'He was so protective. You know, when I was away from him or when he was overseas he was always asking me, "Where are you? Who are you with?" If he didn't believe me, he would make me send photos or he would phone my home phone to see if I'm home or he would phone my sister to see where I am. Often I used to see his friends at the same restaurant I was at, so I don't know if maybe he wanted them to check up on me and who I was with, but definitely, you know, it was very strange to me.'

And Taylor spoke about Oscar's gun as if it was a third party in their relationship. 'He's very stringent with his gun. He keeps it on him all the time, he's always got it around him; he sleeps next to it, so he was obsessive with his gun, he always had it on him,' she said.

Did she ever think he was capable of shooting another human being with it?

'There were many times, like I said in my statement, where the gun was a little bit scary. I think that even though it's a very dangerous weapon, he often handled it like it wasn't really much and there were times that I hid his gun from him. So, I didn't ever think he would shoot someone, but I did know that having a gun around, anything can go wrong.

'There was a time that I did hide his gun under his bed when he was drunk because he got quite aggressive, so I needed to just be cautious, if anything,' she said, referring to an incident that she had detailed in her affidavit. 'We had some friends over that night and he was a little bit drunk and he jumped onto his friend's back, but the floor was wet and they both slipped and Oscar chipped his tooth. So his mouth was bleeding. We said, "It's time-out now, let's all go to bed," and by the time we had gone to bed, he didn't realise that he had fallen, I think he thought that I had beaten him up,' she said astonishingly. 'I hid the gun from him and the next day he was looking for the gun and I had to tell him what happened but I don't think he had any recollection of what he had done.'

When asked if she thought he was capable of physical abuse, Taylor said she took the view that it was safer to indulge and ignore, than to stand up and provoke him.

'You know, I think any man that's angry or has a short temper could be abusive and every woman would react differently. In my position, I'm the type of girl if I'm shouted at, I wouldn't retaliate, I wouldn't provoke someone because I know that it would only get worse. I would probably cry if I was shouted at. And another woman's perspective would be to retaliate or become abusive, so in my position, I definitely would not have provoked someone who is already angry.'

Another 'problem' Taylor said recurred throughout her relationship with Oscar was the persistent presence of his ex-girlfriend Jenna Edkins.

'She kept contacting him and eventually she ended up contacting me. She was a very big problem in our relationship. That girl was such a problem. I've had contact with Jenna, I've told her to back off, I've told her … I've had to, as the girlfriend of Oscar, I should not have to be messaging his ex-girlfriend, saying, "Leave my boyfriend alone; stop contacting him." And as much as she was contacting him, he was obviously contacting her back.'

Taylor's voice rose in pitch as she exclaimed that she had to send Jenna messages 'all the time!'

She elaborated: 'She sent me messages saying he cheated on her all the time.

It's normal in their relationship. So for her, it's normal for him to be with other girls because she knows that she'll still have him when he falls back ... I know she had a connection with his mother, so ... she kind of ... probably feels that she needs to be supportive there.'

Taylor painted a picture of a relationship between Jenna and Oscar that would not be extinguished, despite its turbulence – one that she claimed ran in parallel to any other relationship that Oscar entered into.

'I think they had a problematic relationship, if anything. I think it was one of those relationships that you are stuck in for years and you never get out and I think every time he had a girlfriend and, like in my case it was a year and a half – he was with Jenna before me, he was with Jenna during me, he was with Jenna after me. He was with Jenna before Reeva, he was with Jenna while he was dating Reeva and he's probably still with Jenna now. So ... that girl is always going to be in his life and ... you know, that's why he can't be with other women, because that's cheating!'

It didn't surprise Taylor when we revealed to her that Jenna was present in Oscar's life the evening before he shot Reeva. That Oscar had spent nearly ten minutes on the phone to Jenna before the shooting. And that he had made telephonic contact with her on several occasions after he had a fallout with Reeva.

'Typical!' Taylor exclaimed. 'I would not be surprised. At all. At all!' It was as if a missing piece of the puzzle had dropped for Taylor.

'You know, we both suffer from insomnia. Often I would wake up and he would be sitting on his phone. I often saw her name, although it was not saved under "BabyShoes" at the time. It was "Jenna Edkins". I often saw her name. If he was showing me a photo on his phone and her WhatsApp message would pop up – we fought over that a lot. She was a very big problem in our relationship, a huge problem,' Taylor repeated.

And then, as if a floodgate had been opened, she detailed her thoughts on the extent of the relationship. 'I can confirm that she was at his house. I used to find products that only ladies would use. We bought a puppy, well he wanted a puppy and I was with him at the time so it kind of became like our little baby and at the time I found a photo of Jenna with the dog and I know when we got the dog so I know it was when we were together. So that's caught red-handed. Lying on his bed with our dog. I had problems with Jenna our whole relationship.'

But surely Oscar and Jenna could simply be friends and there might be no romantic involvement? After all, they shared a powerful history together and one that linked Oscar to his late mother? Was Jenna only an emotional crutch or was there more to it? Taylor claimed it was the latter.

'When we started dating he told me that they were kind of still friendly. They had just ended their relationship, they were kind of still friendly and the reason why they spoke was because she was there to support him. Her mother knew his mother and obviously which I understand and which I respected – is that his mother passed away while he was very young and if there's any attachment to your mother, you would want that in your life. So I think having Jenna, always there in his life, he just knew that his mother was still kind of in his life, which I respected. I said to him, "If you want to be friends with her, that's fine with me." But again, in my eyes, if you are messaging your ex-girlfriend, or seeing your ex-girlfriend with intentions, that is cheating. He didn't want me to know that he was in contact with Jenna, which was already sneaky. If they were just friends, why was Jenna never around? With me, I said, "If you are just friends with Jenna then why can't I come with you to see her?"'

During Oscar's holiday to Cape Town in December 2012 – before Reeva flew in to join him and their friends Justin and Samantha – Taylor claimed that Edkins posted a photo of herself and the athlete to her Instagram feed and then apparently took it down hours later. Taylor pointed to this photograph as evidence of her claim that Jenna and Oscar were still involved, although the photograph could also simply be evidence of a good friendship, as Edkins insisted in her response to our questions.

Taylor laughed at the 'Babyshoes' term of endearment Oscar used to refer to Edkins on his phone contact list. It was a moniker he had used for her too. 'I know we always used to joke because my feet are so small compared to his.' But the most common term of endearment they had shared was 'Baba' – the same name Oscar and Reeva adopted for one another.

• • •

Towards the middle of 2012, Oscar left South Africa for four months to train in Italy and compete in the Olympic and Paralympic Games. He had been dating Taylor for a year and their relationship could not have been better.

'Things were good and I think the first month he was over there things were really good with us. Obviously it's like dating over Skype and it was quite tough but it was okay, it was working. And then … thereafter … after about a month, I think, I started realising he was acting a bit weird,' said Taylor.

Her mother Trish elaborated. 'Before he went away, everything was fine. He came to stay with us. He used to come stay with us quite often. It was probably the best their relationship was, before he left, it was really, really going well.'

But then, all of a sudden, everything changed. 'Early on while he was still in Italy, long before he went to London, he phoned me out of the blue one day. Crying and crying and crying on the phone. And it took me a while to realise like, shit, Oscar's crying, and then from that phone call onwards it was just ongoing phone calls, SMSes, emails,' revealed Trish. 'He was literally crying for help in so many ways.'

In one of the emails Oscar sent from Italy to 'Samantha and the Taylor family' in July 2012, he poured out his heart and apologised for the pain he had caused. He explained that the email was difficult to write as he was confronting issues he had been denying to himself for years:

> *Peoples first impression of most often one of 2 ways. It's what they have heard through friends of friends or what they have read or seen in the media. Both having positive and negative connotations mostly due to my personal actions. In the past when someone [took] me for the positives I was all quick to allow myself to be content. When the negatives came up I put my guard up and tried to defend myself. In my career which was the one I have become accustomed to defending this came naturally. Although I often get sick of it it is something that I have realised that I'll have to deal with. On a personal front when people have judged me negatively, I haven't been able to be all so comfortable. Partly due to me not wanting to believe the truth at times, often because I didn't feel I had to explain myself or my actions as I hadn't had anyone to answer too from a young age and other times because I saw people's perceptions of me made up already.*

On 17 July, just a few days after sending the email, Oscar sent an extended BBM message to Taylor, which featured these lines:

> ... I have got many flaws. I'm far from perfect. I'm sorry for being a fuck up and for not making you feel appreciated like you deserve. That's the last thing I would've wanted ...

Once he was in London, the situation deteriorated even further. Taylor switched on her phone one morning to see on Twitter that her boyfriend allegedly had a new girlfriend. UK tabloid reports had splashed that the Blade Runner was dating Russian model Anastassia Khozissova. The pair had reportedly met in New York and was spotted holding hands while out and about in Chelsea.

'I saw oh, Oscar has a girlfriend and it wasn't me. So that was when I ended it with him the first time. I didn't really want to speak to him because I was angry, so we were emailing each other all the time and … that's when I started dating Quinton,' she said, referring to her highly publicised relationship with the TV producer and mining billionaire Quinton van der Burgh.

'It was really tough because, obviously I loved Oscar and I wanted things to work but I knew at that time it just wasn't going to work for me. So while he was over at the Olympics, he was obviously very upset and he invited me to go over to the Olympics and he wanted to organise me a visa and a flight and everything, but I just felt at that time I definitely wasn't in the right place to give him a chance.

'We were communicating over email but I was just so angry that I didn't want to speak to him, so he was phoning my family all the time. He was phoning my sister, probably ten, twenty times a day. He was phoning my mother in the middle of the night and messaging my brothers. He was checking up on me, he was asking my friends where I was and who I'm with. It was really exhausting. We had broken up, but he wouldn't acknowledge that we had broken up. I think on everyone's behalf it was very exhausting,' said Taylor.

It was around this time, during the Paralympics, that teammate Arnu Fourie moved out of the room they shared. Fourie told broadcaster David O'Sullivan that this was because Oscar was constantly screaming on his phone. Fourie later denied this, but Taylor confirmed that it was indeed her on the other end of Oscar's telephone tirades.

Just two days after Oscar's blowout over the length of Brazilian sprinter Alan Oliveira's blades at the Paralympics, he sent several more BBMs to Taylor. In the exchange, Oscar appeared to raise his concerns about Taylor seeing Van der Burgh and admitted to cheating on Taylor with Jenna Edkins during their relationship:

5 September: I know it is unacceptable. I'm sorry I didn't know what to say when you called and went off at me. I was called Jen last night and spoke for a long time with her. I told her that I had been seeing you since September .. I told her that in the beginning I enjoyed spending time with you and after a couple of months I started falling for you. I know that at times I played with your emotions because I was too scared to let go of Jenna. I'll be honest with you because you deserve that. The last time I did anything with her was in January. We drifted apart and on her birthday I toke her for dinner, we had had a rough time and I know it wasn't right but I was a coward and lonely and went running back to her. I tried to make things work …

The last messages between Oscar and Taylor were sent on the same day that the athlete and his 4 x 100 metres relay teammates, including Arnu Fourie, celebrated winning gold and breaking the world record.

Trish also allegedly bore the brunt of the emotional outpouring over this time, fielding phone calls from Oscar at all hours. 'He was so emotionally unstable. By this stage I also knew that he had an angry streak in him, I'd seen and heard about things that had gone wrong. He cried continuously. I was worried … I was worried … I thought he was going to commit suicide when he was away, and so often on the phone I'd keep him in the phone until he stopped crying, or … he calmed down and we'd often end up laughing or joking … or I'd say to him, "Your race tomorrow is going to be okay, it's going to be fine," and then when I felt he was okay, then the conversations would end.'

For Trish, it was difficult to reconcile the Oscar who was the face of the Olympics and riding the wave of international celebrity with the man on the other end of the phone.

'I couldn't speak to anyone about it. If it got into the media, we were just going to be trashed and my daughter would just be so badly trashed by the media. We were trapped in his secret. We were actually trapped. It was terrible – this started before the Olympics and carried on all the way through the Olympics and all the way through the Paralympics. It carried on for months. You know what it's like, everyone loved Oscar, so we had to keep everything a secret.

'I kept saying, "Oz, you have to see a psychologist, you have to." He used to promise all the time, "No, I know I need help, I promise you, Trish, I promise you I will go to a psychologist." He never did. In every conversation, he'd promise me he'd see a psychologist. He did book one in London, but he never went to the appointment.'

When Oscar returned from the Olympics, he and Samantha got back together again, despite his behaviour while he had been away. 'Towards the end of his London season, we were contacting each other again and we were just trying to work through issues more than anything, so we were going back and forth speaking to each other about everything, and the both of us decided, if we're going to make this work, it's got to work from both sides, so both of us have to put the work into the relationship, and that's when I decided, you know what, I'm not going to be half-hearted about a relationship, and I had ended things with Quinton,' explains Taylor.

It was a few weeks later that the couple went to the Seychelles to be featured on *Top Billing*. Despite presenting a picture of happiness, Taylor and her mother were still terribly concerned. Trish said the phone calls continued and Oscar's behaviour became increasingly volatile. She thought Oscar was going to combust.

'What would happen is he would cry, cry, cry for like a week and then out of the blue, when things went well, he would go on an absolute high and then suddenly he'd be with women, drinking, fast cars, and then a few days later he would go on with this crying – it was too extreme. His emotions were too extreme,' said Trish, completely identifying with the defence concept of the 'Two Oscars'.

Towards the end of October, the relationship between Taylor and Oscar was on the skids. It was around this time that the now infamous confrontation between Oscar and Van der Burgh took place. As Taylor explained, it was on the morning before the couple went to Sun City for a weekend during which the relationship really fell apart.

'The altercation had happened that day that we had left for Sun City. I was actually, I was at his house, I was packing for the both of us to leave for Sun City for the weekend, and he told me he would be home by about three o'clock. I think it was about four o'clock and we had to be in Sun City by six o'clock. So by four o'clock I had phoned him and his phone was off and then I got a phone call from a friend of mine who was at the race track, and he said to me, "Do you know what happened with Quinton and Oscar?"

'I sent Oscar a message and I said to him, "Why are you causing shit in our relationship. Why … why did you feel the need to confront Quinton?" He went crazy, you know, he told me, "I'm your boyfriend, you should have been sticking up for me but you turn around and you're sticking up for Quinton." It definitely caused another issue and that's why Sun City was just a rough ride for the both of us because all those past issues came up again.'

Although Oscar later testified in court they broke up that weekend, Taylor believed they formally remained a couple. 'I think we both just had a very rough weekend and he flew back with me to Cape Town because he had a meeting in Cape Town and I came to see my family in the winelands. I think we were emailing back and forth up until that night of the Sports Awards, so I think in our minds we both kind of knew the relationship was over, but there was no … there was no confirmation because our emails were so back and forth.'

But Taylor knew it was over once and for all when she switched on the TV and saw Oscar and Reeva on the red carpet at the awards. 'I was so heartbroken. I mean, obviously in my mind, we were fighting and I think we both knew the relationship was coming to an end again, but I never knew he would go to that extreme to spite me and take another girl to the awards, so I think at that moment I knew I never wanted to see him again.'

It was then that she also claimed to have received a phone call from Darren Fresco, 'threatening' her and warning her to stay out of Oscar's space.

This infuriated and terrified Taylor's mother. 'I said to him, "Something is going to go wrong before the end of this year." And that was already, I think it was already October or November,' recalls Trish.

'I said, "Something is going to go wrong and it's going to go wrong soon." In my mind I thought he's either going to commit suicide or he's going to have a car accident, because he was speeding everywhere. And I said to him, "It's going to go wrong soon and I can't see a way out for you because you are sitting in the middle of your own web of lies, and everything around you is collapsing."'

Trish's forecast, of course, proved to be prophetic. Something terrible did go wrong. And when she heard the news on Valentine's Day, she said it broke her heart.

'I thought he had committed suicide. Then when we found out that he had shot someone, I was just ... I was so sad. I just thought, why did no one ... why didn't his family stop this? Why did no one – I couldn't have been the only person that knew that things were so bad. His family must have known. His coach must have known. His manager must have known. Why was no one getting him help? People must have known.'

Reasonably, Possibly True

'Your version is so improbable that nobody would ever think it is reasonably possibly true.'

This became the state's dictum when attacking Oscar's version of events, and was repeated by prosecutor Gerrie Nel when he questioned elements of the timeline of events on the morning of Valentine's Day. Nel cross-examined Oscar for nearly five days and jumped around to the various themes and topics raised in Oscar's evidence-in-chief; it was never chronological or tackled in the manner it was presented by the accused.

In one session Nel would question Oscar on the moments in the bathroom just before the shooting, and then jump to the scene at Tashas; on another occasion he would quiz Oscar on the dinner he said he had with Reeva the night before the shooting, and then switch to dealing with crime in the area. The technique was designed to throw the witness off, to test his memory.

Nel was clear about what he thought of Oscar's version of events. 'I am saying that your version of events is in fact untrue. Mr Pistorius, I say that you have a concocted version, which you have tailored to fit the state's case and you are tailoring your version as you are sitting there.'

Amongst the difficulties Nel had with Oscar's version was how he was able to recall fine detail about everything he did leading up to the shooting – what he saw and heard, how quickly or slowly he was moving, where his hands were placed – yet when it came to that critical moment in the bathroom when he pulled the trigger, his memory wasn't nearly as reliable.

Nel argued that to believe Oscar, one would have to accept that Reeva got out of bed without saying a word to the accused; that she slipped down the passage without him seeing her; that she took her phone with her; and that she never once screamed when he shouted at intruders.

The prosecutor seemed puzzled that the couple who had allegedly just spoken to each other about their sleep troubles did not communicate further. In answering Nel's persistent questions, Oscar asserted that Reeva never asked where he was going when he got out of bed, or why he was getting out of bed, and he never told her he was going to collect the fans. Perhaps most importantly, he says Reeva did not say she was going to the toilet.

> Nel: *Would you have expected that kind of conversation between the two of you? Why would she not, why would she not ask you where you were going?*
>
> Accused: *I do not know, M'Lady.*
>
> Nel: *It is because your version is improbable. One would expect her to say, ask where you are going. Would you not expect her saying that?*
>
> Accused: *I do not think so, M'Lady.*
>
> Nel: *Why? Would you expect her not to say a thing when you get up in the middle of the night, if she is awake?*
>
> Accused: *I do not know what I would expect, M'Lady. I do not know ...*

Nel did not believe Oscar's explanation that fetching his firearm and confronting the threat was the only option available to him. Nel suggested that Oscar could have called Reeva and then fled the bedroom, or even hidden from the intruder.

> Nel: *You both could have been on her side of the bed, with your view on the passage.*
>
> Accused: *My Lady, I did not want harm to come to Reeva. So I wanted to put myself, as I said, between the harm and Reeva. If I had stuck next to Reeva, it would have put her in harm My Lady. So I did not think of ... I told her to get down and call the police. I could have done a host of things. But at that time, that was the decision that I made.*
>
> Nel: *You see, I am ... Mister, you know that it is my view that your version is not correct and it is improbable that you would act in that way ...*

Nel explored what had often been the topic of public debate – why would Oscar believe that an intruder who had just broken in to his house would hide inside his toilet?

> Nel: If there is an intruder, do you think he would go into the toilet
> and close the door?
>
> Accused: I am not sure what an intruder would do, My Lady, if he was
> caught off guard. I do not know … I cannot be expected to
> answer that question.
>
> Nel: Standing, now you are standing there, you, Mr Oscar Pistorius
> standing there, thinking: he came through that window, he went
> into that toilet. That is what you thought.
>
> Accused: That is correct. It was a possibility, My Lady.
>
> Nel: No, it cannot, it is so far-fetched that it would happen, Mr
> Pistorius. It is improbable that you would even think that an
> intruder would run into my toilet and lock the door and close the
> door.

Nel did not believe for one minute that Reeva had remained silent throughout the time the accused said he was calling out to her to warn her about the
intruder and to call the police. Oscar recalled standing at the entrance to the
bathroom shortly after peering inside to check whether he could see anyone.
With his firearm out in front of him, he said he again screamed for Reeva to call
the police and kept on shouting.

> Nel: Just a moment. Of your whole version, Mr Pistorius, this is the
> most improbable. Reeva at that stage is three metres away from
> you in a toilet.
>
> Accused: I did not know that, My Lady. I thought that she was in the
> bedroom.
>
> Nel: No, no. In fact, I am talking about the fact. At that stage when
> you shouted and screamed at Reeva to phone the police, she is
> three metres away from you in a toilet.
>
> Accused: That is correct, My Lady.
>
> Nel: And she never uttered a word.
>
> Accused: That is correct, My Lady.
>
> Nel: It is not probable. She would be scared. She would shout out and
> talk to you. You are in the same room.
>
> Accused: My Lady, I agree with Mr Nel. She would have been terrified, My
> Lady, but I do not think that would have [led] her to scream out.
> I think that she would have kept quiet for that reason … I was
> shouting and I was approaching the toilet and she was in the, I

was approaching the bathroom and she was in the toilet. Then I
presume that she would think that the danger is coming closer to
her. So why will she shout out?

Nel: *Because you are in the room, sir! Mr Pistorius, you are now*
in the room, you are shouting. She is three metres away from
you behind that particular door. There is no way that you will
convince the court that she stood there, saying nothing.

In an effort to show that Oscar's version was a lie, Nel picked apart every detail, every step Oscar said he took that morning. It was relentless cross-examination that often took its toll on the accused, but elicited little sympathy from Nel.

Oscar vacillated from confidence when dealing with the firearm-related charges to tears when pressed on the moments he killed his girlfriend. It was widely believed that Nel was going to be tough on the athlete, but the prosecutor's tactics proved to be ruthless and devoid of any sensitivity whatsoever. Oscar would have to sustain this scrutiny for five long days in the witness box.

Contaminated, Disturbed, Tampered

Q uestions surrounding the police's handling of the crime scene emerged in the bail application mere days after the shooting and cast a shadow over the police's integrity. In light of the South African public's cynicism about the capabilities of the police service, this wasn't entirely surprising. Former investigating officer Hilton Botha was accused of entering the crime scene without the appropriate protective bootees covering his shoes. Although anyone close to the case would claim that this was not relevant because the accused had already admitted to killing the victim, it was the principle that was being tested. It was a 'how dunnit' rather than a 'who dunnit'. But then more details of irregularities emerged, some by the police's own admission and others voiced by Oscar himself. The accused stated in his plea explanation that he would use this to argue his innocence:

> It will also be demonstrated during this trial, whilst Botha was the investigating officer and tasked with preserving the scene, that the scene was contaminated, disturbed and tampered with. This feature of the State's case will be dealt with when Botha, amongst others, gives evidence.

At the time, the defence team assumed Hilton Botha would take the stand and were sharpening their knives in anticipation. But this wasn't the way the trial ultimately played out. Instead, the state called the former Boschkop station commander and the first police officer to arrive on the scene, Colonel Schoombie van Rensburg.

The veteran policeman has a Friar Tuck-like appearance, with a shiny bald patch on the top of his head and neatly trimmed greying hair around the back and sides. Recently retired, he had subsequently followed his passion to coach sport.

Van Rensburg explained how it came to be that he and a Constable Christelle Prinsloo were the first police officers to arrive. He had found Oscar in a very emotional state in the kitchen, where he was being consoled by a woman later identified as Carice Viljoen, the daughter of neighbour Johan Stander.

Nel led the witness through his observations when he arrived on the scene: who was there, what were they doing, what did they say and how did he react? The answers set out the timeline of events, plotted the movements of key players in the police and the accused, and explained what had informed the police's rationale to arrest Oscar on a charge of murder.

Van Rensburg said he confined Oscar to the kitchen, where he observed the athlete retching at times. When Hilton Botha arrived, Van Rensburg showed the investigating officer Reeva's body, and together they followed the blood trail up the stairs, down the passage into Oscar's bedroom, past the cupboards and into the bathroom. Nel referred to the crime scene pictures along this path, which the policeman described and confirmed was indeed the state in which he had observed them. He was asked to comment on specific items in the bedroom:

> Nel: *Now that view of the bedroom, can you still remember that as the view you got the day you entered?*
>
> Van Rensburg: *That is correct, M'Lady. That is as it was.*
>
> Nel: *When you got to the scene, was that door open or closed?*
>
> Van Rensburg: *The door was open, M'Lady.*
>
> Nel: *What was the condition of the curtains, when you got to the scene?*
>
> Van Rensburg: *The curtains were drawn open as they were there. They were not closed.*
>
> Nel: *Now before we carry on, Colonel, since the time that you arrived at the scene, did anybody go upstairs, up until the time that you and Botha went up?*
>
> Van Rensburg: *After I had arrived on the scene, M'Lady, until I went up with Botha, nobody else entered that scene.*

The state was pre-empting the defence case. Nel was also laying the foundations for a much later exchange with Oscar, when he would take the accused through the state of the bedroom in order to discredit his version.

Van Rensburg further confirmed that when he arrived the grey duvet was on the floor in front of one of the fans; a pair of denim jeans was lying next to the duvet; a pair of white flip-flops was found on the left side of the bed close to an overnight bag on a chair; a firearm holster was found on the left bedside table; the two fans were found as they were pictured; and a box of eight luxury watches was found on top of a speaker in the room.

With the photograph of the bathroom up on screens in the courtroom, Van Rensburg described the state in which he found the room: the shattered wood panels, bullet shells, the cricket bat, shards of bullet fragments, the open window, the silver pistol with the hammer pulled back, and two cellphones. A black iPhone, lying closest to the firearm, had come out of its silver case, which to Van Rensburg created the impression it was two phones on top of each other. He said it was only later, while he was not present and while moving items in the bathroom, that police discovered the second phone, a white iPhone, under a towel closest to the bath.

Van Rensburg stated that after inspecting the crime scene and establishing from Oscar that only he and Reeva had been in the house at the time of the shooting, he immediately viewed the athlete as a suspect. Oscar was then moved from the kitchen to the garage where his brother Carl and Advocate Kenny Oldwadge had access to him. The cop insisted that from the time he arrived at the house, access control was implemented and a barrier erected. In the days that followed, the house was locked up with numbered and tagged tamper-proof seals that were documented.

When the police's photographer Bennie van Staden arrived, Van Rensburg and Botha led him through the crime scene, from Reeva's body up to the bathroom where the shooting had taken place. He insisted only the three of them went upstairs and that no one else had access to the first level of the house. Only later did he allow Oscar's sister Aimee and Carice Viljoen to go to the bedroom to fetch clothes, but Van Staden accompanied them.

Van Rensburg said he had specifically asked Van Staden to take a picture of the watchcase as he had realised that the watches were valuable and might be tempting for someone to steal. Because of blood smears on the mirror on the inside lid, the case was also considered evidence. At some stage after Oscar was removed from the scene and the forensics team was upstairs gathering evidence, Van Rensburg entered the room and noticed that one of the watches was missing. Van Staden had told him that Aimee had taken one. And then, a short while later when he was downstairs, Van Staden told him that another watch had in the interim been removed from the box. 'Immediately I gave the instruction that everybody had to come to the garage,' said Van Rensburg.

'We body searched everyone. We searched all the bags each and every forensic expert had on his possession. We searched the whole house through again. Again went back to the main bedroom. We even searched the vehicles of all the forensic experts on the scene without giving anyone permission to leave. We could not find the watch.'

Van Rensburg said he opened a case of theft and personally returned the remaining six watches to Oscar some time later. The incident prompted stricter access control to the house; and every person entering and exiting was searched.

This, however, wasn't the only incident of blatant police bungling, as Van Rensburg further explained. He said that after the photographer had finished in the bathroom, the ballistics expert, a lieutenant, was allowed in to conduct investigations and seize the firearm. While talking on his phone, Van Rensburg said he heard the firearm being cocked and turned his head towards the sound. 'The ballistic expert had the firearm in his hand, without gloves. He took out the magazine. The magazine was in his hand and the firearm was in his hand,' he said.

The lieutenant, realising what he had done, apologised before placing the handgun back on the floor, pulling on a pair of gloves, and picking it up again.

Technically, the error didn't make much difference because there was no dispute about who had handled the firearm and pulled the trigger. But it was a reflection on the professionalism and conduct of the South African police. While a fingerprint-contaminated firearm would make no difference in this case, how many other cases were lost because evidence was damaged or altered as a result of an investigator's negligence? The confession by the police officer contributed to the larger argument by the defence – what else was 'contaminated, disturbed and tampered with'?

While this evidence was being led in court, top brass at police headquarters in Pretoria were ready for the backlash. Nel and the prosecution team had informed detective head Lieutenant-General Vinesh Moonoo, who had attended proceedings almost every day, what the witness would be asked to testify about. Moonoo, in turn, briefed his counterpart at the police's Forensic Science Laboratory, as well as the national police commissioner, Riah Phiyega. The police were ready to spin. And yet, despite their preparedness, one investigator admitted that the revelations of theft and bungling did not receive the attention they had all anticipated. It appeared that the momentum of the trial and details relating to Oscar himself, the inside of his house and the police's first encounters with the accused had overshadowed the conduct of the police.

Of course, it also showed how blasé South Africans had become about such incidents.

...

The defence wanted Hilton Botha in the box and Roux was agitated that he didn't get him. Instead, though, he tackled Van Rensburg on the reason he believed the state had called him to testify – that he was there to give evidence on matters far wider than he was able to, and that his evidence was designed to take the place of Botha. While the witness denied the claim, Roux was not wrong. The state was indeed doing everything it could to avoid calling Botha to the stand because they knew he would prove to be a liability.

Van Rensburg confirmed he and Botha were the first to venture upstairs and that no other policeman went upstairs before them.

Roux walked Van Rensburg back through his evidence about Oscar's room; he repeated what he had told the court about the location of the duvet, the fans, the state of the curtains and the door. He said the pair moved carefully through the crime scene. 'You did not disturb anything in the bathroom?' asked Roux.

> *Van Rensburg: Nothing at all.*
> > *Roux: You did not see Mr Hilton Botha disturbing anything in the bathroom?*
> *Van Rensburg: Nothing.*
> > *Roux: Picking anything up, or moving anything?*
> *Van Rensburg: Nothing. We did not touch anything, nothing.*

The suggestion from Roux's line of questioning was clear.

Van Rensburg said the bathroom was photographed as they found it. 'The first priority is to take photos as you receive it. Afterwards then you start with the investigation. Then you start touching in the room, because it has to be seized, you cannot just leave it there and you have to investigate further.'

Van Rensburg said he eventually left Botha and Van Staden to continue their investigation, but again made it clear that only he and the two others had access to upstairs until the photos were taken.

With the deft subtlety of an experienced advocate, Roux produced a piece of evidence to blow Van Rensburg out the water: an affidavit signed by another police officer, Sebetha, who had said in his statement he arrived on the scene together with a Constable Khoza. He said that when he arrived the paramedics were still working on Reeva. Sebetha was also responsible for writing the so-called A1 statement, usually made by the first person to arrive on the scene. So why didn't Van Rensburg write it if he was first on the scene? The witness dismissed the contradiction, but provided no explanation for it.

Roux read from Sebetha's affidavit: 'I proceeded to the upper building where I noticed droplets of blood come from the upper building upstairs.'

'Amazing,' said Van Rensburg. 'I say amazing.'

'What is "amazing"? Could you explain?'

'Because he did not went up there. He was not before me on the crime scene.'

'Yes. Well, let us read ...'

Sebetha described finding a 'stainless 9 mm Taurus in the main bathroom' – a claim that appeared damning in that it blatantly contradicted Van Rensburg's version of events. 'The only explanation that I can give to M'Lady is that he got information and he wrote his statement, the A1 statement on hearsay. He was not in the bathroom.'

In fact, Van Rensburg was so sure he was the first police officer on the scene he urged the court to obtain the AVL records from the police vehicles. The AVL system is a satellite tracking system that shows the exact location of police vehicles at any given time.

Despite Roux going to great lengths to raise questions as to whether Van Rensburg had been first on the scene, both Oscar and neighbour Carice Viljoen testified that Van Rensburg was the first officer to walk in and introduce himself.

Roux took issue with a number of the photos taken at the scene, adamant that they revealed aspects of police tampering during the investigative process. One of those images was of the colonel kneeling on the right side of Oscar's bed fiddling with the cables – one that would become crucial later in the trial.

Roux also had problems with the photos taken of the white iPhone and that they did not state in the caption that a towel had had to be moved in order for the phone to be visible. The problem for the advocate was the defence's ability to rely on photos presented by the state as a true reflection of the crime scene in its untouched state. He referred to pictures of the duvet – the first merely listed the date, while the photo of it folded out made it clear in the caption that it had been moved. Without an explanation in the caption, who was to know that a scene had been altered?

Van Rensburg took pains to emphasise, however, that these were not part of the first set of photos taken at the scene and were thus not representations of the untouched scene. The scene was preserved for the original photos and then the investigation started. 'So then you move stuff to complete your investigation,' he stated.

Nel was quick to correct the discrepancies. After all, his case against Oscar relied heavily on the photographs. He showed that all electronic photographs contain metadata, an electronic signature. And the photos the defence was using were not from the official photographer. This metadata proved key to leading police photographer Bennie van Staden through his evidence-in-chief and the timing of his movements that morning.

• • •

Bennie van Staden's fair hair is thinning on the top. He has 21 years' experience in the police service, eight of these years as a photographer. When he arrived on the scene he found Oscar in the garage with his brother Carl.

Van Staden's evidence was a tedious exercise, but necessary in a criminal trial in order for the prosecution to gather details of each photograph on the record. The photographer had put together a total of 1 147 photos spanning 15 albums, and he had retrieved the metadata for just about every album he compiled.

Van Staden was also responsible for collecting a primer residue sample from Oscar to establish whether the accused had in fact discharged a firearm. Despite Oscar confirming he had washed his hands – after obtaining permission from Van Rensburg – Van Staden attempted to retrieve samples from Oscar's hands and arms. He then proceeded to photograph the accused.

Starting with photo 155 in the first album, which covered the untouched crime scene as police claimed to have found it when they arrived, the photographer walked the court through the images.

Van Staden took his first photo that morning at 05:12am, depicting Oscar standing in the garage, his shorts soaked in Reeva's blood, and his prosthetic legs spattered too. The next few pictures in the album, focusing on the prosthetic legs, were taken at 7:39am – two and a half hours later. It became clear that while the pictures appeared in a numbered sequence, they were not necessarily in chronological order.

The series of pictures from here followed from the entrance to the house, into a sitting area and then to where Reeva's body lay at the bottom of the staircase. There were close-up photos taken of Reeva's head, bruised eye, elbow and hip as well as the marks on her back. The timeline shows it took nearly 15 minutes for the police to roll her body into different positions to get the shots. The tour of the house following the blood trail resumed and Van Staden carried on up the stairs, snapping photographs as he went. At 5:58am the photographer captured an image of the bedroom looking towards the balcony door. In the foreground was the grey duvet crumpled on the floor and a pair of denim jeans folded inside out. A silver tripod fan could be seen blocking the exit to the balcony – Van Staden stated that when he found it, it was switched off. There was light outside, dawn had arrived.

Picture 68 became the centre of a contentious argument between the state and the defence and was key to allegations of crime-scene tampering, as well as alleged discrepancies in Oscar's version. It was a tight frame of the grey duvet lying on the floor, the pair of denim jeans and, to the right in the picture, a small black fan, unplugged with its cord coiled up next to it. The next picture in the sequence, with the caption 'duvet cover spread open by me in the main bedroom', was taken at 7:34am. Subsequent pictures show close-ups of blood spatter on the duvet.

The photographer followed the trail into the bathroom and captured images of the bat, the blood, a crumpled mat and the silver weapon, its hammer cocked back and the safety mechanism off.

Close-ups were taken of the black phone found next to the firearm, followed by photos of the white phone, initially not visible, that was found underneath bloodied towels. Van Staden said he had picked up the towels, after he had photographed the area, as part of his investigation of the scene to check whether there were any exhibits. He did the same with the cricket bat – after photographing it as it was found, he turned it over to reveal the signatures on the other side.

He then moved on to the inside of the toilet cubicle. A wooden door panel had come to rest close to the wall on the right, while a magazine rack was positioned closest to the back wall, with one of its legs in a pool of blood. The position of the magazine rack proved critical later in the trial because, according to the defence, it was the cause of the 'third startle' that triggered Oscar to shoot reflexively.

The toilet lid was up – the underside of which was spattered – but the toilet seat was down. This is where Reeva came to rest with her right arm and head. Van Staden photographed the three ricochet cracks against the tiles and small shards of projectile on the floor before he finished documenting this section of the house.

The sun had risen significantly over the horizon when Van Staden took a picture of the side entrance to Oscar's house at 6:27am. He also photographed several buckets of paint near a service entrance, evidence of renovations that had been taking place at the house. Oscar's two dogs – a light brown American pit bull terrier named Silo, and Enzo, a black-and-white bull terrier – made an appearance in one image as they ate pellets from a silver dish near a back door. Another photo, taken from the garden, looks up at the bathroom window where Oscar believed an intruder had gained entry. Below the window on the paving was, inexplicably, a pair of blue denim jeans – a curious sight that piqued interest on social media but was never questioned in court. There was also a photograph that featured several ladders stacked on top of one another in the backyard. This was the last picture in the album.

Van Staden said he had asked Botha to clear the scene before he went through the house taking the pictures, and while he was doing his work upstairs he was alone. At one point Aimee and Carice Viljoen joined him upstairs when they collected clothes for Oscar from a passage cupboard but they were prohibited from entering the bathroom.

· · ·

Was Van Staden really on his own on the morning of 14 February, enjoying undisturbed access to the scene while taking photographs? That was top of Roux's questions for the policeman because he did not believe him. He worked to show the court why.

Van Staden disputed Hilton Botha's claim in his affidavit that the photographer arrived on the scene shortly after 5:00am – he said he checked his watch to establish that he arrived at 4:50am. Van Staden said he greeted Botha, who explained what they believed had happened, before he showed him around the house. After that he proceeded to the ground floor where he found the accused.

Roux questioned his process in determining which photos made it into the album. During an overnight adjournment Roux asked that Van Staden fetch his master copies of the scene photos to present them in court. The officer arrived with 16 CDs with his photos stored on them. Van Staden's testimony thus became an intense game of 'Spot the Difference' as he was repeatedly shown two images of a scene, with items displaced in one of the photographs, in an attempt to prove that there had been tampering. It had become evident during the photographer's evidence-in-chief that his albums did not represent a chronology of events. Without the captions with picture times, an uninformed viewer could look at one picture and then the next in which something had moved and deduce that the scene had been altered. It wasn't clear that in some instances 90 minutes elapsed between the pictures – one set represented the untouched scene, while the other documented the investigative process. It appeared that, to some degree, the defence had inadvertently, without knowledge of the timeline of when the images were taken, deduced that there had been tampering in some scenarios.

Roux quizzed the photographer about an image that showed the cricket bat lying face down in front of the basin with bloodied towels to the left of it. A spent cartridge was also visible near the bat's handle. Along the spine of the bat was the brand name 'Lazer'. Roux asked Van Staden to identify which letter in the brand name intersected with the line created by the tile grouting beneath the bat – 'E', said the witness.

Roux then requested Van Staden to look at the same area but in a different picture. The wider shot showed the bat in the far top-right corner and included the firearm and cellphones on the mat in front of the shower. Which letter intersected with the tile line in this photo? 'R', responded the witness.

'Someone must have moved it,' said Roux, convinced he'd proven that the scene had been tampered with.

But chatter in the gallery indicated otherwise as reporters struggled to understand why the witness hadn't pointed out to the advocate the scientific fault in his argument – he was dealing with a parallax error. Nel quickly dispensed with this argument in re-examination.

Roux then asked the witness to study two separate images, both of the firearm on the grey mat, but from different angles and framing. The advocate drew Van Staden's attention to a fold in the mat in the first picture, and asked him to compare it to the location of the same fold in the second picture.

'If you look at it carefully you will see that the butt sits on a different position in relation to the fold and the line. Take your time. Can you see it?' asked Roux.

Van Staden could. Roux also pointed out that in the first picture, the black butt of the handgun was clean, but in the second picture, taken just three minutes later, a splinter had found its way on to it.

> Roux: Who changed the firearm position?
> Van Staden: The firearm as such was not changed, M'Lady. The carpet underneath the firearm could have been shifted, M'Lady.
> Roux: Who put the splinter, the wooden splinter on the butt?

Van Staden: No one placed it there, M'Lady. It could have been transferred.
Roux: Who moved the mat?
Van Staden: The mat could have been shifted whilst I was trampling upon it
when I came to take a photograph of the firearm.

Although a translation from Afrikaans to English, 'trampling' in relation to the crime scene is not what the state wanted to hear. It was not obvious that the firearm had been moved, but the splinter visible on the pistol's handle indicated that something had happened.

Roux asked again if Van Staden was alone upstairs when he took the pictures and he insisted he was.

The defence then went on to suggest that he wasn't. Roux asked Van Staden if he knew a Colonel Makhafola? He was the photographer's commander, said Van Staden, and he had been on the scene that morning, but he couldn't recall when.

What about a Colonel Motha, an officer from the ballistics section? Roux explained the defence had been handed photos by Motha that started, according to the metadata, at 5:56am.

Roux said the defence had studied the photographs and compared their times to Van Staden's photos in Album 1, which showed a 'great overlap' in the times he claimed he was working alone upstairs.

Roux read out the times of several of Motha's pictures, and they coincided with Van Staden's movements and locations. Van Staden insisted again he did not see Motha and that he was alone upstairs.

An official picture showed Oscar's handgun with the caption 'firearm in the main bathroom after it was made safe by Constable Msiza'. Van Staden said he had only learnt after returning inside that Motha had handled the firearm. When he found out he reprimanded the colonel and asked that he leave the scene. Msiza subsequently made the firearm safe before Van Staden took the photograph of it.

Another of Motha's photos, at 6:57am, showed the hammer on the firearm forward. A photo with a corresponding time placed Van Staden in the bathroom.

As Roux compared the timestamps on sets of pictures taken on separate cameras, the obvious question was how accurate this comparison was. For the evidence to be of any value, Roux would have to show that Motha's and Van Staden's cameras were synched – that the built-in electronic clocks were set at the same time. But Roux hadn't done this and was working off the assumption that they were.

Nel later pointed out that Colonel Motha was not visible in any of Van Staden's pictures to disprove the claim they were working upstairs together at the same time. Curiously, Nel never sought to question whether the two cameras were synched.

Roux also questioned the quality of some of the official pictures. Instead of a wide shot of the entire box of watches, for example, the best Van Staden had was one showing only half of it. His response was that his focus had been on the blood spatter on the inside mirror, and not the box itself.

The criticism of Van Staden's photographic skills, in the forensic context, was not limited to the courtroom. Police officers on the sidelines of proceedings explained to us that there was not a single shot, or series of shots, that could be used to portray accurately an uninhibited view of an entire room. One investigator explained that it is helpful if a photographer goes into each corner of a room and takes a wide shot looking inward. In that way a full perspective of the area is provided. Van Staden's pictures frustrated investigators, but all they could do was to work with what they had available.

Roux wanted to know more about Album 7, featuring state ballistics expert Colonel Gerhard Vermeulen and his investigations into the marks made on the door by the cricket bat – in particular, the third mark, which he did not investigate. Roux produced an image from the bundle handed over by the state, which appeared to show that Vermeulen had indeed investigated the third mark and Van Staden had in fact taken photos of him doing so. So why weren't they included in the album? The suggestion from the advocate was that the police were deliberately withholding information that did not corroborate their case.

Van Staden had no explanation other than that he compiled the album after consulting with the person who was conducting the investigation, which in this particular case was Vermeulen.

• • •

In Oscar's plea explanation he stated that it would be demonstrated that the crime scene had been 'contaminated, disturbed and tampered with'. A starting point is to understand exactly what those terms mean in the forensic sense. 'Contaminated' implies that evidence is introduced to the crime scene; 'disturbed' means items on the crime scene are changed or moved; and 'tampered' is the intentional moving or changing of items on the crime scene.

Was this why Oscar was pleading 'not guilty'? He said it was part of the reason, but not the entire reason for his defence, and that he had pleaded not guilty because 'what I'm accused of didn't happen'. Oscar stated that his defence team got to learn that the crime scene had been 'contaminated, disturbed and tampered with' when they studied the photographs provided by the state. Nel wanted to know specifics in terms of where the crime scene had been tampered with?

'My Lady, I am advised through my counsel that there will be people that will come forward. I have seen many of the photos that the state has handed to me where there are massive inconsistencies, where items have been moved, where things were not as they were left on previous photos.'

But Nel pressed the witness – he wanted answers. 'It is unfortunately not that easy. Really it is not that easy. I am asking you. It is your plea explanation, you are in the box. You tell me, sir, where was the scene tampered with?'

Oscar replied:

> *My Lady, we can go through the photo files and I can show you many things that were changed … Throughout the photos there were many things that moved. There were cellphones in my bathroom that moved. My firearm had moved. The cricket bat had moved in the bathroom. The discs in my room had moved. The fan's cord had moved. The curtains had moved.*

Nel took notes as the witness listed the items. The prosecutor started with the cellphones. Oscar claimed that blood marks on the floor next to his cellphone matched up to blood on the phone, which proved it had been moved. He added that different photos showing the cellphone with its cover on and then with it off indicated there was an attempt to make it appear like a misunderstanding about the number of phones in the bathroom.

And Reeva's phone?

> Nel: *Reeva's cellphone on the scene, was that at a different position as where you left the cell phone?*
> Accused: *I do not remember where I left the cellphone, My Lady. What I am saying is that between photos that were taken and tendered to us by the state, things changed.*
> Nel: *Okay. So you looked at photographs and you say the state tampered with it? That is all? You cannot remember where you put down Reeva's phone after you used it?*

The question posed a problem for the witness: he didn't have an independent recollection of the crime scene. Oscar was making allegations based on the study of crime scene photographs, not on his memory. But he was confident of his case. 'Various things were disturbed and various things were tampered with. I do not have the knowledge of what it was, but I know that the experts that will come and testify, these things did happen,' he said.

Nel wanted to know exactly who the defence intended calling to support his tampering claims. Oscar said he didn't know the experts by name. It was an odd claim – surely the accused would have consulted with them?

Nel asked about the location of the fans. Van Staden's pictures showed the silver tripod fan in front of the sliding door, while the smaller black floor fan was unplugged and to its right, near the chest of drawers. Both devices were switched off. Oscar said he remembered that the fans were running that night because it was warm. The policemen had testified the fans were switched off and Oscar had deduced the fans had been tampered with. He also said the fans were moved from where he had left them to different points around the room.

A picture of Oscar's side of the bed that showed part of the tripod fan, an extension cable and a pair of hair clippers was displayed on the screen. The accused was unable to comment on the location of the clippers, but confirmed he plugged the device into the same adapter as the tripod fan. Nel asked if Oscar could see the problem with this photograph. 'There is no place for the other fan,' said Nel, as the magnified picture showed there was no third socket on the adapter.

The accused hesitated, now unsure whether he had actually plugged the floor fan into this adapter, and suggested he may have tripped over the cord causing it to unplug, before telling the court he didn't have an independent recollection of where the fan was plugged in.

This was a problem for the defence.

One minute Oscar was sure; the next minute, after being presented with problematic evidence, he was unsure. Oscar believed it was insignificant.

'It is not so insignificant, Mr Pistorius,' said Nel. 'It will show that you are lying and it is very significant.' Nel was slowly building his 'baker's dozen' of inconsistencies in Oscar's version, which would be presented in closing argument.

An argument followed about the length of the cable of the small black fan, and whether it was long enough to have been plugged into a socket behind the chest of drawers. Nel said it was impossible; Oscar said it was, but he couldn't be sure.

This was important for Nel because it proved to the state that Oscar was tailoring his evidence and adapting his version. In his bail application statement Oscar made reference to only one fan collected from the balcony that morning. The inference now was that, on studying the crime scene, the accused had to factor the second fan into his story in an effort to explain its presence.

Oscar said the fan was probably moved unintentionally when the police made space to spread out the duvet to take pictures. 'This is not where I moved the fan that evening. I do not walk and put the fan in the corner of the room with the plug out,' he said. Oscar was also adamant he did not put the grey duvet on the floor and that somebody must have put it there. He remembered it being on the bed.

The cops had testified that when they arrived on the scene, the duvet was on the floor. The state argued that the duvet would have been directly in his path when he moved around in the dark on his stumps. Oscar said he remembered it being over Reeva's legs when he got out of bed to fetch the fans, and seeing it again after the shooting when he was putting on his prosthetic legs.

Oscar said he put the tripod fan with one of its feet on the balcony and the other two inside the room, with the smaller floor fan beneath it on the floor. He said he first brought the small fan in and then the larger fan in before closing the door, blinds and curtains. Looking at photos of the bedroom, he said 'the fan could not have possibly been there, because it is in the way of the door's opening'.

'Indeed. Indeed,' agreed Nel.

'I would have run out on to the balcony My Lady and where I shouted for help, that fan would have been in the way. So it was …'

Nel interrupted the witness: 'It never happened!'

'So it must have been moved, My Lady,' said Oscar, concluding his deduction.

'It never happened, because now you see it. That fan in the position where it is there, would have blocked you … would have made it difficult for you to close that door.' Nel sounded triumphant, like he'd forced the concession he was chasing. He was building to his crescendo.

'You see because, Mr Pistorius, your version is a lie.'

Oscar finally agreed that with the items in the positions as photographed, his version could not be true. But the scene had been tampered with, he insisted. And yet, despite this, his defence counsel had not put questions about these specific items being moved to the two officers who would have been the likely suspects – Van Rensburg and Van Staden.

Nel seemed to summarise his objection to the accused's contention: 'That is why you have to come up with things because now we have to look for a policeman that did the following: that moved the duvet to the carpet, that moved the fan back, that moved the curtain more open. Those three things, am I right?' asked Nel.

'That is correct, My Lady,' confirmed the witness. Could it be this was the first time Roux and the defence team were hearing these claims? 'You see, Mr Pistorius,' said Nel, 'It was never moved … Nobody moved anything.'

Nel used two markers to prove the duvet had to have been on the floor where it was found by the police. The first was the location of the pair of inside-out jeans. Pointing to a photograph, Nel said it appeared that part of the jeans had come to rest on top of the corner of the grey duvet – these were the pants Oscar said he picked up to block a blue LED light that was bothering him, but dropped them when he heard a noise in the bathroom. For the jeans to be on the top of the duvet, the duvet had to be there first. Oscar didn't see this as a problem, claiming that if various items had been moved around the room, it wouldn't be surprising if the jeans were also moved.

Roux also objected, saying it merely appeared that the jeans were on the duvet, but this was not necessarily so. It appeared he may have identified a parallax error, but one not as obvious as the cricket bat in the bathroom.

The second marker was found in the same photograph. When Oscar was carrying Reeva, a jet of blood had spurted from a wound at about 90 degrees out to her left – which meant it was squirting forward relative to the way she was being carried. This spurt trail is most visible on the walls down the flight of the stairs and in the kitchen, where it sprayed from her location at the base of the stairwell. But it appeared that when Oscar carried Reeva down the bathroom passage, her heart pumped, sending a jet of blood into the bedroom towards the balcony door. Nel asked Van Staden to magnify the picture, and there on the carpet were the fine drops in a line leading up and onto the duvet. The blood on the bedding lined up with the blood on the floor, which to Nel was irrefutable proof that the duvet must have been on the floor at least from the time Oscar passed there with his dying girlfriend in his arms. Oscar said the blood could have transferred to the duvet when he went to collect his phones from the bedside table, like the blood that transferred to the wall above the bedside table.

• • •

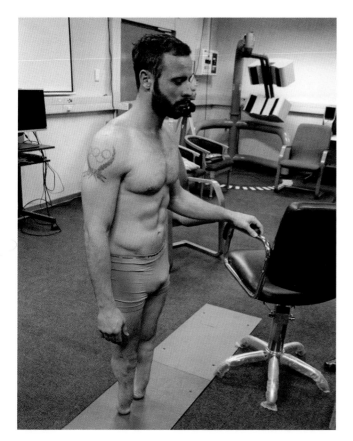

LEFT: Oscar, on his stumps, balances himself using a chair while waiting to have his measurements taken at Ergonomics Technologies in Centurion. SAPS

BELOW: Oscar extends his arms as if holding a firearm while having his measurements taken at Ergonomics Technologies in Centurion. SAPS

RIGHT: Captain Mangena holds up a tape measure while Colonel Vermeulen holds the cricket bat against the door during their investigations. SAPS

BELOW: Police investigators erected a 1:1 scale model of the toilet cubicle and fitted the actual meranti door taken from Oscar's bathroom. BARRY BATEMAN

ABOVE: Oscar, on his stumps, demonstrates at Arnold's house how he approached the perceived threat with his firearm drawn. This video was leaked the weekend before the defence closed its case.
SCREENGRAB FROM
CHANNEL 7 DOCUMENTARY

LEFT: Oscar at a friend's party in April 2013. To his right is Glenn Agliotti.

ABOVE: Oscar and Reeva on
Christmas Eve in December 2012.
DARREN FRESCO

BELOW: While Oscar was
testifying, his ex-girlfriend Sam
Taylor reacted on Twitter to some
of his claims. TWITTER

Samantha Taylor
@samraytay

Last lies you get to tell.. You better make it
worth your while

← Reply ⇄ Retweeted ★ Favorite ← Storify ••• More ꕤ HootSuite

RETWEETS FAVORITES
71 12

10:35 AM - 8 Apr 2014

Jenna Edkins @JennaEdkins · 15 Feb 2013
I would just like to say , I have dated Oscar on off for 5 YEARS, NOT ONCE has he EVER lifted a finger to me , made me fear for my life..
422   76

Jenna Edkins @JennaEdkins · 15 Feb 2013
All I am saying is let him speak , let his side be heard without jumping to conclusions.. Love and thoughts to Reevas famiy..
85   25

Jenna Edkins @JennaEdkins · 15 Feb 2013
You have all my familys love and support #loveandsupportoscar
25   20

Jenna Edkins @JennaEdkins · 15 Feb 2013
People must stop jumping on the bandwagon with such hurtful allegations. Os is the loving , amazing inspirational person we know him to be..
64   26

LEFT: Soon after the shooting, Oscar's former girlfriend Jenna Edkins took to Twitter to defend him. TWITTER

BELOW: Edkins gave Oscar this collage as a birthday present. Police found it in the upstairs TV room. SAPS

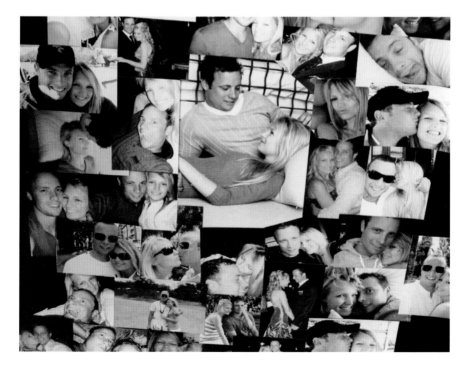

ABOVE LEFT AND RIGHT:
Reeva and Darren Fresco
in a playful mood.
DARREN FRESCO

RIGHT AND BELOW:
Reeva and Samantha
Greyvenstein were close
friends. SAMANTHA
GREYVENSTEIN

ABOVE: Oscar arrives at court with his 'bodyguards' – his uncle Arnold's sons-in-law Dieter Kruger (left) and Johan van Wyk (right).
ANTOINE DE RAS

LEFT: Oscar tries to leave the High Court in Madiba Street while surrounded by the media and the public.
ANTOINE DE RAS

BELOW: Reeva's mother June, accompanied by her legal representative, Advocate Dup de Bruyn, arrive at the High Court.
ANTOINE DE RAS

ABOVE: Prosecutor Gerrie Nel removes his glasses as he waits for a witness to respond to a question. ANTOINE DE RAS

RIGHT: Judge Thokozile Masipa presides over the trial of Oscar Pistorius. To her right is assessor Advocate Janette Henzen-du Toit and to her left is Advocate Themba Mazibuko. SCREENGRAB

BELOW: Oscar leans over the dock to speak to his family. From left are his brother Carl, sister Aimee, cousin Loa Visagie, aunt Amanda Pistorius and uncle Arnold. ANTOINE DE RAS

ABOVE: Barry Roux addresses the court, as Kenny Oldwadge takes notes. KEVIN SUTHERLAND

BELOW: Defence Advocate Kenny Oldwadge addresses the court. IHSAAN HAFFEJEE

ABOVE: Investigating officer Captain Mike van Aardt asked by Nel to conduct a demonstration in court using the door and toilet cubicle mock-up. ANTOINE DE RAS

LEFT: Police ballistics expert Colonel Gerhard Vermeulen demonstrates how he believed Oscar struck the door with the cricket bat. WERNER BEUKES

TOP: Prosecutor Gerrie Nel demonstrates how a person would wield a firearm as he puts questions to a witness. ANTOINE DE RAS

ABOVE: Defence expert witness Roger Dixon handles the prosthetic leg Oscar used on the night he shot Reeva. SIPHIWE SIBEKO

LEFT: A doodle from Nel's notebook – the prosecutor maintains his focus by scribbling intricate patterns in his notebook.

Oscar retches in the High Court during evidence related to the injuries Reeva sustained. THEMBA HADEBE

ABOVE: Defence ballistics expert Wollie Wolmarans demonstrates the concepts used to determine bullet trajectory. CHRIS COLLINGRIDGE

RIGHT: Police ballistics expert Captain Chris Mangena. LEON SADIKI

The defence legal team, from left Rohan Kruger, Kenny Oldwadge, Barry Roux and Brian Webber. ANTOINE DE RAS

Barry Roux consults with his client during a break in proceedings. The pair often engaged in intense conversation. ANTOINE DE RAS

TOP: Oscar and Aimee share a moment as a court orderly looks on at the end of the day's court proceedings.
ANTOINE DE RAS

RIGHT: Oscar consults with his legal team during an adjournment. From the left are Brian Webber, Barry Roux, Roxanne Adams and Kenny Oldwadge.
ANTOINE DE RAS

BELOW: Oscar is flushed and sweats profusely after a bout of retching in the High Court.
BONGIWE MCHUNU

TOP: Security at the Weskoppies Psychiatric Hospital, to which Oscar was referred for a 30-day evaluation.
BARRY BATEMAN

LEFT: Henke Pistorius embraces his son as attorney Brian Webber looks on. Henke attended trial proceedings for the first time during closing arguments.
HERMAN VERWEY

BELOW: Barry Steenkamp made his first court appearance at the trial for closing arguments. He sat alongside his wife June and other family supporters.
HERMAN VERWEY

ABOVE: A mass of reporters, photographers and members of the public throng Oscar's vehicle as he leaves after the first day of judgment. PHILL MAGAKOE

BELOW: Barry Steenkamp, Reeva's father, stares at Oscar while Judge Masipa reads her judgment. PHILL MAGAKOE

Oscar accepted that if the items depicted in the pictures were in an unaltered location, then his version of events could not be true.

The state's argument was that for Oscar's version to be true, a policeman would have had to:

- move the duvet to the carpet
- move the bigger and smaller fans
- move the curtain
- place the denim jeans on top of the duvet.

And this would have had to have been done without knowing what the accused's subsequent story would be in terms of how events in the early morning had unfolded. In the end, Oscar had offered possible explanations for the location of the items, like the possibility that he might have kicked the fan or tripped over the cable, but admitted that he simply couldn't remember.

'Ja. It is because it never happened. That is why you cannot remember it,' said Nel, goading the witness.

'In the beginning of my evidence, I said that I remember everything from when I woke up to the time that I discharged my firearm, my memory after that is not very clear. There are things that I do not remember. This is one of them. So I am not looking for an excuse.'

Before Nel could respond, Oscar continued talking. His speech picked up pace and his voice trembled. 'If I do not remember it, I do not remember it, My Lady.'

'Mr Pistorius, are you okay? You are not emotional?' asked Nel, hinting at his suggestion that the accused used his apparent anguish to avoid difficult questions.

'No, I am fine, My Lady …' said Oscar, belying what was evident to the court. 'If I kicked the fan it would have been in my favour to say I kicked the fan, to explain where the small fan landed up. But I cannot say that because I do not remember it.'

Again, the prosecutor tried to get a word in, but the witness continued his emotional gallop. '… So there are things that are in my favour if I say them, but I do not remember.'

'Are you getting emotional?' asked Nel, finally able to speak to the accused who sat flustered, trembling in the box.

Accused: Yes, I am very emotional, My Lady.
   Nel: Why?
Accused: Because it is a difficult time for me to remember.

> *Nel: But why would this question make you emotional?*
> *Accused: Because this was the night I lost the person that I cared about. I do*
> *not know how people do not understand that.*

Oscar was exasperated and frustrated at the prosecutor's stubbornness and unwillingness to believe him. The accused turned his gaze from Masipa and dropped his head forward as he continued to cry.

The judge called for an adjournment and Aimee rushed to support her brother.

• • •

Oscar had spoken with confidence about the 'experts' and 'specialists' who had pored over the photos and identified clear evidence that the scene had been tampered with. He listed Wollie Wolmarans as one of the witnesses who would present this evidence to the court. But when Wolmarans testified, he never said a word about the crime scene being 'contaminated, disturbed and tampered with'. And neither did the defence team's other expert, Roger Dixon.

In fact, Oscar was the only defence witness to make any mention of the police's alleged mishandling of the crime scene. And with no expert to support his claims that items had been moved, and himself further conceding that for the most part he had no independent recollection of where he had left certain items, the defence's position had fallen flat. Roux and Oldwadge would have to focus their attention elsewhere – on vulnerability and Oscar's psychology.

But Oscar had made what was thought to be a significant concession: if the duvet on the floor was in its true location, with the denim jeans lying on top of it and if the curtains were wide open, with the fan in front of the door and the light switched on – as depicted in the official photographs – his version of events could not possibly be true.

Zombie Stopper

Picture 136 was minimised, ready to be expanded and displayed across the computer screens in the courtroom when the cue came from the prosecutor. 'What we can see there is the effect the ammunition had on a watermelon. It exploded. Am I right?' asked Nel.

'That is correct, My Lady,' agreed Oscar, having just watched a video of himself shooting a high-powered revolver at the red and mushy-centred fruit, before declaring on tape, 'It's a lot softer than brain, but fuck it's like a zombie stopper.'

The Smith & Wesson 500 he was using that day is touted by the manufacturer as 'the world's most powerful handgun'. A camera placed beside the target shows how the .50 calibre bullet, equivalent to 12.7 mm in diameter, caused the watermelon to explode, sending chunks of the fruit and fine spray in every direction.

'You know that the same happened to Reeva's head? It exploded,' spat Nel, with his gaze fixed firmly on the accused. He had a menacing tone to his voice. 'Have a look. I am going to show you, Mr Pistorius, it had the exact same effect. The bullet that went into her head.'

The close-up picture of the right side of Reeva's face flashed across the courtroom screens. Brain matter spoilt her blood-soaked hair. A collective gasp of disbelief broke the stunned silence as the prosecutor waited for an answer. Hands reflexively shot up to cover mouths. While Aimee and Carl shook their heads with tears rolling down their cheeks, unable to protect their sibling from the state's opening salvo, June Steenkamp and her entourage sat with their heads bowed, not looking up. They had been fully briefed about what was to come and knew to keep their eyes away from the screens. The live television feed from Court GD featured the banner 'Graphic Evidence. Viewer discretion is advised'. It was 12:03pm on 9 April when the world was shown what Oscar did to Reeva.

'Have a look there, Mister Pistorius,' said Nel, his tempo and aggression increasing as he goaded the witness. 'I know you do not want to, because you do not want to take responsibility, but it is time that you look at it! Take responsibility for what you have done, Mr Pistorius!'

The witness snapped. 'My Lady, I have taken responsibility. By me waiting … I am not wanting to live my life, but waiting for my time on this stand to tell my story for the respect of Reeva and for myself, I have taken the responsibility,' said Oscar, with his head and eyes pointed directly at the judge, unwilling to look at Nel or the image of his dead girlfriend on the screen.

'I will not look at a picture where I am tormented by what I saw and felt that night! As I picked Reeva up, my fingers touched her head, I remember. I do not have to look at a picture! I was there!' His voice had reached a crescendo of tempo and pitch, lending credence to his counsel's claim that when anxious he sounds like a woman.

'It is the same thing as the watermelon! You had it now in practice, Mister Pistorius,' said an unrelenting Nel, as Roux stood to object to the line of questioning. The defence advocate was not objecting to Nel's style, but rather that the suggestion that watermelon was the same as brains was 'unfair' and 'there was no evidence that it had the same effect'.

Oscar broke down in the dock as Masipa asked that the picture be removed from the screen. His sobs turned to loud wails when court was adjourned to allow him to regain his composure. Aimee rushed across the courtroom to comfort her brother, making a remark in the direction of Advocate Johnson as she passed the prosecution bench – it's not known what she said, but her disdain was unmistakeable.

Members of the defence team were similarly disgusted at Gerrie Nel's conduct during the trial and the approach he took with the accused. Says one member: 'I was very upset, totally upset, I couldn't even speak at how upset I was. To make a comparison between a human head, a watermelon and that of a zombie! I think it worked because it would have upset me as well. I've got great respect for both Gerrie Nel and Barry Roux, but with this tactic of Nel I was shocked and very disappointed with his line of attack.'

A relative of the athlete voiced his disgust at Nel's astonishing tactic. 'Do you know what is a lunatic? That is a lunatic!' said the family member about Nel and the watermelon incident.

Despite the vociferous criticism, this approach was a carefully orchestrated opening act from the prosecution team. And Nel succeeded in doing precisely what he intended: rattling the witness. No amount of consultation and rehearsing of questions and answers could have prepared Oscar for that. And now, under cross-examination, he was alone. He could not speak to Roux, Oldwadge or his attorneys.

It was no coincidence that the team managing the live broadcast had changed the banner to display the graphic image warning. An investigator said that the prosecution team had met with June Steenkamp during the 11am tea break, warning her about what was to come. It's understood that she told them to do whatever they felt was in the best interests of the case and that she trusted them. The plan to show Oscar the photo was conceived when the video footage of the accused shooting the watermelon and making the 'zombie stopper' statement was broadcast on Sky News.

The challenge for Nel was to convince the court to allow the state to play the video. When the prosecutor had earlier asked Oscar whether he knew what a zombie stopper was, he said he had no idea:

> Nel: *Have you never been in the presence of any person using the word 'zombie stopper'?*
> Accused: *Not that I can recall, M'Lady.*
> Nel: *Have you ever seen a video of yourself in the presence of people, referring to a 'zombie stopper'?*
> Accused: *I have never seen a video of myself where someone in the video has referred to a 'zombie stopper' in my ... as far as I can remember, M'Lady.*
> Nel: *If there was such a video on Sky News, showing you shooting and somebody saying, talking about a 'zombie stopper', would you be surprised?*
> Accused: *I am ... I would not be surprised. I am saying I cannot remember. You can show me a video like that and I am in the presence of that person, then I can agree with that.*
> Nel: *Gladly. Can we show that video please?*

Nel's response to the witness's request to watch the video was as quick as an angler's backward jerk on his rod when a darting line indicates the fish has taken the bait. The prosecutor and Roux sparred over the admissibility of the video, but it was eventually allowed to be played.

Introducing the video of Oscar at the shooting range served a dual purpose. Not only did it allow the prosecutor to rattle Oscar, it also showed his attitude towards firearms. In the footage, he and his friends appeared flippant, revelling in the sight of the aftermath of the exploded melon. This was contrary to the claim he presented to the court, that he bought a firearm to protect himself. He was fearful of crime and felt particularly vulnerable and wanted to be in a position to ward off a threat if he was ever placed in such a situation. But his desire to own a firearm extended beyond protection. He was in the process of amassing an assortment of weapons as a collector. So did his love of weapons and eagerness to use them feed off his vulnerability? Or was this vulnerability merely an excuse to try to explain why he fired four shots through a closed toilet door?

Full Combat Recon Mode

It was at Sean Rens's shooting range that Oscar was filmed shooting the Smith & Wesson revolver at the watermelon. Rens was also the arms dealer who had procured the same model of firearm for Oscar, along with five other guns. Oscar was in the process of obtaining a firearm collector's licence. Rens said Oscar had approached him requesting a specific type of revolver – the S&M 500 – and they discussed firearms in general. 'He had a great love and enthusiasm for them, My Lady.'

An invoice submitted to the court listed the items of which Oscar was waiting to take delivery. The document showed that R48 500 had already been paid towards the R52 500 bill for six firearms and 580 rounds of ammunition:

- Smith & Wesson 500 revolver
- Vector LM6 (a civilian and law-enforcement semi-automatic variant of the R6 assault rifle)
- Winchester Defender pump-action shotgun
- Mossberg Maverick pistol-gripped pump-action shotgun
- Mossberg semi-automatic shotgun
- Smith & Wesson .38 Special revolver.

The deal was cancelled after the shooting of Reeva.

Rens also handled Oscar's competency exams for his firearms, in which he was required to fill out a questionnaire that proposed several scenarios to the future gun-owner and tested how the person understood he or she should act in relation to the law. In one scenario:

You are at home alone in an isolated area far from police or security ser-
vices. You happen to look out of your window, and you see two strange
men jumping over your wall and make their way towards your house.
You do not know these men and you are not expecting any form of visi-
tor, because it is very late at night. Have they committed an offence that
justifies the use of lethal force against them?

Oscar correctly answered 'No', he would not be justified to use lethal force.

The scenario was then changed, putting the intruders inside the gun-owner's home and in the process of stealing personal items. Could lethal force be used? Oscar, again, correctly answered 'No'.

The scenario went even further, that the burglars threaten to kill the home-owner who is standing behind a locked security gate. 'Can you discharge a fire-arm at them because you fear for your life?' Once again, the athlete correctly answered 'No'.

Only when the scenario changed to put the home-owner in direct contact with the intruders, with no security gate to protect him, and the assailants armed with a knife and a firearm and advancing towards the home-owner, did Oscar correctly state that he may discharge his firearm and use lethal force to defend himself.

The hypothetical scenario had an uncanny resemblance to the situation Oscar claimed he had found himself in on the morning he shot and killed Reeva. Of course, this immediately raised questions about his conduct in relation to the law. It was not in dispute that Oscar fired his weapon blindly through the locked toilet door. He made no attempt to establish the identity of the intruder and he was not under any direct threat of attack. It was quickly noted in public dis-course that it's a lot easier to know the law when sitting for an exam; it's consid-erably different when faced with a perceived threat in one's home.

In his competency exam, Oscar also correctly listed some of the legal require-ments that must be met to justify using lethal force. Nel asked Rens to read them in to the record. 'Attack must be against you, it must be unlawful. It must be against a person.' None of these requirements had been met in the shooting in question.

Rens discussed various other aspects related to the exam that required the future firearm owner to understand the terms of the law and the safe operation of a weapon. By all indications, Oscar was a competent and knowledgeable fire-arm owner who met the requirements to acquire more weapons.

But, as Rens would confirm, Valentine's Day was not the first time Oscar had unholstered his firearm and prepared to confront an intruder in his house. This incident was further confirmed by Oscar's tweet on 27 November 2012, which was deleted from the athlete's account after the shooting:

> Nothing like getting home to hear the washing machine on and thinking its an intruder to go into full combat recon mode into the pantry! waa

With Rens in the witness box, Nel wanted to know what Oscar had told him about the washing machine incident he had tweeted about. 'He went to what we call code red or combat mode. In other words, draw his gun and go and clear the house as anyone would if they heard a noise inside the house, and when he came to the source of the noise, it was the laundry or something in the laundry, M'Lady,' he said. Rens said he taught self-defence and how to clear a house from room to room in a series of colour codes.

There were other incidents too.

Oscar's friend Dexter Azzie told a BBC3 documentary about a separate incident that occurred when he was spending the night at the athlete's home just before Christmas. 'It was quite a hot evening so I woke up to put a fan on and after bumping it over … it made quite a loud bang … within a minute, he ran outside. He didn't have his prosthetic legs on. He was on his stumps. He had his 9 mm in his hands. He asked if everything was alright. I responded "Yes" and then he went back to his room.'

Another occurred just days before Reeva's death when the couple was at Justin and Samantha's Johannesburg house watching a movie. Oscar got a fright and 'levitated' off the couch.

'It was the Sunday before Reeva was killed. They had come over to our house and we were watching a movie, *Zero Dark Thirty* or some or other war movie,' recalls Greyvenstein. 'Oz had fallen asleep. There was some shooting scene and it woke him up and he got a fright. He jumped up off the couch and he ran through to the dining room and you could just see he had got a fright. He had to walk around and calm down. He just started pacing to calm down. Justin went up to him and said, "Calm down, it's just a movie. Chillax." Reeva just thought it was funny. She laughed and said, "Are you alright?" She was still awake and he had fallen asleep next to her.'

Roux also sought to dispel the suggestion Nel was making that Oscar's intention to obtain a collector's licence and to obtain several and varied kinds of firearms meant that he was irresponsible.

'Then I am not a collector of firearms, so I do not know, but your experience with people collecting firearms, would they be seen as upstanding people, as reckless people?' asked Roux.

'No, they would be upstanding people, M'Lady.'

'It is just that you have some people that have a love for firearms and collecting them and others not?'

'Correct,' said Rens, before adding that there is no connection between being reckless and being a firearm collector and that in his experience the contrary is true.

The gun-dealer's evidence shed further light on Oscar's enthusiasm for firearms of all shapes and sizes: he owned a 9 mm pistol, but was in the process of acquiring the most powerful revolver; he was buying two shotguns, including a semi-automatic – as fast as he could pull the trigger it would fire; and he had his sights on a semi-automatic assault rifle, the same as that used by the South African Police Service.

The evidence also showed that Oscar was familiar with self-defence techniques and appeared to know what techniques to employ when dealing with a threat in the home, and further that he knew the legal obligations placed on a gun-owner related to when exactly deadly force may or may not be used.

The Imagined Intruder

For someone to be so fearful of crime and to believe that someone had broken into their home in a secure estate, they must have had a valid reason. The state called Boschkop police station's Warrant Officer Hendrik Maritz from the Crime Information Office, whose job was to analyse the crime reported in the area and identify trends and hotspots.

Using Oscar's identity number, Maritz first established that the accused had never opened a crime-related case at the police station. Oscar said he had never opened cases because in one instance he did not have insurance so thought there was no need. He also said he did not trust the police, believing that they would not give the matters any attention or be able to do anything about the cases.

Maritz analysed the incidents of crime over a three-year period in the Silver Lakes area and plotted it on a map using red, yellow and blue spots as a record of all crimes committed, specifically house robberies and armed robberies. A single dark-blue dot on the map indicated the Valentine's Day murder docket currently being tried in court.

A closer look at the records, and narrowing them down to the Silver Woods estate, showed that besides the shooting at Oscar's house, the only other reported house robbery or burglary was on 24 October 2011.

Roux made the point that Maritz could only inform the court of the crimes that were reported to the police – he would obviously have no record of unreported incidents, like those to which his client would claim to have fallen victim. The policeman also confirmed that, in general, living in a secure estate did not mean a person was immune to crime – on the morning of this shooting police were dealing with an armed robbery at an estate elsewhere in the capital.

On the face of it, the numbers showed that Oscar lived in a secure complex with very few incidents of crime. Even the neighbourhood in which he lived showed very few occasions of violent crime. His terror at believing an intruder had broken into his home seemed at odds with the reality of living where he did.

So what did Oscar fear so terribly that drove him to react the way he did – going into 'full recon' mode and pumping four bullets into a closed door? What did he believe was lurking beyond and what consequences did he fear?

It has many names. 'The fear of the other', 'the imagined intruder', 'the invisible witness'. It is the faceless, nameless criminal without a conscience or a consequence who perpetrates the violent crimes that feature in the country's media.

It is what drives many South Africans into high-security enclaves such as Silver Woods, with round-the-clock security, guards who patrol 24 hours a day, alarm systems, laser beams, emergency response cars and guard dogs. In some instances, it is what drives individuals to arm themselves with personal handguns or an arsenal of firearms.

Generally, though not necessarily in relation to Oscar, this has been referred to by some writers as *die swart gevaar* ('the black danger/ peril').

In the run-up to Oscar's trial, South African crime novelist Margie Orford wrote about this force, in a column for the *Sunday Times*:

> *This imaginary body, of the paranoid imaginings of suburban South Africa, has lurked like a bogeyman at the periphery of this story for the past year. It is the threatening body, nameless and faceless, of an armed and dangerous black intruder.*
>
> *The figure of the threatening black stranger has driven many South Africans into fortress-like housing estates, surrounded by electric fences, armed guards and the relentless surveillance of security cameras.*
>
> *This figure is the reason almost every middle-class home has a panic button on both sides of the double bed in the master bedroom, a red button that will summons armed guards to the house within minutes. So, the accepted logic goes, of course a man would simply shoot.*

Orford asked the questions: What is this fear? Where does it come from?

> *The estate where Pistorius lived and where Steenkamp died is the contemporary version of the laager. Except this one is very expensive; it has state-of-the-art security; it had no history of crime, let alone violent home invasions.*

*But for a year this man who was not there, the one who Pistorius did
not shoot, has lurked in the shadows of this relentlessly covered story. Is
it a kind of possession, this fear of an intruder that compels a man to
unthinkingly and without hesitation fire a gun through a locked door?
Or is it nothing more than the reclaiming of the old white fear of the
swart gevaar (black peril) as Pistorius' only defence against the charge
of the premeditated murder of Steenkamp? What is this irrational fear
that has sunk so deep into the psyche?*

*It is perhaps the most atavistic of white South African fears. Under
Apartheid, the threat of the swart gevaar was used to excuse any and all
kinds of violence. In the pernicious narrative of 'us' against 'them', these
dangerous strangers, these 'intruders' in the land of their own birth, had
to be obliterated. In that unyielding construct of threat and danger, of
your death or mine, there is no middle ground, no compromise and no
space for thought or language.*

*If Pistorius was not shooting to kill the woman with whom he had
just been sharing a bed, those four bullets fired indicate that there is still
no middle ground. Because whoever Pistorius thought was behind that
door, firing at such close range meant that when he finished there would
be a body on that bathroom floor.*

What Margie Orford described is what Gareth Newham, head of the Governance,
Crime and Justice programme at the Institute for Security Studies, calls the 'fear
of the other' that is so pervasive in South Africa. This fear is entrenched, despite
crime statistics showing a decrease.

'Overall crime has come down, and violent crime has come down by about 25
per cent. Crime in South Africa, as recorded by the South African Police Service
(SAPS), peaked in 2002/2003. About 2.1 million crimes were reported to the
SAPS – it's dropped to about 1.6 million in the most recent figures. So we've seen
quite a big shift.'

While holistically crime levels have come down, it is the kinds of crime that
South Africans fear the most that have increased in frequency. According to the
national *Victims of Crime Survey 2012*, the crime that people in the country fear
most is housebreaking or burglary. About six in every ten (59.3 per cent) households perceived housebreaking/burglary to be one of the most common types of
crime, followed by home robbery (46.2 per cent). Housebreaking/burglary was
the most common crime experienced at least once in 2011 by 5.4 per cent of the
households. It was followed by home robbery (1.5 per cent) and theft of livestock

(1.3 per cent). Theft of personal property (2.5 per cent) was the most common crime experienced by selected individuals aged 16 years and older, followed by assault (1.3 per cent).

This explains the high walls, security fences, 24-hour security and private security estates. Newham says there's a huge gap in the reality of one's risk and the perception that the wealthier you are, the more risk you face.

'When it comes to home invasions and business robberies and car hijackings, we've seen different patterns there. We saw a big increase starting in about 2005 with home invasions, about a 100 per cent increase in house invasions and we've seen about 300 per cent increase in business robberies. Now robberies mean violent attacks. Armed gangs of usually two or three or four go into a house, go into a business with the intent of stealing from that place and that property, and so there's direct contact between the victim and the perpetrators, and the perpetrators are most often armed,' says Newham.

According to the 2012/2013 crime statistics released by the South African Police Service, robberies at residential properties were deemed a 'stubborn' crime that has increased by 69.8 per cent over the past nine years. The stats show that per 100 000 households in the country, 34.3 fell victim to this type of crime in the year that Oscar shot Reeva.

These are often very traumatic experiences for the victims and the media will report on the most violent cases in which people are shot, wounded or raped, which perpetuates the fear. 'That generally tends to build a sense that all house robberies are going to result in some sort of severe injury when, in fact, docket analyses that are taken by the police show that in almost 90 per cent of the time, the victims are physically unharmed. In about 2 per cent of the cases, there is a murder and in about 4 per cent of the cases, there is a rape. So basically it's a crime of economics,' says Newham.

While fear continues to pervade society, crime is not as prevalent as people think. In total there are around 17 000 house robberies a year in South Africa – Newham says that when one considers there are around 8 to 10 million houses, the likelihood of being a target is fairly low, although those in wealthy areas are more likely to be targets. 'So the chances of being a victim are actually quite small, but the thing is it's hitting the middle classes, so people who sometimes have quite a high profile in the community – business people, leaders sometimes become victims to these kind of crimes, so it has quite a big impact in driving fear. It is targeting more wealthier houses, so for instance, the number of houses robbed in Sandton is about six times higher than the number of houses that get robbed in [the poorer township of Alexandra] because if you rob a house in

Alex, you're going to get a lot less out of it than you are going to get in Sandton.'

However, when one looks at South Africa's murder rate, the majority of those killed are murdered by someone they know and not in anonymous robberies.

'Violent crime affects poorer people in South Africa at a far greater rate than wealthier people. If you look at how murder and assault happen in South Africa, a vast majority of those cases are between people who know each other and live in the same communities. According to the police research and a lot of other research, violent crime is mostly between males while under the influence of alcohol. The argument could be about girlfriends, money, sports teams, it turns very violent very quickly and somebody gets shot, stabbed or beaten to death. That is what drives our murder rate. But what happens is people will get these statistics that come out from the police every year, see "Oh, we have 45 murders a day!" or whatever it is and … read about a murder in a house robbery and make this connection that there's just this rampant, random murder going on. It's not like that,' stresses Newham.

He also points out that, despite popular belief, the vast majority of South Africans don't own firearms. 'If you consider that there are approximately 1.8 million firearm owners and about 36 million people over the age of 18 who could legally own a licensed firearm, you have 5 per cent of the population – adult population – carrying firearms. Ninety-five per cent don't, so it's not really correct to think of South Africa as a gun-happy place or that there is generally a culture of using firearms, of carrying firearms; it's actually quite a small number of people who do use or keep firearms legally. Some of the estimations [are] that there is maybe twice that number, or another 1 million or so that are illegal.'

In her article 'The Invisible Witness' for Yahoo Sports, journalist Nastasya Tay said: 'As several commentators pointed out, after Pistorius and his friends took a gun into a busy bistro and discharged it by accident they simply apologised to the manager and left. If a group of young black men had done the same, the consequences would have undoubtedly been more severe, with police being called to the scene.'

Tay added:

> *Public fury has been unleashed at the possibility of a man who murdered his lover in cold blood; yet there has been little anger directed toward Pistorius for wanting to maim or kill the imaginary intruder, whom he had yet to even see.*
>
> *It is an easy narrative, one with undeniable dramatic panache: the Valentine's morning killing of a beautiful woman, by her lover, an*

international sporting icon and double amputee.

Yet it bypasses what is at the heart of the story: the unsaid assumption by a man whose insistence that if it were an intruder, the shooting – without warning, without identification, and through a closed meranti door – would somehow be more acceptable.

State of Mind

It was inevitable that the court would venture into Oscar's state of mind, and explore his psychology leading up to the shots that killed his girlfriend.

The Oscar the world knew was a triumphant athlete, arms thrust into the air after running a record-breaking time on a track or confidently posing in an advert for a global brand. But the world had also been exposed to the angry Oscar who felt he'd been cheated during the Paralympics. What had emerged in court was a fearful Oscar, a man who claimed he faced lifelong exposure to crime and felt vulnerable because of his physical condition. While he kept a firearm with him almost every waking moment, he wanted more weapons. This enthusiasm seemingly blurred the lines of vulnerability. Then there was the emotional Oscar, debilitated by violent episodes of heaving and retching.

It was a complex question of not just who is Oscar, but who was Oscar? The defence team would have to take the court beyond the morning of 14 February and delve into his mind before most would believe his story of an intruder in the house. What made Oscar tick? What ticked Oscar off? What was his mother like? What happened to his father? What effect did being raised without legs have on the growing boy's sense of security? How well did he adapt to global stardom?

Once this was established, the court could then explore the question of how this person could reasonably be expected to act when faced with the prospect of a deadly threat in his own home, and whether that response could mitigate his legal responsibility for Reeva's death.

• • •

Oscar's mental well-being was a starting point for his evidence-in-chief. After a tearful apology to Reeva's family, he told the court he had been prescribed a concoction of sedatives, antidepressants, anti-anxiety and mood stabiliser medications since February 2013. His biggest problem was an inability to sleep and being plagued by nightmares, visions of the events as they unfolded that morning. 'I wake up and I smell ... I can smell blood and I wake up to be terrified,' he said as he grappled to time his sentences between uncontrollable heavings of his chest. 'If I hear a noise I wake up, just in a ... in a complete state of terror, to a point that I would rather not sleep, then I fall asleep and wake up like that.' His sister Aimee, whose contorted face bore the evidence of anguish she'd witnessed first-hand in her sibling, matched his emotions in the gallery. Oscar stated that for weeks after the shooting he could not sleep at all, which led to a significant amount of weight loss. At that stage he moved in to his uncle Arnold's house where he was in the care of his family.

Oscar paused for about 20 seconds when he was asked to describe an episode he'd recently had. 'I woke up in a panic and I ... I am ... I am blessed that my sister stays on the same property as I do, so I can phone her in the middle of the night, which I often do to come and sit by me, and on that particular night ... I do not obviously ever want to handle a firearm again or be around a firearm, so I have got a security guard that stands outside of my front door at night. But I woke up and I was terrified and I ... I for some reason could not calm myself down, so I climbed into the cupboard and I phoned my sister to come and sit by me for a while which she did ... My Lady.'

The purpose of this revelation was twofold: first to illustrate just how emotionally distraught the accused is and that he is still suffering the emotional effects of being responsible for killing his girlfriend; and to show that he continues to harbour an inescapable and incapacitating fear of crime to the point that he has a security guard posted at his bedroom door. These two themes, of remorse and vulnerability, were central to the defence team's case and the basis for trying to prove that Oscar's conduct in the moments leading up to the shooting was reasonable, and that his state of mind after the event was inconsistent with a man who planned to kill the woman he loved.

It was a carefully crafted prologue that concluded with a timed pause from the advocate to allow the court to reflect on what they'd just heard. Roux then changed stride by casting the court's mind back to 22 November 1986. 'Mr Pistorius, going to your background, when were you born?' Oscar discussed his childhood growing up in a loving home, but with a father who wasn't often around because he worked away from home and a 'soft heart-natured' mother who was a fantastic parent. After his parents separated when he was six years old, the three children and their mom struggled financially, but a supportive extended family made sure they were never in want. Oscar said they moved around quite a lot.

Roux asked about the 'difficulty with his legs'.

'I would not say there is a difficulty with my legs,' Oscar said after a brief hesitation, reluctant to concede he is disabled, reminiscent of the man who had fought for parity in the athletic arena. 'I would say that I am ... I have got prosthetic legs that allow me to ... help me to overcome those disabilities or those difficulties, yes a difficulty would be when I do not have my legs on. I do not have balance. I have very limited mobility.'

Oscar described the medical condition with which he was born, how at the age of 11 months his legs were amputated, he received his first pair of prosthetic legs two months after that procedure, and had since been mobile on those legs. Despite his obvious handicap, his parents didn't see this as something that should hold the boy back. Oscar said his parents, particularly his mother, treated him like any other child. While he was bullied on occasions, he ably stood up for himself as he was taught to do by his mother.

From a young age he was very active, participating in a variety of sporting activities without letting his disability impede him. Oscar explained how he had been injured in high-school rugby and how he made his way into disabled athletics.

Oscar also revealed that his mother was particularly concerned by crime, so much so that she slept with a handgun in a padded pouch under her pillow at night. This fear was exacerbated by the lack of a man in the house and that they often lived in areas hard hit by crime. Oscar said at night when his mother got scared, she would call the police. 'On a couple of occasions, they did break into our home, but more often than not, it was just her being scared and so she had come, you know, at night and call us to go and sit in her room and many times we would just wait for the police to arrive,' he said.

Oscar said his mother's death when he was 15 years old was devastating. 'Everything we learnt in life, I learnt from her and when she passed away it was very unexpected.'

Oscar discussed the state of his stumps and the effect they have on his mobility. It was the first time the world was hearing intimate details related to the athlete's stumps. These parts of his body are rarely visible, and when they are they're covered in socks and seen for seconds as he changes between prosthetic legs and his running blades. Oscar said that when his legs were amputated, doctors transplanted the heel pad from his foot onto the end of the stump. 'As I grew, the bone below my knee grew and so the heel pad was supposed to stay at the bottom, but it has rotated as the bone has grown around the back and it is worse on the left side, to the point that I have spoken to my surgeon over the last couple of years to redo the left stump, move the heel pad so that there is soft tissue on the bottom of the bones that I can walk on my stumps better.

'The right stump is about a centimetre longer than the left, but because of the heel pad moving on the left stump, I cannot place weight on my left stump, so I have to rotate my entire leg, my knee joint out to the left when I walk without my prosthetic legs on,' he said.

These problems affect his balance. He can stand on his stumps, but cannot stand still on them. To stand still, he has to hold on to something, as was evident in the pictures taken at Ergonomics Technologies in Centurion, when he had his measurements taken following his arrest. While on his stumps, Oscar has to hold on to a chair, unlike his ability to stand when wearing his prosthetic legs.

As expected of any toned, professional athlete, Oscar's thighs are muscular and bulky, but this appearance ends just below the knee. On the back of his legs, just below the crease where the knee bends, there is a bulk of muscle that appears to be what's left of his calves. The profile changes dramatically as the skin hugs the bone and becomes considerably thinner. Vertical scars extend from the heel pad up the back of this section almost to the point where these calf muscles start. In the photos, scabs and cuts characterise the front of his stumps, evidence of the difficulties he faces wearing prosthetic legs. The left pad is visibly different to the right one, appearing to have a greater surface area and shifting towards the inside of his leg.

When Oscar removes his prosthetic legs, he likes to keep them close by. He lets them air at night and often places them on top of each other with a pair of pants or another garment covering them. 'In many disabled people, it is an extension of your body. I would not leave my prosthetic legs lying around. I do not really want to be seen without them or just, you know, having them lie around. So, I would leave them close to my bag or in a bag,' he said, referring to how he would treat them when at the athletics track.

'I think everybody in South Africa has been exposed to crime at some point, I think,' said Oscar. But not every South African has been exposed to the sheer volume of crime that he claims. Misfortune appears to have followed him throughout his life. He stated that growing up his family was exposed to break-ins during which members of the family were tied up and assaulted. As a young boy, the family returned from a holiday to find that his dad's house had been burgled – 'what was not taken was destroyed'. Oscar said his father has been hijacked twice and 'many other' members of his family have been victims of housebreakings and violent crimes.

Later in his testimony Oscar described how the female members of his family are not permitted to drive alone at night. 'They have all got run-flat tyres and smash-and-grab on their windows and most of them have automatic cars, so that they cannot stall if there is a smash-and-grab or an attempt hijacking and I did not want Reeva to drive alone at night. It is not safe,' he said.

Oscar claimed to be a victim too: he said his house was burgled in 2005 while at an athletics event in the UK; on another occasion a stranger crept into his garden and kicked his dog.

Oscar told the court about an incident when he was driving at night on the N1 highway through Centurion back from an interview in Joburg. 'A car came up behind me and it was going a lot faster than I was and I changed lanes and it came past me and it slowed down a couple of car lengths in front of me and I just saw a muzzle flash, it was dark and I saw the muzzle flash and I could hear the bang coming from the vehicle,' he said.

The athlete said he pulled off the highway and found parking at a nearby restaurant from where he called a friend and was eventually picked up. He said he could not remember who he called.

It was not the last time Oscar was followed or harassed while on the road – he recalled an incident with ex-girlfriend Samantha Taylor when he believed he was being followed to his estate. 'I jumped out of the car and I distanced myself from the car and I had my firearm by my side. I did not draw it but I had my hand on it, on my hip and the two gentlemen in the car sped off.'

And, he continued, '[there] had been other occasions where similar cars, or the same looking car has followed me for a couple of days at a time and I was not sure of who it was or what it was, but I phoned my agent and informed him'.

Then just a month before Oscar shot dead his girlfriend, he did in fact pull his gun out. He had witnessed three occupants of a minibus taxi force another driver off the road, pull him from his vehicle and assault him with bricks.

'I jumped the light and I hooted until I pulled up. I drew my firearm and I pointed it at the three people and they jumped in the taxi and they sped off. I called Netcare. I phoned the police and at this point maybe 30 people had come up from the shopping centre ... the situation seemed to be contained, so I left. I got in my car and I left,' he said.

Oscar said he was the victim of an assault in December 2012 after receiving threats. He said he reported the matter to the Hawks, who arranged a meeting between him and the other party so the matter could be resolved.

Oscar said that since he bought his house at the Silver Woods estate in 2007, there had been constant development and upgrades to the security system in an effort to thwart persistent attempts by criminals to gain entry to the property. Oscar knew of several neighbours who had been burgled or robbed. In one instance, a ladder was used to gain entry to a property. In February 2013 Oscar was in the process of renovating his house in preparation to sell it so he could move to Joburg. The house had damp issues, needed a new coat of paint on the exterior, had a broken window downstairs and the air-conditioning was not working.

Oscar had two dogs, which he bought as protection, but said they didn't have the right personality for that. 'They were very placid and they are loving dogs. They are quite calm, contrary to the names of the animals, my pit bull and bull terrier I always leave around, you know, if I had friends over they would interact and if they would play with kids; they were not at all aggressive. They were not vicious dogs. They were not trained to be attack dogs,' he said.

In the lead-up to the trial many people asked why Oscar would have believed an intruder managed to climb into his bathroom when he had two dogs, and why he never considered that the fact there was no barking indicated that there was no intruder. Oscar's evidence about his dogs thus explained how a stranger would have unhindered access to the property and why they wouldn't react. After the shooting, family friends in Tzaneen adopted the dogs.

Oscar said religion was very important to him, partly because of his mother's influence. Sheila Pistorius was an Anglican who sang in the church choir and participated in a particular kind of religious dancing. 'My mother taught me that … you know … we grew up just knowing that religion is … God is, you know, our refuge and it does not matter what may come of life, but you can always turn to the Lord. When my mom passed away I struggled a bit with my faith. But I always knew that the Lord was part of my life,' he said.

Oscar's faith was revived in 2011, and he started placing more and more trust in God to get where he wanted to be. Then he met Reeva. 'She was a very strong Christian. She would pray for me at night. We would pray about everything. Pray about my training. Pray about all the small things I had in my life. You know we would pray before we eat and ja, I mean … I think religion is maybe … or it definitely is, God is the thing that has got me through this last year,' he said. The behaviour of Oscar and his siblings holding hands, heads bowed together in prayer in the courtroom, was evidence of this.

At this stage of his life, Oscar didn't appear to consider his disability much of a factor in his vulnerability. He felt that when fitted with his prosthetic legs, he was equal to his able-bodied counterparts, but without them he was at a significant disadvantage. Add to that a person who appears to have been disproportionately affected by crime, from a young age with a single mother who slept with a handgun under her pillow, to an adult who was randomly shot at on the highway, followed home and allegedly burgled. All these factors combined made for a fearful Oscar when he found himself without his legs and believing someone had broken into his home. It was a narrative the state did not believe.

When Oscar led the court through his version of events, when it came to that critical moment in the bathroom when he stood on his stumps with his firearm pointed at the door, his only explanation for what happened was: 'and then I heard a noise from inside the toilet what I perceived to be somebody coming out of the toilet. Before I knew it, I had fired four shots at the door.'

Roux didn't stop his client here in order to explore this further or for him to describe to the court exactly what he meant. That was left to Nel.

· · ·

Gerrie Nel wanted Oscar to apologise for what he had done and to accept that his conduct had led to the death of another human being.

'You are a model for sportsmen, disabled and able-body sportsmen all over the world,' suggested Nel, testing the Blade Runner on how he regarded himself now that he was accused of murder.

> Accused: *I think I was, M'Lady. I made a terrible mistake and …*
>
> Nel: *You … you made a mistake. You killed a person, that is what you did. Is it not?*
>
> Accused: *I made a mistake.*
>
> Nel: *You killed Reeva Steenkamp, that is what you did.*
>
> Accused: *I made a mistake, M'Lady.*
>
> Nel: *You repeating it three times, what was your mistake?*
>
> Accused: *My mistake is that I took Reeva's life, M'Lady.*
>
> Nel: *You killed her. You shot and killed her. Will you not take responsibility for that?*
>
> Accused: *I did, M'Lady.*
>
> Nel: *Then say it then. Say yes. I killed … I shot and killed Reeva Steenkamp.*
>
> Accused: *I did, M'Lady.*

While Nel accepted this response, the accused didn't say, 'I shot and killed Reeva Steenkamp,' and he never did in his evidence. For Nel it was about account-ability, getting the accused to take responsibility for his actions and to verbalise such conduct in active language. Oscar would say Reeva 'lost her life', refer to her death as her 'passing', that he 'took her life', and in his apology to her parents he referred to the 'tragedy', but he never once said, 'I killed Reeva.'

For a full five days, the prosecutor worked on Oscar in a deliberate attempt to snare him. He would spend a short period on one subject and, just as Oscar was growing in confidence, Nel would divert to another topic only to return to the original issue when it was least expected.

At times, Oscar became frustrated at the repeated questions and became argumentative. Simple prompts resulted in long answers and explanations that didn't help the accused at all. 'Let us just answer the questions,' said Nel at one point early in the cross-examination:

> Nel: *I know you want to say a lot of things and it is interesting. You are arguing, you are not answering. Why are you arguing and not answering?*
> Accused: *I am sorry, My Lady.*
> Nel: *No, not sorry. Sorry does not answer the question of 'why'. The question is: Why. Sorry is not an answer to why.*

It was quintessential Nel.

Oscar stated that many thoughts went through his mind when he heard the window sliding open, which he believed to have been caused by an intruder gaining access to the bathroom. Top of his mind was his vulnerability. 'I did not have any way of defending myself without my prosthetic legs on. So I ran for my firearm,' he said.

The athlete also confirmed that that morning he was in 'full combat recon mode', in which he is trained to 'go and seek the perceived threat'. 'That is what I tried to do. I did not have my prosthetic legs on, like I had when I had been trained,' he said.

Being on his stumps meant Oscar could not flee the bedroom, as Nel had suggested. 'My Lady, I have very, very limited mobility on my stumps on a hard surface like tiles,' he said. It was important for the state to try to get to exactly what Oscar meant when he said 'before I knew it, I had fired four shots at the door' and why he opened fire, so the prosecutor returned to this question on several occasions throughout the cross-examination.

Oscar provided several different answers and versions to the questions related to what happened in the bathroom in those seconds leading up to the shots. Various exchanges between Nel and Oscar unfolded as follows:

> Nel: *So you never intended to shoot the intruders?*
> Accused: *I never intended to shoot anyone, My Lady. I got a fright from a noise that I heard inside the toilet. I perceived it to be somebody coming out to attack me. That is what I believed.*

[...]

> Nel: *The fact is, did you shoot at the intruders with the intention to shoot them?*
> Accused: *My Lady, I shot because I was at that point with that ... that split moment I believed somebody was coming out to attack me, that is what made me fire my ... out of fear. I did not have time to think. I discharged my firearm.*

[...]

> Nel: *Mr Pistorius, did your gun accidentally go off, or did you fire at the intruders? It is easy.*
> Accused: *My Lady, my firearm was in my possession. I was ... I had my finger on the trigger ... it was an accident what happened. I agree with that. I did not intend to shoot anyone. I shot ... I fired my firearm before I could think. Before I even had a moment to comprehend what was happening, I believed someone was coming out the toilet.*

[...]

> Nel: *Why did you fire?*
> Accused: *Because I heard a noise coming from inside the toilet. That I interpreted at that split moment as somebody coming out to attack me, M'Lady.*
> Nel: *We ... luckily this is all on record. So ... and when you heard that ... you just started shooting?*
> Accused: *That is ... [interrupted]*

> Nel: *Or accidentally your fingers pulled the trigger.*
> Accused: *I started shooting at that point, M'Lady.*
> Nel: *At the intruders?*
> Accused: *At the door, M'Lady.*
> Nel: *But in your mind, at the intruders.*
> Accused: *It is what I perceived as a intruder coming out to attack me, M'Lady.*

On several occasions Oscar said he genuinely believed his life was in danger, that he was going to be attacked and that he was protecting Reeva. In the bail application Oscar stated, 'I heard movement inside the toilet,' which precipitated him firing the shots. Nel wanted to know exactly what this movement or sound was that prompted him to open fire. This noise would be described later by one of the athlete's expert witnesses as the 'third startle' and what prompted him to respond by pulling the trigger:

> Accused: *At that point, My Lady I was standing in the bathroom with my firearm pointed at the door. My eyes were going between the open window and the door and I heard a noise from inside the toilet.*
> Nel: *What noise?*
> Accused: *It sounded like wood, My Lady, like wood moving.*
> Nel: *Wood moving?*
> Accused: *That is correct, My Lady.*
> Nel: *Is that all you heard? Wood moving?*
> Accused: *I thought I heard the door opening, My Lady.*

> *[...]*

> Nel: *Is that what you heard? Is that a wood moving sound?*
> Accused: *Well, it is a wood abrasion noise or sounded ... I did not ... M'Lady, I heard a noise come from the toilet which I perceived as being the door opening. So ...*
> Nel: *Sir, I am not ... I am not interested in your perceptions now or what you perceived. I am interested in what you heard, please. What did you hear?*
> Accused: *I guess in retrospect, M'Lady, I probably heard the magazine rack moving.*

The problem with Oscar's version here was that the magazine rack was found next to the toilet against the back wall. According to Mangena's reconstruction of what took place behind the door, Reeva fell on top of the magazine rack – it did not move before the shots. Both the defence experts – Dixon and Wolmarans – confirmed the location of the rack by highlighting a clean area where there was no blood present caused by one of the legs of the rack pressing against the floor around which blood had pooled. In other words, if you lifted the rack, there would be no blood where its foot had rested on the floor, indicating that it had not been moved prior to the gunshots and the victim bleeding.

Pointing at a photograph of the scene, Oscar said he found Reeva where the magazine rack was in the picture, indicating that that rack itself was to the far right of the cubicle, positioned close to the wall, when he broke through the door.

While Oscar could merely explain what he experienced and how he perceived certain events on the morning of the shooting, it was going to be up to his defence experts to explain his thinking and what led him to that point when he pulled the trigger. It was the introduction of evidence related to a possible psychiatric disorder that took the proceedings in an unexpected new direction.

Generalised Anxiety Disorder (GAD)

State social worker Yvette van Schalkwyk was never part of the defence strategy. But when she came knocking on their door on the eve of election day, they resolved to put her in the witness box a mere two days later. This took many observers by surprise. Van Schalkwyk in fact asked to testify after she had heard negative things said about Oscar in the media and she wanted to correct the impression. At the time, there had been speculation in the press that he had gone for acting lessons – a claim slammed by his PR agent. Roux explained he called the witness because the state questioned the sincerity of the accused.

Van Schalkwyk, a social worker and probation officer, was the state employee assigned by the Magistrate's Court to monitor Oscar's behaviour during his bail application and offer him emotional support. She told the court she was 'upset' by what she had read about the accused and wanted to tell her version of what she had observed a year earlier in the days after the shooting. 'What upset me was the fact that they said he had acting training, he just put on a show, started crying when it was needed. That upset me,' she said.

The social worker described the accused as she observed him in the holding cells at the Pretoria Magistrate's Court as a man who was 'heartbroken about the loss. He cried; he was in mourning; he suffered emotionally. He was very sorry about the loss, especially for her parents. The suffering they are going through.'

The court appointed Van Schalkwyk as Oscar's probation officer when he was released and ordered her to compile weekly reports on his well-being, more specifically on his mental health and emotional state. She compiled four such reports until the bail conditions were successfully appealed.

Van Schalkwyk reported that Oscar was undergoing intensive therapy with psychologist Lore Hartzenberg to help him deal with trauma and anxiety. She concluded: 'The accused is very heartbroken and he still has a lot of emotions and stress. But this are all in context with the incident that happened. His emotional stress are dealt with by the psychologist.'

By week four she reported that Oscar was slowly improving and coping with the situation, and meeting regularly with Hartzenberg. But, by Van Schalkwyk's own admission, her reliability as a witness in this case was called into question.

> Van Schalkwyk: M'Lady, I just want to explain ... when I saw an accused, I usually saw accused for a probation officers report, for a pre-sentence report or a pre-trial report. Never directly after arrest.
>
> Nel: So you have never seen any other accused in a family murder matter just after arrest?
>
> Van Schalkwyk: That is correct, M'Lady.
>
> Nel: So the answer to the question is, you have not seen any adult accused after arrest, shortly after arrest.
>
> Van Schalkwyk: That is correct, M'Lady.
>
> Nel: You have seen one and that is accused before court.
>
> Van Schalkwyk: That is correct, M'Lady.

Nel argued that the extreme emotional state the social worker observed was consistent with someone who had been traumatised by the killing and then being arrested and hauled off to court. She did not have the experience to dispute the prosecutor's claim. Nel focused on what the accused did not say in those holding cells – he did not say, 'I'm sorry, I did it.'

• • •

Professor Merryll Vorster sports short brown hair with hints of grey and sharp facial features. As a registered forensic psychiatrist, she has worked for decades at state mental institutions and at the time of the trial was associate professor in the Department of Psychiatry at the University of the Witwatersrand. She is no stranger to the courtroom and is regularly called to testify in cases through her private medico-legal practice. She is known to most in the legal fraternity, who all have a 'Merryll story' to offer. Vorster's evidence and diagnosis of Oscar set the trial in an unexpected direction that had not been anticipated by the defence.

When, at the request of the defence, Vorster evaluated Oscar in May 2014, she consulted not only the report of psychologist Richard Holmes dated 18 February

2014, but also the Milpark Hospital medical records following the 2009 boat accident and the affidavits from his friend Justin Divaris and Divaris's girlfriend Samantha Greyvenstein, as well as that of Oscar's cousin Graham Binge. Vorster also interviewed Oscar's brother Carl, sister Aimee, his manager Peet van Zyl and coach Ampie Louw, as well as his maternal aunt – his mother's sister – Dianne Binge.

Vorster said the amputation of Oscar's limbs when he was just 11 months old, at a pre-language stage of his life, would have been interpreted by the child as traumatic assault – because he was too young to communicate, he would not have been able to comprehend and understand the type of procedure and the associated pain.

The accused was then fitted with prosthetic limbs and was encouraged to live a normal life and was supported by his family, but Vorster said this meant Oscar was never able to allow himself to be seen as disabled and was encouraged to see himself as normal.

Oscar's mother Sheila became his primary attachment figure, but when Oscar was six she divorced Oscar's father Henke.

Vorster stated that growing up and going through school Oscar appeared to lead a relatively normal life; although he was teased on occasion, he was able to stand up for himself or alternatively had Carl there to defend him. At the age of 15, the death of Oscar's mother led to an increase in his anxiety levels, and what he described as a very stressful period in his life.

The psychiatrist found that from about a year later the young athlete's career took off, until the age of 21 when he cut ties with his father Henke. That divide was still clearly evident during the bail application and later during the trial – Henke remained absent from court right until closing arguments.

Vorster said Oscar started spending significant amounts of time overseas, but became anxious about reports of the high levels of crime back home in South Africa, so he bought a firearm for his own protection.

She believed that Oscar had developed an anxiety disorder, which he worked hard to try to control by managing external factors such as his environment and being well-prepared for events. 'In a way, his strict training regime and his diet helped him to alleviate his levels of anxiety. On the other hand, as he became more and more exposed to being famous and having media attention, he would have had to prepare more and more to not embarrass himself in any way and in that way, to manage his levels of anxiety,' she said.

Vorster said Oscar exhibited many features of anxiety and there was a clear history of anxiety in his mother, brother and sister. She said that the encouragement to behave as a normal child while he was growing up had a significant detrimental impact on his development:

> He became increasingly unwilling to reveal his stumps publicly and this gradually extended to family members and friends. He would keep on his prostheses during the day, only removing them at night when he went to bed. He gradually developed a poor self image, feelings of inadequacy about his amputations.
>
> By concealing his disability, this rendered him less able to access the emotional support he required to manage his vulnerability and self-esteem issues.

Vorster explained how living this life only compounded the problem. Day after day, it became more difficult to keep his anxiety under control, and as the levels of anxiety increased so would his insecurities about his personal safety. She said this led Oscar to improve security at his house as reports of break-ins and other crime heightened his fear; he was hyper-vigilant, suffered sleep disturbances and would wake up believing there was someone in the house. Oscar constantly looked around, scanning his surroundings for any potential threat, with Vorster describing him as a distrustful and guarded person.

Vorster stated that during their consultation Oscar was asked to take off his prosthetic legs and, while he was embarrassed to do so, he complied. She said his ability to walk and balance on his stumps was poor and that his physical vulnerability was immediately apparent. These physical limitations fed into Oscar's mental well-being. 'His physical vulnerability makes him more anxious. His anxiety makes him want to conceal his physical vulnerability,' she said.

It was at this stage that crucial evidence was introduced – and no one saw it coming. Vorster said she had diagnosed the accused with a Generalised Anxiety Disorder (GAD), adding that he had a long history of this disorder and it had probably commenced with the amputation of his limbs at the age of 11 months.

> These factors were all operating at the time of the offence under discussion and would have been compounded by Mr Pistorius's psychical vulnerability and the additional pressure of perceiving his environment as hostile and unsafe.
>
> When exposed to a threat, Mr Pistorius is more likely to respond with

> *a fight response rather than a flight response as his psychical capacity for*
> *flight is limited.*

An aspect of Oscar's defence was taking shape. Roux was trying to explain why his client behaved the way he did on Valentine's morning – Oscar does not possess a flight response because his physical limitations make that impossible. Vorster said the court should consider Oscar's incapacity as an amputee together with his GAD condition, which would have been present at the time of the shooting.

• • •

What exactly did Vorster mean when she requested the court to take into account Oscar's diagnosis of GAD on the morning in question? Did this affect his ability to distinguish between right and wrong or his ability to act in accordance with his understanding of right and wrong? Vorster said she merely suggested that the court takes into account these factors when considering the conduct of the accused on the morning.

Nel, however, had appeared in a previous case in which a similar set of circumstances around a finding of GAD had taken place. This meant he was able to think on his feet and react, and he promptly referred the professor to section 78 of the Criminal Procedure Act that deals with 'mental illness or mental defect and criminal responsibility'. With her vast court experience, Vorster knew where Nel was headed.

'Do you say it is possible that he had diminished responsibility at the time?' the prosecutor asked.

Vorster was reluctant to give a straight answer; instead she skirted the simple yes or no response Nel was seeking. 'I am not saying that this constitutes a mental illness,' she said.

Then what was she saying? The accused doesn't suffer from a mental illness and his ability to determine right from wrong was not affected. So why was Vorster called, Nel wanted to establish.

She couldn't have it both ways.

The prosecutor called the defence's bluff, arguing that if Vorster said there was just the mere possibility that Oscar suffered from diminished capacity, then in terms of section 78 he should be referred for mental observation. The witness was reluctant to commit, saying instead that that would be a decision for the court to make.

The court would indeed have to make a decision, as Nel launched an application to have Oscar sent for 30-day psychiatric evaluation.

Nel based his application on his interpretation of the section 78(2) of the Criminal Procedure Act:

> *If it is alleged at criminal proceedings that the accused is by reason of mental illness or mental defect or for any other reason not criminally responsible for the offence charged, or if it appears to the court at criminal proceedings that the accused might for such a reason not be so responsible, the court shall in the case of an allegation or appearance of mental illness or mental defect, and may, in any other case, direct that the matter be enquired into and be reported on in accordance with the provisions of section 79.*

Section 79, the next section in the Act, to which Nel refers, sets the guidelines and basis for a panel to be established to conduct a psychiatric evaluation of an accused. By this time Roux and the attorneys were flipping through their thick legal textbooks and case law to establish whether Nel's argument had merit. It was the defence team's decision to introduce mental health as a possible defence, so Nel felt that the law then compelled him to act on it.

It was an interesting strategy by both sides. Nel was shutting down a possible defence for Oscar and closing a potential hole for an appeal down the line. But the other side of the coin was an acquittal based on mental incapacity. Not to mention that Roux ran the very high risk of his client becoming a 'state patient' for the rest of his life, committed to a medical facility without the option of ever leaving.

Nel argued that the court was compelled to refer the accused to the Weskoppies Psychiatric Hospital for observation. Oscar remarked to a journalist during a tea break that Nel's application was 'a joke'. The possibility of Oscar being an 'outpatient' and only undergoing evaluation during the day was mooted but commentators thought it an unlikely scenario because it was so unusual.

• • •

Tension filled the gallery the next morning as Oscar and his family waited for Masipa to deliver her ruling. Proceedings still hadn't started by the usual 9:30am as counsel was called to the judge's chambers. Roux emerged several minutes later and walked directly to Oscar who was standing in the dock. He appeared resigned; with terse lips he was shaking his head. Arnold shuffled past the tightly packed bodies in the gallery to join the conversation. When he returned to his spot, he released a long sigh before speaking to his wife Lois and Aimee. Like a game of broken telephone, whispered conversations made their way down the row of Pistorius supporters.

Despite Roux's rigorous attempt to oppose the application, Judge Masipa agreed with the state's interpretation of the law and that the court had no discretion in this regard. The judge said the basis for the application was the evidence of the defence's own witness.

'The accused may not have raised the issue that he was not criminally responsible at the time of the incident in so many words, but evidence led on his behalf clearly raises the issue and therefore cannot be ignored,' said Masipa. 'Not only that, but the allegations have been properly substantiated by the evidence of Dr Vorster.'

Masipa chose the unlikely 'outpatient' option for Oscar and ordered that he report to Weskoppies every weekday, starting 26 May, for no more than 30 days. A panel of three psychiatrists – doctors Leon Fine, Herman Pretorius and Carla Kotze – and a psychologist – Jonathan Scholtz – was given the task of establishing whether Oscar 'by reason of mental illness or mental defect, was at the time of the commission of the offence, criminally responsible for the offences charged, whether he was capable of appreciating the wrongfulness of his act, or of acting in accordance with an appreciation of the wrongfulness of his act'.

The 'Two Oscars'

Reporters, camera operators and outside broadcast vans lined the road leading to the entrance of Weskoppies Psychiatric Hospital. Established in 1892, and originally called the Krankzinnigengesticht te Pretoria (Pretoria Lunatic Asylum), its main Edwardian-styled building is tucked away behind a forest of pine trees along a ridge west of Pretoria. The state facility has hosted some of the country's most notorious criminals, including the so-called 'Modimolle Monster' Johan Kotze – convicted of orchestrating the gang rape of his ex-wife and murdering her son – and convicted child molester 'Advocate Barbie' Cezanne Visser. Police officers were called in to assist with security at the entrance to the hospital. Oscar arrived shortly before 9am in a black compact sedan, far less conspicuous than the usual SUV in which he arrived at court. He would spend the next four weeks reporting to the facility as and when required, where he was put through dozens of tests and interviewed numerous times by the panel of experts.

Court resumed on 30 June. The psychiatrists' report found:

> At the time of the alleged offences, the accused did not suffer from a mental disorder or a mental defect that affected his ability to distinguish between rightful or wrongful nature of his deeds and a mental disorder or mental defect did not affect his ability to act in accordance with the said appreciation of the rightful or wrongful nature of his deeds.

Psychologist Jonathan Scholtz supported this finding:

> Mr Pistorius did not suffer from a mental defect or mental illness at the

time of the commission of the offence that would have rendered him criminally not responsible for the offences charged.

Mr Pistorius was capable of appreciating the wrongfulness of his act and or acting in accordance with an appreciation of the wrongfulness of his acts.

Amongst the findings in the psychologist's report was that Oscar did not suffer from significant anxiety, nor did he suffer from a clinically diagnosable anxiety disorder. Scholtz found that the accused presented with an elevated risk of suicide, but his religious beliefs and strong family ties mitigated against this possibility. His study found no evidence to indicate that Oscar had a history of abnormal aggression or explosive violence, and those who knew him described him as gentle, respectful and conflict-avoidant.

The psychologist interviewed Oscar for a total of 19 hours and spoke to 16 people close to him, including his family members and friends such as his mom's sister Dianne Binge, his former Pretoria Boys High School principal Bill Schroder and his coach Ampie Louw. The only ex-girlfriend amongst those interviewees was Jenna Edkins, described as being in a relationship with Oscar between 2008 and 2011, 'with intermittent breaks of short duration and still friends with him'.

Scholtz discovered what he believed was a split in Oscar's personality, what he referred to as the 'Two Oscars': 'The one a vulnerable, scared disabled person; the other a strong physical person achieving beyond expectation.'

He said that at various phases of his life Oscar was unfortunate enough to experience incidents when he was exposed to crime, directly and indirectly. These included a burglary at his home, the hijacking of a family member in 2011, and the attack on the man by assailants who jumped out of a taxi. 'He became increasingly safety conscious and fearful. He became known for his nervousness and anxiety about safety in South Africa,' said the psychologist.

Scholtz believes that the construction of the Two Oscars came fully into being when the accused was a young adult:

The one Oscar being an international superstar, more confident and feeling more in control at 1.84 m tall. That part of him falling back on his physicality and 'never say die' attitude that had served him so well.

The other Oscar being a vulnerable and fearful disabled person, at less than 1.5 m tall once his prostheses were removed and he was alone at night. That part of him falling back onto his anxiety and fear, not feeling in control.

> *With his prostheses on any people can damage him but without them*
> *he feels defenceless. 'I am stuffed without my legs on.' For this reason*
> *he acquired a weapon and even searched for one that was lighter and*
> *smaller so that he could always keep it with him.*

Scholtz said Oscar was immediately taken with Reeva when she entered his life, to the extent that he even took her to his grandfather's funeral and introduced her to his uncle Arnold – apparently, the first girlfriend to have met him, although Sam Taylor would later dispute this. Scholtz found that 'their relationship shows none of the characteristics associated with an abusive relationship', and that they had a 'normal, loving relationship where the athlete exhibited genuine feelings towards Reeva'.

While the reports cleared Oscar of any mental illness or disorder that could have affected his ability to determine right from wrong – he wasn't insane and was thus still criminally liable – they did present a psychological profile of someone completely different from the gold-medalist Paralympian. Weak and insecure on his stumps, Oscar used his prosthetic legs as a prop to exude confidence, and to further compensate for growing insecurity he acquired another prop – a firearm.

Anatomy Lesson

Orthopaedic surgeon Dr Gerald Versfeld has known Oscar for most of the young man's life. It was to Versfeld that Oscar's parents turned when he was a baby, seeking advice on how best to deal with the congenital deformities of his legs. It was Versfeld who advised them to amputate below the knee and performed the procedure that would define Oscar's life. The soft-spoken man continued to treat Oscar throughout his life, so he is intimately familiar with his type of amputation and the difficulties the athlete faces with his stumps.

Part of the defence team's contention related to Oscar's vulnerability is his lack of mobility on his stumps. Versfeld was called to explain in a clinical manner precisely why Oscar experiences such difficulties and what effect these have on his mobility.

Oscar can't stand still on his stumps; he has to move around to retain his balance. He is also far better walking on soft surfaces – such as carpets as opposed to tiles – and has better balance in the light as opposed to the dark. He needs his arms to be able to balance on his stumps and often fell over.

Versfeld presented X-rays to the court and asked Masipa to have a look at them as he explained what they showed, but he also asked that the judge have a closer inspection of the stumps.

Masipa and her assessors made their way down from the bench to where Oscar was seated, just behind Nel. Masipa leant on a court orderly for support.

Oscar had pulled up his pants and taken off his prostheses, exposing the bony extensions below his knee that are almost always kept hidden. Like in Rembrandt's *Anatomy Lesson of Dr Nicolaes Tulp*, the surgeon drew the attention of the small crowd that had gathered to the subject's stumps. While Oscar sat upright with his eyes closed, bearing the humiliation of being prodded and inspected, Versfeld, who was kneeling down, gently moved the heel pad around on the stump to demonstrate its mobility.

> *If you consider your own heel, you would know that the heel is very firmly fixed to the bone, so this, you can see that the soft tissue is very, very mobile and what is happening is that the main heel pad is at the back here. If the foot is put down in an incorrect position, the heel pad slips backwards and he puts the weight on where there is no heel pad and therefore that, that creates pain and instability and it often causes him falling.*

As the doctor continued his demonstration, Nel remained seated in front of his lectern doodling in his notebook and didn't once look back to see what Versfeld was demonstrating to the court. The prosecutor was indifferent; it didn't matter because it wasn't his case. Oscar's mobility and the problems he experienced with his stumps had no bearing on the state's version of events – of the argument that led to the shooting.

• • •

Nel set out a timeline and offered to the court his own reason for why Versfeld was called at such a late stage in the trial. The doctor first consulted with Oscar on 7 May 2014, nearly a month after he had finished his own testimony.

'You have seen a person for whom it was very important to indicate severe vulnerability and inability to walk. What will you say if I tell you that?' asked Nel.

'I cannot dispute that. I think that is fair,' said Versfeld, making the concession.

Nel questioned the doctor's ability to make a finding on Oscar's vulnerability in relation to his physical disabilities. His point was that in Oscar's own version he ran on his stumps, he moved fans, he walked on tiles, he fired his handgun and he never once fell over despite doing it all in the dark. The athlete's version was thus in stark contrast to what his experts wanted the court to believe in relation to his mobility.

> *Nel: Based on your version, and I am not accepting that, I am just saying, running back from the bathroom, in the pitch dark, would you expect the accused to fall, if it is pitch dark, he is running,*

> *he cannot really concentrate on how to put his stumps down or*
> *things, on your version?*
>
> Versfeld: *It would be difficult.*
>
> Nel: *What would be difficult?*
>
> Versfeld: *To run in the pitch dark, holding on to a weapon and he would be*
> *at high risk for falling.*
>
> Nel: *And in all probability he would fall, if you just look at the*
> *probabilities, from where you are standing.*
>
> Versfeld: *He would have a high risk of falling, yes.*

Nel was determined to expose the lie, that Oscar's version was so improbable and the fact that he had called witnesses at such a late stage was merely an attempt to bolster a version that had come under significant attack during his cross-examination. Roux, however, countered the claims by stating that all the while Oscar moved in the dark he either had one hand on the floor or was leaning against a wall.

The Jerry Maguire Factor

Oscar's agent Peet van Zyl was another late addition to the witness list. He was called on the Saturday after the legal teams had received the psychiatric assessment report – which found that the accused did not suffer from an anxiety disorder – and was told to be at Barry Roux's chamber to consult to be a witness. Until that week, Van Zyl had not been part of the defence strategy. But his presence on the stand inadvertently opened the door for the state to address the court on character evidence – evidence it was not permitted to adduce, but can question a witness on if presented by the defence team.

Van Zyl described his relationship with the accused, having met him in 2004 at the Athens Paralympic Games and establishing a business relationship two years later. When Roux asked about Oscar's vigilance, it was soon clear why the defence had called the agent.

'It was very evident that … he had a heightened sense of awareness,' said Van Zyl. He recalled how Oscar would speed in his car to the airport for fear of being hijacked; he would choose well-lit parking spaces with easy access; and recalled how in a New York street Oscar grabbed his arm in fright after a loud bang.

Even in his own home, Van Zyl said, Oscar was always looking around, asking his housekeeper whether the front door was locked and where the dogs were. When they went for coffee, the manager said his client would choose a table that had clear access and a view of the exit.

Significantly, Van Zyl only recalled two incidents when Oscar lost his temper: once in 2009 at the Barcelona Airport when a group of reporters confronted him about the controversy related to his blades and called him a cheat; and the second time during the London Olympic Games when Oscar walked off a BBC radio interview at the presenter's suggestion that the athlete was an embarrassment for South African athletics administrators.

He described Oscar's relationship with Reeva as 'loving and caring', and that he had been asked to arrange that she accompany Oscar to athletics meetings in Brazil and the UK. 'He has never asked me for anything like this, to have one of his girlfriends in the past accompany him on any trips to an athletic competition' he said, adding later that plans were also in the pipeline for the couple to travel to Italy in July 2013.

· · ·

It was Werner Swart of the *Sunday Times* who, days after Van Zyl stepped down from the witness box, drew the comparison between Oscar's agent and the main protagonist of the movie with the same name *Jerry Maguire*.

Just as Maguire hopped, skipped and jumped for American footballer Rod Tidwell – 'Show me the money!' – Nel tried to show the court that Van Zyl was doing the same dance for Oscar, that he was there to protect his client's interest at all costs and not say 'negative things about Oscar'.

Van Zyl told us outside court one morning that he kept out of Oscar's private life and that their relationship was strictly business. 'I was making a ton of cash out of South Africa's new Posh and Becks,' he said.

Van Zyl said he had made no mention in court of the infamous incident at the London Games when Oscar complained about Brazilian Alan Oliveira after he beat him simply because he had not been there and rather specifically referred to incidents that happened in his presence. While he conceded that Oscar lost his temper, he said there was a history to the affair that related to the length and design of the blades Oscar's competitor had been using. It was the first public outburst from the athlete that many believed, in hindsight, provided some insight into his personality.

Then there was the incident with fellow athlete Arnu Fourie, as told to former Talk Radio 702 presenter David O'Sullivan. Fourie had just won the bronze medal in the 100 metres when O'Sullivan asked what it was like sharing a room with Oscar. 'He told me he had been forced to move out, because Oscar was constantly screaming in anger at people on the phone.'

On the witness stand Van Zyl said he had not been specifically informed of the details of the issue, other than that Fourie wanted to leave the room because of problems with his client and that he believed it had been dealt with at a team level. Van Zyl, in his cross-examination, gave a stronger indication that all was not right between the two teammates, saying there had been 'a situation', but it had been dealt with.

Later, after Van Zyl's evidence, Fourie issued a statement via Twitter:

> *Just to clarify..*
>
> *I approached our medical Doctor at the London 2012 Paralympic Games to find out if the isolation room was available 2 nights before our 100 m Final. It was one of the most important races of my life and I wanted to rest and recover well on my own time in preparation for the race. I cherish all the moments we shared at the London Games.*
>
> *Arnu Fourie.*

Notably absent in the statement was any denial of the allegations that Oscar 'was constantly screaming in anger at people on the phone'.

The South African Paralympic team doctor, Wayne Derman, was also asked about this when he came to give evidence. He confirmed that two nights before the 100 metres final, Fourie came to him complaining that he had symptoms of an upper respiratory tract infection. To avoid the illness spreading, Fourie was placed in an isolation room reserved for this purpose. Derman insisted he knew nothing about the request being related to Oscar screaming on the phone.

But beyond the courtroom, O'Sullivan stuck to his version of the conversation. After the matter was raised in court, O'Sullivan was contacted by a number of individuals, including Paralympic athletes, who were present at one of Oscar's angry outbursts in the Village. They refused to be publicly identified because they didn't want to get embroiled in the saga, but they did – according to O'Sullivan – provide further details about the fight.

He says they confirmed that Oscar was fighting with his then girlfriend Samantha Taylor. 'The athletes said Oscar was heard threatening the man who had dared to invite his girlfriend out. They spoke about Pistorius's rage, how he had cried and shouted and stormed out of the Village. As one of them put it: "Oscar went tilt" – South African slang for losing control. A person close to the situation said the throat infection was, in fact, a ruse to get Fourie away from Pistorius,' says O'Sullivan.

The same night Fourie issued his Twitter statement, Samantha Taylor made contact with the prosecution team. She told them that Fourie had asked to be moved because Oscar had been arguing with her on the phone. She confirmed the same to us: 'There was a lot of screaming and shouting and crying and making up. I know Arnu Fourie said in a statement that he moved out because he had a race and he needed to concentrate on it, but ... I mean I think he also feels like he didn't want to put himself in the position to "out" Oscar in a way.'

Taylor also produced an email that Oscar sent to her on 18 July 2012 that appeared to show that Reeva wasn't the only girlfriend he planned to take overseas to competitions.

> *When I invited you I was so excited to tell you because I knew we had had some hard days behind us. I had asked Peet to do everything he could last week to find you a ticket ...*
> *... I don't even feel like going to London now that you wont be there with me.*

In court, Nel also referred to an email Oscar sent to his agent on 12 September 2012 that included copies of Taylor's passport:

> *Here is Sams Passport. Please keep it on file, think we sorting shit out.*
> *:)*
> *Oz*

Van Zyl was adamant Reeva was the first girlfriend Oscar asked to accompany him to a competition, and after studying the email with the passport presented in court he said he could not remember receiving it.

Van Zyl said he kept Taylor's passport on file as it was later used to make travel arrangements for the Seychelles trip the couple were featured on for local TV magazine show *Top Billing*, but reiterated no knowledge of Taylor ever being invited to the London Olympic Games. Nel argued that if Van Zyl has no recollection of this significant request – to take a girlfriend to the Olympic Games – then it must be a lie by the accused. The prosecutor believed it was an example of the agent protecting his client, that he wanted to testify that Reeva was the only girlfriend he ever invited overseas.

It was hard to see what value Van Zyl's evidence had brought for the defence team; it was anecdotal at best.

The 'Third Startle'

The defence team saved a big gun for last with sports scientist Professor Wayne Derman, who rounded off Oscar's defence. He brought together the elements of the heightened anxiety, Oscar's fear of crime and his training as an athlete, and attempted to explain what triggered Oscar's reaction on that Valentine's morning. Derman submitted a 53-page report that started off with a disclaimer that he was giving evidence in his personal, private and professional capacity and not as a representative of any institution or organisation. He wanted to make it clear he wasn't speaking for the University of Cape Town, where he's employed, or as the chief medical officer for the South African Paralympic Team that went to London in 2012.

The professor had known Oscar for six years, conducting periodic health assessments of the athlete and making direct observations during medical consultations. Derman said he got to know Oscar better by spending time with him during the 2008 Beijing and 2012 London games, but he has also remained his treating physician outside of his role as team doctor.

Derman said Oscar's most significant medical issue over the years has been his stumps, which were chronically problematic, particularly the left one. This meant he was unable to bear full weight on that stump, had poor balance and walking was difficult – in other words, Derman was echoing the observations of Oscar's orthopaedic surgeon Dr Gerald Versfeld.

In terms of his patient's psychological well-being, the professor noted:

> *My observations relating to aspects of Mr Pistorius' interactions with myself, is that he is an anxious individual. I have found him to be anxious during most interactions, with myself and others within the*

Paralympic village and other environments particularly related to competition. He has a tremor of the hands. He also presents with a sleep disorder, a disorder for which I have previously had to medicate him.

Derman referred to a study that looked at markers of psychological stress, particularly anxiety and depression, which found these indicators higher in athletes with disabilities as opposed to a control group of able-bodied athletes. He said Oscar's results for this same test were higher than the average for the group, which meant he exhibited higher levels of anxiety and depression in relation to this test:

I also found Mr Pistorius to be hyper vigilant. I have observed this behaviour particularly with him rapidly looking around the room and scanning when we are in the dining hall setting, the team setting and even during one on one consultations in my rooms.

He presents with a very exaggerated startled response which I have observed a number of times at opening or closing ceremonies when the events were marked by fireworks. Whilst I have seen this exaggerated response in a number of the Paralympics athletes, Mr Pistorius exhibits an excessive response which involves him covering his head and ears and cowering away until the noise ends.

Derman pulled these threads together by concluding that, in his experience, the levels of anxiety and fear as well as the startle response, and fight-or-flight response, is increased in certain people with a disability.

He explained this response as how the body prepares itself for strenuous physical activity in the face of an emergency or stressful situation. To add to this, he found that the fight-or-flight response featured more prominently with people with disabilities, particularly those with mobility impairment. The professor further differentiated between these responses: the startle is the stimulus, usually auditory or visual, that triggers the fight-or-flight response.

Derman then produced academic literature that further showed that the startle response, which triggers the fight-or-flight response, was also exaggerated in individuals with high anxiety. It was becoming clear where the defence was going with this witness: the court would have to place Oscar in the bathroom, consider all the factors related to his psychology and then trigger this response.

Derman explained the anomaly that Nel had identified, that despite Oscar's claim that he felt vulnerable, he went towards the danger. 'Well, in this context, M'Lady, fleeing is not an option. The individual has no lower legs, so to flee is not an option and if one finds oneself without the ability to flee, the other option is to fight. So to approach the danger is an understandable physiological phenomenon,' he said.

Under cross-examination, when questioned about those seconds before he pulled the trigger, Nel had challenged Oscar on his evidence that 'I was not thinking'. Derman referred back to his explanation about how the unconscious part of the brain comes into play in such a situation, and how that part of the brain has even greater control over the conscious part of the brain in individuals who present with higher anxiety. He argued that this accounted for Oscar's apparent inability to think in that moment.

Applying this to Oscar's version, Derman identified three auditory events that constituted the triggers for the startle that led to the fight-or-flight response.

- The bathroom window opening.
- The toilet door slamming shut.
- The noise inside the toilet cubicle – the magazine rack.

Derman believed the court should consider Oscar's significant disability when passing judgment on his reaction on the morning of the shooting. Without his prosthetic legs fitted he did not have the option to take flight when presented with a threat; he has a lifetime of real and learnt vulnerability; a profound fear of crime; added to that his hyper-vigilance that results in an exaggerated startle response, and heightened anxiety that results in a significant fight-or-flight response; and his training as an athlete to be primed to react to the auditory stimulus of the starter's gun:

> It is my considered view, having regard to my knowledge and experience of Mr Pistorius, my knowledge and experience of disability and athletes with disability and my knowledge of the physiological responses under stressful conditions, all of which render it probable that his version of having experienced auditory stimuli, which he perceived to be life threatening to both himself and Ms Steenkamp, resulted in a significant startle and the flight and fight response, as he is not able to flee, due to his disability, his fight response dominates his behaviour, as it has in the past, and he approaches the perceived danger.
>
> Further sounds then lead to further potentiated startles and in the

setting of the complexities mentioned above, resulted in an exaggerated
fight response, which culminated in this horrific tragedy.

Derman's evidence set out one possible defence of the accused; it explained why he fetched his gun instead of running away, as Nel had suggested he could have done, and it explained why he said he did not intend to shoot, but he did 'by accident'. But would the judge accept it and how would the prosecution react?

• • •

The prosecution's first problem with Derman was whether he could in fact be seen as an expert witness – he conceded he had never testified in a criminal matter. The prosecutor's second issue was whether the professor could be considered unbiased, with a duty towards the court, when the accused was also his patient. Nel argued there was a conflict of interest, in that as a medical practitioner the witness would have an obligation towards his patient. The cross-examination was thus characterised by several tense exchanges between the prosecutor and the witness, with the judge having to step in on several occasions. The questions were not about the science of the responses Derman described, but rather about their application in this particular scenario.

Derman consulted with Oscar first before the trial started and for a second time before he was referred for psychiatric observation. Nel questioned the witness on the information Oscar had provided to him about the incident, and tested him on his thoroughness.

> Nel: *Now, you ... I am sure you still have your notes of all these*
> *consultations you have had and if somebody would ask you,*
> *specifically what happened the first and second occasion, you*
> *would be able to tell the court?*
>
> Derman: *Well what I can tell you, Mr Nel, M'Lady, is that I asked Mr*
> *Pistorius, what happened on that night. It was very important*
> *that I heard from him first-hand, to which he described that to*
> *me. I did not take any notes about that. I listened carefully to*
> *him and when I spoke to him subsequently to that, I again spoke*
> *to him. I wanted to make sure that there ... some of the things in*
> *the record that I read, did not make sense to me and again, I did*
> *not take specific notes about this. I made sure that I understood*
> *it as it was here.*

Nel argued that an expert witness, expected to give evidence in a criminal trial in a High Court, would have taken notes of the meetings he had with the accused. He also wanted details of the original version of events given by Oscar to Derman. Oscar had only given the explanation of the magazine rack noise triggering his reaction under cross-examination and Nel implied it was a new invention.

Derman said Oscar told him about the magazine rack at their first meeting.

When Nel questioned the time period during which a person would be less in control of the conscious part of their brain, Derman explained that on the first startle – the window opening – Oscar froze.

'Ja, so now he froze,' said Nel. 'So whatever he done after that, that was him being in control of himself, thinking what he is doing?'

'Well, I know that the … his next response is, he told me was to go and get the gun next to his bed,' said Derman.

Nel's issue with this version was the apparent contradiction of the startle response being a freeze, and then the accused fetching his firearm. 'You cannot now freeze and then fight,' he argued. The prosecutor was attacking the defence that Oscar was not consciously thinking about his actions when he fetched his firearm and stormed the perceived threat in the bathroom. 'Okay but, what you will … what you are able … what you will concede is, there is an element of thinking,' said Nel.

'There is indeed,' answered Derman. 'Because he realised he has to get a gun.'

The prosecutor zeroed in on the effect that time has on this type of response:

> Nel: Now in an incident like this, where there is a startle with … the accused finding a gun, knowing where it is. Getting the gun to fire, going to the bathroom, killing someone. Would that still make sense to you, if there was just one startle?
>
> Derman: No, there would need to be more startles.
>
> Nel: Okay. Good now there we are. Why?
>
> Derman: Because of the period of time that elapsed between that first startle and the reaction.

The point Nel was making is that over a period of time the physiological response to the startle would diminish, so for Oscar to claim this defence he would have to have experienced those additional startles.

Nel tested the witness on his understanding of Oscar's intentions when he approached the danger:

> Nel: Now with a gun in front of me the confrontation is, shoot. Am I right?
>
> Derman: Yes I would say if one has a gun in front then the intention is to shoot.
>
> Nel: So at least we can say that walking down the passage even in your … even on your version being in the fight mode, his intention was to shoot, whoever he would come across … if he comes across someone?
>
> Derman: Yes I would say to shoot to protect one self, I agree with that statement.
>
> Nel: You see, professor my statement is not shoot and protect but to shoot and you agree with that statement. His intention is to shoot?
>
> Derman: Yes. That is correct, if one is walking out with a gun outstretched in front of you.
>
> Nel: Even in the fight mode the accused on this night, the intention, the clear intention was to shoot if he came across something. Am I right?
>
> Derman: I suppose if you come across an intruder or danger you would shoot, I do not know.

This was the evidence the defence did not want to hear because it contradicted Oscar's own claims that he never intended to shoot anyone.

The second startle was the toilet door being closed, but Derman couldn't tell the court exactly what this caused Oscar to do. 'My memory is a bit fuzzy on this …' he said, which highlighted Nel's concerns about the expert witness not taking notes.

Derman said the crucial third sound – the so-called third startle, the magazine rack moving – culminated in the shooting. He agreed with Nel's proposition that Oscar fired at the sound but could not explain why, merely stating that that was his fight-or-flight response. He did, however, concede that when he fired at the sound it was to nullify any threat. It is there where Nel ended his cross-examination and asked that the matter adjourn until the Monday to allow himself time to consult with an expert. The court agreed.

• • •

By the Saturday afternoon, word was spreading quickly on social media that an Australian TV network had obtained exclusive footage of Oscar re-enacting the events of Valentine's Day. Channel 7's investigative show *Sunday Night* had obtained secret footage filmed by American forensic and crime scene reconstruction experts, The Evidence Room.

Oscar's defence team hired the Cleveland, Ohio-based company run by Scott Roder in October 2013, but no evidence or witnesses from the company had been presented in court. The footage was broadcast on the Sunday, about midday South African time, and showed Oscar on his stumps, in a blue Nike vest and black pants, acting out various aspects of his version some eight months after the killing.

In one scene, the athlete moved quickly towards the camera with his arms stretched out in front of him as if holding a firearm; in another he was asked to run as quickly as he could. The awkwardness of his movement was evident, but he was able to move with some speed and without the need to hold on to something, even when pretending to hold a firearm and walking backwards. The footage was filmed at his uncle Arnold's house in Waterkloof.

Oscar was also timed as to how quickly he could put his prosthetic legs on – about 25 seconds. Aimee played the role of Reeva as Oscar demonstrated how he picked her body off the floor of the bathroom and carried her downstairs. In one scene, portraying how Oscar had discovered his girlfriend behind the door, he positioned himself over the toilet bowl illustrating the scene.

Roder told *Sunday Night* that he believed Oscar never intended to kill Reeva. 'Absolutely, the physical evidence is consistent and his story remains unchanged. If you look at the evidence Oscar's clearly not guilty,' he said.

Roder described what the psychologist identified as the Two Oscars. 'When he's on his prosthetics, you know he's very tall broad-shouldered athletic guy; he looks like he can really handle himself. But when he takes his prosthetics off and he's on his stumps uh he's short, the confidence washes away from his face.'

Despite the forensic expert believing Oscar's version of events, the video appeared to show that the accused was far more mobile than the defence team wanted the court to believe. A lot had been said about the difficulties Oscar faced on his stumps, so why not show the court exactly how he is able to move? Speculation suggested that the footage had not been shown because it did not support his case.

That Sunday afternoon defence attorney Brian Webber issued a statement confirming that The Evidence Room had been hired to map visually the events of the morning and in this process videos were made:

*The 'visual mapping' was for trial preparation only and was not intended
to be used for any other purpose.*

*We wish to make it very clear that the material that has been aired
was obtained illegally and in breach of the non-disclosure agreement with
The Evidence Room. Its usage also constitutes a breach of privilege as this
material was produced for trial purposes on the instructions of a commissioner, and the ownership of the copyright vests in the commissioner.*

No permission for the disclosure thereof has been given.

Webber added that the Pistorius family was angry because the broadcast constituted a 'staggering breach of trust and an invasion of the family's privacy'.
But then Webber made a curious comment: that in their discussions with the
Australian channel, 'we received an undertaking that they would not air any of
the material before the end of the trial'.

This raised the question of when exactly they had found out that this footage
had been sold. Nel had unexpectedly asked for an adjournment the previous
Thursday – had the defence thus anticipated wrapping up the case by the Friday
and would have been satisfied if the footage was broadcast that Sunday?

Talk amongst reporters from the various international news agencies indicated they had known about the video for some time because the company was
shopping it around.

Sunday Night's executive producer Mark Llewellyn defended their decision to
broadcast it. 'We would not have run the footage if we thought we had obtained it
illegally. The material shown on *Sunday Night* goes to the heart of both the prosecution and defence cases, including the account provided by Oscar Pistorius,'
he said in a statement.

The pressing question was whether Nel would attempt to introduce the video as
evidence as he had done with the 'zombie stopper' footage. A member of the prosecution team said that while the video appeared to support its case, it would be
too much effort to attempt to introduce it. He said Nel did not want to lose focus
at this late stage of the case. In the end, the video was not introduced and it was
left for the public to debate whether the footage proved or disproved Oscar's case.

• • •

Gerrie Nel had spent the previous Friday consulting with one of the psychiatrists appointed to the panel that had observed Oscar and reported back to
the court. When he returned to his lectern on Monday morning, he was better

prepared to question Dr Derman. The prosecutor wanted to know from the clinician whether he was in a position to interpret and testify on the results of various tests conducted during the psychiatric referral. Derman felt that with his 20 years' experience he could.

Nel returned to Derman's evidence of when he asked Oscar to demonstrate for him how he ran and his mobility on his stumps. The change in the prosecution's stride caught the attention of those in the gallery as it appeared Nel might refer to the leaked video.

> Nel: So, Mr Pistorius in fact described to you how he ran or demonstrated to you how he ran.
> Derman: He demonstrated to me how he ran.
> Nel: He did not say 'I never ran, I moved cautiously'.
> Derman: No, I wanted to gauge what he meant by 'run', because as I explained before, M'Lady, I know that Mr Pistorius cannot run, because in order to run both feet or both lower limb projections have to be off the ground at the same time.
> Nel: Can I just ask you then: Was it ever demonstrated to you that Mr Pistorius was able to walk backwards on his stumps?
> Derman: It was never demonstrated to me.
> Nel: You think it is possible?
> Derman: I have never seen him walk backwards, but I do not see why it should not be possible.
> Nel: Apart from the demonstration in the corridor did you see any other demonstration of the accused running?
> Derman: No, I have a number of times when we have been travelling seen him moving on his stumps from bed to bathroom and around his room. That is the only time I have seen it.

That was the closest Nel came to referring to the leaked video footage, which depicted Oscar walking backwards, unaided with his right hand up as if holding a firearm. Oscar had explained that in the dark of his room and as he shuffled around on his stumps, he would use one hand on the floor to guide himself and remain steady.

The prosecutor thus challenged Derman's evidence that Oscar was vulnerable, as he was a person living in a secure complex with an alarm system, who has a big support group around him that includes family and Derman as his doctor. 'Now, that whole scenario mitigates his vulnerability in his context,' Nel suggested.

> Derman: *I disagree strongly.*
>   Nel: *But we have the person with a gun on the night. If Mr Pistorius*
>   *was vulnerable on that night he armed himself. Am I right?*
> Derman: *He did.*
>   Nel: *At least he will concede with a gun in hand he is less vulnerable.*
> Derman: *He might indeed be less vulnerable, but how much less*
>   *vulnerable I do not know and I cannot think if that would*
>   *reduce his vulnerability absolutely.*

The centrality of the so-called third startle showed itself again as Nel returned to the issue. One of Oscar's hobbies was shooting and he spent a fair amount of time at a shooting range. Why wouldn't the sounds of those shots trigger a startle response? asked Nel.

'M'Lady, as I understand this phenomenon,' explained Derman, 'if one is expecting a sound, and is in control of that sound, then it does not have the same startle response as if you are not expecting a sound.'

It was the answer Nel wanted – standing in the bathroom with the belief that there was someone hiding in the toilet, surely Oscar would have expected a noise to emanate from inside the cubicle. On this expectation, he argued, an auditory stimulus would not have triggered the startle response. And add to that the fact that Oscar was still reacting to the second startle – the toilet door closing – he would have experienced heightened awareness of his surroundings.

Derman disagreed entirely. 'M'Lady, with respect, Mr Nel has got it wrong,' he said. 'It is exactly the opposite. The startle would be potentiated in the fear setting. It is exactly opposite to what Mr Nel said.'

For Nel the most crucial aspect he needed to prove to the court was Oscar's 'intention'. Did he intend to shoot at whoever was behind the door?

Derman ventured his opinon. 'From what I understand, M'Lady, it was his intention to shoot. That is how I understand it,' said Oscar's doctor.

Derman was the final defence witness to be called, his role was to bring together the factors set out by the previous witnesses. He was there to explain Oscar's conduct in the context of his psychological make-up, his physical short-comings, his inherent fears and the physical and emotional environment in which he found himself – in that bathroom, that night, firearm in hand, facing a threat that lurked behind a closed door. Could his response – his impulse to pump four shots through that door – be considered reasonable for such a man in such a position?

Oscar's Changing Defence

When Oscar finally stepped off the stand, following days of gruelling cross-examination and only a brief response from Roux, the defence case was arguably far weaker than before he had testified. Oscar's evidence was heavily criticised by legal experts, who judged him to be forgetful, evasive, combative and contradictory.

On all four charges, he did himself no favours. He denied that the sunroof incident took place at all, despite two other witnesses saying it had happened. On the Tashas shooting he admitted he had Fresco's gun in his hand but claimed the firearm went off without him pulling the trigger. He told the court he was keeping ammunition for his father and yet he hadn't spoken to his dad for years. Crucially, he explained the gun went off in the bathroom but he never intended to fire it, despite his strategy of putative private defence.

Criminal attorney Tyrone Maseko believes Oscar did himself a disservice. 'I was rather perturbed at how he never or very seldom conceded anything, even on questions which had little bearing on his defence. If he had made necessary concessions he would have come across more credible and a more reliable witness,' says Maseko. 'I thought he was a bit argumentative and unnecessarily so. He was quick to correct Nel whenever he misspoke but couldn't answer some questions because "he doesn't remember". He just did not come across as someone who is believable.'

Law lecturer Kelly Phelps is more reluctant to pass judgment on how Oscar performed on the stand, saying that that would be the judge's duty. 'It is fair to say that he performed more strongly in his evidence-in-chief than in cross-examination but that is what you would expect of any witness. No person will endure the kind of aggressive cross-examination that he endured and emerge unscathed. Nor does a court expect a perfect performance – human memory and character are never perfect. It will be a question of balance – taking all of his time on the stand into account does the bench think that the fundamental aspects of his story are true.'

She continued: 'Much was made in the media of Gerrie Nel's accusations that Pistorius was lying – that is the prosecutor's job, to try to convince the court that the accused's version is unsound. However, just because the prosecutor says so, doesn't mean the judge accepts that contention. A judge is not an empty vessel waiting to be filled with the wisdom of the legal teams – she will apply her mind critically to the various allegations made and compare the allegations with all of the evidence on record before deciding which version she believes.'

Oscar's evidence on the stand also led to a perception that the defence team had changed strategy. It was always the belief, from the outset, that Oscar's legal team would argue putative private defence.

'Given Oscar's version of the events one could only really accept that this was his defence (even though never formally stated) and the one which the defence would argue tooth and nail in proving Oscar's innocence,' says litigation attorney David Dadic.

But then the nature and integrity of the defence came under immense pressure. Under cross-examination Oscar seemed to give evidence that pointed to a different legal defence. He told Nel that he shot 'by accident' and it was 'a mistake'. He insisted he never intended to shoot anyone, that the gun just went off in his hand:

> Nel: *You referred in your plea explanation to this incident, or this occurrence as 'an accident'. Is that correct?*
>
> Accused: *That is correct, My Lady.*
>
> Nel: *What was the accident?*
>
> Accused: *The accident was that I discharged my firearm in the belief that an intruder was coming out to attack me, My Lady.*
>
> Nel: *So the discharge was not accidental? Or was the discharge accidental?*
>
> Accused: *The discharge was accidental, My Lady. I believed that somebody was coming out. I believed the noise that I heard inside the toilet was somebody coming out to attack me, or to take my life.*
>
> Nel: *No. Do you know what an 'accidental discharge' is?*
>
> Accused: *Mr Nel, would like to explain to me what an 'accidental discharge' is, My Lady.*

> Nel: *You know ...*
>
> Accused: *My understanding is that I did not intend to discharge my firearm.*
>
> Nel: *Okay, no then you do. So you never intended to shoot the intruders?*
>
> Accused: *I never intended to shoot anyone, My Lady. I got a fright from a noise that I heard inside the toilet. I perceived it to be somebody coming out to attack me. That is what I believed.*

As Nel continued, Oscar confirmed that he shot without thinking:

> Nel: *So now I am asking you and we have five more minutes, Mr Pistorius, did your gun accidentally go off, or did you fire at the intruders? It is easy.*
>
> Accused: *My Lady, my firearm was in my possession. I was ... I had my finger on the trigger ... it was an accident what happened. I agree with that. I did not intend to shoot anyone. I shot ... I fired my firearm before I could think. Before I even had a moment to comprehend what was happening, I believed someone was coming out the toilet.*

It seemed as though Oscar's defence was switching to what is known as 'sane automatism'. This is the kind of defence used for someone who was sleepwalking or epileptic and was unable to control their actions.

David Dadic comments: 'It seemed that Oscar was desperate to avoid admitting, while under cross-examination, that he intentionally shot at somebody (the "intruder") on the evening (intent is a necessary element in self-defence) and actually went to the point of saying that the gun "went off by mistake" when he heard the sound in the bathroom which he assumed to be the door opening.'

Dadic continued: 'Now at the time I believed Oscar had simply chosen a poor manner of speaking in responding to the barrage of questions in his attempt to avoid admitting any form of intent. But unfortunately for Oscar statements in the box do not go without repercussion, and when he uttered this comment Nel pounced all over it, accusing Oscar of now changing his defence to one of involuntary act or automatism. The defence of automatism means that the defendant was *not aware* of his or her actions when doing the particular deed that constituted the illegal act. It's also a well-known defence in our law but one that's not easily accepted by our courts and usually very difficult to prove.'

Wits professor James Grant agrees that a claim of 'accident' amounts in law to a claim of involuntariness. 'Automatism is a term used by lawyers to sound fancy. It is a reference to the absence of a fundamental requirement of liability that one's conduct must be voluntary. It simply means that the accused was acting involuntarily. Examples of involuntariness include movements in an epileptic seizure, movement made by virtue of overwhelming physical force, such as if one is blown by a hurricane through your neighbour's glass door. Sleepwalking is also a well-recognised instance of involuntariness. The essence of the defence is that your mind did not direct or control your conduct. His testimony seems to be raising this defence … A claim to involuntariness is a difficult one because our courts assume that ordinary conduct is voluntary.'

Grant acknowledges that the interpretation of 'accident' is very technical. 'It is understandable that an accused who is unfamiliar with the law and the legal implications of what he is saying may make this mistake. This is not, in my view, the problem. The problem is that he seems unclear as to what his defence is. On a charge of murder, there is nothing inconsistent with innocence to intentionally kill someone – so long as you think you are doing so lawfully (such as in private defence). But if this is your defence, it makes no sense to deny having intended to kill anyone. An accused who does so would appear to be unclear about his/her defence. For me this gives rise to a crucial question: why would an accused be so unclear about his defence that it seems to change as he testifies on the stand?'

The more significant change in defence came when forensic psychiatrist Merryll Vorster was called to the stand in an effort to show that Oscar didn't act beyond the bounds of reasonableness in the moment, in killing the 'intruder', and the defence wanted to give insight into his extremely fearful state of mind.

'Professor Vorster was principally called to give evidence on a report she had done on Oscar only weeks prior to taking the stand in which she diagnosed him to have a psychiatric condition known as Generalised Anxiety Disorder [GAD]. She essentially said that, even though Oscar was not criminally insane, in that he knew the difference between right and wrong, he may, consequent to his condition, not have been able to act in accordance with such knowledge on the night and in the moment, a legal defence known as non-pathological incapacity,' explains Dadic. 'This defence suggests that in certain circumstances a person can be of such temporary impaired state of mind, while committing the act, that he may be acquitted of it. In this case it was suggested that his GAD caused him to be more fearful and more hyper-vigilant than the ordinary man and thereby caused him to do what he did.'

The thinking was that the defence had changed to a third strategy: that of 'pathological incapacity'.

'Vorster diagnosed the accused with a psychiatric disorder (Generalised Anxiety Disorder) and insisted that this did not constitute a mental illness for the purpose of a defence of pathological incapacity. The issue then turned on whether the condition that Vorster diagnosed did constitute a mental illness. A mental condition or disorder must constitute a mental illness (or defect) to form the basis of a pathological incapacity defence. The obvious question then is what is a mental illness or defect?' says Professor Grant.

'In the Pistorius case the court was confronted with testimony of a well-respected mental health expert to the effect that Pistorius suffered from a mental disorder that would (indirectly) make him dangerous and took the view that this may reasonably possibly constitute a mental illness. Once that was recognised and coupled with Vorster's testimony that Pistorius's capacity for self-control at the time of the conduct in question may have been affected, the court had no choice. It had to refer him,' adds the law professor.

That third potential defence fell away following Oscar's evaluation at Weskoppies Psychiatric Hospital. Barry Roux was forced to place on record that, in fact, the defence was one of putative private defence. However, in closing arguments the issue became blurred once again. The defence asked in its heads of argument to consider the alternatives:

> If the honourable court were to find that the accused did not discharge the shots in a reflexive response, consequent upon an exaggerated startle, which made him incapable of acting in accordance with the appreciation of right and wrong or incapable of acting, then the alternative finding can only be that the accused intentionally discharged the shots in the belief that the intruders were coming out.

But the prosecution believed the defence was still attempting to apply two defences, when that is simply not allowed. During oral argument, Nel stated:

> M'Lady, it is two, two concepts, two defences that you can never argue, never, M'Lady, with the utmost respect. If you put any reliance on your client's version, if you say to this court: I do not put any reliance on my client's version, I am just looking at all the facts, that is, I do not want to say: perhaps possible, but let me rather say: more possible than when you want to rely on the accused's version. M'Lady, I did not act, but if

you find I did, please accept that I did so intentionally with a reason.
M'Lady, those two defences cannot be argued. An accused must at least
have a defence but, M'Lady, this will show how the accused tailored his
version, how one defence was not possible and not because of anything
but the weak performance of this accused during cross-examination.

Judge Masipa would have to decide whether this vacillation between defences would impact on her findings. 'It's important to note that vacillation between defences, if accepted by the court, can be damning for an accused, because it can seem tailored in that it may give the court the impression that you are making up your story as you go along, dependent on the evidence that's been led,' says Dadic.

High-profile litigator Ian Levitt believes Oscar's performance and the change of versions could be detrimental when it comes to judgment. 'I think he performed very poorly. He changed his version in material aspects, mainly the two versions that came through. Now those two versions don't have anything that can coincide with each other; they are mutually destructive. I think this materially affects his credibility and whether any version should be believed at all. I think it would be difficult for any court faced with two versions to try to believe anything that he says when he contradicts himself in such a material way. Assuming that they knew that Pistorius was not going to do well in the box, all they could do was try their best to discredit the police, to discredit the crime scene, to attack every witness that the state brought to testify.'

Opinion was that it could ultimately emerge that Oscar could be the master of his own downfall. His own testimony could trip him up.

I Put it to You –
Closing Arguments

After a month-long hiatus, everyone returned to their seats in Court GD as if they had never left. But they had – foreign correspondents had spent the month away from the human drama of the Oscar Pistorius trial to cover violent conflict in Gaza, an Ebola outbreak in West Africa, the escalating tension in the Ukraine following the shooting down of a Malaysian Airlines plane and the kidnapping of some 200 schoolgirls by Boko Haram in Nigeria.

But on the morning of 7 August, they were all there to witness two masters of their craft wrapping up their cases. It was Day 40 of the trial and there was an air of relief and an atmosphere of finality as the case entered its last stretch prior to judgment.

For the first time both fathers appeared at the trial. Barry Steenkamp, a large hulking man with a thick white beard, uncomfortable in a suit, arrived with his wife June, who had attended each day. He shared a warm embrace with the ANC Women's League's Jacqui Mofokeng, who had been a pillar of support for the family, both emotionally and financially.

Barry had indicated a week earlier in a Sunday newspaper that he felt duty-bound to be in court for his daughter. He hadn't attended previously because of ill-health, suffering a stroke a few weeks before the trial started. Barry took up a seat next to June, while to his left was the couple's advocate Dup de Bruyn. June's cousin Kim Martin, another regular supporter of the family, was also there.

The Myers sisters and their mother were in their usual places, towards the middle of the front bench, effectively a buffer between the Steenkamp and Pistorius camps.

The extended Pistorius family filed in: all the uncles, Theo, Leo and Arnold, with their spouses, as well as several cousins. Oscar's father Henke arrived and shook the hands of the male relatives and greeted the women with a hug and a kiss. He and Arnold did not appear to acknowledge one another, a testament to the strained relationship Henke has with his family. However, Aimee did give her father a warm embrace and seemed emotional to see him arrive. Oscar did greet his dad, but only later during a break. When Henke thrust his arms around his son, Oscar didn't budge, cementing his hands to the wooden dock as he was awkwardly hugged.

The one notable absence was Oscar's brother Carl. He had been seriously injured in a car accident in Limpopo just days before. He had spent several days in the Intensive Care Unit of a Pretoria hospital with multiple broken bones and was unable to attend.

By the time Oscar took his seat in the dock of the courtroom, in a dark suit and dark-framed eyeglasses, both the defence and the prosecution were set to present closing arguments. The timeframe had been set down for two days. Each side had handed in its 'Heads of Argument', written summaries of their cases, but this was an opportunity for the senior counsel of each party to argue before Judge Masipa and the two assessors. It was inevitable that Gerrie Nel and Barry Roux would play to the public, that their arguments would be theatrical, that the legal proceedings had the potential to deteriorate into a pageant. In closing argument, often the man with the best oratory ability will appear more convincing, particularly in this arena, which was the first South African trial to be broadcast live.

Nel went first and he opened by setting the scene with a quote from his favourite defence advocate, the fictional Horace Rumpole from the television series *Rumpole of the Bailey*: 'With all due respect to Your Ladyship, I was thinking that a criminal trial is a very blunt implement for digging out the truth.'

He explained himself: 'Now, M'Lady, and it was evident in this matter. It was not the matter that the truth was just there, it was a case that we had to work on, worked on days, worked on hard, both the state and the defence, but we are confident, M'Lady, that, although blunt, it always leads to getting to the truth and, I think, in this matter it also did.'

As a prosecutor, Nel is an expert in 'packaging' his arguments, relying on analogies and metaphors for ease of understanding complex matters. He used three such devices as he made his case: the analogy of an athlete dropping the 'baton of truth'; a destroyed 'mosaic'; and a 'baker's dozen' of inconsistencies in Oscar's version.

He opened with the first of these analogies: 'The State will expose how he stumbled over his lies and deceit and in the process dropped the baton and he was unable to complete the race. It is the State's case that the accused was a deceitful witness and that the court should have no difficulty in rejecting his core version of events.'

Nel immediately went on the offensive, attacking Oscar's credibility as a witness, accusing him of being incapable of taking responsibility for any wrongdoing and playing the role of the 'victim' of circumstance. He argued that the accused was a deceitful witness who had tailored his evidence and used 'well-calculated and rehearsed emotional outbursts to deflect the attention and avoid him having to answer questions'.

Nel posed a burning question. Just what is Oscar's defence? 'Is it putative self-defence? Is it an act of sane automatism? Did he have criminal capacity to act? Or was it all an accident (as in Tashas restaurant) where he had the gun in his hand and it purportedly discharged itself?'

The state believed an objective evaluation of the facts showed that there had been no real threat to the accused. 'The perceived imminent attack was nothing more (on his version) than a sound. The door was locked. There was no evidence that there was even an attempt to open the door from within the toilet cubicle.' This meant he could not argue he was acting in self-defence.

'It is our argument that, on his own version, the accused acted so unreasonably that his version could never be accepted as reasonably possibly true,' said Nel.

He argued that even if the court did accept Oscar's version, he should still be convicted of murder. 'He cannot escape a finding that he acted with *dolus eventualis* by arming himself and, whilst approaching the "danger", foresaw the possibility that he may shoot and kill someone but reconciled himself with this possibility by walking into the bathroom and then without objective or subjective cause, fired four shots into a small toilet cubicle whilst anticipating that someone was in the cubicle and likely to be killed.'

Nel moved to negate the defence that Oscar was suffering from anxiety and that he felt vulnerable. 'There will be argument about the anxiety of the accused, that he was an anxious person. Now what is interesting, M'Lady, is that the anxiety did not present itself when they were stopped by the Metro Police officers on the way back from the Vaal, not at all, quite the opposite. He was not anxious, he challenged the Metro Police officers, he engaged with the police officer about what he was doing with his gun, not an anxious person being worried and scared of the police being there and finding my firearm. We say, M'Lady, that the anxious nature of what the accused would want the court to believe is anxiety-on-call, when I need to be anxious, when I need somebody to accept my anxiety, I have it on call, anxiety-on-call,' said Nel somewhat disparagingly.

Nel floated the concept of a 'mosaic of proof', arguing that the objective facts create 'a rather gruesome mosaic'. 'We will argue that the accused destroyed his mosaic with his unconvincing contradictory evidence. Each separate piece of circumstantial evidence, viewed in isolation, may be argued to only weigh as much as a feather but all the feathers together on the scale will convincingly balance the scale in favour of the State.'

It was an approach Nel had taken before in a case in which he could rely on only circumstantial evidence – the case against former police chief Jackie Selebi: the belief that it is the weight of all the feathers, all of the individual pieces of evidence, that will outweigh the defence's case.

Nel also made another subtle reference to Selebi, who he once referred to as the worst witness to ever testify in a court. Nel suggested Oscar was not far behind the former police chief.

'It is our respectful submission that the accused was an appalling witness. We cannot argue that he was the worst witness ever, that honour belongs to someone else. The accused was, however, demonstrably one of the worst witnesses ever encountered. The accused did not present as someone striving to give a truthful version, but rather as someone who was tailoring a version and was more concerned with the implications of his answers than the truth thereof.'

In the case of Selebi, Nel had used the device of 'Selebi's Five Big Lies'. Now, he created 'Oscar's Baker's Dozen' exposing the major discrepancies, contradictions and in the state's view, deceitfulness exposed during Oscar's evidence.

Number 1 – Nel challenged Oscar's answers to questions posed to him around the infamous 'zombie stopper' video. Initially Oscar testified that he had no idea what it was but was then shown a recording of himself using the phrase.

Number 2 – Nel claimed Oscar realised he needed to be inside his bedroom to rely on a sound he had heard in the bathroom, but he 'forgot his version under oath in the bail application'. Nel also accused Oscar of resorting to blaming his counsel for his contradictory versions.

Number 3 – Nel argued Oscar had to create time to allow Reeva to get to the toilet and because he had to be inside the room to hear the sound in the bathroom, he created a version that included a second fan – but had only mentioned one fan in his bail application statement. Nel argued that this 'destroyed some of the pieces of the mosaic as the accused had to adapt his version because there was no space for a further electrical plug in the extension cord'.

Number 4 – Nel stated that 'with the mosaic pieces falling from the canvas', Oscar 'turned his version of events into a farce', claiming he apparently moved the fans to where the duvet was. Nel had argued that the placement of the objects showed that Oscar's version could not be true, but the defence had argued the scene was tampered with. 'He also had to create a version that would make it possible for him to go onto the balcony to shout for help. The snowball effect of a lie becomes quite evident.'

Number 5 – Nel believed the tailoring of evidence by Oscar had a 'domino effect' and if 'one piece of the mosaic is moved the rest have to as well to keep the picture intact'. He argued that with the fans having been moved, Oscar had to create an untrue version about the duvet.

Number 6 – Nel claimed Oscar had to explain why the police would have moved the smaller fan into the corner of the room and then thrown the duvet onto the floor, followed by a pair of Reeva's jeans. All of this would have had to have been done before the photographs were taken at 05:58 without knowing Oscar's version.

Number 7 – Oscar's failure to deal with the duvet on the floor 'led to the accused having to adapt his version to place the duvet on the bed which in turn led to a contradiction (Number 8) of when he last saw the deceased'.

Number 8 – During the bail application, Oscar claimed he never saw Reeva get up as his head was in his hands and it was pitch black and she was behind him. Nel argued that Oscar then gave several contradictory versions about the duvet, including 'Reeva had the duvet over the bottom part of her legs' and 'I could see the duvet going up, that is all I could make was a silhouette … I presume that it was her legs under it …'

Number 9 – The state argued Oscar's version about him wanting to cover the blue LED light emitting from the amplifier is so improbable it cannot be reasonably possibly true. 'He had to ensure that he remained with his back to the bed in an attempt to explain why he did not see the deceased leave the bed.'

Number 10 – Nel believed the time-and-position adaptation created a further domino effect more devastating to Oscar's version than he could have foreseen. 'It must be impossible on his version for the denim, which he had in his hands, to land on top of the duvet if the duvet had not already been on the floor.'

Number 11 – Nel insisted it would be 'inconceivable' that Oscar would have failed to mention in the bail application that he spoke to Reeva when he got up. He believed this must be a tailored version to 'avoid a negative inference from the improbable version that he woke up and never ascertained where the deceased was'.

Number 12 – On the state's version, Oscar's mosaic continued to fall apart when he tried to explain his warning to Reeva. 'At first the accused allegedly whispered to Reeva, however, this changed to – "I did not whisper at her, M'Lady. I said it in a soft manner." He realised that "whisper" would imply closeness as part of the normal meaning of the word.'

Number 13 – Nel criticised Oscar's unconvincing evidence about the activation and deactivation of his house alarm. 'Viewed in the light of all the other inconsistencies and contradictions, it becomes significant with the real question being why the accused would even have bothered to deactivate the alarm.' Nel contended that if Oscar was so traumatised from previous events, he would have triggered the alarm. He pointed to a cellphone charger downstairs as evidence that Oscar had gone downstairs to charge his phone.

In short, through the illustration of the baker's dozen, the state was arguing that Oscar's version would have to be rejected because it simply did not make sense.

'M'Lady it was just so many lies in such a short period that the snowball effect became so evident. He tells one lie and he has to continuously build on it, build on it and it just pick up so ridiculously,' exclaimed Nel. 'We will argue that the court reject his version that he heard a sound which he perceived to be an intruder. We argue that there was no moving of fans. The fan was in the doorway, the curtains open and the deceased fled to the toilet with her cellphone. Without the moving of the fans and the closing of the curtains the accused's version is just not reasonably possibly true but in fact false.'

Nel believed that all of this showed Oscar was guilty of murder. 'If the accused's elaborate false version is rejected, the court will have no option but to accept that the accused knew the deceased was in the toilet and fired four shots with *dolus directus* to kill her.'

To even consider Oscar's version, Nel argued the court would have to accept that:

- Reeva decided to relieve herself and did so without saying a word to the accused.
- For no apparent reason, she opened the bathroom window.
- She took her cellphone with her to the bathroom.
- She decided not to switch on any of the lights.
- She did not utter a word whilst the accused was screaming, not even when he was in the bathroom.
- The deceased got up from the toilet to close and lock the door.
- The deceased dressed herself before she was shot.

- The deceased did not hide as a result of all the screaming but stood upright facing the danger.

Nel's delivery was theatrical, his voice low but elevating occasionally as he emphasised a point, picking his foot up on the chair next to him and swinging his glasses around. He laughed at times, as he trailed off sentences, emphasising the incredulity of the claims made by Oscar or his witnesses. But he was sure to maintain decorum, punctuating each remark with the words 'with the utmost respect'.

His baker's dozen delivered, Nel focused on the reason why Oscar shot, the screams, the neighbours and the gastric content of Reeva's stomach. He also asked the questions that had been asked in every hairdressing salon and around ever water cooler and dinner table in the country: why did Reeva take her cellphone to the toilet with her and why didn't she scream when Oscar screamed at her to call the police?

The state anticipated the defence would argue that emphasis should be placed on Professor Derman's testimony about the so-called 'third startle'. This would explain Oscar's reflex action to shoot when he heard what Derman and Oscar suggested was the magazine rack scraping across the floor. In an attempt to discredit Derman's evidence about Oscar's impulse to shoot on hearing the sound of wood moving, Nel argued that Derman was biased and unconvincing. On the state's version there was no startle to trigger the shooting.

'We have four well-grouped shots by the accused. Somebody that is in control not somebody that is not in control. He wants us … he wants the court to believe that he was … acted automatically, did not know what he was doing. When he heard the sound it was exactly when it started and he just fired. He did not, M'Lady. There is four shots, grouped shots and the angle would indicate, M'Lady, that it is all aimed at the toilet bowl,' argued Nel. He was also heavily critical of defence forensic experts Wolmarans and Dixon, suggesting that they were in his experience the worst expert witnesses to testify in a trial.

For Nel, it was crucial to substantiate the state's claim that Oscar and Reeva had had an argument. With no direct evidence, he had to rely on separate pieces of circumstantial evidence. This included the testimony of pathologist Gert Saayman that Reeva had eaten at around 1am, that Estelle van der Merwe heard what she thought was an argument, that Mrs Stipp testified that the bathroom light was on and that the WhatsApp messages on Reeva's phone revealed a turbulent relationship.

Nel also anticipated the defence would spend significant time trying to cast doubt on the neighbours called as witnesses for the state. This was undeniably one of the prosecution's strongest cards – the claims that the neighbours heard the blood-curdling screams of a woman and then gunshots.

He emphasised their reliability as credible witnesses. 'None of them have ever met the accused or the deceased. Furthermore it can safely be argued that other than where these witnesses are each other's spouses, the others have never met each other. They have made their statements independently and the corroboration is exceptional. Not only do they corroborate each other's versions but the objective facts and circumstantial evidence corroborates detailed aspects of their evidence. They all remain steadfast and even explained why they didn't believe it was a man they heard screaming.'

Nel acknowledged that their evidence was not perfect but argued that 'imperfections and possible imperfections are expected of people who witnessed an event without an idea that they were later going to be cross-examined about minute detail and it clearly indicates the absence of a conspiracy to prejudice the accused'.

He insisted that if the court found that the bathroom light was on immediately after or even before the shots were fired, as Mrs Stipp claimed under oath, 'then the accused's version will crash dramatically'. This would show that Oscar and Reeva were awake and likely arguing.

He believed the fact that Reeva must have eaten between 01:00 and 03:17, coupled with the evidence of Estelle van der Merwe that she heard an argument, had to be viewed together. 'It cannot be a mere coincidence that on the same morning that the accused shot and killed the deceased, that Van der Merwe heard a woman's voice as though engaged in an argument and that this argument ended with the gunshots.

'This is a good example of something that seems insignificant if seen in isolation but becomes significant if evaluated with the other evidence. The trial court has to step back and evaluate the mosaic as a whole.'

On the WhatsApp messages extracted from Reeva's phone, Nel argued that they provided the court with insight into the relationship. Bizarrely, he used a quote from an interview clinical psychologist Leonard Carr had done on a radio station. Carr had responded to Roux's suggestion that 90 per cent of the messages were of a loving nature – the psychologist said this equates with arguing that only 10 per cent of your body has cancer.

Judge Masipa, who was largely quiet during proceedings, observing and absorbing, spoke up at this point:

> Court: *But Mr Nel.*
>
> Nel: *Yes, M'Lady?*
>
> Court: *Can you really rely on these Whatsapp messages? Can you really make a proper inference one way or the other?*
>
> Nel: *M'Lady, with the utmost respect, yes M'Lady, because we just read what she wrote. She wrote it. It is not in dispute.*
>
> Court: *No, no, no, I hear what you are saying, but aren't relationships dynamic?*
>
> Nel: *Indeed, indeed.*
>
> Court: *Yes.*
>
> Nel: *Up and down, no problem.*
>
> Court: *The fact that you are unhappy today, does not mean tomorrow you will not be.*

Nel believed that in the absence of anyone other than Oscar saying the couple was happy, the court had to accept the messages.

The state's approach to the gun-related charges was similar to that of the main charge. The intention was to attack Oscar and his version, accusing him of shirking responsibility.

'In summary, he avers that he has done nothing wrong as far as count 3 (sunroof) is concerned. His stance is that the two witnesses gave false evidence against him. He will argue that they have conspired to lie against him. As far as count 2 (Tashas) is concerned he will admit he had the gun in his hand, he will accept that the gun cannot fire without the trigger being pulled but never the less he claims that it did. In this instance he would have the court believe that the impossible inexplicably occurred.'

In wrapping up his argument, Nel became increasingly animated and urged Masipa to convict Oscar. He argued that even if the court accepted Oscar's version that he thought there was an intruder in the toilet, he must be convicted of murder with *dolus directus* – a direct intention to kill.

He also argued that should the court accept Oscar's version of events as reasonably possibly true, he cannot escape a conviction on culpable homicide. 'A reasonable man, armed with a firearm, facing a closed door would not have fired four shots through the door if "provoked" only by a sound.'

It was the state's argument that Oscar was guilty of a premeditated murder.

• • •

When Nel took his seat he left a major question open – one that Roux eagerly attempted to capitalise on. Crucially, Nel had given no explanation whatsoever for the first sounds (at 3:12am) that some of Oscar's neighbours had apparently heard. On the defence version, these were the shots. On the state's version, they seemed simply not to exist. Instead, the state argued the shots had been at 3:17am. It was the defence's contention that the second set of noises was Oscar breaking the door down with the bat.

But if the state believed the shots happened at 3:17am, it would leave Oscar only two minutes to leave the bathroom, discover Reeva was missing, find his cricket bat, break down the door and pull out his dying girlfriend before phoning Johan Stander at 03:19am.

It was the timeline that was out of kilter and this was Barry Roux's focus when he got to his feet to argue his client's case. Roux was indignant. His argument was impassioned and his voice, usually high in pitch, was even squeakier than usual. He was at pains to argue his case, appearing astounded by the state's version.

He used two clear strategies to cast doubt on the prosecution's case. After all, the onus was not on him to prove Oscar's case, only to create reasonable doubt about the state's argument. He turned to what he called the 'objective facts' of the case and showed how the state's version, on flimsy circumstantial evidence, could not be the only inference drawn – there could be other possible inferences. He built his case around a timeline that had been meticulously constructed from the evidence. He plotted the events of Valentine's Day morning to show how the defence's version was the only one that made sense. He coupled this with a blistering attack on Dr Stipp, calling his credibility into doubt and effectively accusing him of lying.

Secondly, he focused significant attention on police incompetence and the credibility of the police experts who testified. He was not claiming 'conspiracy', but rather that the policemen had disrupted the crime scene through folly and that this could not be held against Oscar.

But the most significant issue Roux had with the prosecution was why Nel did not give an explanation for the first set of sounds. 'We were waiting for the state to tell the court, what were those first shots? And you will not find the answer in his heads of argument and you will not find the answer in his argument and one thing you cannot do in a criminal trial, you cannot ignore a serious material objective fact. You cannot do that and the state has done. I know why the state has done it, because it will cause a nosedive of their case on the 03:17 description, what they described as shots. They also do not deal with the cricket bat striking the door, because they cannot. But we will deal with that,' argued Roux.

He rebutted Nel's suggestion that Oscar was anxious on command and not at all times. 'An anxious person and a vulnerable person does not walk around and show his anxiety and his vulnerability all the time. That will come to the fore when there is danger, or a perceived danger,' argued Roux and reminded the judge of Professor Scholtz's idea of the 'Two Oscars' – one confident and one anxious. 'One that you will see, that is everything fine and the other one, that you will not necessarily see when he is vulnerable.'

Roux also focused on the state's failure to call former investigating officer Hilton Botha to the stand to testify. This was ironic because the prosecution had been so critical of the defence for not calling witnesses to back up its claims on the screams.

The bulk of the defence's argument was, however, moulded around the timeline that was carefully constructed. On the defence's version, the timeline appeared as follows:

- 02:20: Security activated guard track next to the house of the accused
- Approximately any time between 03:12–03:14: First sounds
- Approximately 03:14/5: Accused shouting for help
- Approximately any time between 03:12–03:17: Screaming
- ±03:15: Accused seen walking in the bathroom
- 03:15:51 (duration 16 seconds): Dr Stipp's telephone call to security
- 03:16 (duration 58 seconds): Mr Johnson's call to Strubenkop Security
- 03:16:13: Mr Michael Nhlengethwa's first call to security – did not go through
- 03:16:36 (duration 44 seconds): Mr Michael Nhlengethwa's second call to security
- 03:17: Dr Stipp's attempted call to 10111
- 03:17: Second sounds
- 03:19:03 (duration 24 seconds): Accused's call to Johan Stander (Exhibit ZZ8)
- 03:20:05 (duration 66 seconds): Accused's call to 911
- 03:21:33 (duration 9 seconds): Accused's call to security
- 03:22:05 (duration 12 seconds): Security's (Pieter Baba's) call to the accused
- 03:22 Security (Pieter Baba) arrived at the house of the accused
- Approximately 03:22: Johan Stander and Carice Viljoen arrived at the house of the accused
- Approximately 03:23/24: Dr Stipp arrived at the house of the accused
- 03:27:06: Johan Stander's call to 911 in the presence of Dr Stipp
- 03:27:14 (duration nil): Dr Stipp's attempted call to security

- 03:41:58: Ambulance arrived at security gate of Silver Woods estate (Photo YYY)
- Approximately 03:50: Declaration of death by paramedics (Record 2187 – Carice Viljoen) and accused going upstairs to collect identity document of the deceased
- Approximately 03:55: Police arrived at the house of the accused

Using this timeline, Roux attempted to show the court that only the defence's version could make sense. He also suggested the court should place more weight on the evidence of the neighbours who were closest to Oscar's house, such as the Nhlengethwas, as they were more believable. In addition, he defended the decision not call a witness to testify that Oscar sounds like a woman when he is anxious because, he argued, the nearby neighbours had done the job. So too had acoustics expert Ivan Lin.

Attached to the heads of argument was a 26-page document effectively aimed at destroying Dr Stipp's version of events. In an attempt to undermine his credibility, it criticised him heavily for the timing of events he gave during his testimony.

'He was then the only one saying oh, no, that help, help, help, was after the security guards had came to me and after I had made a call at 03:27 and after they had left a few minutes later, which was after 03:30, I heard a man shouting help, help, help and we say, really? Really, because at that time Dr Stipp was at the house of the accused. At that time the accused was … on all the evidence unchallenged, in the foyer with the deceased and with Carice Stander and Johan Stander standing outside, and Dr Stipp examining him. So … examining the deceased. So it cannot be. But I will show you many things about Dr Stipp that cannot be, many many things and Ms Stipp,' bristled Roux.

Stipp claimed he had seen someone walking in Oscar's bathroom after 3:30 – at the same time that, by the accounts of Stander, his daughter Carice and the security guard Baba, Stipp was already inside Oscar's home. The defence was adamant that Dr Stipp, based on the objective evidence, was already out of his own house by 3:27am.

Roux argued that for Stipp to see Oscar through the window, the athlete would have to be wearing his prostheses. This meant Stipp indirectly confirmed that Oscar had attached his legs before he struck the door with the cricket bat, the version the athlete had presented to the court.

The defence counsel also attempted to cast doubt on the testimony of the other neighbours who had testified for the prosecution. He was of the view that

Michelle Burger and Charl Johnson had tailored their versions and that it was unlikely the couple would not have collaborated on them. He also undermined Estelle van der Merwe, stating that her claim that she had heard what sounded like a woman arguing was speculative.

To counter Van der Merwe, Roux pointed out that Mrs Stipp, who was awake just before 3:00am, didn't hear any kind of argument and that the security guards did not notice any disturbance when doing their rounds in the hours before the shooting.

For Roux it was important to cast doubt over any kind of inference that Oscar and Reeva were awake and possibly arguing before the shooting because this suggested a 'motive' for the murder. But this also meant attacking Saayman's testimony on gastric emptying, promptly challenging Saayman's evidence by reminding the court that it was not an absolute, but rather that the pathologist had only 'suggested' that Reeva could have eaten two hours before her death and not definitively – there could be a couple of hours variance either way.

To neutralise the contentious WhatsApp messages, Roux directed the court to the Valentine's Day card Reeva had written to her boyfriend. In it she said it was a good day to tell him she loved him. On the defence's version, this was evidence enough to prove the couple was in a loving relationship.

Roux challenged Nel's argument that Oscar was standing in front of the toilet door, talking to Reeva when he shot. 'The accused was not standing in front of the door. Why, if he wanted to shoot someone in an argument, would he remain in the entrance as if he is scared of whoever was in the toilet? That is far more consistent that he was scared, that he did not trust whoever was in the toilet. Otherwise, yes, walk into the bathroom stand right in front of the door,' said Roux.

He also argued against the contention that it had been a 'good grouping' of shots. 'My Lady, what he should say to you and I am not a shot, I have not touched a firearm for many, many, many years, but if you put me two metres from a door and ask me to fire four shots, I am pretty sure I can get a better grouping. If you say to me aim and fire from two metres, My Lady, it is from here where Ms Johnson is sitting, there fire four shots in the door. We must be careful when we look at that grouping and think that is a person 100 or 150 metres away, then it is a brilliant grouping. But two metres away, is that a good grouping for two metres away?' asked Roux rhetorically.

The defence counsel methodically worked through Nel's 'baker's dozen' of inconsistencies, dismissing them with disregard. 'M'Lady, if that is a baker's dozen, I do not want to eat those cookies. Because it is not a good one. It is really not a good one,' he said emphatically to the amusement of some in the courtroom.

Roux explained it was expected there would be discrepancies between Oscar's bail application and his evidence in the witness box. He also explained Oscar's apparent memory loss under pressure: 'This man suffers from a severe depression in that witness box. Not my evidence, the psychiatrist report. Professor Scholtz's report. Major stress. You cannot just ignore that. So when he tells you: "My memory is not very good at the moment." It makes sense. Do not criticise him for that. It makes sense.'

He also dismissed questions about Reeva's behaviour that had been posed by the state. He didn't think it odd that she had taken her phone to the toilet – it could have been used for light or to look at social media. 'M'Lady, if you work through the WhatsApp messages, you will find WhatsApp messages from the deceased in the toilet at night. I can understand it. You take it to give you light there. People do it all the time when they get up, with their cellphones. All the time. That does not defy logic. Why must you switch on a light, you walk with your cellphone, especially the younger generation. They ... I want to say like battery and torch, but they gel so well with their cellphones, that it is not strange.'

Roux also explained it wasn't unusual that Reeva had not shouted out when she heard Oscar scream because she did not want to give her position away to a possible intruder.

'She could have done two things. She could have given her position away, she heard him screaming intruders in the house, they must get out. Or she can think I must hide, I must keep quiet. I do not want them to get to me. It works both ways, there is no special potion there. There is no special answer there, there is no special probability.'

Having to his mind answered the state's case, Roux went on the offensive and began to deal with the law. It was important for him to explain what was potentially viewed as Oscar's changing defence or different versions. He also had to prove to the court that it was not the athlete's intention to kill anyone, but that he felt threatened and was acting on reflex.

Oscar could not be considered a 'reasonable man' by the conventional test, he stated. 'The law is not that reasonable man from 1960 in his grey suit and his grey shoes. We have moved away. We ... we referred to the case to say it has moved on. You have to look at the person in the same position with the same abilities/disabilities,' Roux insisted. He argued that in discharging the firearm, Oscar did so because of an increased startle response. The startle response was reflexive and Oscar could not be held accountable because he lacked capacity in the involuntary reflexive response. He also emphasised that the startle response was exaggerated or increased due to the 'slow burn' effect of his disability over years and his consequent increased vulnerability.

Roux pointed to Professor Derman's evidence to back this up and criticised Nel for questioning his credibility. 'He is highly, highly, highly qualified. He is the most qualified person in the country. Whatever he was saying to the court, he backed up with research, with authoritative articles, publications on that very point. He was not saying something because he says that is what I am thinking.'

The defence counsel then proffered a risky analogy in comparing Oscar to a woman who had been abused over a long period of time and who had then snapped and killed her abuser. He used this to demonstrate his theory on 'slow burn'. But Judge Masipa, a known advocate for women's rights, was quick to question the analogy:

Court: *You spoke about the 'slow burn'. I understand it when you speak about an abused woman situation, how does it apply to the accused in this case?*

Roux: *I will explain it and that is fully dealt with in the evidence of Professor Derman, but I am going to sum it up and also refer to: you are a little boy without legs, you experience daily that disability and the effect of this. You experience daily that you cannot run away. I am not talking about abuse here. You know I cannot run away. I cannot run away. I do not have a flight response. We all know that we have three responses: freeze, fight and flight, primal. What Professor Derman was at pains to explain, is to say that is well known in research and his ... also his experience with that disability, over time you get an exaggerated fight response, that is why he would go and not run away. That is the 'slow burn effect'. Not abuse. It was just a brilliant ... the word was for the first time used in relation to abuse. So that constant reminder I do not have legs, I cannot run away, I am not the same, that is with him. He can pretend ... he can pretend that he is fine and he is wonderful with his legs on and we see this athlete and that is what Professor Scholtz was saying, and I will invite you to look at that part, when he says we have two Oscars ... we must understand that 'slow burn' and the anxiety. If you are anxious and if you are vulnerable, and if you have the 'slow burn effect', you do not go to bed and cannot sleep, lie awake, but the moment you are confronted with danger, or perceived danger, it comes to the fore. Then ... then you are*

> *compromised because of the 'slow burn', because of the anxiety,*
> *because of your real position in that sense and it was in that sense*
> *that I say, the abuse is different, but it is the same. Without legs,*
> *abuse. Abuse, abuse. So ultimately when that woman picks up that*
> *firearm … we can use the common word, I have had enough, I am*
> *not shooting you because you have just assaulted me, not because*
> *of one punch with a fist in my face, I would never have shot you*
> *because of one punch with a fist in my face, but if you have done it*
> *60, 70 times, that effect of that over time it filled the cup to the brim*
> *that is … in that sense, My Lady.*

Essentially, the defence case was that, in the face of danger, Oscar had to choose between fight, freeze or flight and over time the fight reflex had become exaggerated because, with his disability, 'flight' was not an option. Roux went so far as to demonstrate this by slamming the desk in front of him for effect. 'You are vulnerable. You have the effects of the "slow burn" over many years. You are anxious. You are trained as an athlete to react to sound, sprinters. We all know him. You are trained. He says, take all those factors into account and he stands now with his finger ready to fire if necessary, and he stands there and then …' Roux banged his hand on wood.

Roux stressed that he was not putting forward contradictory defences and explained what he was asking of the court in his heads of argument:

> *If the Honourable Court were to find that the Accused did not discharge*
> *the shots in a reflexive response, consequent upon an exaggerated star-*
> *tle, which made him incapable of acting in accordance with his appre-*
> *ciation of right and wrong, or incapable of acting, then the alternative*
> *finding can only be that the Accused intentionally discharged the shots,*
> *in the belief that the intruder/s was/were coming out of the toilet, to*
> *attack the Accused and the Deceased.*

But Roux did make one significant concession during his closing argument. This was around the shooting incident at Tashas. Oscar took partial responsibility. 'He is guilty, My Lady, he is guilty on the first alternative, that he negligently used that firearm and causing the discharge. It must be like that. He says that in so many words. He says, "I made a mistake,"' said Roux, raising the question as to why Oscar did not plead guilty on this charge from the outset. This would have negated the need to call several witnesses who discredited his character.

Roux persisted with his client's innocence on the sunroof charges and suggested that Darren Fresco and Samantha Taylor had conspired against Oscar. He insinuated that Fresco had testified to save himself and that Taylor's motive was to get back at Oscar as she believed he had cheated on her. He even argued that Fresco should not be granted indemnity from prosecution, a decision Masipa had to make.

With Oscar's father in the public gallery, having allegedly refused to give a statement to the defence to back up his son's claim on the ammunitions charges, Roux persisted with his client's version. Oscar did not believe he should be convicted for keeping his father's ammunition in his safe.

In closing, Roux urged the judge to consider Oscar's position: the 'slow burn' of his disability over his lifetime, his startle response, his anxiety.

> *It comes down to that split second, that one minute or 20 seconds, I do not know how long it was, or 30 seconds in the accused's life, where he was standing at the entrance to the bathroom, firearm pointed at the door, that is what this case is all about.*
>
> *Should he have … in the event if the court not finding reflexive, should he have discharged the shots. Not confusing it with dolus, as a reasonable person in his position.*
>
> *If the answer is yes, that is the end of the case. If the answer is no, then all the other aspects would only be mitigation, he must be convicted.*
>
> *We have explained in the heads of argument, why we believe in those peculiar circumstances he was not negligent. We ask you to consider it and then in your discretion, you and the learned assessors consider that crucial point, taking into account three o'clock in the morning. Knowledge of danger of people entering the house, standing with the firearm. Should he have discharged the firearm, yes or no. We have made our submissions then, M'Lady, and we say this is what the case is all about.*

• • •

Late on the Friday afternoon, both men had made their cases. They had invested all of themselves in their closing arguments. Oscar, watching the display of expertise and performance from a prime seat in the courtroom, knew there was no more to be done. The arguments had been made.

It had been an excruciating six months for those who had packed the public gallery day after day, most notably the extended Pistorius family, Reeva's parents and the Myers. And then, in what was seen as a final act of resistance, Oscar's aunt Lois Pistorius, glowered at Nel and asked in Afrikaans: '*Kry jy nie skaam nie?* [Aren't you ashamed?],' *Beeld* newspaper reported. Nel didn't hear her and didn't respond.

Later that afternoon, Oscar tweeted his gratitude to those who had walked with him over the past few months:

> Thank you to my loved ones and those that have been there for me, who have picked me up and helped me through everything.

Over the 39 court days of the trial, a total of 37 witnesses had taken the stand. Thousands of pages of court transcripts had been produced and dozens of exhibits introduced.

Judge Masipa, a 66-year-old former social worker and journalist, held in high esteem by her contemporaries despite her limited experience as an advocate, now had to take it all away and mull it over. She and her two assessors had to deliberate and determine whether the version put forward by the state was the only reasonable, possible version of events – did the prosecution meets its 'burden of proof'? Did a global superstar – reckless and gun-toting, incapable of taking responsibility for his actions – deliberately, intentionally, kill his beautiful model girlfriend in cold blood in a premeditated murder? Alternatively, she had to consider whether enough doubt had been cast by the defence in posing its version. Did a vulnerable, anxious young man, affected by a lifetime of disability and a turbulent upbringing, fearful of violent criminals, desperately try to protect the love of his life in the only way he could, and was he now suffering through the most monumental tragedy?

There was also a murky grey area between these two polarised perspectives, which Masipa would have to navigate by considering complex legal interpretations and nuanced understandings of the law to reach a final verdict.

The Scales of Justice

There is a perception in South Africa that money and influence can buy justice. This notion has been reinforced by a series of legal decisions over the past few years that have been highlighted in the media.

National Police Commissioner Jackie Selebi was convicted of corruption, sent to prison for 15 years, spent less than a year in the hospital wing of a correctional facility and was then released on medical parole, suffering from kidney problems.

A decision was taken by the acting head of the National Prosecuting Authority to withdraw corruption charges against President Jacob Zuma based on so-called spy tapes alleging political interference. This was despite Zuma's financial adviser Schabir Shaik being convicted on a reverse charge of corruption. Shaik was also released on medical parole, having been diagnosed with hypertension.

But perhaps the case that has most entrenched this perception, rightly or wrongly, is that of Fred van der Vyfer who was acquitted of murdering his girlfriend, Stellenbosch student Inge Lotz. With their wealth, the Van der Vyfers were able to fly in the very best international forensic experts to expose what was widely considered the questionable practices of the police investigators. They were able to lay bare what appeared to be a conspiracy against Fred; he was found not guilty of the murder and to this day no one has been convicted of the crime.

Stephen Tuson, associate professor at the School of Law at the University of the Witwatersrand, believes that this perception is based in reality. 'I think it is absolutely true if you can hire a competent defence. But not only that but competent investigators and competent science and forensic investigators, competent reports from all sorts of specialists – you will be able to counter everything the state raises against you, and there is absolutely no doubt in my mind that money buys you a better quality of justice, without exception. Because you can afford to make all the preliminary applications for all the documentation and evidence and forensics you want. All of these processes and all of these investigations cost an enormous amount of money and the attorney's time costs a lot.'

• • •

While the perception remains that money and influence do indeed buy a better quality of justice, research appears to show differently. Rather, Oscar's status and celebrity could have a detrimental effect to his right to justice.

In fact, at the close of the defence case, Barry Roux told the court: 'We were unable to call a number of witnesses because they refused, and didn't want their voices heard all over the world.' Of course, the defence could have exercised its right to subpoena the witnesses to testify, but that did not happen. 'It's not Barry's style,' as one source close to the defence team put it.

As an example, Samantha Greyvenstein told us that while she did consult with the defence team in chambers, she ultimately chose not to testify for them. 'Everything that I said in my statement was true and I didn't feel that I had anything else to contribute. Everything else would have been an elaboration. I wanted to stay completely neutral and I didn't want to be in the limelight. I prefer not to throw myself and my family into the media,' said Greyvenstein.

Oscar's lawyers had opposed the application to have the trial broadcast and, in the end, believed that televising the trial counted against him. They argued this would lead to an unfair trial and create a media circus and that Oscar's trial should be treated like any other. The concern was that televising proceedings would allow witnesses to tailor their evidence – an allegation that emerged several times during Roux's cross-examination.

This notion was again highlighted when the media juxtaposed the massively high-profile Oscar Pistorius murder trial with the case underway in the courtroom alongside Court GD. Thato Kutumela was on trial for raping and murdering his pregnant model girlfriend Zanele Khumalo in 2011. While Oscar's fate was being decided next door, Judge Johan Kruger sentenced the 28-year-old to 20 years in prison.

Law expert Kelly Phelps says that despite widely held public beliefs, research actually suggests that, if anything, fame of the accused leads to harsher treatment by the courts. 'With regards to money – people seem to assume that money buys a miscarriage of justice. This is grossly unfair. If anything, money levels the playing field between the state and the defence, rather than tilting the scales in favour of the accused. The state has huge resources available to it in prosecuting cases that far outweighs the resources of most accused persons. The focus should be on getting poor people access to justice to the same extent that wealthy people have access to justice, not on removing the access to justice of wealthy people. The fact that wealth evens the playing field is a universal reality in all legal systems, not something unique to South Africa.'

And research tends to back up what Phelps says. In 'Professional Athletes Held to a Higher Standard and Above the Law: A Comment on High-Profile Criminal Defendants and the Need for States to Establish High-Profile Courts', LN Robinson examined the treatment of professional athletes. The study found that professional athletes' celebrity status and the national media coverage that accompanies their cases mean that some athletes are singled out as sacrificial lambs while allowing other athletes to receive preferential treatment.

'High-profile defendants, although occasionally above the law, nevertheless frequently find themselves subject to increased scrutiny due to their status and visibility, and that as a result a special court system is necessary to protect their right to a fair trial.'

With that said, however, the study also found that when an athlete is actually sentenced to jail, the system often provides that person with preferential treatment while the sentence is being served:

> For instance, while in jail awaiting trial, it was reported that OJ Simpson received special treatment not afforded to other inmates. He received a hot shower every day, was given unlimited visitation privileges, hot dinners, extra time out of his cell to stretch his legs, more access to the telephone, private no-contact visits with his girlfriend and children, and visitors on Christmas Day.

A recent study out of Warwick University, entitled 'Celebrity Adjudication: Comparative Analyses of United States Verdict Rates for Celebrity Defendants', examined celebrity status as an outside influence on judicial decision-making. The researcher examined 303 celebrity verdicts from 1998 to 2010 in order to shed light on whether celebrities are adjudicated in the same or a similar manner as non-celebrities. The findings suggest that celebrities do not receive any special treatment at trial, and are in fact convicted at a 12.1 per cent higher rate than non-celebrity defendants.

One possible explanation for this outcome is the idea of betrayal. 'We put our faith in these people, we emulate them in many sociological ways; we dress like them, we eat what they eat, and we tend to admire them. When they fail to live up to our lofty ideals for their behaviour we feel betrayed and take our revenge.' Another possible explanation is envy. 'So, though we admire celebrities, we may secretly want them to fail because they frequently have the status, wealth, and attention we do not. When given the opportunity, we punish them.'

Much of the research focuses on cases in the United States where juries decide guilt or innocence. In South Africa, of course, trained judicial officers and assessors make the decision and not juries of laypeople.

• • •

Despite the research, reading the public temperature in South Africa, the assumption was that with his own wealth and that of his family, Oscar would be able to hire the very best experts in the world, that he would turn to foreigners to assist him and that his own forensic team would vastly outsmart the local policemen and investigators.

While the defence did go to American company The Evidence Room to help in recreating the events of Valentine's Day in 3D animation, no foreign expert or world-renowned authority was called as a witness for the defence.

However, it did emerge that during a two-week adjournment in April, the legal team contacted US forensic expert Alexander Jason, who referred them to acoustics expert Susan Witterick at dBx Acoustics in the UK. Witterick stated on her online blog that she was briefed by Oscar's defence team and was put on standby to get on a plane to be in the witness box within a fortnight. She said, in the end, the team opted to use Ivan Lin because 'they couldn't afford to use me'.

It also appeared as though even the initial experts they approached didn't remain involved. It seemed that the defence then had to make do with what they could and those they approached only conducted tests well after the trial had begun. In fact, defence counsel Mannie Witz went as far as to call the defence 'lastminute. com' and 'Johnny Come Lately' when commenting on the team's preparation.

During the course of the trial, both the defence and prosecution teams drew criticism from commentators for their tactics and strategy. This was inevitable when the trial was being so closely scrutinised and being broadcast blow by blow. The legal fraternity in South Africa is a small one, and behind the scenes of the High Court theatre, a fascinating version of how things may have played out could be heard. Most lawyers see it as unethical to criticise their colleagues in public, particularly in a field dominated by ego and competition. Instead, they would only speak anonymously. And despite the chatter in legal circles and the extensive speculation about what was going on behind closed doors, only those within the legal teams truly knew the circumstances. That didn't stop the sharpest legal minds from volunteering an opinion.

• • •

What was potentially going on behind the scenes within Oscar's legal team? Was it all about who was calling the shots and who held the real power?

'I know for a fact there is massive infighting between Roux and Oldwadge over the instructions which they give to Oscar,' comments a top criminal defence attorney. 'They speak to Oscar about a specific incident and then Kenny kind of takes over and says this is important. Kenny took over. He's hired because Oscar's brother was defended by Kenny in other matters.'

A source close to the defence team, who does not want to be identified, confirms there was a disagreement between Oldwadge and Roux. 'There was a serious fallout. I don't know what it was about but they had a big fight. They spent an hour behind closed doors and when Kenny came out he was furious.'

The attorney believes that the root problem is Oscar's choice of attorney. Brian Webber has very little experience in criminal cases and primarily practises in corporate litigation. 'I don't think that Oscar's lawyer has done a criminal matter in the last 20 years. It's an enormous misconception that the lawyer just sits there in the back – he's the one who sits down with his client and goes through the case. The buck has to stop somewhere. I prepare the living shit out of a guy. Barry wasn't briefed properly on this. Barry needs to feel heavily supported.'

A senior advocate with decades of experience fully agrees with this notion. 'Advocates carry out the instructions of the attorney. They can give advice but can't tell you what to do. An advocate's job is to prepare a case for litigation and litigate. They can determine strategy, but they can only advise. I can say to you, these are your options, having heard your version, but I can't adapt your version or panel beat it. Your attorney in discussion with you will give instructions and the advocate must do it. If a client says, "I want you to stand on your head and wear pink underwear," then you fucking do it. But you can't withdraw for nebulous reasons. If you're available, you have to take it. It's called the cab-rank rule. Ethically you're not supposed to choose – some people would never get represented if that were the case.'

Just about every lawyer we spoke to was of the opinion that the defence strategy was wrong from the outset and that such a detailed version should never have been put on record at the bail application.

'Remember what his rights are, to say fuck all. He had already verbally told the police his version. They're calling the doctor to the funeral to be honest,' says the attorney.

The senior advocate agrees: 'I thought they dealt with it very poorly. That statement is deadly. It amounts to a confession for murder. I presume that they felt cornered. The state only opposed bail to get a version. All you need to do is give a version, very bland, as non-committal as possible. You don't even have to give a version at all. I would have stuck with "intruder, big fright, fired shots. It's the morning after, I actually don't even know, my client is not able to depose to a statement, and we're considering hospitalising him." I'm sure Barry was livid with that statement.'

However, it is understood that Roux did play a role in settling on the affidavit.

The attorney believes Roux allowed Nel great latitude in cross-examination. 'You can't allow Gerrie to stand up and go on and on and on. Barry could have jumped up. Gerrie will cross-examine an innocent or honest person into looking very bad. He is the representative of the people and his duty here is to get the truth in front of court. Nothing is going to stop him. Gerrie is fucking unstoppable. He gave Oscar the hiding of his life.'

Another top advocate, who has defended many a criminal, says the problem from the outset was that 'the tail wagged the dog' and the 'fuck-up of a bail application'. It all came down to strategy.

'In the plea explanation, it was putative private defence. When they saw it didn't tie in, then they went with temporary, non-pathological incapacity. It's what they do in road rage cases – if I lost my temper to the point that I couldn't control myself, I get off. It's an "emotional storm".

'They took a principled decision right in the beginning not to use automatism because they denied the argument. But there's no hybrid. The public and the courts didn't see it coming and then Vorster came and it changed for the third time. They wanted to keep both doors open but they could have cut a deal right in the beginning.'

Advocate Mannie Witz was willing to go on record about what he thought of the strategy of both the prosecution and the defence. He assisted Darren Fresco in drawing up his statement and has been a prominent commentator throughout the trial. Witz says Oscar's legal team had no choice but to go with the intruder defence as they were 'married to it', because it was what Oscar had told Dr Stipp and the Standers in the minutes after the shooting.

'They must have been aware that their client, when they got instructions, must have told them that Stipp was there. He had told Stipp that he had made a mistake and he had told Stander. I think he had to stick to that version. Especially when a guy like Dr Stipp is a person who is a complete independent – he's got nothing to do with any of the parties – if he's going to come along and say that, I think you're married to that version. I think what the defence tried to do, they tried to taper that version in with a very difficult defence, which is putative private defence.'

Witz thinks they were trapped into the bail application statement. 'There's been a lot of criticism going around about the bail application statement, and I mean he's got very experienced guys who appeared for him. The defence knew from the beginning that what they set out in the bail application was going to be used eventually, but I think the state was actually quite cunning and quite shrewd in that bail application.'

Witz says he's been surprised at how tardy the defence appears to have been in preparing witnesses. 'A lot of the witnesses have been after-the-event witnesses. Like Professor Merryll Vorster. Merryll is a very competent woman, very experienced and she knows this game, and I mean they only got hold of her after Oscar had given his evidence and after everything, and then she then came out with this anxiety disorder. I found it a bit strange. They never gave the reports to the state, so the state was really caught unawares and a lot of these reports were done after the event.'

Like the other lawyers we interviewed, Witz is of the opinion that the core problem is an attorney who isn't experienced in criminal law and a potential fallout within the defence team.

'Brian's not a criminal lawyer. It's the second one he's ever done in his whole life and the last one. Brian used to do all the Pistorius family stuff and do all the endorsement and the civil stuff and commercial work when they needed an attorney. He just said to me this is the second and the last in his whole career and he has been on the go for 35 years,' says Witz.

He has also heard about the friction within the defence team. 'There's talk about it. There's a lot of talk around the chambers about what's going down and what happened, etc. No one knows what the real truth is.'

Regardless of the speculation in legal circles, it seems as though the reality is different. A source close to the defence legal team rubbished many of these speculations.

'There was really not a fallout at all between Barry and Kenny. They work very well together and have a good relationship. Barry calls the shots and Kenny does the groundwork. Barry will never be intimidated by Kenny.

'The real fallout was between Brian and Kenny. For a day or two there was a bit of sulking. Kenny felt that some of the things he asked from Brian were not forthcoming quickly enough. To say that Kenny and Uncle Arnold are big mates is not true. Arnold was sort of interfering and Kenny took no nonsense. Arnold was saying "do this, do that" and Kenny didn't like it.'

The source suggests criticism of Webber's lack of experience was, however, spot on. 'Brian was just out of touch with the criminal aspects, the strategies, he was lacking the experience.'

The source is quick to explain the defence team's strategy around the bail application statement, saying that criticism is simply unfair. It's also understood that Oscar was keen to take the stand at the bail application already but he was stopped by his lawyers.

'We all know in a bail application that you stay clear of the merits. Oscar wanted to tell his story. He wanted to give evidence at the bail application already. Barry knew he would not have coped. He wanted his version out there, understanding the dangers. He wanted to tell the truth. He didn't want them later to say that he's coming up with a version. He insisted on giving evidence and the legal team said "No". They would rather take the route of an affidavit. In fact, in giving that version, the legal team believed it would save his credibility ultimately in the trial. There will always be contradictions in a version but the material gist remained the same throughout all his versions. Ultimately, the judge would have realised that Oscar's version is not a fabricated afterthought premised on a reading of the docket and trial preparation.

'Barry didn't like it but felt that once Oscar's version was confirmed by the experts, that it was not unsafe to go that route.'

Why didn't the defence choose to go with overseas forensic experts, as it was widely thought would happen?

'There were huge time limitations to get experts and the only people they could get were Wollie and Dixon. With Dixon, for example, Barry never anticipated he would go beyond the agreed ambit of his evidence. They couldn't go internationally to bring in expert witnesses due to financial constraints,' said the source.

And why did it appear that so much was done at the very last minute? The source states that this is not true and the defence was never in disarray, as has been suggested by observers.

'The only witness that was instructed belatedly was Merryll Vorster, for two reasons – the one was that another witness became unavailable very late and when they considered Oscar's evidence, they realised that the role that his anxiety played should be explained. They realised they had no choice but to call another expert witness and that's why they went to Merryll.

'With Van Schalkwyk, the social worker, she went to the legal team after

Oscar's evidence, telling them that it was unfair what was being said in cross-examination that it was "all about Oscar". She said she wanted to testify to correct that perception and Barry called her so quickly because the next expert witness was not available the following day and, rather than standing down and waste court time and money, he put the witness on the stand. They thought she was a great witness.

'Dixon's and Wolmarans's tests weren't done late. Barry wasn't happy with the cricket bat test and he sent them back to redo it again. It's not a criticism of Barry's but of the efficiency of the defence witnesses.'

While colleagues are highly critical of Roux's apparent failure to protect the accused while he was on the stand and not object as actively as he could have done, those close to the defence legal team suggest this was an intentional move by the senior counsel. He had read the judge and did not want to provoke her.

'There were many instances where objections to the cross-examination of Nel would have been justified. However, it was felt that the judge would see right through what was taking place and that the unfair cross-examination would be converted into a negative for the state as it was obvious that the judge was not impressed with Gerrie's style of cross-examination. The defence also did not want to be seen to protect Oscar in his evidence all the time as that in itself would create a negative perception.'

A source close to the legal team is dismissive of gossip and baseless speculation and was ready to hit back, taking a swipe at Advocate Witz, a regular on TV during the trial. Those in the defence team have also all heard the rumblings that have been going on in chamber corridors, 'always by the same people, who should not necessarily be in a position to criticise.

'Any experienced lawyer will realise that he or she does not know the full facts and the complexity of the facts and to sit on the sideline and to shoot from the hip is not only dangerous but outright stupid. It's for that very reason that you would not see prominent counsel on television shows as they know that it would not only be improper but that they are not privy to the full facts and the difficulties in the matter. However, those wanting to improve their image would revel in the attention,' says the source. 'You'll never see Barry doing that.'

• • •

While the prosecution team did not appear to be struck by the same internal politics and wrangling, it wasn't without its problems. During the course of the trial Gerrie Nel's style of cross-examination shocked many. Commentators described it as a 'scorched earth approach', 'win at all costs' mentality and suggested that deliberately humiliating or laughing at a witness was 'atrocious behaviour'.

However, the real criticism of the prosecution would only come after judgment when it appeared to many that the state had got its tactics wrong. The sentiment was that they had overreached, been too greedy and gone for too much right at the outset.

An experienced criminal advocate, who doesn't want to be named, has strong views on the prosecution's approach. 'I think their strategy was poor. I think they went for a big hallelujah and they didn't have to. If they had just gone quietly for murder and not dressed it up as anything more than just a murder, then it would have been different. There wouldn't have been all this confusion with different kinds of *dolus*. But they had to go with a thing called premeditated murder, which doesn't exist in South Africa, and conflated the issues. We didn't have to have sobbing and screaming and neighbours coming by and trajectories and *kak*. None of that was necessary.

'Murder in South Africa is not a big deal – we get convictions for murder every day. They put so much extra stuff in to try and dress it up like the number one murder in the world when in fact it isn't. The personalities are irrelevant.'

A source within the state's team disagrees, saying they were never distracted by the personalities or the media attention. 'It was a case like any other. Honestly, it was just a case and I think our reaction was more that we would want to do it because, even before we went to court and were listening to the media and everyone speculating about oh poor Oscar and poor Oscar, we were just thinking oh those could have been our daughters. Is her life now less important because someone important would have killed her? No way. And for us we just went to court. That's it. We didn't know it would get the kind of attention it did. We knew it would get media attention, but it wasn't important.'

The criminal advocate says that while decisions would have been made by the whole team, the lead prosecutor's style does have an impact. 'It's Gerrie's style to go for the big thing and we've seen it happen so many times. It's a common error in prosecution. It is his style to go for broke, like he did with Jackie Selebi. This case is simple – it's just a murder. There was a human being in a very small, enclosed place. Another human being fired a gun into an enclosed space – on his own version expecting another human being to be there. That is murder.'

Litigation attorney David Dadic agrees that the state was overly ambitious and its tactics backfired. 'I do believe that the evidence never got to the point of where they wanted it to get to regarding a conviction of premeditated murder. Should the same energy and resources have been spent entirely on proving *eventualis* rather than the difficult convention of premed, we may have seen a different result.'

In the same way that commentators say the defence was 'married' to Oscar's bail version, so too was the prosecution 'married' to its approach to the bail process.

'When the bail hearing happened, Nel wanted it to be a Schedule 6 premed because he wanted a version from Oscar in bail. He wanted to attach him to a version. He left himself with that difficulty. It was a good move at the time to get a version from Oscar, but it backfired because he had to stick by that charge and prove it. He couldn't leave it as a tactic,' says Dadic.

Like the criminal advocate, Dadic says the court would not have got confused if the prosecution had not led unnecessary evidence. 'It would have been less confusing in the court's mind. The waters were very coloured by over-evidence – WhatsApp messages and iPhones and all these things that at the end of the day didn't even come into bearing.'

Kelly Phelps says she has never been able to understand why the state persisted with a premeditated murder charge. 'I have never doubted the sincerity of their belief and their approach, but I have always been absolutely confounded as to what that sincerity of belief is based on. There has never ever been any substantial evidence. If you read the defence's heads of argument, where they have trawled through all the evidence and built up this chronology based on incontrovertible facts, it's the one thing that you can't dispute. I don't see how anyone can read that timeline and not be utterly convinced.'

By presenting a premeditated murder case to the court under the context of massive media hype and live broadcast, the state might also have influenced the 'court of public opinion'. Those laypeople watching, who don't understand the law, have drawn their own conclusions and these could be incredibly difficult to shift.

Phelps believes it is unfair to Pistorius and to Steenkamp's family. 'I think it's forever changed public opinion and I don't think it will ever be reversed. I think they've absolutely prosecuted the case in the media,' she says. 'How many people are ever going to read those heads of argument? I think this really has been trial by media. You cannot prosecute a case on a hunch. It's a disservice to the victim's family because it creates white noise.'

As is inevitable with any criminal case, especially one run so openly and so intensely scrutinised, everyone will always believe their view to be right. The law can also be open to interpretation and so it was with the State vs OLC Pistorius. Everyone had an opinion.

Judgment Day

The back door to courtroom GD swung open, revealing two elevated moon-boots and a wheelchair. It was carefully steered down the carpeted slope past the teeming public gallery, avoiding several armed officers in bulletproof vests, and through the cordoned-off main courtroom area, before coming to a stop in an open space next to the defence counsel's desks.

Carl Pistorius was parked, ready for judgment. The incongruity of the image of Oscar's brother, one arm in a plaster cast and clearly incapacitated from a bad car accident he had been involved in weeks earlier, contributed to the surreal nature of the entire picture and the almost circus-like atmosphere at play in and around the High Court in Pretoria.

Outside, a fried-chicken stand did a roaring trade to international journalists who had jetted in for the big story. A woman with a quirky tulle hairpiece held up a painted banner reading, 'Oscar you were, you are, will always be inspiration, a HERO'. Another, advertising herself as Mrs United Nation Limpopo, clutched a large poster featuring newspaper clippings of herself with rhinos, alongside pictures of Oscar and Reeva. A drunk Afrikaans-speaking man in khaki and a red hat danced with ANC members in yellow overalls parading signs calling for Oscar to rot in jail if found guilty. We had gone down the rabbit hole and emerged into this madness.

Inside, the extended Pistorius clan packed into the front row – aunts, uncles, cousins, doting sister Aimee and father Henke, panama hat in hand. Barry and June Steenkamp sat in the same row on the other side of the courtroom, flanked by their advocate and, as usual, members of the ANC Women's League; Barry's brother Mike and his wife had joined the family for the first time, making this the biggest Steenkamp showing since the start of the trial. The Myers family sat a few seats away. Darren Fresco paced anxiously up and down; his wife, in a short leopard-print dress, sat in the Steenkamp camp. Marc Batchelor, his peroxide hair gelled to a peak, sat in the back benches. The court orderly, responsible for announcing the judge's entrance, manned the front door. The feisty prosecutor, the calculated defence counsel, the team of forensic investigators, the clerk, the stenographers, the journalists who had been following the twists and turns of the case: all the characters were in place, bar one …

• • •

A mere two years earlier the Blade Runner had been paraded on the global stage of the Olympic Games, an icon who had overcome adversity to inspire and be lauded worldwide.

It was for a different reason that Oscar was now walking through the media, four rows deep on either side, spilling over with onlookers and journalists and their cameras on ladders, into the courtroom to face judgment in his murder trial. He strode through the pack, his game face on, the image of concentration – a flashback to him on the track moments before the starter's gun fired.

Escorted by his ever-present entourage of familial bodyguards, Oscar stopped to greet various relatives. However, his focus was clear as he headed to the wheelchair and Carl, making for the brother who had been by his side through-out his life, and who had not allowed time in intensive care to prevent him from witnessing this momentous event.

Oscar bent down, kissed Carl on the cheek and gave him a hearty hug, embrac-ing his brother for several seconds. As he stepped back, Oscar's face momentar-ily betrayed him. Tears weren't far away, but for now he held them in, composed and focused, as he walked to the dock where he took his seat as the accused. The final act of this drama was about to begin.

• • •

'*Staan in die hof!* Stand in the court!'

As she did for each session of the trial, Judge Thokozile Masipa carefully made her way towards her chair, leaning against the wall for support. A stand had been placed on the bench in front of her seat, a thick wad of paper perched on it. Without any introduction, she launched straight into business. The only diver-sion was first to tell the accused that he could remain seated until she instructed him to rise.

Oscar gave little away, staring intently at Masipa as she began to read from the bundle of white paper on the stand in front of her. 'In 2013 the accused stayed at house number 286 Bush Willow Street ...'

The expectation had been that Masipa's ruling would be dull and dense, containing summaries of the evidence of each of the witnesses who had testified and extensive reference to case law and precedent. The thinking was that she would deliver her judgment over two days and keep her cards close to her chest, only revealing towards the end which way she was going to rule.

Masipa ran through her summary of the facts of the matter, those issues that were not in dispute and Oscar's plea explanation at the start of the trial six months earlier. The court was hushed, but for the incessant hammering on laptop keyboards. Some people scribbled away on notepads. Masipa first set out 'the issues', explaining that these were limited to whether 'at the time when the accused shot and killed the deceased, he had the requisite intention and if so whether there was any premeditation'.

She did not see the need to summarise all the evidence placed before her. 'It shall not be possible, nor will it serve any purpose, to rehash the evidence in detail,' she explained. 'It shall also be fruitless to repeat every submission by counsel. This court has, however, taken all the evidence and that includes all the exhibits and all submissions by counsel into consideration.'

The first significant issue tackled was Oscar's claim in his plea explanation that the defence would show the tampering and contamination of the crime scene. He had promised under oath that witnesses would be called to back up this allegation, but that did not happen. Masipa found that three issues arose around this topic: was the scene tampered with, how long was a missing extension cord and were the police pictures authentic?

'This court is of the view that these issues have paled into insignificance when one has regard to the rest of the evidence,' she said. For Masipa, all the talk of tampering and contamination had come to naught and was of no consequence. She cleared that issue off the table and moved on quickly, much faster than expected.

Immediately, Masipa began to address the state's main case of premeditated murder. Speculation in legal circles ahead of the judgment had been that the prosecution had probably not done enough to actually prove this charge, despite dedicating a large portion of its case to it.

The state contended that there had been an argument in the early hours of Valentine's Day, that in a fit of rage Oscar had armed himself and chased a fleeing Reeva into the bathroom before intentionally shooting and killing her through the closed toilet door. To attempt to prove this, the state had relied heavily on the testimony of neighbours Estelle van der Merwe, Michelle Burger and her husband Charl Johnson, as well as Johan and Annette Stipp. It had also pointed to the evidence of pathologist Gert Saayman on Reeva's stomach contents as evidence that she was awake and eating in the hours before she was killed. In addition, the state used WhatsApp messages exchanged between Oscar and Reeva to illustrate rocky moments in the relationship and to suggest that the two of them could have had an argument.

To counter, the defence carefully crafted a timeline of events constructed around objective facts, most notably the phone records. It had pointed to this timeline as evidence that the state's version of what had happened simply could not be true. Crucially, the defence differed from the prosecution on the sequence of events and on the contentious dispute about the two sets of noises.

How would Masipa deal with the state's lack of explanation around the first set of noises? In setting out her ruling, the judge said, '[The] nub of what is in issue can be divided into three neat categories: gunshots, sounds made by a cricket bat striking against a door and screams in the early hours of the morning.'

Masipa established that it was clear that there was a misinterpretation of some of the sounds. Some witnesses had heard more than four shots; some neighbours might have missed some of the sounds because they had been asleep or because their attention was focused elsewhere, for example, if they were on the phone at the time. It could also have been because they were in a sleepy haze or simply too far away from the scene.

Cutting straight to the chase, Masipa rejected the evidence of two of the most crucial state 'earwitnesses': Burger and Johnson. The couple, who live in the neighbouring Silver Stream estate, came forward after the bail application, claiming to have heard the blood-curdling screams of a woman before the shots. 'The evidence of this witness, as well as that of her husband Mr Johnson who sought to corroborate her evidence, was correctly criticised in my view as unreliable,' found Masipa.

However, she did not think Johnson and Burger had lied about what they had heard: 'I do not think that Mr Johnson and Ms Burger were dishonest. They did not know the accused or the deceased so they had no interest in the matter. They also did not derive any pleasure in giving evidence.'

Masipa warned that the court approached the evidence of these witnesses with necessary caution. 'It is easy to see why the witnesses would be mistaken about the events of that morning. The distance from which Burger and Johnson heard the noises put them at a distinct disadvantage.'

At issue was the identification of voices and whether or not the witnesses had truly heard a woman screaming that morning. Masipa made the point that none of the witnesses had ever heard Oscar cry or scream when he was anxious, and thus had no model against which to compare what they had heard. Even ex-girlfriend Samantha Taylor conceded under cross-examination that she had never heard Oscar scream under life-threatening circumstances. Masipa also relied on the evidence of defence acoustics expert Ivan Lin to show that, from a distance, the neighbours would not have been able to differentiate conclusively between the screaming of a man and of a woman.

The judge sought to establish whether it was possible that it could have been Reeva screaming between the shots being fired, and for this she relied on the evidence of Professor Gert Saayman. As she read from the postmortem report, Oscar quietly sobbed and Barry Steenkamp, who had not been in court for Saayman's testimony, leaned forward on the bench, resting on his arm. June bent over to check on him as the more graphic details were touched on.

Crucially, Masipa found that the shots had been fired in quick succession. 'In my view, this means that the deceased would have been unable to shout or scream. At least not in the manner described by those witnesses who were adamant that they had heard a woman scream repeatedly. The only other person that could have screamed is the accused. The question is, why did he scream?' Masipa asked rhetorically. Oscar's version was that he screamed when he realised Reeva was not in the bedroom, and the judge found that that claim had not been contradicted.

She again questioned the reliability of neighbours' testimonies and explained why most witnesses 'got their facts wrong'. She echoed what had been said by many commentators critical of the live broadcast of the trial, an unprecedented event in South African judicial history.

Some witnesses had conceded that they knew what happened in court before taking the stand. 'I am of the view that the probability is that some witnesses failed to separate what they knew personally from what they had heard from other people or from what they had gathered from the media,' said Masipa.

Roux had paid special attention to discrediting the evidence of Dr Stipp and his recollection of times, contending that Stipp had moulded his evidence to suit the state's case. But Masipa disagreed, commenting: 'Dr Stipp had no interest in the matter and therefore would have no reason to tailor his evidence to assist the state. I do not believe that he coloured his evidence against the accused. On the contrary, he showed no bias.' What she did concede, though, was that Stipp could, of course, have been mistaken in elements of his testimony.

She spoke of the 'difficult terrain that the court had to traverse to reach a conclusion', explaining why ultimately she chose not to rely on any of the subjective testimony of any of the neighbours who came to testify. 'It would be unwise to rely on any evidence by the witnesses … who gave evidence on what they heard that morning without testing each version against objective evidence. Human beings are fallible and they depend on memory, which fades over time.'

Instead, as the defence had suggested in its closing argument, she chose to look solely at the objective evidence available, most specifically the phone records, to confirm the sequence of events on Valentine's morning.

Masipa's focus shifted to the pivotal timeline of events. The defence had spent considerable time building this timeline during the trial and Roux had formulated his closing argument around it. He had also been critical of Gerrie Nel's failure to explain the sequence of events properly. Masipa, too, took issue with this. 'There was no address from the state to disturb the timelines set out hereunder,' she pointed out.

She then set out her own chronology of events based on objective facts and it read remarkably like the one presented by Roux in closing argument. Crucially, she confirmed that she agreed with the sequence as set out by the defence: the first set of noises was the gunshots and the second was the cricket bat striking the door. This fundamentally contradicted the prosecution's claim that the second set of noises was the shots that had followed Reeva's screams.

'An analysis of the evidence, using the timelines as a basis, will also assist this court to determine whether the state has proved beyond reasonable doubt that the accused had direct intention and premeditation to kill the deceased.'

Masipa was deconstructing the state's premeditation case. She had showed her hand incredibly early on. Then, just as she had hit her straps, she called for a brief adjournment.

During the break Oscar leaned forward and wiped his eyes, rubbing them with the tips of his fingers as attorney Brian Webber had a word with him. Journalists took the opportunity to tweet some atmosphere and analysis.

Aislinn Laing, the southern African correspondent for the *Telegraph* titles, tweeted:

> Have seen judges give points to the defence then find against them before, and we're only 40 minutes in, still a long way to go.

The BBC's Andrew Harding gave perspective on Masipa's ruling so far:

> We're seeing Masipa's logic and style here – gentle, tolerant of error from witnesses, but razor sharp.

It was evident Masipa did not buy the argument that the screams the neighbours had heard were those of a woman. Rather, she found they were those of Oscar in the moments after firing his gun. The defence had done enough to cast doubt over the state's version of events.

On her return to her seat, Masipa picked up precisely where she had left off. She reiterated that she agreed with the defence's timeline and set out why.

She took issue with the fact that while Van der Merwe had said she had heard a woman crying, her husband had told her that it was Oscar. 'This piece of evidence is enough to throw some doubt on the evidence of the witnesses who were adamant that they heard a woman screaming,' commented Masipa. She found that the Nhlengethwas' version – that the crying occurred shortly after the first sounds – 'has a ring of truth to it' when set against the timeline of the phone calls. Lending credence to this was the evidence of Burger and Johnson, who had said that the screaming occurred between 3:12 and 3:17. Masipa also reached the conclusion that Annette Stipp's times seemed to have been wrong. She seemed to place little weight on the evidence of Rika Motshuane as she had 'guessed' at her times and, although being an immediate neighbour, had not heard the first set of sounds.

Having dealt with the screams and the gunshots, Masipa then kicked out the next leg of the prosecution's theory that an argument between Reeva and Oscar had led to the shooting.

In support of this theory, the state had pointed to, amongst other things, that Reeva had taken her phone with her into the bathroom and had locked herself in the toilet cubicle.

'In my view there could be a number of reasons why the accused felt the need to take her cellphone with her to the toilet. One of the possible reasons is that the deceased needed to use her cellphone for lighting purposes, as the light in the toilet was not working. To try and pick just one reason would be to delve into the realm of speculation.'

The state had also led evidence of WhatsApp messages to try to show that the relationship was 'on the rocks' and that the 'accused had a good reason to want to kill the deceased'. In response, the defence had placed messages on the record that showed the relationship was a loving one. Masipa had already indicated during the trial that she might not be convinced by the messages and confirmed this position in her verdict.

'In my view none of this evidence from the state or from the defence proves anything. Normal relationships are dynamic and unpredictable most of the times while human beings are fickle. Neither the evidence of a loving relationship, nor of a relationship turned sour can assist this court to determine whether the accused had the requisite intention to kill the deceased, found the judge. 'For that reason this court refrains from making inferences one way or another in this regard.'

With her dismissal of the WhatsApp messages, the inference could be drawn that even if the prosecution had been aware of Oscar's phone call to his former girlfriend Jenna Edkins on the evening before the shooting and sought to argue that it might show some discord in his relationship with Reeva, it may have been seen by the judge as inconsequential to the case.

The state had relied on pathologist Gert Saayman's testimony to suggest that Reeva had eaten at least two hours before the shooting, as the stomach contents could have buttressed the theory that she was awake and arguing with Oscar. This was tied in with the evidence of neighbour Estelle van der Merwe to try to prove the state's claim.

Masipa found that the court could not rely on the premise of gastric empty-ing because it was not an 'exact science' and evidence before the court remained inconclusive. 'However, even if this court was to accept that the deceased had something to eat shortly before she was killed, it would not assist the state as the inference sought to be drawn from this fact is not the only reasonable inference. She might have left the bedroom while the accused was asleep to get something to eat,' Masipa found.

She also said that what complicated the situation further was that 'it's not clear when and if the alarm was activated that evening or that morning'. In addi-tion, she stated: 'There is nothing in the evidence of Mrs Van der Merwe that links what sounded like an argument to her to the incident at the house of the accused.' Instead, Masipa placed weight on the fact that security guard Pieter Baba had patrolled past Oscar's house before the shooting at 2:20am and had found nothing untoward.

It was becoming clear that the judge was not buying the state's version that an argument had led to a premeditated shooting. After having heard weeks of detailed testimony from neighbours and forensic experts, in a few minutes she had dismissed the screams, the timeline, the stomach contents, the WhatsApp messages and any suggestion that there had been fighting.

Masipa then applied her mind to the defence case and to Oscar's version and how he vacillated about his intentions in the moments before he shot.

'A perusal of the evidence of the accused shows the number of defences or apparent defences. On the version of the accused it was not quite clear whether he intended to shoot or not. This was exacerbated by the fact that Dr Merryll Vorster, called on behalf of the accused, placed in doubt the accused's culpability at the time of the incident. Dr Vorster's evidence was that the accused suffered from a general anxiety disorder which may have affected his conduct at the time of the incident.'

This comment spoke to the 'changing defence' that so many legal commentators had written about during Oscar's time in the witness box.

Masipa carefully scrutinised the testimony of the accused and selected certain extracts from his evidence. She showed how he moved from it being an accident, to how he never intended to shoot anyone, to how he pulled the trigger when he heard the noise, that he did not purposefully fire into the door, that he shot out of fear, that the discharge was accidental and that he never aimed at the door, amongst others. She made special mention of the fact that although Oscar said that at no stage was he ready to discharge the firearm, he had released the safety mechanism on the gun and it was in a ready mode.

'The accused stated that he never thought of the possibility that he could kill people in the toilet. He considered, however, that thinking retrospectively it would be a probability that someone could be killed in the toilet. He stated that if he wanted to shoot the intruder, he would have shot higher up and more in the direction of the opening of the door, to the far right of the door and at chest height. I pause to state that this assertion is inconsistent with someone who shot without thinking.'

And just as Masipa was on the brink of revealing whether or not she believed the state had a case of premeditated murder against Oscar, she abruptly adjourned for tea. It was cliffhanger stuff.

At this point, the sentiment from the police investigators and the state's team was that while they'd lost the possibility of a conviction on premeditated murder, they were still holding out for a potential guilty verdict on murder *dolus eventualis*.

At the same time, relief was beginning to seep into the defence camp, but no one was celebrating prematurely. 'I hate judgments,' despaired a stressed-looking Barry Roux, rocking back on his chair. In response to a comment from us that the judgment seemed to be going in Oscar's favour, a member of the Pistorius family responded swiftly, 'It has nothing to do with favour; it's about the truth.'

• • •

Masipa took her seat again and immediately picked up with the defence's case.

The defence had pointed to the evidence of Professors Derman, Vorster and Scholtz to confirm that Oscar had discharged his firearm in reflex because he felt vulnerable and was fearful. Masipa said this evidence, along with the versions presented by the accused while on the stand, showed that 'we are dealing with a plethora of defences'.

She worked her way through each of these, starting with 'criminal capacity', which emerged during the course of the trial. 'The inevitable question therefore was whether the accused could distinguish between right and wrong and whether he could act in accordance with that distinction. Though not clearly expressed in so many words the defence had the hallmarks of temporary non-pathological incapacity.' This was the defence that emerged when Professor Vorster was on the stand and the result was that Oscar was referred for psychiatric evaluation.

The judge referred to the report of the panel constituted to analyse Oscar while at Weskoppies Psychiatric Hospital, and that of the psychologist, which found that he did not suffer from a mental illness that would have rendered him criminally not responsible. She also spoke to the defence's contention that Oscar suffered from an increased startled response as described by Professor Wayne Derman and that Oscar had shot with a reflex impulse.

'I disagree with this submission. There is a huge difference, as submitted by state counsel, between a reflex action and involuntary action. The latter has a hallmark of a defence of non-pathological insanity as it gives the impression that the accused had no control over his action when he fired the shots at the door. That this cannot be is clear from the steps that the accused took from the moment he heard the sounds of the window opening until the time he fired the four shots. There was no lapse of memory or any confusion on the part of the accused. On his own version, he froze, then decided to arm himself and go to the bathroom. In other words he took a conscious decision. He knew where he kept his firearm and he knew where his bathroom was. He noticed that the bathroom window was open, which was something that confirmed his correctness about having heard the window open earlier,' read Masipa.

She found that this behaviour was inconsistent with lack of criminal incapacity and continued: 'In any event the experts have already pronounced on this defence and this court has not been given any reason not to accept their evidence. This court is satisfied that at the relevant time the accused could distinguish between right and wrong and that he could act in accordance with that distinction. It is also clear that the defence of non-pathological insanity has no foundation.'

The feeling in the courtroom was that the scales of justice could be tipping back in the state's favour. 'This is a roller-coaster ride,' whispered one journalist. 'My nerves are frayed,' said another, riding the judgment wave through peaks and troughs. Oscar was no longer crying but looking straight ahead at Masipa through heavy eyelids.

Masipa then moved on to the next of Oscar's suggested defences – putative private defence. Did he genuinely believe there was an intruder in the house and that he and Reeva were under real threat?

Oscar's defence team had relied on his testimony to show that he shot because he believed an intruder was about to attack him and Reeva. However, Masipa's view was that this testimony was contradictory and she referred to extracts from the accused's testimony to show this. She also reminded those in the courtroom that in evaluating putative private defence, the court applies a subjective test as opposed to an objective test, which means the court needs to consider the accused's state of mind and perception.

She found that Oscar deliberately armed himself with a loaded weapon and moved towards the perceived danger. 'It would be absurd, for instance, to infer from the accused's conduct that he was going to hit the intruder over the head with it as he could easily have used a cricket bat for that purpose.' She agreed with Professor Derman's view that Oscar is a 'fight' rather than a 'flight' reaction person. 'This court also accepts that a person with an anxiety disorder as described by Dr Vorster would get anxious very easily, especially when he's faced with danger. It is also understandable that a person with a disability such as that of the accused would certainly feel vulnerable when faced with danger.'

But she hastened to add that Oscar was not unique in this respect. 'Women, children, the elderly and all those with limited mobility would fall under the same category. But would it be reasonable if without further ado they armed themselves with a firearm if threatened with danger? I do not think so as every case would depend on its own merits.'

Masipa believed Oscar clearly wanted to use the firearm and the only way he could have used it was to shoot at the perceived danger. 'The intention to shoot however, does not necessarily include the intention to kill,' continued the judge. Oscar's chest shifted up and down as he took a deep breath.

'Depending on the circumstances of each case the accused could be found guilty of *dolus eventualis* or culpable homicide. In this case there is only one essential point of dispute and it is this: did the accused have the required *mens rea* [guilty mind] to kill the deceased when he pulled the trigger? In other words, was there intention? The essential question is whether, on the basis of all the evidence presented, there is a reasonable doubt concerning the accused's guilt.'

Roux rested his cheek on his fist and stared at his water bottle. Nel continued doodling in his notebook. Oscar shut his eyes as Masipa continued: 'The accused was a very poor witness. While during evidence-in-chief he seemed composed and logical, with the result that his evidence flowed and made sense, while giving his version under cross-examination he lost his composure.' This comment sent the pendulum of expectation firmly to the prosecution's side.

The defence had explained Oscar's poor performance by saying he was suffering from enormous emotional stress, had been traumatised by the incident and was under medication when taking the stand. 'This argument does not make sense in my view,' found Masipa.

'What we are dealing with here is the fact that the accused was amongst other things an evasive witness. In my view there are several reasons for this. He failed to listen properly to questions put to him under cross-examination giving an impression that he was more worried by the impact that his answers may cause rather than the questions asked. Often a question requiring a straightforward answer turned into a point of debate about what another witness did or said. When contradictions were pointed out to him … he often blamed his legal team for the oversight.'

Reinforcing the perception that the tide was turning against Oscar, Mapisa posed several questions that were top of mind for many who had been watching the trial, and had been raised by Magistrate Nair as 'improbabilities' at the bail hearing.

'In the current case, the accused was killed under very peculiar circumstances. There are indeed a number of aspects in the case that do not make sense,' noted the judge. Why didn't Oscar ask Reeva whether she had heard anything when he heard what he thought was the window opening? Why didn't he check to see whether Reeva had heard him before making his way to the bathroom? Why didn't Reeva communicate with Oscar when she was in the toilet and he just a few metres away? Why didn't she phone the police as Oscar had asked her to? Reeva could have done this irrespective of whether she was in the bedroom or the toilet because she had her phone with her. Why did Oscar fire not one, but four shots before running back to the bedroom to try to find Reeva?

'It makes no sense to say she did not hear him scream, "Get out" – the accused version is that he screamed on top of his voice when ordering the intruders to get out,' continued the judge.

'These questions unfortunately will remain a matter of conjecture. What is not conjecture, however, is that the accused armed himself with a loaded firearm when on his own version he suspected that an intruder might be coming in through the bathroom window. He was not truthful when asked about his intentions that morning as he armed himself with a lethal weapon. The accused was clearly not candid with the court when he said he had no intention to shoot at anyone as he had a loaded firearm in his hand, ready to shoot.'

Masipa reminded the court that the onus rests with the state and not with the defence to prove the case beyond reasonable doubt. She also commented that, should Oscar's version be found to be reasonably possibly true, he would be entitled to an acquittal.

Unexpectedly, Masipa appeared to be reaching a climax in her ruling as she summed up the circumstantial evidence with respect to the murder charge and Oscar's explanation. The prosecution had hoped that the weight of all the individual feathers of evidence together could be enough to prove its case, but would it be?

'The timelines as set out in the chronology of events tip the scales in favour of the accused version in general. Viewed in its totality, the evidence failed to establish that the accused had the requisite intention to kill the deceased let alone with premeditation. I am here talking about direct intention. The state clearly has not proved beyond reasonable doubt that the accused is guilty of premeditated murder. There are just not enough facts to support such a finding.'

BREAKING #OscarPistorius NOT GUILTY of Premeditated Murder

• • •

With the premeditated murder charge ruled out, Judge Masipa swiftly moved on to the murder charge. Here she had to deal with several dense legal concepts that leave much open to interpretation and were ultimately the source of debate and dispute surrounding her ruling.

Essentially, the state had argued that even if Oscar thought he was shooting at an intruder, he should still be convicted of murder because by shooting through the closed door he had intended to kill a human being and that all the elements of murder *dolus eventualis* had been met. In turn, the defence had contended that the state was trying to reintroduce the concept of 'transferred malice', which is not part of South African law.

Masipa took some time explaining two separate legal concepts that are sometimes confused: *aberratio ictus*, which literally translated means 'going astray of the blow', and *error in objecto*, 'error as to the object'.

As Professor James Grant explains, *aberratio ictus* applies when a shooter 'misses a target'. 'If I shoot a gun at a particular person, but I miss, the law recognises that the bullet may easily come to rest in a wall, a tree, or fall harmlessly to the ground somewhere. It could also, of course, strike another person – and this is where things get interesting. Our law used to take the view that this was no defence – you had still killed a human being. It used to do this by "transferring intent" from the intended victim to the actual victim. But we have now shifted to the position that recognises that, if you miss your target, whether you are liable for murder – if the bullet happens to strike another person and kill him or her – must depend on whether you had intention (in law, at least foresight) of this prospect.'

This is very different from scenarios of *error in objecto*. In this case, it doesn't matter if you intended to kill one person but killed another instead, so the identity of the victim makes no difference.

An example of this would be if you wait in a parking lot to shoot Jim; you see who you think is Jim walking towards his car, you fire and the target is killed. But it's not Jim; it's actually Bob who happens to look a lot like Jim.

The problem is that it's easy to confuse these two legal principles.

Professor Grant consistently stated from the outset that this case was not one of *aberratio ictus* as the defence claimed; rather, it was one of *error in objecto*. 'Oscar did not miss his target. He fired at and killed whoever was behind the door. It is therefore not a case of *aberratio ictus*. It is, at best, an immaterial/inessential error (*in objecto*) – no defence,' Grant explains.

Judge Masipa's ruling was in agreement with this viewpoint. She ruled that Oscar's case was not one of *aberratio ictus* and said: 'My view is here we are not dealing with *aberratio ictus* as there was no deflection of the blow. It would therefore serve no purpose to say anything more about this. We are clearly dealing with *error in objecto* or *error in persona* in that the blow was meant for the person behind the toilet door, who the accused believed was an intruder. The blow struck and killed the person behind the door. The fact that the person behind the door turned out to be the deceased and not an intruder is irrelevant.'

This took Masipa back to what exactly Oscar's intention was: did he have the intention to kill the person behind the toilet door who he mistook for an intruder?

'The accused had intention to shoot at the person in the toilet but states that he never intended to kill that person. In other words, he raised the defence of putative private defence.'

Masipa explained that murder requires 'intention' and that the test to determine this intention is subjective. 'In the present case the accused is the only person who can say what his state of mind was at the time he fired the shots that killed the deceased,' she said.

'The accused has not admitted that he had the intention to shoot and kill the deceased or any other person for that matter. On the contrary, he stated that he had no intention to shoot and kill the deceased. The court, however, is entitled to look at the evidence as a whole and the circumstances of the case to determine the presence or absence of intention at the time of the incident.

'In the present case, on his own version, the accused suspected that an intruder had entered his house through the bathroom window. His version was that he genuinely although erroneously believed that his life and that of the deceased was in danger.'

Importantly, Masipa was convinced that Oscar's belief was an honest one – he really did think there was an intruder in the house. This, she said, was due to a number of reasons: 'The bathroom window was indeed open so it was not his imagination at work when he heard the window slide open. He armed himself with a loaded firearm and went to the direction of the noise. He heard a door slam shut. The door [to the] toilet was indeed shut when he fired four shots at it after he heard a movement inside the toilet. On his version he was scared as he thought the intruder was coming out to attack him. There is no doubt that when the accused fired shots through the toilet door he acted unlawfully, there was no intruder.'

Then Masipa made one of the most crucial statements of her judgment, the one that would be most closely scrutinised by legal analysts. She asked the question she believed to be central to the murder charge (although many believe it was the wrong question): 'The question is (1.) Did the accused subjectively foresee that it could be the deceased behind the toilet door? and (2.) Not withstanding the foresight, did he then fire the shots thereby reconciling himself to the possibility that it could be the deceased in the toilet?'

Those critical of her judgment argue that the question should not have been about whether or not Oscar foresaw that *Reeva* was behind the door – but rather whether he foresaw that it could have been any human being behind the door.

As Masipa moved towards finality on the murder charge, Oscar heaved in the dock, racked by sobs.

'The evidence before this court does not support the state's contention that this could be a case of *dolus eventualis*,' ruled the judge.

Barry Steenkamp sighed and leaned forward on the bench in front of him; his advocate leaned across to June and whispered in her ear. Gina Myers covered her mouth with her hand and wept.

Masipa had believed that Oscar's story was reasonably possibly true and, in support, pointed to his behaviour in the minutes after the shooting and the various versions he presented during his bail application, plea explanation and on the stand. Ironically, it was arguably the greatest criticism of the defence lawyers from their colleagues – that they had given such an extensive explanation at the bail application – that had come to be their saving grace.

'On the contrary, the evidence shows that from the onset the accused believed that at the time he fired shots into the toilet door, the deceased was in the bedroom while the intruders were in the toilet. This belief was communicated to a number of people shortly after the incident,' said Masipa.

Oscar had given this version to Johan Stander when he phoned him; he said the same thing to Carice Viljoen when she arrived at the house, and to Dr Stipp when he tried to help save Reeva. He also said as much to the police officers when they arrived on the scene.

Masipa agreed with the defence that it was highly improbable that he would have made this up so quickly and be so consistent in his version. He had presented this same story at the bail application before he had access to the police docket and before he was privy to the evidence that was later led in court.

As the judge spoke, Kenny Oldwadge leaned back in his chair and looked skyward. For all the criticism he had drawn from his colleagues for 'inviting the doctor to the funeral' and for giving such a detailed statement, it seemed that the judge had vindicated him.

Nel continued doodling in his notebook.

Masipa asked the question that underlay the charge. 'Did the accused foresee the possibility of the resultant death yet persisted in his deed, regardless whether death ensued or not?

'In the circumstances of this case, the answer has to be "No". How could the accused reasonably have foreseen that the shots he fired could kill the deceased? Clearly he did not subjectively foresee this as a possibility that he would kill the person behind the door, let alone the deceased, as he thought she was in the bedroom at the time. To find otherwise would be tantamount to saying that the accused's reaction after he realised that he had shot the accused was faked, that he was play acting, merely to delude the onlookers at the time.'

Ironically, it was Dr Stipp, who the defence had spent much time trying to discredit, who proved to be their most valuable asset. Masipa accepted Stipp's evidence as an independent witness, who had described Oscar's emotional distress, that Oscar 'looked genuinely distraught as he prayed to God and pleaded with him to help save the deceased'.

'It follows that the accused's erroneous belief that his life was in danger excludes *dolus*. The accused therefore cannot be found guilty of murder (*dolus eventualis*),' Masipa ruled. Oscar heaved, mucus streaming down his face.

BREAKING #OscarPistorius NOT GUILTY of Murder (*dolus eventualis*)

'That, however, is not the end of the matter as culpable homicide is a competent verdict,' Masipa said, before breaking for lunch. Although culpable homicide is still a serious crime with a potential maximum 15-year jail term, the relief in the Pistorius camp was palpable.

Oscar spent some time huddled in the dock, Carl and Aimee clustered around him, their arms interlinked as they prayed. The poignant moment was broken when attorney Brian Webber walked over and slapped Oscar twice on the arm – his relief evident.

In the lunch break that followed, journalists were all a bit shell-shocked and a storm of confusion broke on social media, with legal experts called in to help explain the nuances of what had just happened.

The confusion was fuelled by a delay in Judge Masipa's return. Roux and Nel both disappeared into her chambers, the prosecutor with a thick purple legal text-book under one arm. They were accompanied by Darren Fresco's advocate Riaan Louw, possibly there to address Masipa on Fresco's indemnity from prosecution.

When Masipa returned to her seat, it was to hand down her ruling on culpable homicide and it took a mere 13 minutes.

Culpable homicide refers to 'negligence', so Masipa would have had to decide whether she thought Oscar was negligent or not. For this Masipa had to apply the reasonable person test.

The defence had argued that Oscar's disability had rendered him vulnerable and that someone in his circumstances and with his ability could not be found guilty. Masipa did not agree. 'Vulnerability is not unique, as millions of people could easily fit into that category,' she pointed out.

She said there were several other options open to Oscar for him deal with the danger. He could have picked up his cellphone to call security or the police; he could have run to the balcony and screamed as he did after the shooting; there was no reason why he couldn't do so before he ventured into the bathroom with a loaded firearm – calling security and running to the balcony would probably have taken as much time if not less than it had taken to go to the bathroom and discharge those four shots. 'It is also significant that at the time that he heard the window slide open, he was nearer to the balcony than to the bathroom,' she added.

The defence had also argued that growing up in a crime-riddled environment and in a home where his mother was paranoid and always carried a firearm, placed Oscar in a unique category of people. 'I agree that the conduct of the accused may be better understood by looking at his background; however, the explanation of the conduct of the accused is just that, an explanation. It does not excuse the conduct of the accused. Many other people have experienced violent crime and have not resorted to sleeping with firearms under their pillows,' Masipa dismissed the argument.

'If the accused, for example, had awoken in the middle of the night and in darkness saw a silhouette hovering next to his bed and had in a panic grabbed his firearm and shot at that figure only to find that it was the deceased, his conduct would have been understandable and perhaps excusable. In such a case he would not have been expected to call security,' judged Masipa.

But, she said, in this instance this was not the case. 'The accused had reasonable time to reflect, to think and to conduct himself reasonably. On the facts of this case, I am not persuaded that a reasonable person with the accused's disability in the same circumstances would have fired four shots into that small toilet cubicle.

'Having regard to the size of the toilet and the calibre of the ammunition used in the firearm, a reasonable person with the accused's disability and in his position would have foreseen that if he fired shots at the door the person inside the toilet might be struck and might die as a result. The accused knew that there was a person behind the toilet door; he chose to use a firearm which was a lethal weapon [and] he was competent in the use of firearms as he had undergone some training.'

In drawing to a close, Masipa asked the questions critical to this charge. Would a reasonable person in the same circumstances as Oscar have foreseen the reasonable possibility that if he fired shots, whoever was behind the door might be struck by a bullet and die as a result? Would a reasonable person have taken steps to guard against that possibility? 'The answer to both questions is "Yes", ' she said.

'He failed to take any step to guard against the resultant death. I am of the view that the accused acted too hastily and used excessive force. In the circumstances it is clear that his conduct was negligent.'

Masipa stopped short of making a ruling on culpable homicide at that point, although her direction was clear as she adjourned for the day.

Oscar was overcome with emotion. Well after the courtroom had emptied, and with a massive throng of journalists awaiting his exit, he spent around half an hour seated in the far corner of the courtroom. Aimee sat half on his lap, half on the arm of his chair, stroking his head as he scrolled through his phone. Finally, after what must have been an excruciatingly emotional day, he walked out. When asked how he felt the day had gone, he looked straight ahead, said nothing and kept walking.

• • •

Did Oscar 'escape' a murder charge? Did he 'walk free'? Many people thought so. Legal experts piled into the debate, with many believing Judge Masipa had made a fundamental error in law in her application of *dolus eventualis*. Opinions were offered on social media, in traditional media and all across the country.

Attorney David Dadic tweeted:

> He is a bad witness but believes his version regarding his intent not to shoot? Huh?

Constitutional law professor Pierre de Vos tweeted:

> Surely if you shoot into a door of small toilet and know somebody behind door you foresee and accepts possibility of killing. Not sure rejection of dolus eventualis is correct here. #OscarTrial

The sense from criminal defence advocates we spoke to was that Masipa had 'conflated' the concepts of reasonable foreseeability and *dolus eventualis*.

'I've had colleagues phone me today gobsmacked, literally saying, "Do I not understand the law? I would be amazed if Gerrie doesn't appeal!"'

In Grant's opinion, Masipa got all the complicated 'legal stuff' right but made an error in applying it. 'What she did was she got the principles of this difficult stuff right. But she hashed the application of *dolus eventualis* to *error in objecto*. There should have been a finding of intention to kill, but there could have been conceivably a finding of lack of intention with respect of unlawfulness. It's conceivable that he could have been mistaken that he was entitled to kill. That would have been a sound foundation for an acquittal on murder.

'I'm saying that she acquitted on the wrong grounds. The problem is that she gets the difficult theory right, but, in applying *dolus eventualis* to this theory, asks the wrong question. She should have asked: did he foresee the possibility of killing *whoever* was behind the door? Instead, she asked, did he foresee the possibility of killing *Reeva*? She set about answering the wrong question to start with.'

Essentially Masipa's critics were arguing that if Oscar could have foreseen that someone could die when he shot, he should be convicted of murder.

Criminal attorney Ulrich Roux summarised this best in a piece he wrote for *The Guardian*:

> *In delivering her ruling, Judge Thokozile Masipa said that 'a reasonable person would have foreseen if he fired shots at the door, the person inside the toilet might be struck and might die as a result', which suggests a classic case of dolus eventualis.*
>
> *But the judge seems to have cleared him of this charge because she felt that, to be guilty of common-law murder, Pistorius needed to have foreseen that his actions would kill a specific person – Reeva Steenkamp.*
>
> *The state tried to prove that Pistorius was aware that it was Steenkamp behind the toilet door but the judge accepted the defence's claims that he thought it was an intruder. She put a lot of weight on the genuine remorse he showed after the fact, saying there's no way he could have faked that.*

Dadic distilled the storm of criticism into one simple comparison. 'Jub Jub the rapper gets in his car. He's drunk and he's drag racing. He gets convicted of *dolus eventualis* because the court decides he must have foreseen a negative consequence to his act. Oscar Pistorius is sober with a gun and shoots four shots into a closed door. He is acquitted of *dolus eventualis* because the judge is of the view that he didn't foresee and is convicted of culpable homicide because he should have foreseen. In my opinion the test has been misapplied by the judge as it is difficult to legitimately believe that a person who shoots at someone four times does not on some level wish to kill that person – that is intent.'

But, as is the case with any contentious judgment, some legal minds believe Masipa got the law exactly right.

University of Cape Town law expert Kelly Phelps explains: 'As I see it, there were always going to be problems for the state with *dolus eventualis*. The one pertains to the actual boundaries of the definition itself and the other pertains to this legal rule that they were trying to evoke in *error in objecto*. This is such a technical part of the law. This is not the type of debate you see in courts every day. It's nuanced esoteric debate that academics have amongst themselves. I'm not surprised that people are missing the nuance.

'The state tried to argue *dolus eventualis* in a variety of *indeterminatus* and what that means in laypeople's words is "general intention", meaning "I didn't particularly care or know who I was going to kill but I foresaw the possibility that I would kill someone but I proceeded none the less". So when the state put to Oscar but you didn't know who was behind the door, there could have been a child or a homeless man, he said "Yes". The problem for the state was that if it had been a child, or a homeless man, Oscar would be guilty of murder because he hadn't excluded the possibility that it was either a child or an intruder and proceeded anyway. However, he had excluded the possibility in his mind that it could be Reeva in the bathroom; therefore he cannot have *dolus eventualis* with respect to killing her because he subjectively, genuinely did not foresee the possibility that she could die and proceeded nonetheless. It's not fulfilling the legal boundaries of *dolus eventualis*. I think the finding is exactly right,' says Phelps.

Writing on The Law Thinker website, editor Brad Cibane backed up Masipa's ruling, pointing a finger instead at what he called Gerrie Nel's 'cockup':

> In Oscar's case, the State failed to prove this 'actual reconciliation' beyond a reasonable doubt. In fact, it was not the State's case that Pistorius foresaw that he was going to kill the 'intruder' and reconciled itself to that possibility. Instead, quite befuddlingly, Advocate Nel (the State prosecutor) opted for what most of us thought was an impossible route – proving that Pistorius intended to kill Steenkamp.
>
> It is worth noting that saying Pistorius 'should have foreseen' that opening fire at the 'intruder' would lead to the intruder's death is negligence, not intention. That is a 'reasonable man' or objective standard. A subjective standard is what Pistorius actually foresaw and actually reconciled himself to, as the consequence of his actions.

In South Africa, while there is no jury system, there is an appeal system. This means that Masipa's decision could be taken on appeal to a higher court, the Supreme Court of Appeal in Bloemfontein, and ultimately, if applicable, to the Constitutional Court in Braamfontein.

However, the state can only appeal a ruling after sentencing is finalised and if a judge is found to have made an error of law and not an error of fact. In the wake of the verdict, most commentators insisted an appeal was inevitable. But some believe that Masipa's so-called error was one of fact and not law, rendering an appeal impossible. Cibane is one of these. 'What Pistorius actually thought is a factual finding. Therefore, it will be extremely difficult, if not utterly impossible, to overturn Masipa J's findings on the facts as presented or proven by the State,' he wrote in his blog.

For the defence to appeal a culpable homicide conviction also comes with risk and potential complications because a higher court could overturn Masipa's judgment and impose a murder conviction.

At the time of going to print, it was unclear whether either side would appeal Judge Masipa's verdict.

• • •

On the morning of the second day of judgment, newspapers trumpeted the previous day's news – Oscar Pistorius would be acquitted of murder. However, the dailies were also filling column space with quotes from legal experts debating the merits of Masipa's judgment. She, in the meantime, was likely cocooned away from all the noise, as she seemed to have done successfully throughout the trial. As her blue-light cavalcade brought her down Madiba Street shortly after dawn, it's possible she had no idea of the dust she had kicked up.

The previous afternoon Masipa had stopped short of convicting Oscar of culpable homicide and there was still space for her to acquit him entirely. What would her final verdict be? She also had to make a finding on the three gun-related charges Oscar faced: the sunroof incident, the Tashas shooting and the ammunition charge. In addition, Masipa would have to make a finding on Darren Fresco's indemnity and whether he had been a truthful witness with regards to the Tashas incident.

When Masipa took her seat on the bench, she went straight to Count Two – the alleged sunroof shooting – and summarised the facts. Two witnesses had been called to testify to this charge: Oscar's ex-girlfriend Samantha Taylor and Darren Fresco. Their versions had differed considerably and Oscar had accused them of conspiring against him. He denied that the shooting had happened at all.

Masipa agreed that Taylor and Fresco's versions of how, where and when the incident happened were so dissimilar that 'one may be tempted to think they were talking about different incidents'. The judge emphasised she had to approach their evidence with caution.

She found that Fresco was not an impressive witness on this particular count. 'In fact, he was proved to be a dishonest witness,' said Masipa, referring to the photograph produced by Roux during cross-examination that showed that Fresco was driving the car when he had claimed it was Oscar. She noted that Fresco couldn't say with certainty where the incident had happened, and he told an 'unlikely story'. With regard to Taylor, Masipa said it was clear that she had been hurt by the manner in which the relationship had terminated. But this didn't mean 'she was out to falsely implicate the accused'. In fact, Masipa found that it was Taylor's version rather than Fresco's that had 'a ring of truth' to it.

But this was not enough – the state had to prove its case beyond a reasonable doubt and, because of crucial contradictions by the state witnesses, Masipa found: 'The evidence placed before this court falls short of a conviction in a criminal matter. This court's conclusion is that the state has failed to establish that the accused is guilty beyond reasonable doubt and has to be acquitted.'

BREAKING #OscarPistorius NOT GUILTY on sunroof shooting charge

Masipa moved on to Count Three, the discharge of a firearm at the Tashas restaurant in Melrose Arch. Boxer Kevin Lerena had testified on this charge, so too had Fresco who had been offered indemnity for his potentially incriminating evidence. Roux had already accepted a degree of guilt on behalf of his client during closing argument so a finding of guilty was likely.

There had been some dispute about whether or not Oscar had actually pulled the trigger or what had caused the gun to go off, but Masipa was not distracted by this.

'In my view it really does not matter what caused the firearm to discharge as that will not assist this court in determining whether the accused was negligent. No one has submitted that there was intention on the part of the accused. What is relevant is that the accused asked for a firearm in a restaurant full of patrons and that while it was in his possession it discharged. He may not have intentionally pulled the trigger; however, that in itself does not absolve him of negligently handling a firearm in circumstances where it creates a risk to the safety of people and property and not to take reasonable precautions to avoid the danger.'

Masipa found that Fresco's version was materially supported by Lerena. 'Lerena was a good witness and I did not detect any indication of bias against the accused. This court was given no reason to reject his evidence and that evidence is accepted in total as true and reliable. It follows also that this court accepts the evidence of Fresco in this regard.' Sitting in the front row of the gallery, Fresco ran a hand through his hair and let out a deep sigh – his indemnity was likely now.

Pointing to the testimony of firearms trainer Sean Rens, Masipa established that it was clear that Oscar had been trained in handling firearms responsibly. 'He should not therefore have asked for a firearm in a public place such as a restaurant full of patrons, let alone handle it,' said Masipa. It was her view that the state had proved its case on this count beyond reasonable doubt.

BREAKING #OscarPistorius GUILTY on Tashas shooting charge

Lastly, Masipa addressed the charge of illegal possession of ammunition – the rounds in his safe for which he did not have a licence and he claimed belonged to his father.

Masipa referred to the law regarding what licence Oscar required in order to keep the ammunition. She focused on 'intention' and whether this was necessary on this charge, suggesting that it was. She also mentioned that the state had made much of the fact that Henke Pistorius had refused to give a statement to support Oscar's claim that the ammunition belonged to his father. 'In my view this does not assist the state,' said Masipa.

'The accused version was that the ammunition belonged to his father and that he had no intention to possess it. The fact that there is no corroboration for the accused version does not assist at all. Accordingly, what the state needed to do was to introduce evidence to the contrary. It did not do so. The accused version remains uncontroverted. The state has failed to prove that the accused had the necessary intention to possess the ammunition. Therefore he cannot be found guilty on this count,' ruled the judge.

BREAKING #OscarPistorius NOT GUILTY of illegal possession of ammunition

Those in the Steenkamp camp had maintained a dignified silence throughout the ruling, but when not guilty verdicts emerged on the additional gun-related charges, there was much murmuring and muttering on these benches.

Masipa had effectively taken the sting out of her judgment of the previous day. Now that she neared the climax of her ruling, her verdict was a foregone conclusion.

She ran through a summary of her findings, starting with the murder charge. 'Evidence led by the state on this count was purely circumstantial. It was not strong circumstantial evidence. Moreover, the evidence of various witnesses who gave evidence on what they heard, on what sequence and when, proved to be unreliable.

'The accused gave a version that could reasonably, possibly be true. In criminal law that is all that is required for an acquittal as the onus rests with the state throughout. There was no basis on which this court could make inferences of why the accused would want to kill the deceased. In addition, there is objective evidence in the form of phone records; this too supports the version of the accused. Furthermore, the conduct of the accused shortly after the incident is inconsistent with the conduct of someone who had the intention to commit murder.

'It cannot be said that the accused did not entertain a genuine belief that there was an intruder in the toilet who posed a threat to him. Therefore he could not be found guilty of murder *dolus directus*,' said Masipa.

Reeva's mother June, stoic throughout, kept her composure while her husband shifted his hulking frame. He had gone a deep shade of red and leaned hard on the bench in front of him, clasping his hands on the wood. Next to him, advocate Dup de Bruyn scribbled notes. The rest of the Steenkamp family, each with a black-and-white picture of Reeva pinned to their lapels, looked distraught. In the row behind them, Gina and Kim Myers were crying. Oscar calmly stared ahead. He appeared far more composed and controlled than he had the previous day.

'This court has already found that the accused cannot be guilty of murder *dolus eventualis* either on the basis that, from his belief and his conduct, it could not be said that he foresaw that either the deceased or anyone else for that matter might be killed when he fired shots at the toilet door. It also cannot be said that he accepted that possibility into the bargain,' Masipa went on.

'Evidential material before this court however showed that the accused acted negligently when he fired shots into the toilet door knowing there was someone behind the door and that there was very little room in which to manoeuvre. A reasonable person therefore in the position of the accused with similar disability would have foreseen that possibility that whoever was behind that door might have been killed by the shots and would have taken steps to avoid the consequences and the accused in this matter failed to take those consequences [sic]'.

Judge Masipa raised her glass of water and shifted her documents to one side.

'Mr Pistorius, please stand up.'

Oscar stood, adjusted his microphone vertically and clasped his hands in front of him. The last six months of trial had culminated in this moment.

June appeared tense. Barry glanced across the row of spectators at his daughter's boyfriend and killer, his look possibly reflecting a second heartbreak, that the legal outcome had somehow diminished his daughter's death.

Having regard to the totality of this evidence, in this matter, the unanimous decision of this court is the following:

On Count One ... the accused is found 'not guilty' and is discharged.
Instead he is found 'guilty' of culpable homicide.
On Count Two ... the accused is found 'not guilty' and is discharged.
On Count Three ... the accused is found 'guilty' of the second alternative.
On Count Four ... the accused is found 'not guilty' and discharged.

Oscar took his seat.

Masipa still had to address the issue of Fresco's indemnity. His attorney Riaan Louw appeared before her as she handed down her decision.

'It was clear that Fresco was not out to falsely implicate the accused. He merely stated a fact, which was that the firearm discharged while in the possession of the accused. He was fair to the accused and gave him credit where it was warranted. It is the opinion of this court that Mr Darren Fresco answered frankly and honestly all questions put to him. Accordingly he's discharged from prosecution for the offence specified as Count Three.'

An ANC Women's League member in her green jacket, sitting alongside Fresco, grabbed his hand in support. His wife smiled and gave a slight clap.

Masipa stood and left the court, leaving behind her a room heavy with emotion.

The Steenkamp's family advocate bowed his head towards June, explaining the verdict from the notes on his yellow legal pad. Reeva's cousin Kim Martins broke down and was consoled by an equally emotional Gina Myers, while Barry walked over to Fresco and slapped him on the shoulder. Those on the benches marked 'Steenkamp Family' seemed dazed and confused. 'She didn't get what she deserved,' said one close friend. Another remarked, 'I don't mind that he only got culp as long as he goes to jail for a very long time.'

The state legal team and police forensic experts appeared deflated. 'How are you doing?' we asked. 'Not good,' said one. 'What is the point of my job?' said another. Gerrie Nel packed up his sketchpad full of six months' worth of doodles, his face giving nothing away.

Although their relief was evident, the Pistorius family maintained their dignity, choosing not to celebrate or claim victory in any way. Aimee walked over to Oscar, who remained seated in the dock, and kissed him on the cheek and hugged him. Moments later his uncle Arnold made his way over and spoke to his nephew for several seconds before the men shared a long embrace.

It was clear that there was still a long road to travel. Culpable homicide is by no means an escape and a potential jail term would loom large.

Arnold Pistorius later addressed the media at an impromptu press conference inside the courtroom. With his wife next to him, he read off a handwritten statement:

> *On behalf of the family, we would really like to show how deeply grateful we are for Judge Masipa who has found Oscar not guilty of murder and it's a big burden for us off our shoulders and Oscar. We always knew the facts of the matter and we had never any doubt in Oscar's version of this tragic incident. At this stage, however, the matter remains before the court. Arguments in aggravation and mitigation for sentence still need to be delivered. It would be highly inappropriate for the family to make any further statements at this stage regarding merits of the case and findings of the court. We respect the fact that the legal process is not over and must always be run in the course of justice. And furthermore, a tragic event like this, there is no victors in this. We as a family remain deeply affected by the devastating tragedy event and it won't bring Reeva back but our hearts still go out for her family and friends.*

Shortly after court had been adjourned, the National Prosecuting Authority issued a statement of its own:

> *The National Prosecuting Authority of South Africa respects the findings of the court today. However, it is important to mention that from the very beginning the prosecutors held the view that there was sufficient evidence to secure a successful prosecution on the charges that were preferred against the accused. We respect the court decision to convict the accused on culpable homicide, which is in fact a serious crime. We are, however, disappointed that we were not successful in securing a conviction on the original charge of premeditated murder, negligent discharge of a firearm and possession of ammunition. NPA will await until the matter is concluded and will then comment on any further legal steps that might be envisaged. Further, NPA is satisfied with the manner in which the prosecution team prosecuted the case. They displayed the highest degree of professionalism and their ethical conduct could not be faulted throughout the trial. They have served as good ambassadors for the National Prosecuting Authority of South Africa and the fight for justice.*

The Myers family also released a brief statement:

> *Nothing will ever bring Reeva back. That's what's sad. The fact remains that she is gone. We will forever be heartbroken. Today we are disappointed to say the least. But as Ghandi says: 'There is a higher court than the courts of justice and that is the court of conscience.'*

June and Barry Steenkamp gave their views on Masipa's judgment through an exclusive interview with broadcaster NBC, saying 'justice was not served'. They expressed 'disbelief' at the verdict.

'I just want the truth. Reeva died a horrible, painful, terrible death,' said June. 'He shot through the door and I can't believe that they believe it was an accident. I really don't care what happens to Oscar. It's not going to change anything because my daughter is never coming back. He's still living and breathing and she's gone, you know, forever.'

Having run the race of his life, Oscar Pistorius, the Blade Runner who had inspired so many and had achieved so much, who had fallen so spectacularly from the highest peak of fame and stardom, emerged out of the Pretoria courthouse into the circus-like bedlam that had characterised his trial for months, running the gauntlet of the media once again. A roar of screams went up from the crowd as he was bundled by his bodyguards into a sedan and driven off down Madiba Street, leaving the detritus of many lives, including his own, in his wake.

Sequence of Events

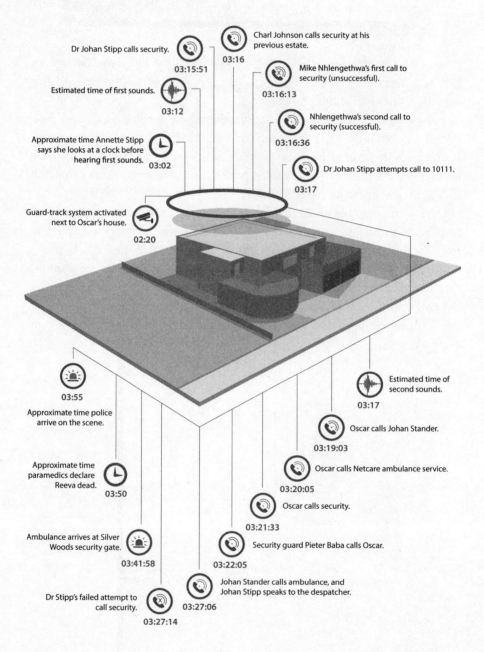

Dr Johan Stipp calls security. 03:15:51

Charl Johnson calls security at his previous estate. 03:16

Mike Nhlengethwa's first call to security (unsuccessful). 03:16:13

Estimated time of first sounds. 03:12

Nhlengethwa's second call to security (successful). 03:16:36

Approximate time Annette Stipp says she looks at a clock before hearing first sounds. 03:02

Dr Johan Stipp attempts call to 10111. 03:17

Guard-track system activated next to Oscar's house. 02:20

Estimated time of second sounds. 03:17

Approximate time police arrive on the scene. 03:55

Oscar calls Johan Stander. 03:19:03

Approximate time paramedics declare Reeva dead. 03:50

Oscar calls Netcare ambulance service. 03:20:05

Oscar calls security. 03:21:33

Ambulance arrives at Silver Woods security gate. 03:41:58

Security guard Pieter Baba calls Oscar. 03:22:05

Johan Stander calls ambulance, and Johan Stipp speaks to the despatcher. 03:27:06

Dr Stipp's failed attempt to call security. 03:27:14

Floor Plan of the Crime Scene

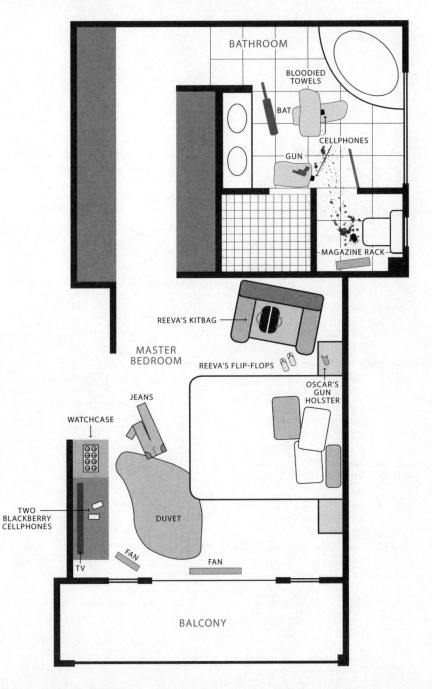

BATHROOM

BLOODIED
TOWELS

BAT

CELLPHONES

GUN

MAGAZINE RACK

REEVA'S KITBAG

MASTER
BEDROOM

REEVA'S FLIP-FLOPS

OSCAR'S
GUN
HOLSTER

JEANS

WATCHCASE

TWO
BLACKBERRY
CELLPHONES

DUVET

FAN

FAN

TV

BALCONY

References

Valentine's Day

Pages 24–25 'The Ex-Lead Investigator of the Oscar Pistorius Murder Case: "He Shot Her – That's It"', *Vanity Fair*, 1 May 2012.

A Lioness's Legacy

Pages 33–34 Reeva Steenkamp, 'Bucket Babe: Reeva Steenkamp', The Bucket (blog site), 29 September 2011.

Page 34 Shaanaaz de Jager, 'PE Beauty Vies for R1-million Prize in TV Show', *Weekend Post*, 8 September 2012.

Pages 35–36 Hagen Engler, 'The Reeva I knew', Daily Maverick, 14 February 2013.

Page 39 'Reeva Steenkamp's Final Message of Love', ZAlebs, 15 February 2013.

Page 41 Clayton Morar, 'Reeva was Smitten with Oscar, Says Childhood Friend', *City Press*, 15 February 2013

Page 42 'Eish, is our Blade Runner a Player?', *City Press*, 10 November 2012.

Page 43 'Oscar Pistorius: Shots in the Dark', produced by James Stolz, Kim Kennedy, Marcie Spencer, Patti Arnofsky, Sarah Carter, Taigi Smith and Avi Cohen, CBD News, 16 June 2014.

Page 52 Petro-Ann Vlok, 'Tragic Love Match', *YOU*, 28 February 2013.

Page 52 Gabi Mbele, 'Sweet Tweets, then Arguing in Public', *Sunday Times*, 17 February 2013.

Page 52 'Oscar Pistorius', *Carte Blanche*, 24 February 2013.

Pages 53–54 Nicki Güles, 'Reeva Feared "Lies" Could Ruin her Relationship with Oscar', *City Press*, 21 February 2013.

Page 54 Barbara Jones, 'Oscar Killed our Golden Girl Reeva So Now He Must Pay Us Blood Money: Barry and June Steenkamp's First Newspaper Interview about their Daughter and Pistorius', *Daily Mail*, 29 June 2013.

Page 56 'Reeva Steenkamp's Final Message of Love', ZAlebs, 15 February 2013.

Pages 56–57 Sarah Evans and Sally Evans, 'Oscar Pistorius: Valentine's Day of Despair', *Mail & Guardian*, 15 February 2013.

The Bullet in the Chamber

Page 60 Oscar Pistorius, *Blade Runner*, Virgin Books, 2009.

Page 62 Donald McRae, 'Oscar Pistorius: South Africa's

Symbol of Hope Shattered', *The Guardian*, 15 February 2013.

Page 67   'Leaked Reports that Pistorius' Carbon Fibre Prosthetic Limbs Provide a "Considerable Advantage"', *The Science of Sport*, 19 December 2007.

Page 69   Craig Timberg, 'Double Amputee Allowed to Compete for Olympic Bid', *The Washington Post*, 17 May 2008.

Page 70   Awo Sarpong, 'South African Double-Amputee Makes History', *Jamati*, 19 May 2008.

Page 70   Sean Gregory, 'The World's Most Influential People 2012', *Time*, 18 April 2012.

Page 71   Sally Evans, 'Oscar out of Intensive Care', *The Times*, 25 February 2009.

Pages 72–73   Rebecca Davis, 'Did Oscar Pistorius Lie on the Stand?', Daily Maverick and Eyewitness News, 23 April 2014.

Page 74   Glynnis Underhill, 'Prior Assault Claim Stalks Oscar Pistorius', *Mail & Guardian*, 1 March 2013.

Pages 76–77   Gareth A Davies, 'Oscar Pistorius Storms out of BBC Interview after "Insulting Question"', *The Telegraph*, 6 September 2011.

Page 77   'Oscar Pistorius', *Carte Blanche*, 24 February 2013.

Page 78   Jeff Eisenberg, 'Kirani James Swaps Number with Oscar Pistorius after 400 meters Semifinal', Yahoo! Sports, 5 August 2012.

Page 79   Simon Hart, 'Oscar Pistorius "Sorry" for Criticising Alan Oliveira's Blades after Paralympics 200m Defeat', *The Telegraph*, 3 September 2012.

Page 80   Andy Bull, 'Oscar Pistorius Angry at Shock 200m Paralympic Loss', *The Guardian*, 3 September 2012.

Page 82   David O'Sullivan, 'Oscar Pistorius: Not the Boy I Knew', *The Sunday Telegraph*, 17 February 2013.

Page 83   'Oscar Pistorius: What Really Happened', BBC Television Documentary, March 2013.

Page 83   CNN Interview with Graeme Joffe, 7 March 2012.

Pages 83–84   Michael Sokolove, 'The Fast Life of Oscar Pistorius', *The New York Times*, 18 January 2012.

Pages 84–85   Jonathan McEvoy, 'Inside Oscar's Bedroom: One Cricket Bat, Baseball Bat, Revolver and Machine Gun', *The Daily Mail*, 14 February 2013.

Page 85   Jonny Steinberg, 'Oscar Pistorius: The End of the Rainbow', *The Guardian*, 24 May 2013.

Page 89   Charis Labuschagne, 'Ons Superstar Oscar: Roem nie Altyd Great', *Sarie*, 21 February 2013.

Pages 89–90   Gabi Mbele and Werner Swart, 'Oscar was "Worried about Reputation" after Altercations: Reeva', *The Sunday Times*, 13 April 2014.

Page 91   Charis Labuschagne, 'Ons Superstar Oscar: Roem nie Altyd Great', *Sarie*, 21 February 2013.

Breaking News – Barry Bateman
Page 93   Charis Labuschagne, 'Ons Superstar Oscar: Roem nie Altyd Great', *Sarie*, 21 February 2013.

Fall from Grace – Mandy Wiener

Page 100 Mandy Wiener, 'When the Media Circus Moves on, Reeva Steenkamp Will Still be Dead', Daily Maverick, 15 February 2013.

The Legal Teams

Page 108 'Pistorius Prosecutor Nel has "Integrity Beyond Reproach"', Mail & Guardian, 20 February 2014.

A Weekend in Jail

Page 125 Aislinn Laing, 'Oscar Pistorius' Father Blames South African Gun Culture on the ANC', The Telegraph, 3 March 2013.

Pages 125–126 Aislinn Laing, 'Oscar Pistorius Shot Reeva Steenkamp "on Instinct", his Father Says', The Telegraph, 16 February 2013.

Page 127 Adriaan Basson, 'Exclusive: The Case against Oscar', City Press, 17 February 2013.

Pages 126–127 Nick Parker, 'Steroids Found at Blade Runner's Mansion', The Sun, 18 February 2013.

Pages 127–128 'Pistorius' Future Races Cancelled – Agent', City Press, 18 February 2013.

Saying Goodbye to Reeva

Page 130 'Reeva's Death Leaves a Void, Says Family', iol, 19 February 2013.

Page 130 'Why Did Oscar Pistorius Kill Our Daughter?', Channel 5, June 2013.

From Investigating Officer to Accused

Page 149 'Pistorius Detective Faces Attempted Murder Charges', The New Age, 21 February 2013.

Page 151 Charis Labuschagne, 'Ons Superstar Oscar: Roem

nie Altyd Great', Sarie, 21 February 2013.

Life Carries On

Page 171 'Oscar Pistorius: What Really Happened', BBC Television Documentary, March 2013.

Page 172 'Oscar Pistorius Spotted Jogging around Athletics Track', London Evening Standard, 4 April 2013.

Page 172 'Oscar Wants to Train: Agent', The Times, 3 April 2013.

Page 173 Werner Swart, 'Oscar Parties, Flirts, Shops', The Sunday Times, 14 April 2013.

Page 174 Werner Swart, 'Partying Oscar Hits on Reeva Double just 52 days after Shooting Girlfriend', The Times, 20 July 2014.

Page 177 Alex Crawford, 'Pistorius: Images Show Bloody Scene of Killing', Sky News, 31 May 2013.

Facing the Law

Pages 182–183 Stephanie Findlay, 'Oscar Pistorius Hires Dream Team Ahead of Murder Trial', Time, 7 February 2014.

Page 187 Definition of 'murder' occurs in J.M. Burchell, Principles of Criminal Law, 4th edition, Juta, 2013.

Page 192 Gavin Hood (dir.), A Reasonable Man, Africa Media Entertainment, M-Net, Movieworld, August 1999.

Page 194 Rebecca Davis, 'Analysis: Why Oscar Pistorius Has No Other Choice but to Testify', Daily Maverick, 25 March 2014.

The State vs OLC Pistorius

Page 201 Schalk van Zuydam, 'Oscar Pistorius Murder Trial in Pictures', Yahoo! News, 3 March 2014.

Page 203 'Reeva Steenkamp's Heartbroken Mother Talks

about Attending Trial – and "Forgives" Oscar Pistorius', *Hello!*, 5 March 2014.

My Lady
Page 206 Jane Thandi Lipman (dir.) and Ruth Cowan (creator), *Courting Justice*, Morris and Ruth B. Cowan Foundation, 2010.

Page 209 Norimitsu Onishi, 'From Apartheid-Era Jail Cell to the Bench in Pistorius Case: Oscar Pistorius Trial Judge Overcame Apartheid', *The New York Times*, 6 August 2014.

A Plea of Not Guilty
Page 215 Herman Scholtz, 'Oscar Saak: Twee Swaargewigte en 'n Groentjie', *Rapport*, 9 August 2014.

What the Neighbours Heard
Page 249 David Smith, 'Oscar Pistorius Denies Trying to Intimidate Reeva Steenkamp's Friend', *The Guardian*, 6 May 2014.

The Last Meal
Pages 258–259 Jason Payne-James, Anthony Busuttil and William Smock (eds), *Forensic Medicine: Clinical and Pathological Aspects*, Greenwich Medical Media, 2002.

The Bat
Page 289 Alexander Jason, 'Oscar Pistorius Door: Cricket Bat vs Gunshot Sounds: Analysis', YouTube, 8 March 2014.

ContraDixon
Page 296 Shain Germaner, 'Oscar Trial: Now for Damage Control', *The Star*, 15 April 2014.

Page 306 David Smith, 'Pistorius's Expert Witness Says He was Joking about his Destroyed Reputation', *The Guardian*, 17 April 2014.

Pasta, with a Side of Gunfire
Pages 340–341 'Oscar Pistorius in the Seychelles', *Top Billing*, Tswelopele Productions, 10 October 2012.

The Secrets of the Missing Apple
Page 371 Jim Cymbala, *Breakthrough Prayer: The Power of Connecting with the Heart of God*, Zondervan, 2003.

Page 381 Oscar Pistorius, *Blade Runner*, Virgin Books, 2009.

Trapped in a Secret
Page 419 'Oscar Pistorius in the Seychelles', *Top Billing*, Tswelopele Productions, 10 October 2012.

Full Combat Recon Mode
Page 449 'Oscar Pistorius: What Really Happened', BBC Television Documentary, March 2013.

Page 449 Kathryn Bigelow (dir.), *Zero Dark Thirty*, Columbia Pictures, Annapurna Pictures, First Light Production, 11 January 2013.

The Imagined Intruder
Pages 452–453 Margie Orford, 'Imagined Threat of Black Stranger at Heart of Defence', *Sunday Times*, 3 March 2014.

Page 453 *Victims of Crime Survey 2012*, Statistical release P0341, Statistics South Africa, 27 September 2012.

Pages 455–456 Nastasya Tay, 'The Invisible Witness', Yahoo! Sports, 2 April 2014.

Generalised Anxiety Disorder (GAD)
Page 468 David K Li, 'Pistorius Took "Acting Lessons" before Crying on Stand', *New York Post*, 20 April 2014.

Page 468 'Oscar Pistorius Trial: Spokeswoman Denies Athlete

Took Acting Lessons', *The Guardian*, 22 April 2014.

The Jerry Maguire Factor

Page 482   Werner Swart, 'Oscar's Agent Shows He's No Jerry Maguire', *Sunday Times*, 7 July 2014.

The 'Third Startle'

Page 491   *Sunday Night* (The Evidence Room footage), Channel Seven, 6 July 2014.

I Put it to You –
Closing Arguments

Page 501   Graeme Hosken, 'A Tale of Two Fathers', Times Live, 8 August 2014.

Page 518   Marida Fitzpatrick, 'Nou vir die Uitspraak', *Beeld*, 9 August 2014.

The Scales of Justice

Page 520   Lisa Davies, 'Oscar Pistorius and Thato Kutumela: A Tale of Two Murder Trials', *Sydney Morning Herald*, 8 March 2014.

Page 521   LN Robinson, 'Professional Athletes Held to a Higher Standard and Above the Law: A Comment on High-Profile Criminal Defendants and the Need for States to Establish High-Profile Courts', *Indiana Law Journal* 4(8), 1998.

Page 521   Maria M Wong, 'Are Celebrities Charged with Murder Likely to be Acquitted?', *North American Journal of Psychology* 3, 2010.

Page 521   Bruce A Carroll, 'Celebrity Adjudication: Comparative Analyses of United States Verdict Rates for Celebrity Defendants', *Entertainment and Sports Law Journal* 11, 2013.

Judgment Day

Page 549   Ulrich Roux, 'Oscar Pistorius Verdict: Judgment Seemed to Support Charge of "Dolus Eventualis"', *The Guardian*, 12 September 2014.

Page 550   Brad Cibane, 'Judge Masipa Got It Right: Oscar Pistorius and the Intention to Kill', The Law Thinker, 12 September 2014.

Page 557   'Myers Family: "We are Disappointed with the Verdict"', The Juice, 12 September 2014.

Page 557   'Oscar Pistorius: Reeva Steenkamp's Parents Say "Justice was not Served"', *NBC News*, 12 September 2014.

Acknowledgements

Writing and publishing a book, particularly one of this nature and scale, is no easy feat. It requires extraordinary amounts of time, commitment, investment, passion and attention to detail. This would not have been possible without the outstanding team at Pan Macmillan.

Andrea Nattrass, thank you for holding our hands, for the incredibly long hours, for your high standards, for the whip-cracking and the patience. You really are our favourite publisher.

Thank you Terry Morris for your trust in us and for ensuring we have felt so welcome as part of the Pan family. Laura Hammond, your tireless efforts to get the monkeys dancing are always appreciated.

Sean Fraser, your meticulous editing has earned you those whiskies. Thank you also to Sally Hines, Kevin Shenton and Michiel Botha for your outstanding work on this project.

To the team at Webber Wentzel, especially Dario Milo and Stuart Scott, we appreciate your time and your careful attention to this text. Your advice and guidance have been invaluable.

This book would not be a reality without the relentless support of our editor-in-chief at Eyewitness News, our 'Number 1', Katy Katopodis. Katy has repeatedly allowed us to drop off the news diary and disappear to research and write. You, Katy, are a mentor and a leader who deserves the immense loyalty you inspire.

Thank you also to Terry Volkwyn and Primedia Broadcasting for backing this project and allowing us time to complete it. To the rest of the wonderful Eyewitness News team – particularly Benita, Camilla, Sheldon, Alex, Stephen, Gia, Christa, Reinardt, Landi and Pippa – we appreciate your patience as we dropped off the news planet.

Thanks, too, to the legal experts – Kelly Phelps, Professor James Grant, Tyrone Maseko, Ian Levitt and David Dadic – who took the time to assist us and to read the text.

Rebecca Davis's on-point coverage of the trial on Daily Maverick and on Twitter must be acknowledged as a continued source of both courtroom developments and of grounding perspective in a media storm of madness.

To those sources who gave of their time and their knowledge and who cannot be publicly acknowledged, thank you for your trust and for giving us custodianship of your stories.

Mandy Wiener and Barry Bateman
September 2014

• •

My co-author Barry 'Batman' Bateman has immersed himself in this story with a commitment that is without comparison. His detailed and wide-ranging knowledge about the case is astonishing. I know that my perfectionist, A-type personality doesn't make for the best traits in a co-author, so thanks, Barry, for dealing with me so graciously. At times it felt like those early-morning writing sessions would never end, but I have so enjoyed travelling this journey with you, one egg breakfast at a time.

Sarah-Jane Olivier has been my sounding board and 'first reader'. Thank you for being so circumspect, for providing perspective and for transcribing hours of interviews under pressure. Your insight is beyond measure.

Katy, you have encouraged, inspired and motivated me every step of the way. I couldn't ask for a better mentor.

I'm grateful for the advice and guidance of David O'Sullivan and Jenny Crwys-Williams, both of whom are a constant source of wisdom.

Each book I have written has coincided with a major life event. This time around, I thought I'd step it up a gear and try to write this one in the months after the birth of my first baby whilst still in 'The Darkness' of new motherhood. The trial began one week after I gave birth to our son. It made for interesting times.

I would not have survived were it not for the incredible support structure around me. Never more have I subscribed to the belief of Ubuntu, that it takes a village to raise a child. There are too many people to thank individually, but I must acknowledge Dr Rubi Gordon, Symonah, Dr Neli Stoykova, Sister Sam, Bridgette, Gil, Ang, Marie, the Gloss girls, Brett, Thendo and the staff at Billi Bi.

Thanks, too, to my friends who are always there to celebrate my success and check in to see whether I was surviving the pressures of motherhood and deadlines – Louise, Nadine, Shelley, Steve, Sim, Sarah, Kim, Dov, Glenda, Emma, Debs, Zas, Mand, Sue, Jimbo and Justin.

Annika, Nicci and Cindy, I would not have made it through those early weeks without you. Thank you for keeping me sane, feeling normal and for being just a WhatsApp away.

Judy, the comfort of listening to my boy giggling with you while I laboured to finish this book has made it so much easier. Thank you for looking after him as if he were your own. To Loretta, thank you for always making sure I am looked after so well!

Raymond and Marcelle, I cannot thank you enough for your love and support and for being such generous grandparents, with both your time and your energy. To the Meisels – the whole mad lot of you – I love being a part of your family.

Angie and Lili, thank you for being Meisels with me and for always being on the end of the phone.

To my own parents, enjoy these naartjies too. Thank you for leading the fan club and for always taking such pride in what I do. Elian and Janine, thank you for the Skype calls, the phone calls, the messages, the dinners and the unwavering love and support. I'm so proud of you both.

Finally, to my boys, Sean and Sam. You are my everything.

Sam, you have brought such light into my life and taught me how to live and to love in a way I never knew I could. Being so ridiculously cute and distracting really made this book difficult to complete. The first six months of your life have been a pretty wild ride for us all and it's only going to get more awesome from here. (I'm sorry for all the live Oscar Pistorius Trial Channel I made you watch in your first weeks on earth.)

Sean, I would not have wanted to do life with anyone else, and being on a team with you makes it all possible. I am so grateful for all those hours of daddy daycare you put in while I was typing away. Love you to there and back.

MW

· · ·

I never hesitated when the opportunity arose to embark on this project with Mandy Wiener, and my expectations of what I would learn from her have been far exceeded. Mandy transformed my often dry, hard-fact accounts of events into colourful, gripping narrative. I have been the pain in her neck on the odd occasion, but I got there eventually through her patience and guidance (at least the last chapter didn't require too much hacking). Thank you would not be complete without a full appreciation for your family – Sean and little Sam – who have been without a wife and mommy for those long hours behind the desk.

I thank all my journalist colleagues, particularly those in Pretoria, who have helped me grow and develop as a professional through the years. While we are competitive and want to scoop each other on the next big break, we're also a strong community, bonded by shared experiences. I consider many of you my friends and I value the time we spend working together on stories – whether we're numbing our arses on hard court benches or being burnt to a cinder under the harsh sun at a crime scene waiting for a police briefing. Thanks to Phil, Charl, Graeme, Zelda, Fanie, Hanti, Gerhard,

Cornel, Danielle and all the others who slog at it daily, gathering news and producing incredible content.

My Eyewitness News colleague Gia Nicolaides deserves special mention for her tireless coverage of the trial, which allowed me to remain inside court as she dashed out on the hour every hour to cross live and file.

To develop as a professional you require a mentor who understands your personality, who is able to nudge you when you need direction, pick you up when you trip and give you freedom to grow – my editor Katy Katopodis does all that and more.

I would not have survived the weeks of sitting in courtroom GD if it weren't for the humour and conversation in row two – Paul, Nastasya, Andrew (pass the biscuits, please), Aislinn and Alex.

Covering this trial allowed to me to develop my career in a direction I had not really considered, thanks to the vision and commitment of *Carte Blanche* producer George Mazarakis. DStv's Oscar Pistorius Trial Channel 199 was a South African first and I was part of that. Easing in to television work was made a breeze by the professionalism and cool on-air presence of John Webb. Producer Graham Coetzer and the competent team he assembled for the project kept everything under control at our 'rooftop position'. What set the #OscarTrial apart from other stories I've covered were the tweeps, all 200 000 of you, who followed @barrybateman for the latest on this developing story. I've thoroughly enjoyed every 140-character debate, your commentary and your criticism.

To my parents, Geoff and Linda, there isn't enough space in this book to explain how much I love you and appreciate the sacrifices you've made to enable me to find direction and grow. My little brother, Colin, who has watched my back in so many ways, you epitomise the character that bonds siblings.

With me for every step of this journey have been my three girls – Sholain, Isobel and Aishwari.

My little girls, your smiles, giggles and mischief replenish that joy deep inside my heart that is too often tarnished by the world I report on every day. The adoration I see in your eyes every time you look up at me makes me want to be the best father ever.

My dear wife, it has been a year in which you have allowed me to immerse myself in a story like no other and disappear for days into the study to focus my full attention on this trial. I know how tough it is keeping a handle on our two little rats on your own, but you relieved me of this duty so often. Thank you for listening, for understanding, for consulting, for counselling and, most importantly, for laying down the law. I love you, Sholain, and I don't go a day without appreciating that you love me.

BB